POVERTY, U. S. A.

THE HISTORICAL RECORD

ADVISORY EDITOR: David J. Rothman

Professor of History, Columbia University

RURAL POOR
IN THE GREAT DEPRESSION

Three Studies

Rural Youth
Bruce L. Melvin and Elna N. Smith

Migrant Families
John N. Webb and Malcolm Brown

Rural Families on Relief
Carle C. Zimmerman and Nathan L. Whetten

Arno Press & The New York Times
NEW YORK   1971

Reprint Edition 1971 by Arno Press Inc.

•

Reprinted from copies in
The State Historical Society of Wisconsin Library

LC# 70—137177
ISBN 0—405—03133—5

POVERTY, U.S.A.: THE HISTORICAL RECORD
ISBN for complete set: 0-405-03090-8

Manufactured in the United States of America

RURAL YOUTH

THEIR SITUATION
AND PROSPECTS

WORKS PROGRESS ADMINISTRATION
DIVISION OF SOCIAL RESEARCH

Publications
of the Division of Social Research
Works Progress Administration

Research Monographs

Special Reports

WORKS PROGRESS ADMINISTRATION
Harry L. Hopkins, *Administrator*
Corrington Gill, *Assistant Administrator*
DIVISION OF SOCIAL RESEARCH
Howard B. Myers, *Director*

RURAL YOUTH:
THEIR SITUATION AND PROSPECTS

By

Bruce L. Melvin
and
Elna N. Smith

•

RESEARCH MONOGRAPH XV

1938
UNITED STATES GOVERNMENT PRINTING OFFICE, WASHINGTON

Letter of Transmittal

WORKS PROGRESS ADMINISTRATION,
Washington, D. C., July 15, 1938.

SIR: I have the honor to transmit an analysis of the present situation and future prospects of rural youth. The report is based on a comprehensive survey of the field studies and general literature dealing with rural youth.

Although there is already a "surplus" of rural youth, their numbers will increase steadily until some time between 1940 and 1945. Even assuming a considerable urbanward migration of farm youth, it appears that there will be over 1,000,000 more youth in rural territory in 1940 than there were in 1930. With economic opportunities in rural areas already far from adequate to meet the demands of youth, the gravity of the situation is evident. Moreover, young people in rural areas are definitely handicapped with respect to educational and recreational facilities.

Many agencies, both governmental and nongovernmental, are providing services and opportunities for rural youth, but their largely uncoordinated efforts reach only part of the rural young people who need assistance. Fundamental amelioration of the situation calls for united efforts in behalf of equalizing opportunities.

This study was made in the Division of Social Research under the direction of Howard B. Myers, Director of the Division. The data on which the report is based were collected and analyzed under the supervision of T. J. Woofter, Jr., Coordinator of Rural Research.

The report was written by Bruce L. Melvin and Elna N. Smith. It was edited by Ellen Winston. Special acknowledgment is due the personnel of the National Youth Administration and of the Office of Emergency Conservation Work both for data and for constructive criticism.

Respectfully submitted.

CORRINGTON GILL,
Assistant Administrator.

HON. HARRY L. HOPKINS,
Works Progress Administrator.

Contents

ILLUSTRATIONS

Figures

Photographs

Rural Youth:
Their Situation and Prospects

IX

INTRODUCTION

Y OUTH IS a period of economic and social adjustments. As the transition period from childhood to maturity it has tended progressively to expand as civilization has advanced. It is here defined as including all young people 16 through 24 years of age. In a democracy it is society's obligation to make certain provisions for this transition period. Schools have been made available on the secondary and college levels to prepare youth for making their adjustments, since it has been assumed that economic opportunity is open to the youth who are prepared through education to take advantage of it. Despite the expansion of educational facilities, however, present economic opportunities are so limited that large numbers of young men and women are unable to establish themselves in a field that may be expected to lead to economic security. As a result the problems of youth have become serious and far-reaching in their implications and effects.

Lack of economic opportunity with the resultant social consequences of unemployment, underemployment, or employment at work which is unsuited to individual temperament or capacity has, of course, not been limited to youth in recent years. But the demoralizing psychological effects of idleness, discouragement, and frustration during periods of economic stress are particularly far-reaching and lasting for youth.

In recent years unemployment has been widespread among rural as well as urban youth, although more notice has been taken of the latter. Too often the rural youth situation has been dismissed with the statement that at least the young people on farms need not starve. Such summary disposition of the matter fails to take account of the other necessities of human living or of the fact that there are thousands of rural young people in small towns who are just as desperate as their city cousins for a chance to develop their capacities and to banish the spectre of insecurity.

Many individuals and organizations are interested in the welfare of rural youth. Numerous programs are being planned in an attempt to meet their problems. To guide this planning there has been a distinct need for a comprehensive statement of the general situation faced by youth in rural areas as well as a digest of what is known about the condition of youth in specific areas. Before new studies and programs are undertaken, it is important to know what information past surveys, other studies, and census data have yielded.

A great deal of miscellaneous material of varying quality is available, including some studies made on a State basis. The usable data on many topics are exceedingly scanty, however, and point to the need for further research. An effort has been made in this report to summarize such data as are available and to supplement them with an evaluation of the situation and prospects of rural youth.

Chapter I discusses the distribution of youth; chapter II deals with their economic situation; chapter III treats of their educational status and opportunities; chapter IV takes up the marital condition of youth; while chapter V summarizes their recreational opportunities. Chapter VI discusses what governmental agencies and some nongovernmental agencies with programs for rural youth are doing in attempting to meet the situation faced by youth. The final chapter attempts to interpret the general situation and to point out the implications of the data presented in the preceding chapters for future programs and policies.

Resettlement Administration (Jung).

What Does the Future Hold?

SUMMARY

DURING THE early thirties, when economic opportunity was at a minimum, more youth were maturing in the United States than ever before. In 1935 there were in this country approximately 20,800,000 youth, 16–24 years of age, almost 10,000,000 of whom were in rural areas—a record figure in each case. Moreover, it is estimated that by 1940 the total will have increased to more than 21,500,000 with well over 10,000,000 youth in rural areas.

DISTRIBUTION OF YOUTH

Youth is the principal age of migration just as it is the period of occupational and marital adjustment. In the past migration to the cities has tended to take care of the surplus population of rural areas. The checking of this migration during the depression, as economic opportunities in urban areas were sharply curtailed, resulted in the "piling up" of youth in rural areas and the emergence of a major rural youth problem.

During the decade from 1920 to 1930 the net migration from farms totaled 6,300,000 persons of whom about 2,000,000 were youth 16–24 years of age. Girls left at an earlier age than boys, and more young people left the poor agricultural areas than the better farm lands. Southern Negroes moved in large numbers from farms to the cities in their own section as well as to the cities of the North. At the same time there was a steady migration from cities to farm areas close at hand, causing the largest population increases for the period to occur in the territory close to industrial and commercial centers.

Of the rural youth reported by the 1930 Census, over 40 percent lived in nonfarm areas. In the largely nonagricultural New England, Middle Atlantic, and Pacific Divisions nonfarm youth constituted over one-half of the rural total. In the dominantly agricultural areas the problems of farm and nonfarm youth are similar, but in primarily industrial areas the problems of rural-nonfarm youth may have little relation to agriculture. In the South race questions complicate the situation since Negro youth form an important proportion of the rural population, larger in the farm than in the nonfarm group.

Even at the beginning of the depression the pressure of farm youth on employment opportunities was more acute than that of rural-nonfarm youth. Pressure on the land as measured by replacement rates of rural-farm males was particularly heavy in the Southern States. The excess of country youth was accentuated between 1930 and 1935 as rural-farm youth increased much more rapidly than rural-nonfarm youth. While all rural youth increased approximately 13 percent, farm youth increased almost 19 percent to a record total of 6,107,000.

The checking of the cityward flow after 1930 contributed greatly to the increase by 1935 of 1,150,000 in the number of rural youth, while the youth population in the cities was declining. The net migration varied from State to State. Apparently more youth migrated to than from farms in the New England, Middle Atlantic, and East North Central States, reflecting the shutdown in industry in those regions. In other regions youth left the farms in spite of the limitations of industrial and commercial opportunities. Where farm income has normally been very low and where drought and dust storms have been severe, youth have migrated in large numbers.

The extent of migration to cities within the next few years will have an important effect on the rural youth problem through its effect on the pressure on employment opportunities in rural areas. Without such migration there would be almost 2,000,000 more rural youth in 1940 than in 1930. Even with the expected migration there will be between 500,000 and 600,000 more rural-farm youth and 500,000 more rural-nonfarm youth in 1940 than in 1930.

ECONOMIC SITUATION OF RURAL YOUTH

In the past, economic security in rural society has been measured chiefly by property ownership. The farm youth expected to acquire a good farm free of debt and the village youth ultimately to own a business or to attain a secure position in some profession or skilled trade. The large-scale development of lumbering, mining, and textile industries introduced a wage-earning class into this system, and there has been an increasing trend toward dependence on wages for part or all of the income. Meanwhile, youth have been "piling up" on the home farm where they receive little or no return other than subsistence for their labor.

With more and more youth accumulating on the home farms, and as the possibility of finding economic security through migration to urban areas decreases, their situation becomes of course less tolerable. In poor land areas, like the Lake States Cut-Over, the trouble is acute on account of the extremely small return for their work and the large proportion of youth who have no work at all. Even on good land the increased number of youth of employable age who cannot find a living away from the home farm is affecting the economic balance.

The situation of young women forced to remain on the home farm is probably more precarious than that of the young men since little but housework and farm labor are available to them. In general, it appears that young women working at home are less likely to receive wages from parents than are young men, and in the poorer areas their role is regularly that of unpaid servants.

Probably not less than 2,000,000 rural youth have been members of relief households at some time since 1930. The peak in the number of households was reached in February 1935 when approximately 1,370,000 rural youth were receiving aid. By October the number of youth on relief had declined to 625,000. Most of those removed from the relief rolls had been transferred to the Civilian Conservation Corps or with their families to the Resettlement Administration so that the decline in the number receiving some form of Government aid was probably not great. Young men left the general relief rolls more rapidly than young women, and older youth found more opportunities for going off relief than did those under 20 years of age.

Developments of recent years have greatly reduced the opportunities of rural youth for attaining economic security. Progress toward farm ownership is hindered and frequently prevented by the growing burden of debt, the increase in tenancy, the decreased demand for farm laborers, the trend toward large-scale ownership of land, mechanization of agriculture, and the development of large areas of agricultural maladjustment. The children of owner-operators therefore start as laborers, like their parents, but unlike their parents they often remain permanently in that or the tenant class.

The alternatives presented to underprivileged farm youth appear to be three—to remain in the country at a low level of living, to go to the cities to compete for jobs at very low wages, or, if their need is sufficiently great, to obtain jobs provided by one of the governmental agencies. There is no longer new acreage to be opened up, and much hitherto cultivated land is no longer profitable.

Nonagricultural employment, instead of offering possibilities for the greatly increased number of maturing rural youth, has reduced its labor requirements, and the supply of local labor already trained is usually sufficient for its needs. Untrained rural youth going to industrial or urban areas ordinarily find opportunities only in the hardest and most menial work, which is also the most poorly paid.

EDUCATIONAL STATUS AND OPPORTUNITIES OF RURAL YOUTH

Rural youth are definitely handicapped in comparison with urban youth by the lack of educational facilities. Because of comparative lack of taxpaying ability rural States have the most meager provisions for public education. Hence the areas with the largest proportions of children have the poorest schools.

Largely because of the differences in educational facilities rural youth do not attend school to the same extent as do urban youth. Rural-farm youth attend school in smaller numbers proportionately and leave school earlier than do rural-nonfarm youth, also primarily because of variations in educational opportunity. School attendance alone does not measure the educational situation, however, and many rural youth, particularly in the South, are greatly retarded with respect to grade attainment. Moreover, although marked progress has been made, illiteracy is still prevalent in States with large reservoirs of surplus youth and with large numbers of Negro or Mexican youth. As late as 1930 about 1 out of every 20 rural-farm youth in the United States was still unable to read and write.

High school attendance increased during the period when employment was hard to find, the gain occurring in both town and country. The National Youth Administration and other relief agencies have contributed to this development in recent years by assisting youth in the lowest income groups to continue in school. In rural areas where the educational handicap has been severe even in normal times, similar aid over a long period appears advisable.

Where facilities are available, a large proportion of all rural youth attend school, from which it may be assumed that with adequate opportunity a substantial increase in rural attendance can be expected. Much Federal and local effort has been expended in extending rural high school facilities and especially vocational training in agricultural and homemaking courses. One of the most significant phases of the vocational agricultural work has been the development of the organization known as Future Farmers of America with its emphasis on practical farming experience.

The desirability of nonagricultural training for farm youth is made apparent by the shortage of farm work and by the usual unfitness of such youth to compete for urban employment.

MARRIAGE OF RURAL YOUTH

In farm life especially, marriage represents an economic as well as a social adjustment since the farm home and the farm business are one. It does not necessarily involve a comparable economic adjustment for rural-nonfarm youth since the young man may have become established in some occupation long before his marriage.

The proportion of youth married is greater for both sexes and for all years among rural than urban youth. At each year of age more young women than young men are married in both urban and rural territory. Early marriage of girls is particularly frequent in rural areas.

More rural-nonfarm than rural-farm youth of both sexes were married in 1930. The higher rate among the rural-nonfarm group seems to be associated with large rural-industrial populations. Moreover, most of the States with particularly high rural-nonfarm marriage rates are Southern States in which marriage rates among youth in general are high. Color also influences the proportion of youth who are married, relatively more Negro than white youth being married in all residence groups.

Between 1910 and 1920 there was an upward trend in the percent married among both rural and urban youth. In the twenties there was little change in the proportion of youth married, but during the early years of the depression (1929–1932) the marriage rate for the entire country fell, the decline appearing to be greater in urban than in rural areas. As the rural depression had begun in the twenties, and the reduction in the marriage rate was then negligible, it seems doubtful whether depression conditions have any marked effect in causing farm youth to postpone marriage. In 1933 the marriage rate began increasing and continued through 1934, returning practically to the 1929 level. This recovery was general among both rural and urban States.

USE OF LEISURE TIME

The social adjustments of youth largely determine the patterns of their adult lives. Hence it is particularly important for a wide variety of wholesome recreational activities to be available for them. Within recent years there have been many changes in the kinds of recreation in which rural youth indulge, as automobiles, motion pictures, and the radio have become generally available. The rural community has frequently become disorganized and as a result has less and less control over the behavior of individual members.

So far rural communities have been slow to realize the social and recreational needs of youth and have made few attempts to meet them. On the other hand, a large proportion of rural youth do not participate in such institutions and organizations as have been developed. Except for the church and Sunday school, organizations in rural areas have attracted a relatively small percentage of those eligible for membership and have often failed to meet the needs of those who did become members. The extent to which youth participate in social organizations apparently depends largely on their economic status and educational attainments.

In addition to the church and other organizations there are many informal activities which absorb the leisure time of rural young people. The extent to which youth attend motion pictures and dances, belong to athletic groups, play games, read, etc., varies widely from one section to another. The amount and type of reading is largely determined by the availability of library facilities. Recreation within the home is still of major importance and has received new stimulation and development as a result of the depression. The lack of recreational

84015°—38——2

activities is particularly acute in poor land areas. The various Federal emergency agencies established during the depression of the early thirties have made an important contribution through making available to rural areas some of the facilities for wholesome recreation, such as playgrounds, swimming pools, and community centers, which are taken for granted by city dwellers.

PROGRAMS TO AID RURAL YOUTH

Many organizations, both governmental and nongovernmental, have developed definite and constructive programs for aiding rural youth. The Cooperative Extension Service of the United States Department of Agriculture, operating through the State colleges of agriculture, promotes its work for youth through the 4–H Club program and through organizations for young adults. The 4–H Club membership is composed primarily of young people below the youth group and includes chiefly young people in school from farm homes. The program for older groups, which is still largely in the experimental stage, emphasizes the promotion of better farming and the development of leadership in educational and cultural guidance and in recreational activities.

The federally-aided high schools with courses in vocational agriculture have expanded their part-time and evening classes in agricultural education since the depression of the early thirties. Unemployed and out-of-school youth have been given training to equip them for work when the opportunity comes. The Office of Education has pioneered in many programs of value to rural areas, such as conservation, radio, and public forums.

The National Youth Administration has a varied program which covers a far more extensive group than the relief group for which it was organized primarily. Its present services to youth include aid to those who cannot attend school without help, special courses at agricultural colleges for farm boys and girls, work projects for out-of-school youth, and vocational guidance and job placement. Through these various programs hundreds of thousands of youth are being aided.

The Civilian Conservation Corps has the threefold purpose of conserving natural resources, providing employment for needy young men, and giving vocational training. By January 1, 1938, approximately 900,000 rural youth from low-income or relief families had spent one enrollment term or more in camp.

The Works Progress Administration, while it has no program especially designed for youth, has reached a considerable number of rural youth through its educational projects, work projects, and provision of recreational facilities. The Farm Credit Administration through its production credit associations to finance crop and livestock production and, more recently, through its program for giving youth opportunities to rent farms is helping young men get a start in farming. The Agricultural Adjustment Administration and, more recently, the Soil Conservation and Domestic Allotment Act through assisting rural families have aided the youth in those families. Similarly the Resettlement Administration, now the Farm Security Administration, has aided rural youth through helping their families. However, direct assistance to youth in making their own economic adjustments has not been rendered by these agencies.

The United States Employment Service helps young people as well as older workers to secure jobs. So far, data on the extent to which the USES functions with respect to rural youth are not available.

Nongovernmental agencies serving youth are numerous and varied. Those which have been developed in rural areas with definite programs for out-of-school youth include the junior programs of the Farm Bureau and the Farmers Educational and Co-operative Union, the National Grange which embraces the entire family in its membership, the Wisconsin Farm Short Course for farm boys, and cooperative youth clubs. In addition there are many localized projects with varying characteristics scattered throughout the country. Often experimental in nature, they are performing important functions in widening the opportunities and outlook of rural youth.

In spite of excellent work on the part of various agencies, governmental and nongovernmental, the problems of rural youth as a whole are still far from being solved. Although much has been accomplished to ameliorate conditions resulting from the depression, probably the majority of rural youth have not had the advantages of any specialized program.

THE LONG-TIME PROBLEM

The long-time rural youth problem is that of an excess in numbers in relation to a dearth of rural opportunities, a situation which becomes greatly aggravated during "hard times." Yet rural youth need not necessarily face constricted opportunities if society assumes its full responsibility for this great human resource.

While equality of educational opportunity is generally accepted as a fundamental democratic principle, the fact must be clearly faced that there is not equality of educational facilities in rural America. Because of such inequalities, there are thousands of out-of-school rural youth inadequately prepared to cope with the problems of modern life. In view of the limited financial resources available in many rural areas, it seems clear that the Federal Government must extend greatly increased support if the democratic ideal of equality in education for rural youth is to be realized.

No amount of education will be of much benefit to rural youth, however, if adequate opportunities for gainful employment are lacking. Agriculture cannot begin to absorb the increasing number of rural youth. Migration to urban centers will not meet the situation unless it is carefully directed. Even with guided migration cities are unlikely to be able to absorb the vast numbers of rural youth who ought, under present conditions, to leave rural territory. While agricultural developments point toward even further restrictions in opportunities for youth on farms, the expansion of the field of service occupations holds possibilities for large numbers of young people. This development, however, is contingent on rural areas being able to support the social services they so badly need.

The consequences of inequality are nowhere more apparent than in the social and recreational life of young people. Dull and uneventful communities do not necessarily breed antisocial behavior, but they may yield lethargic and restricted personalities. Society must accept the responsibility of providing not only educational and economic opportunities for rural youth but also adequate recreational and social facilities if well-rounded personalities are to be developed.

Society must recognize the exploitation and waste of its young manhood and womanhood which now exist. A concerted frontal attack has yet to be made on the long-time factors responsible for the widespread destitution and restricted social opportunities of rural youth.

Chapter I

DISTRIBUTION OF YOUTH

THE INTENSITY of the difficulties that rural youth encounter in making their adjustments into adult society at any particular time and place largely depends on the rate at which youth reach maturity and the extent to which they move into or out of the community. A population of one hundred may create pressure on a given number of acres of poor land but be well adjusted if on good land. In rural areas of ample opportunities the concentration of numbers—particularly of youth—does not create serious difficulties except in times of widespread unemployment. On the other hand, concentration in areas of limited economic opportunities and of restricted health, recreational, and educational facilities creates continuous maladjustment which becomes greatly aggravated in times of general economic depression.

Manifold problems confront the youth of rural America today. The problems of rural youth are, moreover, closely related to those of youth in cities, and the maladjusted situations in which the youth of the two groups have found themselves in recent years have been due both to long-time trends and to the depression.

In the Nation as a whole, in spite of slackening birth rates and restricted immigration, there were more youth in 1935 than ever before. In that year some 20,800,000 persons, or one-sixth of the population, were in the youth group (16–24 years of age). The number had steadily increased from 1930 to 1935, the period during which opportunities were at a minimum. Almost half of these youth were living in rural districts, and the growth in numbers had been greatest in rural territory.

EFFECT OF FERTILITY RATES ON THE DISTRIBUTION OF YOUTH

The number of youth at any given time depends primarily on the number of births 16 to 24 years previously. The trend of births in the United States rose until 1921 when the peak was reached, with a second lower peak coming in 1924 (appendix table 1). Barring the

1

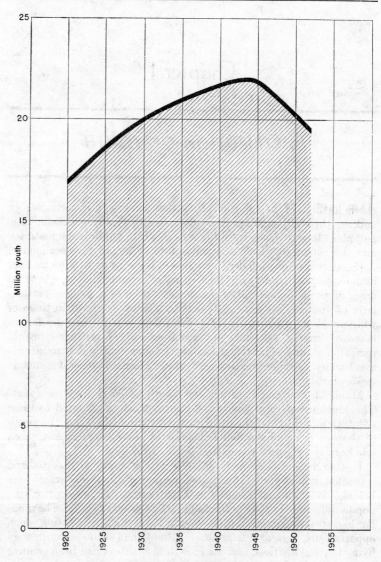

FIG. 1-TREND IN NUMBER OF YOUTH IN
THE UNITED STATES
1920-1952

Source: Appendix table 2.   AF-2647, WPA

possible effects of change in immigration policy and assuming a constant death rate, there will be more youth in the United States about the period 1942 to 1944 than at any other period prior to that time (appendix table 2). The total number of youth will begin to decrease shortly thereafter because the number of births per year in the United States has declined almost steadily since 1924 (fig. 1).[1]

Table 1.—Percent of Total Population and of Total Youth Population in Urban and Rural Areas, by Geographic Division, 1930

Geographic division	Total population		Total youth population	
	Urban	Rural	Urban	Rural
United States	56.2	43.8	56.1	43.9
New England	77.3	22.7	78.7	21.3
Middle Atlantic	77.7	22.3	79.6	20.4
East North Central	66.4	33.6	68.6	31.4
West North Central	41.8	58.2	42.1	57.9
South Atlantic	36.1	63.9	35.9	64.1
East South Central	28.1	71.9	28.3	71.7
West South Central	36.4	63.6	36.4	63.6
Mountain	39.4	60.6	39.3	60.7
Pacific	67.5	32.5	67.9	32.1

Source: Bureau of the Census, *Fifteenth Census of the United States: 1930*, Population Vol. II, U. S. Department of Commerce, Washington, D. C., 1933, pp. 611, 671, 674, and 694.

Although more children have been born and reared in the country than in the cities, migration to the cities has balanced the deficit of births in urban territory so that in 1930 the percent distribution of

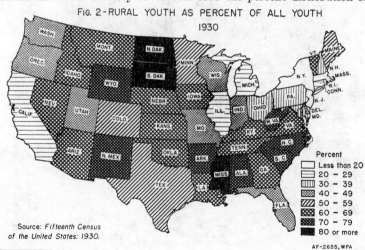

FIG. 2-RURAL YOUTH AS PERCENT OF ALL YOUTH
1930

Percent
☐ Less than 20
≡ 20 - 29
▥ 30 - 39
▨ 40 - 49
▧ 50 - 59
▦ 60 - 69
▩ 70 - 79
■ 80 or more

Source: *Fifteenth Census of the United States: 1930.*

AF-2655.WPA

[1] There will be a slight upswing again in the number of youth from about 1960 through 1965. At that time the children of women born during the high birth rate years of 1921–1924 will be entering the youth group. National Resources Committee, *Population Statistics, 1. National Data*, Washington, D. C., October 1937, p. 9.

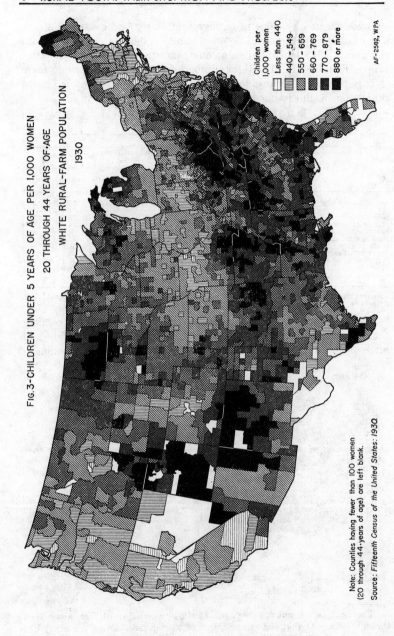

FIG. 3 – CHILDREN UNDER 5 YEARS OF AGE PER 1,000 WOMEN
20 THROUGH 44 YEARS OF AGE
WHITE RURAL-FARM POPULATION
1930

Children per
1,000 women

Less than 440
440 - 549
550 - 659
660 - 769
770 - 879
880 or more

AF-2582, WPA

Note: Counties having fewer than 100 women
(20 through 44-years of age) are left blank.

Source: Fifteenth Census of the United States: 1930.

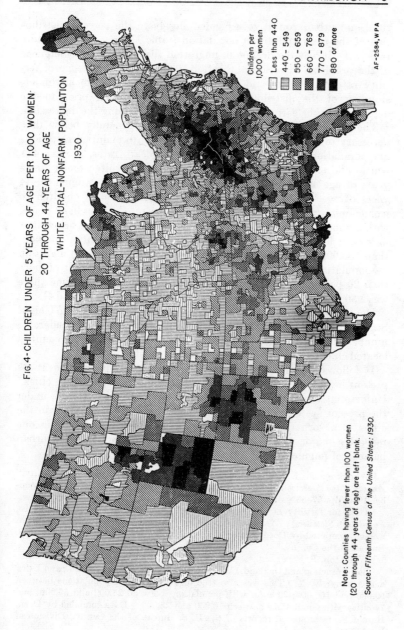

Fig. 4 - CHILDREN UNDER 5 YEARS OF AGE PER 1,000 WOMEN·
20 THROUGH 44 YEARS OF AGE
WHITE RURAL-NONFARM POPULATION
1930

Children per
1,000 women

Less than 440
440 - 549
550 - 659
660 - 769
770 - 879
880 or more

AF-2584, WPA

Note: Counties having fewer than 100 women
(20 through 44 years of age) are left blank.

Source: Fifteenth Census of the United States: 1930.

rural and urban youth corresponded closely to the percent distribution of the rural and urban population (table 1, fig. 2, and appendix table 3). It was the decline in migration that caused the emergence of the problems of rural youth after 1930. Some knowledge of fertility rates [2] in urban and rural territory is essential to an understanding of the distributive process which operated prior to the depression of the early thirties and was checked during the depression.

The fertility rate of the large cities is now generally below that necessary to maintain their population. Even to maintain a stationary population it was necessary, with 1930 death rates, to have 444 white children under 5 years of age for each 1,000 white women 20–44 years of age and 499 Negro children per 1,000 Negro women 20–44 years of age.[3] According to this standard the ratio of children to women in the native white population of the United States in all places with a population above 10,000 in 1930 was on the average below that necessary for replacement.[4] Only 1 city with a population of more than 100,000 in 1930 had a fertility rate sufficiently high to maintain its population. The large cities had on the average a deficit of more than 20 percent in the number of children. At the same time there was a 50 percent surplus of children in rural territory (figs. 3 and 4).

Deaths already exceeded births in 1935 in 6 cities in the United States with more than 100,000 population [5] as well as in a considerable number of smaller cities. The same situation existed in 130 counties located chiefly in the Northeast and the far West.

It follows that in order to maintain the urban population at its present level there must be a movement of rural people to the cities.[6] Unfortunately or fortunately, depending on the point of view, under the present system there are not enough economic possibilities in the cities to absorb the entire rural population surplus. Hence in one respect a major youth problem is the maintenance of a rural-urban balance of population.

---

[2] Whelpton, P. K., "Geographic and Economic Differentials in Fertility," *Annals of the American Academy of Political and Social Science*, Vol. 188, November 1936, pp. 37–55.

[3] Data for fertility of white women from National Resources Committee, *Population Statistics, 1. National Data, op. cit.*, table 14; data for fertility of Negro women computed by Dorn, Harold F., based on life tables prepared by the U. S. Bureau of the Census.

[4] Whelpton, P. K., *op. cit.*, p. 46.

[5] San Francisco and Oakland, Calif.; Portland, Oreg.; Seattle, Wash.; and Utica and Albany, N. Y. This was also true of 12 cities with populations between 50,000 and 100,000; 20 cities with populations between 25,000 and 50,000; and 74 cities with populations between 10,000 and 25,000. Data compiled by Dorn, Harold F., from special reports of the U. S. Bureau of the Census, Division of Vital Statistics.

[6] Baker, O. E., "Rural-Urban Migration and the National Welfare," *Annals of the Association of American Geographers*, Vol. XXIII, June 1933, p. 73.

EFFECT OF MIGRATION FROM 1920 TO 1930 ON THE DISTRIBUTION OF YOUTH

Between 1920 and 1930 the total rural-farm population declined from 31,358,600 to 30,157,500, a decrease of almost 4 percent. During this decade, however, the number of persons 15–24 years of age in the rural-farm population rose from 5,750,400 to 5,855,200, an increase of about 2 percent.[7] This accretion occurred in spite of the heavy migration of youth from farms during the decade.

Limited data suggest that in the decade 1920–1930 migration was relatively heavier from the poorest land than from the good land.[8] During the depression, however, the flow of population from submarginal land was reversed, the population returning to these poor lands from the cities.[9] This necessarily caused a "piling up" of youth in submarginal areas. Moreover, during the 5-year period 1930 to 1935 there was an actual migration from regions of commercial crop production.[10]

The total net migration from farms between 1920 and 1930 was 6,300,000, of which approximately one-third, or, conservatively estimated, about 2,000,000, were youth 15 to 25 years of age.[11] In total numbers this group exceeded the age group under 15 years, the group between 25 and 35 years of age, and the group 35 years of age and over.

These data establish youth as the principal age of migration. Just as it is the period of occupational adjustment and marital adjustment so it is the period of adjustment to new communities.

The estimate that one-third of all the migrants from farms between 1920 and 1930 were youth is conservative since 25 percent of all persons who left the farms between 1920 and 1930 were 10–14 years of age in 1920 and 23 percent were 15–19 years of age in 1920 (table 2). The figures also indicate that many migrants are children who move with their families. On the other hand, the large majority of youth probably migrate independently of their families as is shown by a

[7] Bureau of the Census, *Fifteenth Census of the United States: 1930*, Population Vol. II, U. S. Department of Commerce, Washington, D. C., 1933, table 16, pp. 588–589. Fifteen-year-olds are included in this tabulation because the 1920 Census did not give the farm population by single years.

[8] Analysis of the migration of rural population made in the Division of Social Research, Works Progress Administration, Washington, D. C.

[9] Goodrich, Carter, Allin, Bushrod W., and Hayes, Marion, *Migration and Planes of Living, 1920–1934*, Philadelphia: University of Pennsylvania Press, 1935, p. 71. See also Woofter, T. J., Jr., "Rural Relief and the Back-to-the-Farm Movement," *Social Forces*, Vol. 14, 1936, p. 382 ff.

[10] Folsom, Josiah C. and Baker, O. E., *A Graphic Summary of Farm Labor and Population*, Miscellaneous Publication No. 265, U. S. Department of Agriculture, Washington, D. C., November 1937, p. 31. See also National Resources Committee, *Population Statistics, 1. National Data, op. cit.*, p. 65.

[11] Baker, O. E., *The Outlook for Rural Youth*, Extension Service Circular 223, U. S. Department of Agriculture, Washington, D. C., 1935, p. 4.

comparison of the age distribution of the rural-farm and urban populations (table 3). If the population under 15 years of age is classed as children, those 15 to 24, inclusive, as youth, those 25 to 64 as the mature productive group, and those 65 and over as aged, and if comparisons are made of the percentages of the total population belonging to these age groups on the farms and in the cities in 1930, the years of migration become even more obvious. In the farm population 36 percent are children as against 26 percent in the city.

Table 2.—Estimated Percent Distribution of Migrants From Farms, by Age and Sex, 1920–1930

Age			Male	Female
1920		1930		
	Total:	Number	2, 805, 000	3, 368, 500
		Percent	100	100
Under 5 years		10-14 years	5	6
5-9 years		15-19 years	7	13
10-14 years		20-24 years	25	25
15-19 years		25-29 years	26	20
20-24 years		30-34 years	13	9
25-29 years		35-39 years	6	4
30-34 years		40-44 years	4	3
35-39 years		45-49 years	3	3
40-44 years		50-54 years	1	3
45-49 years		55-59 years	2	3
50-54 years		60-64 years	2	3
55-59 years		65-69 years	2	3
60-64 years		70-74 years	2	2
65-69 years		75-79 years	2	3

Sources: Bureau of the Census, *Fifteenth Census of the United States: 1930*, Population Vol. II, U. S. Department of Commerce, Washington, D. C., 1933, pp. 588–589; and Dorn, Harold F. and Lorimer, Frank, "Migration, Reproduction, and Population Adjustment," *Annals of the American Academy of Political and Social Science*, Vol. 188, November 1936, p. 287.

There is a close correspondence in the youth group, but the city population has 51 percent in the productive ages as against 40 percent in this age group in the farm areas. Thus the 15–24 year age group is the period when an excess of children on the farms is being converted into an excess of persons in the productive ages in the city.

Certain generalizations may be made about the youth contingent of migrants. In the first place girls left the farms at a younger age than boys, and in the second place more young people migrated from the

Table 3.—Population of the United States, by Age and Residence, 1930

Age	Rural				Urban	
	Farm		Nonfarm		Number	Percent
	Number	Percent	Number	Percent		
Total	30, 158, 000	100. 0	23, 663, 000	100. 0	68, 954, 000	100. 0
Under 15 years	10, 862, 000	36. 0	7, 408, 000	31. 3	17, 787, 000	25. 8
15-19 years	3, 421, 000	11. 3	2, 116, 000	8. 9	6, 015, 000	8. 7
20-24 years	2, 434, 000	8. 1	2, 016, 000	8. 5	6, 420, 000	9. 3
25-64 years	11, 880, 000	39. 5	10, 546, 000	44. 6	35, 142, 000	51. 0
65 years and over	1, 552, 000	5. 1	1, 558, 000	6. 6	3, 524, 000	5. 1
Unknown	9, 000	*	19, 000	0. 1	66, 000	0. 1

*Less than 0.05 percent.

Source: Bureau of the Census, *Fifteenth Census of the United States: 1930*, Population Vol. II, U. S. Department of Commerce, Washington, D. C., 1933, pp. 587–589.

Surplus Youth Must Migrate.

poorer agricultural areas than from the better farm lands. Of the farm girls 10–14 years of age in 1920, 43 percent had migrated by 1930 while of the farm boys of the same age group 33 percent had migrated. For the next older age class, 15–19 years in 1920, 43 percent of both sexes had migrated by 1930.[12] In some States the migration was much more extensive. In Michigan, for example, 37.4 percent of the males on farms 10–14 years of age in 1920 and 58.8 percent of the females in this category had migrated by 1930.[13]

Migration was especially toward the larger cities.[14] According to a study in New York State for the period from 1917 to 1930,[15] the factors determining the migration from the farms in addition to age were opportunity, size of farm, education, distance, and capital.

Not all of the young migrants were white. The movement of Negroes from the farms of the South included many young people. It is estimated that almost 1,000,000 more Negroes left farms than moved to farms between 1920 and 1930. This number was equal to about three-fourths of the natural increase of Negroes in the United States during the same period.[16] The Negro as well as the white

[12] Dorn, Harold F. and Lorimer, Frank, "Migration, Reproduction, and Population Adjustment," *Annals of the American Academy of Political and Social Science*, Vol. 188, November 1936, p. 280.

For discussions of migration see Anderson, W. A., *Mobility of Rural Families. I*, Bulletin 607, Cornell University Agricultural Experiment Station, Ithaca, N. Y., June 1934, and *Mobility of Rural Families. II*, Bulletin 623, Cornell University Agricultural Experiment Station, Ithaca, N. Y., March 1935; Smick, A. A. and Yoder, F. R., *A Study of Farm Migration in Selected Communities in the State of Washington*, Bulletin 233, Washington Agricultural Experiment Station, Pullman, Wash., June 1929; Hamilton, C. Horace, *Rural-Urban Migration in North Carolina, 1920 to 1930*, Bulletin No. 295, North Carolina Agricultural Experiment Station, Raleigh, N. C., February 1934, and "The Annual Rate of Departure of Rural Youths from Their Parental Homes," *Rural Sociology*, Vol. I, 1936, pp. 164–179; Goodrich, Carter, Allin, Bushrod W., and Hayes, Marion, *op. cit.*; Zimmerman, Carle C., "The Migration to Towns and Cities," Nos. I and II, *American Journal of Sociology*, Vol. XXXII, 1926, pp. 450–455, and Vol. XXXIII, 1927, pp. 105–109, No. III with Duncan, O. D. and Frey, Fred C., *American Journal of Sociology*, Vol. XXXIII, 1927, pp. 237–241, No. IV with Duncan, O. D., *Journal of Farm Economics*, Vol. X, 1928, pp. 506–515; Gee, Wilson, "A Qualitative Study of Rural Depopulation in a Single Township: 1900–1930," *American Journal of Sociology*, Vol. XXXIX, 1933, pp. 210–221; Gee, Wilson and Runk, Dewees, "Qualitative Selection in Cityward Migration," *American Journal of Sociology*, Vol. XXXVII, 1931, pp. 254–265; and Reuss, Carl F., "A Qualitative Study of Depopulation in a Remote Rural District: 1900–1930," *Rural Sociology*, Vol. 2, 1937, pp. 66–75.

[13] Thornthwaite, C. Warren, *Internal Migration in the United States*, Philadelphia: University of Pennsylvania Press, 1934, p. 33.

[14] Zimmerman, Carle C., Duncan, O. D., and Frey, Fred C., *op. cit.*

[15] Young, E. C., *The Movement of Farm Population*, Bulletin 426, Cornell University Agricultural Experiment Station, Ithaca, N. Y., March 1924, p. 88.

[16] Dorn, Harold F. and Lorimer, Frank, *op. cit.*, p. 283.

youth in the Southeast went not only to the cities in their own section but also to cities in other sections. Moreover, even with the migration of Negroes from rural territory as heavy as it was during the decade prior to 1930, it was not sufficient to reduce the proportion of total youth that was rural below the figure for the proportion of the total population that was rural.

So far the discussion of rural migration during the twenties has been in terms of the net movement to urban areas, but the return flow from cities during these years was likewise of considerable significance. The destination of this counter movement was principally farms [17] and the area immediately surrounding the large cities. This flow to the peripheries of the cities is shown by the fact that the counties that had the largest population increases through immigration between 1920 and 1930 were in the neighborhood of large cities.[18] The increase in the number of rural-nonfarm youth amounted to 21 percent between 1920 and 1930.[19]

DISTRIBUTION OF YOUTH, 1930

The migratory trends left the youth population of the United States in 1930 divided between urban and rural territory about as the total population was divided (table 1 and appendix table 3), 44 percent rural and 56 percent urban. Of the 11,300,000 urban youth 62 percent were in the New England, Middle Atlantic, and East North Central Divisions. Of the 8,800,000 rural youth, 65 percent were in the Southern and West North Central Divisions (appendix table 4). Before 1930 when the numbers of city youth were not being replenished by maturities to the age 16 in the city, there was a constant flow from rural to urban areas and from the farm sections of the Nation to the industrial sections. This rearing of a substantial part of the urban

Table 4.—Residence of Rural Youth in the United States, by Geographic Division, 1930

Geographic division	Total rural		Rural-farm	Rural-nonfarm
	Number	Percent		
United States	8,844,643	100.0	58.1	41.9
New England	261,745	100.0	27.7	72.3
Middle Atlantic	856,346	100.0	29.1	70.9
East North Central	1,240.852	100.0	54.2	45.8
West North Central	1,232,814	100.0	67.7	32.3
South Atlantic	1,814,478	100.0	58.7	41.3
East South Central	1,272,379	100.0	71.7	28.3
West South Central	1,412,705	100.0	69.7	30.3
Mountain	365,483	100.0	51.1	48.9
Pacific	387,841	100.0	42.1	57.9

Source: Bureau of the Census, *Fifteenth Census of the United States: 1930*, Population Vol. II, U. S. Department of Commerce, Washington, D. C., 1933, p. 674.

[17] Bureau of the Census, *Fifteenth Census of the United States: 1930*, Agriculture Vol. IV, U. S. Department of Commerce, Washington, D. C., 1932, p. 12.

[18] Thornthwaite, C. Warren, *op. cit.*, p. 28.

[19] From 3,409,100 in 1920 to 4,131,600 in 1930, Bureau of the Census, *Fifteenth Census of the United States: 1930*, Population Vol. II, *op. cit.*, p. 589. Fifteen-year-olds were included in this tabulation because the 1920 Census did not give the rural-nonfarm population by single years.

population on the farms represents a notable financial contribution by rural areas to the urban labor market.

The location of rural youth is further shown by comparing the concentration of rural-nonfarm youth with that of rural-farm youth. Over 40 percent of all rural youth in the United States in 1930 were classed as rural-nonfarm (table 4). In three of the nine geographic divisions—New England, Middle Atlantic, and Pacific—nonfarm youth made up more than 50 percent of the rural youth population. These regions are for the most part comprised of dominantly nonagricultural States, such as Massachusetts, New York, Pennsylvania, and California (fig. 5).

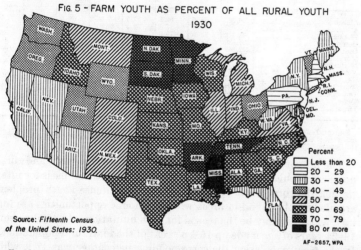

FIG. 5 - FARM YOUTH AS PERCENT OF ALL RURAL YOUTH
1930

Percent
Less than 20
20 - 29
30 - 39
40 - 49
50 - 59
60 - 69
70 - 79
80 or more

Source: Fifteenth Census of the United States: 1930.

AF-2657, WPA

In the dominantly agricultural States the problems of rural-nonfarm youth are closely related to the problems of farm youth. In the States that are primarily industrial, however, such as West Virginia, in which a large proportion of the rural population is engaged in mining, or Pennsylvania, which has both mining and manufacturing, the conditions confronting the rural-nonfarm youth may have little relation to agriculture.[20]

In the South race further complicates youth's situation. In 13 States Negro youth formed a considerable segment of both the farm and nonfarm rural youth population in 1930, although their residential distribution differed widely among the various States. On the whole, Negroes made up a larger percentage of the farm youth than of the nonfarm youth (table 5). In three States—Arkansas, Mississippi, and South Carolina—Negro youth comprised more than 50 percent of all farm youth. In two additional States—Georgia and

[20] For a discussion of industrial villages see Brunner, Edmund deS., *Industrial Village Churches*, New York: Institute of Social and Religious Research, 1930.

Louisiana—more than 40 percent of all farm youth were Negroes. Negro youth constituted as much as 40 percent of all rural-nonfarm youth in only one State, which signifies that the problem of the young Negro in rural territory is more likely to be localized on farms than in the villages.

Table 5.—Color of Rural Youth in 13 Southern States, by Residence, 1930

State	Rural-farm				Rural-nonfarm			
	Total		White	Negro	Total		White	Negro
	Number	Percent			Number	Percent		
Alabama	246,797	100.0	62.1	37.9	107,057	100.0	65.4	34.6
Arkansas	206,027	100.0	47.8	52.2	61,866	100.0	80.0	20.0
Florida	47,972	100.0	70.2	29.8	74,866	100.0	61.1	38.9
Georgia	267,889	100.0	58.5	41.5	115,440	100.0	63.0	37.0
Louisiana	152,863	100.0	54.2	45.8	78,849	100.0	65.0	35.0
Maryland	38,015	100.0	79.4	20.6	65,465	100.0	80.0	20.0
Mississippi	255,916	100.0	42.6	57.4	57,926	100.0	59.2	40.8
North Carolina	292,768	100.0	65.4	34.6	141,656	100.0	74.5	25.5
Oklahoma	187,114	100.0	85.5	14.5	95,855	100.0	89.7	10.3
South Carolina	172,764	100.0	43.2	56.8	91,066	100.0	62.5	37.5
Tennessee	215,544	100.0	84.7	15.3	90,743	100.0	85.9	14.1
Texas	438,507	100.0	69.7	30.3	191,624	100.0	75.0	25.0
Virginia	162,200	100.0	71.9	28.1	118,171	100.0	73.1	26.9

Sources: Bureau of the Census, *Fifteenth Census of the United States: 1930*, Population Vol. II, U. S. Department of Commerce, Washington, D. C., 1933, pp. 681–686; and special tabulation by U. S. Bureau of the Census.

The proportion youth form of the total rural, rural-farm, and rural-nonfarm population, respectively, affords an additional basis for interpreting the rural youth situation. The more intense youth problems are likely to be found in areas where economic opportunities are limited, whatever may be the reason for such limitation. In 1930 persons 16–24 years of age made up 16.4 percent of the total rural population.[21] In the farm population the corresponding percentage was 17.1, while for the nonfarm population it was 15.6. Thus, even at the beginning of the depression the nature of the population structure was such that the pressure of farm youth for employment opportunites was more acute than that of the nonfarm group within their respective areas.

REPLACEMENT RATES OF RURAL-FARM MALES

The replacement rate of males in a specified segment of the population provides an objective measure of the pressure of youth on the older age groups. This replacement rate is a percentage relationship between the number of males 18 years old and 18 to 64 years of age, inclusive. It is obtained by subtracting from the total number of males becoming 18 years of age in any given year the number of males becoming 65 years of age and the number of deaths during that year of males 19 through 64 years of age. The result is then computed

[21] Bureau of the Census, *Fifteenth Census of the United States: 1930*, Population Vol. II, *op. cit.*, pp. 599–600.

as a percentage of the number 18 through 64 years of age to secure the annual replacement rate (table 6).[22]

Table 6.—Replacement Rates of Males 18 Through 64 Years of Age in the Rural-Farm Population, 1920 and 1930

Item	1920	1930
Number 18 years of age	336, 827	363, 793
Number 65 years of age plus deaths 19–64	160, 165	162, 390
Excess maturities	176, 662	201, 403
Age group, 18–64	8, 363, 674	8, 263, 405
Annual replacement rate	2. 1	2. 4

Source: Woofter, T. J., Jr., "Replacement Rates in the Productive Ages," *The Milbank Memorial Fund Quarterly*, Vol. XV, 1937, p. 350.

The replacement rate is also a measure of pressure on opportunity, which in farming areas means pressure on the land. In the country as a whole the replacement rate for rural-farm males was higher in 1930 than in 1920, indicating that competition for opportunity between those becoming 18 years of age and those who were older was growing increasingly severe. This competition was particularly acute in three geographic divisions—South Atlantic, East South Central, and West South Central—in which replacement rates were considerably above the United States average in 1930 and in which a substantial increase in the rate occurred between 1920 and 1930 (table 7 and fig. 6).

Table 7.—Replacement Rates of Males 18 Through 64 Years of Age in the Rural-Farm Population, by Geographic Division, 1920 and 1930

Geographic division	1920	1930
United States	2. 1	2. 4
New England	−0. 1	0. 4
Middle Atlantic	0. 3	0. 8
East North Central	1. 4	1. 4
West North Central	2. 0	2. 0
South Atlantic	2. 6	3. 2
East South Central	2. 4	2. 8
West South Central	2. 8	3. 1
Mountain	1. 5	1. 7
Pacific	0. 5	0. 7

Sources: Bureau of the Census, *Fourteenth Census of the United States: 1920* and *Fifteenth Census of the United States: 1930*, U. S. Department of Commerce, Washington, D. C. Special tabulation from the Bureau of the Census for age 65 for 1920. The number of deaths 19 through 64 years of age was obtained by applying rates from Dublin, Louis I. and Lotka, Alfred J., *Length of Life*, New York: The Ronald Press Company, 1936.

The replacement rate varied widely among the different geographic divisions and States, the rates generally being much higher in those divisions and States that are agricultural than in those that are industrial (appendix table 5). Even in the Dakotas, prior to the visitation of the droughts, there were more than twice as many young men becoming 18 years old as could possibly be absorbed by the economic opportunities being opened through death and senescence.

[22] Woofter, T. J., Jr., "Replacement Rates in the Productive Ages," *The Milbank Memorial Fund Quarterly*, Vol. XV, 1937, pp. 348–354.

FIG. 6 - REPLACEMENT RATES OF MALES 18 THROUGH 64 YEARS
OF AGE IN THE RURAL-FARM POPULATION

1920

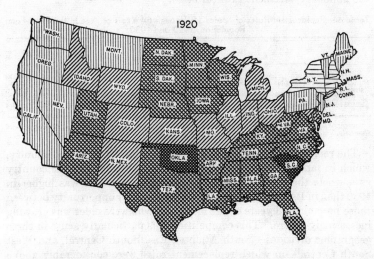

1930

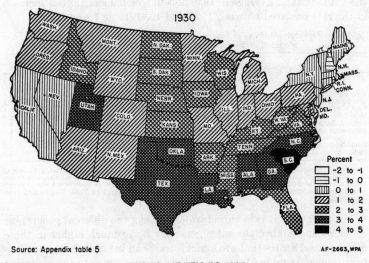

Percent
-2 to -1
-1 to 0
0 to 1
1 to 2
2 to 3
3 to 4
4 to 5

Source: Appendix table 5

AF-2663,WPA

RURAL YOUTH IN 1935

The number of rural youth increased about 13 percent during the 5-year period ending in 1935, reaching an estimated total of 9,991,600 (table 8). The increase was greatest in the industrial States of New England and in the Middle Atlantic and East North Central Divisions. The variation among the States ranged from a 1 percent decrease in South Dakota to a 30 percent increase in Nevada [23] (appendix table 6).

There were an estimated 6,107,000 rural-farm youth in 1935, which represented an increase since 1930 of 18.8 percent. This increase likewise was greatest in the three industrial regions, the New England, Middle Atlantic, and East North Central Divisions, and undoubtedly may be accounted for largely by the fact that numbers of families in industrial areas turned to the land during the depression.

Table 8.—Number of Rural Youth in 1930[1] and Estimated Number in 1935,[2] by Geographic Division and Residence

Geographic division	Total rural			Rural-farm			Rural-nonfarm		
	1930	1935	Percent increase	1930	1935	Percent increase	1930	1935	Percent increase
United States	8,844,643	9,991,600	13.0	5,140,910	6,107,000	18.8	3,703,733	3,884,600	4.9
New England	261,745	304,700	16.4	72,388	106,600	47.3	189,357	198,100	4.6
Middle Atlantic	856,346	1,002,100	17.0	249,071	365,000	46.5	607,275	637,100	4.9
East North Central	1,240,852	1,479,500	19.2	672,382	885,200	31.7	568,470	594,300	4.5
West North Central	1,232,814	1,329,600	7.9	834,861	910,100	9.0	397,953	419,500	5.4
South Atlantic	1,814,478	2,085,500	14.9	1,065,628	1,300,800	22.1	748,850	784,700	4.8
East South Central	1,272,379	1,433,500	12.7	912,120	1,056,700	15.9	360,259	376,800	4.6
West South Central	1,412,705	1,530,900	8.4	984,511	1,080,300	9.7	428,194	450,600	5.2
Mountain	365,483	393,100	7.6	186,701	206,600	10.7	178,782	186,500	4.3
Pacific	387,841	432,700	11.6	163,248	195,700	19.9	224,593	237,000	5.5

[1] Bureau of the Census, *Fifteenth Census of the United States: 1930,* Population Vol. II, U. S. Department of Commerce, Washington, D. C., 1933, p. 674.
[2] For method of estimation see appendix B.

The increase in the number of farm youth varied widely among the several States (appendix table 6). For example, although the increase for the United States as a whole was less than 19 percent, in Pennsylvania it was 51 percent and in West Virginia and Michigan it was around 48 percent. Virginia and Maryland likewise showed large gains. Kentucky and Tennessee in the Appalachian Area had the highest percentage increases in the number of youth on farms of all the South Central States. In the West, Utah, Washington, and Oregon likewise experienced a considerable increase in the number of farm young people.

The percent change in the number of rural-nonfarm youth during the 5-year interval was much less than for farm youth, particularly if Rhode Island and Nevada are excluded. Both of these States have unusual population characteristics which make the estimation of their respective nonfarm populations for 1935 exceedingly problematical. Though the other States presented variations ranging

[23] The New England States are not referred to specifically in the discussion of the increase in number of farm youth because there is some question about the accuracy of the 1930 Census of Agriculture for some of the New England States. The data for Connecticut are known to be incorrect. Though the percentages calculated are misleading, they are included for what they are worth to complete the tabulation. Their inclusion has no appreciable effect on the percent change for the United States as a whole.

from a 4.4 percent decrease in Idaho to a 16.8 percent increase in Delaware, the variation by divisions appears to have been very slight—only a little more than 1 percent (table 8). It would be hazardous to draw conclusions from the figures for the rural-nonfarm youth population since the estimates were made on a purely arbitrary basis.[24]

TRENDS IN THE NUMBER OF YOUTH AFTER 1930

The increase in the number of youth in rural areas, especially on farms, between 1930 and 1935 helped to accentuate the phenomenon which has been designated as the rural youth problem. The flow of young people from the farms to the cities that prevailed during the twenties was checked with the coming of the depression of the early thirties while greater and greater numbers of boys and girls were coming into the youth group (16–24 years).

There were probably about 700,000 more young people in the United States in 1935 than in 1930 (table 9). It is estimated that by 1940 the accretion will amount to twice that number (table 11, p. 20). The checking after 1930 of the cityward flow of young people which characterized the twenties was an impelling factor in changing the trend of the distribution of youth and contributed greatly to the increase of 1,150,000 in the number of youth in rural territory by 1935. There would have been 200,000 more youth in rural areas had there not been a net migration of youth from the farms to the cities of about that number. The tremendous increase of youth in rural territory was due largely to the "piling up" process on the land.

Table 9.—Youth Population of the United States, by Residence, 1930[1] and 1935[2]

Residence	1930	1935	Increase or decrease
Total	20,126,800	20,786,700	659,900
Urban	11,282,200	10,795,100	−487,100
Rural	8,844,600	9,991,600	1,147,000
Farm	5,140,900	6,107,000	966,100
Nonfarm	3,703,700	3,884,600	180,900

[1] Bureau of the Census, *Fifteenth Census of the United States: 1930*, Population Vol. II, U. S. Department of Commerce, Washington, D. C., 1933, pp. 598–600.
[2] For method of estimation see appendix B.

Exactly the opposite trend was manifest in the cities where the number of youth declined by more than 450,000 from 1930 to 1935. This decline in the number of youth in the cities during the depression did not prevent the rise of a youth problem of critical proportions, but the problem would have been even greater if there had been more young people coming in from the farms and if the birth rate in the cities had not dropped so precipitately some years ago.

The interfarm-city migration varied somewhat for individual years from 1930 to 1935 and involved in it was a considerable contingent

---

[24] For method of estimation see appendix B.

of young workers from industrial centers who sought refuge on farms.[25]
The movement of population from cities to farms was greater than
the reverse flow only in 1932, however.[26] Beginning in 1933 the
number going to urban centers has been greater than the outward
trek. Probably relatively few people who migrated to the cities in
1933 when the tide of migration first turned were youth going to the
city for the first time.[27] Furthermore, the movement of youth has
no doubt varied considerably the country over. Some indication of
the variation may be gained from a survey made in October 1934 of
the mobility of the rural and town population in 139 counties scattered over the United States. "Sixty [counties] reported the existence of significant population shifts at the time the survey was made.
In 35 of these the dominant movement was from open country to
villages and towns, in 13 it was from villages and towns to the open
country, while the 12 remaining counties reported the 2 types of
movement to be approximately equal in volume."[28]

Table 10.—Estimated Migration of Youth to and From Farms, by Geographic Division, 1930–1934[1]

Geographic division	Net migration of youth from farms, 1930–1934	Net migration of youth to farms, 1930–1934
United States	274, 300	77, 900
New England	—	17, 100
Middle Atlantic	—	42, 600
East North Central	—	18, 200
West North Central	78, 900	—
South Atlantic	55, 400	—
East South Central	43, 000	—
West South Central	75, 700	—
Mountain	20, 000	—
Pacific	1, 300	—

[1] Based on data from the U. S. Department of Agriculture, Bureau of Agricultural Economics.

The net migration varied considerably among the different geographic divisions (table 10). Thus, during the 5 years since 1930
apparently more youth migrated to than from farms in the New
England, Middle Atlantic, and East North Central States, reflecting
the shutdown in industry in these regions which forced people to take
refuge on the land. In Michigan, for example, youth 15–24 years of

[25] State Emergency Welfare Relief Commission, "Age, Sex and Employment
Status of Gainful Workers in Five Types of Communities," *Michigan Census
of Population and Unemployment*, Lansing, Mich., July 1936, p. 6. See also
Goodrich, Carter, Allin, Bushrod W., and Hayes, Marion, *op. cit.*, p. 62.

[26] Bureau of Agricultural Economics, *Farm Population Estimates, January 1,
1936*, U. S. Department of Agriculture, Washington, D. C., release of October 27,
1936.

[27] Baker, O. E., *The Outlook for Rural Youth, op. cit.*, p. 6.

[28] Division of Research, Statistics, and Finance, *Mobility of Rural and Town
Population*, Research Bulletin F–7, Federal Emergency Relief Administration,
Washington, D. C., April 16, 1935, p. 1.

age made up 17.2 percent of the total population in the rural townships in 1930 but in 1935 they made up 22.8 percent of the total.[29]   In the other divisions of the country, despite the limitations in industrial opportunity, youth were forced to leave the farms.   In the South Atlantic and East South Central Divisions, where the average farm income is notoriously low, and in the West North Central and West South Central States, where the ravages of drought and dust storms have been most severe, youth left the land in large numbers.   This movement in the 2 latter divisions conformed to the decline in the farm population in the 10 drought States between 1930 and 1935.[30]

Data gathered in North Carolina show that young people from relief families did not leave home as rapidly as did children from nonrelief families during the years 1931 to 1934.[31]

Evidence is conflicting in regard to the pattern of youth migration during the early thirties.   According to mobility studies in certain sections of Ohio it adhered to the general pattern of the twenties with respect to age and sex.[32]   Other evidence suggests that the young women have been remaining in rural territory in larger proportions than formerly and in greater proportions than the young men.   The increasing proportion of young women in rural relief households is one evidence of this.[33]   Moreover, the National Youth Administration reports show that during several months in 1937 there were more young women than young men employed by this agency.[34]

The increase in the number of rural-nonfarm youth between 1930 and 1935 was estimated at a little less than 200,000.[35]   It seems

[29] Calculated from base tables secured from the State Emergency Welfare Relief Commission, *Michigan Census of Population and Unemployment,* Lansing, Mich.

[30] Taeuber, Conrad and Taylor, Carl C., *The People of the Drought States,* Research Bulletin Series V, No. 2, Division of Social Research, Works Progress Administration, Washington, D. C., March 1937, p. 25. See also Goodrich, Carter, Allin, Bushrod W., and Hayes, Marion, *op. cit.,* p. 62; and Hill, George W., *Rural Migration and Farm Abandonment,* Research Bulletin Series II, No. 6, Division of Research, Statistics, and Finance, Federal Emergency Relief Administration, Washington, D. C., June 1935.

[31] Hamilton, C. Horace, *Recent Changes in the Social and Economic Status of Farm Families in North Carolina,* Bulletin No. 309, North Carolina Agricultural Experiment Station, Raleigh, N. C., May 1937, pp. 123–125.

[32] Lively, C. E. and Foott, Frances, *Population Mobility in Selected Areas of Rural Ohio, 1928–1935,* Bulletin 582, Ohio Agricultural Experiment Station, Wooster, Ohio, June 1937, p. 33.

[33] Melvin, Bruce L., *Rural Youth on Relief,* Research Monograph XI, Division of Social Research, Works Progress Administration, Washington, D. C., 1937, pp. 17–20.

[34] Division of Research, Statistics, and Records, *Report on Progress of the Works Program, December 1937,* Works Progress Administration, Washington, D. C., table 40, p. 65.

[35] The estimate for the rural-nonfarm youth was made on the assumption that there had been no migration from rural-nonfarm territory. See appendix B.

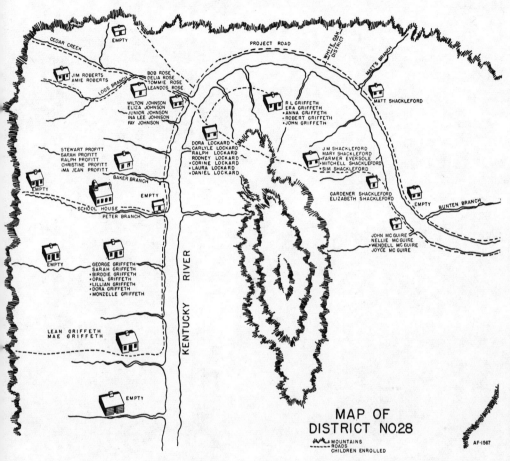

CEDAR CREEK

EMPTY

PROJECT ROAD

WHITE OAK DISTRICT

MATTS BRANCH

JIM ROBERTS
AMIE ROBERTS

LOGS BRANCH

BOB ROSE
DELIA ROSE
TOMMIE ROSE
LEANDOS ROSE

MATT SHACKLEFORD

WILTON JOHNSON
ELIZA JOHNSON
• JUNIOR JOHNSON
INA LEE JOHNSON
FAY JOHNSON

R L GRIFFETH
ERA GRIFFETH
• ANNA GRIFFETH
• ROBERT GRIFFETH
• JOHN GRIFFETH

STEWART PROFITT
SARAH PROFITT
RALPH PROFITT
CHRISTINE PROFITT
• MA JEAN PROFITT

DORA LOCKARD
• CARLYLE LOCKARD
RALPH LOCKARD
RODNEY LOCKARD
• CORINE LOCKARD
• LAURA LOCKARD
• DANIEL LOCKARD

J M SHACKLEFORD
MARY SHACKLEFORD
• FARMER EVERSOLE
• MITCHELL SHACKLEFORD
• SIM SHACKLEFORD

EMPTY

BAKER BRANCH

EMPTY

SCHOOL HOUSE

PETER BRANCH

GARDENER SHACKLEFORD
ELIZABETH SHACKLEFORD

EMPTY

BUNTEN BRANCH

EMPTY

EMPTY

GEORGE GRIFFETH
SARAH GRIFFETH
• BIRDDIE GRIFFETH
• OPAL GRIFFETH
• LILLIAN GRIFFETH
• DORA GRIFFETH
• MONZELLE GRIFFETH

JOHN MC GUIRE
NELLIE MC GUIRE
• WENDELL MC GUIRE
JOYCE MC GUIRE

KENTUCKY RIVER

LEAN GRIFFETH
MAE GRIFFETH

EMPTY

MAP OF
DISTRICT NO.28

MOUNTAINS
ROADS
CHILDREN ENROLLED

AF-1567

That mountain children must still go long distances to school is illustrated by this sketch of a typical school district in Kentucky. The distance from the McGuire house on the right to the school house on the left is approximately 5 miles. If the weather permits, Wendel McGuire can save about 2 miles by going across the mountain on foot or horseback and fording the river. Other distances are in proportion. Until recently the "Project Road" was little more than a narrow mountain trail, at times impassable, but it has been improved somewhat through the emergency work programs. The roads across the mountain and up the creek hollows are mere trails.

probable that the natural increase in the number of youth, that is, the aging of those 11–14 in 1930, on the fringes of the cities would by itself account for most of this. In fact, limited evidence indicates that there was a decline in the number of youth in agricultural villages. One study in Wisconsin states, "The depression has evidently sent village people to the farm and it has certainly kept farm young people from going to the village and city." [36]

Enumerations made in 45 agricultural villages during the summer of 1936 also showed that on the whole there had been a decline in the number of youth since 1930.[37] Had there been no migration from 1930 to 1936 there would have been 4,994 youth 15–19 and 4,910 youth 20–24 years of age in these villages in 1936, whereas the numbers were actually 4,379 and 3,568, respectively. Thus, for these two age groups there were only 88 percent and 73 percent, respectively, of the number there would have been without emigration. If this situation can be regarded as typical, the "piling up" of youth in rural agricultural territory has been largely on farms.

In 16 of the 45 villages a detailed study was made of the present residence of high school graduates of the classes of 1930–35. It was found that 62.9 percent of the graduates who were residents of villages at the time of graduation still resided in their own or other villages on June 1, 1936. On the other hand, of the graduates who were residents of the open country at the time of graduation, 73.4 percent were living in the open country on June 1, 1936.[38]

The studies of part-time farmers bear out the conclusion that the increase of youth in the rural-nonfarm population has been due to natural increase and not to the movement of youth from the cities to their peripheries. The part-time farming movement apparently has consisted largely of persons above the youth age.[39]

[36] James, J. A. and Kolb, J. H., *Wisconsin Rural Youth, Education and Occupation*, Bulletin 437, Wisconsin Agricultural Experiment Station, Madison, Wis., November 1936, p. 13.

[37] These are 45 villages selected from the 140 villages used by Brunner, Edmund deS. and Lorge, Irving for their study reported in *Rural Trends in Depression Years*, New York: Columbia University Press, 1937. Data on population will be given in a forthcoming monograph by Melvin, Bruce L. and Smith, Elna N., *Youth in Agricultural Villages*, Division of Social Research, Works Progress Administration, Washington, D. C.

[38] Melvin, Bruce L. and Olin, Grace E., "Migration of Rural High-School Graduates," *The School Review*, Vol. XLVI, 1938, table 3, p. 281.

[39] Salter, L. A., Jr. and Darling, H. D., *Part-Time Farming in Connecticut: A Socio-Economic Study of the Lower Naugatuck Valley*, Bulletin 204, Connecticut State College, Department of Agricultural Economics, Storrs, Conn., July 1935, p. 25. See also Beck, P. G., *Recent Trends in the Rural Population of Ohio*, Bulletin 533, Ohio Agricultural Experiment Station, Wooster, Ohio, May 1934; and Morison, F. L. and Sitterley, J. H., *Rural Homes for Non-Agricultural Workers— A Survey of Their Agricultural Activities*, Bulletin 547, Ohio Agricultural Experiment Station, Wooster, Ohio, February 1935.

The extent of cityward migration within the next few years will have much to do with the rural youth problem in so far as it may be defined as a pressure of people for opportunity on the land and otherwise. Without heavy migration from the farms there will be a greater "piling up" of youth on the farms by 1940 than in 1930 [40] (table 11). At the same time, without migration the number of urban youth will be almost 600,000 less in 1940 than in 1930. If the "piling up" in rural territory above the number in 1930 is not to occur, the cities must absorb between three and four times the decline that would occur in the cities without migration. In fact, without migration there would be almost 2,000,000 more rural youth in 1940 than in 1930. Even with the expected migration there will be over 1,000,000 more youth in rural areas in 1940 than there were 10 years previously.[41]

Table 11.—Youth Population in 1930 [1] and 1940 [2] With No Rural-Urban Migration Assumed for the Decade, by Residence

Residence	1930	1940	Increase or decrease
Total	20,126,800	21,526,800	1,400,000
Urban	11,282,200	10,696,200	−586,000
Rural	8,844,600	10,830,600	1,986,000
Farm	5,140,900	6,627,000	1,486,100
Nonfarm	3,703,700	4,203,600	499,900

[1] Bureau of the Census, *Fifteenth Census of the United States: 1930*, Population Vol. II, U. S. Department of Commerce, Washington, D. C., 1933, pp. 598–600.
[2] For method of estimation see appendix B.

[40] Because of the acceleration of migration during the later thirties, it is estimated that there will be somewhat fewer youth on farms in 1940 than there were in 1935. This decline, however, will have little effect on the current problem of population pressure on the land.

[41] Since data at hand show that some migration is in process, it seems reasonable to make certain assumptions from which to forecast the distribution of rural and urban youth in 1940. It has already been indicated that the net emigration of farm youth from 1930 through 1934 was almost 200,000. Assuming that one-third of the net migration from farms to cities was youth, there was a cityward movement of approximately 125,000 farm youth during the year 1935 and 150,000 during both 1936 and 1937. If 150,000 continue to migrate each year during the years 1938 and 1939, the total migrating for the 5 years, January 1, 1935, to January 1, 1940, will be approximately 725,000. If the 200,000 migrating between 1930 and 1935 are added to this number, an estimated total of 925,000 youth will have left the farms between 1930 and 1940. Subtracting this total from the estimated increase in the number of youth on farms between 1930 and 1940, assuming no migration, there will still be between 500,000 and 600,000 more youth on the land in 1940 than in 1930. At the same time there will be an increase of 500,000 rural-nonfarm youth. Thus, even with the expected migration of farm youth there will still be over 1,000,000 more youth in rural territory in 1940 than there were in 1930. For total number migrating see Bureau of Agricultural Economics, *Farm Population Estimates, January 1, 1936, op. cit.*; and Taeuber, Conrad, "Farm Population Decreases During 1936," *The Agricultural Situation*, Vol. 21, U. S. Department of Agriculture, Bureau of Agricultural Economics, Washington, D. C., July 1, 1937, pp. 17–18.

Chapter II

THE ECONOMIC SITUATION OF RURAL YOUTH

TRADITIONALLY, economic security in rural society has been measured by property ownership. Farm youth who expected to be farmers looked forward to possessing an adequate amount of land free of debt. Youth who were reared in villages expected to own some business or to attain a secure and relatively independent position in some profession or skilled trade. With the passage of time, however, such industries as lumbering, mining, and textiles were developed on a large scale in rural territory, and a wage-earning class was created. In rural America the trend in recent years has been toward dependence on wages for work. The idea of having a job has become dominant, particularly among the younger generation.

Any analysis of the economic situation of rural youth must recognize this trend as well as the traditional background both of the rural economic system and of the economic relationship between parents and children. The economic status of rural young people who are living with their parents and working at home can be but partially measured by money income, by property owned, or by whether or not they receive wages for their work. It must frequently be measured by the prospects for ultimately owning a farm or business in the community or becoming established in a profession, in a secure salaried position, or in a skilled trade.

Statistical statements concerning the number of unemployed youth, especially farm youth, in rural territory will not be of much value until the term *unemployment*, as it may be applied legitimately to rural people, is clearly understood. One discussion of methods of making unemployment estimates contains the following statement: "All family farm labour (employables in the farm family who work on the farm without receiving a stated wage) * * * are included as employed persons. Thus, gainful workers who have moved from cities to farms to live with and help their families and relatives, or to

21

engage in subsistence farming, are counted among the employed."[1] This definition of employed would include many farm youth in relief households who were working on the home farm. Moreover, it would consider as employed a mass of surplus rural youth just above the relief level who were working at home with little or no economic return, merely because they could not migrate. Furthermore, whether to include people who are working on subsistence farms as employed when they have no regular source of cash income is an open question.

Consequently, in analyzing the opportunities of rural youth for obtaining economic security it must be borne in mind that in rural territory this does not necessarily mean a job with wages. Many studies of youth have been made on the assumption that the job criterion was applicable to rural young people without qualification, and this has resulted in much confusion among the data of the various studies. In order to interpret the situation of rural youth fully, it is necessary to analyze such studies in terms of opportunities for farm youth to attain farm ownership or a satisfactory tenant status, if they remain in rural territory, or for village youth to become permanently established in some nonagricultural occupation. At the same time some attention must be given to the possibility of these youth finding security through migration to urban areas.

Rural youth may be grouped into three economic categories: (1) those gainfully and advantageously occupied or otherwise advantageously situated; (2) those who have remained above the relief level but whose situation is precarious; and (3) those who are at the relief level. Unfortunately, data are not at hand to show in any comprehensive quantitative way the number, residence, or occupation of those who belong to the first two categories, although objective information is available regarding their economic condition in general. Where rural conditions were particularly unfavorable, thousands of families were forced on relief, and it is from this group that the third category of youth is recruited. Considerable data are available for this latter group.

EMPLOYMENT AND INCOME

Farm youth between 15 and 24 years of age form the bulk of the unpaid family labor and a large proportion of the hired labor on farms, and these two categories comprise most of the agricultural workers within these ages (table 12 and fig. 7). To be specific, over 95 percent of all the young men 15–19 years of age and over 70 percent of those 20–24 years of age listed in the 1930 Census as agricultural workers belonged to one or the other of these two groups, which together totaled over 1,843,000 youth. By 1935 probably 500,000 [2]

---

[1] Nathan, Robert R., "Estimates of Unemployment in the United States, 1929–1935," *International Labour Review*, Vol. XXXIII, January 1936, p. 54.

[2] See ch. I.

more young men in this age group had "piled up" on the farm, which sharpened the competition for available farm labor jobs and no doubt greatly increased the number of unpaid family workers. It is significant that the predominant shift of the young men from unpaid family labor appears to come between the ages of 15 and 24 years and the shift from hired labor between 20 and 30 years. If the shift is not made from hired labor during this time, the young men tend to remain in that status.

Table 12.—Type of Employment of Workers in Agriculture, by Age and Sex, 1930

Age	Total workers		Farm operators		Unpaid family workers		Wage workers	
	Male	Female	Male	Female	Male	Female	Male	Female
Total	9,562,059	909,939	5,815,626	263,608	1,184,784	475,008	2,561,649	171,323
10–14 years	224,084	95,173	—	—	196,474	87,187	27,610	7,986
15–19 years	1,080,008	172,149	49,043	—	608,141	140,431	422,824	31,718
20–24 years	1,156,936	112,811	344,438	4,845	239,143	77,494	573,355	30,472
25–29 years	902,211	70,047	497,771	7,965	62,032	42,002	342,408	20,080
30–34 years	825,680	57,883	575,773	13,145	25,838	29,467	224,069	15,271
35–39 years	895,899	68,689	691,690	23,901	14,175	28,658	190,034	16,130
40–44 years	849,079	65,157	682,340	30,163	8,277	21,407	158,462	13,587
45–49 years	844,949	67,113	687,713	36,467	5,723	18,805	151,513	11,841
50–54 years	802,094	61,344	660,557	39,153	4,493	12,844	137,044	9,347
55–59 years	662,246	46,234	547,392	33,321	3,864	7,484	110,990	5,429
60–64 years	539,104	38,200	442,800	29,106	4,273	4,673	92,031	4,421
65–69 years	385,893	26,198	314,196	21,009	4,461	2,576	67,236	2,613
70–74 years	241,862	16,063	198,398	13,584	4,156	1,124	39,308	1,355
75 years and over	147,369	12,440	121,133	10,777	3,551	726	22,685	937
Unknown	4,645	438	2,382	172	183	130	2,080	136

Source: Bureau of the Census, *Fifteenth Census of the United States: 1930*, Population Vol. V, U. S. Department of Commerce, Washington, D. C., 1933, pp. 118 and 352.

Since a large proportion of all farm laborers are youth, data on the wages of farm laborers provide one measure of the income of farm youth. In 11 counties studied in 1936 the average annual earnings among male agricultural workers per county ranged from $178 among Negro cotton pickers in Louisiana and $125 among white workers in a Tennessee county to $347 among white laborers in Pennsylvania and $748 among orientals in Placer County, Calif.[3] In some cases this represented cash income over and above board and room but in a large proportion of cases board and room were not furnished. These data on low annual earnings of wage workers in agriculture are substantiated by monthly data published by the U. S. Department of Agriculture.[4]

The most common types of cash income of farm youth in southern New York were found to be: first, spending money or irregular contributions from parents; second, wages earned at home; third, receipts from the boys' own property; and fourth, wages earned away from

[3] Vasey, Tom and Folsom, Josiah C., "Farm Laborers: Their Economic and Social Status," *The Agricultural Situation*, Vol. 21, U. S. Department of Agriculture, Bureau of Agricultural Economics, Washington, D. C., October 1, 1937, p. 15.

[4] U. S. Department of Agriculture, *Agricultural Statistics, 1936*, Washington, D. C., p. 349.

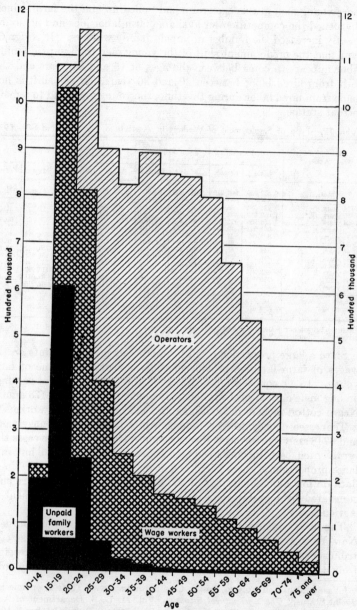

FIG. 7-NUMBER OF MALE WORKERS IN AGRICULTURE, BY
TYPE OF EMPLOYMENT AND AGE, 1930

Source: *Fifteenth Census of the
United States: 1930.*

AF·2619, W P A

home.[5] Only a very small percentage of farm boys have any understanding with their fathers respecting a definite return for their labor on the farm. Hence, an Iowa study made in the summer of 1934 of 1,107 out-of-school farm youth showing that only 286 of them reported that they received wages [6] does not mean necessarily that the remaining 821 were unemployed.

The employment and the income of rural youth, when used as measures of their economic welfare since the depression of the early thirties, generally show a widespread lack of gainful employment. In Tompkins County, N. Y., only 42 percent of the unmarried rural young men 15 to 29 years of age, not in full-time day school, were employed full time in 1935, leaving 58 percent employed part time, at home, or not at all. Indeed, 30 percent were unemployed or were working only occasionally. Even on farms 21 percent of the young men were unemployed. Of the total employed in both village and open country, farm laborers, unskilled laborers, and skilled mechanics were most numerous in descending order of importance. The average weekly earnings of the entire employed group were $13.[7]

Of 110 married young men in the same county 81 percent were employed full time, 11 percent were employed part·time, 3 percent were in school, 1 percent were occupied at home, and only 4 percent were out of school and unemployed.[8] "The average weekly earning of the 101 young men who reported weekly remuneration was $18 * * * 21 percent received less than $15 a week * * * 54 percent received between $15 and $24 a week * * *." Incomes of village youth were somewhat higher than those of farm and nonfarm youth of the open country.[9]

In 5 Connecticut townships the average money income of 282 unmarried rural young men and women, 182 of whom were out of school, was $221 for 12 months ending in the spring of 1934.[10] The range in average income of the young men was from $112 for those 16–17 years old to $378 for those 21–25 years old. The sources were

[5] Beers, Howard W., *The Money Income of Farm Boys in a Southern New York Dairy Region*, Bulletin 512, Cornell University Agricultural Experiment Station, Ithaca, N. Y., September 1930, p. 13.

[6] Starrak, J. A., *A Survey of Out-of-School Rural Youth in Iowa*, Committee on Education, Iowa State Planning Board, Des Moines, Iowa, 1935, p. 10.

[7] Anderson, W. A., *Rural Youth: Activities, Interests, and Problems, II. Unmarried Young Men and Women, 15 to 29 Years of Age*, Bulletin 661, Cornell University Agricultural Experiment Station, Ithaca, N. Y., January 1937, pp. 10–16.

[8] Anderson, W. A., *Rural Youth: Activities, Interests, and Problems, I. Married Young Men and Women, 15 to 29 Years of Age*, Bulletin 649, Cornell University Agricultural Experiment Station, Ithaca, N. Y., May 1936, pp. 10–11.

[9] *Ibid.*, pp. 18–19.

[10] Brundage, A. J. and Wilson, M. C., *Situations, Problems, and Interests of Unmarried Rural Young People 16–25 Years of Age*, Extension Service Circular 239, U. S. Department of Agriculture, Washington, D. C., April 1936, pp. 14–16.

work at home, work away from home, allowances, and gifts, including spending money. In addition to the money income many of the Connecticut young people had board, lodging, and clothing provided. The authors of the report remark that "the young people studied were well provided for from the standpoint of funds to care for their social and recreational needs." The question might be raised, however, as to whether the maximum average income here shown is adequate for a young man who wishes to marry. Even so, the situation in Connecticut at the time this study was made appears unusually favorable in the light of other studies and of the widespread rural destitution at that time.

A recent survey of unmarried young people conducted by the Cooperative Extension Service of the Department of Agriculture in Arkansas, Maryland, Iowa, Utah, and Oregon yielded significant data on employment.[11] Of the young men who were out of school, only 26 percent were not dependent upon their father's farm for employment; 36 percent were needed on the home farm and were operating it or replacing a hired man; while 38 percent were dependent on the home farm but were needed only for seasonal labor or were not needed at all.

In 9 townships in Ohio information was gathered in the spring of 1932 on 300 unmarried young men and women 16 to 24 years of age. "These young people were unable to obtain remunerative employment. Subsistence was essential. Even though these youth were of legal age and no longer in school their parental families stood willing to provide that subsistence, but not much more. In a few cases the parental business was in such a state that it could utilize the labor of such youth and pay wages. In most cases the young people were forced to be content with subsistence plus whatever else the parents felt able to give, which frequently was nothing at all."[12] This study also showed that only a small proportion (31 percent) of the young men not attending school received cash according to any definite plan.

The welfare of young people in such a category as that indicated above, while obviously not as problematical as that of youth in marginal or relief families, nevertheless presents a serious challenge.

Low incomes of youth may be a reflection of the "piling up" process discussed in the previous chapter. In a study made in Douglas

[11] Reported by Joy, Barnard D., Extension Studies and Teaching Section of the Division of Cooperative Extension, U. S. Department of Agriculture, at the conference of State leaders in charge of developing older rural youth programs in the State Extension Service, held during the annual meeting of the Land-Grant College Association, Washington, D. C., November 14–17, 1937.

[12] Lively, C. E. and Miller, L. J., *Rural Young People, 16 to 24 Years of Age, A Survey of the Status and Activities of 300 Unmarried Individuals in Nine Ohio Townships*, Bulletin No. 73, Ohio State University and Ohio Agricultural Experiment Station, Columbus. Ohio. July 1934, p. 7.

County, Wis., which is one of the poorest counties of the State,[13] unemployment was found to be serious among 857 young people 16–28 years of age.[14] About three out of four of these young people reported that they were unemployed at the time of the survey, the fall of 1934. They probably meant that they were not receiving wages. In Wood County of the same State, where 2,176 young people replied to a questionnaire in the winter of 1934–35, the proportions which were not self-supporting ranged from 88 percent for those 15–19 years of age to 39 percent for those 25–29 years of age. When the study was made, only 23 percent of the young men and 17 percent of the young women were employed with pay. This indicates a high percentage of idleness since only a little over 21 percent of the youth were in school.[15]

The economic handicap of youth in submarginal land areas, such as the cut-over regions near the Great Lakes, is typified by the case of the Harvey family. Three boys 15–25 years of age "worked out" whenever they could. During 1932 they worked in a logging camp and at odd jobs until they earned in all practically $100.[16] In Mc-Cracken County in the poor land area of Kentucky it was found that of 242 out-of-school rural young men 15–24 years of age, 173, or 71.5 percent, were farming at home and only 18.6 percent were farming away from home in 1936.[17] In Breathitt County of the same State data were gathered in 1935 on 104 young men and 75 young women. Only 13 were working for a cash wage although 121 were doing some work.[18]

These examples illustrate the situation in the poor land areas, but even on good land the effect on economic opportunities of the "piling up" of youth is also manifested. In Nebraska,[19] for example, it was found that of 6,232 young men, all but 437 of whom were 16–24 years of age, 4,449, or 71.4 percent, were working on the home farm in 1935.

[13] Kirkpatrick, E. L. and Boynton, Agnes M., *Wisconsin's Human and Physical Resources*, Research Section, Resettlement Administration, Region II, Madison, Wis., July 15, 1936, pp. 4, 12, and 17.

[14] Wileden, A. F., *What Douglas County Young People Want and What They Are Doing About It*, Rural Youth and Rural Life Series, Extension Service, University of Wisconsin, Madison, Wis., December 1935, p. 4.

[15] Kirkpatrick, E. L. and Boynton, Agnes M., *Interests and Needs of Rural Youth in Wood County, Wisconsin*, Rural Youth and Rural Life Series, Extension Service, University of Wisconsin, Madison, Wis., January 1936, p. 4.

[16] Kirkpatrick, E. L., Tough, Rosalind, and Cowles, May L., *How Farm Families Meet the Emergency*, Research Bulletin 126, Agricultural Experiment Station, University of Wisconsin, Madison, Wis., January 1935, p. 20.

[17] Woods, R. H., *A Study of the Status of Rural Youth in Ten Counties in Kentucky*, Heath High School, McCracken County, Ky., 1936, p. 1.

[18] Office of the County Schools, *Programs for Which Out-of-School Young People in Breathitt County, Kentucky Are Asking*, Jackson, Breathitt County, Ky., 1935.

[19] Nebraska Vocational Agriculture Association, *Summary of the 1935 State Study of the Educational Needs of the Out-of-School Group of Farm Boys in Nebraska*, Lincoln, Nebr., p. 1.

It has already been shown how the underemployment of young people in Iowa, one of the best agricultural States, has pushed itself into the realm of rural problems. Similarly in Michigan, "in the rural townships, over half of the male workers in the 15–19 year class and over one-quarter in the 20–24 year class were working without pay for relatives."[20]

These studies indicate that rural youth were probably receiving little return when working at home and, at the same time, had little opportunity to work away from home. Indeed, farm youth in dominantly farm territory are limited in the number of jobs they may be able to secure away from the farm. In Connecticut, however, where opportunities away from the farm are more frequent, only 37 percent of the young men studied in the spring of 1934 [21] were engaged in farm work away from home. Other leading occupations in order of percentage employed were road work, millwork, and day labor.

Lack of opportunities for earning more money obviously constitutes a serious problem among farm boys. Increased incomes for youth dependent on farms are inextricably linked with increasing farm income as a whole since many of the farms upon which these young people are living could not be increased either in size or in number of enterprises, "particularly because national policies emphasize agricultural conservation on a historical base."[22]

The situation of the rural young women who have been forced to remain at home is probably more precarious than that of the young men. The traditional job of the woman on the farm is housework or farm labor. The farm offers little else to the unmarried young woman although the villages do afford some opportunity for remunerative employment. Anderson found in Tompkins County, N. Y.,[23] that of 161 out-of-school rural young women who were single, 50, or 31 percent, had no work of any kind. The chief occupations of those working were homemaking, teaching, and office and stenographic work. He states: "Remunerative work for young women was scarce, and, if these figures are typical, the problem of employment was more difficult for young women than for young men." Of those considered employed, 49, or 30 percent, were doing housework, usually at home, and very few received regular wages.

Wileden points out, however, that in Douglas County, Wis., the average income of young women was more than twice that of young

[20] State Emergency Welfare Relief Commission, "Age, Sex and Employment Status of Gainful Workers in Five Types of Communities," *Michigan Census of Population and Unemployment*, Lansing, Mich., July 1936, p. 26.

[21] Brundage, A. J. and Wilson, M. C., *op. cit.*, p. 20. See also data reported by Joy, Barnard D., *op. cit.*, for young people in five other States.

[22] Joy, Barnard D., *op. cit.*

[23] Anderson, W. A., *Rural Youth: Activities, Interests, and Problems, II. Unmarried Young Men and Women, 15 to 29 Years of Age, op. cit.*, p. 11.

Learning to Farm.

Topping Sugar Beets.

men, $266 and $130, respectively, for the preceding year. This difference is accounted for by the fact that a considerable number of the young women in the upper ages were teachers.[24]

Young women are, on the whole, more dependent on the generosity of their parents than are young men. Thus, in Connecticut [25] only 2 percent of the girls reported receiving wages for work at home although 11 percent received an allowance averaging $87 for the previous year and 50 percent received gifts from their parents averaging $83 for the year. Of the boys 16 percent received wages for work at home but only 7 percent had an allowance and only 29 percent received gifts from their parents. The annual average from the latter two sources was $69 and $58, respectively. Eighty percent of the boys but only fifty-seven percent of the girls had incomes from wages for work away from home.

In Wisconsin one study showed that 65 percent of the girls depended on their parents for spending money and only 20 percent reported themselves as being economically independent.[26] Lively found in Ohio that 82.8 percent of the girls 16–24 years of age were not gainful workers.[27] It has been pointed out that the role of the girls in the tobacco and cotton farm families of the South is that of an unpaid servant.[28]

The restricted opportunities of young women in rural areas to obtain remunerative employment make their plight particularly distressing.

YOUTH ON RELIEF

The large number of rural youth who had to be assisted directly or indirectly by the Government during the depression of the early thirties indicates the seriousness of their situation. Probably not less than 2,000,000 rural youth have been members of relief households since 1930. The peak in the number of households on general relief was reached in February 1935 when approximately 1,370,000 rural youth—14 percent of all rural youth—were receiving aid.[29] By October of that year the number had declined to approximately 625,000.

[24] Wileden, A. F., *op. cit.*, p. 4.

[25] Brundage, A. J. and Wilson, M. C., *op. cit.*, p. 14.

[26] Kirkpatrick, E. L. and Boynton, Agnes M., *Interests and Needs of Rural Youth in Wood County, Wisconsin, op. cit.*, pp. 4 and 6.

[27] Calculated from Lively, C. E., *The Status of Rural Youth, 16–24 Years Old, in Selected Rural Areas of Ohio*, Preliminary Research Bulletin, Ohio State University and Ohio Agricultural Experiment Station, Columbus, Ohio, November 1, 1935, p. 4.

[28] Miller, Nora, *The Girl in the Rural Family*, Chapel Hill: University of North Carolina Press, 1935, pp. 50 and 61.

[29] Melvin, Bruce L., *Rural Youth on Relief*, Research Monograph XI, Division of Social Research, Works Progress Administration, Washington, D. C., 1937.

This did not mean that 700,000 youth became self-supporting, although the general improvement in agricultural conditions undoubtedly took some rural households containing youth off the relief rolls. The decline was chiefly due to the expansion of the Civilian Conservation Corps enrollment and to the transfer of rehabilitation families, among which were several hundred thousand youth, from the Federal Emergency Relief Administration to the Resettlement Administration.

Certain facts about the relief situation of rural young people provide a further basis for evaluating the economic problem presented by these youth. There was an increase between February and October 1935 in the relative proportion that young women constituted of the total number of youth on relief because enrollment in the Civilian Conservation Corps and most agricultural labor and other opportunities were available only to young men. During the same interval there was a tendency toward more concentration in the age group 16–19 years than in the age group 20–24 years, as such opportunities were more generally available to the older than to the younger age group. There appeared to be greater need for assistance to the youth in the villages than to those in the open country. This does not signify, however, that youth in the open country were better off economically than village youth. They may have been living on a mere subsistence level in the open country where some food could be produced on the land. As was to be expected, youth on relief were found in greater numbers proportionately in poor than in good land areas.

In relief families less than one-half of the young men and slightly more than one-tenth of the young women who were out of school had some employment. They were employed chiefly as farm laborers, domestic servants, and unskilled laborers.

Unlike urban youth most young men in rural areas and about one-half of the young women who were in the labor market had had work experience. This experience of rural youth on relief, however, was of such a limited nature that it qualified them only for jobs at the bottom of the occupational ladder.

EMPLOYMENT OPPORTUNITIES

Rural youth obviously must find their employment opportunities within the prevailing economic system. According to the American tradition the youth in agriculture climbs the agricultural ladder—that is, by beginning as a farm laborer, becoming a tenant, and then a farm owner. The village youth likewise progresses in some occupation, gradually attaining increased responsibility. Eventually he shares in a business and perhaps owns it or has a secure position in one of the professions or trades. Are the trends in rural life increasingly restricting the chances of youth to start at the bottom and climb these ladders?

Within Agriculture

Several factors have combined to make it more and more difficult for young people to pass up the rungs of the agricultural ladder. Chief among these are: (1) the growing burden of debt on farms; (2) the increase in tenancy; (3) the decreased demand for farm laborers; (4) the trend toward large-scale ownership of land; (5) the mechanization of agriculture; and (6) the development of areas of general agricultural maladjustment. These will be discussed in order.

Farmers are steadily losing the ownership of the land they cultivate. The equity of the farm operators dropped from 54 percent of the value of all farm real estate in 1900 to 42 percent in 1930. It is probable that this equity was considerably less in 1935 than in 1930. The equities of farm operators in 1930 ranged from an average of less than 30 percent in Illinois, Iowa, and South Dakota to an average of over 70 percent in Maine, New Hampshire, and West Virginia.[30]

Two kinds of debts burden the farmer—long-time and short-time. The short-time debts bear very heavy interest rates. Of the landlords interviewed in a study of landlord and tenant relations in the South, 52 percent had short-term debts. The interest rates ranged from 10 percent on Government loans to 15 percent on bank loans and 16 percent on merchant accounts. For tenants and croppers interest rates were still higher.[31]

The growing number of farms operated by tenants, especially in good land areas, makes it constantly more difficult for youth to rise on the agricultural ladder. A permanent tenant class is developing from which relatively few are able to emerge into ownership.[32] Tenancy has increased from 25 percent of all farmers in 1880 to 42 percent in 1935.[33] Between 1930 and 1935, depression years, the percentage of the total number of farms operated by tenants in the country as a whole declined slightly, but the actual number of tenants increased. Because the increase in the total number of farms was sufficient to offset the increase in tenants, the statistics show a slight percentage decline in tenancy.

This increase in tenancy seems to be occurring in all sections of the country. In the South, for example, "Since bad years outnumbered good in the 25 years ending in 1935, the net shift was down the [agricultural] ladder, with losses in ownership and independent renting and large gains in the helpless sharecropper class, fixing the insti-

[30] Turner, H. A., *A Graphic Summary of Farm Tenure*, Miscellaneous Publication No. 261, U. S. Department of Agriculture, Washington, D. C., December 1936, p. 1.

[31] Woofter, T. J., Jr., *Landlord and Tenant on the Cotton Plantation*, Research Monograph V, Division of Social Research, Works Progress Administration, Washington, D. C., 1936, pp. xxv-xxvi.

[32] National Resources Committee, *Farm Tenancy*, Report of the President's Committee, Washington, D. C., February 1937, p. 54.

[33] *Ibid.*, p. 3.

tution of tenancy more firmly in the southern agricultural organization." [34] In some sections of the South, such as the Mississippi Delta, the proportion of tenancy has now reached 90 percent; in the Red River Bottoms it is 80 percent; and in the Black Belt, 73 percent.[35] Some tenancy is not incompatible with a healthy state of agriculture, but when it reaches such high proportions, a serious condition begins to develop.

That the problem of tenancy was becoming serious for youth even before the depression is shown by a study in the Middle West. "In Wisconsin the farmers who acquired their farms 30 to 50 years ago were tenants, on an average, some 4 or 5 years. Those acquiring farms recently have been tenants 6 or 7 years * * *. In recent years, 1912–1922, somewhat over one-fifth of those reporting had been tenants 10 or more years. In Kansas the same change has occurred except that the early tenant stage of 4 years has stretched out to 9 years. In Nebraska, starting with about the same period of tenancy in the early years it has recently lengthened to more than 10 years."[36]

The difficulties encountered by tenants in becoming owners are paralleled by the even greater difficulties of farm laborers in moving to the next rung of the agricultural ladder. This is especially important in an analysis of the outlook for rural youth since they usually are destined to start on the lowest rung. As one author puts it, "The children of owner-operators [in the Cotton States] start in as laborers or sharecroppers at the bottom of the agricultural ladder, and in increasing numbers remain to swell the lower ranks. The rest of the country appears to become progressively less immune to the same general influences that render ownership difficult in the Cotton States." [37]

This condition is further illustrated by the fact that while the number of all agricultural workers in the United States declined 1.8 percent from 1920 to 1930, the paid agricultural laborers increased 17.0 percent. But in this interim the number of unpaid family laborers dropped 10.3 percent (table 13).[38] The increasing number of hired farm laborers between 1920 and 1930 was concomitant with the growing commercialization of agriculture, which is especially marked by intensive production requiring seasonal labor. Added to

[34] Woofter, T. J., Jr., *op. cit.*, p. 14.

[35] Odum, Howard W., *Southern Regions of the United States*, Chapel Hill: University of North Carolina Press, 1936, p. 61.

[36] Hibbard, Benjamin H. and Peterson, Guy A., *How Wisconsin Farmers Become Farm Owners*, Bulletin 402, Wisconsin Agricultural Experiment Station, Madison, Wis., August 1928, p. 33.

[37] Watkins, D. W., "Agricultural Adjustment and Farm Tenure," *Journal of Farm Economics*, Vol. XVIII, 1936, p. 469.

[38] The figures for 1920 and 1930 are not exactly comparable since the 1920 enumeration was made as of January 1, a slack time for farm labor, and the 1930 enumeration as of April 1, a peak period for farm labor.

this situation is the fact that the depression seemingly forced many persons who at one time were farm owners, tenants, or croppers into the status of agricultural laborers.[39]

Table 13.—Workers in Agriculture [1] in the United States, 1920 and 1930

Type of worker	1920	1930	Percent increase or decrease
Total	10,665,812	10,471,998	−1.8
Farm operator	6,479,684	6,079,234	−6.2
Farm laborer [2]	4,186,128	4,392,764	+4.9
Wage worker	2,336,009	2,732,972	+17.0
Unpaid family worker	1,850,119	1,659,792	−10.3

[1] 10 years of age and over.
[2] The figures for 1920 and 1930 are not exactly comparable since the 1920 enumeration was made as of January 1, a slack time for farm labor, and the 1930 enumeration as of April 1, a peak period for farm labor.
Source: Bureau of the Census, *Fifteenth Census of the United States: 1930*, Population Vol. V, U. S. Department of Commerce, Washington, D. C., 1933, p. 40.

During the depression the total number of farm laborers, including both wage hands and unpaid family workers, increased from 4,393,000 in April 1930 to an estimated 5,919,000 in January 1935.[40] In addition to the effect of the variation in the dates of the 1930 and 1935 Censuses, the number of hired laborers declined rapidly because of lessened demand. In 1935 there were only an estimated 1,646,000 hired laborers while unpaid family laborers had increased to 4,273,000.

The tendency for ownership of the land to become concentrated in the hands of corporate landlords also makes for an even larger number of laborers and tenants. Corporate ownership of land in Iowa, where this movement has been studied intensively, reached 11.2 percent in January 1937, an increase of 3.3 percent since September 1933.[41] In Emmet County, Iowa, in which it was estimated that over 70 percent of all farms were operated by tenants in 1936, 40 percent of all farms so operated were corporately owned.[42] In 1934, 14 percent of the land area of Montana was owned by corporations.[43] This represents an increase of 18 percent in this type of

[39] National Resources Committee, *Farm Tenancy, op. cit.*, p. 63.
[40] Bureau of the Census, *Fifteenth Census of the United States: 1930*, Population Vol. IV, U. S. Department of Commerce, Washington, D. C., 1933, p. 25; and Folsom, Josiah C. and Baker, O. E., *A Graphic Summary of Farm Labor and Population*, Miscellaneous Publication No. 265, U. S. Department of Agriculture, Washington, D. C., November 1937, p. 6.
[41] Murray, W. G. and Bitting, H. W., *Corporate-Owned Land in Iowa, 1937*, Bulletin 362, Iowa Agricultural Experiment Station, Ames, Iowa, June 1937, p. 95.
[42] Schickele, Rainer and Norman, Charles A., *Farm Tenure in Iowa, 1. Tenancy Problems and Their Relation to Agricultural Conservation*, Bulletin 354, Iowa Agricultural Experiment Station, Ames, Iowa, January 1937, p. 181.
[43] Renne, Roland R., *Montana Land Ownership*, Bulletin No. 322, Montana Agricultural Experiment Station, Bozeman, Mont., June 1936, pp. 17–29, and *Readjusting Montana's Agriculture: IV. Land Ownership and Tenure*, Bulletin No. 310, Montana Agricultural Experiment Station, Bozeman, Mont., February 1936, p. 17.

ownership between 1925 and 1934. In the Southeastern Cotton States large banks, insurance companies, and mortgage companies began to take over vast acreages during the boll weevil period through foreclosures. During the twenties the trend was well under way and the depression of the early thirties increased the corporation holdings still more.[44]

In addition, mechanization has been rendering unnecessary the presence of large numbers of unpaid farm laborers—the farmer's own sons—as well as paid laborers. With modern machinery the farm operator can manage more acres with less help than formerly, especially on the large commercial farms. While the total number of farms in Kansas, for example, rose from 166,600 in 1890 to 174,600 in 1935, the number of farms of 500 to 1,000 acres increased from less than 4,000 in 1890 to more than 15,000 in 1935. Farms of 1,000 acres and over increased from a few more than 1,000 to over 5,000 during the 45 years. At the same time the number of small farms, those having less than 50 acres on which little machinery could be used, increased, and the number of farms having 50 to 174 acres, those that would compete with the larger farms in commercial production, declined.[45]

The average amount of cropland per worker will continue to increase as the tractor and other power machinery are perfected and displace horsepower, if judgment can be based on what has happened in the past.[46] In 1930 there were about 920,000 tractors on farms, but by 1935 the number had increased to approximately 1,175,000.[47] Because of this mechanization process the agricultural output per worker increased 23 percent from 1919 to 1929.[48] For example, by 1933 in the wheat producing areas of the Great Plains only about 25 percent as much man labor was required to produce 1 acre of wheat as was required in 1919,[49] and the labor requirements of many other crops have also been sharply reduced.[50]

[44] Woofter, T. J., Jr., op. cit., p. 20.

[45] Bureau of the Census, United States Census of Agriculture: 1935, Vol. III, U. S. Department of Commerce, Washington, D. C., 1937, p. 96. Comparison of the number of farms with 50 to 499 acres was made for 1900 and 1935.

[46] Hurst, W. M. and Church, L. M., Power and Machinery in Agriculture, Miscellaneous Publication No. 157, U. S. Department of Agriculture, Washington, D. C., April 1933, p. 8.

[47] Cooper, Martin R., "Displacement of Horses and Mules by Tractors," The Agricultural Situation, Vol. 21, U. S. Department of Agriculture, Bureau of Agricultural Economics, Washington, D. C., June 1, 1937, p. 22.

[48] Ezekiel, Mordecai, $2,500 a Year, New York: Harcourt, Brace and Company, 1936, p. 24.

[49] Cooper, Martin R., "Mechanization Reduces Labor in Growing Wheat," The Agricultural Situation, Vol. 21, U. S. Department of Agriculture, Bureau of Agricultural Economics, Washington, D. C., April 1, 1937, p. 12.

[50] National Resources Committee, Technological Trends and National Policy, Washington, D. C., June 1937, pp. 99–101.

The mechanization of farming is a mark of progress in that machine labor is substituted for human labor. Since the demand for food products is relatively stable, little expansion of the demand for agricultural products can be expected unless there is a tremendous increase in their use in industry. Hence, what is to become of those whose labor is displaced by technological changes? Unless the present preoccupation with commercial agriculture is modified, only three courses seem open to these people: they may remain in rural territory at a low level of living; they may go to the cities, usually to work at miserably low wages; or they may go on relief or take jobs provided by one of the governmental agencies.

All of these trends in rural America, impinging on the steadily growing number of rural youth, have created a pressure for land and opportunity unprecedented in American history. Youth can no longer "go West." This pressure is becoming more and more severe in the face of already existing widespread areas of intensive economic maladjustments.

Early in the depression it was found that there were six extensive rural areas in the United States in which poverty was rampant, with 20 to 30 percent of the families in many counties on relief. These areas were: (1) the Appalachian-Ozark, (2) the Lake States Cut-Over, (3) the Spring Wheat, (4) the Winter Wheat, (5) the Western Cotton, and (6) the Eastern Cotton.[51]

The Appalachian-Ozark Area represents an extreme in maladjustment. Already overpopulated in 1930, particularly on submarginal land, both population and the number of farms increased between 1930 and 1935. In this area there was a migration to the land during the earlier years of the depression.[52] Here, too, many people who were in nonfarm occupations previously turned to farming.[53] For some time it has been recognized that the principal problems of the region as a whole involve the excess of population in relation to the economic opportunities available under prevailing conditions. There are large numbers of persons, particularly among the younger generation, who will welcome opportunities for employment elsewhere.[54] It has been estimated that the area has a surplus of at least 340,000 people.[55]

[51] Beck, P. G. and Forster, M. C., *Six Rural Problem Areas, Relief—Resources—Rehabilitation*, Research Monograph I, Division of Research, Statistics, and Finance, Federal Emergency Relief Administration, Washington, D. C., 1935.

[52] Goodrich, Carter and Others, *Migration and Economic Opportunity*, Philadelphia: University of Pennsylvania Press, 1936, pp. 73–74.

[53] Hamilton, C. Horace, *Recent Changes in the Social and Economic Status of Farm Families in North Carolina*, Bulletin No. 309, North Carolina Agricultural Experiment Station, Raleigh, N. C., May 1937, pp. 57–59 and 69.

[54] Gray, L. C. and Clayton, C. F., in *Economic and Social Problems and Conditions of the Southern Appalachians*, Miscellaneous Publication No. 205, U. S. Department of Agriculture, Washington, D. C., January 1935, p. 5.

[55] Goodrich, Carter and Others, *op. cit.*, p. 122.

The Cotton Belt with its excess of population is an area of disorganized agriculture, characterized by extensive waste of human ability and energy as well as of land and resources. It has been estimated that nearly 3,000,000 young people matured into the age group 15–25 years between 1930 and 1935 in the rural districts of 11 Southern States. "Hardly a half million of these stepped into places vacated by deaths of their elders, hardly a half million remained in school, about a quarter of a million are cared for in the increases in farms—mostly subsistence farms." [56]

Youth in the other three areas also face restricted opportunities because of general conditions. The Lake States Cut-Over Area is suffering on the one hand from an exhaustion of its natural resources and on the other from a turning to the land both of persons in the area previously engaged in nonagricultural occupations and of others induced to settle there by colonization promoters.[57] The two Wheat Regions belong to the drought area in which there is probably an excess of 900,000 people over the number who can profitably inhabit these Plains States.[58] This area has been characterized of late years by intensive distress and important fluctuations in population.[59]

The proportion of youth in relief families in these areas is generally high. In addition there is a mass of young people in marginal families, some on good land, more on poor land, but all continually on the borderline of distress. This large number of marginal youth is an impelling force operating to cause the spread of areas of maladjustment. Under present conditions the farm population of America is already above the maximum needed for maintenance of the agricultural output. Hence, unless unusual demands for labor develop in the cities, more and more rural youth may look forward to living only on a self-sufficing basis.[60]

Outside of Agriculture

Can the nonagricultural fields of employment absorb the excess number of rural youth? If these fields are to solve the problems of rural youth, they will have to provide employment in 1940 for ap-

[56] Woofter, T. J., Jr., "Southern Population and Social Planning," *Social Forces*, Vol. 14, 1935, p. 19.

[57] Beck, P. G. and Forster, M. C., *op. cit.*, pp. 11–15.

[58] Goodrich, Carter and Others, *op. cit.*, p. 243.

[59] Taeuber, Conrad and Taylor, Carl C., *The People of the Drought States*, Research Bulletin Series V, No. 2, Division of Social Research, Works Progress Administration, Washington, D. C., March 1937, p. 52.

[60] See Kolb, J. H. and Brunner, Edmund deS., "Rural Life," ch. X in *Recent Social Trends*, New York: Whittlesey House, McGraw-Hill Book Company, Inc., 1934; and Nelson, Lowry and Hettig, T. David, "Some Changes in the Population of Utah as Indicated by the Annual L. D. S. Church Census, 1929–1933," *Utah Academy of Sciences, Arts and Letters*, Vol. XII, 1935, p. 107 ff.

One Type of Seasonal Employment.

proximately 1,400,000 more rural youth than they did in 1930.[61]   Two barriers, however, stand in the way of absorption of this potential rural labor supply: namely, competition of the older age groups and the labor situation in the cities which is complicated by many factors.

During the depression of the early thirties industries kept many of their workers with families on part-time employment.   When industry began to pick up, naturally these part-time workers were put on full time and those who had been released but were still employable and available were taken back.   Consequently, many youth who had reached maturity during these years could not find employment.   This is one manifestation of the competition of youth with the older age groups which must remain intense for many years. Even for some years after 1944 the increase in the number of persons in the productive ages above 24 years will be proportionately more rapid than the decline in the number of youth.

The continued expansion of technology [62] is one force that constantly complicates the labor situation that rural youth face in trying to find employment in industry.   For rural youth technology acts as a two-edged sword.   The harvester-thresher combine, tractor, and corn-husker displace farm wage earners, but the industries that manufacture such machinery obviously do not absorb these same laborers. Unless there is a greater demand than now appears probable[63] on the part of industry for agricultural products to be used in manufacturing, displaced farm labor is forced to turn to nonagricultural occupations for a livelihood.   But at the same time the introduction of labor-saving machinery in industry inevitably forces men to seek other jobs.   Rural youth who go to the cities, therefore, find themselves competing with this displaced group for work.

The increasing advance of technology has made the expansion in production of manufactured goods possible but in recent years the introduction of new or improved machines has not been accompanied by increased employment.   In 1935 the volume of total employment was 18 percent below the 1920 level, but the volume of production was 14 percent higher.   Taking the employee man-years per unit of production in 1920 as 100, the unit labor requirement index in 1935 was 72.[64]   The trend toward restriction of the number needed to produce

[62] National Resources Committee, *Technological Trends and National Policy, op. cit.*

[63] *Ibid.*, pp. 103 and 133.   See also Goodrich, Carter and Others, *op. cit.*, pp. 404–408.

[64] Weintraub, David and Posner, Harold L., *Unemployment and Increasing Productivity*, National Research Project, Works Progress Administration, Philadelphia, Pa., March 1937, pp. 19–20.   See also *Federal Reserve Bulletin*, Board of Governors of the Federal Reserve System, Washington, D. C., January 1938, p. 44.

manufactured goods is further shown[65] by the fact that during the third decade of this century production in the manufacturing industries increased about 40 percent, but the number employed decreased about 2 percent from 1919 to 1929.

While such changes in productivity and employment must be qualified by the fact that over a period of time there are changes in the relative importance of different products and different industries, with their varying labor requirements,[66] they do show that the manufacturing field is not absorbing an increasing number of rural youth. Moreover, new machines and new processes are constantly being developed,[67] which will result in extensive changes in labor demands in the future. In the cases where the change involves displacement of labor, unemployed persons are continually being thrown on the labor market automatically to become competitors of youth seeking employment for the first time.

During the twenties much of the unabsorbed labor that previously would have gone into manufacturing turned to "service" industries—trade, professional service, public service, and personal and domestic service. In 1920 persons employed in the service industries comprised 30 percent of all those gainfully employed. By 1929 this percentage had risen to 38 percent of the total. Though this percentage fluctuated in the years following 1929, it had reached 42 percent by 1935.[68] Whether the long-time trend in this field can continue is an open question. On the other hand, the need for the services of more teachers, doctors, recreation leaders, etc., is unquestioned.

Technology is not the only force that has made it difficult within the last few years for youth of both country and city to obtain employment in nonagricultural occupations. In many localities the exhaustion of natural resources, such as timber and minerals, has left a substantial segment of the rural population in those localities without their chief source of income. Other localities have felt the effects of the increased tendency to substitute materials, such as scrap iron and plastics, for raw materials formerly in use and have consequently experienced a lessened demand for their products. The general economic depression also brought in its wake a decrease in demand for many manufactured articles as well as for many services, and the attendant widespread unemployment has exercised particular hardships on youth.

[65] Weintraub, David and Kaplan, Irving, *Summary of Findings to Date, March 1938*, National Research Project, Works Progress Administration, Philadelphia, Pa., 1938, p. 23. See also Goodrich, Carter and Others, *op. cit.*, p. 469.

[66] Weintraub, David and Kaplan, Irving, *op. cit.*, p. 23.

[67] Ezekiel, Mordecai, *op. cit.*, p. 20.

[68] Weintraub, David and Posner, Harold L., *op. cit.*, p. 26. See also Goodrich, Carter and Others, *op. cit.*, pp. 490–491.

In the South, where the oversupply of rural youth is especially large, the outlook for labor outside of agriculture appears inauspicious. The cotton factories that have afforded employment for youth as well as others from the country have apparently reached their peak in the number of workers needed.[69] "With few alternative avenues of employment the southern labor supply must take its choice of agriculture or the cotton mill * * *. The labor advantage has tended to mask in the balance sheets the symptoms of disorganization in the industry, and its factors of decadence thus have passed unnoticed and uncorrected." [70]

In a sample studied in Detroit, Mich., in 1934, 50 percent of the out-of-school youth were unemployed when the index of employment was higher than it had been for 4 years.[71] In a study of youth in Denver, Colo., in 1935, 27.5 percent were in school full or part time, but 31 percent were out of school and unemployed with only 19.1 percent employed full time.[72] Of the remainder 8 percent were employed part time and the rest were either occupied at home or were unable to work or attend school. In New York City an estimated 390,000 young people were unemployed in the 5 boroughs in 1935 with 140,000 of them never having had a job.[73]

It has been the experience of the United States Employment Service that it is more difficult to place youth than persons in the older age groups. Thus, for the year ending July 1, 1936, youth below 25 years of age constituted 34 percent of all applicants but only 21 percent of all persons placed.[74] Furthermore, of the total number of applicants those with past experience in agriculture, forestry, and fishing formed the largest segment. These facts reflect the widespread unemployment of rural youth.

The problem of unemployment of urban young people seems to be somewhat concentrated in the age group below 20 years. In the Michigan study of unemployment 25.3 percent of the male workers and nearly 21 percent of the female workers under 20 years of age in the 14 largest cities (first-class cities) were seeking work for the

---

[69] Allen, R. H., Cottrell, L. S., Jr., Troxell, W. W., Herring, Harriet L., and Edwards, A. D., *Part-Time Farming in the Southeast*, Research Monograph IX, Division of Social Research, Works Progress Administration, Washington, D. C., 1937, p. 90.

[70] Vance, Rupert B., *Human Geography of the South*, Chapel Hill: University of North Carolina Press, 1932, p. 297.

[71] Stutsman, Rachel, *What of Youth Today*, Detroit Youth Study Committee, Detroit, Mich., 1934, p. 46.

[72] *Survey of Youth in Denver*, University of Denver Reports, Vol. 12, No. 4, 1936, p. 10.

[73] Matthews, Ellen Nathalie, "Unemployed Youth of New York City," *Monthly Labor Review*, Vol. 44, 1937, p. 270.

[74] Computed from reports of the U. S. Employment Service.

first time.[75]   According to the survey of workers on relief made in
March 1935, 49 percent of all urban workers 20 years of age and
under were inexperienced workers in comparison with only 14 percent
of those 21 to 24 years of age.[76]   Such data are significant because
youth have supplied a large percentage of the urban-bound migrants
from rural territory.   Under present circumstances such migrants are
likely to find the labor market already glutted with young people of
their own age.

Undoubtedly there was an improvement in opportunities for the
employment of youth in urban territory prior to the business recession
of 1937–38, but it is well to examine the types of opportunities which
seemed to be most numerous.   According to the director of the
National Youth Administration for the State of Illinois [77] youth who
were willing to perform hard physical labor could find work.   In the
service fields, including hotels, restaurants, and household service
work, it was thought that about two out of three seeking such employment in the spring and summer of 1937 would find jobs.   The same
held true for factory employment, but only two applicants out of
every seven were considered likely to find employment in white-collar
jobs.   This suggests that the chief employment even in cities will
be unskilled labor.[78]   To rural youth will fall the lot of performing
the most menial and unremunerative types of labor in the cities
because their city cousins refuse to accept the pitiably low wages
paid for such work and because few rural youth are trained for skilled
work.

Even with a substantial increase in urban employment it is doubtful
if there will be a demand for workers approaching the available supply.
Faced with restricted opportunities in urban areas rural youth can
no longer solve their economic problems by leaving the village or the
farm.

[75] State Emergency Welfare Relief Commission, "Age, Sex and Employment
Status of Gainful Workers in Five Types of Communities," *Michigan Census of
Population and Unemployment, op. cit.*, p. 26.

[76] Calculated from data given in Hauser, Philip M., *Workers on Relief in the
United States in March 1935* (Abridged Edition), Division of Social Research,
Works Progress Administration, Washington, D. C., 1937, table 7, p. 15.

[77] Report based on a 30-day study of youth employment in Illinois by the
National Youth Administration.   Released for the newspapers June 8, 1937.

[78] Leybourne, Grace G., "Urban Adjustments of Migrants From the Southern
Appalachian Plateaus," *Social Forces*, Vol. 16, 1937. p. 242.

Young Loafers in a Mountain Town.

Chapter III

EDUCATIONAL STATUS AND
OPPORTUNITIES OF RURAL YOUTH

THE PRESENT educational system in America is based on the assumptions of the necessity for equality of opportunity, freedom of thought and inquiry, and the inevitableness of economic and social change. In this connection three fundamental questions are raised in this chapter: To what extent are rural youth being reached under our present educational organization? Are they being adequately prepared for farm living? Are they being adequately prepared for nonfarm living?

AVAILABILITY OF SCHOOL FACILITIES IN RURAL AREAS

The educational facilities available to large numbers of rural youth are meager. Paradoxically, the best and most adequate educational facilities are concentrated in areas where there are the fewest children in relation to the total population and where under present conditions there will continue to be the fewest children in the immediate future.[1] On the other hand, in the submarginal territory of the Appalachian-Ozark Area and in other parts of the South where the birth rates are high and the educational needs great, school facilities are far from adequate. The Southern States rank lowest in the value of school property per pupil enrolled, in the average salary of teachers, and in per capita expenditures for public day schools.[2]

This low ranking is due to the inability of these States to support education as there are great differences in the relative ability of the States in this regard. Some of the richest States have a per capita taxpaying ability at least six times greater than the poorest States. Mississippi, Alabama, South Carolina, Arkansas, Georgia, and Ken-

---

[1] Osborn, Frederick, "Significance of Differential Reproduction for American Educational Policy," *Social Forces*, Vol. 14, 1935, pp. 23–32.

[2] Odum, Howard W., *Southern Regions of the United States*, Chapel Hill: University of North Carolina Press, 1936, pp. 103 and 105. See also *Report of the Advisory Committee on Education*, Washington, D. C., 1938.

tucky, all highly rural States, are at the bottom of the list in taxpaying ability. It is, therefore, not surprising to learn that they rank 44th, 45th, 40th, 48th, 47th, and 42d, respectively, in opportunity for education as reflected in per pupil expenditures.[3]

In many States it would require more than 100 percent of the available tax resources to bring the amount spent per child for education even up to the national average. The disparities among communities in ability to cope adequately with the burden of child care and education are apparent when the distribution of the national income is considered. The farmers of the Southeastern States have to support more than 13 percent of the Nation's children 5–17 years of age but receive only 2.2 percent of the national income, whereas the adult nonfarm population of the Northeastern States supports only about twice as many children (27 percent) on its share of the national income which is almost 42 percent.[4]

Table 14 shows concretely that rural areas are at a marked disadvantage in comparison with urban areas with regard to school expenditures and length of school term. Moreover, the South Atlantic, East South Central, and West South Central Divisions lag behind the others.

Accessibility of high school facilities is reflected in part by statistics on enrollment in rural public high schools. In 1930 about 30 percent of the rural population in the United States 14–17 years of age, inclusive, were in high schools in rural communities.[5] This percentage varied considerably among the States for several reasons. In the New England and Middle Atlantic States town and city schools are frequently readily accessible to rural youth. Consequently, on the whole, they do not attend rural high schools in the same proportion as in some other States. It has been estimated that 13 percent of the enrollment in the urban high schools of the country come from rural territory.[6] The percentage of rural youth 14–17 years of age in rural high schools in 1930 was above the United States figure in the States of the East North Central and West North Central Divisions except in Wisconsin which barely approximated it. Rural schools are more readily accessible in these States than in some of the other States.

[3] *Hearings Before the Committee on Education and Labor, United States Senate,* 75th Cong., 1st sess., on S. 419, "A Bill to Promote the General Welfare Through the Appropriation of Funds to Assist the States and Territories in Providing More Effective Programs of Public Education," p. 23.

[4] National Resources Committee, *The Problems of a Changing Population,* Washington, D. C., May 1938, pp. 206–207.

[5] Gaumnitz, W. H., "The Place of the Small School in American Secondary Education," *Economical Enrichment of the Small Secondary-School Curriculum,* Department of Rural Education, National Education Association, Washington, D. C., 1934, p. 16.

[6] *Ibid.,* p. 15.

The Mountain and Pacific States with the exception of New Mexico and Arizona also exceeded the national average, but most of the South Atlantic, East South Central, and West South Central States were considerably below the average. In these States there are not enough high schools to care for all youth. Moreover, in many sections of these States the lack of transportation facilities makes school attendance at a distance impracticable.[7] Walking long distances day after day is not conducive to sustained school attendance.

Negro youth in rural territory are especially handicapped by lack of available high schools. The United States Office of Education estimated that in the early 1930's at least 900,000 Negroes of high school age were not in school. In two States—Arkansas and Mississippi—

Table 14.—Comparative Average Expenditure per Pupil and Length of Session in Urban and Rural Schools, by Geographic Division, 1933–34

Geographic division and residence	Number of counties, towns, and parishes reporting rural schools and number of urban school systems	Total current expenses per pupil	Average number of days in school session
UNITED STATES			
·Urban	145	$86.42	181.7
Rural	440	43.10	156.2
NEW ENGLAND			
Urban	11	106.96	185.6
Rural	83	78.47	174.9
MIDDLE ATLANTIC			
Urban	11	121.69	189.3
Rural	12	75.02	177.4
EAST NORTH CENTRAL			
Urban	23	85.30	178.6
Rural	43	62.46	167.7
WEST NORTH CENTRAL			
Urban	18	79.86	182.2
Rural	70	64.31	167.2
SOUTH ATLANTIC			
Urban	10	49.96	174.3
Rural	55	31.16	149.9
EAST SOUTH CENTRAL			
Urban	10	50.13	179.9
Rural	81	24.66	144.0
WEST SOUTH CENTRAL			
Urban	14	54.27	176.9
Rural	21	34.39	159.1
MOUNTAIN			
Urban	26	75.81	178.6
Rural	54	77.83	175.2
PACIFIC			
Urban	22	105.32	183.2
Rural	21	73.41	176.8

Source: Herlihy, Lester B., "Urban and Rural School Expenditures," *School Life*, Vol. 21, 1936, p. 272.

[7] For the situation in southwestern Texas in 1924–25, see Works, George A. and Others, *Organization and Administration*, Texas Educational Survey Report, Vol. I, Texas Educational Survey Commission, Austin, Tex., 1925, p. 224.

only 4.7 percent of the Negro population of high school age are actually enrolled in high school. In 5 other Southern States the percent is below 10. In 15 Southern States there are 230 counties having a population of 159,000 Negroes 15–19 years of age and having no high school facilities for colored pupils within their boundaries. In the same States there are 195 more counties, with nearly 200,000 Negroes of high school age, which have no 4-year high schools for Negroes.[8]

The effect of lack of educational opportunity is reflected not only in general statistics on school attendance but also in specific instances. The situation in Breathitt County, Ky., is typical of a large section of the mountainous, submarginal Appalachian Area. During the 5-year period, 1931–36, more than 2,000 of the 2,443 youth who finished the elementary schools of Breathitt County did not go to high school because of their poverty and the difficulty of reaching the 1 county high school.[9]

In areas where facilities are available, a large proportion of all rural youth attend school.[10] Of 300 young unmarried persons 16–24 years of age interviewed in rural Ohio in the spring of 1932,[11] 179 were still in school, including practically all who were 16 years of age. Over 50 percent of those out of school were high school graduates. A study in a number of rural counties in Indiana showed a substantial relationship between attendance and the adequacy with which high schools are provided when measured on the basis either of population or of area.[12] Hence it may be assumed that given adequate opportunity for public school attendance a substantial proportion of persons of school age will take advantage of this opportunity if they can possibly do so. There are always some, however, who, like 50 percent of the out-of-school youth interviewed in Taylor County, Wis., will be unable to go on to school because of "lack of funds" while others will be "needed at home" and therefore cannot continue their education.[13]

[8] Caliver, Ambrose, *Secondary Education for Negroes*, Bulletin, 1932, No. 17, National Survey of Secondary Education, Monograph No. 7, U. S. Department of the Interior, Office of Education, Washington, D. C., 1933, pp. 14–15 and 27.

[9] Gooch, Wilbur I. and Keller, Franklin J., "Breathitt County in the Southern Appalachians," *Occupations*, Vol. XIV, 1936, p. 1027.

[10] Dawson, Howard A., *Satisfactory Local School Units*, Field Study No. 7, Division of Surveys and Field Studies, George Peabody College for Teachers, Nashville, Tenn., 1934, pp. 31–32.

[11] Lively, C. E. and Miller, L. J., *Rural Young People, 16 to 24 Years of Age, A Survey of the Status and Activities of 300 Unmarried Individuals in Nine Ohio Townships*, Bulletin No. 73, Ohio State University and Ohio Agricultural Experiment Station, Columbus, Ohio, July 1934, pp. 7–8.

[12] *Report of the Indiana Rural Education Survey Committee*, Indianapolis, Ind., March 1926, pp. 26–32.

[13] Gessner, Amy A., *Young People in Taylor County*, Rural Youth and Rural Life Series, Extension Service, University of Wisconsin, Madison, Wis., October 1936, p. 5.

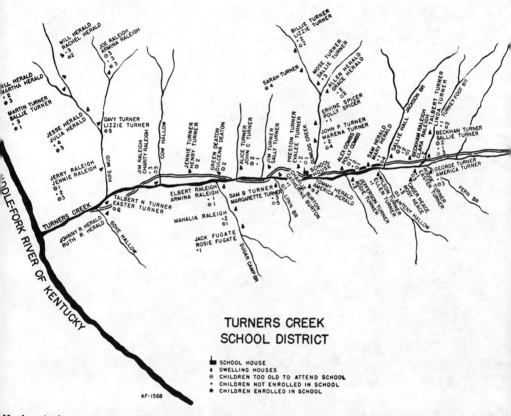

TURNERS CREEK
SCHOOL DISTRICT

▪ SCHOOL HOUSE
▲ DWELLING HOUSES
⊕ CHILDREN TOO OLD TO ATTEND SCHOOL
• CHILDREN NOT ENROLLED IN SCHOOL
✳ CHILDREN ENROLLED IN SCHOOL

AF-1568

Nowhere is the pressure of population on physical resources more clearly demonstrated than in Turners Creek School District. Thirty years ago this small valley provided a meager living for four families. Now worn-out, eroded hillsides, denuded of their forest cover 2 decades ago, and the narrow valley must give sustenance to almost 10 times that number since there is practically no means of securing supplemental income.

SCHOOL ATTENDANCE OF RURAL YOUTH

Largely as a result of differences in educational facilities, rural youth do not attend school to the same extent as do urban youth. During the school year 1929–30 more than 6 out of every 10 youth 16 and 17 years of age in urban territory were attending school in comparison with little more than 5 out of every 10 in rural territory (table 15). More urban than rural youth in the older ages also were attending school. Boys were in school to a greater extent than girls in urban areas while the reverse was true in rural areas. The only group in which rural youth were on an equal footing with urban youth with respect to school attendance was among girls 18–20 years of age.

Table 15.—School Attendance of Youth 16 Through 20 Years of Age, by Residence and Sex, 1929–30

Residence and sex	Age in years			
	16–17		18–20	
	Total number	Percent attending school	Total number	Percent attending school
Total urban	2,373,283	60.5	3,744,064	22.5
Male	1,149,003	62.2	1,736,338	25.4
Female	1,224,280	58.9	2,007,726	20.0
Total rural	2,289,854	53.9	3,071,646	19.9
Male	1,190,067	51.1	1,594,208	19.1
Female	1,099,787	56.9	1,477,438	20.9
Rural-farm	1,432,010	52.0	1,838,904	19.1
Male	766,663	48.1	990,221	17.3
Female	665,347	56.5	848,683	21.2
Rural-nonfarm	857,844	57.2	1,232,742	21.3
Male	423,404	56.6	603,987	22.0
Female	434,440	57.7	628,755	20.6

Source: Bureau of the Census, *Fifteenth Census of the United States: 1930*, Population Vol. II, U. S. Department of Commerce, Washington, D. C., 1933, p. 1099.

The situation with regard to high school attendance is even more unfavorable to rural youth than is total school attendance.[14] According to a recent report, "In urban areas (1931–32) one school child in four was attending high school, while in rural areas only one in seven of the school population was in high school. The difference is a product primarily of difference in opportunity rather than difference in native ability or even in interest."[15]

Comparison of school attendance in 1929–30 of rural-farm youth 16 and 17 years of age and of rural-nonfarm youth of the same age shows the advantage to be with nonfarm youth in all geographic divisions of the United States except the South Atlantic and the East South

[14] Gaumnitz, W. H., *op. cit.*, pp. 15–17.
[15] *Human Resources*, report submitted to the National Resources Committee by the American Council on Education, Washington, D. C., January 1936, pp. 55–56.

84015°—38——5

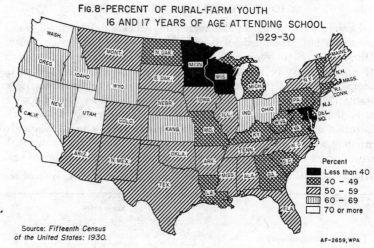

FIG. 8-PERCENT OF RURAL-FARM YOUTH
16 AND 17 YEARS OF AGE ATTENDING SCHOOL
1929-30

Percent
- Less than 40
- 40 – 49
- 50 – 59
- 60 – 69
- 70 or more

Source: *Fifteenth Census
of the United States: 1930.*

AF-2659, WPA

Central (appendix table 7). Among the 18- to 20-year-olds farm
youth had the advantage in school attendance in the South Atlantic,
Mountain, and Pacific Divisions.

In some States the difference between the two rural groups in school
attendance was marked. In Michigan, for example, 62.2 percent of
the nonfarm 16- and 17-year-olds were attending school in 1929–30
while only 47.5 percent of the farm youth of the same age were in
school (figs. 8 and 9 and appendix table 7). An even greater discrepancy existed in Minnesota where 70.9 percent of the nonfarm
youth but only 39.9 percent of the farm youth were in school. In
both States the proportion of nonfarm youth in school exceeded the

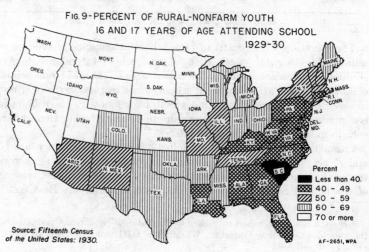

FIG. 9-PERCENT OF RURAL-NONFARM YOUTH
16 AND 17 YEARS OF AGE ATTENDING SCHOOL
1929-30

Percent
- Less than 40
- 40 – 49
- 50 – 59
- 60 – 69
- 70 or more

Source: *Fifteenth Census
of the United States: 1930.*

AF-2651, WPA

United States average while the proportion of farm youth was well below the average. In the Northern States, in general, where a large percentage of the rural-nonfarm population is concentrated in agricultural villages and in areas immediately surrounding the cities, rural-nonfarm youth were attending school in greater relative numbers than were rural-farm youth.

The various States show a wide disparity with respect to the percentage of farm youth attending school. In Minnesota and Wisconsin, where much of the Cut-Over Area is located, 39.9 and 34.3 percent, respectively, of the farm youth 16 and 17 years of age were in school in 1929–30. The only other State in which the proportion in school was less than 40 percent was Maryland (37.0 percent), largely because of the low attendance rate among Negroes. The highest percentages were in Utah (80.0 percent), Washington (72.1 percent), and California (71.8 percent).

In most of the southeastern section of the United States, comprising the South Atlantic and East South Central Divisions, the school attendance of the 16–17 year old farm group was below the national average of 52.0 percent. Exceptions were Florida, Tennessee, and Mississippi.

Negro youth in rural areas were at an especially great disadvantage with respect to school attendance. According to the 1930 Census only 46.4 percent of Negro farm youth 16 and 17 years of age and 39.7 percent of the nonfarm youth of that age were in school.[16]

School attendance alone does not measure the educational situation since many rural youth, particularly in the South, are greatly retarded. While in such States as Minnesota and Wisconsin most of the youth 16 and 17 years of age attending school are in high school, in Georgia and South Carolina or Tennessee and Mississippi many youth in this age group, white as well as Negro, are still in the grades. In fact, in Wisconsin in 1930 over 30 percent of the rural youth 14–17 years of age were in high school in comparison with only 15 percent in Georgia.[17]

ILLITERACY AMONG RURAL YOUTH

The educational situation of rural youth is clearly revealed by the incidence of illiteracy.[18] About 1 in 20 rural-farm youth 15–24 years of age was illiterate in 1930. The comparable proportion for the rural-nonfarm group was 1 in 33 (appendix table 8). In contrast less than 1 in 100 urban youth 15–24 years of age was illiterate in 1930.

Illiteracy is especially prevalent in the States with large reservoirs of surplus youth and with large numbers of Negro or Mexican youth (figs. 10 and 11). In the South Atlantic States over 8 percent of all

[16] Bureau of the Census, *Fifteenth Census of the United States: 1930*, Population Vol. II, U. S. Department of Commerce, Washington, D. C., 1933, table 10.

[17] Gaumnitz, W. H., *op. cit.*, p. 16.

[18] The U. S. Bureau of the Census defines as illiterate any person 10 years of age and over who is not able to read and write, either in English or in some other language.

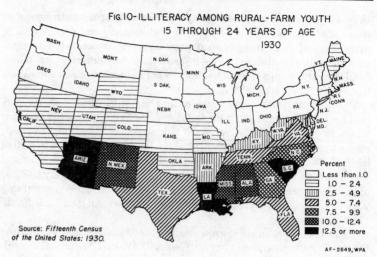

Fig. 10-ILLITERACY AMONG RURAL-FARM YOUTH
15 THROUGH 24 YEARS OF AGE
1930

Percent
☐ Less than 1.0
1.0 — 2.4
2.5 — 4.9
5.0 — 7.4
7.5 — 9.9
10.0 — 12.4
■ 12.5 or more

Source: *Fifteenth Census
of the United States: 1930.*

AF-2649, WPA

rural-farm youth 15–24 years of age were illiterate in 1930. More than 1 out of every 10 youth on farms in South Carolina, Alabama, Mississippi, Louisiana, New Mexico, and Arizona were illiterate. Percentages of illiteracy among nonfarm youth in these same States were also far above the average. Except in the three Southern and the Mountain Divisions illiteracy rates were slightly higher among rural-nonfarm than among rural-farm youth.

The increased school attendance during the decade prior to 1930 had an important effect in reducing the incidence of illiteracy in the younger age group in comparison with those 20–24 years of age in 1930 (table 16). Moreover, since 1930 the work of the adult educa-

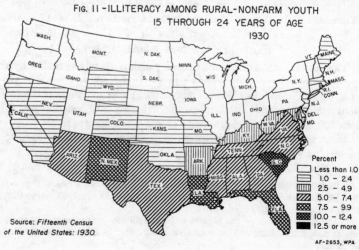

FIG. 11 -ILLITERACY AMONG RURAL-NONFARM YOUTH
15 THROUGH 24 YEARS OF AGE
1930

Percent
☐ Less than 1.0
1.0 — 2.4
2.5 — 4.9
5.0 — 7.4
7.5 — 9.9
10.0 — 12.4
■ 12.5 or more

Source: *Fifteenth Census
of the United States: 1930.*

AF-2653, WPA

tion program of the Works Progress Administration and the education program of the Civilian Conservation Corps, as well as locally sponsored programs, have contributed to reducing illiteracy among young people in rural areas.[19]

Table 16.—Illiteracy Among Rural Youth 15 Through 24 Years of Age, by Residence, 1930

Residence	Age in years			
	15–19		20–24	
	Total number	Percent illiterate	Total number	Percent illiterate
Total rural	5, 536, 704	3. 3	4, 450, 070	4. 9
Rural-farm	3, 420, 969	4. 0	2, 434, 241	5. 9
Rural-nonfarm	2, 115, 735	2. 3	2, 015, 829	3. 7

Source: Bureau of the Census, *Fifteenth Census of the United States: 1930,* Population Vol. II, U. S. Department of Commerce, Washington, D. C., 1933, p. 1227.

EDUCATIONAL ATTAINMENTS OF OUT-OF-SCHOOL RURAL YOUTH

Farm youth apparently attend school less regularly and leave school earlier than village youth, especially in dominantly agricultural areas. Consequently, they have a lower grade attainment than rural-nonfarm youth. In five counties of Wisconsin 71.3 percent of the young men on farms, 20–25 years of age, had not completed any work above the eighth grade in comparison with only 30.0 percent among village young men. Among farm young women 60.2 percent in contrast to 21.0 percent of the village young women had completed only the eighth grade or less.[20] The lower grade attainment of farm youth is substantiated by other studies in Wisconsin [21] and in Iowa.[22]

As indicated by the data for Wisconsin, young men in rural America do not receive as much formal education as do young women. A recent study of unmarried youth in Tompkins County, N. Y., revealed that 72 percent of the single young men in comparison with 81 per-

[19] The Education Division of the Works Progress Administration estimated in September 1937 that the literacy program had reached approximately 200,000 persons of all ages in rural areas (based on unpublished data). The Education Division of the Civilian Conservation Corps reported that 2.7 percent of the enrollees between April 1 and October 1, 1936, were illiterate, amounting to approximately 9,000 men. This percentage has remained practically constant among enrollees of the past year.

[20] James, J. A. and Kolb, J. H., *Wisconsin Rural Youth, Education and Occupation,* Bulletin 437, Wisconsin Agricultural Experiment Station, Madison, Wis., November 1936, p. 5.

[21] Kirkpatrick, E. L. and Boynton, Agnes M., *Interests and Needs of Rural Youth in Wood County, Wisconsin,* Rural Youth and Rural Life Series, Extension Service, University of Wisconsin, Madison, Wis., January 1936, p. 3.

[22] Starrak, J. A., *A Survey of Out-of-School Rural Youth in Iowa,* Committee on Education, Iowa State Planning Board, Des Moines, Iowa, 1935, table VII.

cent of the single young women 15–29 years of age, who were out of school, had received some high school or college training.[23]   Surveys made in both Waushara County [24] and Wood County,[25] Wis., as well as in Ohio [26] and Virginia,[27] give further evidence of the fact that young women in rural areas tend to stay in school longer than young men.

The poor land areas show the worst conditions with respect to educational attainment.   Data gathered from seven southern Appalachian counties show that 54.0 percent of the out-of-school rural youth 16–18 years of age in 1932 had not gone beyond the sixth grade and 93.4 percent had not gone beyond the eighth grade (table 17).[28]

Table 17.—Grade Completed by Out-of-School Youth in 7 Submarginal Counties,[1] by Age, 1932

Age	Total		Grade completed									
	Number	Percent	3 or less	4	5	6	7	8	9	10	11	12
Total___	1,165	100.0	9.3	13.4	13.1	18.2	23.7	15.7	2.6	1.4	2.3	0.3
16 years_____	381	100.0	13.6	15.8	13.1	16.5	22.3	14.2	2.1	1.3	0.8	0.3
17 years_____	413	100.0	8.7	13.8	13.6	18.4	25.7	14.3	1.9	1.5	1.9	0.2
18 years_____	371	100.0	5.4	10.5	12.7	19.7	22.9	18.9	3.8	1.3	4.3	0.5

[1] Lumpkin County, Ga.; Jackson and Wolfe Counties, Ky.; Macon County, N. C.; Monroe County, Tenn.; and Mercer and Pendleton Counties, W. Va.

Source: Computed from schedules provided through the courtesy of W. H. Gaumnitz, U. S. Department of the Interior, Office of Education, Washington, D. C.

In Virginia's poor land and mountain areas "many of the present generation of young people are not getting much more formal training than did their parents.   *   *   *   The children of unskilled laborers, subsistence farmers, and miners are the ones most prone to drop out of school in the earlier grades." [29]

[23] Anderson, W. A., *Rural Youth: Activities, Interests, and Problems, II. Unmarried Young Men and Women, 15 to 29 Years of Age*, Bulletin 661, Cornell University Agricultural Experiment Station, Ithaca, N. Y., January 1937, pp. 5–6.

[24] Kirkpatrick, E. L. and Boynton, Agnes M., "Rural Young People Face Their Own Situation," *Rural Sociology*, Vol. 1, 1936, p. 156.

[25] Kirkpatrick, E. L. and Boynton, Agnes M., *Interests and Needs of Rural Youth in Wood County, Wisconsin, op. cit.*, p. 3.

[26] Johnson, Thomas H., *A Study of Rural Youth, 18 to 25 Years, Out of School and Unmarried*, College of ·Education, Ohio University, Athens, Ohio, May 1935, p. 34.

[27] Magill, Edmund C., *Handbook on Out-of-School Youth Education in Virginia*, A Summary of the Minutes of the Out-of-School Youth Training Conference, National Youth Administration and Virginia Polytechnic Institute, Blacksburg, Va., August 1935, p. 8.

[28] Computed from schedules provided through the courtesy of W. H. Gaumnitz, U. S. Department of the Interior, Office of Education, Washington, D. C.

[29] Garnett, W. E., *A Social Study of the Blacksburg Community*, Bulletin 299, Virginia Agricultural Experiment Station, Blacksburg, Va., August 1935, p. 61.

One of the 132,000 One-Room Schools.

A Modern Rural School.

HIGH SCHOOL ATTENDANCE SINCE 1930

High school enrollments increased during the depression of the early thirties in both rural and urban territory although an upward trend was already in evidence prior to 1930. In that year 58.0 percent of all urban youth and 39.5 percent of all rural youth 14–17 years of age were in high school; by 1934 these percentages had risen to 67.9 and 60.5, respectively.[30] Not only did more young people attend high school but also a larger proportion was graduated. One study found that of 1,000 pupils in the fifth grade in 1910–11 only 139 were graduated from high school in 1918, whereas of 1,000 pupils in the fifth grade in 1928–29, 383 were graduated in 1936.[31]

Comparative data for the school years 1931–32 and 1933–34 show that the percentage increase in school attendance was almost twice as great in rural as in urban high schools (appendix table 9). The aggregate number enrolled in urban high schools actually declined in the South Atlantic and West South Central Divisions. Only the New England Division showed a decline in the number attending rural high schools. The increase in high school enrollment for the United States as a whole between the school years 1933–34 and 1935–36 was only about half as great as between the years 1931–32 and 1933–34. During the more recent period, however, the percentage increase in rural areas was almost three times as great as in urban areas. Only in the urban areas of the Pacific Division was there an actual decrease in enrollment. In spite of the greater proportionate increase in each period, however, youth in rural areas were still not attending high school to the same extent as were those in urban areas.

Although the expansion of high school enrollment during depression years was in conformity with a general trend, at the same time it was apparently due partially to the "piling up" of youth in rural territory. Youth who would normally have gone to the cities remained in rural areas and attended high school. Moreover, high school facilities for rural youth and transportation facilities between the open country and towns have been constantly increasing so that expanded facilities have also operated to increase enrollments. The growing tendency for high school graduates to take postgraduate high school work before, or in lieu of, college work accounted for the increase in this type of student from 686,355 in 1931 to an estimated 945,000 in 1936 for the country as a whole.[32] No doubt the high school graduates in rural territory were well represented among this number.

---

[30] Cook, Katherine M., *Review of Conditions and Developments in Education in Rural and Other Sparsely Settled Areas*, Bulletin, 1937, No. 2, U. S. Department of the Interior, Office of Education, Washington, D. C., 1937, p. 7.

[31] Foster, Emery M., "School Survival Rates," *School Life*, Vol. 22, 1936, p. 14.

[32] *Ibid.*, p. 14.

Without critical analysis figures on rising school attendance may obscure the influence of economic maladjustments on the education of young people. Although there is no reliable information on the extent to which youth in low income or relief families have been forced to leave school, there are data which indicate that rural youth in the lowest economic classes are greatly retarded educationally.[33] Furthermore, it is a well-known fact that, on the whole, youth from the lowest income classes drop out of school very shortly after they reach the maximum compulsory school age. Rural youth are no exception.[34]

The activities of the Federal Emergency Relief Administration, the Works Progress Administration, and the National Youth Administration have helped to ameliorate the devastating effects of the depression for many youth in the lowest income groups by making it possible for them to remain in school. These agencies helped either the family of the youth or the youth himself. In those rural areas having an excess of youth, however, where young people have been severely handicapped even in normal times and where school attendance has always been exceedingly low, aid similar to that which has been extended during the depression must be continued and expanded if youth are not to be permanently underprivileged.

VOCATIONAL TRAINING IN RURAL SCHOOLS

Many of the high schools that do exist in rural areas offer no vocational training and hence do not adequately meet the needs of youth who will enter either agricultural or nonagricultural occupations. Those which do offer vocational training are usually limited to agricultural and/or home economics courses and therefore do not provide for youth who will enter nonagricultural occupations.

Regardless of whether girls seek employment outside the home, it is important that they be adequately trained for homemaking. No published data are available on the number of rural high schools including home economics courses in their curricula. When a check was made about 1933 [35] on the location of the Smith-Hughes high

---

[33] Melvin, Bruce L., *Rural Youth on Relief*, Research Monograph XI, Division of Social Research, Works Progress Administration, Washington, D. C., 1937, ch. IV; and Hummel, B. L. and Bennett, C. G., *Education of Persons in Rural Relief Households in Virginia, 1935*, Rural Relief Series, No. 8, Virginia Polytechnic Institute, Blacksburg, Va., January 1937, p. 10 ff.

[34] For example, see Nelson, Lowry and Cottam, Howard R., "A Comparison of Educational Advantages and Achievements of Rural Relief and Nonrelief Households of Two Counties in Utah," *Utah Academy of Sciences, Arts and Letters*, Vol. XII, 1935, p. 128; and McCormick, T. C., *Comparative Study of Rural Relief and Non-Relief Households*, Research Monograph II, Division of Social Research, Works Progress Administration, Washington, D. C., 1935, pp. 33–34.

[35] Information obtained from U. S. Department of the Interior, Office of Education, Division of Home Economics, Washington, D. C.

schools teaching home economics, it was found that approximately 75 percent were in places of less than 2,500 population.

Federally-aided schools reached about 196,000 girls in 1936 in their full-time day school courses and an additional 37,000 in part-time classes for employed girls. Classes for adults had an enrollment of better than 142,000, many of whom no doubt were young wives and mothers seeking guidance in meeting their homemaking problems more intelligently, efficiently, and economically.[36] In addition there were thousands of girls taking homemaking courses in schools operated under State plans, but there is no way of knowing how many of them were rural.

Vocational agriculture was included in approximately 40 percent of the rural high schools of the United States by 1934. It was estimated at that time that 14 percent of the farm boys 14–20 years of age who were in school were being reached by this vocational work.[37] Since that time the number of federally-aided vocational agricultural schools has increased considerably, but because of the provision that every dollar of Federal money must be matched by State funds, the schools are not always located on the basis of need or of farm population.

By 1936 there were 5,612 of these day schools. Computing the average number of farm males 14–20 years of age per school in the various States,[38] it becomes apparent that these schools have been located without enough regard to the number of farm youth that ought to be served. While Massachusetts and Connecticut average about 360 and 370 farm males of this age group, respectively, per school and the Middle Atlantic and East North Central States average 340 and 350, respectively, such highly rural States as West Virginia, Georgia, Iowa, North Dakota, South Dakota, Tennessee, Alabama, Arkansas, and Oklahoma average approximately 550, 660, 640, 930, 640, 620, 700, 620, and 710, respectively. Missouri, Wisconsin, and Minnesota, though less rural than the other States mentioned, nevertheless have almost one-half of their population classified as rural, and these States have an average of 590, 600, and

[36] Vocational Division, *Digest of Annual Reports of State Boards for Vocational Education to the Office of Education*, Fiscal Year Ended June 30, 1936, U. S. Department of the Interior, Office of Education, Washington, D. C., p. 53.

[37] Office of Education, *Vocational Education and Changing Conditions*, Bulletin No. 174, U. S. Department of the Interior, Washington, D. C., 1934, p. 106. See also Hamlin, Herbert M., "Our Dual System of Rural Education," *School Review*, Vol. XLIV, 1936, p. 181.

[38] Vocational Division, *Digest of Annual Reports of State Boards for Vocational Education to the Office of Education, op. cit.*, table 1; and Bureau of the Census, *Fifteenth Census of the United States: 1930*, Population Vol. II, *op. cit.*, were used as the basis for this computation for the purpose of illustration although it is recognized that the number of persons 14–20 years of age has increased considerably since 1930.

670 farm boys, respectively, 14–20 years of age for every school giving courses in vocational agriculture.

A survey in seven Southern States in 1933 showed that the departments of vocational agriculture already established constituted about 57 percent of the number needed. It was believed then that other regions might have an even lower percentage of rural schools providing this instruction in comparison with the total number operating under such conditions as to indicate a need for this type of work.[39]

By the fall of 1937 the number of federally-aided vocational agricultural high schools had increased to almost 7,000,[40] and as a result of the passage of the George-Deen Act in 1936 [41] providing for the further development of vocational education in the several States and territories a still further expansion of vocational agriculture will undoubtedly take place.

One of the most significant phases of the vocational agricultural work in rural high schools has been the development of the organization known as Future Farmers of America. This organization is now more than 10 years old and includes more than 120,000 boys between the ages of 14 and 21 enrolled in vocational agricultural courses in the federally-aided high schools of the country. Active membership may be retained 3 years after the boy has completed his systematic instruction in vocational agriculture and high school.[42] While the members secure practical experience in farming through their agricultural instruction and membership in the organization, the ultimate objectives are chiefly educational.[43] Since the distribution of the local chapters is restricted to schools including vocational agriculture in their curricula, this program is denied a large mass of rural boys who do not have access to a Smith-Hughes high school or who do not attend high school.

A parallel organization, called New Farmers of America, for Negro boys enrolled in the approximately 600 federally-aided Negro high schools had a national membership of 47,000 in 1937.[44] The upper age limit for membership is slightly higher than for white boys.

Not all rural or even farm boys are to become farmers, however. A large proportion have for many years gone into nonagricultural occupations, and for the good of agriculture as an industry under the

---

[39] Office of Education, *Vocational Education and Changing Conditions, op. cit.*, p. 106.

[40] Office of Director of Vocational Agriculture, U. S. Department of the Interior, Office of Education, Washington, D. C.

[41] Public, No. 673, 74th Cong., approved June 8, 1936.

[42] *Future Farmers of America, Revised Manual*, 1936, p. 9.

[43] Ross, W. A., "What Do You Mean—F. F. A?" *School Life*, Vol. 21, 1935, pp. 94–97.

[44] Office of Executive Secretary of the New Farmers of America, U. S. Department of the Interior, Office of Education, Washington, D. C.

An FFA Boy's Test Plot of Hybrid Corn.

present system the proportion leaving farm territory ought to be greater. Vocational openings are not easily found by graduates of rural high schools in fields other than agriculture.[45] Inadequate as the vocational training is for farm boys and girls who are to become farmers or wives of farmers, the chances of obtaining training for other occupations are almost nonexistent for rural young people within reasonable distance and at a reasonable cost. A count was made of the number of federally-aided schools in three States—Alabama, Minnesota, and California—having vocational agriculture and at the same time offering instruction in trade and industry. The first of these States had 175 federally-aided schools, white and colored, teaching vocational agriculture in 1936. Of these 16 white and 9 colored, or one-seventh of the total, also offered courses in trade and industry. Only 6 of the 25 were in places having a population of less than 2,500. Minnesota had 114 federally-aided vocational agricultural high schools but not a single school offered instruction in trade and industry. California had 15 federally-aided schools that provided vocational training in agricultural and nonagricultural fields but only 1 was in rural territory, that is, in a place having a population of less than 2,500.[46]

The desirability of vocational training other than agricultural training for rural young people has been recognized by many. Galpin stated the problem concisely as follows: "The fact is that not all children of farmers are to be farmers and housewives on farms. The need of guidance in the matter of vocational careers among farm youth is especially urgent, just because so many farm youth as a necessity must select rationally or else drift ignorantly into a great variety of occupations." [47]

Vance has recently emphasized the importance of providing training for white and Negro youth in the direction of more flexible skills which may open the way to a choice of jobs in the more complex urban environments. This is necessary because many southern farm youth must inevitably go to the cities for employment.[48]

[45] Frayser, Mary E., *Attitudes of High School Seniors Toward Farming and Other Vocations*, Bulletin 302, South Carolina Agricultural Experiment Station, Clemson, S. C., June 1935, pp. 30–31.
[46] Computed from lists of the federally-aided schools giving instruction in vocational agriculture and in trade and industry provided through the courtesy of the U. S. Department of the Interior, Office of Education, Washington, D. C.
[47] Galpin, C. J., "The Need of Guidance Among Farm Youth," *The Vocational Guidance Magazine*, Vol. IX, 1930, p. 25.
[48] Vance, Rupert B., *New Orleans Item-Tribune*, April 12, 1936.

Chapter IV

MARRIAGE OF RURAL YOUTH

FOR ALL youth marriage is a major social adjustment; for farm youth it is usually both a social and an economic adjustment. In agricultural society marriage may well mark the time in life when the young man begins to operate a farm for himself. The young woman submerges her economic role within that of her husband rather than embark on or continue an independent career. Traditionally the farm home and the farm business are one. For rural-nonfarm youth, however, marriage does not necessarily involve a comparable economic adjustment since the young man in the small town may have been on the way to becoming established in business, in a profession, in a secure salaried position, or in a skilled trade for some time prior to his marriage.

The normal sequence for American boys is school, employment, marriage, and a new family.[1] The sequence for girls is similar except that employment is not a necessary requisite to marriage. A break in this cultural pattern is certain to have significant consequences. Previous chapters have shown that rural young people on the whole are handicapped—more in some regions than in others—in securing a satisfactory education and that the problem of employment and becoming established in a life work is acute in some sections. Youth who leave school at a relatively early age face a fairly long period of enforced leisure before they find regular employment.

The marriage rate in the United States has been declining more or less steadily since the early twenties; the decline was greatly accentuated early in the depression,[2] affording evidence of widespread postponement of marriage among youth as a result of unemployment or underemployment. That the postponement of marriage may have

[1] May, Mark A., "The Dilemma of Youth," *Progressive Education*, Vol. XII, January 1935, p. 5.

[2] Stouffer, Samuel A. and Spencer, Lyle M., "Marriage and Divorce in Recent Years," *Annals of the American Academy of Political and Social Science*, Vol. 188, November 1936, pp. 58–59.

serious effects upon the birth rate has been shown[3] and that it affects the emotional life of those unable to marry as well as the sex mores is generally accepted. What are the facts regarding the marriage of rural young people, and what are their implications for the future of rural life?

PROPORTION OF YOUTH MARRIED

Youth is the period during which the majority of all marriages occur. The proportions of youth which are married, however, vary importantly by residence, sex, age, and color.

Rural and Urban Youth Compared

A larger percentage of the total rural than of the total urban population is married. If the farms and the cities having a population above 500,000 had had the same age distribution of the total population 15 years of age and over in 1930, there would have been 15 percent fewer persons married in the big cities than on the farms. The percent of young people below 20 who were married was about twice as great on farms as in the large cities, and among those 20–24 years of age the percent was about one-third higher on farms than in cities.[4]

The proportion of youth married in 1930 was greater for both sexes and for all years among rural than urban youth (table 18 and fig. 12). At each year of age there is a considerable difference between the sexes, many more young women than young men being married in both urban and rural territory. Apart from the fact that rural as well as urban young women marry earlier than men, there is the additional fact that early marriage for girls is the custom in many rural communities. At the age of 24 years a little less than one-half

Table 18.—Percent Married of Total Youth Population, by Age, Residence, and Sex, 1930

Age	Urban		Rural	
	Male	Female	Male	Female
16 years	0.1	2.7	0.2	6.1
17 years	0.4	7.1	0.9	13.2
18 years	1.5	14.9	3.0	24.5
19 years	4.3	23.6	7.4	35.5
20 years	9.3	32.4	14.2	45.5
21 years	16.8	40.1	23.3	53.1
22 years	25.2	47.8	32.2	60.2
23 years	34.3	54.8	41.2	66.4
24 years	42.4	60.4	48.8	71.4

Source: Bureau of the Census, *Fifteenth Census of the United States: 1930*, Population Vol. II, U. S. Department of Commerce, Washington, D. C., 1933, p. 851.

[3] Stouffer, Samuel A. and Lazarsfeld, Paul F., *Research Memorandum on the Family in the Depression*, Bulletin 29, New York: Social Science Research Council, 1937, p. 5.

[4] Ogburn, William F., "Recent Changes in Marriage," *American Journal of Sociology,* Vol. XLI, 1935, p. 290.

(48.8 percent) of the young men but almost three-fourths (71.4 percent) of the young women in rural areas were married. Among the urban youth of this age 42.4 percent of the young men and 60.4 percent of the young women were married in 1930.

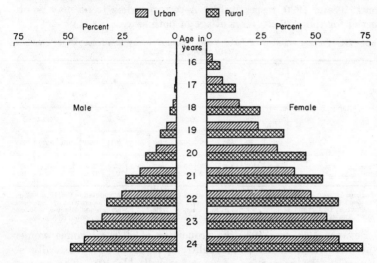

FIG. 12- PERCENT MARRIED OF TOTAL YOUTH POPULATION
1930

Source: *Fifteenth Census of the United States: 1930.*   AF-2677, WPA

The difference between the sexes in the percent married in 1930 was considerably greater for rural youth than for urban youth, particularly in the lower age range. Of the young men and women in urban territory 20 years old in 1930, 9.3 and 32.4 percent, respectively, were married. In comparison, of the rural young men and women of the same age 14.2 and 45.5 percent, respectively, were married. Since young women migrate to the cities at an earlier age than young men,[5] it is probable that a larger proportion of the girls remaining in rural territory marry than would otherwise do so, many of them taking husbands older than themselves.

In this connection attention should be called to the fact that between 1910 and 1920 the trend in the percent married of both sexes was upward for both urban and rural youth. Thus 1.4, percent of the rural young men 15–19 years of age were married in 1910, but by 1920 the corresponding percent was 2.4.[6] During the same interval the percent of the rural young women of the same age who

---

[5] See ch. I.
[6] Stouffer, Samuel A. and Spencer, Lyle M., *op. cit.*, p. 60.

were married rose from 10.2 to 14.5 (table 19). Among the urban youth 15–19 years of age 0.7 percent of the young men were married in 1910 but by 1920, 1.7 percent of this age were married. Of the young women of the same age the percents married were 7.7 and 10.4 for 1910 and 1920, respectively. A corresponding trend may be observed for those 20–24 years of age of both sexes.

Table 19.—Percent Married of Total Youth Population, by Residence, Age, and Sex, 1910, 1920, and 1930

Residence	Age in years											
	15–19						20–24					
	Male			Female			Male			Female		
	1910	1920	1930	1910	1920	1930	1910	1920	1930	1910	1920	1930
Urban	0.7	1.7	1.3	7.7	10.4	10.2	20.6	25.8	25.8	42.4	47.6	47.1
Rural	1.4	2.4	2.2	10.2	14.5	15.5	27.3	31.1	31.2	57.5	58.4	58.8

Sources: Bureau of the Census, *Fifteenth Census of the United States: 1930*, Population Vol. II, p. 848 and *Fourteenth Census of the United States: 1920*, Population Vol. II, p. 516, U. S. Department of Commerce, Washington, D. C.; and Stouffer, Samuel A. and Spencer, Lyle M., "Marriage and Divorce in Recent Years" *Annals of the American Academy of Policital and Social Science*, Vol. 188, November 1936, p. 60.

Between 1920 and 1930 the proportion of all rural young women who were married increased slightly, but there was practically no change in the proportion of young men (table 19). The percent change among urban youth in both age groups was negligible for this decade. The fact, however, that in rural areas there was even a slight increase in the percent of young women married and no decrease in the percent of young men married during the decade 1920 to 1930, when the price level of farm products was already much below that of industrial products, suggests that rural youth may not postpone marriage to any great extent under adverse economic conditions.

Rural-Farm and Rural-Nonfarm Youth Compared

When the number of married rural youth was analyzed with respect to residence, it was found that with the exception of boys below 20 years of age and of girls 16 years of age, proportionately more rural-nonfarm than rural-farm youth of both sexes were married in 1930 (table 20, fig. 13, and appendix table 10). This situation is difficult to interpret since little is known about the marital status of the various segments of the rural-nonfarm population, such as the population of agricultural villages, industrial villages, and the peripheries of cities. However, an examination by States and by divisions of the percent of rural-nonfarm youth of both sexes married suggests a tentative explanation.

Rural-nonfarm youth 20-24 years of age were married in greater proportions in those States in which there was a large contingent of rural-

Table 20.—Percent Married of Rural Youth Population, by Age, Residence, and Sex, 1930

Age	Rural-farm		Rural-nonfarm	
	Male	Female	Male	Female
16 years	0.3	6.1	0.2	6.1
17 years	1.0	12.8	0.8	13.8
18 years	3.2	23.7	2.6	25.7
19 years	7.4	33.7	7.3	37.9
20 years	13.9	43.8	14.7	47.7
21 years	22.5	51.2	24.4	55.3
22 years	30.8	58.8	34.0	61.8
23 years	39.1	65.4	43.7	67.5
24 years	46.3	70.4	51.5	72.3

Source: Bureau of the Census, *Fifteenth Census of the United States: 1930*, Population Vol. II. U. S. Department of Commerce, Washington, D. C., 1933, p. 851.

industrial population than in other States. For example, in West Virginia with its coal mining settlements 71.3 percent of the young women and 39.3 percent of the young men 20–24 years of age were married in 1930, whereas the corresponding percentages for this age group in the United States as a whole were only 60.8 and 33.7, respectively. This explanation probably holds likewise for Kentucky which also has many coal settlements, for Oklahoma with its coal, oil, and natural gas settlements, and for Texas with its oil and natural gas settlements, all three States having high percentages of both sexes in this age group married. The proportions married of the younger age

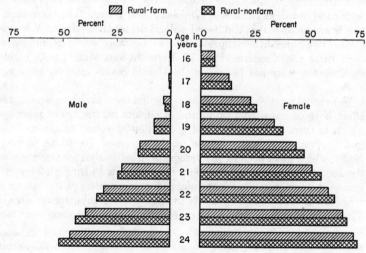

Fɪɢ. 13-PERCENT MARRIED OF RURAL YOUTH POPULATION
1930

Source: *Fifteenth Census of the United States: 1930.*
84015°—38——6

AF- 2679, WPA

group in the rural-nonfarm population in these same States also exceeded the comparable United States percentages.

In most other States in which the percent of the rural-nonfarm youth of both sexes married exceeded the United States figure,[7] a considerable proportion of the rural-nonfarm population is composed of inhabitants of mining, lumbering, or other types of nonagricultural settlements. While the industrial composition appears significant, it is important to note that most of the States with particularly high rural-nonfarm marriage rates are Southern States in which marriage rates among youth in general are high.

The percentages of rural youth married by sex and age groups varied widely from one section of the country to another (appendix table 10). Thus, of the rural-nonfarm women 20–24 years of age the proportions married ranged from 48.1 percent in New England to 67.1 percent in the West South Central States while the same two regions yielded the two extremes for the same age group of farm young women, namely, 43.0 percent and 65.3 percent, respectively.

New England and the Pacific States had the lowest percentages of both rural-farm and rural-nonfarm young men 20–24 years of age who were married. The other extreme was provided by the East South Central States, a highly rural division.

In New England, where the population is concentrated heavily in industrial centers, the young people marry, on the whole, later than in such rural States as Arkansas, Louisiana, and Texas. The same variation is apparent within the New England States themselves. Whereas Connecticut and Massachusetts had exceedingly low percentages of their rural youth married in 1930, Vermont and Maine, both highly rural States, were not far below the United States total for each age group.

Individual studies bear out the generalizations above regarding the effect both of industrialization and of custom on the age of marriage which in turn are related to the proportion of young people married in any given rural area. In the rural sections of Tompkins County, N. Y., which have been in the process of urbanization for many years, the age of the married young men, ranging from 15 through 29 years, averaged 28 years while for the married young women of the same age range the average was 24 years.[8] In contrast, in a submarginal area in Virginia, well removed from the cities, "Reports on the age of marriage

---

[7] For example, Indiana, New Mexico, Louisiana, Alabama, North Carolina, South Carolina, Tennessee, Georgia, and Florida. Mississippi and Arkansas both exceed the United States figure but the percent of rural-farm youth married in both age groups exceeds the percent of rural-nonfarm youth. Both States are highly agricultural and have a negligible rural-industrial population.

[8] Anderson, W. A., *Rural Youth: Activities, Interests, and Problems, I. Married Young Men and Women, 15 to 29 Years of Age*, Bulletin 649, Cornell University Agricultural Experiment Station, Ithaca, N. Y., May 1936, p. 7.

for 501 women showed that 21.6 percent married at 16 or younger, 10.8 percent at 15 or below, and 38.3 percent between 17 and 20. Slightly over a fifth of the men were married by the time they were 20." [9]

White and Negro Youth Compared

Color and residence both influence the proportion of youth of the various ages which is married. In 1930 relatively more Negro than white youth were married in all segments of the population—urban, rural-farm, and rural-nonfarm (table 21). While more Negro young men in rural-farm than in rural-nonfarm territory were married, the reverse was true for Negro young women with the exception of those 24 years of age.

Table 21.—Percent Married of Total Youth Population, by Age, Residence, Color, and Sex, 1930

Age	White		Negro	
	Male	Female	Male	Female
URBAN				
16 years	0.1	2.3	0.3	7.1
17 years	0.3	6.3	1.2	15.7
18 years	1.3	13.5	4.4	27.7
19 years	3.8	21.9	10.4	38.9
20 years	8.4	30.6	19.9	47.3
21 years	15.7	38.6	31.3	54.5
22 years	23.8	46.6	40.6	58.7
23 years	33.1	53.8	49.3	63.3
24 years	41.4	59.7	55.2	65.9
RURAL-FARM				
16 years	0.2	5.6	0.5	8.2
17 years	0.8	11.7	1.6	17.5
18 years	2.7	21.4	5.5	31.8
19 years	6.3	31.5	13.6	42.2
20 years	11.9	41.3	24.8	51.7
21 years	19.0	49.6	40.7	58.0
22 years	27.0	57.3	51.0	63.6
23 years	35.4	64.5	59.7	68.3
24 years	42.9	69.9	65.6	72.1
RURAL-NONFARM				
16 years	0.2	5.5	0.5	11.2
17 years	0.7	12.8	1.5	21.8
18 years	2.4	24.3	4.7	34.8
19 years	6.8	36.5	12.2	46.8
20 years	14.0	46.4	21.6	54.4
21 years	23.3	54.5	35.4	60.7
22 years	33.1	61.2	43.5	64.9
23 years	43.2	67.1	52.0	69.5
24 years	51.5	72.2	66.2	71.6

Sources: Special tabulation by the U. S. Bureau of the Census of the number of married youth; and Bureau of the Census, *Fifteenth Census of the United States: 1930*, Population Vol. II, U. S. Department of Commerce, Washington, D. C., 1933, pp. 598–601.

In 13 Southern States, where a high proportion of all youth was married, there was a general tendency for more Negro than white youth in rural areas to be married. This was true of both young men and young women in the rural-farm and rural-nonfarm groups (table 22), although there were numerous exceptions, particularly among females. In almost all of the Southern States and among both sexes more Negro youth in rural-nonfarm than in rural-farm territory were married.

[9] Garnett, W. E., *A Social Study of the Blacksburg Community*, Bulletin 299, Virginia Agricultural Experiment Station, Blacksburg, Va., August 1935, p. 16.

Table 22.—Percent Married of Rural Youth Population in 13 Southern States, by Residence, Color, and Sex, 1930

State	Rural-farm				Rural-nonfarm			
	White		Negro		White		Negro	
	Male	Female	Male	Female	Male	Female	Male	Female
Alabama	21.9	43.6	23.8	39.1	27.3	50.3	31.1	53.6
Arkansas	22.3	48.0	30.0	53.4	25.8	51.1	29.6	52.1
Florida	13.9	37.9	19.7	40.1	21.7	52.2	28.8	60.5
Georgia	19.2	40.7	26.1	41.3	23.0	43.7	33.7	51.9
Louisiana	19.5	43.3	25.7	46.7	22.3	46.7	26.5	51.0
Maryland	10.4	29.8	10.5	31.1	16.8	40.8	16.4	37.8
Mississippi	21.5	44.6	31.1	51.5	22.2	44.4	31.1	53.9
North Carolina	16.8	36.4	18.6	33.4	26.8	45.8	24.5	41.1
Oklahoma	19.2	45.7	20.9	45.1	25.0	52.1	25.4	49.8
South Carolina	16.7	36.6	21.2	33.8	25.9	46.4	33.5	48.2
Tennessee	19.5	40.4	24.2	43.5	27.4	48.7	23.0	41.8
Texas	17.8	40.8	25.3	46.2	22.0	48.4	28.5	50.6
Virginia	12.7	30.4	12.1	29.2	20.8	44.5	19.1	37.3

Source: Special tabulation by the U. S. Bureau of the Census.

MARRIAGE DURING THE DEPRESSION OF THE EARLY THIRTIES

The marriage rate for the country as a whole fell from 10.1 per 1,000 population in 1929 to 7.9 per 1,000 population in 1932, the lowest point in the recorded history of marriage in the United States (appendix table 11). Since the bulk of all marriages occurs within the youth group, it is fair to assume that approximately the same decrease occurred in the marriage rate of young people 16–24 years of age. Many youth postponed marriage during the depression of the early thirties. Among 13,500 youth 16–24 years of age interviewed in Maryland approximately 20 percent of those over 20 years of age stated that their marriage had been delayed. More than one-half of this group gave some economic reason as the cause of the delay, while others reported such causes as no opportunity, family objections, or personal illness.[10]

Two conclusions drawn from limited evidence seem tenable: the decline in the marriage rate was not consistent in all States, and it tended to be greater in urban than in rural States. It is very difficult to judge the effects of the depression on the marriage rate among the farm population because the depression for farmers really began in the early 1920's.[11] Hardships of farmers during this period, however, apparently did not cause farm youth to postpone marriage. Consequently, it is an open question whether the general depression beginning in 1929 was the primary cause of the drop in the marriage rate in rural areas.

The decline in the rate of marriage in the urban population was not

[10] Bell, Howard M., *Youth Tell Their Story*, American Youth Commission of the Council on Education, Washington, D. C., 1938, p. 43.

[11] For a discussion of research on rural life from this approach see Sanderson, Dwight, *Research Memorandum on Rural Life in the Depression*, Bulletin 34, New York: Social Science Research Council, 1937.

consistent, if the situation in Philadelphia is typical.[12] It was found in this one city that the effect of the depression of the early thirties was not uniform on all groups or classes of the population. In some areas the rates fell, in others they rose, and in still others they were stationary.

Though a study in rural areas in North Carolina seems to demonstrate clearly a relationship between a decline in marriage rates and economic conditions,[13] it is not known whether similar studies in other rural sections would yield the same relationship of these two factors. It seems unlikely that the effect of the depression would be any more uniform in rural territory than it was found to be in the urban study just referred to.

A comparison among the States further confirms the two conclusions drawn above. According to the United States Census of 1930 there were 21 States in which more than one-half of the population was urban. Eleven of these States had an average marriage rate for the period 1926–1929 above the national average for that period. In 1932 the rate was above the national rate in only nine of these States (table 23). Whereas among the 27 rural States there were 14 in which the average marriage rate for the period 1926–1929 was above the national average, by 1932 this number had increased to 17.

Trends in marriage rates among the States were not consistent, but on the whole they tended to confirm the statement that the decline was less in rural than in urban areas. In 10 States—New Hampshire, South Dakota, Nebraska, Virginia, South Carolina, Kentucky, Oklahoma, New Mexico, Arizona, and Nevada—the rates were higher in 1932 than the average of their respective rates from 1926 to 1929. Only one—New Hampshire—is more than 50 percent urban. Of the remaining 38 States that experienced a decline in 1932 from their marriage rate for the 1926–1929 period, 18 had rates below the national figure both in 1932 and for the period 1926–1929. Of these 8 were dominantly rural—Maine, Vermont, Minnesota, Iowa, North Dakota, North Carolina, Idaho, and Wyoming—and 10 were urban— Massachusetts, Rhode Island, Connecticut, New Jersey, Pennsylvania, Ohio, Michigan, Wisconsin, Delaware, and Oregon. In the other 20 States, equally divided between the rural and urban categories, the marriage rates were, with a few exceptions, above the national rate both in 1932 and for the period 1926–1929.

Marriages began increasing in 1933 and continued through 1934,[14] when the national rate was only 0.4 per 1,000 below the 1929 level

---

[12] Bossard, James H. S., "Depression and Pre-Depression Marriage Rates: A Philadelphia Study," *American Sociological Review*, Vol. 2, 1937, pp. 686–695.

[13] Hamilton, C. Horace, *Recent Changes in the Social and Economic Status of Farm Families in North Carolina*, Bulletin No. 309, North Carolina Agricultural Experiment Station, Raleigh, N. C., May 1937, pp. 146–148.

[14] Stouffer, Samuel A. and Spencer, Lyle M., *op. cit.*, pp. 58 and 63. The 1934 rate is given as 10.28 and that for 1935 as 10.41 per 1,000 population.

Table 23.—Marriage Rate per 1,000 Population in Urban [1] and Rural [2] States, 1926–1929 and 1932

State	Rate per 1,000 population	
	Average rate 1926–1929	1932
United States	10.1	7.9
NEW ENGLAND		
Urban:		
New Hampshire	10.7	11.6
Massachusetts	7.1	5.3
Rhode Island	7.6	5.9
Connecticut	7.5	5.6
Rural:		
Maine	7.9	7.0
Vermont	8.0	6.7
MIDDLE ATLANTIC		
Urban:		
New York	10.2	8.1
New Jersey	7.6	5.5
Pennsylvania	7.3	5.8
EAST NORTH CENTRAL		
Urban:		
Ohio	9.0	4.4
Indiana	13.1	11.0
Illinois	11.1	8.4
Michigan	8.3	5.7
Wisconsin	5.8	4.7
WEST NORTH CENTRAL		
Urban:		
Missouri	10.6	9.6
Rural:		
Minnesota	8.9	6.7
Iowa	8.7	3.2
North Dakota	6.3	5.3
South Dakota	9.2	10.3
Nebraska	7.1	8.5
Kansas	11.0	8.9
SOUTH ATLANTIC		
Urban:		
Delaware	4.8	3.8
Maryland	15.7	13.8
District of Columbia	10.5	10.0
Florida	15.7	10.0
Rural:		
Virginia	8.8	10.1
West Virginia	11.1	10.5
North Carolina	7.2	3.6
South Carolina	14.0	14.6
Georgia	9.9	8.9
EAST SOUTH CENTRAL		
Rural:		
Kentucky	11.6	12.0
Tennessee	12.8	6.8
Alabama	11.5	9.4
Mississippi	16.3	11.1
WEST SOUTH CENTRAL		
Rural:		
Arkansas	14.8	13.8
Louisiana	10.2	9.0
Oklahoma	12.6	13.9
Texas	13.0	6.7
MOUNTAIN		
Urban:		
Colorado	11.6	6.3
Utah	11.3	11.2
Rural:		
Montana	9.8	9.2
Idaho	9.0	3.4
Wyoming	7.9	3.4
New Mexico	13.0	20.6
Arizona	12.7	17.1
Nevada	41.1	76.2

See footnotes at end of table.

Table 23.—Marriage Rate per 1,000 Population in Urban and Rural States, 1926–1929 and 1932—Continued

State	Rate per 1,000 population	
	Average rate 1926–1929	1932
PACIFIC		
Urban:		
Washington	12. 1	10. 1
Oregon	8. 4	6. 9
California	11. 2	7. 3

¹ With at least 50 percent of the population living in centers of 2,500 or more.
² With at least 50 percent of the population living in the open country or in centers of less than 2,500.

Source: Bureau of the Census, *Marriage and Divorce*, Annual Reports, U. S. Department of Commerce, Washington, D. C.

(appendix table 11). The recovery from the low rate of marriage was general among both rural and urban States.

If judgment can be drawn from the situation in North Carolina, the rate of marriage was somewhat higher among the rural nonrelief population than among the rural relief population during the depression years of 1932 to 1934, inclusive.[15] "* * * the marriage rate of the nonrelief population rose substantially in 1933; whereas, the marriage rate of households (to be on relief in 1934) continued to decline."[16]

Data are not sufficient to determine to what extent the findings in North Carolina are applicable to the country as a whole. Taking all the youth on relief in October 1935 the percent married was slightly greater than was the case in the total rural youth population in 1930. Of all the youth on relief in October 1935, 41 percent of the young women and 20 percent of the young men were married, while in 1930 in the total rural population 39 percent of the young women and 17 percent of the young men were married.[17]

The abnormal marriage rates in some States are undoubtedly due somewhat to State laws or other special circumstances.[18] In North Carolina, for example, the couples go from their home State to Virginia and South Carolina to avoid conforming to laws requiring publicity and certificates of physical fitness prior to marriage. As a consequence the rate in North Carolina was extremely low in 1932 and for some years previous in comparison with neighboring States (appendix table 11). Nevada's tremendous increase is related to the large

[15] Hamilton, C. Horace, "The Trend of the Marriage Rate in Rural North Carolina," *Rural Sociology*, Vol. 1, 1936, p. 455.

[16] *Ibid.*, p. 461.

[17] Melvin, Bruce L., *Rural Youth on Relief*, Research Monograph XI, Division of Social Research, Works Progress Administration, Washington, D. C., 1937, ch. III.

[18] Bureau of the Census, *Marriage and Divorce: 1932*, U. S. Department of Commerce, Washington, D. C., p. 14.

number of divorces and subsequent remarriages that take place in that State.

A summary review of the statutes of the various States in order to determine, if possible, whether or not there is any relation between the laws regarding the minimum age of marriage and marriage rates yielded the following results: Of the 23 States where the minimum age for marriage of girls is 16 years or above, 12[19] are urban according to the classification in table 23 and 11[20] are rural. Of the remaining 25 States where the minimum age of marriage is below 16 years, 9[21] are urban and 16[22] are rural. That is, on the whole there is a tendency for rural States to have a lower minimum age of marriage than urban States. There probably is some connection between the laws of the rural States and the fact that larger percentages of rural than of urban girls in the younger ages are married. Only in New Hampshire is the minimum age fixed by statute at 18 years.[23]

The period of delay before marriage has been instituted by only one-third of the rural States but by more than one-half of the urban States. The rural States taking this precaution against hasty and unwise marriages of young people are Georgia, Maine, Minnesota, Mississippi, Montana, Tennessee, Texas, Vermont, and West Virginia; the urban States are California, Connecticut, Delaware, Maryland, Massachusetts, Michigan, New Hampshire, New Jersey, New York, Ohio, Oregon, and Wisconsin.

The limited data available for the depression years indicate that in spite of fluctuations in rates the fundamental factors in the marriage situation of rural youth have remained about the same. Rural youth do marry at a somewhat earlier age on the average than urban youth; but this is associated with the cultural pattern in rural areas where early marriage is socially approved. It is also a well-known fact that early marriages are characteristic of the lower economic groups and hence of the groups with the lowest standards of living and the most limited educational attainments. Because such large proportions of rural youth are underprivileged in these respects, a high rate of mar-

---

[19] California, Connecticut, Delaware, Illinois, Indiana, Massachusetts, Michigan, New Hampshire, New York, Ohio, Pennsylvania, and Rhode Island.

[20] Arizona, Kansas, Maine, Minnesota, Montana, Nebraska, Nevada, New Mexico, Vermont, West Virginia, and Wyoming.

[21] Colorado, Florida, Maryland, Missouri, New Jersey, Oregon, Utah, Washington, and Wisconsin.

[22] Alabama, Arkansas, Georgia, Idaho, Iowa, Kentucky, Louisiana, Mississippi, North Carolina, North Dakota, Oklahoma, South Carolina, South Dakota, Tennessee, Texas, and Virginia.

[23] Heisterman, Carl A., "Marriage Laws," *Social Work Year Book*, New York: Russell Sage Foundation, 1933, pp. 276–278. These and other data on marriage laws were brought up to date, October 1937, by the Legal Section of the Division of Social Research, Works Progress Administration, Washington, D. C.

What Is Their Chance for Security?

Resettlement Administration (Shahn).

Perplexed Young Parents.

riage naturally occurs. Yet these youth have such limited economic opportunities that they face appalling handicaps in their efforts to attain a reasonable economic base for family life.

The factors which are associated with early marriage are also conducive to high birth rates. It is not only the lowest economic groups in general but these groups in rural areas in particular which are contributing far more than their proportionate share of births. Modern methods of birth control are as yet little known in most rural areas. Moreover, it is in such areas, where economic need is greatest and birth rates are highest, that opposition to artificial family limitation is strongest.

The inevitable result of having a large proportion of rural youth married, with the attendant high birth rate, is increased population pressure on submarginal land areas and hence an increase in the number of economically marginal and submarginal families. Under conditions which might provide a satisfactory minimum standard of living for small families, the economic situation of large families becomes intolerable. Hence this is a vicious circle in which poverty begets poverty.

Escape by migrating to better land or through industrial opportunity is becoming possible for a constantly decreasing proportion of rural young people. Consequently, it has been observed in some mountainous areas that a new cabin is built by a young couple farther up the hollow where there are already too many cabins, and another family is started on its tragic cycle.

The situation is not limited to farm youth. Through their high marriage rate rural-nonfarm youth are augmenting the number of families on the poverty level in rural-industrial areas just as are farm youth in submarginal open country areas. The fact cannot be too strongly emphasized that rural youth need guidance and assistance under present circumstances in making the economic and personal adjustments associated with successful family life.

Chapter V

THE USE OF LEISURE TIME

THE CONSTRUCTIVE use of leisure time is of more importance to the individual during youth than during any other equal number of years of his life. Social adjustments that have permanent consequences to the individual are largely made through the social and recreational activities of these years. Such activities follow three general lines: (1) participation in the programs of the institutions and organizations of the community, such as the church, the Farm Bureau, and the Grange; (2) recreation through organized community facilities, such as community houses, playgrounds, and swimming pools; and (3) spontaneous group and individual activities, such as reading, dancing, visiting, fishing, or going to motion picture shows. It is important that youth have the opportunity to secure adequate recreation through these three channels. Crime, to say nothing of restricted personalities, is too often the result of inadequate recreational facilities.

RURAL CHANGE AND THE USE OF LEISURE TIME

Within recent years a number of forces active in rural life have brought about great changes in the kinds of recreation in which rural youth indulge. Among these the most important are: (1) the breakdown of the social solidarity of old neighborhoods and communities; (2) new methods of transportation and communication with the consequent more intensive contact with the city; (3) the expansion of commercialized forms of recreation, such as dance halls, roadhouses, and movies, in rural areas; and (4) the increase of rural recreational activities. Along with these forces has come an increasing belief in the value of recreation, although rural communities have been much slower than urban communities to recognize the need for leisure-time activities planned solely for pleasure. In some rural areas marriage is still "frequently accepted as the end of 'good times'," [1] but this idea is now much less widespread than it once was.

---

[1] Frayser, Mary E., *The Use of Leisure in Selected Rural Areas of South Carolina*, Bulletin 263, South Carolina Agricultural Experiment Station, Clemson, S. C., March 1930, p. 58.

The community of 25 years ago, now largely disorganized [2] and in a state of change, provided the means of recreation in its natural environment and institutional life and exercised rather sharp approval or disapproval of what youth might do. Leisure-time pleasures of youth were closely associated with the family and·the activities about the farm. Family recreation consisted on the one hand of games, practical jokes, and "roughhouse," and on the other hand of associations with friends and neighbors. Hunting and fishing were both individual and neighborhood affairs. Opportunities for the association of young men and young women were provided through visiting and the assemblages of the community institutions.

The church performed a distinct function as a social and recreational institution, although its supporters frequently would have resented such an implication. Young people went to church and attended church suppers and other events in order to be together. Seasons of protracted meetings provided the approved social and psychological settings for the association of the sexes. The spelling bees of the school, the programs of the old literary societies, and the special activities of the Grange were all very important in the lives of the youth. In a social and recreational way the community was a closed corporation. Its standards of conduct brooked little variation; the behavior of individuals followed socially approved patterns.

The rural community is no longer a closed unit. Its boundaries have been broken. Its institutions and organizations have changed. In many cases the rural churches have died. Some schools have declined and others have been consolidated. Economic and educational organizations, such as the cooperatives and the clubs that cooperate with the extension services of the States, have arisen in community life.

Probably the automobile and motion pictures have been the most potent forces in changing community boundaries and in expanding the social and recreational activities of young people. Isolation no longer exists for the rural youth who has the use of an automobile; he has access to the best that Hollywood produces. How many of the 15,273 motion picture theaters in the United States in January 1935 [3] were in definitely rural areas or what proportion of the weekly attendance consisted of rural youth is not known, but young people from the country frequently drive many miles to participate in this

---

[2] See Melvin, Bruce L., *The Sociology of a Village and the Surrounding Territory*, Bulletin 523, Cornell University Agricultural Experiment Station, Ithaca, N. Y., May 1931.

[3] *The 1935 Film Daily Year Book of Motion Pictures*, p. 762. The number of theaters has decreased during the depression. In 1931 there were 22,731 theaters according to Steiner, Jesse F., "Recreation and Leisure Time Activities," *Recent Social Trends*, New York: Whittlesey House, McGraw-Hill Book Company, Inc., 1934, p. 940. In 1930 the weekly attendance was estimated at 100,000,000.

form of diversion. Moreover, the automobile is itself a form of social life since "just riding around" is now one of the important types of recreation for a large number of youth.[4]

The growth of transportation facilities has also been a major factor in developing commercialized forms of amusement other than motion pictures in rural areas. Casual observation attests to the fact that the dance hall, the tavern, the roadhouse, all of varied type and cost, are now scattered on main roads throughout wide stretches of rural territory. Whether these places are attended primarily by the young people from the cities or from the country is an open question. But inevitably they must influence the leisure-time activities of rural young people.

The radio, too, has frequently invaded the most isolated homes. "Popular dance orchestras no longer furnish entertainment to their immediate patrons alone; their reputations are national; their music is relayed to the most distant places * * *; the people throughout the entire country may hear the roar of the crowd and share in the thrill of great sporting events * * * ."[5]

Aside from the extension of commercialized recreational facilities, such facilities as public parks, playgrounds, swimming pools, and community and recreational centers have recently been greatly expanded in both rural and urban territory. The proportionate distribution of these facilities in rural areas cannot be determined, but definite effort has been made through the programs of the various Federal emergency agencies to enrich rural life by making available some of the facilities for wholesome recreation which are taken for granted by city dwellers. Casual observation of empty swimming pools and unfrequented community halls in some rural sections raises a legitimate doubt, however, regarding the extent to which these new facilities were bolstered by an adequate community organization to foster their proper utilization.

In view of the numerous changes that are influencing rural society, there arise certain fundamental questions which help define more

[4] Substantiating data will appear in a forthcoming monograph by Melvin, Bruce L. and Smith, Elna N., *Youth in Agricultural Villages*, Division of Social Research, Works Progress Administration, Washington, D. C. See also Frayser, Mary E., *The Play and Recreation of Children and Youth in Selected Rural Areas of South Carolina*, Bulletin 275, South Carolina Agricultural Experiment Station, Clemson, S. C., June 1931, p. 34.

[5] Steiner, Jesse F., *op. cit.*, pp. 941–942. For more detailed treatment of the subject by the same author, see *Americans at Play*, New York: McGraw-Hill Book Company, Inc., 1933.

The study in four rural counties in South Carolina showed that in 1931 "Radio sets were found in relatively few of the homes of the young white people * * * ." See Frayser, Mary E., *The Play and Recreation of Children and Youth in Selected Rural Areas of South Carolina, op. cit.*, p. 20. This is undoubtedly not general since radios are widespread in the farm homes of good land areas.

clearly the problem of youth's expenditure of leisure time. Are the youth of low-income families able to take advantage of the new opportunities for social and recreational life? Are rural institutions and agencies providing opportunities for social life and recreation for rural youth by performing deliberately functions which they once performed in the course of their regular activities? Are rural youth being regimented and standardized in their leisure-time activities so that the spontaneity that once accompanied rural recreation is being lost? And if so, does it matter, or is it even desirable?

PARTICIPATION OF YOUTH IN RURAL ORGANIZATIONS

Data on the activities of rural youth yield a few tenable conclusions. In the first place communities have not been sufficiently aware of the social and recreational needs of youth. In the second place a great mass of rural youth are in no way participating in the work or programs—social, recreational, or otherwise—of such community institutions and organizations as have been developed. These statements may require slight modification in view of the activities of the various emergency agencies in recent years, but by and large they still hold.

The church probably has more youth in its membership than any other rural institution, but it is doubtful if it is reaching many youth in a social and recreational way. In Virginia it was estimated that less than 20 percent of the rural young people between 15 and 24 years of age were being reached by young people's religious organizations.[6]

The role of the church in a community's social and recreational life, however, seems to be variously interpreted. Fewer than a dozen of all the churches in 140 villages studied in 1936 had well-rounded programs of recreation, adult education, or welfare. In one of the villages studied "a socially-minded pastor, concerned over the obvious revolt of youth against moral conventions and mores, initiated a program of activities and discussion for the young people of the community. To compete with roadhouses, weekly dances were included. The response of the youth was almost unanimous. Immediately, quite unanimous opposition arose from the other churches. Proselyting was charged. The program was, therefore, discontinued; and the youth problem rapidly assumed more serious proportions. In another village, a young people's program in a well-equipped community building was offered to the WPA recreation officials; but the building was closed and the program discontinued when it was discovered that WPA leadership meant that persons of any church could be admitted." [7]

The extent of church attendance and membership varies greatly with

---

[6] Hamilton, C. Horace and Garnett, W. E., *The Role of the Church in Rural Community Life in Virginia*, Bulletin 267, Virginia Agricultural Experiment Station, Blacksburg, Va., June 1929, p. 88.

[7] Brunner, Edmund deS. and Lorge, Irving, *Rural Trends in Depression Years*, New York: Columbia University Press, 1937, pp. 314–315.

When Urban Amusements Come to Rural Communities.

the locality. In Douglas County, Wis., about 40 percent of the young people reported attending church and 27.5 percent were members.[8] These proportions were lower than those for the other Wisconsin counties where youth surveys were conducted. In these counties almost 40 percent of the youth were church members and a slightly larger percent attended church services and church functions.[9] In parts of rural Ohio the church seems to play a larger role in the lives of the young people. Practically two-thirds of 300 young people interviewed replied that they held a church membership, but the survey also showed that outside of church and Sunday school their organizational affiliations were very meager.[10] Even higher percentages for participation in church activities were reported in Iowa,[11] in Genesee County, N. Y.,[12] and in Connecticut.[13] No doubt still higher percentages would be reported for youth in the rural South were comprehensive data available for youth separate from adults. One study in South Carolina, for example, showed that church attendance ranged from 90 to 100 percent for young people between the ages of 14 and 21.[14]

Some studies point out that more girls than boys attend church, and there are indications that the church, as well as other community organizations, plays a part in the lives of more village than open country young people.[15] An exception to this generalization appears

[8] Wileden, A. F., *What Douglas County Young People Want and What They Are Doing About It*, Rural Youth and Rural Life Series, Extension Service, University of Wisconsin, Madison, Wis., December 1935, p. 5.

[9] Kirkpatrick, E. L. and Boynton, Agnes M., *Interests and Needs of Rural Youth in Wood County, Wisconsin*, Rural Youth and Rural Life Series, Extension Service, University of Wisconsin, Madison, Wis., January 1936, p. 9; and Gessner, Amy A., *Young People in Taylor County*, Rural Youth and Rural Life Series, Extension Service, University of Wisconsin, Madison, Wis., October 1936, p. 7.

[10] Lively, C. E. and Miller, L. J., *Rural Young People, 16 to 24 Years of Age, A Survey of the Status and Activities of 300 Unmarried Individuals in Nine Ohio Townships*, Bulletin No. 73, Ohio State University and Ohio Agricultural Experiment Station, Columbus, Ohio, July 1934, pp. 8–15. See also Johnson, Thomas H., *A Study of Rural Youth, 18 to 25 Years, Out of School and Unmarried*, College of Education, Ohio University, Athens, Ohio, May 1935, pp. 12–13.

[11] Starrak, J. A., *A Survey of Out-of-School Rural Youth in Iowa*, Committee on Education, Iowa State Planning Board, Des Moines, Iowa, 1935, p. 10.

[12] Thurow, Mildred B., *Interests, Activities, and Problems of Rural Young Folk: I. Women 15 to 29 Years of Age*, Bulletin 617, Cornell University Agricultural Experiment Station, Ithaca, N. Y., December 1934, p. 38.

[13] Brundage, A. J. and Wilson, M. C., *Situations, Problems, and Interests of Unmarried Rural Young People 16–25 Years of Age*, Extension Service Circular 239, U. S. Department of Agriculture, Washington, D. C., April 1936, p. 25.

[14] Frayser, Mary E., *The Play and Recreation of Children and Youth in Selected Rural Areas of South Carolina, op. cit.*, p. 54.

[15] Punke, Harold H., "Leisure-Time Attitudes and Activities of High-School Students," *School and Society*, Vol. 43, 1936, p. 887; Kirkpatrick, E. L. and Boynton, Agnes M., *op. cit.*, p. 9; and Dennis, W. V., *Organizations Affecting Farm Youth in Locust Township, Columbia County*, Bulletin 265, Pennsylvania State College Agricultural Experiment Station, State College, Pa., June 1931, p. 38.

in New York State, however, where the greatest need for organizations is among the village and nonfarm married young people.[16]

Except for the church and Sunday school, organizations in rural areas have succeeded in attracting a relatively small percentage of those eligible for membership[17] and have often failed to meet the needs of those who did become members. One survey states that 56 percent of the young men and 46 percent of the young women who were not married did not belong to any organization, while 62 percent of the young men and 54 percent of the young women who were married indicated that they received no benefits from organizations. The young men and women out of school indicated in much larger proportion than those in school that they received no benefits from the organizations of which they were members.[18] One writer makes the statement in regard to a rural section of Pennsylvania that the young people "participated to a very limited extent in the organizational life of the community. The clubs, lodges, and other organizations set up by the community either were not attempting to attract the youth, or their purposes and programs were not of sufficient interest to young people." [19]

Scattered surveys report the membership of specific organizations. One-fourth of all the unmarried young people interviewed in Connecticut were members of the Grange.[20] Less than 2 percent of the young men were members of other farm organizations and less than 1 percent of the young women belonged to a home demonstration group. There are, however, no comparable data for married young people of the same age in the same locality. Communities in Iowa varied widely in the percentage of out-of-school youth belonging to organized groups, the extremes being 10 and 35 percent. Outside of

[16] Anderson, W. A., *Rural Youth: Activities, Interests, and Problems, I. Married Young Men and Women, 15 to 29 Years of Age*, Bulletin 649, Cornell University Agricultural Experiment Station, Ithaca, N. Y., May 1936, p. 47.

[17] Garnett, W. E. and Seymour, Aja Clee, *Membership Relations in Community Organizations*, Bulletin 287, Virginia Agricultural Experiment Station, Blacksburg, Va., June 1932, p. 22. See also Kirkpatrick, E. L., "Forgotten Farmers," *Rural America*, Vol. XI, May 1933; and Frayser, Mary E., *The Play and Recreation of Children and Youth in Selected Rural Areas of South Carolina, op. cit.*, pp. 25–26 and 65–66.

[18] Anderson, W. A., *Rural Youth: Activities, Interests, and Problems, II. Unmarried Young Men and Women, 15 to 29 Years of Age*, Bulletin 661, Cornell University Agricultural Experiment Station, Ithaca, N. Y., January 1937, pp. 27 and 29, and *Rural Youth: Activities, Interests, and Problems, I. Married Young Men and Women, 15 to 29 Years of Age, op. cit.*, p. 38. See also Sones, Ellwood, *A Study of 100 Boys and Girls in Centre County, Pennsylvania*, Master's thesis, Pennsylvania State College, State College, Pa., 1933.

[19] Dennis, W. V., *Social Activities of the Families in the Unionville District, Chester County, Pennsylvania*, Bulletin 286, Pennsylvania State College Agricultural Experiment Station, State College, Pa., April 1933, p. 21.

[20] Brundage, A. J. and Wilson, M. C., *op. cit.*, p. 26.

religious organizations (other than church and Sunday school) which claimed about 6 percent of the total, 4–H Clubs had slightly more than 4 percent, lodges had more than 2 percent, and Future Farmers of America and women's clubs each had a little more than 1 percent of the total in their memberships. Only 23 percent of the total surveyed belonged to any organized group.[21] There is no indication in any of these studies whether the various types of organizations were available to all of the youth surveyed.

It is possible that youth are being reached in equal proportions with other groups since the factors bringing change to rural areas are influencing the whole of the rural population as well as the youth. A recent study in Connecticut shows that "There has been a movement toward the abandonment, the realignment, and the centralization of many rural social, economic, and professional agencies, and much of this movement has been cityward." [22] The attractions of rural institutions may be about as great for youth as for the older population. On Muscatine Island in Iowa, for example, the few young people on the Island attended Island organization meetings in much the same proportion as did the older people.[23]

In Wisconsin the extension program in community activities, including drama, discussion, music, and recreation, was analyzed to find what age groups were furnishing the leadership. This survey comprised a sample of 383 of the 1,500 volunteer local and county leaders of all ages working on all of the various phases of this project. The age group furnishing the greatest proportion of leaders was assumed also to be providing the greatest proportion of participants. It was found that about 50 percent of the drama leaders and about 31 percent of the discussion leaders were in the 15 to 30 age group. This is significant when we find that only about 25 percent of the rural-farm population and 22 percent of the rural-nonfarm population in Wisconsin fall in this 15 to 30 age class. These figures indicate that this kind of program as a whole in Wisconsin is reaching youth 15 to 30 years of age more extensively than it reaches any other corresponding age group.[24]

Youth's participation in social organizations apparently depends to a large extent on two factors: economic status and educational attainment. In Pennsylvania it was found that the children of farm owners

[21] Starrak, J. A., *op. cit.*, p. 11.

[22] Hypes, J. L., *Social Participation in a Rural New England Town*, Teachers College, Columbia University, New York City, 1927, p. 1.

[23] Wakeley, Ray E. and Losey, J. Edwin, *Rural Organizations and Land Utilization on Muscatine Island: A Study of Social Adjustments*, Bulletin 352, Iowa Agricultural Experiment Station, Ames, Iowa, December 1936, p. 103.

[24] Wileden, A. F., " 'Neglected' Youth—What About Them?" *Rural America*, Vol. XII, May 1934, p. 10.

had more varied and more extensive social activities than the children of farm tenants and laborers. The latter had very little share in the organized social life of the community.[25] Although data on the relationship of education to social participation are not available for youth separately, it is likely that the relationship is the same as for groups composed of all ages. In Illinois it was found that the participation of farm people in community activities was directly related to the extent of their formal schooling. While 90 percent of the high school graduates took an active part in the organizations of which they were members, only 60 percent of those with less than an eighth grade education were active members. Voluntary organizations, such as the church, farm and home bureau, 4-H Clubs, cooperatives, social clubs, and lodges, drew their support chiefly from the most stable members of the community, farm owners who stayed on the same farm over a long period of years and who had at least some high school education.[26]

In certain selected rural areas of South Carolina there appeared to be a more or less close relationship between educational attainment and economic status and the types and uses of leisure. The disparity was especially marked between Negroes and whites.[27] Even the church does not serve all occupational groups equally. According to conclusions drawn from one Virginia study, farm and labor groups "either do not care to participate in church activities as much as other groups or [they] do not have the advantage of as much or as efficient church service as do other occupational groups."[28] A survey of the community participation of a relatively immobile group of hired farm laborers in 11 selected counties yielded the conclusion that they did not participate in organizations to any appreciable extent but that they did take some part in the social and informal community life, such as visiting, motion pictures, religious meetings, and shopping trips.[29]

In Arkansas it was found that age and automobile ownership had more effect upon the participation of farm people at religious, social, and recreational events than any other factors tested. "When other things were equal, youth and automobiles each multiplied attendance by three. If age and automobile ownership had been the same in each tenure class, there would have been no significant differences between the attendance of farm owners, tenants, and laborers. As it was, however, farm owners attended 2.5 times as often as laborers and 1.4

[25] Dennis, W. V., *op. cit.*, p. 22. See also Lindstrom, D. E., *Forces Affecting Participation of Farm People in Rural Organization*, Bulletin 423, Illinois Agricultural Experiment Station, Urbana, Ill., May 1936, pp. 103 and 110.

[26] *Ibid.*, pp. 110 and 125.

[27] Frayser, Mary E., *The Use of Leisure in Selected Rural Areas of South Carolina*, *op. cit.*, pp. 76–80.

[28] Hamilton, C. Horace and Garnett, W. E., *op. cit.*, p. 97.

[29] Vasey, Tom and Folsom, Josiah C., *Survey of Agricultural Labor Conditions*, U. S. Department of Agriculture, Farm Security Administration and the Bureau of Agricultural Economics, Washington, D. C., 1937.

A Village Joint.

times as often as tenants." [30]   In one section the highest attendance
rate at religious, social, and recreational events was found among
members of farm owners' families under 25 years of age with automobiles, and the lowest rate was among members of farm laborers'
families under 25 years of age without automobiles.[31]   Thus, social
stratification may play a major role in determining the recreational
opportunities of rural youth.

Organizational life for youth is particularly limited in poor land
areas, such as the Blue Ridge, Cumberland, and Allegheny Plateaus,[32]
and in other parts of the South.[33]   In some of these communities the
only social contacts are those obtained at church gatherings and
funerals and through informal house-to-house visits.   In one community it was deemed inadvisable to have social gatherings of young
people because of the drinking of the young men.[34]   In many sections
of the country youth are passing into maturity after having had little
influence exerted upon them by the regularly established institutions
and organizations of rural life.

The foregoing discussion very largely applies to the social and recreational participation of farm youth.   Limited data suggest that conditions vary so widely in the rural-nonfarm population that specific
generalizations may be made only about particular groups.   Thus, in
agricultural villages youth who are in high school on the whole engage
in numerous social and recreational activities both within and without
the school.   Those out of school, however, show a very low degree of
social participation in comparison with those in school.[35]   There seems
to be a decided drop in the participation of youth in social and recreational activities when their school careers close.

Among the youth of part-time farming families, who may be
considered rural-nonfarm from some points of view, a fairly high

[30] McCormick, T. C., *Rural Social Organization in the Rice Area*, Bulletin No.
296, Arkansas Agricultural Experiment Station, Fayetteville, Ark., December
1933, pp. 37–38. See also McCormick, T. C., *Rural Social Organization in Washington County, Arkansas*, Bulletin No. 285, Arkansas Agricultural Experiment
Station, Fayetteville, Ark., May 1933, pp. 37–40, and *Rural Social Organization in
South-Central Arkansas*, Bulletin No. 313, Arkansas Agricultural Experiment
Station, Fayetteville, Ark., December 1934, pp. 29–34.
[31] McCormick, T. C., *Rural Social Organization in South-Central Arkansas*, *op.
cit.*, p. 34.
[32] Garnett, W. E., in *Economic and Social Problems and Conditions of the
Southern Appalachians*, Miscellaneous Publication No. 205, U. S. Department of
Agriculture, Washington, D. C., January 1935, p. 164.
[33] Raper, Arthur F., *Preface to Peasantry*, Chapel Hill: University of North
Carolina Press, 1936, chs. XVIII, XIX, and XX. See also McCormick, T. C.,
Farm Standards of Living in Faulkner County, Arkansas, Bulletin No. 279, Arkansas Agricultural Experiment Station, Fayetteville, Ark., October 1932, pp. 9–11.
[34] Garnett, W. E., in *Economic and Social Problems and Conditions of the Southern
Appalachians, op. cit.*, p. 164.
[35] Melvin, Bruce L. and Smith, Elna N., *op. cit.*

proportion of young people participate in such social activities as are available. In a study of part-time farming in the Southeast it was found that young people's organizations, for example, were available to 83 percent of the part-time farms with 40 percent of the families having one or more members participating in such organizations. This percent of participation was higher than for nonfarming industrial families studied in the same area, about two-fifths of whom were living in towns, villages, or the open country. Young people's organizations were available to 88 percent of the families but participated in by one or more members of only 24 percent of the families.[36]

INFORMAL LEISURE-TIME ACTIVITIES OF RURAL YOUTH

Outside of the church and other organizations found to a greater or less extent in rural territory, there is quite a gamut of activities that may absorb the leisure time of young people. These range from organized group recreation, such as athletic teams promoted by some local agency or by youth themselves, parties, and picnics, to individual activities, such as swimming, reading, and attendance at motion pictures, public dance halls, and roadhouses.

The literature presents a very confusing picture of the leisure-time pursuits of young people the country over outside of organizations. At one extreme is the statement for one section of the South: "The majority of both races find nothing to do but to sit idly around, tramp off to their neighbors, or while away the time at the store. Their houses are unattractive and their minds unstimulated."[37] At the other extreme is the situation among the unmarried rural youth in five Connecticut townships where the young people enjoyed social activities of a diversified character.[38] Attendance at movies was reported by 93 percent of this group with an average of 28 times a year. Three-fourths of the young women reported attending dances and averaged 22 dances a year, and two-thirds of the young men attended dances on an average of 26 times a year. Between these two situations lie all degrees of extent of recreational activities.

In Ohio the 10 most widespread activities reported were reading, attending shows, automobile riding, playing cards, attending parties, playing basketball, friendly visiting, listening to the radio, attending picnics, and swimming.[39]

[36] Allen, R. H., Cottrell, L. S., Jr., Troxell, W. W., Herring, Harriet L., and Edwards, A. D., *Part-Time Farming in the Southeast*, Research Monograph IX, Division of Social Research, Works Progress Administration, Washington, D. C., 1937, p. 67.

[37] Raper, Arthur F., *op. cit.*, p. 401.

[38] Brundage, A. J. and Wilson, M. C., *op. cit.*, pp. 25–28.

[39] Lively, C. E. and Miller, L. J., *op. cit.*, p. 15. See also Kirkpatrick, E. L. and Boynton, Agnes M., *op. cit.*, pp. 7–8; Gessner, Amy A., *op. cit.*, pp. 5–7; and Anderson, W. A., *Rural Youth: Activities, Interests, and Problems, II. Unmarried Young Men and Women, 15 to 29 Years of Age, op. cit.*, pp. 20–23.

Recreation within the home is still of great importance. In Taylor County, Wis., where 90 percent of the young people indicated that their recreational needs were inadequately met, "Almost two-thirds of these boys and girls found some recreation in their homes * * *. Homes of friends were also important agencies of recreation providing for about 45 percent of the boys and girls. The movie theater is fourth in importance as an agency of recreation." [40]

One important form of recreation in the home is reading but the extent to which this is indulged in varies from locality to locality. Comparable studies made in Illinois and Georgia indicate that the high school youth of Illinois spent more time reading than did the youth of Georgia while the reverse was true of attendance at athletic games. [41] Reading is, however, almost always high on the list of leisure-time activities, [42] although the type of reading matter ranges from newspapers and magazines of varying caliber to books, mostly fiction. [43]

Both the amount and the type of reading on the part of young people are probably largely determined by the availability of a library to any given group. That rural people are on the whole seriously handicapped by lack of library service has been long recognized by the American Library Association. In 1935 it was said that 37 percent of the Nation's population—slightly more than 45,000,000 people— were still without library service. Of these 88 percent lived in the open country or in villages of less than 2,500 population. Moreover, the 40,000,000 rural people who lived outside library service areas formed 74 percent of the total rural population. There are still more than a thousand counties in the United States without a single library within their boundaries. [44]

Surveys in individual States yield the same contrast in library service to rural and urban people. In South Carolina 39.6 percent of the population lived in library areas in 1930–31. But whereas 94 percent of the urban residents of the State had some kind of book service, only 25 percent of the rural people were so favored. [45] In Missouri almost 95 percent of the rural population receive no service from public libraries, while more than 95 percent of the urban population of the State have such service. [46]

[40] Gessner, Amy A., op. cit., p. 5.

[41] Punke, Harold H., op. cit., p. 885.

[42] Gessner, Amy A., op. cit., p. 6.

[43] Anderson, W. A., Rural Youth: Activities, Interests, and Problems, II. Unmarried Young Men and Women, 15 to 29 Years of Age, op. cit., pp. 24–26.

[44] "Contrasts in Library Service," Bulletin of the American Library Association, Vol. 29, 1935, p. 249.

[45] Frayser, Mary E., The Libraries of South Carolina, Bulletin 292, South Carolina Agricultural Experiment Station, Clemson, S. C., October 1933, pp. 7–8.

[46] Morgan, E. L. and Sneed, Melvin W., The Libraries of Missouri, A Survey of Facilities, Research Bulletin 236, Missouri Agricultural Experiment Station, Columbia, Mo., April 1936, p. 15.

In recent years the emergency agencies have done a great deal to help equalize library service. Under the Works Progress Administration about 2,500 free libraries have been established where such services had either been discontinued or had never existed, and 2,000 traveling libraries are providing services for about half a million persons in sparsely settled rural areas, especially in Arkansas, Ohio, Virginia, Georgia, and Texas.[47] In this work the National Youth Administration has had an important part.[48]

The American Library Association indicates that at present there are about 300 tax-supported, county-wide library systems serving the people in the open country and in villages. There are also a number of experiments under way in service to areas larger than a city or county. In the last 2 years State aid for rural library development has been an important factor in building up this service.

One study shows that the leisure-time activities engaged in by both young men and young women are predominantly of the indoor passive type, such as reading, card playing, checkers, chess, and other games, and listening to the radio, but the young men stated that they would prefer to engage in more outdoor activities.[49] Another study also indicates a wish to shift from the more common activities to other activities for which opportunities are often largely lacking, such as tennis, swimming, boating, golf, and camping.[50] This lack in rural areas has been poignantly described as follows: "What I have seen has frequently saddened and distressed me. In some places the country lacks cultural privileges today quite as much as it did a century ago, and the young men and women of farming districts must look to the cities for whatever of social life and amusement and entertainment it is their fortune to purchase. As long as this is the case we cannot make a well balanced race of agriculturalists; we cannot make of country life a life worth living."[51] That lack of opportunities for wholesome recreation is particularly acute in the poor land areas, where there is a "surplus" of youth, is a matter of common observation.

There is a more hopeful side, however. In the 1936 report of the Youth Section of the American Country Life Association the young people stated that "Wiser use of leisure, including recreational programs, activities and facilities seems to be an outstanding need in the

[47] Division of Research, Statistics, and Records, *Report on Progress of the Works Program, June 1937*, Works Progress Administration, Washington, D. C., p. 61.

[48] National Youth Administration, *Facing the Problems of Youth*, Washington, D. C., December 1936, pp. 27–28.

[49] Anderson, W. A., *Rural Youth: Activities, Interests, and Problems, II. Unmarried Young Men and Women, 15 to 29 Years of Age, op. cit.*, p. 36.

[50] Hubbard, Frank W., "Today's Youth Problems," *The Journal of the National Education Association*, Vol. 25, 1936, p. 21.

[51] Beattie, Jessie Louise, "Recreation Experiments in Rural Communities," *Recreation*, Vol. XXIX, 1936, p. 537.

Bringing Books to Rural Youth.

local community * * *." [52] This group recommended the development of various forms of group recreation already carried on successfully in different communities, such as softball leagues; drama and music festivals; folk games and songs; development of art appreciation; hobbies, such as marionettes, metalcraft, and weaving; and discussion and other educational meetings.[53] In some instances the depression has caused rural people, especially youth, to use their initiative in developing recreational activities at home.[54] "With the depression has come almost universally a home talent, home-grown social and recreational life the like of which we have not seen for decades. A little checking up indicates that this program is manned and participated in largely by young people themselves." [55]

While the lack of adequate facilities or programs for wholesome recreation is no doubt partially due to the lack of financial resources in an area, it is not infrequently due to the lack of awareness in communities of the recreational needs of youth. It is often assumed that youth will adopt the practices of adults. The fact that the young people have not accepted the adult patterns of recreation and use of leisure time does not seem to have discouraged community leaders in adhering to this belief. The recreational interests of young people need to be studied as a problem in community organization, and an effort should be made to find ways and means of interesting them in activities that at least will not be harmful.[56] This would apply with equal force to communities that have been overrun with cheap commercial types of recreation and to communities where drunkenness and disorder accompany such social activities as are attempted.[57]

CRIME AND DELINQUENCY IN RURAL AREAS

Urban studies of youth have revealed that the key to the problems of many young people lies in the use they make of their leisure hours.[58]

---

[52] *Education for Living in the Rural Community*, National Conference, Student Section, American Country Life Association, Kalamazoo, Mich., August 10–13, 1936, p. 2.

[53] *Ibid.*, p. 5.

[54] The part that the social and recreational program sponsored by the Works Progress Administration has played in meeting the needs of rural youth during the depression is discussed briefly in ch. VI.

[55] Wileden, A. F., "What Kind of Rural Life Have Young People Reason to Expect in the United States?" speech at Ninth National 4–H Club Camp, Washington, D. C., June 13, 1935, p. 4.

[56] Hoffer, C. R., "Youth as an Object of Sociological Study," *Sociology and Social Research*, Vol. XX, 1936, p. 420.

[57] Gooch, Wilbur I. and Keller, Franklin J., "Breathitt County in the Southern Appalachians," *Occupations*, Vol. XIV, 1936, pp. 1011–1110.

[58] Thrasher, Frederic M., *The Gang*, 2d ed., Chicago: The University of Chicago Press, 1936, p. 79.

It has also been found that the wholesome use of leisure time plays an important role in preventing crime and delinquency. There is no reason to believe that this relationship is any less effective in rural than in urban areas.

The frequency of youthful crime is appalling. J. Edgar Hoover says "Persons who are little more than children form one-fifth of our most dangerous heritage. It appears inconceivable; yet it is a stark fact that our misguided boys and girls are thieving, robbing, holding up banks and stores, and shooting down employees, proprietors and the police who attempt to capture them." [59] In 1934 the United States Census Bureau gathered information from 116 State and Federal prisons, reformatories, and camps and found that 20 percent of the total commitments were under 21 years of age. [60] From 1932 through 1934 the number of youth 19 years of age arrested outnumbered any other age group, but in the last half of 1935 youth 21–23 years of age constituted the largest number. The single age group having the largest number of arrests during 1936 and the first quarter of 1937 was the 22-year-olds. [61]

Crimes of youth were on the increase during the early part of the depression. According to one statement the number of youth below 21 sent to reformatories and prisons was 11 percent greater in 1930 than in 1929, and for those 21 to 24 years of age the increase was more than 15 percent. [62] The survey of youthful crime in Breathitt County, Ky., confirms the fact of an increase for that particular section of mountainous territory. [63]

Table 24 seems to show that youthful crime measured by the number of young people received by Federal and State prisons and reformatories from the courts increased through 1931 but that thereafter there was a consistent decline for all ages until 1935 when those 20 years of age and 21–24 years of age showed a slight increase. While these figures do not by any means measure the extent of criminality among youth, [64] they are useful in indicating the trend.

A number of attempts have been made in the past to discover whether or not there was any relation between crime and economic conditions. These studies and the few studies on the depression of

[59] Speech at a Boys' Club dinner, Chicago, Ill., November 9, 1936.

[60] Johnston, James A., "The First Line of Defense," *School and Society*, Vol. 44, 1936, p. 43.

[61] Federal Bureau of Investigation, *Uniform Crime Reports*, U. S. Department of Justice, Washington, D. C., Second Quarterly Bulletin, 1936, pp. 82–83, and First Quarterly Bulletin, 1937, p. 39.

[62] Office of Education, *Vocational Education and Changing Conditions*, Bulletin No. 174, U. S. Department of the Interior, Washington, D. C., 1934, p. 82.

[63] Gooch, Wilbur I. and Keller, Franklin J., *op. cit.*, p. 1052.

[64] Shalloo, J. P., "Youth and Crime," *Annals of the American Academy of Political and Social Science*, Vol. 194, November 1937, p. 81.

the early thirties were recently summarized.[65] The conclusion drawn was that on the whole there appears to be little correlation between crime and economic conditions.

Difference of opinion exists in regard to the prevalence of crime among youth in rural territory. One authority believes that conditions in rural areas are more serious than statistics would indicate.[66] Attorney General Lutz of Indiana asserts that "there is more crime in proportion in the country than in the city; that arch criminals learn their first lessons of crime in the country, for instance, John Dillinger * * *."[67] On the other hand, studies in five institutions located in California, Michigan, New Jersey, Ohio, and New York, exclusive of New York City, indicate that crime in rural communities is not as great as in urban centers.[68]

Table 24.—Prisoners 15 Through 24 Years of Age Received From Courts by Federal and State Prisons and Reformatories, 1929–1935

Age	Rate per 100,000 population of same age [1]						
	1929	1930	1931	1932	1933	1934	1935
15–17 years	44.8	46.1	49.3	41.0	37.9	39.4	37.9
18 years	146.4	154.1	164.5	150.5	138.0	138.6	130.0
19 years	180.1	194.5	207.8	199.3	174.0	168.2	165.9
20 years	166.8	187.7	210.2	183.9	170.7	155.0	165.7
15–20 years	103.9	111.5	120.9	108.6	98.7	96.3	95.5
21–24 years	152.8	171.2	193.6	184.7	167.0	155.8	159.2

[1] Calculations based on population July 1, of each successive year estimated by the Bureau of the Census.

Source: Bureau of the Census, *Prisoners in State and Federal Prisons and Reformatories*, U. S. Department of Commerce, Washington, D. C., 1929–1935.

The types of crime most prevalent in urban and rural areas appear to differ significantly. Of the rural arrests reported for the first quarter of 1937, 10.5 percent were offenses against the person (homicide, rape, aggravated assault) but only 4.2 percent of urban crimes were of this type.[69] It is well to remember, however, that rural areas are not policed as adequately as the more populous areas; hence only the most serious crimes are brought to justice. These would most likely be offenses against the person. In cities the proportionate

[65] Sellin, Thorsten, *Research Memorandum on Crime in the Depression*, Bulletin 27, New York: Social Science Research Council, 1937, ch. III.

[66] Letter from L. J. Carr, University of Michigan, Ann Arbor, Mich., May 6, 1936.

[67] Lutz, Philip, Jr., "Cooperation in Curbing Crime on Indiana Farms," radio address, February 13, 1936. Obtained from Attorney General's Office, Indianapolis, Ind. See also Thompson, Dave, "Farm Stealing Must Stop!" *The Prairie Farmer* (Indiana edition), Vol. 108, February 29, 1936, pp. 1–2.

[68] Bowler, Alida C. and Bloodgood, Ruth S., *Institutional Treatment of Delinquent Boys*, Bureau Publication No. 230, U. S. Department of Labor, Children's Bureau, 1936, Part 2, p. 35.

[69] Federal Bureau of Investigation, *Uniform Crime Reports, op. cit.*, First Quarterly Bulletin, 1937, p. 14.

percentage is decreased by the greater frequency of other types of crimes.

Generalizations from much of the statistical data are extremely questionable because of variations in legal practice. A study conducted near Nashville, Tenn., in an agricultural county containing a small town shows that most of the juvenile cases up to a certain degree of seriousness had been settled by the judge and the families involved and not even a record was kept unless a commitment was made. But when psychiatrists and social workers were brought in they made the local leader conscious that there was a youthful crime problem.[70] Furthermore, definitions of crimes are inconsistent. In a west Tennessee county chicken stealing is a crime but drawing a knife on another person is not. Thus deliquency is largely a function of the cultural pattern of a community.[71]

When this is recognized, as well as the fact that much of the crime in rural sections, as in urban, may be explicable in terms of under-privilege, obviously the major methods of attack will be through education and personal and vocational guidance. This was perceived by the workers on the Child Welfare Survey of Missouri [72] who repeatedly pointed out that youth and children in particular rural counties were in need of supervision and guidance because of behavior problems.

Surveys of youthful crime in rural territory indicate that the solution lies largely in providing better economic opportunities, guidance for living, and provisions for wholesome social expression of maturing personalities through participation in organizations and through satisfying recreation. Furthermore, conditions of rural living outside the areas that are strongly affected by urban influences seem to provide values that are the antithesis of crime.[73] A recognized method of combating youthful crime whether in rural areas or city centers is the provision of wholesome social and recreational life.

[70] Reckless, Walter C., "Juvenile Delinquency and Behavior Patterning," *Proceedings, Second Biennial Meeting, Society for Research in Child Development*, National Research Council, Washington, D. C., October 31, 1936.

[71] *Ibid.*

[72] Child Welfare Survey conducted by the Civil Works Administration in 1934 in a number of rural counties in Missouri.

[73] Mann, A. R., "Some Foundations for a Philosophy of Country Life," *Rural America*, Vol. X, June 1932, pp. 8–11; and Baker, O. E., *Farming as a Life Work*, Extension Service Circular 224, U. S. Department of Agriculture, Washington, D. C., October 1935, p. 6.

Chapter VI

MEETING THE PROBLEMS OF RURAL YOUTH

VARIOUS ORGANIZATIONS are expanding and adjusting their programs to aid in solving the problems of rural youth. The most important agency in rural society whose function has been, and still is, to prepare youth to make their adjustments into adult life is the public school. The school, like other agencies, has been expanding its program. Since chapter III is devoted to a discussion of the problems of education with emphasis on the public schools, however, attention is focused in this chapter on the special activities of agencies directed primarily toward meeting the needs of out-of-school young people.[1] These agencies, both governmental and nongovernmental, are performing valuable service in pointing out new paths to follow in assisting youth to meet the many problems with which they are confronted in the present-day world.

The major concern of this chapter is not with the number and proportion of rural youth being reached by the various agencies but rather with the type of work that is being promoted. Furthermore, activities designed to help rural youth have been studied with specific attention to the fact that the complex situation confronting rural youth is not a phenomenon of the depression of the early thirties alone and that remedial measures must be designed to meet the long-time situation.

GOVERNMENTAL AGENCIES

Both old and newly established governmental agencies are taking special cognizance of the problems of out-of-school rural youth and have developed constructive programs to meet some phases of their problems. Probably more than 7,000,000 young men and women,

---

[1] The U. S. Office of Education in cooperation with the States fulfills an important function in teaching vocational education in the Smith-Hughes high schools (see ch. III). The organization, Future Farmers of America, is also discussed in chapter III since membership is restricted to boys who are or have been enrolled in vocational agricultural courses in federally-aided high schools.

16 through 24 years of age, living in rural territory, are out of school.[2] Youth in school are occupied and, on the whole, may be said to be adjusted. With leaving school, either through graduation or by dropping out, there comes the anxious period of striving to find a place in the economic world. At least two regular agencies—the Cooperative Extension Service of the United States Department of Agriculture and of the State colleges of agriculture and the federally-aided high schools with regular courses in vocational agriculture—and three emergency agencies—the Civilian Conservation Corps, the National Youth Administration, and the Education Division of the Works Progress Administration—have performed special educational functions for out-of-school youth during the depression as well as providing their regular programs of work. The Office of Education in the Department of the Interior has done much to promote the cause of education for this group.

Education is not the only channel, however, through which services are available to rural youth to help them meet their problems of adjustment and development. The Works Progress Administration, the Agricultural Adjustment Administration, and the Resettlement Administration have been playing important roles in this respect but in such a way that it is very difficult to differentiate the particular benefits accruing to youth from those received by the general population. The United States Employment Service attempts to finds jobs for youth as well as for their elders. The Farm Credit Administration has tried to help youth in a financial way. All of these agencies have been accumulating experience along various lines that should be of great value in formulating future policies and programs.

Cooperative Extension Service

The Cooperative Extension Service of the United States Department of Agriculture and of the State colleges of agriculture promotes its work for youth through the 4–H Club program and through organizations for young adults. The membership of the 4–H Club begins with boys and girls 10 years of age and includes about 1,000,000 young people below 21 years of age. Only 20 percent of the total membership is composed of youth 16 years of age and over,[3] and apparently there is no tendency for the proportion in this age group to increase.[4]

---

[2] According to the 1930 Census (Population Vol. II, pp. 1184–1185) 22.6 percent of the rural youth 16–24 years of age were in school. Applying this percentage, even though it is conservative, to the estimated number of rural youth in 1935 (table 9) yields more than 2,000,000 of the almost 10,000,000 rural youth in school.

[3] Calculated from figures for 1935 provided through the courtesy of the U. S. Department of Agriculture, Office of the Cooperative Extension Service, Washington, D. C.

[4] Joy, Barnard D., *Statistical Analysis of Trends in 4-H Club Work, With Special Reference to 1935*, Extension Service Circular 247, U. S. Department of Agriculture, Washington, D. C., August 1936, p. 16.

A Typical 4–H Club Project.

Furthermore, an analysis of the 4–H Club members 16–20 years of age shows that the out-of-school youth are not being reached proportionally since more than two-thirds of the members of this age are in school while only approximately one-third of the rural young people 16–20 years of age are in school.[5]

The 4–H Club work is organized primarily for boys and girls whose families make their living from agriculture [6] and largely fails to reach the nonfarm segment of the youth population.   Moreover, if the situation in Illinois is typical, it draws its members primarily from the homes having the greater economic and social advantages,[7] thus not serving the lower income groups.   Apparently, difficulty has been encountered in developing a program of 4–H Club work which appeals to youth above the sixteenth year except to those in positions of leadership.[8]

The failure of the 4–H Club program to hold rural youth in the upper age group has caused the extension service to promote a program outside the 4–H Clubs especially designed to appeal to this age. The work thus far is largely in the experimental stage.   The principal lines of activity have been the promotion of better farming and the development of leadership in educational and cultural guidance and in recreational activities.[9]   In 1935 there were more than 1,800 older youth groups with an enrollment of nearly 45,000.[10]   By 1936 the number of groups had increased to approximately 2,000 with a total enrollment of 51,000.[11]

These clubs are widely scattered, and the total enrollment in any one State is not large.   In only 2 States, Illinois and Arkansas, was the membership more than 4,000 in 1936 (table 25).   In some States the groups have arisen spontaneously while in others they have been fostered by the State extension service.   It is encouraging to see that this work is being carried forward in the States with large areas of submarginal land as well as in those in which fertile farming areas predominate.

[5] *Ibid.*, p. 17.

[6] Harris, T. L., *Four-H Club Work in West Virginia*, Bulletin 241, West Virginia Agricultural Experiment Station, Morgantown, W. Va., April 1931, p. 15.

[7] Lindstrom, D. E. and Dawson, W. M., *Selectivity of 4-H Club Work: An Analysis of Factors Influencing Membership*, Bulletin 426, Illinois Agricultural Experiment Station, Urbana, Ill., August 1936, p. 255; and Duthie, Mary Eva, *4-H Club Work in the Life of Rural Youth*, Ph. D. thesis, University of Wisconsin, Madison, Wis., 1935, p. 95.

[8] Wileden, A. F., " 'Neglected' Youth—What About Them?" *Rural America*, Vol. XII, May 1934, pp. 10–11.

[9] Statement by Graham, A. B., U. S. Department of Agriculture, Cooperative Extension Service, Washington, D. C.

[10] Wilson, M. C., *Statistical Results of Cooperative Extension Work, 1935*, Extension Service Circular 244, U. S. Department of Agriculture, Washington, D. C., June 1936, p. 7.

[11] Calculated from reports in the U. S. Department of Agriculture, Office of the Cooperative Extension Service, Washington, D. C.

Table 25.—Young People Reached by the Cooperative Extension Service of the United States Department of Agriculture Through the Older Young People's Program, by Geographic Division and State, 1936

Geographic division and State	Number of groups organized	Number of members		
		Total	Young men	Young women
United States	1,981	50,733	24,530	26,203
New England	71	3,083	1,450	1,633
Maine	3	108	34	74
New Hampshire	20	452	220	232
Vermont	14	1,043	476	567
Massachusetts	11	755	333	422
Rhode Island	4	88	35	53
Connecticut	19	637	352	285
Middle Atlantic	81	2,108	1,200	908
New York	39	1,268	777	491
New Jersey	14	238	102	136
Pennsylvania	28	602	321	281
East North Central	309	13,990	7,341	6,649
Ohio	62	3,530	1,825	1,705
Indiana	66	2,401	1,190	1,211
Illinois	92	6,029	2,992	3,037
Michigan	27	736	444	292
Wisconsin	62	1,294	890	404
West North Central	185	5,813	2,791	3,022
Minnesota	35	1,148	606	542
Iowa	40	1,912	980	932
Missouri	24	614	308	306
North Dakota	41	772	165	607
South Dakota	3	145	92	53
Nebraska	10	161	71	90
Kansas	32	1,061	569	492
South Atlantic	571	10,770	4,507	6,263
Delaware	3	90	43	47
Maryland	26	751	356	395
Virginia	65	1,256	285	971
West Virginia	87	1,920	954	966
North Carolina	91	1,790	762	1,028
South Carolina	40	500	233	267
Georgia	203	3,894	1,732	2,162
Florida	56	569	142	427
East South Central	244	4,761	2,110	2,651
Kentucky	46	914	467	447
Tennessee	53	1,398	642	756
Alabama	26	613	198	415
Mississippi	119	1,836	803	1,033
West South Central	407	8,373	4,363	4,010
Arkansas	268	5,124	2,520	2,604
Louisiana	9	446	204	242
Oklahoma	32	1,704	798	906
Texas	98	1,099	841	258
Mountain	99	1,506	571	935
Montana	9	226	109	117
Idaho	6	68	68	—
Wyoming	3	43	11	32
Colorado	6	59	18	41
New Mexico	42	581	211	370
Arizona	—	—	—	—
Utah	32	517	149	368
Nevada	1	12	5	7
Pacific	14	329	197	132
Washington	2	33	10	23
Oregon	5	103	64	39
California	7	193	123	70

Source: U. S. Department of Agriculture, Office of the Cooperative Extension Service, Division of Extension Studies, Washington, D. C.

There is at the present time a committee known as the Older Rural Youth Committee of the Extension Section of the Land-Grant College Association whose duty it is to promote the organization of such groups. It is the policy of this committee to "help young people to analyze their own problems and to formulate their own programs." In accordance with this position the committee recently made the following suggestions to the several States:[12]

"(1) At present, our primary interest should be with young men and women who are out of school, at home on farms, and are not yet married, or are not farming on their own account.

(2) The Director of Extension should appoint a college older rural youth committee.

(3) At each college, two persons, one representing agriculture and the other home economics, should be designated by the Director as leaders for the program on older rural youth.

(4) A few demonstration counties should be selected in each State in which to institute this program.

(5) When there are less than 25 interested youth members in a county, a county organization should be formulated. When the number grows sufficiently to warrant them, local units may be formed.

(6) Each unit of young persons should have its own officers, counselors, and leaders.

(7) Two other organizations are needed: (a) a county council of officers of the local units of young people; (b) a county committee of counselors and leaders and the extension agents.

(8) Additional studies of the interests, activities, and problems of the young people should be made."[13]

The diversity of approach in the various States is well characterized by the situation in the Northeastern States where "Some States are concentrating on honor clubs or outstanding 4–H members; others are broadening the field to include all farm youth, regardless of 4–H experience; and others are opening the field up to all rural youth. In some cases the young men organize separately from the young women, although provision is usually made for bringing the two groups together. Again, the approach occasionally has been along father-and-son lines."[14]

A few examples of the interests of these older youth groups will suffice to illustrate further the scope of the programs being promoted. In Illinois, for more than 2 years, these youth groups have been holding forum discussions on present-day problems. The development of

---

[12] From the report of the committee presented by L. R. Simons, Chairman, at the meeting of the Land-Grant College Association, Washington, D. C., November 17, 1937.

[13] Ibid.

[14] Kendall, J. C., "Integration of Extension Programs in Order to Present a Continuing Program Through 4–H Clubs, Older Youth Groups, Young Married Groups, and Adult Organizations," paper read at the Land-Grant College Association, Washington, D. C., November 17, 1937.

the programs has been largely in the hands of the young people themselves with the Extension Service offering advice and suggestions for the conduct of the meetings. In Indiana a small group has been studying methods of agricultural cooperation. In Montana the programs consist of four phases: economic and social improvement; general education, largely through the medium of group discussion; social and recreational programs for both the clubs and the community; and special community service.[15] The young people of Missouri have held institutes dealing with farm problems. During the winter of 1933-34 instruction in typewriting, farm and home record keeping, and amateur dramatics was given in the South Dakota clubs.[16] Dramatics have a prominent place in many of the young people's groups.[17] In the Utopia Clubs of Kentucky emphasis has been given to such projects as landscaping, farm accounts, clothing budgets, poultry, and other subjects, following the pattern of the 4-H Clubs.[18] Study groups also make up the bulk of the activity of the group in St. Louis County, Mo., where the members meet one night each week to study dramatics, chorus work, orchestra, English, and public speaking under instruction secured from the Adult-Education Service of the State. But social hours are also indulged in after the regular business meetings are concluded.[19]

Of particular promise is the direction being taken by an Iowa club. In September 1937 some of the members of the Boone County Rural Young People's Club were hosts to a group of representatives of the Boone Junior Chamber of Commerce from the county seat, Boone, a town of 12,000 inhabitants and the only one of any size in the entire county, at a meeting called for the purpose of discussing plans for cooperative community activities. A joint rural-urban committee was appointed to arrange the details of a plan of action.[20]

At least three States—Iowa, Kansas, and Missouri—maintain a regular service at the State college of agriculture for sending out material to assist youth in the development of programs. Fourteen States have a person attached to the extension staff of the State college of agriculture whose particular duty it is to promote these

[15] Extension Service, *Organization and Programs for Farm Young People*, Extension Service Circular 229, U. S. Department of Agriculture, Washington, D. C., December 1935, p. 19.

[16] *Ibid.*, p. 27.

[17] For a statement concerning the rural arts program of the Extension Service in the various States, see Patten, Marjorie, *The Arts Workshop of Rural America*, New York: Columbia University Press, 1937. This book does not refer specifically to older youth groups but surveys the general program which benefits young and old alike.

[18] Extension Service, *Organization and Programs for Farm Young People, op. cit.*, p. 9.

[19] *Ibid.*, p. 18.

[20] Rural Youth Section, *Over the State With Rural Youth Organizations*, Extension Service, Iowa State College, Ames, Iowa, October 1937, p. 6.

older youth groups. In some cases this person is attached to the 4–H Club office, and in other cases he reports to the director of the extension service in the State.

Office of Education and the Federally-aided High Schools

The federally-aided high schools with courses in vocational agriculture have for many years promoted part-time and evening classes in agricultural education. This work has been greatly expanded during and since the depression of the early thirties.[21] This program of work was designed to assist those who were out of school and unable to find employment by giving training which would equip them for work when the opportunity came.[22]

In some cases the plans called for informal instruction in agriculture, agricultural shopwork, and community activities. One of the most comprehensive State-wide programs of this kind was set up in Louisiana for farm boys 14–25 years of age without regard to previous schooling.[23] The purpose was threefold: to assist boys to establish themselves as farmers on a satisfactory basis; to assist those interested in related work, such as farm shop, blacksmithing, sirup making, etc.; and to provide training for participation in home and community improvement. An individual program was worked out for each boy.

In Ohio there were, in 1935, 167 part-time classes in vocational agriculture for out-of-school boys 16–25 years of age. The Ohio plan has been followed successfully for some years.[24] It begins with "finding surveys" to get in touch with out-of-school farm youth. These surveys are followed by home surveys of needs and resources which form the basis for planning what phase of instruction is to be taken up in the group meeting once a week. The instruction period is followed by a period of recreational activities. The completion of the unit course of instruction frequently leads to the formation of a Young Farmers Association, thus giving continuity to the program from year to year.

Part-time classes for out-of-school young men in Catchings, Miss.,[25] combine vocational agricultural training with individual business pro-

[21] Vocational Division, *Digest of Annual Reports of State Boards for Vocational Education to the Office of Education*, Fiscal Year Ended June 30, 1935, U. S. Department of the Interior, Office of Education, Washington, D. C. Data for 1936 show a slight decrease in enrollment in part-time and evening classes in vocational agriculture.

[22] Swanson, H. B., *Youth . . . Education for Those Out of School*, Bulletin 1936, No. 18–III, U. S. Department of the Interior, Office of Education, Washington, D. C., p. 1.

[23] *Ibid.*, p. 59.

[24] *Ibid.*, p. 58.

[25] Waller, T. M., "Things Done With Out-of-School Boys in Catchings School District," *Mississippi Vocational News*, Vol. XVI, No. 12, 1935, p. 3.

grams designed to establish the youth in farming. Trades related to agriculture are also taught.

The horizon of activity of the public schools is being expanded more and more to include the out-of-school group. This tendency shows itself in the increasing emphasis on nursery schools and kindergartens and on the subject of parent education, both of which are particularly helpful to young parents. The development of these two phases in rural territory has, as usual, lagged behind the cities. While programs for part-time training of young people who have either dropped out of school or been graduated have most frequently emphasized the vocational motive, some progress has been made in orienting part-time education toward other important objectives, such as good citizenship, improved home membership, and worthy use of leisure time. In the vanguard of this movement has been the Office of Education of the Department of the Interior, which in addition to its usual services to the field of education, has pioneered in conservation education, radio, and public forums.[26] Each of these fields needs further development in rural territory.

National Youth Administration

The National Youth Administration came into existence on June 26, 1935. It has four major objectives:[27]

"(1) To provide funds for the part-time employment of needy school, college, and graduate students between 16 and 25 years of age so that they can continue their education.

(2) To provide funds for the part-time employment on work projects of young persons, chiefly from relief families, between 18 and 25 years of age, the projects being designed not only to provide valuable work experience but to benefit youth generally and the communities in which they live.

(3) To encourage the establishment of job training, counseling, and placement services for youth.

(4) To encourage the development and extension of constructive leisure-time activities."

---

[26] *Annual Report of the Secretary of the Interior, For the Fiscal Year Ending June 30, 1937*, Washington, D. C., pp. 262–263. See pamphlets prepared by the Committee on Youth Problems which functioned in the U. S. Department of the Interior, Office of Education, from the fall of 1934 to the spring of 1936. The Committee's activity was made possible by a grant from the General Education Board. The pamphlets are: *Youth . . . How Communities Can Help*, Bulletin 1936, No. 18–I; Glover, Katherine, *Youth . . . Leisure for Living*, Bulletin 1936, No. 18–II; Swanson, H. B., *Youth . . . Education for Those Out of School*, Bulletin 1936, No. 18–III; Kitson, Harry D., *Youth . . . Vocational Guidance for Those Out of School*, Bulletin 1936, No. 18–IV; Harley, D. L., *Youth . . . Finding Jobs*, Bulletin 1936, No. 18–V; and Jessen, Carl A. and Hutchins, H. Clifton, *Youth . . . Community Surveys*, Bulletin 1936, No. 18–VI.

[27] National Youth Administration, *Facing the Problems of Youth*, Washington, D. C., December 1936, p. 8.

Although the National Youth Administration was established primarily to assist youth of relief status, in its operation it has helped many others. This discussion therefore is oriented toward the broader rather than the restricted service [28] that this organization has rendered through the several phases of its program. The work has been accomplished largely through State organizations, the National Office and National Advisory Committee functioning primarily as coordinating and advisory units. The program operates in each State with the advice of a State Advisory Committee.

Student aid is extended on a work basis to youth who cannot attend school without financial assistance. Local school authorities select the youth and supervise the work for which the students are paid. A total of 404,700 secondary school, college, and graduate students were being helped in April 1936, the peak month of that year.[29] Of this number 275,500 were in high school, but there is no way to determine accurately how many of these were rural youth.

The peak month during the following year was also April when the total number receiving student aid reached almost 444,000.[30] The next year the number of students receiving student aid was cut one-third, chiefly because of the reduction in funds made available to the National Youth Administration.

The wages paid have been for "Clerical and office work; library, museum, and laboratory assistance; the conducting of forums, adult education classes, and other civic ventures; special research; grounds and building maintenance * * *." [31] The youth going to high school may receive no more than $6 a month. The maximum that may be paid in any one month to a student receiving college aid is $20, while those in graduate schools may not earn in excess of $40 in any one month.[32] The pay has been low but it has enabled thousands of youth who were close to the poverty line to continue their education.

An analysis of the NYA student aid quotas for 1936–37 indicates that rural youth may be receiving more than their proportionate share of this type of assistance. About 18 percent of the total was allocated to counties having no incorporated place with more than 2,500 population. According to the 1930 Census only 13 percent of the

[28] See Melvin, Bruce L., *Rural Youth on Relief*, Research Monograph XI, Division of Social Research, Works Progress Administration, Washington, D. C., 1937, ch. VI, for a discussion of the National Youth Administration as an agency for meeting the needs of youth in rural relief families.
[29] A small number of grade school pupils were included who were 16 years of age and over.
[30] Division of Research, Statistics, and Records, *Report on Progress of the Works Program, December 1937*, Works Progress Administration, Washington, D. C., p. 64.
[31] National Youth Administration, *Facing the Problems of Youth, op. cit.*, p. 14.
[32] National Youth Administration, *School Aid 1937–1938*, Bulletin 9, p. 4, and *College and Graduate Aid 1937–1938*, Bulletin 10, p. 5, Washington, D. C., 1937.

total population of the country lived in these counties. Another 23 percent was allocated to counties having incorporated places with populations of from 2,500 to 10,000. These counties contained 21 percent of the country's population.[33]

This apparent advantage of rural youth [34] may reflect the disadvantages in educational opportunity which rural youth face and which the National Youth Administration, despite certain handicaps, is helping to overcome. The regulations for giving student aid do not limit the expenditures to youth on relief. This is one of the few emergency activities that was not restricted to the relief group and can thus contribute to the solution of the larger problem of making up the deficit in education among the youth of all underprivileged rural groups.

In 1937 a new educational program for out-of-school young people was initiated by the National Youth Administration in cooperation with the Department of Agriculture and various agricultural schools and colleges. This is a Nation-wide resident training project which is making it possible for boys and girls from low income farm families to spend from 6 weeks to 6 months at the State agricultural colleges, working for their subsistence while taking courses in agriculture and home economics. The students are selected with the assistance of the local county agents and vocational agricultural instructors. By October 3,300 students from families receiving some form of public relief were attending 40 schools in 10 States.[35]

Approximately half of each student's time is devoted to work on projects established in connection with the schools. These consist of various forms of construction work about the school property, such as the construction of workshops and cooperative dormitories, maintenance of demonstration plots and plant nurseries, work in the barns and dairies, assistance to farm and home demonstration agents, and similar tasks. Students earn a monthly sum not exceeding one-half of the Works Progress Administration security wage prevailing in the region but sufficient to cover their expenses for room, board, medical care, and equipment. In addition, they earn from $5 to $10 each month with which to meet personal needs. The monthly payments per student range from $18 to $28, depending on the locality.[36] To reduce costs to a minimum the students cooperate in doing most of the work in connection with their living arrangements, even raising a considerable portion of the food in some instances.

[33] Melvin, Bruce L., op. cit. There is so little difference between the percent of the population 15 through 24 years of age and of the total population living in these residence groups that separate calculation of the total youth by residence was unnecessary.

[34] It is not known how many youth in the second group of counties were rural.

[35] Division of Research, Statistics, and Records, Report on Progress of the Works Program, December 1937, op. cit., p. 67.

[36] Office of the Director of the National Youth Administration, Washington, D. C.

NYA Trains Prospective Farmers.

NYA Gardening Project.

Because many of the students selected have had less than a high school education, the bulk of the training is given through demonstration methods in such fields as farm practices, soil conservation, soil chemistry, dairying, poultry raising, crop diversification, and care of farm equipment. Girls are trained with a view to instilling certain standards of home maintenance and are instructed in personal hygiene, cooking, marketing, home gardening, and food preservation. The course of study is reduced to as practical terms as possible, and methods of instruction are informal.

The NYA has also established many youth training centers designed to provide inexperienced youth with a knowledge of and training in occupations found in their home communities. These centers are widely scattered over the United States; the extent to which rural youth are reached depends on the location of a particular project. The setup at Passamaquoddy Village, Maine, affords an excellent example of the methods and objectives followed.

The first year of the Passamaquoddy experiment ended on October 30, 1937. Each of 225 young men had been provided work experience for 5 to 6 weeks on 3 different types of jobs. Among the score or more types of occupational experience provided were painting, electrical work, carpentry, plumbing, steam fitting, and automotive work. Besides being given the chance to acquire occupational experience, these youth were also afforded an opportunity to acquire sound work habits. Supplementing the industrial training were classes in mathematics, science, and English closely associated with their work activities.[37]

The work projects of the National Youth Administration are confined to out-of-school youth who have been certified as eligible for employment on the Works Program and who have registered with the United States Employment Service. An analysis of the distribution of work among 2,120 counties in the United States in January 1937 showed that 18 percent of the youth employed on work projects were in counties having no incorporated place with over 2,500 population although only about 13 percent of the total population of the United States live in the 1,400 counties belonging to this class. The counties that have incorporated places of 2,500 to 10,000 population had about 16 percent of the employment although this group of counties has 21 percent of the total population of the country.[38]

The work projects upon which youth are engaged are related in so far as possible to the training, skills, and aptitudes of the individuals. The development of skills is perhaps one of the most important

[37] Brown, Richard R., "NYA Uses Quoddy in Education Test," *New York Times*, October 24, 1937.

[38] Melvin, Bruce L., *op. cit.*, ch. VI. This chapter calls attention to the obstacles encountered in the operation of the National Youth Administration program in rural areas.

phases of this work since almost 50 percent of those working on the projects of the National Youth Administration have had no previous work experience. An analysis of the work being done in the latter part of 1936 by 180,703 youth on work projects showed that 24 percent were assigned to recreation and community service projects, 10 percent to construction projects where skills in trades, such as carpentering and bricklaying, were taught, and 14 percent to public service projects. Other projects provided activities in sewing, domestic science, guide service, agriculture, land development, and highway beautification. The last three types were in operation especially in rural areas. The average pay per month for all youth employment on work projects was $15.46, the range being from $10.44 per month in Kentucky to $21.28 in California.[39] Since then the average monthly earnings have been a little higher, fluctuating between $16 and $17.[40]

The all time peak in employment on NYA work projects was in April 1937 when more than 192,000 youth were employed. The number fluctuated between 180,000 and 190,000 during the first 5 months of 1937, after which the number steadily declined. Several factors combined to bring about this decline. Funds for the operation of the program were reduced somewhat. The effect of this curtailment was not as serious as it might have been, however, since at the same time there was a temporary increase in employment opportunities in both regular and seasonal occupations because of the temporary improvement in economic conditions.

Another analysis was made of the type of experience being obtained by these youth during the first part of October 1937. Unfortunately the categories used are not identical with those used in 1936, which makes comparison difficult. This analysis shows that 30 percent were employed on professional and clerical projects among which clerical projects predominated. Goods projects occupied more than 16 percent of the youth (10.8 percent working on sewing projects and 5.6 percent on workshop projects). About 13 percent of the youth worked on the development of recreational facilities and almost 12 percent were recreational leaders in parks and play centers. Public buildings jobs occupied more than 10 percent of the youth. Other construction activities (highway, road, and street projects and conservation projects) were less important. At that time there were about 123,000 young men and women employed.[41]

How many of these youth were rural is not known. If the same percentage applied in October 1937 as applied roughly to an analysis of NYA employment in June 1936, then slightly more than one-fifth were

[39] National Youth Administration, *Administrative and Program Operation of the National Youth Administration, June 26, 1935–January 1, 1937*, Washington, D. C., pp. 6 and 32.

[40] Division of Research, Statistics, and Records, *Report on Progress of the Works Program, December 1937*, op. cit., p. 66.

[41] *Ibid.*, pp. 65–66.

rural young people.[42]   Included among these would be the youth from farms who participated in the resident training projects previously mentioned.[43]   How many additional farm youth were employed on other types of projects is not known.   The resident training projects were developed particularly for farm youth.   There was a definite need for this type of training program for out-of-school young people who were forced to remain in rural areas.   The usual type of work projects was difficult to operate in many rural areas where the young people who are eligible for employment by the NYA often live scattered over wide areas, thus making the cost of transportation and supervision prohibitive.   These educational projects cannot entirely take the place of regular work projects for needy farm young people since the maximum cash income on the resident vocational training projects is $5 per month.

The National Youth Administration may be reaching a larger percentage of the rural-nonfarm than of the rural-farm youth.   This is of particular importance since youth in industrial villages as well as their elders have been among the most intense sufferers during the depression.   Furthermore, since youth are probably among those having the least opportunity to receive special training for a vocation, the NYA program of uniting work and training is a distinct service to a much neglected group.   Its functions, however, might well be extended to others than those certified as eligible for employment under the Works Program.

The Junior Placement Service of the National Youth Administration operates in conjunction with 65 offices of the United States Employment Service in as many cities where junior placement counselors concentrate on placing youth in jobs.   Efforts are made to place the youth in positions for which they are adapted.[44]   Through these offices and others of the Federal and State employment services youth are being aided in finding jobs, but the proportion of those placed who are rural residents cannot as yet be determined.

Unfortunately for rural youth these counselors are usually located in cities with the result that their efforts are necessarily confined to job opportunities in the cities.   Hence this service can be taken advantage of by rural young people only when they come into the city.   Moreover, the fundamental need for the migration of some youth from rural areas of limited resources, though recognized in the abstract, has not been incorporated into the policy of the Junior Placement Service.   It has been felt that rural young people coming into

---

[42] Melvin, Bruce L., *op. cit.*, p. 51.

[43] See p. 96.

[44] Division of Research, Statistics, and Records, *Report on Progress of the Works Program, December 1937, op. cit.*, p. 68.   See also *Hearings Before the Subcommittee of the Committee on Appropriations, House of Representatives, in Charge of Deficiency Appropriations*, 75th Cong., 1st sess., January 13, 1937, pp. 56–57.

the cities in any considerable number would jeopardize the opportunities of the excess unemployed youth already in the cities, and the chances for success or security of the rural youth migrants would be restricted by the competition of the unemployed urban youth.

Vocational guidance is an important function being performed by the National Youth Administration to assist youth—especially out-of-school youth—to make occupational adjustments. The guidance consists largely of giving information about various fields of work, training required, pay and promotional possibilities, and relative availability of jobs. This work is usually promoted by cooperation with sponsors of work projects, individual guidance bureaus, and other agencies that advise youth on occupational opportunities. In many States special bulletins on occupations and occupational opportunities have been prepared. This service operates in practically every State in one form or another and in varying degrees of extensiveness.[45]

Apprentice training has also been promoted by the National Youth Administration through the Federal Committee on Apprentice Training. While this should contribute somewhat to broadening employment opportunities for young people, its chief purpose is to set up standards to safeguard those entering the skilled trades. This work was made a permanent function of the Department of Labor by a congressional act signed August 16, 1937.[46] Since industry is located chiefly in urban centers, the bulk of the apprentices will naturally be drawn from urban youth. The proportion of the apprentices in the Nation's industrial establishments which comes from the farms and small towns is not known. A realistic approach to the problems of the "surplus" of youth in some regions [47] would involve more intensive exploration of the possibility of extending opportunities for apprenticeships to rural young people.

It must be remembered, however, that the term *apprentice* is being defined in a very restricted sense [48] and that those occupations which either have or could have apprentices in this restricted sense include probably little more than 10 percent of the gainfully employed persons in the United States. The apprenticeship system does not,

[45] National Youth Administration, *Report on the Placement and Guidance Program*, Washington, D. C., February 1938.
[46] Public, No. 308, 75th Cong., 1st sess.
[47] See ch. I.
[48] Special Release No. 3, U. S. Department of Labor, Federal Committee on Apprentice Training, March 1938, defines the term to mean "A person at least 16 years of age who is covered by a written agreement with an employer, and approved by the State Apprenticeship Council or other established authority, which apprentice agreement provides for not less than 4,000 hours of reasonably continuous employment for such person, for his participation in an approved schedule of work experience through employment and for at least 144 hours per year of related supplemental instruction."

therefore, safeguard the training period—varying from a few weeks to a few months or a year or two—of the other thousands of young people who must enter the labor market every year with no assurance of advance or ultimate security. Rural youth are more likely to be found engaged in occupations other than those protected by apprenticeship, if indeed they are fortunate enough to obtain employment at anything but unskilled labor.

During 1936–37 the National Youth Administration experimented with setting up educational work camps for young women.[49] This phase of the program was discontinued after a year's trial, chiefly because of the high per capita cost of maintenance.[50]

Civilian Conservation Corps

The Civilian Conservation Corps, initiated in 1933, was created originally "for the purpose of relieving the acute condition of widespread distress and unemployment * * * and in order to provide for the restoration of the country's depleted natural resources and the advancement of an orderly program of useful public works * * * " [51] Though the original act did not contain any provision as to the ages of the men to be employed, executive and administrative action in the early days of operation determined that the emergency conservation work should be primarily a young man's program.[52] The types of jobs performed by the youth in the CCC camps fall into 10 general classifications: [53] (1) structural improvements (including bridges, fire towers, service buildings, etc.); (2) transportation improvements (including truck trails, minor roads, airplane landing fields, etc.); (3) erosion control (including check dams, terracing, terrace outletting, vegetative covering, etc.); (4) flood control, irrigation, and drainage (including dams, channel work, ditching, riprap, etc.); (5) forest culture (including planting of trees, stand improvement, nursery work, seed collection); (6) forest protection (including fire fighting, fire prevention, and presuppression, pest and disease control, etc.); (7) landscape and recreation (including public camp- and picnic-ground development, lake- and pond-site clearing, landscaping, etc.); (8) range (including stock driveways, elimination of predatory animals, etc.); (9) wild life (including stream improvement, stocking fish, emergency wild life feeding, food and cover planting,

---

[49] Melvin, Bruce L., *op. cit.*, ch. VI.

[50] Office of the Director of the National Youth Administration, Washington, D. C. This program was an outgrowth of the camp program for women begun under the Federal Emergency Relief Administration in 1934. The emphasis in the earlier camps was on workers' education, whereas in the NYA camps the emphasis was on work projects.

[51] Public, No. 5, 73d Cong.

[52] World War veterans were also enrolled.

[53] *Annual Report of the Director of Emergency Conservation Work, Fiscal Year Ending June 30, 1936*, Washington, D. C., p. 4.

etc.); (10) miscellaneous (including emergency work, surveys, mosquito control, etc.).

In the Act of June 28, 1937, extending the life of the Civilian Conservation Corps 3 more years, the additional purpose of providing general educational and vocational training was written into the act. By the end of 1937, 1,800,000 unemployed, unmarried young men from 17 through 28 years of age had been enrolled in the camps.[54] The regular period of enrollment is 6 months although many youth have had two or more periods. The new act limits the enrollment to 2 years [55] but specifies that enrollment need not be continuous. The peak in the number of men in the camps was reached in August 1935 when there were 427,300 enrolled juniors,[56] that is, unemployed single men 17 through 28 years of age. The camps were established principally for the benefit of this age group. Since July 1, 1937, the enrolled strength of the Corps may not exceed 300,000 at any one time, of which not more than 30,000 may be World War veterans.[57]

In September 1935 the age limit for enrollment was reduced from 18 to 17 years. This caused a considerable increase in applications since a great many youth 17 years of age are out of school and unemployed. The bulk of the enrollment is composed of young men under 21 years of age. During the year prior to April 1937, 75 percent of the enrollees had not reached their twenty-first birthday. Well over one-half of the juniors selected during that year were 17 or 18 years of age.[58]

It is probable that 50 percent of all junior enrollees who have passed through the CCC camps have come from rural territory.[59] This would mean that by January 1, 1938, about 900,000 young men from low income or relief families in rural areas had spent varying periods of time in a camp. This is a substantial proportion of the

---

[54] Information from Office of the Director of Emergency Conservation Work, Washington, D. C. See also Persons, W. Frank, "Selecting 1,800,000 Young Men for the C. C. C.," *Monthly Labor Review*, Vol. 46, 1938, pp. 846–851.

[55] The length of the service to be counted from July 1, 1937, the effective date of the act.

[56] *Annual Report of the Director of Emergency Conservation Work, Fiscal Year Ending June 30, 1936, op. cit.,* p. 2; and Melvin, Bruce L., *op. cit.,* pp. 96–97.

[57] See Section 7 of the Act of June 28, 1937, which provided for additional Indian enrollees as well as territorial and insular possession enrollees. These had also been enrolled since the beginning of the Civilian Conservation Corps.

[58] *Fourth Anniversary Report to the President*, Director of Emergency Conservation Work, Washington, D. C., April 5, 1937, p. 10. Evidence of the need of 17- and 18-year olds for the type of training and experience available in CCC camps continues to be borne out by later enrollments. See CCC Office, *Quarterly Selection Report, Covering the January 1938 Enrollment of the Civilian Conservation Corps,* prepared by the U. S. Department of Labor, March 4, 1938, pp. 2–3.

[59] Information from Office of the Director of Emergency Conservation Work, Washington, D. C.

more than 2,000,000 rural youth who have been on relief rolls since 1933 when the Federal Government first began dealing officially with the problem of destitution.[60]   The percentage of youth in the camps from rural territory has steadily increased since early in the history of emergency conservation work.   Whereas in the beginning the bulk of the enrollment came from the cities, by January 1937 rural youth made up 54.7 percent[61] of the total enrollment.   By that time, therefore, the young people from rural areas were in the camps in numbers disproportionate to the percentage they constituted of the total youth population.   In 1930, according to the census, the proportion of all youth who were rural was 43.9 percent and in 1935, according to estimates, it was approximately 48 percent.[62]

In January 1937, when an analysis was made of the place of origin of the youth then in the camps, the Civilian Conservation Corps had an enrollment of 350,350.   Seventy-five percent, or 262,760, were from the open country or from centers with less than 25,000 population.   Of these 191,494 were rural, but of this rural group only a little over one-third, 35.9 percent, were from farms.   The others, approximately two-thirds (64.1 percent), were rural-nonfarm youth. This indicates that the Civilian Conservation Corps is reaching a much greater relative proportion of rural-nonfarm youth than farm youth.   Furthermore, if the number of rural-nonfarm youth is added to the number of youth in centers from 2,500 to 25,000 population, it is found that this group constitutes 55 percent of all enrollees.[63] Thus, more than one-half of the enrollees at the time of the survey came from 35 percent of the total population.[64]

At least two hypotheses may be offered for this situation.   One is that the publicity about the Civilian Conservation Corps may not reach the open country youth as it does the youth of the villages and towns; the other is that poverty-stricken families from the open country have been going to the county seats as well as to other towns and small cities because they could no longer subsist on the farms or could not get farms to operate and that the youth from these families constituted a large proportion of those who went to the CCC camps from places of this size.

The January survey of the enrollees in the camps previously referred to revealed the fact that the Negro enrollees remained in the camps for much longer periods of time than the white boys.   Whereas

[60] Melvin, Bruce L., *op. cit.*, ch. VII.

[61] *Annual Report of the Director of Emergency Conservation Work, Fiscal Year Ending June 30, 1937*, Washington, D. C., p. 35.

[62] See ch. I, tables 1 and 8, and appendix table 2.

[63] Calculations made from data contained in *Annual Report of the Director of Emergency Conservation Work, Fiscal Year Ending June 30, 1937, op. cit.*, p. 34.

[64] Bureau of the Census, *Fifteenth Census of the United States: 1930*, Population Vol. II, U. S. Department of Commerce, Washington, D. C., 1933.

the median period of enrollment was 8.9, 9.9, and 9.6 months, respectively, for white enrollees classified according to place of origin as rural, small city, and large city, the corresponding percentages for Negro enrollees were 16.2, 15.8, and 11.5 months.[65] The holding power of the Corps for Negro youth, most of whom come from the rural South, may be indicative of the fact that opportunities for Negroes in their home communities were exceedingly restricted and that in many cases subsistence was not even available at home. As a result many Negroes re-enrolled two or more times.

It is not unlikely that the same type of factor operating in a different way may have played a part in swelling the number of rural-nonfarm enrollees in the camps at the time of the survey. When the average white farm boy left the camps, he returned at least to subsistence on the home farm if he did not have remunerative employment awaiting him after his discharge, whereas the village boy returning to his family without prospect of employment became an extra drain on the family's financial resources. Hence, the village boy might elect to re-enroll in a greater number of cases than the farm boy. By January 1937 this process of re-enrollment on the part of the nonfarm youth may have meant that there were at that time a considerable number of long-term nonfarm enrollees augmenting the number of new enrollees from nonfarm residences that came into the Corps at each succeeding enrollment period.

The statute under which the Civilian Conservation Corps operated during the first 2 years of its existence did not contain specific language restricting enrollment to men of relief status. In practice, however, enrollment was limited primarily to persons in this category since there were more than enough of them to fill up the Corps. Beginning in April 1935 a relief requirement for the selection of enrollees was in force until June 30, 1937. The Act of June 28, 1937, states that "The enrollees in the Corps * * * shall be unmarried male citizens of the United States between the ages of seventeen and twenty-three years, both inclusive, and shall at the time of enrollment be unemployed and in need of employment." Doing away with the relief restrictions has made it possible for the youth in economically marginal families to take advantage of the work and training provided by the Civilian Conservation Corps though the great bulk of enrollees still comes from families which are receiving some form of public assistance or are eligible for such assistance.

The words *unemployed and in need of employment* are not defined in the act. By administrative action priorities have been established

---

[65] The median length of enrollment of juniors in all of the camps at the time of the survey was 9.7 months. The median for the total in each of the three categories—rural, small city, large city—did not vary appreciably from this figure. Information from Office of the Director of Emergency Conservation Work, Washington, D. C.

which attempt to give a preferred selection status in the Corps to youth from families below the normal or average standard of living in their home communities. The determination of what constitutes a normal or average standard of living is the responsibility of the local selection agents who, because of their familiarity with local conditions, are the best judges of which boys should be given the opportunity of the camp experience.

Since the new act went into effect there has been a steadily increasing pressure for enrollment in the Corps. By the time of the October 1937 enrollment there were many youth wishing to enroll than were needed to fill the approximately 130,000 vacancies. This was the third largest number of vacancies in the history of the Corps and was followed in January by one of the smallest enrollments in the history of the Corps at which time there were several times as many young men wishing to go to the camps as could be selected.[66] This increased demand for enrollment was undoubtedly a reflection of the increase in unemployment, the effects of which began to be felt by October and became increasingly noticeable in the succeeding months.

Many of the young men who enter the camps have never had any work experience of any kind, and a significant proportion of those who could claim some experience had not had it in any line or under circumstances that would fit them for steady employment in the future. It is apparent, therefore, that the opportunity to obtain worth-while work experience through Civilian Conservation Corps employment is doing much to take up the slack of unemployment between leaving school and securing work. That the need for employment immediately following a young man's leaving school is widespread in economically marginal families is accepted. When enrollment was restricted to youth from families certified for relief, it was found that during 1 year 25 percent of the youth selected had had no employment prior to entering the camp. The importance of a program which helps break the vicious circle of jobs being unavailable to young persons without experience and experience dependent upon jobs cannot be overemphasized.

The enrollees are at work on national, State, and private forest lands, on State and national park lands, on eroded agricultural lands, on drainage and reclamation projects, and on overgrazed portions of the public domain.[67] From the enumeration of the major categories into which the more than 150 types of work undertaken may be listed,[68] it can readily be seen that the work of the Corps has contributed im-

[66] Information on October 1937 enrollment supplied by the U. S. Department of Labor, CCC Office. See also CCC Office, *Quarterly Selection Report, Covering the January 1938 Enrollment of the Civilian Conservation Corps, op. cit.*, p. 2.

[67] Statement of Robert Fechner, Director, CCC, before the United States Senate Special Committee to Investigate Unemployment and Relief, March 15, 1938, p. 7.

[68] See p. 101. See also *Annual Report of the Director of Emergency Conservation Work, Fiscal Year Ending June 30, 1937, op. cit.*, pp. 8–9.

measurably to the conservation of our natural resources at the same time that it has been a force in disseminating knowledge about conservation methods.

The work experience given the youth through this broad program is designed to provide instruction in the jobs being performed, such as auto mechanics, steam shovel operation, concrete construction, clerical work, surveying, stonemasonry, etc. The thousands of enrollees who participate in this job-training program not only receive instruction from the foreman while on the job but also attend at least one class a week dealing with the subject related to their job.[69]

The educational work is a significant aspect of the service being rendered youth by the Civilian Conservation Corps. Special vocational training and regular formal schooling are offered. During the first 4 years of operation approximately 50,000 youth have been taught to read and write. More than 500,000 enrollees have taken work in grade school subjects; 400,000 have received high school instruction; and some 50,000 have taken college work. Cultural training is furthered through the promotion of dramatic clubs, circulation of books, the formation of music groups, and arts and crafts production.[70] In these activities the youth are being taught constructive use of leisure time. The new act specifies "That at least 10 hours each week may be devoted to general educational and vocational training" which will make possible a broader development of this aspect of the camp experience.

Works Progress Administration

The Works Progress Administration, independent of the National Youth Administration, has aided youth both directly and indirectly in its various programs. Most persons employed on WPA projects are the chief breadwinners of their families. Many young persons who have such responsibilities have been thus aided through obtaining employment in this agency. In a few selected States for which accurate data were available (table 26), a tabulation of the age distribution of those employed on all WPA projects showed that persons 16–24 years of age constituted from about 3 to 12 percent. Relatively more young women than young men were employed.

Most of the projects promoted by the Works Progress Administration have been in the field of construction, such as highways, roads and streets, public buildings, parks and other recreational facilities, conservation, sewer systems, and airports.[71] In addition projects for

---

[69] Office of Education, *Semi-Annual Report of CCC Educational Activities (July 1– December 31, 1936)*, U. S. Department of the Interior, Washington, D. C., p. 3.

[70] *Fourth Anniversary Report to the President, op. cit.*, p. 18.

[71] For a discussion of the work of the Works Progress Administration see Division of Research, Statistics, and Records, *Report on Progress of the Works Program, June 1937, op. cit.*

CCC Boys Going to School.

Study Hour in a South Dakota High School Dormitory.

white-collar workers and in the fields of public health, the arts, education, and recreation have been put into operation. The latter type of projects probably has been of greatest significance for young people.

Table 26.—Number and Percent That Youth Constituted of All Workers on WPA Projects in 9 Selected States, November 10, 1937

State	Total persons employed	Youth		Male			Female		
		Number	Per-cent of total	Total	Youth	Per-cent of total males	Total	Youth	Per-cent of total females
Georgia	21,984	2,708	12.3	15,064	1,984	13.2	6,920	724	10.5
Louisiana	21,882	2,007	9.2	17,794	1,372	7.7	4,088	635	15.5
Maine	3,041	312	10.3	2,442	247	10.1	599	65	10.9
Minnesota	33,631	2,971	8.8	27,920	2,217	7.9	5,711	754	13.2
Oklahoma	40,415	3,471	8.6	33,390	2,947	8.8	7,025	524	7.5
Oregon	10,060	344	3.4	8,080	247	3.1	1,980	97	4.9
Pennsylvania	154,781	19,409	12.5	133,894	15,002	11.2	20,887	4,407	21.1
Wisconsin	34,148	2,821	8.3	29,617	1,784	6.0	4,531	1,037	22.9
Wyoming	1,717	172	10.0	1,007	75	7.4	710	97	13.7

Source: Special tabulation, Division of Social Research, Works Progress Administration, Washington, D. C., February 7, 1938.

The Education Division of the Works Progress Administration, for example, has conducted a variety of educational projects, including the so-called emergency colleges,[72] with the cooperation of the State boards of education and local educational authorities. At least 4,000,000 adults have availed themselves of the opportunities thus provided during the past 3 years.[73] Though the program does reach rural areas, no estimate is available of the relative proportion of the students in rural and urban localities except for the literacy classes.[74] Nor is there any estimate of the number of students in the youth group attending these education classes. It is reasonable to suppose, however, that a considerable percentage consists of youth.

One of the most helpful educational phases of the emergency program begun by the Federal Emergency Relief Administration and continued by the Works Progress Administration and National Youth Administration in South Dakota is the establishment of the high school dormitory system. Buildings in a number of small towns and villages have been equipped as boarding and rooming establishments where young people from the surrounding rural territory may live while attending the local high school. This is the result of the joint efforts of the local school boards and the Government agencies. Almost 6,000 youth of high school age were being assisted when the program was at its peak in 1936.[75]

---

[72] Swanson, H. B., *Youth . . . Education for Those Out of School, op. cit.,* pp. 5–15.

[73] "Education Program of Works Progress Administration," *Monthly Labor Review,* Vol. 45, 1937, p. 140.

[74] See ch. III, p. 49.

[75] Information from the Women's Division, Works Progress Administration, Washington, D. C.

A still further contribution of the Works Progress Administration to the needs of youth is in the recreation field. Not only have many communities been supplied with physical facilities for wholesome recreation, such as swimming pools, baseball diamonds, tennis courts, parks and picnic grounds, and recreation and community centers, but also great strides have been made in promulgating a philosophy concerning the place of recreation in modern life and in emphasizing the relation of recreation to community organization and community vitality. As a result of the recreational program undertaken, many youth have shared in the training for leadership roles in the recreation field in particular and in community life in general. In the country as a whole approximately 20 percent of all persons employed on recreational projects at that time were young persons under 25 years of age.

Aside from giving work to youth the recreational program has made available to all youth, not just those in relief families, recreational activities that otherwise might never have been developed in many communities. In an analysis of the recreational work promoted by the Works Progress Administration in 320 selected counties in the United States in August 1937 it was found that participation hours of persons 16 to 24 years of age were approximately 25 percent of the total hours.[76]

Farm Credit Administration

The Farm Credit Administration has a definite program for helping young men to get started in farming, although it is doubtful if its benefits are sufficiently widespread. Under its supervision about 550 production credit associations have been established in the United States [77] which have as part of their function lending money to small groups of boys to finance crop and livestock production. In 1936 approximately 200 groups, including about 2,500 boys, secured money from this source. The chief requirement for the youth to secure a loan is that a responsible sponsor have charge. Though the lending has been confined primarily to groups from 4–H Clubs and Future Farmers of America, other groups may secure aid.[78]

The Farm Credit Administration, through the Federal Land Banks, has another plan that is being tried out in cooperation with teachers of vocational agriculture. Promising young students from the classes in vocational agriculture are given an opportunity to rent a farm which has come into the hands of the Administration with a view to accumulating money and buying the farm. As yet there is no wide-

---

[76] Williams, Aubrey, "Rural Youth and the Government," *Rural Sociology*, Vol. 3, 1938, p. 8.

[77] *The Fourth Annual Report of the Farm Credit Administration*, Washington, D. C., 1936, p. 42.

[78] Information from Farm Credit Administration, Washington, D. C.

spread program of this nature, but the undertaking is well along in the experimental stage.[79]

Agricultural Adjustment Administration

The Agricultural Adjustment Administration has initiated constructive measures which are assisting youth in an indirect manner. The provisions of the act which established the original AAA in 1933 "related to the purchasing power of a group of commodities, to the establishment of a price relation between agricultural and urban products, and to the economic status of farm producers as a group * * * "[80] The second act, passed to take the place of the original act invalidated by the Supreme Court and known as the Soil Conservation and Domestic Allotment Act, has five specified purposes: preservation of soil fertility, diminution of soil exploitation, promotion of the economic use of land, protection of rivers and harbors against the results of soil erosion, and the attainment of parity income for agriculture.[81] This program was not, of course, designed primarily for youth. It will help thousands of youth by assisting their families although it cannot solve the problems of other thousands on poor land nor can it enlarge a farm to make room for two boys when the farm has only enough acres to require the care of one.

Resettlement Administration

The Resettlement Administration, now the Farm Security Administration, has promoted a varied program which also has indirectly aided youth in the families assisted. Two phases of the program—rehabilitation and resettlement—could be of special significance for youth if directed toward helping young people make their adjustment into farming. The rehabilitation work has consisted largely of making loans and direct grants to families on the relief level in order to give them a new start. The work of resettlement proper has consisted in taking families from poor land areas and resettling them on good land.[82] As a long-time measure it would be more advantageous to help youth obtain good land when they begin to farm rather than to rehabilitate or resettle them and their families later.[83] In one or two of the resettlement units the families selected have been chiefly young

[79] Pearson, James H., "Progressive Establishment of Young Men in Farming Occupations," *American Vocational Association Journal and News Bulletin*, Vol. XI, 1936, p. 146.

[80] Agricultural Adjustment Administration, *Agricultural Adjustment, 1933 to 1935*, U. S. Department of Agriculture, Washington, D. C., 1936, p. 7.

[81] U. S. Department of Agriculture, *Report of the Secretary of Agriculture, 1936*, Washington, D. C., p. 11.

[82] Resettlement Administration, *First Annual Report*, Washington, D. C., 1936, pp. 9–18 and 33–40.

[83] See discussion of this suggestion in Rainey, Homer P. and Others, *How Fare American Youth?* New York: D. Appleton-Century Company, Inc., 1937, ch. VI.

couples below 30 years of age. The selection of such families, however, did not constitute a definite policy on the part of the Resettlement Administration.

United States Employment Service

The years since 1933 have seen an enormous development of the Federal and State machinery for assisting the citizens of the country to find work. While almost every county in the United States had some persons registered as seeking work,[84] there are still no data on how far the service is really able to deal with unemployment in rural territory in the light of the factors that have been complicating the employment situation during the last decade.

Though the problem of obtaining employment is serious for the older workers, the difficulties of the young people appear even more pressing, according to Employment Service experience.[85] Mention has already been made of the presence of junior counselors in some employment offices and of their probable effectiveness in dealing with the problems of unemployment among rural young people. In offices where there are no junior counselors the young people must take their chances in competition with older workers.

NONGOVERNMENTAL AGENCIES

Nongovernmental agencies serving youth are numerous and varied—character building, religious, political, fraternal, civic, cultural, social, and recreational [86]—but it is doubtful that many are penetrating very far into rural territory.[87] Attention has therefore been directed only to a few which are designedly working in rural territory and definitely fostering programs for out-of-school rural youth. This is admittedly an incomplete list. There have been no definite criteria for the selection of those that have been included. Some are mentioned because they seem particularly suggestive and promising; others are discussed because of their timeliness or their extensiveness.

Farm Bureau

The Junior Farm Bureau has recently been formed under the direct guidance and sponsorship of the American Farm Bureau Federation. The primary purpose of this developing organization is to supply the

---

[84] In July 1936 the active files of the registrants in 37 States and the District of Columbia comprised between 9 and 18 percent of the total number gainfully employed in 1930, and in 6 States more than 18 percent of the total gainfully employed were registered. U. S. Employment Service. *Who Are the Job Seekers?* U. S. Department of Labor, Washington, D. C., 1937, pp. 17–18.

[85] *Ibid.*, p. 41.

[86] Chambers, M. M., "Non-Governmental National Youth-Serving Agencies and Organizations," *School and Society*, Vol. 44, 1936, pp. 544–547.

[87] Douglass, H. Paul, *How Shall Country Youth Be Served?* New York: George H. Doran Company, 1926.

At the Employment Office.

need for "social, recreational and educational development of rural young people * * *." [88] In order to realize this purpose the Farm Bureau Federation has perfected a standard plan of organization consisting of local and county units. The members of the county organization consist of young persons living on farms who have reached the age of 18 years or who are former members of 4–H Clubs or Future Farmers of America or similar organizations. Membership is automatically terminated at the age of 25 years or at the time youth establish homes or engage in farming on their own account. The promotion of social and recreational activities and educational work on agricultural problems [89] will be of value to the youth, but the sponsoring agency has an institutional purpose also in securing Farm Bureau membership. It would "develop an intelligent, constructive leadership in the ranks of the Junior Farm Bureau, who would be prepared to take up the responsibilities of leadership for the Farm Bureau when they became members." [90] In Ohio and Indiana this means leadership in the promotion of the cooperatives fostered by the Farm Bureau. Hence, youth who go to the Farm Bureau camps in these States are given thorough instruction in the theory and organization of cooperatives. [91]

Farmers Educational and Co-operative Union

The Farmers Educational and Co-operative Union is particularly strong in the Dakotas, Minnesota, Wisconsin, Montana, and Oklahoma but functions also in several other States, chiefly in the Middle West. Membership of the entire family in the organization is encouraged. To this end the Farmers Union has organized the Juveniles, children of members who are under 16, and the Juniors, those between the ages of 16 and 21. Not until they are 21 years of age do the boys become dues-paying members. At the same time the girls become honorary members. The Juniors have all of the rights of dues-paying members; they may hold office in the local organization, vote, and be sent as delegates to county or State conventions. They study social problems, legislation, and cooperation and enter contests in essay writing and speechmaking. In some States they attend summer camps for a period of intensive study and training in leadership. [92]

[88] Strayer, George, "The Junior Farm Bureau," address before the Midwest Rural Youth Conference, Ames, Iowa, July 23, 1936.

[89] Vaniman, V., "Relationship Between the Junior Farm Bureau and the Farm Bureau Movement," address before the Midwest Rural Youth Conference, Ames, Iowa, July 23, 1936.

[90] *Ibid.*

[91] Letter of August 3, 1937, from the Extension Sociologist, State College of Agriculture, Columbus, Ohio, and letter of August 13, 1937, from Office of State Farm Bureau, Indianapolis, Ind.

[92] Edwards, Gladys Talbott, *The Farmers Union Triangle,* Farmers Educational and Co-operative Union of America, Jamestown, N. Dak., 1935, pp. 54–59.

The history and methods of cooperation are emphasized, but instruction is also given in the various aspects of economic problems that touch the farmer's interest, such as money, credit, and taxation, as well as in conservation of natural resources, handicraft, and social and recreational leadership.

Like the plans of the Farm Bureau for its youth the work of the Farmers Union on behalf of the Juniors is designed to prepare youth to take their part in furthering the basic program and philosophy of the parent organization. The Junior program is a development of the last 10 years, having received official recognition at the national convention of the Farmers Union in 1930.

National Grange

Like the Farmers Union the National Grange also embraces in its membership the entire family though the children must be 14 years of age to be voting members. The national office estimates that 35 percent of the membership is less than 30 years of age.[93] The 1936 membership was said to include 800,000 persons in 35 States.[94] No special effort has been made on a national scale to enlarge the program of the Grange to meet the needs of young people although in some States the youth problem has been recognized.[95] The educational and social services rendered youth by this organization are therefore through the medium of the regular program.

Wisconsin Farm Short Course

The Wisconsin State College of Agriculture provides a Farm Short Course each year from the middle of November to the middle of March for young men from the farms. There are no entrance requirements or examinations. Most of those who have attended thus far ranged from 19 through 26 years of age. Since the course is adapted from the Danish Folk School program, it is founded on the theory that "The satisfactory solution of many of our agricultural problems will be greatly aided by the education of our farm youth. This education should be in the economic and social fields which train for better rural organization and able rural leadership as well as in the arts and sciences of agriculture."[96] Unlike the Danish schools, however, there

[93] The National Grange Publicity Bureau, Springfield, Mass. All locals do not present this picture. In 1 farm community in Pennsylvania only 15 out of a total membership of 91 were less than 30 years of age and these were between 25 and 30.

[94] The National Grange Publicity Bureau, *Official Roster*, Springfield, Mass., 1936.

[95] Volunteers for Youth Service and Department of Sociology, *Michigan Youth*, Vol. I, No. 2, Michigan State College, East Lansing, Mich., November 1933.

[96] Christensen, Chris L., *An Educational Opportunity for Young Men on the Farm*, University of Wisconsin, Madison, Wis., June 1935, pp. 3 and 11.

is no course for girls. Classes are held in principles and practices of business cooperation, the social sciences, and the humanities. The maximum enrollment of 325 was reached in the 1936 term.

Cooperative Youth Clubs

With the growth of the cooperative movement in America there have developed a number of youth clubs in various parts of the country. These clubs act as educational and cultural centers for youth in localities where there already are cooperative societies and aid in the formation of consumers' clubs in places where there is as yet no cooperative society or enterprise.[97] In two sections of the country youth clubs have been united into leagues—The Northern States Cooperative Youth League with headquarters in Superior, Wis., and The New England Federation for Cooperative Clubs with headquarters at Gardner, Mass.[98] While most of the cooperative youth clubs are not rural, they are to some extent reaching rural youth in their respective localities. Their extension is definitely linked with the progress of the consumer movement in rural territory. The most significant rural development in the direction of cooperation is the educational and cultural programs for youth promoted by the Ohio [99] and Indiana Farm Bureaus through their summer camps.

Douglas County, Wis.

In Douglas County, Wis., the young people themselves requested the establishment of a forestry camp during the winter of 1934–35. The camp was financed under the forest crop law [100] and was attended by 60 young men. Although the project lasted only 1 year, it was considered unusually successful because: (1) it provided employment for young men who were idle; (2) it gave opportunity for a practical type of education for that county; and (3) it was a feasible method of promoting reforestation and conservation.[101]

Breathitt County, Ky.

Breathitt County, Ky., is an area in which youth are especially handicapped by poverty and lack of opportunity. In an attempt to ameliorate the adverse situation a program of study and planning was begun in 1934 with the specific purpose of building up a guidance

---

[97] Letter from secretary-treasurer of Massachusetts League of Cooperative Clubs, October 1936.

[98] Letter from The Cooperative League of the United States of America, 167 West 12th Street, New York City, November 15, 1937.

[99] Jones, Inis Weed, "Not by Bread Alone," *Good Housekeeping Magazine*, July 1937, pp. 38–39.

[100] Wileden, A. F., *What Douglas County Young People Want and What They Are Doing About It*, Rural Youth and Rural Life Series, Extension Service, University of Wisconsin, Madison, Wis., December 1935, p. 7.

[101] Letter from A. F. Wileden, April 8, 1936.

program. The experiment has been under the direct guidance and control of the County Planning Board in which the moving spirit has been the County Superintendent of Schools. The Alliance for the Guidance of Rural Youth—formerly known as the Southern Women's Educational Alliance with headquarters at Richmond, Va.—has been helpful in planning and advising on certain phases of the program.

The first step in this undertaking was to gather basic facts on economic and social conditions in the county with special reference to the problems which the youth themselves were facing. Although the county has approximately 2,700 out-of-school youth, the educational, occupational, and recreational opportunities are greatly limited.[102] In an economic way this program is helping the youth to adjust occupationally both within and without the county in so far as this has been possible. Socially it is stimulating the youth to individual initiative and self-reliance, to develop a better way of life under adverse economic conditions. Educationally it is assisting in building up opportunities for youth who are out of school as well as for those who are in school.

Rockland County, N. Y.

A unique experiment in building and maintaining a unified county-wide program of guidance in 47 schools in the semirural county of Rockland, N. Y., was initiated in a modest way in 1929.[103] Two years later the County Board of Supervisors, in accordance with the authority granted by State law, appointed a county vocational and extension board and authorized the employment of a county director of guidance, but, because of the straitened circumstances of county finances at that time, only limited funds were available for the experiment. Despite financial handicaps, however, a twofold program was embarked upon: first, a series of community surveys was undertaken for the purpose of revealing pertinent information about the county, characteristics of its population, and its educational, health, and occupational situation; and second, a county-wide program of guidance was promoted as well as guidance programs in such individual school systems as contracted for the services of the county director of guidance.

On the basis of the knowledge gained and interest aroused through the various surveys, and by pooling the resources of the State, foundations, and local institutions, a mental hygiene program has been initiated. Teachers have been given the opportunity of obtaining some training in guidance. A Junior Placement Service has been inaugu-

---

[102] Gooch, Wilbur I. and Keller, Franklin J., "Breathitt County in the Southern Appalachians," *Occupations*, Vol. XIV, 1936, p. 1027.

[103] Gooch, Wilbur I. and Miller, Leonard M., "Vocational Guidance in Rockland County," *Occupations*, Vol. XIV, 1936, pp. 835–911.

rated and a service providing guidance and training in household employment and child care has also been set up.

This program has been credited with bringing together many diversified interests in the county, vitalizing the curriculum of practically the entire school system from the elementary grades through the high school, and broadening the outlook of pupils and citizens alike in regard to the forces operating to produce the unemployment situation in Rockland County. To many of the pupils now in the secondary schools in this county, or recently graduated, the selection of an occupation has been presented as an orderly, logical, and thoughtful process instead of a haphazard chance process with its attendant human waste in occupational misfits and in feelings of frustration and futility. Though the system has been attached in its initial stages directly to the public schools and serves, therefore, the in-school group primarily, there is a follow-up of those who leave school or are graduated. Moreover, the placement service is intended to serve more than merely the in-school group.

Private Institutions Serving Rural Areas

Scattered throughout some of the underprivilegea areas of rural America are private schools or settlement centers of varying character and purpose, many of which are rendering valuable service to specific communities. Some of them have labored under severe handicaps, but in many communities they have rendered the only social service available to the people. In some communities they have blazed trails of economic and social rehabilitation, trails which too often have later been neglected for want of resources to render the programs really effective. Because their sphere of activity is restricted, they know their people and their community background as few social leaders do who are entrusted with the development of broad programs. Their personnel, often seasoned by years of self-sacrificing labor, are eager to cooperate with any agency that can help raise the standards of living of the poverty-stricken folk among whom they work.

Some of these private endeavors lay special emphasis on youth though they maintain the general community approach. This is certainly true of the Campbell Folk School at Brasstown, N. C.,[104] the Farm School at Asheville, N. C.,[105] and the Ashland Folk School at Grant, Mich. Another interesting rural community development under way in Michigan is known as the Hartland Area Project. Financed by a foundation, it has markedly enriched the lives of the young people of the community.[106] Pine Mountain Settlement School

[104] "The People of an American Folk School," *Survey Graphic*, Vol. XXIII, 1934, pp. 229–232.

[105] White, Edwin E., *Highland Heritage*, New York: Friendship Press, 1937.

[106] Western State Teachers College, *The Educational News Bulletin*, Vol. VII, Kalamazoo, Mich., October 1936, p. 20.

in Harlan County, Ky., is still another type of school performing an educational service for the young people who come to stay at the school's quarters and to younger children in the community who come as day pupils. In addition the school's leaders are ministering to the social needs of the community and assisting in planning for its economic enrichment.[107] These illustrations do not exhaust the roster of private institutions affecting the lives of rural young people, but they suffice to suggest that a significant service is being rendered by this type of organization.

[107] Glyn A. Morris, Director of Pine Mountain Settlement School, Pine Mountain, Ky.

Chapter VII

CONCLUSIONS

Youth is an adjustment period. It is the age when most young people leave school. It is the time when they strive for economic adjustment, which frequently involves migration from one community to another. It is a short period in the life of each individual when marriage and preparation for marriage and other social adaptations into adult life are made. During these transition years most of life's patterns are fixed. Society's maladjustments are of particular concern when they intensify the problems of youth. To the extent that these maladjustments make a permanent imprint on the personalities of large numbers of youth, their consequences will be lasting—enduring for at least a generation.

The plight of rural youth is not a problem of the country alone. It is of vital significance to the cities as well. In one respect the crux of the rural youth problem is the relation of rural youth to city youth. Except in periods of severe depression it is probable that urban youth could make their economic adjustments with relative ease, at least on a minimum subsistence level, if they did not face the competition of rural youth who migrate to the cities. Death among the older city dwellers opens opportunities about as fast as urban youth mature. But the long-time rural youth problem is that of an excess in numbers in relation to a dearth of rural opportunities, a situation which becomes greatly aggravated during "hard times." Hence, rural youth must go to the cities in large numbers as long as there is any hope of employment.

During the next 15 to 20 years there will be a continual increase in the working population of the entire country. The number coming into the productive ages and automatically competing for employment opportunities, particularly with workers immediately older than themselves, will for some years be much greater than the deaths within the productive ages. As a result the intensification of the problems of youth in making their economic adjustments is likely to continue for some time.

While most rural young people encounter some difficulties in making their economic adjustments and in obtaining an adequate education

117

and the opportunity for satisfactory personal and social development, those encountered since 1930 have been more acute than ever before. This does not mean that the majority of all rural youth have been on relief or that all have faced insurmountable handicaps in "getting a start," but it does mean that great numbers of young people have faced serious obstacles in making their transition into adult activities. Moreover, without definite public policies directed toward aiding young people, America is facing the prospect of successive generations of youth, among which many young people will be seriously maladjusted and some will be idle or only partially occupied throughout their mature years.

The future of American rural life, and to a large extent of urban life, rests on increased industrial production, a closer integration of industry and agriculture, and an expansion of the cultural and human services so badly needed in rural society. Rural youth as they approach the threshold of citizenship responsibility need not necessarily face contracting opportunities. It is the responsibility of a democratic society to see that these new citizens receive a fair share of the national income in order that they may become effective consumers as well as producers and thus contribute in just measure to the prosperity of both agriculture and industry.

Rural America must choose between two courses. One is the active planning for the conservation of its human resources, recognizing the fact that with no age group will the planning produce greater returns than with young people. The other is to let present trends continue. Until free land in the West was exhausted and the cities ceased their mass absorption, youth could escape from their home communities. But the problems of rural youth can no longer be wholly transferred to other communities. Never has this country been faced so forcefully with the necessity of charting a course for its rural youth.

THE NEED FOR EDUCATION AND GUIDANCE

The ability of the individual youth to make his economic adjustment when opportunities are available depends largely upon the education and guidance that may have been afforded him. That education gives an advantage in the struggle for security and that equality of educational opportunity is an inherent right of youth are traditions in American life. The fact must be clearly faced, however, that there is not equality of educational facilities in rural America and that the areas which supply the largest portion of the oncoming generation are those in which educational opportunities are most severely restricted.

A heavy increase in rural high school enrollment has occurred during the same years that the most serious problems of rural youth have emerged. While this enrollment may have been partly due to expanded school facilities, it undoubtedly has been in large measure a result of present-day employment conditions. In numerous instances youth have gone to school because there was nothing else to do. Moreover, during recent years there has been a definite movement to keep youth in school longer. This raises certain questions. Will the fact that youth attend school for longer periods solve the problems of rural youth? Or does continued attendance in the average public school of today only postpone the time when the same problems must be faced, with little better chance for successful solution? To what extent have the schools been shock absorbers for the depression? How effective have they really been in assisting youth to make their social and economic adjustments?

These queries cannot be answered categorically. They point, however, to the desirability of a redefinition of the functions of the rural schools in terms of current conditions, especially with respect to vocational education and guidance.

Guidance toward occupations is almost entirely lacking in rural areas. Youth commonly pass through the rural school curriculum with the hazy assumption that they are being prepared to enter adult life. But the preparation they receive other than that core of knowledge recognized as general fundamental training too often has only indirect relation to their future work. Most youth enter adult occupations by chance. Giving them greater opportunities for both general and specific occupational training and for learning more about occupational openings is a special need facing rural America.

Rural schools are responsible for the training and guidance of three broad groups of pupils: those who will go into commercial agriculture; those who will enter nonagricultural occupations in either rural or urban areas; and a third large group comprising those who under present circumstances are destined to remain in rural territory living on the land on a more or less self-sufficing basis. It is being increasingly recognized that one of the first duties of the school is the discovery of the particular potentialities and aptitudes of the developing pupil so that on reaching the youth age the individual has some idea of the vocation or vocations in which he or she could reasonably expect to succeed if given additional and proper training. It is, of course, not to be expected that every rural high school can be equipped to train youth in a wide variety of skills, but there are certain fields in which they must provide training if a large proportion of rural young people are to have any vocational training at all. Vocational training in agriculture is doing much to prepare youth for farming, but with all the efforts in this direction it is doubtful if at present enough youth are being trained in high schools and colleges to provide an adequate number of farmers to raise the agricultural products needed for market at the highest possible level of efficiency and at the same time to operate their farms in accordance with the best principles of soil conservation.

That does not affect the fact that there is a "surplus" of youth on the land; it only indicates that youth are not being prepared in sufficient numbers to engage in scientific agriculture.

The rural-nonfarm youth who will enter nonagricultural occupations and the farm youth who will leave the farms receive little special consideration in the educational system. These two groups together constitute considerably more than half of all rural youth. Usually these groups can secure only the general education provided by a standard curriculum. Moreover, it is usually a curriculum built on the assumption that at high school graduation the young people will go on to college. This is in spite of the fact that many of the professions and white-collar occupations for which young people are being trained are at present overcrowded when judged in relation to the economic demand.

Schools have not been sufficiently aware of the fact that for youth in economically marginal families—and in recent years in families that have been on relief—the problems of social and economic adjustment are intensified. Though some of this group of rural youth will migrate, the large number that will remain presents a continuing challenge to the schools to teach them a better way of life in their home communities.

In analyzing the educational needs of rural youth, it must be kept constantly in mind that high school facilities are not readily available for all rural youth. The above discussion respecting vocational education does not apply to many areas because even general secondary schools are lacking. Despite past and pending commendable efforts to remedy the gross inequalities in educational opportunity, the goal is far from being reached. There has been a justified movement to place better schools in these areas through extending Federal support. In view of the limited financial resources available in many rural areas, it seems clear that unless the Federal Government does extend support, the democratic ideal of equality in education will remain unrealized for rural youth.

Because inadequacies and inequalities in educational opportunity do exist, there are thousands of out-of-school rural youth poorly prepared to cope with modern life. It has been the function of the National Youth Administration and the Civilian Conservation Corps to provide some education and training for this group. These two agencies have done more than merely help the youth from underprivileged families. They have provided experience from which to project permanent policies to aid such out-of-school youth. Unfortunately, limitation of funds has prevented them from meeting fully the needs of this mass of young people, who constitute the bulk of all rural youth and who need above all both training and guidance for occupational adjustment.

Consideration of the youth group, whether in or out of school, whether employed or unemployed, should be a definite and integral part of a program of social planning. Such a program should go hand in hand with economic planning whether under Federal, State, or local auspices. In areas that are predominantly rural the unit for local planning is likely to be the county, though any particular type of plan that might be set up should be adapted to the particular situations of the communities concerned. Representatives of such agencies as the extension service with its county farm and home demonstration agents; women's and business men's organizations of the villages and towns; the welfare agencies; the farmers' organizations, such as the Farm Bureau, the Grange, and the Farmers Union; the National Youth Administration; land banks; the Civilian Conservation Corps wherever possible; employment services; the schools, including particularly the county superintendent, principals, and vocational education teachers; the churches; and other special groups in particular counties that may be interested in youth's welfare could well constitute county planning councils to deal with the problems of youth.

Such councils could have at least three functions: planning for the general welfare of the youth of the county; acting as channels through which information on opportunities for work could be given to the youth of the county; and providing for adequate guidance for youth. Such guidance involves encouraging youth to remain in school as well as helping them to make their adjustments when they leave school. The efforts of such county councils would be increased in effectiveness if coordinated and guided by State-wide councils organized on somewhat the same basis. The programs for such councils might be developed along somewhat the following lines.

In each State a division of occupational information and guidance with paid leadership and responsible financial backing could be established through the cooperation of such agencies as the State college of agriculture, the State department of education, the National Youth Administration, the Civilian Conservation Corps, the employment services, the State department of public welfare, and other governmental and nongovernmental agencies concerned with the problems of youth. In fact, occupational information is now being gathered in many States.[1]

---

[1] The National Youth Administration, for example, has already made industrial and occupational studies in Florida, Georgia, Illinois, Indiana, Kentucky, Ohio, Texas, West Virginia, and Wisconsin. Among the industrial studies made are those of aviation manufacturing, air transportation, baking, candy making, canning, cotton growing, furniture making, insurance, and millinery. The occupational studies include aviation, beauty culture, diesel engineering, forestry, photography, plant pathology, radio service, soil science, school teaching, and salesmanship (data secured from the Office of the National Youth Administration, Washington, D. C.).

Through this office to the county planning councils would pass the results of the work of the many agencies that are working with youth and are assembling data on available opportunities and personal characteristics necessary for success in various occupations. With the passage of time a State agency of this type would be able through both personal representation and literature to render assistance to county councils or other county organizations that deal with youth problems.

With the available facts about occupational opportunities at hand, together with the school records and a working knowledge of the interests and aptitudes of the youth, the county planning councils would be in a position (1) to help youth locate employment opportunities; (2) to advise them as to whether or not they should accept some job that might be available in the community or vicinity or go to urban centers; and (3) to recommend whether or not they should seek further education (with assistance from the National Youth Administration if necessary), go to a Civilian Conservation Corps camp, seek an apprenticeship in industry, take advantage of one of the training centers established by the National Youth Administration, or enroll in part-time training courses available through the schools. Through this mechanism, moreover, the migration of youth either to cities or to other rural areas could be directed, thereby reducing the hazards of seeking to become established economically in a strange community.[2]

Both the National Youth Administration and the Civilian Conservation Corps have been making their programs of training more and more practical. Both agencies have demonstrated their usefulness in assisting youth to make their adjustment from the public school into an occupation. It appears essential that these agencies be allowed to plan on a more permanent basis, thereby increasing both their efficiency and their effectiveness.

In connection with advising young men about going into farming it would be well to emphasize the desirability of expanding the plan now being fostered by the Division of Vocational Agriculture of the United States Office of Education and by the Farm Credit Administration to place graduates of vocational high schools on good farms and to provide agricultural guidance until they are able to assume full responsibility for their farming operations. By this method the

---

[2] State and county councils have been organized in New York State on a voluntary basis. Efforts are now in progress to establish these councils on a legal basis. The movement is a result of cooperation between the State department of education, the State college of agriculture, and the National Youth Administration. While this plan differs in certain details from the one suggested here, the chief objectives are the same. See mimeographed statement of New York State Advisory Committee of the National Youth Administration, 30 Lodge Street, Albany, N. Y., February 11, 1938.

The Rural Community Must Plan for Its Youth.

youth is given a chance to help himself and, if he is successful, in time he can purchase the farm from the Farm Credit Administration. To the extent that rural youth can be started on good farms at the beginning of their careers they will be spared the destitution and failure that have been the lot of so many tenant, laborer, and share-cropper families.

Another educational activity which needs expansion is the discussion and evaluation of the problems of youth by the youth themselves. This is being done to some extent on other age levels by the forum method in both rural and urban areas. By this means farmers themselves are planning soil conservation and crop control programs and becoming acquainted with the broad aspects of agricultural problems in America through the help of the State colleges and of the United States Department of Agriculture. Agencies dealing with rural youth might well embark on the promotion of discussions to help the youth understand their own problems. Youth want to talk about their own problems and the problems confronting the world. A democracy is obligated to give to its youth the facts about the complex economic and social world in which they live and which is so largely responsible for the difficulties they face in making their own adjustments. Moreover, the solution of problems in a democracy must be a continuing process. The discussions may not produce immediate results in economic and social changes, but the conclusions reached by youth today are likely to form the groundwork for the programs of tomorrow.

THE BAFFLING ECONOMIC SITUATION

In the past rural youth entered farming or found work in a town or city as a matter of course. There was never any question on the part of themselves or their parents about opportunities being available when adulthood was reached. If the individual wanted to work, he could find employment at home, in a city, or on new lands. The person who failed was generally considered to do so because of indolence.

"Go West, young man," was a guiding principle for decades. While agricultural areas were expanding, it was almost traditional that one son would take over the father's farm, a second go West, and a third go to the city. During the first quarter to a third of the present century, while these traditional avenues were narrowing, education came increasingly to be looked upon as a necessary prerequisite to satisfactory adjustment into adult life. No amount of education and training, however, will be of much benefit to youth if adequate opportunities for gainful employment are lacking. In spite of increasing pressure on the land in both good and poor farming areas many youth not needed for agricultural work have been forced to remain on farms, and many rural youth in nonfarm territory have turned to the land for a meager living.

Farm youth who are fortunate enough to be members of one- or two-child families and live on a family-sized farm largely free of debt in a good land area have the prospect of future security. They stand a chance of coming into ownership through inheritance and of making the adjustments in their operations that may be required by developments in technology and commercial production. Not so fortunate are youth who belong to large families, particularly in poor land areas, or who are the children of tenants, sharecroppers, and farm laborers.

More emphasis could well be placed on settling young married couples from this group, who want to go into farming, on land which will provide them a decent living and which they ultimately can expect to own or to hold under an equitable long-time lease and on giving them whatever assistance and supervision may be necessary to place their farming operations on a sound basis, instead of waiting until they have lived half or more of their lives on poor land. Bases for programs to establish qualified youth on good land are supplied by the experience of the Farm Credit Administration and the Division of Vocational Agriculture in the plan already referred to for starting youth in agriculture, as well as by the experience of the Farm Security Administration. The experience of the latter agency in selecting farm families in the lowest income class and supervising their agricultural activities has shown that with proper supervision and with the provision of other badly needed assistance many of these families can attain economic self-sufficiency. The youth of these families if properly taught and supervised can likewise succeed.

Unless present trends are checked and specific action taken to start youth on the road to farm ownership, more and more rural youth will never climb above the first or second rung of the agricultural ladder. The difficulties of getting started in nonagricultural occupations also appear to be increasing. There is need of definite policies to prevent the logical consequences of these trends from blighting the lives of thousands of rural young people.

It must be remembered that probably less than one-half of the youth in agricultural territory today can be placed on good commercial farms. Consequently, the other half face one of two alternatives, accepting a lower standard of living or going into nonagricultural occupations. This latter course involves either migrating to the cities or entering nonfarming occupations in rural territory. Such trends as increasing mechanization of agriculture, removal of submarginal land from cultivation, and limited foreign markets for farm products are factors restricting the opportunities for rural youth which have been discussed sufficiently (ch. II). Introduction of new types of agricultural production and wider use of farm products already grown may offer some possibilities. For example, soy beans are being utilized for purposes other than food. Cornstalks are used in insulation and synthetic materials of many kinds. This is all to the good. But farm products, it is well to remember, are largely consumed as food and fibers, and the expansion in consumption of both occurs very slowly. Increase in consumption depends upon an expanding population and the ability of that population to buy. As long as population was increasing rapidly in this country through the excess of births over deaths and immigration, the increase in demand for farm products was greater than the increase in production per man. Since population is no longer rapidly increasing, this outlet for farm products cannot be expected rapidly to augment the opportunities for commercial farming.

Owing to the fact that the solution of the problem of "surplus" youth on the land would appear to lie in the direction of expansion of opportunities in other fields than agriculture, brief consideration is given to a few possibilities. Migration to urban centers of those not having economic opportunities in rural territory is one method of relieving the situation and preventing the increase of the lowest income group.[3] If it proceeds too rapidly or on too large a scale, however, migration to the cities is fraught with dangers both to the migrants and to laborers already there. Rural migrants are frequently in the position of having to accept work at any wage and under any conditions. Untrained persons going from submarginal areas to the cities tend to follow unskilled occupations, and of unskilled laborers the cities already have an oversupply. These newcomers find it difficult to establish themselves while facing desperate competition in a strange environment. Frequently these young people have no way of effectively relating themselves to other workers, to employers, and to society.[4] Hence, thousands of young people who have sought work in urban centers within the last few years have been advised by employment agencies and employers to return to their home communities.

Directed migration could prevent in large measure the waste attendant upon unsuccessful search for urban employment and at the

[3] For a full discussion of migration see Goodrich, Carter and Others, *Migration and Economic Opportunity*, Philadelphia: University of Pennsylvania Press, 1936.
[4] A study in Cincinnati, Ohio, on the adjustments of migrants from the Kentucky mountains to the city showed that in comparison with residents of the same urban neighborhoods and of the same social class more highlanders worked at low-skilled occupations and more earned less than $1,000 a year. In slack times they were laid off earlier and were rehired later. See Leybourne, Grace G., "Urban Adjustments of Migrants From the Southern Appalachian Plateaus," *Social Forces*, Vol. 16, 1937, pp. 238–246.

same time smooth the way for those who are able to enter the skilled trades, services, and professions. It appears unlikely, however, that the cities will be able to absorb the vast numbers of rural youth who are now pressing for a start in life and who ought, under present conditions, to leave rural territory. While a limited number were being directed to satisfactory adjustments outside of rural territory, there would still be the problem of the adjustment of the remaining surplus. Some of these should be enabled to prepare themselves for skilled trades and services so badly needed in rural communities. This should be paralleled by definite steps to make possible the utilization of these trained persons for the benefit of rural society.

It has frequently been proposed that this surplus, or part of it, might be satisfactorily provided for through part-time farming combined with employment away from the farm. The system has long been in operation in New England, and the industrial villages of the Southeast were frequently laid out on the assumption that the workers could tend small plots of land in their off-time from industrial employment. This practice of living on the land and securing a wage from some source other than farming is common near cities and in rural industrial areas. It has several distinct advantages, such as low cost of housing, home ownership, and the production of a more adequate food supply than might be purchased, all of which supplement wages. However, without an extension of opportunities for industrial labor with hours adapted to some work on the land, the expansion of this way of life to meet the needs of more youth appears unlikely. Industry must evince additional signs of actual decentralization into more widely scattered areas of rural territory before this combination may be encouraged on a significant scale, except in connection with labor made available through conservation and forestry programs and such other occupations as may be developed in hitherto undeveloped rural areas. The prospects for expansion of the principal rural industries, such as mining and small manufacturing plants, do not in general seem promising.[5] Development of commercial services is becoming increasingly noticeable along extensions of hard-surfaced highways into remote rural territory, but neither the nature nor the extent of such possibilities has as yet been accurately gauged.

While developments in scientific agriculture and mechanization of the farming process in the years to come promise to restrict even further opportunities for youth in agriculture and expansion in industrial opportunity appears problematical, the field of service

[5] See Allen, R. H., Cottrell, L. S., Jr., Troxell, W. W., Herring, Harriet L., and Edwards, A. D., *Part-Time Farming in the Southeast*, Research Monograph IX, Division of Social Research, Works Progress Administration, Washington, D. C., 1937; and Creamer, Daniel B., *Is Industry Decentralizing?* Philadelphia: University of Pennsylvania Press, 1935.

occupations holds possibilities for absorbing large numbers of young people if adequate financial provision can be made for supplying more adequate social services in rural areas. There is a distressing need for more doctors, nurses, and teachers. Society could also use more librarians, social workers, and recreational leaders. The field of personal services is only beginning to be exploited in rural areas.

In recent years the Nation has been awakened to the consequences of unrestrained exploitation with its attendant waste of the country's natural resources. It is time society recognized the cruel exploitation and waste of its young manhood and womanhood which now exist.

The foregoing analysis may have a pessimistic outlook. The task of absorbing this surplus labor is not as easy as it might seem, nor can it be done with the facility that is implied when expansion or decentralization of industry is so glibly prescribed as the remedy for unemployment. Talk alone does not bring about either of these developments. One prerequisite to a solution of the problem is the recognition on the part of both urban and rural society that the problem is a mutual one and that both need to appreciate the complementary relationship the other bears to the solution. The difficulty in bringing about a full realization of the situation rests in the fact that temporary remedial measures are in danger of obscuring the long-time trends which were causal factors in the depression of the early thirties. However, America will choose during the next few years between letting more and more of her rural youth drift into debilitating poverty and making provisions for them to travel a road to economic security.

THE SOCIAL AND RECREATIONAL SITUATION

The consequences of inequality of opportunity are nowhere more apparent than in the social and recreational life of young people. Since apparently rural youth marry at almost as great a rate in bad times as in good and in even greater proportions in the States with large destitute rural populations than in States with the higher rural incomes, it is clearly important to provide, in low as well as high income areas and in bad times as well as good, an environment conducive to wholesome family life and individual development. It has been said that greater emphasis should be given "to values of family life, to ways of living which promote physical vigor, and to conditions which guarantee a larger measure of economic security, especially to young couples during the early reproductive years."[6] While education in its broader sense can do much to develop a more wholesome family life and is exceedingly important both to insure a wide selection of the marriage partner and as training for parent-

---

[6] Lorimer, Frank and Osborn, Frederick, *Dynamics of Population*, New York: The Macmillan Company, 1934, p. 348.

hood, economic security is fundamental to the promotion of family welfare. The attainment of economic security for a substantial proportion of the families now in the marginal or submarginal class economically, in either rural or urban society, must occur through a process of social and economic evolution at times painfully slow.

Some of the debilitating effects of inequality of economic opportunity may be offset by more adequate provision for wholesome social and recreational life. Youth who cannot afford commercialized recreation because of their poverty may in the long run be better off if they can be guided to use their leisure time in pursuing interests that will provide a chance for full activity and self-expression. Moreover, as already suggested, leadership in the field of wholesome recreation would afford opportunities for employment for some of the "surplus rural youth" if a program, along the lines of that now carried on by the Works Progress Administration, could be greatly expanded and placed on a more permanent basis.

Regardless of what the future holds in the way of recreation in rural areas, a fundamental question remains: To what constructive use is the leisure time of youth being put? Too often youth in rural communities are looked upon as a "floating population," meaning that they are past the age of high-school activities and have not yet reached the age for joining adult organizations.[7] This period in a young person's life should be bridged not only by wholesome individual activities but also by group activities that will both train and encourage him to enter into and assume responsibilities for the success of adult social-civic organizations.

Youth's participation in adult organizations outside the church is negligible if the entire bulk of the rural youth population is considered and is, moreover, definitely conditioned by social status. This, in turn, is usually conditioned by economic status. While some of the farm organizations have made noteworthy attempts to appeal to the younger generation, they appear, with few exceptions, to have succeeded better with the juvenile age group than with youth. Moreover, they serve only a fraction of the rural population and chiefly those in the higher income brackets.

There are many factors in the situation. The fault lies not entirely with either the adults or the young people. In some cases the older generation may not take cognizance of the desire of youth to be effective participating members of local community organizations. In other cases young people may scatter their energies over such wide areas in pursuit of commercialized urban amusements or the cheap counterpart which has invaded the countryside that there is no time or desire to join with the older folk to consider community

[7] Office of Education, *Young Men in Farming*, Vocational Education Bulletin No. 188. U. S. Department of the Interior, 1936, p. 101.

problems or to participate in such group recreation as there may be. Roadhouses, "beer joints," and other "hangouts" in many cases provide the meeting places for the younger generation. In some communities the tradition of what recreation should be restricts the actions of the young people with the result that they go to more distant places to do as they please. Those young people who do not have transportation facilities are then dependent upon communities that all too frequently have meager opportunities for recreation. In those isolated rural areas where most of the families are at the poverty level, very few of the young people are able to seek diversion outside of the local community. These are precisely the communities that have a dearth of facilities for constructive leisure-time activities with no financial resources to remedy the situation. It is not surprising therefore that in some areas of this type the principal forms of recreation indulged in by youth are drinking and fighting.

The attack on the problem of leisure-time activities cannot be uniform but must vary with the community. In some areas the first need is the provision of physical equipment, such as parks, swimming pools, tennis courts, baseball diamonds, recreational centers, and libraries. The emergency agencies have made a beginning in this direction. Not only have they placed facilities for recreation in hundreds of communities but they have also provided motivation for orderly behavior by providing work projects for young people. These absorb the energy and interest of youth, and they yield a small money income. They also give youth a vision of what constructive activity can mean to the individual, and they offer the hope that life need not always be drab, monotonous, and tragic. Local leaders in backward rural areas have many pathetic tales to tell of the hardships that some young people endure in order to be able to get to the county seat from their homes to participate in a shopwork or mechanics training project. A major result of the work of the National Youth Administration has undoubtedly been a reduction in the volume of crime among young people. Moreover, a boy's experience in a Civilian Conservation Corps camp often does much to change his attitude toward life and to give him an appreciation of constructive recreation. This avenue of experience should certainly be kept open, and it probably should be extended to girls

Dull and uneventful communities do not necessarily breed antisocial behavior, but they may yield lethargic and restricted personalities that are no asset to the community and that make the execution of progressive programs in any sphere of endeavor extremely difficult. Individuals with such personalities are almost sure to lack social insight and even the elementary understanding of the workings of present social, economic, and political institutions which is so necessary as a background for a fundamental attack on local problems. In vitalizing young people who were in imminent danger of being set in the mould of a dwarfed personality, the programs described in the preceding chapter have been of great benefit.

In rural areas that are not economically underprivileged, where there are or could be adequate recreational facilities, the approach is less obvious and may involve a change in idealogy of both youth and adults.[8] In these areas youth must be encouraged to appreciate the wholesome value of community endeavors and neighborly fun as over against the doubtful, expensive, and ephemeral value of the mere seeking of diversion and thrills. Adults must be willing to relinquish some of their control of local affairs and accept younger people into their councils. All this requires skillful leadership among both adults and youth, leadership which must, in large part, be consciously developed within the community, if not actually imported. In an earlier day satisfactory rural leadership may have evolved naturally. Today, however, there are too many hazards in the path of developing socially-minded rural leadership to risk trusting it to spontaneous growth.

Society must, therefore, accept the responsibility not only of providing opportunity for adequate physical and mental development on the part of maturing young people but also of providing trained leadership. Moreover, it must accept responsibility for bringing within the reach of the "other half" the means for developing rounded personalities, well equipped and eager to contribute to the life of their community.

Rural communities, and the youth who live within them, hold the power to solve their leisure-time problems. The youth themselves can do it if given direction. In addition to direction, of course, it may be necessary for help to be extended in providing facilities. There are very few young people who would not rather engage in sports than sit around and plan mischief. The principle of keeping active young bodies engaged in wholesome physical recreation is just as applicable to maturing youth as to adolescents. One fundamental principle to follow, however, in developing activities among youth for the wholesome use of leisure time is to give the youth themselves a chance at leadership. Questions have been raised frequently respecting the competition of the roadhouse and other forms of commercialized amusement with community activities. Often the commercial agencies win. It seems probable, however, that when this is the case programs have not been built with and by the youth but have been imposed by well-meaning adults.[9]

---

[8] Lindeman, Eduard C., "Youth and Leisure," *Annals of the American Academy of Political and Social Science*, Vol. 194, November 1937, pp. 59–66, especially p. 65.

[9] For a discussion of this point see George, William R., *The Adult Minor*, New York: D. Appleton-Century Company, Inc., 1937.

○

MIGRANT FAMILIES

WORKS PROGRESS ADMINISTRATION

DIVISION OF SOCIAL RESEARCH

Publications
of the Division of Social Research
Works Progress Administration

Research Monographs

I. Six Rural Problem Areas, Relief—Resources—Rehabilitation
II. Comparative Study of Rural Relief and Non-Relief Households
III. The Transient Unemployed
IV. Urban Workers on Relief
V. Landlord and Tenant on the Cotton Plantation
VI. Chronology of the Federal Emergency Relief Administration, May 12, 1933, to December 31, 1935
VII. The Migratory-Casual Worker
VIII. Farmers on Relief and Rehabilitation
IX. Part-Time Farming in the Southeast
X. Trends in Relief Expenditures, 1910–1935
XI. Rural Youth on Relief
XII. Intercity Differences in Costs of Living in March 1935, 59 Cities
XIII. Effects of the Works Program on Rural Relief
XIV. Changing Aspects of Rural Relief
XV. Rural Youth: Their Situation and Prospects
XVI. Farming Hazards in the Drought Area
XVII. Rural Families on Relief
XVIII. Migrant Families

Special Reports

Legislative Trends in Public Relief and Assistance, December 31, 1929, to July 1, 1936
Survey of Cases Certified for Works Program Employment in 13 Cities
Survey of Workers Separated From WPA Employment in Eight Areas During the Second Quarter of 1936
A Survey of the Transient and Homeless Population in 12 Cities, September 1935 and September 1936
Areas of Intense Drought Distress, 1930–1936
The People of the Drought States
Relief and Rehabilitation in the Drought Area
Five Years of Rural Relief
Age of WPA Workers, November 1937
Survey of Workers Separated From WPA Employment in Nine Areas, 1937
Workers on Relief in the United States in March 1935, Volume I, A Census of Usual Occupations
Urban Housing: A Summary of Real Property Inventories Conducted as Work Projects, 1934–1936

WORKS PROGRESS ADMINISTRATION

F. C. Harrington, *Administrator*

Corrington Gill, *Assistant Administrator*

DIVISION OF SOCIAL RESEARCH

Howard B. Myers, *Director*

MIGRANT FAMILIES

By

John N. Webb

and

Malcolm Brown

•

RESEARCH MONOGRAPH XVIII

1938

UNITED STATES GOVERNMENT PRINTING OFFICE, WASHINGTON

Letter of Transmittal

WORKS PROGRESS ADMINISTRATION,
Washington, D. C., December 27, 1938.

SIR: I have the honor to transmit a report on the characteristics and activities of the depression migrant families which received relief from the transient program of the Federal Emergency Relief Administration.

A high degree of population mobility is a basic necessity in America. As long as the American economy continues to expand, population redistribution to fit the changing concentration of resources will be essential. Rapid changes in industrial technique require a continual shifting of workers among the industrial areas of the country. Varying birth rates in different parts of the country produce a population flow from the regions of high natural increase toward the regions where the increase is less. Soil erosion and the increasing mechanization of agriculture are constantly releasing great numbers of small farmers and agricultural workers for industrial employment in the cities. In the West large-scale agriculture requires an army of migratory agricultural workers who travel great distances to piece out a year's work at short-time harvest jobs.

During good times, when migrants reestablish themselves in a new community with little difficulty, the desirability of population movement is not questioned. During a depression, on the other hand, the same sort of population movement frequently entails a relief problem. As a result, distress migration is generally disapproved by the resident population. This disapproval is expressed concretely in the multifarious State legal residence requirements that exclude newcomers from the usual types of relief benefits in the local governmental units.

In 1933, recognizing that the State residence requirements created a no man's land in which large numbers of needy migrants were ineligible for relief, the FERA set up a uniform requirement of 1 year's residence for general relief throughout the United States. Through the Federal transient program the FERA assumed responsibility for those persons who could not meet this requirement. On this basis the transient program gave care (in addition to the unattached) to some 200,000 different migrant families, containing approximately 700,000 individuals, during the 2 years of its operation.

By examining the experience of the transient program, this report has been able to isolate a number of widely-held misconceptions about transients and transient relief. Analysis of the reasons why migrant families left home and of their subsequent travels reveals that they were not—as is so commonly believed—irresponsible and degraded groups addicted to chronic wandering. On the contrary, a large majority of them were habitually settled and self-supporting families dislodged by the depression and seeking reestablishment elsewhere. The families left home not only because they were in distress but also because of a reasonable expectation of an improved status at their destination. Their travels rarely took them beyond the region with which they were familiar and frequently took them no farther than into an adjoining State. Half the families had moved no more than once before receiving transient relief; afterwards, a large majority remained in the same transient bureau where they had first registered until they found work.

Of particular significance in this connection is the evidence in this study that migrant families were reabsorbed from the transient relief program at a rate considerably higher than the rate for workers on general relief. This fact suggests that the migration of the families studied aided them materially in working out their economic problems, even though public assistance was temporarily required in the process.

The report finds that the transient relief problem is essentially an urban-industrial problem which has in recent years been complicated by migration of destitute drought-refugees. In spite of the belief that depression migration is a one-way movement in which certain States are exclusively contributors, while other States are exclusively recipients, it is revealed that the migration of the families studied usually involved a more or less balanced interchange between the States.

The report concludes from the evidence presented that future efforts toward providing relief to nonresidents should recognize that migrants in need are not essentially different from residents in need. The solution of the transient relief problem would therefore appear to lie in the direction of making the regular work relief and general relief programs accessible to nonresidents by means of reducing or eliminating State legal settlement requirements which artificially create the "transient" as a separate category. The experience of the past, however, warns against the presumption that the initiative in working out this solution will come from the individual States. Transiency is a national problem, and Federal leadership is essential in achieving a solution which would take into account both the needs of distressed migrants and the interests of the individual States.

The study was made by the Division of Social Research under the direction of Howard B. Myers, Director of the Division. The collection and analysis of the data were supervised by John N. Webb, Coordinator of Urban Surveys. The report was prepared by John N. Webb and Malcolm Brown. Special acknowledgment is made to M. Starr Northrop and Jack Yeaman Bryan, who assisted in the analysis of the data, and to Katherine Gordon, who assisted in the preparation of the tables.

Respectfully submitted.

CORRINGTON GILL,
Assistant Administrator.

COL. F. C. HARRINGTON,
Works Progress Administrator.

Contents

Migrant Families

INTRODUCTION

DISTRESS MIGRATION was one of the problems that confronted the Federal Emergency Relief Administration when in 1933 it undertook the wholly new task of active cooperation with the States in extending aid to the unemployed. Through the transient relief program the FERA made available—for the first time on a national scale—immediate and adequate assistance to the needy nonresident. Little was known at that time of the nature of depression migration, and one of the important, though incidental, services of the transient program was to call attention to the problem of the migrant unemployed and to provide a means by which this problem might be studied.

The background of this study is the transient relief program of the Federal Emergency Relief Administration. The principal purpose of this report is to make available information—parallel in its details to the discussion of unattached transients in *The Transient Unemployed* [1]—about the migrant families which registered at transient bureaus. In addition the report attempts to relate the distress migration of families to the larger fields of labor and population mobility.

NONRESIDENT FAMILIES IN NEED

Although transiency has been a recognized social problem for a generation, the problem of nonresident families in need was not clearly demarked until the operation of the transient program. Prior to the transient program it was not generally known that any considerable number of needy families were migrating, and depression migrants were believed to consist almost entirely of unattached men and boys. So little was known of family migration that the early plans for the transient relief program were principally for providing congregate shelters in cities and camps outside the cities for unattached men. The relatively small proportion of family registrations and cases under care in transient bureaus (see ch. IV) during 1934 was, in large part, the result of a lack of facilities for family care.

[1] See Webb, John N., Research Monograph III, Division of Social Research, Works Progress Administration, Washington, D. C., 1935.

XIII

The underestimation of family distress migration during early years of the depression partly grew out of the fact that family mobility was less spectacular than the mobility of unattached persons. Needy families did not ride the freight trains or congregate at the railroad yard limits where they would have attracted attention at every town along the main-line railroads. Instead they moved largely by automobile so that, except for the general state of disrepair of their cars and the frequent protrusion of personal belongings from the sides, they differed little in appearance from many nonmigrant travelers on the highways.

Another reason for the failure to note family migration was the cautious nature of their travels. All the families studied here were interstate migrants; yet, in the majority of cases they moved relatively short distances. More often than not they migrated within the same general area in which they had been residing. Usually they went to places where they were known or had relatives and friends who might help them. Accordingly, migrant families did not appear as strangers completely unfamiliar with the country.

Most important of all is the fact that a substantial proportion of the families which received aid from transient bureaus made their application for assistance after the completion of migration. These families had often lived in the new community for several months before they found it necessary to ask for aid. Before the initiation of the transient program, the problem of these families would have been known only to social service workers.

The transient relief program brought the problems of needy migrant families to light by granting assistance not only to (1) the migrants who were in need while en route but also to (2) those whose need developed after they had reached their destinations but who could not get resident relief before the expiration of the time required for establishing legal residence in the new community. For this latter group of families transient relief was, in effect, little different from resident relief. Their appeal for special assistance did not arise out of distress connected with the act of migration itself, but from the fact that some specified period of time had not yet been served in the new community.

IMPLICATIONS OF GOVERNMENT AID

The registration figures of the transient relief program justify an estimate that—in addition to the unattached transients—some 200,000 different migrant families, containing approximately 700,000 individuals, were assisted by the transient program during the slightly more than 2 years in which the program was operated. Even granting that many families later returned to their original place of residence, it is clear that the families assisted by the transient program made up a population movement of considerable importance.

The role of the Government in assisting these needy migrant families had little or no effect in initiating their mobility. Very few of the families (or the unattached either) migrated for the purpose of obtaining transient relief. The effects of the transient program upon population movement were felt after migrants were already on the road and frequently after their migration had been completed. The transient program did not create depression mobility, but it was itself created to cope with the fact of depression migrants in need.

The basic purpose of the transient program was to relieve a particular category of distressed persons. The depression demonstrated that people will migrate regardless of the danger that they may become ineligible for normal relief assistance. The difficulty of obtaining local public assistance did not "prevent" the migration of distressed families before the initiation of the transient relief program; it did, however, increase the distress of the migrants who failed to establish themselves at their destination. Because the Federal Government extended assistance to migrants who failed to reestablish themselves after leaving home, it did indirectly affect the population movement itself. In that respect the migration studied here differs from the unassisted distress mobility before 1933 and in previous depressions, when aid to transients was meager and was given with reluctance.

RELATION BETWEEN NORMAL AND DEPRESSION MIGRATION

Basically, migration represents population movement in response to real or fancied differences in opportunity. In periods of prosperity this fact is never questioned. Migration in good times is obviously the response to a greater opportunity in some community other than the one of residence. In periods of depression, however, the opportunities of prosperous times, and particularly the economic opportunities, approach the vanishing point in all communities. Nevertheless, *relative* opportunity remains the motive force back of depression migration, even though the response on the part of the migrant was largely the result of comparing the fact of no opportunity in the place of residence with the hope of some opportunity in another community. During the prosperous 1920's, for instance, differences in opportunity precipitated a large scale movement of workers from rural areas to the cities, and during the early 1930's many of these workers went back to the land because even the limited opportunities in the country were greater than in the cities.

There are two complementary forces at work in any migration and particularly in a depression migration. In the first place there is the expulsive force in the community of residence, and in the second place there is the attractive force in the place of destination. When unfavorable conditions prevail the expulsive forces receive most attention, and when conditions are favorable the attractive forces are most likely to be noted.

Such expulsive forces as unemployment, underemployment, and low wages were obviously an important cause of depression migration. They were not, however, the only forces at work. The apparent ease with which solvent families move from one community to another during prosperous times has by a careless analogy been carried over and applied to depression migrants. Actually, migration is far from a simple operation even in the best of times; and the force required to uproot a settled family and initiate a migration during a depression is far greater than is generally realized. In the migration studied, an essential part of the motivation was the fact that the families were usually drawn to a particular destination by attractions which gave the appearance of being reasonably substantial.

Trial and error are necessarily involved in most migrations. There is an element of uncertainty in any change of the environment and circumstances under which a living is obtained. Detailed knowledge of the social and economic conditions in the new community (and of their probable development in the future) would be necessary if the element of risk in migration were to be removed; and such information is seldom available to migrants or, for that matter, to anyone else.

The element of uncertainty in migration explains why attempts to find a more desirable place to live frequently end in failure. Undoubtedly the risks of leaving a community that is known for one that is unknown, or less well known, vary with favorable and unfavorable economic conditions; but the risk remains in some degree even in the best of times. There is some wasted effort in migration at any time and the loss increases when conditions become adverse.

The migration under consideration in this report occurred during a period of widespread unemployment. Moreover, the migrants studied had, at the time of observation, been unsuccessful in their efforts at relocation. However, the fact that migration had failed to achieve its purpose does not warrant the conclusion that the migrants studied were a residual group of failures. On the contrary, the evidence suggests that—granted an upturn in employment—most of the families could have been expected to gain the objective of their migration and resume economic self-support. Indeed, there was little to distinguish the families which received relief as transients—in either their behavior or social characteristics—from families in the general population which take part in normal population movements except that transient relief families are temporarily in need of public assistance.

During good times migration in search of economic opportunity liquidates itself without a great deal of need for public assistance.

During a depression, on the other hand, essentially the same sort of population movement entails a relief problem. As a result, distress migration is disapproved by the resident population, and tenuous moral distinctions between normal and distress migration get wide acceptance. These distinctions have little objective basis. The "normal" mobility of prosperity becomes "mobility in trouble" in a period of depression. Transiency has been aptly described as being in essence simply "the trouble function of mobility."[2]

PROBLEMS IN MEASURING MIGRATION

Because of the complexity of motivation, including, for example, the weighing of alternatives by the individual, migration is difficult to explain. Distress alone will not account for the migration of the families assisted by the transient program, nor do the risks of depression migration explain why some distressed families moved and others did not. For some families the distress of unemployment was offset partially by the relative security of local relief; for others, the risks of migration were outweighed by the opportunities that might be found. Only through direct contact with the migrant can the important factor of motivation be appraised.

The term *migration* is applied within a wide range of mobility. At the lower end the range stops just short of absolute stability; i. e., just short of the situation where a person was born, reared, and resided continuously in only one community.[3] At the other end of the range migration approaches the constant mobility of such groups as the migratory-casual workers who live and work on the road from one year to the next.[4] Between these two extremes are to be found the great bulk of the migrants who in the course of time bring about the fundamental changes in population distribution. Obviously then, the

---

[2] Wickenden, Elizabeth, "Transiency=Mobility in Trouble," *The Survey*, Vol. LXXIII, No. 10, October 1937, pp. 307–309.

[3] Moves within a community were excluded from the definition of migration used in the study, although such moves are a special type of migration and deserve more attention than they have received. Clearly, intracity moves could not be excluded on the basis of distance traveled alone, since within large metropolitan areas, such as New York or Los Angeles, it is possible to travel distances greater than those separating many communities from their nearest neighbor. There are good reasons for the decision to exclude moves within cities when the entire country is under consideration. The unit of measurement in spatial changes must necessarily be some recognized civil division, and the city unit serves that purpose without the loss of essential information and without undue complications in statistical tabulation. The city unit also serves as a rough distinction between urban and rural in such important matters as the origins and destinations of migrants.

[4] See Webb, John N., *The Migratory-Casual Worker*, Research Monograph VII, Division of Social Research, Works Progress Administration, Washington, D. C., 1937.

term *migration* covers many types of population movement. It becomes increasingly important that these types be identified and their interrelationship studied.

SOURCE OF INFORMATION

In the main the information presented in this report is based upon a representative sample of 5,489 migrant families selected from the total number receiving care in transient bureaus during September 1935. All the families considered in this report were interstate migrants. The sample was drawn from 85 cities located in 39 States and the District of Columbia (fig. 1). The cities were chosen to provide the wide geographical distribution necessary to the inclusion of all types of migrant families, as well as to take account of differences resulting from variations in size of city and from variations among the States in transient relief programs. The number of families selected in each State was proportionate to the number of families under care in each State during July 1935. A system of random selection was applied within each city to insure freedom from bias in choosing the families to be interviewed.

Through no fault of the method applied in selecting the sample, the families included do not provide a full representation of depression migrants. The unattached persons who received care at transient bureaus are of course excluded. Since the characteristics and behavior of the unattached differed markedly from those of the families, extreme caution must be exercised in applying to the unattached the generalizations that will be drawn from the study of the families.

There was a distinct urban bias in the transient relief population as a whole, and that bias appears in the group of families studied. Transient bureaus were necessarily located in cities and particularly in large cities, because the main routes of travel converge on centers of population. As a result migration involving exchange or redistribution of rural population was much less likely to come into contact with the transient program than was the migration of urban population.

Still another limitation of the sample as representative of all types of depression migration grows out of the fact that these families were selected at a time when the transient relief program had been in operation for about 2 years. During this period of time there was some tendency for families to "pile up" on transient relief in some areas where the slowness of economic recovery retarded their absorption into the resident population. Where this occurred, there was some tendency toward overrepresentation of the less successful depression migrants.

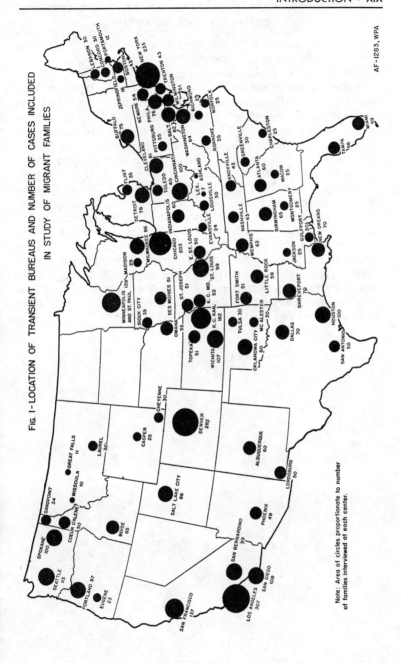

FIG. I - LOCATION OF TRANSIENT BUREAUS AND NUMBER OF CASES INCLUDED IN STUDY OF MIGRANT FAMILIES

AF-1283, WPA

Note: Area of circles proportionate to number of families interviewed at each center.

ORGANIZATION OF THE REPORT

In view of the complexity of motivation in depression migration and its importance to an understanding of this movement, the first chapter deals with reasons for migration. The second chapter examines the origins and destinations of these families with particular emphasis upon the extent to which redistribution of population resulted from the movement of the families studied. For the purpose of determining whether the presence of these families on transient relief was the result of habitual instability, an examination is made in chapter III of the mobility of these families prior to the migration that led to need for transient bureau assistance. With these aspects of migration established, it is possible in chapter IV to consider the effect of the transient relief program upon distress migration. The personal characteristics of migrant families in terms of such familiar social classifications as age, sex, color, and race is the subject of the fifth chapter; and an analysis of their employability, occupational and industrial attachment, and duration of unemployment is presented in chapter VI. In chapter VII the more important findings of the report are reconsidered in terms of the larger problem of population mobility of which the depression migration of needy families is shown to be a distinct and important type.

SUMMARY

ALTHOUGH TRANSIENCY has been a recognized social problem for a generation, the problem of nonresident families in need was not fully realized until the operation of the transient relief program of the Federal Emergency Relief Administration, which gave care to a total of roughly 200,000 families containing approximately 700,000 individuals during 2 years of its operation, from September 1933 to September 1935. The transient program brought to light the full extent of the problem of needy migrant families. It extended aid to the depression migrants who were in need while on the road. It also aided those migrants to a new community whose need arose before the expiration of the time required to establish residence. Transient relief took over the no man's land of responsibility created by the tradition of residence requirements for relief eligibility.

Distress migration is disapproved by the resident population, and as a result tenuous distinctions have been drawn between migration under normal and under distress conditions. These distinctions have little objective basis. There was little to distinguish families which received transient relief—in either behavior or social characteristics—from families in the general population which have taken part in the "normal" mobility which is considered to be a characteristic of the American people. The normal mobility of good times becomes "mobility in trouble" in a period of depression.

REASONS FOR MIGRATION

At first glance it may seem impossible to reduce the causes of so complex an action as migration to simple terms for analysis. The complexity of the descriptions, however, is reduced by the fact that reasons for migration are composed of two complementary factors: the reason for leaving one specific place and the reason for selecting another specific place as destination.

The 5,489 migrant families which were interviewed in transient bureaus to form the basis for this study reported that economic distress was the principal reason for leaving their last settled, self-supporting residence. Unemployment was the most important cause of distress, and as a reason for leaving settled residence it by far out-weighed the combined effects of business and farm failures, inadequate earnings, and inadequate relief. Ill-health requiring a change of climate was second to unemployment as a displacing force.

The complaint that migrant families were on the road to see the country "at no expense" to themselves had little basis in fact. Nearly all the families were in more or less acute distress at the time they left their last settled residence.

Very few of the families with a settled residence set out with no destination at all or with such vague destinations as "eastern Colorado" or "the cotton-fields" in mind. Moreover, those families which did intend to migrate to a specific, predetermined place rarely reported an unreasoning choice of destination. The families generally migrated only when the probability of an improved status appeared to be high. More than half the families chose a destination in which there were close personal connections more or less obligated to assist them. Another large group chose its destination because of such specific facts as letters of recommendation to employers, the purchase of farms or homes, and employment-office direction. Altogether, four-fifths of the families had a definite contact at their destination.

What the families hoped for at their destinations was a solution to the basic problems which had confronted them at their former residence. Four-fifths of the families sought economic betterment, principally employment and, to a less extent, help from relatives. Among the remainder the chief objectives were healthful climate and the desire to rejoin relatives.

The reasons for leaving settled residence and for selecting a destination did not vary greatly in the different sections of the United States. Unemployment was the principal expulsive force in every State except North Dakota and South Dakota, where farming failure was of principal importance. Inadequate earnings and inadequate relief showed no significant regional variation. The principal regional variation in the objectives sought at destination was in the proportion of health-seekers, who were particularly attracted to Arizona, California, Colorado, and New Mexico.

The families were neither particularly adventurous nor, on the other hand, irresponsible in undertaking the migration which later necessitated aid from transient bureaus. The essence of the migration studied is contained in the fact that the families were, in general, distressed groups which saw a reasonable solution to their problems through migration to another community.

ORIGINS AND MOVEMENTS

The FERA records of the 30,000 migrant families under care in transient bureaus on June 15, 1935, show that migrant families tended to move relatively short distances. Only 3 percent of the families made full transcontinental moves. The preponderance of short-distance moves places the much-discussed depression movement to the West coast in a new perspective. Although the transcontinental migrations of families were by far the most spectacular, they were actually much less important numerically then the short migrations in all parts of the United States.

A considerable amount of family mobility consisted of a balanced interchange between the States. Rarely was there a large movement from any given State to another without a substantial counter movement. Net population displacement was thus only a fraction of the population movement. Two-thirds of all the movement resulted in the balance of losses and gains within each of the States, and, in terms of population displacement, was canceled. The remaining one-third of the movement was net displacement.

In the belief that they were moving toward regions of greater opportunity, many of the families moved to communities from which families like themselves were at the same time departing because of a lack of opportunity. It would thus appear that a large part of the movement dissipated itself in waste motion. Such a conclusion is not without value in demonstrating the disparity between desirable social goals and uncontrolled social behavior. This conclusion, however, has little relevance, in view of the concrete realities facing depression-stricken families.

Migrant family displacement showed clear geographical trends. The westward flow of families into Kansas, Colorado, California, Washington, Oregon, and New Mexico far exceeded all other net movement, and the general direction of the net movement for the entire United States, with the exception of the Southeast, was consistently toward the West. In the South the greater part of the net movement was northward to Illinois, Ohio, New York, and Michigan. Negroes played an important part in this movement.

There was a striking similarity between these trends and the displacement of families in the general population between 1920 and 1930. In both periods the predominating tendency was a westward movement, and the chief destination in both was California. The emigration from the Cotton States was principally northward in the two migrations. In both there was a net movement out of the less industrialized Eastern States into the more highly industrialized Eastern States.

The most important differences between the displacement of the general population in the 1920's and that of migrant families were the greater movement of families from the Great Plains States, particularly Kansas and Oklahoma. Washington, Oregon, and Idaho were exceedingly important as migrant family destinations, though they received little net gain from the internal migration of the general population in the 1920's.

Throughout the United States on June 30, 1935, 1 migrant family was under care in FERA transient bureaus for each 910 families in the total population, or 1.1 migrants per 1,000 resident families. Because of the wide variety of social and economic conditions in the various regions of the country, the rate of emigration from many States fell exceedingly far above and below this national average. Nevada, for example, contributed migrant families to other States at a rate 35 times the contribution of New Hampshire. The States from which the families emigrated most readily were mostly Western States. All the States with exceptionally high emigration rates lay west of the Mississippi. Several Southern States, particularly Arkansas and Florida, had family emigration rates above the national average. Migrant families emigrated least readily from the densely populated northeastern and north central regions of the United States.

When the migrant family intake of the various States was adjusted to State population, it was found that Idaho, at one extreme, had 1 family under transient bureau care for each 100 population families, while South Dakota, at the other extreme, had 1 family under care per 30,000 population families. In proportion to the resident population the problem of needy migrant families was most serious in Idaho, followed by New Mexico and Colorado. California ranked as fourth and was closely followed by Washington, Wyoming, and the District of Columbia. Most of the States with the highest rate of immigration were States lying west of the Mississippi River.

Migrant families tended to emigrate most readily from those States which had normally been contributing the greatest proportion of their population to other States before 1930. Migrant families tended to seek out those States into which the population had largely been flowing before 1930. There was, however, no consistent relationship between high family emigration rates and a high intensity of resident relief, nor between high family immigration rates and a low intensity of relief.

The origins and destinations of migrant families were both predominantly urban. The families moved mostly from city to city, rather than from farm to farm or between urban and rural places. The origins and destinations of 56 percent of the families were both urban, but both were rural for only 8 percent.

All States, with the single exception of South Dakota, contributed fewer migrant families from rural places than the rural composition of their population would have warranted. In spite of the 1934 drought and in spite of the chronic agricultural problem in such States as Alabama, Georgia, Oklahoma, and Texas, families from these States originated chiefly in urban places. It would appear, therefore, that in the United States as a whole the migrant family relief problem was basically urban and industrial rather than rural and agricultural.

THE PROBLEM OF "CHRONIC WANDERING"

Chronic wandering, at one extreme of mobility, is the aimless type of movement characteristic of persons to whom stability has become either impossible or unattractive. Migration, at the other extreme, is the purposeful and socially necessary type of mobility which has stability as its immediate object. Plainly, public assistance furthers readjustment more easily among migrants than among wanderers.

Examination of family mobility between January 1, 1929, and the date at which the families first registered at a transient bureau reveals that few of the families were habitual wanderers. Over one-half had maintained one residence for 3 years or more, and four-fifths had maintained one residence for at least 1 year. Thus, not more than one-fifth of all the migrant families could be considered to have been highly mobile before they received transient relief.

When family mobility is considered in terms of moves rather than length of residence, it is found that one-fifth had lived in only one place between 1929 and first transient relief and three-fifths had lived in no more than three places. Very few of the families reported any substantial gaps of mobility between their various residences.

The record of family moves shows that the more recently a family was married, the more mobile it was in relation to the length of time it had been formed. Family mobility tended to be greatest soon after marriage and before the families had gained a foothold in a community.

The families which were settled and self-supporting before 1929 became progressively more mobile between 1929 and 1935. But the families which were not settled were as mobile in 1929 as they were in the years that followed. In part, the consistently high mobility of this small group of families resulted from the pursuit of migratory-casual occupations. Except for this minority group, there is little doubt that the families had by and large been habitually settled and self-supporting until a short time before their first transient bureau registration.

Two-fifths of all migrant families first applied for transient relief in the community where they had been residing. Thus, in spite of the generally accepted belief that the nonresident relief problem is one of assisting persons on the road, actually, a large number of families had already completed their migration before applying for transient relief.

EFFECTS OF THE TRANSIENT PROGRAM

The transient program was frequently condemned for "encouraging transiency." Transient bureaus, it was held, aided migrants to "blithely skip from one camp to another, seeing the country while the Government footed the bill." The wide acceptance of such opinions is not difficult to understand. A small part of the migrant family population did consist of chronic wanderers, and the extreme case, because of the attention it attracted, was accepted as proof that all needy migrants were irresponsible and undeserving. The evidence presented in this report indicates that these opinions were unfounded.

In the first place there was relatively little movement of families from bureau to bureau. At the time this study was made three-fourths of the families had registered only at the transient bureau where they were interviewed, and only one-tenth had registered at three or more bureaus.

In the second place families came into and left transient relief at a fairly rapid rate. Monthly closing rates averaged 30 to 60 families for each 100 families under care in the transient program. This could only mean that the same families were wandering from bureau to bureau or that the migrant family population was continually in process of renewal. Since the movement between bureaus was small, it must be concluded that the migrant family population was rapidly changing in membership. Roughly 20 to 40 percent of each month's family case load left the transient relief program each month. The closing rate on resident relief during the same period was 5.6 percent. Allowing for families closed from transient bureaus to the resident relief rolls, and even for the possibility that many other families may have received resident relief later, the turnover of migrant families through normal economic adjustment would still appear to be many times higher than the turnover rates on resident relief.

Transient relief appears to have been a stabilizing influence upon families uprooted by the depression. It did not encourage wandering. On the contrary, it prevented aimless wandering by relieving the needs which were its cause. Stabilization, however, did not mean unlimited dependence upon the transient program for support. Transient relief provided necessary but interim assistance to migrants who in most instances had definite objectives and who were frequently only temporarily in need. The transient program not only provided immediate relief to a distressed group, but it also assisted materially in the solution of the problems that gave rise to the distress.

In judging the value of the transient program, it should be kept in mind that the transient program defined and took over the no man's land of responsibility which had been created by the tradition of the legal settlement requirements for local relief in the various States. The extent of the needs which would otherwise have been largely unmet can be inferred from a summary of the multifarious and frequently stringent restrictions governing eligibility for resident relief benefits.

Typical poor laws provide that a migrant would not be eligible for local relief unless he had lived within the State continuously, with intent to establish permanent residence, and without public assistance for at least 1 year; and in 10 States the residence must have lasted from 2 to 5 years. The migrant's legal status was further complicated by statutes in 19 States providing for loss of legal settlement in the State of origin. These provisions often caused migrants to lose settlement status in one State before it could be acquired in another. A large number of families were, indeed, without legal residence in any State. This fact does not reflect any particular degree of mobility among the families so much as it demonstrates the efficiency with which the settlement laws operate to penalize needy migrants.

Whether or not severe residence requirements do protect a State from an influx of needy nonresidents is still a debatable question. But in many cases the only reasonable solution of distress is through migration. At this point residence requirements and economic forces meet in a head-on collision, which can only be avoided by broadening the concept that people actually do "belong" in a particular place even though that place may be unable to provide them with the opportunity to make a living.

PERSONAL CHARACTERISTICS

Comparison of the personal characteristics of migrant families with those of families in the general and nonmigrant relief populations reveal several important selective factors at work in the migration studied:

1. Youth was a clearly defined characteristic of the economic heads of migrant families. One-half were under 35 years of age, and four-fifths were under 45. In contrast only one-third of the heads of all resident relief families were under 35, and only three-fifths were under 45. Among male heads of families in the general population about one-half were under 45. This distribution indicates the presence of many infants and school-age children in the migrant families; and, indeed, four-fifths of the children in these families were under 15 and one-third were under 5 years of age.

2. Migrant families were small families. Well over half contained only two or three members. The average family size was 3.1 persons, significantly less than the size of both resident relief families and families in the general population (excluding 1-person families).

3. Migrant families were preponderantly native-born white families. By comparison with the general population, foreign-born and Negro migrant family heads were underrepresented. These two minority groups were overrepresented, however, in the resident relief popu-

lation, showing that although more frequently victims of the depression, these groups nevertheless tended to remain immobile. During recent decades the foreign-born have tended to settle in large industrial centers and to group themselves according to racial or national ties. These ties have acted as deterrents to migration, despite limited economic opportunity and recurring unemployment. Moreover, local prejudice outside the highly industrialized areas makes the migration of distressed foreign-born persons more difficult than of the native-born. Custom and prejudice operate to restrict the mobility of Negro families just as effectively.

4. There was a small incidence of separation, widowhood, and divorce among the family groups. Among migrant family heads the proportion that were separated, widowed, or divorced was less than that found in the general population.

5. Migrant family members had a higher level of schooling completed than the heads of either the urban or rural resident relief population. Some of the difference between the school attainment of migrant and resident relief families is attributable to the youth of the migrant group and to the underrepresentation of Negroes. In any event, it is clear that migration was not caused by lack of education.

OCCUPATIONAL RESOURCES

Well over half of the economic heads of migrant families were fully employable. One-third were employable with certain handicaps, consisting principally of chronic illness, physical handicaps, and age. One-ninth of the economic heads were totally unemployable; women heads with dependent children made up a majority of this group, which also included the aged and totally disabled.

Thus, a majority of the economic heads of migrant families were able to work, willing to work, and within the preferred age-range for private employment. Because of physical handicaps and age, the employability of the next largest group was qualified to some extent. There remained a small group of families with unemployable heads; for these families, it is clear that public assistance through old-age and disability benefits and aid to dependent children was the only means by which stability could be assured.

In terms of main class of usual occupation, migrant family heads were markedly "higher" than the heads of resident relief families, and they compared favorably with the gainful workers 10 years of age and over in the general population. There were fewer unskilled and more skilled workers among migrant family heads than among either the resident relief population or the gainful workers in the 1930 Census. White-collar workers were also overrepresented among migrant family heads by comparison with resident relief workers, though they were greatly underrepresented by comparison with gainful workers in the general population.

The greatest number of skilled and semiskilled migrant family heads were building and construction workers. Among the unskilled migrant family heads, manufacturing, agriculture, and domestic service were represented in about equal proportion. The principal white-collar groups were farm owners, salesmen, storekeepers, musicians, technical engineers, and clergymen.

In terms of usual industry, migrant family economic heads were underrepresented in agriculture by comparison both with the economic heads of resident relief families and with gainful workers in the general population. This underrepresentation reflects the basically urban background of the families in transient bureaus. Migrant family heads reported a larger proportion usually engaged in trade and professional service than heads of resident relief families. Otherwise, the two groups showed about equal representation in the broad industrial classifications.

It is significant that the great majority of the families were not usually migratory workers. The detailed occupational and industrial analysis reveals, however, that a large proportion of the family heads customarily followed pursuits that permitted migration with little loss. There was, for example, a large concentration of skilled workers in building, of semiskilled machine operators, and of unskilled workers, such as restaurant cooks, whose occupations can be followed equally well over a wide area.

Long unemployment involves a deterioration of skill which lowers the probability of reemployment. Accordingly, the information on the family heads' usual occupation and industry is qualified by the lapse of time since they last worked.

The average time elapsed since the migrant family heads' last employment at their *usual* occupation was 18.5 months. It was substantially less than the average duration of 30.3 months as reported in sample studies of urban workers on resident relief in 1934, or the average of 40.6 months for a sample of WPA workers in April 1936. The average time elapsed since the family heads' last job at *any* occupation was 7.8 months. For urban workers on relief the average was 22.7 months, and for WPA workers in the last quarter of 1935 it was 24.0 months. It is indicated that many families, while not usually migratory-casual workers, had turned to migratory-casual work after beginning migration. This fact not only implies low earnings on the road but also a lowered occupational status, and it qualifies to some extent the relatively high distribution of family heads in terms of main class of usual occupation.

The analysis of the occupational resources of migrant families suggests the probability of their return to self-support. Beginning with the families with unemployable economic heads, it is clear that if these families were to be absorbed by the new community of residence, it would be on the basis of a transfer of the relief obligation from the old community to the new. It should not be overlooked, however, that such a transfer was frequently socially desirable.

Many of the families with handicapped economic heads were well-equipped occupationally. Some of these families, however, had migrated to communities where their health might be improved but where the opportunities for securing adequate employment were not promising.

For the remaining and majority group, the fully employables, there appears to be little question that their migration could achieve the purpose of reestablishment in the new community.

Chapter I

REASONS FOR MIGRATION

DURING AND after the operation of the Federal transient program there was widespread public discussion of the effects of distress migration. Usually, however, these discussions have been concerned only with the real and imagined effects of this migration upon the resident population. Little effort was made to understand the real point of view of the migrants themselves. This neglect has given rise to popular acceptance of strange theories about the causes of migration, theories which prevent any understanding and hinder any solution of the problem. It seems plain that an understanding of distress migration must include some knowledge of what it meant to the migrant. The depression migrants' own point of view is clearly revealed in the causes the families reported in explaining their migration.

Although there is a considerable body of information available on the generalized causes of population mobility, little is known of the way in which these causes directly affect individuals. In order to learn the individuals' own explanation for the migration which eventually led to relief at transient bureaus, two questions were asked each of the families interviewed for this study:

(1) Why did you leave the community where you last maintained a settled, self-supporting residence?
(2) Why did you select one particular place, to the exclusion of other places, as your destination?

The answers to these questions are the basis for the present chapter.[1]

---

[1] The reasons for migration could not be determined for about one-fifth of the 5,489 families included in this study. It was impossible, by definition, to derive reasons for the migration of the families which had no settled residence. This group of families consisted of those which had not been settled and self-supporting since 1929 and of those which had not been settled and self-supporting since the time the families were formed, if this event occurred after 1929. Although these families must be excluded from the study of reasons for migration, they are the subject of special analysis in ch. III.

1

At first glance it may seem impossible to reduce the description of so complex an action as depression migration to simple terms for statistical analysis. With a small number of cases this would be true, but examination of many descriptions reveals that they tend to form patterns and that each pattern centers around one common reason that predominates throughout the entire class of similar situations. Moreover, the complexity of the answers which the families gave was reduced by recognizing that the reasons for migration are necessarily composed of two complementary factors: the reason for leaving one specific place and the reason for selecting another specific place.

The problems involved in statistical presentation of the reasons for migration will be evident from an examination of the families' own statements. At the end of this chapter will be found typical reasons reported by 15 typical families. A review of two histories in which particularly complex circumstances are involved will illustrate both the complexity of motivation and the method by which the complexity has been reduced. The Krugers, for example (see history 6, p. 23), migrated from Chicago to San Antonio, Tex., because of (1) unemployment, (2) inability to get resident relief, (3) eviction, and (4) free transportation to San Antonio. The fact that a friend who was driving to Texas was willing to take them with him does not explain the Krugers' move from Chicago, although it *does explain* the selection of their destination. Economic distress arising out of difficulty in obtaining employment or relief and culminating in eviction for nonpayment of rent was the expulsive force that explains why the Krugers were ready to leave Chicago.

The Mosher family (see history 9, p. 23) had long wanted to leave Alabama for the North, but it was not until the death of a brother in Chicago that their move finally took place. The fact that the Moshers had difficulty making a living on an Alabama farm, plus the inadequacy of the relief they received, explains why they wished to leave Alabama; and the death of a relative in the North explains their selection of a particular destination.

The first step in the analysis was to differentiate between the reasons for leaving settled residence and the reasons for selecting a particular destination. The cause of migration always presents two aspects, either directly or by implication. In terms of the place of origin, the cause of migration manifests itself as economic or personal *inadequacies* associated with the community of origin. This aspect may be isolated as the reason for leaving settled residence.[2] In terms of

---

[2] Reason for leaving settled residence was defined as the force, associated with the community of settled residence, which made the families susceptible to the idea of moving.

the place of destination, the cause of migration consists in the expected *advantages* associated with the community of destination. In this aspect the cause of migration is manifested as the reason for selecting a particular destination.[3]

The reason for leaving one place and the reason for selecting another were, of course, two sides of the same coin. It must be remembered that neither reason by itself contains the full explanation of migration. Although the two sets of reasons are tabulated separately, each contains but part of the explanation and the complete explanation must consider both. Moreover, it is important to note that the inadequacies of the place of origin and the advantages of the place of destination were not absolute, but relative to each other. In earlier internal American migrations the "inadequacy" of the places of origin consisted to a large degree in the substantial advantages of cheap land and speculation in new country and in the extensive job opportunities that resulted from the rapid expansion of industry. After 1929, however, this situation was reversed, and destinations frequently came to have advantages only by comparison with the desperate conditions which existed in the communities in which migrants had been settled.

The reasons for leaving settled residence and the reasons for selecting a particular destination, although considered separately, involved special complexities in the reports of many families. In most cases, however, these complexities were merely different aspects of the same general circumstances. In both of the family cases that have been cited, the generic reason for leaving a settled residence was economic distress. For the Krugers, this distress manifested itself as unemployment, inadequate relief, and finally as eviction. Because it was not possible to classify all three of these related circumstances, the one which came last in point of time was selected.[4] The Krugers' reason for leaving settled residence, accordingly, was classified as eviction; and the fact of eviction carries the implication of the other economic difficulties even though they are not specified.[5]

---

[3] Reasons for selection of destination were classified in two ways: first, according to the nature of each family's contact at the destination; and second, according to the basic and secondary objective sought by each family at the destination.

[4] The logic of this distinction lay in the fact that it isolated "the last straw" as a principal reason.

[5] A few families reported a complex reason in which the different factors were not generically related as in the instance cited above. For example, a few families reported that in addition to being unemployed, the health of some member was injured by the climate at the place of settled residence. When such unrelated circumstances were reported, the reason for migration which was classified does not carry the implication of the additional reasons reported by the families. However, a separate tabulation showed only 15 percent of the families reporting this type of complex reason for migration.

REASONS FOR LEAVING SETTLED RESIDENCE

During the depression the transient problem led many newspapers to express the fear that the country was being "overrun" by "deadbeats" who should be promptly "sent home" and made to stay there. The same line of comment was usually accompanied by a special theory that the motivation behind distress migration was the migrants' moral incompetence to maintain stability. The families were said to have left home because they enjoyed travel; and when the FERA transient program reached full operation, the phrase "at Government expense" was added to this explanation.

More realistic answers to the question of why the families migrated are suggested in the 15 case histories. A number of families, as the histories show, had no "homes" at which they could have stayed or to which they might have been returned (see histories 10 and 15, pp. 24 and 25). Nearly all the families which started migration from a settled residence reported frankly that the situation at their settled residence, as far as their own prospects were concerned, had become quite hopeless.[6]

These 15 histories indicate several of the particular sources of this dissatisfaction, such as unsuccessful search for work, inability to earn a living on farms, inadequate relief, unwillingness to be a burden upon relatives, and ill-health. A comprehensive view of the relative importance of these and other basic reasons for leaving settled residence is presented in table 1.

A Distress Migration

The charge that migrant families were out to see the country at no expense to themselves had little basis (table 1). Nearly all the families were in more or less acute distress at the time they left settled residence. Only 6 percent of the families were in no particular difficulties. Of these the majority had jobs that required traveling; the remainder simply left their jobs and businesses and proceeded to another place that appeared to have greater advantages.

Economic difficulty was by far the most important of the basic reasons for migration. More than two-thirds of the families were primarily in economic distress, chiefly through long unemployment, inadequate earnings, the loss of farms or businesses, and inadequate relief. The size of this group clearly stamps the movement as being, above all, a migration of depression-stricken families.

About one-fourth of the families were in personal distress of varying seriousness. The most important single difficulty listed in this group was illness necessitating a change to a different climate or to a com-

---

[6] Migrant families usually protested vigorously against returning to the locality of settled residence (see histories 5, 6, 9, and 11, pp. 22, 23, and 24).

Table 1.—Reason Migrant Families Left Settled Residence

Reason for leaving settled residence	Migrant families
Total	4,247
	Percent distribution
Total	100
Economic distress	69
Unemployment [1]	49
Inadequate earnings [1]	7
Unable to work in particular community [1]	3
Farming failure [1]	8
Business failure [1]	3
Inadequate relief	3
Unwilling to be on relief [1]	1
Evicted from home	2
Relatives unable to continue support	1
Miscellaneous economic difficulties	1
Personal distress	25
Ill-health [1]	11
Domestic trouble [1]	6
Disliked separation from relatives or friends	4
Community disapproval [1]	1
Personal dislike of community [1]	2
Miscellaneous personal difficulties	1
Not in distress	6
Job required traveling	3
Left job	2
Left farm	*
Left business	1
Other	*

* Less than 0.5 percent.
[1] For detailed breakdown see appendix table 1.
NOTE.—81 families, whose reason for leaving settled residence was not ascertainable, are not included.

munity in which medical care was available; and of somewhat less importance were domestic trouble, the desire to rejoin relatives because of homesickness or because the relatives needed help, and the desire to leave a community in which a member of the family had died.

It should be remembered that the hard-and-fast division of the families into those whose distress was primarily either economic or personal often oversimplifies complex motives. Personal difficulties doubtless lay at the root of the economic distress of many families, especially of those which reported that they were ashamed to apply for relief or that their relatives could no longer support them.

It is probable that to an even greater extent economic hardships were the cause of personal distress reported by the families. Much of the domestic trouble shown in table 1 consisted of quarrels between a family and its relatives over the sharing of living expenses. All the families which migrated because of dislike of the community were also unemployed. The instances of desertion and divorce were often directly related to the inability of the economic head to support his family, and community disapproval was more often than not the result of antisocial behavior growing out of unemployment.

Several of the classifications shown in table 1 require detailed analysis and clarification.

Unemployment

Unemployment was the most frequently reported reason for leaving settled residence. Two-fifths of the families migrated primarily because they saw no prospect of further work in the community in which they had once considered themselves permanent residents.

Obviously the fact of unemployment does not by itself explain the migration of these families. Most of the millions of American families which were unemployed during the depression did not go to other States in search of work. An equally important part of the explanation of the migration of these families lies in the advantages they expected at their destinations.

The great majority of the families reporting unemployment as their basic reason for leaving settled residence attributed their unemployment directly to the depression itself, rather than to long-time trends in industry or accidental events (appendix table 1). Almost three-fourths of them explained that they were unemployed because of depression retrenchment at the place they usually worked (see history 5, p. 22) or because of the slack demand for their skill—usually related to construction—in the community in which they had been settled (see history 6, p. 23). The remainder was divided about evenly into two groups. One group of family heads had lost their jobs through events not directly related to the depression—through discharge for cause, the retirement of managers whose favorites they were, or through nepotism (see history 1, p. 21). The other group attributed their unemployment to causes which would probably have necessitated migration regardless of the depression—to the completion of a job of definite duration in seasonal occupations, to the effects of the drought, or to the migration of industry.

Inadequate Earnings

A number of families reported that they had been more or less regularly employed until the time they left their settled residence, but that they were dissatisfied with the amount of their earnings (table 1). Most of these families added that they were actually unable to live on the income their jobs provided. The cause of their low earnings was attributed most frequently to a reduction to part-time work. Less important causes were seasonal employment, lowered occupational status, and reduced wages (appendix table 1).

Unable to Work in a Particular Community

This classification, although relatively unimportant among the other causes of economic distress, is nevertheless significant in that it isolates a special migration problem. The heads of the families included in this group had been definitely eliminated from the labor market in the community where they had been settled, but they were partially or wholly employable in other communities. The greater part of this group consisted of persons who had developed occupational diseases which prevented further work at their usual occupation—of copper miners, for example, who had left Butte because they had developed lung trouble and had been advised by their doctors to try to find lighter work in a warmer climate. A few families included in this category left because the bad name of some member had made it impossible for any of the family to find work (appendix table 1).

Farming Failure

Farm owners and tenants who had been displaced from the land did not comprise a large part of the migrant families studied. As against the 40 percent who reported unemployment, only 8 percent reported displacement from the land as the basic reason for leaving settled residence.

Only slightly more than one-tenth of the families primarily in economic distress were farming failures. More than half of these families were drought refugees. A very small number left farms which had been ruined by floods. The remainder, constituting more than a third of the families reporting farming failure, was made up largely of evicted tenants; all the agricultural regions contributed to this group in about equal proportions (appendix table 1).

Other Economic Difficulties

Another group—slightly larger than the group reporting farming failure as their basic reason for leaving settled residence—migrated because of special problems growing out of all the economic difficulties that have been discussed (appendix table 1). These families were separately recorded because of the fact that their unemployment, failure as farmers, etc., would not have caused migration had it not been for the added difficulties. The largest classification in this group contained those families which reported that they either could not get relief at all or were unable to live on the relief they received (see history 9, pp. 23–24). A somewhat smaller group left settled residence to avoid the embarrassment of being on relief in a community in which they were well known. The rest of this miscellaneous group was made up of families evicted from their homes (see history 6, p. 23), those which had become too heavy a burden upon their relatives (see history 7, p. 23), and a few which left because of such reasons as pressing debts and the high cost of living.

Ill-Health

The psychological, case-work "solution" to the problem of aiding needy nonresidents, as well as the more realistic approach in terms of economic readjustment, both overlook one extremely important cause of the migration of destitute families. As table 1 shows, the second largest single reason for leaving settled residence was ill-health. Approximately one-tenth of the families began migration primarily because of the illness of some member of the family.

It is significant that so many health seekers participated in this depression migration. As recovery began and as the numbers displaced by unemployment declined, the proportion of health seekers—whose distress is only indirectly related to depression—would be expected to increase. Future efforts toward the solution of the transient problem must take this important cause of mobility into full account.

Only about one-eighth of the families reporting ill-health as the primary cause of migration left settled residence to seek medical care in another community. By far the greater part of these families moved because of the climate in the place where they had been settled (appendix table 1). Many families, containing tubercular patients, had been advised to leave damp climates or areas in which there had been severe dust storms. Frequently reported, also, were persons who had to leave high altitudes because of heart trouble, persons with asthma, persons who could not stand severe winters, and families in which members were suffering from malaria.

Domestic Trouble

Domestic trouble was the basic reason for the migration of a relatively small group of families, comprising 6 percent of the total. The majority of these families migrated because of trouble between husband and wife; of these, separations and divorces accounted for nearly all, while desertion was a relatively insignificant cause. Among the rest of this group quarrels between a family and its relatives and the death of husband, wife, or parents were reported with about equal frequency (appendix table 1).

Disliked Separation From Relatives or Friends

Approximately 1 family in each 25 reported that it left its settled residence because of personal distress growing out of separation from its relatives. Often the wife was homesick and wanted to be near her parents. Other families had received word that their relatives were destitute or were ill, and they had left settled residence to rejoin their relatives and to help them.

Other Personal Difficulties

A few families left settled residence for other personal reasons. Some reported that they had been either directly compelled to leave (see history 11, p. 24) or had been made so uncomfortable that they wanted to leave. Another group, comprising 2 percent of all families, reported that they personally disliked the climate, the foreigners, or some other feature of the community. A handful of families reported such other miscellaneous reasons as fear of earthquakes and flight from the Cuban revolution and from vigilante terror in East Arkansas.

REASONS FOR SELECTING DESTINATION

The fact that such a preponderant number of migrant families left their settled residence in distress provides but half the explanation of their migration. It is necessary to turn at this point to the second and equally important half of that explanation contained in the reported reasons for the selection of a particular destination.

Families With No Destination

Actually, the families were seldom literally driven from their homes by adversity. Their migration rarely resulted from a simple choice between either leaving settled residence or facing utter disaster. Despite the hardships which the families reported, only a very few left settled residence without a particular destination in mind. Of the families which began migration from a community in which they had been settled and self-supporting, 92 percent intended to proceed to a specific place (table 2). Only 8 percent set out with no destinations at all or with such vague destinations as "the West," "eastern Colorado," or "the cotton fields" in mind.

Table 2.—Migrant Families With and Without Specific Destination and Reason for No Destination

Destination	Migrant families
Total	4, 328
	Percent distribution
Total	100
Specific destination	92
No specific destination	8
Seeking work	4
Migratory occupation	2
Other	1
Not ascertainable	1

As table 2 shows, one-half of the families without destinations set out to travel from community to community in search of work (see history 5, p. 22). A smaller group left settled residence to follow migratory work, such as cotton picking, sugar-beet work, or carnival and circus work. A third group—made up of health seekers without

specific destination, those trying to find relatives, and those who
simply set out to wander with no particular purpose in mind—comprised only 1 percent of the families.

Type of Contact at Destination

Those families which did intend that their migrations should end in
a specific, predetermined place very rarely reported a capricious and
unreasoning choice of their destination.[7] Migrations based upon a
long and desperate gamble that conditions might be improved were
decidedly not the rule though they were sometimes reported. The
families studied showed a clear tendency to migrate only when the
probability of an improved status appeared to be reasonably high
(table 3).

Table 3.—Type of Contact Migrant Families Had at Destination

Type of contact at destination	Migrant families
Total	3,899
	Percent distribution
Total	100
Definite contact	80
Former residence of family or members of family	12
Residence of relatives or close friends	43
Particular skill of family head in demand at destination	2
Other definite contact [1]	23
No definite contact	20
Heard rumors that locality had advantages	16
Attracted by advertising	1
Chance selection of destination [2]	3

[1] Includes such contacts as letters of recommendation, job transfers, physicians' referral of health cases, purchase or trade of homes or farms, etc.
[2] Includes families which happened to get a ride, which were driven to nearest place of refuge, etc.

NOTE.—429 families, whose type of contact at destination or reason for selecting destination was not ascertainable, which had no destination, or whose place of destination was not ascertainable, are not included.

That the family migrations were essentially cautious rather than
quixotic is indicated in table 3, which shows the types of contact that
attracted the families to the destination they chose. Slightly more
than half of the families chose a destination in which there were close
personal friends or relatives who were more or less obligated to assist
them (table 3). Friends or relatives lived at the destination of 43
percent of the families, and an additional 12 percent, returning to a
place in which they had formerly resided, probably had even more
valuable and numerous contacts at their destination.

[7] Several families driven out by dust storms reported that they had selected
particular places on the Pacific coast as their destinations because they wanted to
live at the greatest possible distance from the Dust Bowl. Such explanations
were very infrequently reported.

During the depression it was a common occurrence for the groups most seriously affected by reduced earnings to double-up within one household. Pooled resources increased the security of all, and the crowding together of many people under one roof reduced the total cost of rent and heat. The large proportion of migrant families moving to places where they had relatives or close friends suggests that the same expedient played a substantial part in setting into motion the families studied. The principal difference between this particular group of migrant families and the nonmigrants who pooled their resources was that the migrants had to cross a State boundary in the process.

In addition to the families which returned to a former residence and those which moved to a community in which relatives or friends resided, a third large group of families also had a definite contact at their destination. This group, comprising 23 percent of the families with destinations, was made up of families which chose their destinations because of such specific entrees as letters of recommendation to employers, the sight-unseen purchase of farms or homes, satisfactory reports of employment opportunity through correspondence, and employment office direction.

Finally, a small group of families with none of the three types of specific contacts discussed had destinations in a community where the special skills of the economic head would in all probability have been in demand. This group included such people as foundry and rolling mill workers who migrated from one steel town to another, textile workers moving to another cotton mill town, and meatcutters moving to Kansas City.

The total number of families with definite contacts at their destination comprised nearly four-fifths of the families. It is thus clear that the families were generally neither foolhardy nor particularly adventurous in undertaking the migration which involved assistance from transient bureaus. Least of all were they intent upon seeing the country at the Government's expense. Instead, they were, in general, distressed groups which saw a reasonable solution to their problems through migration to another community. The essence of the migration studied is contained in this fact.

A minority of the families, comprising about one-fifth of the total group, were an exception to this generalization. As table 3 shows, 20 percent of the families selected a destination with which they had no definite links of any sort. The greater part of these families were attracted by vague rumors that times were good or that the climate was healthful at the place of destination. A few of them were attracted by advertised economic advantages. There were frequent instances of migration to submarginal land that had been incorrectly advertised to be rich, productive soil from which a good living could be made.[8] After making a down payment on the land, the families discovered that it was either worthless or that the cost of improving it was beyond their means; and at the time the families were interviewed, all had abandoned the farms to which advertising had attracted them. Finally, there was a residual group whose definite destinations had been selected through sheer chance. These were families which "happened to get a ride" to a particular place (see history 6, p. 23), those whose destinations were determined by special bus rates, and those which selected their destinations for "no particular reason."

Objectives Sought at Destination

What the families hoped for at their destination was a solution to the basic problems which had confronted them at their settled residence. Accordingly the particular advantages they sought were generally the obverse of the kind of distress they reported as their reason for leaving settled residence. The relative importance of the different objectives reported by the families is shown in table 4.

Economic Betterment

Approximately four-fifths of the families selected their destination primarily in hope of economic betterment. The greater part of these—and indeed the majority of all the families—were seeking employment. Second in importance was a destitute group made up of a substantial number of unemployables (see ch. VI, p. 111) who migrated to the homes of relatives or friends in the expectation that they would be taken in and helped until they were able to support themselves again. These families, together with those seeking employment, made up almost the entire group which reported that they sought economic betterment at their destination.

All other kinds of economic betterment sought are conspicuously small. Only 5 percent of the families intended to take up land as either owners or tenants. About half that number planned to open a small business establishment of their own. Although 4 percent of the families left settled residence primarily because of distress related specifically to relief, only 1 percent of the families had relief as their basic objective at their destination. A handful of families selected their destination in order to be in a place where living costs would be cheaper, in order to look after property, to prospect for gold, or to trap (see footnote 1, table 4).

---

[8] For instance advertising circulars described submarginal land in the two poorest agricultural counties in the State of Washington in this way: "Soil sub-irrigated, black, silt, and sand loam; abundant water supply; numberless trout streams * * *. A farmer can start with small capital and work into a beautiful farmhome with all modern advantages close at hand." A letter in the files of the Works Progress Administration Division of Social Research tells of one farmer "remarking grimly that a certain lumber company [which advertised its cut-over properties as productive farm land] was responsible for more bankrupt farmers in eastern Washington and northern Idaho than the depression itself."

Table 4.—Objectives Sought by Migrant Families at Destination

Objectives sought at destination	Migrant families
Total	4,005
	Percent distribution
Total	100
Economic betterment	79
Employment	57
Promise of work	14
Hoped to find work	43
Farm	5
Had arranged to secure farm	1
Hoped to secure farm	4
Business	3
Had arranged to open business	1
Hoped to open business	2
Help from relatives or friends	11
Relief	1
Cheaper cost of living	1
Miscellaneous economic objectives [1]	1
Personal objectives	21
Healthful climate or medical care	10
To rejoin relatives	8
Sentiment	1
Miscellaneous personal objectives [2]	2

[1] Include such reasons as: to take advantage of special bus rate, to collect debts, to look after property, to buy fruit to peddle, to bet on horse races, to prospect for gold, to trap fur-bearing animals, etc.
[2] Include such reasons as: to seek safety from vigilante mobs, to take a vacation, happened to get a ride, to follow the voice of God, to march in the bonus army, to seek revenge, to put children in school, etc.

NOTE.—323 families, whose place of destination or reason for selecting destination was not ascertainable and which had no destination, are not included.

However cautious the families may have been, the specific economic betterment which they sought was more often hoped for than promised. Table 4 shows how many families left settled residence with the positive assurance that they would find employment, farms, and businesses, and how many were only more or less vaguely hopeful of securing them. While 43 percent of the families *hoped* to find work at their destination, only 14 percent had been promised work; 3 percent hoped to secure a farm, as against 1 percent which had already rented or bought a farm before reaching their destination; and 2 percent *hoped* to open a business, as against 1 percent which had definitely arranged to open a business before moving.

Although this general view of the families' economic prospects shows that few had a definite promise of work when migration began, it must be remembered that the majority of the families had contacts which appeared to promise them a measure of security at their destination. It is significant, moreover, that the families whose prospects for work were least definite tended to migrate most readily to a destination at which they had close personal ties. A separate tabulation showed that well over one-half of the families which merely hoped for work, but only about one-fifth of those promised work, migrated to a former residence or to the residence of relatives.

Personal Objectives

The chief objectives of 21 percent of the families were of a personal nature. Nearly half of these families were health seekers who had been advised by their physicians to move to a specific place for hospitalization or for a particular kind of climate. The only other important group, comprising 8 percent of the total, consisted of families which wished to rejoin their relatives for personal reasons—because of homesickness and loneliness, to nurse relatives who were ill, to be with dying relatives, or to attend the funeral of a relative who had died.

Sentimental reasons occupied an insignificant place among the reasons for selecting a particular destination. Such explanations as "the North always represented freedom and equality to us," or "we always wanted to live in Detroit," or "we always wanted to see the West" were reported, but not frequently. Such reasons were the principal motivation of only 1 percent of the families. Approximately the same number of families reported the usual remarkable assortment of non-classifiable reasons for selecting destination: to take a vacation, to follow the voice of God, to seek revenge, etc. (table 4, footnote 2).

REASONS FOR MIGRATION, BY STATE

The same pattern of causes which governed the migration of the families as a whole was also operative in each of the individual regions of the United States. Except in a few States where obviously peculiar conditions existed, families emigrating from widely dissimilar States reported the same reasons, distributed in much the same proportion. The reasons for selecting destinations, while somewhat more varied, also tended toward similarity in different parts of the United States. The amount of variation in the reported reasons for migration to and from the different States [9] is shown in figures 2, 3, and 4.

Reasons for Leaving Settled Residence, by State

Economic Reasons

Unemployment, the reason for leaving settled residence which was most frequently reported by the families as a whole, was also the most frequently reported reason in 29 of the 30 States and groups of States shown in figure 2. Its importance as the basic unsettling force was generally uniform, even among States with altogether dissimilar economic and social characteristics. For example, in 14 of the 30 groups unemployment accounted for 38 to 43 percent of the emigrating families. Among these 14 groups were such widely diverse

[9] Because of the small number of families moving to and from several States, two or more contiguous States were sometimes combined in figs. 2, 3, and 4. The same combinations used here are also used in ch. II, figs. 5–10.

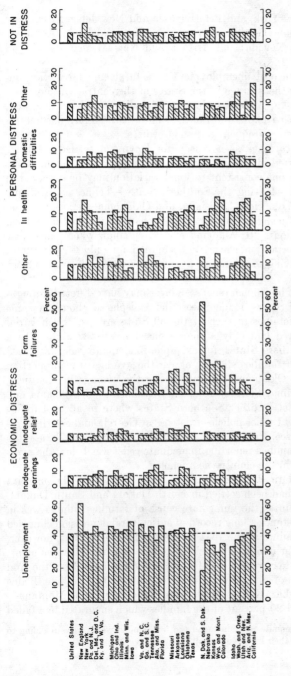

FIG. 2 – REASON MIGRANT FAMILIES LEFT SETTLED RESIDENCE
BY STATE OR REGION OF SETTLED RESIDENCE

Note: Dotted lines represent average for United States.

Source: Appendix table 2.

AF-2851, WPA

sections as New York, and Pennsylvania and New Jersey; Kentucky and West Virginia; Georgia and South Carolina; Oklahoma, Arkansas, and Utah and Nevada; and Arizona and New Mexico (fig. 2 and appendix table 2).

The importance of unemployment as a displacing force was consistently below the average in the States of the central and northern Plains—Nebraska, Kansas, Colorado, Wyoming and Montana, and, above all, North Dakota and South Dakota—where farming failures were reported more frequently than elsewhere.

Inadequate earnings as a reason for leaving a settled residence were also reported in a generally uniform proportion throughout the country. Only one consistent regional variation may be observed in figure 2; families leaving the Southern States—Tennessee, Alabama and Mississippi, Florida, Louisiana, and Oklahoma—reported inadequate earnings in slightly higher proportions than families emigrating from other regions. In Alabama and Mississippi, where this cause was most important, however, it accounted for only 13 percent of the families leaving as against an average of 7 percent for the country as a whole.

Regardless of how much relief standards may have differed throughout the United States, inadequate relief [10] displaced about the same proportion of families in each of the 30 State groups. Such variations as occurred had only a slight consistency by sections. In a number of Southern States, for example, inadequate relief displaced a proportion of families slightly above the average; the proportion was highest in Oklahoma and was above the average in Kentucky and West Virginia, Florida, Louisiana, Arkansas, and Alabama and Mississippi. Yet in other Southern States where in all probability the same resident relief policies existed—in Georgia and South Carolina, in Tennessee, Virginia and North Carolina, and in Texas—the proportion of families reporting inadequate relief was below the average proportion in the country as a whole.

Farming failure displaced slightly more than half the migrant families which had been settled in North Dakota and South Dakota. In these two States the immediate cause of farming failures was in nearly every instance a long record of agricultural depression climaxed by total crop failure in the 1934 drought. It is significant, however, that the drought dominated the movement from the Dakotas alone. In no other State or region did the proportion displaced from the land exceed one-fifth of the total number of emigrants. In five Plains States—Nebraska, Kansas, Colorado, Wyoming, and Montana—between 15 and 20 percent of the families which emigrated had failed

[10] In fig. 2 inadequate relief included the few families which were unwilling to apply for relief in their home communities.

to earn a living on farms. But in Oklahoma the proportion of farm failures was only 12 percent, and in Texas it was only 6 percent.

Other States which contain agricultural subregions lost an insignificant number of families because of farming failure. In Michigan, Minnesota, and Wisconsin, in which the Lake States Cut-Over region lies, the proportion of migrant families which were displaced from the land was well below the national average. In both Arkansas and Missouri farming failure accounted for only one-seventh of all emigrating families. And in the Cotton States the proportion of farming failures varied from 4 percent in Virginia and North Carolina to a high of only 10 percent in Alabama and Mississippi.

Other economic distress, as shown on figure 2, included business failures, inability to work in a particular community, evictions, and other forms of economic distress which were shown separately in table 1. Accordingly, the rather wide variations which appear in this column of figure 2 are the result of several unrelated forces. In Virginia, Kentucky, and West Virginia the proportion of families reporting other economic distress was increased by the emigration of coal miners whose ill-health prohibited any future work in the mines. In Montana there was a similar emigration of many copper miners. The other economic distress in North Dakota and South Dakota consisted chiefly in the bankruptcy of small shopkeepers ruined by the drought. In Pennsylvania and New Jersey the bankruptcy of small merchants, as in lunchrooms or delicatessens, and the high cost of commutation from settled residence to a job once held were the principal forms of other economic explosive forces.

Personal Reasons

In the East ill-health was not a frequently reported cause of migration except in New York, and Pennsylvania and New Jersey, where tuberculosis necessitated a change of climate for many families. It is particularly significant that all Southeastern States except Florida reported a proportion far below the national average.

In the West ill-health was much more important as a reason for leaving settled residence. It caused the migration of 20 percent of the families leaving Wyoming and Montana, where ill-health resulting from severe winters was the chief complaint. The high proportion of health seekers leaving Minnesota also resulted from the cold winters. Health-resort States generally had a high proportion of emigrants reporting ill-health. Nearly one-fifth of the families leaving Arizona and New Mexico were motivated by ill-health, and approximately the same proportion left Colorado, where the high altitude caused heart ailments. The health seekers who left Texas were chiefly families from the urban areas or from the Panhandle which migrated because of tuberculosis.

Domestic trouble was infrequently reported in all States. It displaced 10 percent or less of the families from every geographical division except Georgia and South Carolina, where a high incidence of broken families raised the proportion to 11 percent. Other personal difficulties, including a number of such separate categories as absence of relatives, personal dislike of community, and community disapproval, were about uniformly reported in the different sections of the country.

Reasons for Selecting Destination, by State

Contacts at Destination, by State

In all the States combined, more than one-half the migrant families selected as their destination a community in which they had close personal contacts, and in addition about one-fourth were attracted by some other definite entree. Less than one-fourth had no definite contact at their destination. Against this average, one broad regional variation may be noted (fig. 3 and appendix table 3). Migrant families with destinations in the States east of the Mississippi River showed a more-than-average tendency to select as their destination a community in which they had formerly resided, or in which they had

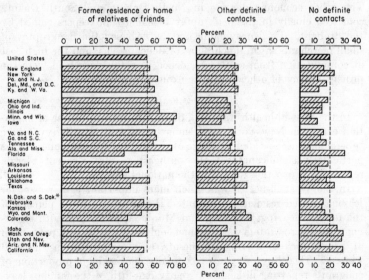

FIG. 3 – TYPE OF CONTACT OF MIGRANT FAMILIES AT DESTINATION
BY STATE OR REGION OF DESTINATION

* Base too small for calculation.

Note: Dotted lines represent average for United States.

Source: Appendix table 3.

AF-2852,WPA

relatives or close personal friends. Conversely, the importance of rumor—indicated in the third column of figure 3—in attracting migrant families was most marked in the West and played a very small part in determining the movement of the families whose destinations were in the East.

As a result of special circumstances a few individual States had their own peculiar variations of this pattern. In Florida and Louisiana the proportion of families migrating to the place in which they had close personal contacts was far below average and the proportion attracted by rumor was very large. In Arkansas and Texas, with a high proportion of families migrating to the oil and cotton fields where seasonal work had been promised, the proportion reporting other definite entree was far above average. Other contact was also important for the families with destinations in Colorado, and Arizona and New Mexico, where the most frequently reported entree was a physician's referral.

Of the families with California destinations, the proportion moving to a community in which they had close personal contacts was 54 percent, approximately equal to the national average. The family movement into California, rather than being unique, thus appears to have been attracted by essentially the same general forces which dominated migrant family movement in the rest of the United States. Idaho, and Washington and Oregon, like California, reported about the average proportion of families attracted to places where they had relatives or close personal friends. It should be noted, however, that in three of these States somewhat more than the average proportion of families were attracted by rumor.

Objectives at Destination, by State

Just as unemployment was the chief reason for migrant families leaving settled residence in nearly every State, so a search for work was almost uniformly the most frequently reported objective of the families at their destination (fig. 4 and appendix table 4). In 27 of the 30 States and State groupings shown in figure 4, employment was the objective of the majority of the families.

Several States containing submarginal agricultural regions reported more than the average proportion of families whose objective was to secure a farm. In New England and Kentucky most of these families came from urban centers hoping to secure a farm to tide them through the depression. In the Mississippi Valley, on the other hand, these families were sharecroppers (as in Missouri and Arkansas) or tenants (as in Oklahoma and Nebraska) who were seeking to improve their status as farmers. The families intending to secure a farm in Idaho, and Washington and Oregon were made up of a heterogeneous group which took up submarginal farms on logged-off land.

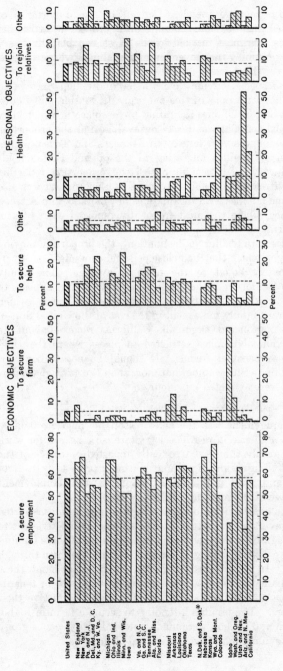

FIG. 4 – OBJECTIVES SOUGHT BY MIGRANT FAMILIES AT DESTINATION BY STATE OR REGION OF DESTINATION

*Base too small for calculation.

Note: Dotted lines represent average for United States.

Source: Appendix table 4.

4F-2853, WPA

In any case, however, the proportion of families seeking a farm was generally very small. Only three of the geographical groupings shown in figure 4 had more than 10 percent of the families reporting the object of securing a farm at their destination, and only in Idaho [11] was the proportion above 15 percent. The preponderance of families seeking employment and the relative insignificance of those hoping to secure farms reflect the essentially urban-industrial perspective of the families which received assistance from FERA transient bureaus.

The proportion of families migrating to secure help from their relatives was far greater in the East than in the West. In the Southeastern States these were principally broken families, and the large proportion shown in figure 4 reflects the high incidence of domestic trouble reported in the Southern States (fig. 2). In the Midwestern States, on the other hand, the proportion of broken families was very small, and the large representation of those seeking help from relatives resulted from the doubling-up of complete families.

The destinations of health seekers made a simple and obvious pattern. Although the need for hospitalization attracted a few families into nearly every State, only six States and State groupings received more than the average proportion of these families. In the East Florida stood out, and in the West almost all States from Texas to California were above average. The highest proportion of all was reported for Arizona and New Mexico, where exactly half the families were health seekers. The next largest proportion was reported by Colorado, with 33 percent. California was third, with 22 percent of the families reporting that they had selected that destination hoping that the climate would improve their health.

FAMILY HISTORIES

1. THE SLADE FAMILY [12] settled in Dalhart, Tex., in 1932. A friend had opened a coalyard there and had invited Mr. Slade to come and manage the business for him. The job promised to be permanent. After a year had passed, however, the owner's destitute nephew arrived in Dalhart, and the owner felt obliged to give him Mr. Slade's job. A long search for another job in Dalhart was without success. The Slades decided that it would be utterly impossible to find work there. Accordingly, they packed their furniture and moved to Denver, where they had formerly lived. Mr. Slade found occasional odd jobs in Denver but could not support his wife and small son on his earnings.

---

[11] In Idaho the sample study was made only in Boise and Sand Point. Practically every transient bureau family under care at Sand Point had come to the community to take up logged-off land. For that reason, Idaho is represented as having a larger proportion of families which hoped to secure a farm at their destination than would have been shown had the migrant families in every Idaho transient center been included in this study.

[12] The names throughout this section are fictitious, and many of the places have been changed to conceal the identity of the families whose histories are described.

When their savings were all spent, they came to the transient bureau for help.

2. JIM KOVICH went to work as a rough carpenter in the Youngstown, Ohio, steel mills in 1925. He had steady work until he was caught in a general layoff in the spring of 1930. After that, his family lived on short-time jobs and savings for 4 years. Finally, in 1934 they had to go on relief. Mr. Kovich was very restless on relief, and when he heard from a friend that he might get work in Flint, Mich., he left his family in Youngstown and went to investigate the rumor. Within a month he found a job, and in March 1935 he sent for his wife and three children. In August he was laid off again. He had been unable to save any money on the job. In September the Koviches came to the transient bureau for help.

3. ROY HARRIS had been a West Virginia coal miner for 30 years. In the summer of 1934 the mine at which he had been working closed down. He was too old to get a job in another mine, and there was no hope of other work. The Harrises applied for resident relief but were unable to live on the allowance they received. Mr. Harris had a brother living in St. Louis. In the spring of 1935 Mr. and Mrs. Harris and the two children moved to St. Louis to try to locate the brother, who they thought could help them find work. When they found Mr. Harris's brother, he was unable to help them, and the family applied for transient relief.

4. HARRY LARSON worked out of Devils Lake, N. Dak., as a brakeman on the Great Northern. He lost his job in 1933. Since Devils Lake is principally a railroad town, there was no chance of finding other work there. Mrs. Larson had formerly lived on a farm in the northern Minnesota cut-over region. The couple believed that the best solution of their problem would be to return to Minnesota and take up a plot of land. This experiment soon failed. The frost ruined their first crop and left the couple stranded. The Larsons then moved to Duluth and went on transient relief.

5. GEORGE PASTOR, 40 years old, had been a cotton-mill worker in the Piedmont for 25 years. In 1928 he found a job in Greenville, S. C., where he remained for 7 years. In January 1935 the mill in which he worked began to lay off workers. Mr. Pastor was first reduced to 3 days' work a week, then to 2. Because there was no prospect that the mill would run full time soon, the Pastors and their two children set out to make the rounds of all the textile mills in the South to try to find work. When they arrived in New Orleans, Mr. Pastor was promised a job in a cotton mill as soon as it reopened a month later. Afraid to risk losing the chance to work, Mr. Pastor would not leave New Orleans. When they ran out of money, they came to the transient bureau for help until the mill reopened.

6. WILLIAM KRUGER had been working as a house painter in Chicago for 10 years. Work became harder and harder to find, and after September 1933 there was none at all. In the summer of 1934 the couple applied for relief, but while waiting for relief to be granted they were evicted from their home. On the same day, learning that a friend was preparing to drive to San Antonio, the couple persuaded him to let them go along. Mr. Kruger was unable to find work in San Antonio and the couple registered at the transient bureau. After 6 weeks they moved to Shreveport, La., where Mr. Kruger found a job driving a caravan of automobiles to Los Angeles. When they registered at the Los Angeles transient bureau, they were promptly returned to Chicago for resident relief. The Krugers were by now completely dissatisfied with Chicago. In June 1935, after 2 months in Chicago, Mr. Kruger found another job driving a caravan to San Francisco. They had been in the San Francisco transient bureau for 3 weeks when interviewed and insisted that they would not return to Chicago. Mr. Kruger had been promised a job as painter, and the couple proposed to settle down in California.

7. MR. AND MRS. ROBERTS were both over 70. Since 1929 they had been living in Kansas City on their small savings, on Mr. Roberts' earnings from light carpentry work, and on the contributions of their son. In 1932 they moved to Council Bluffs, Iowa, to help their son build a house. They lived in Council Bluffs for 3 years. In 1935 the son lost his job and in order not to be a burden Mr. and Mrs. Roberts moved back to Kansas City, where they owned a house that could not be rented. Meanwhile, they had lost their legal settlement status in Missouri, and when they needed relief they had to go to the transient bureau.

8. THE JOHNSON FAMILY raised cattle in Clark County, Kans. The dust storms of 1935 turned the farm into a waste of sand dunes. Moreover, Mr. Johnson and two of the children contracted "dust pneumonia." In desperation they wrote to a Spokane real estate office to inquire whether they could secure a plot of land there with little money. When they were informed that Washington had "good, cheap land and a pleasant climate," they decided to leave for Spokane immediately. The very next day they sold all the livestock for whatever it would bring, paid the grocery bill, piled their furniture in the old Ford truck, and set out for Spokane. When they arrived there in June, their money had run out. They were unable to get any land and were forced to register at the transient bureau within a week after their arrival.

9. THE MOSHER FAMILY, consisting of Mr. and Mrs. Mosher and their eight children, were Negro farm owners in Russell County, Ala. Many of their friends and relatives had moved to Chicago in 1917

and 1918, and the Moshers had long wanted to move North also. After the depression they had an increasingly difficult time managing their farm. By 1933, after they could no longer support themselves on the earnings, they applied for relief. The relief offered them was inadequate. In November 1934 Mrs. Mosher's brother died in Chicago, and she and two of the children were given a ride North to attend the funeral. When they arrived in the North they found it much to their liking. They sent word back to Alabama for the rest of the family to follow them. The Mosher children started North one by one, and by September 1935 six of them had arrived. In August 1935 the family had to apply for transient relief. Chicago social workers were not successful in persuading them to return to Alabama, and the family was to be dropped from the rolls on October 1. Their plans were to try not only to stay in Chicago but also to bring the rest of the family North to join them.

10. "DR." HUNT and his wife had been constantly on the road since they were married in 1930. Dr. Hunt, a quack, had devised a cure for all human ailments. He had been making a living by peddling his nostrums from city to city, and by 1935 he had visited every State with his cures. Feeling an urge at that time to settle down, he stopped off in Pittsburgh. He planned to open a "foot clinic" in Pittsburgh and to establish permanent quarters in which to manufacture his cure for varicose veins. Meanwhile, he applied for relief at the transient bureau.

11. JACK CARSON lost his job as switchman in Nashville in 1931. He and his wife then went into the bootlegging business. In 1933 they were caught by the police and were given a prison sentence, suspended on the condition that they leave the State. In compliance the couple set out on a freight for the Southwest, where they understood they could find work picking cotton. Since 1933 they had been traveling about from place to place as migratory-casual workers picking cotton in Texas and New Mexico and picking berries in Arkansas. They had become extremely dissatisfied with this work, and when they were interviewed in Milwaukee, they declared that they intended to remain there if they had to go to jail.

12. HAZEL SMITH had married Ed Smith in 1932, soon after he arrived in Sand Point, Idaho, looking for a place to farm. The couple moved out to a plot of logged-off land near Sand Point. For 2 years they struggled to make the farm pay, but in 1935 they lost it. The couple and their small child had no place to go except to Mr. Smith's parents in San Diego. Upon arrival in San Diego they found that Mr. Smith's parents were on relief and unable to help. The family then proceeded to San Francisco, where they hoped to find work. There they registered at the transient bureau. Mr. Smith looked for

a job for a month, then suddenly he disappeared. After 3 months he had not been heard from.

13. JOE WATKINS had been a plumber in Tulsa, Okla. In 1934 his wife developed tuberculosis. The family physician told her that she would have to have a change of climate immediately and arranged for her to receive medical care in Phoenix, Ariz. Since Mrs. Watkins was too ill to travel alone, Mr. Watkins quit his job in Tulsa to accompany her. When the couple reached Albuquerque, Mrs. Watkins had a severe hemorrhage and was not able to proceed to Phoenix. After 6 months in Albuquerque their savings were gone, and they had to apply at the transient bureau for relief.

14. THE CAMPBELLS had been living with Mrs. Campbell's parents in Fort Smith, Ark., ever since they were married in 1933. The old folks became more and more insistent that they leave. In February 1935 Mr. Campbell received word from his brother that there were good chances for work in Los Angeles. Accordingly, the couple set out with their baby for Los Angeles. When they arrived they found work as farm laborers near San Bernardino, but when this work was ended, they had to apply for transient relief. The couple insisted that they be permitted to remain in California, which they greatly preferred to Arkansas.

15. THE BISHOPS felt that they had never been settled since they were married. Mr. Bishop had been a hotel clerk in New York, but he lost this job 1 week after his marriage. The Bishops then set out for Jacksonville, Fla., to visit an aunt. After a month in Jacksonville they started toward the Pacific coast. When they were interviewed in the El Paso transient bureau, they stated that they were on their way to California because they had always wanted to see the West.

Chapter II

ORIGINS AND MOVEMENT

DISTRESS AT the place of origin and reasonable expectation of betterment at the place of destination were shown in the preceding chapter to have been the motivation for the depression migration of most of the families studied. The geographical movements produced by the action of these forces are traced in this chapter, and the general trends are described.[1] These trends are then compared with the trends revealed in the record of internal American migration prior to 1930 in order to show the relationship between this distress migration and "normal" predepression population mobility.

Fortunately, there is available a record of the geographical mobility of all migrant families under care by transient bureaus in the United States, as well as those included in the representative sample on which this report is based. The origins and movement of the 29,885 interstate migrant families which were registered in FERA transient bureaus on June 30, 1935, are presented in figures 5–10.[2]

---

[1] It should be noted that the States in which the families were registered in transient bureaus were not necessarily the same States to which the *destination* discussed in the preceding chapter refers. A family's *destination* was the place to which it intended to migrate at the time of leaving a settled residence. The correspondence between the State of destination and the State of transient bureau registration was nevertheless large.

[2] Every 3 months beginning September 30, 1934, each State transient director reported the State of origin of all unattached and family transients under care on the last day of the quarter (FERA Form 304). The Quarterly Census report for June 30, 1935, rather than the sample on which this study is based, was used in drawing the origin and place-of-registration maps (figs. 5–10), the trend maps (figs. 11 and 12), and the rate-of-immigration and emigration maps (figs. 13 and 16). Although tests showed that the origin and place-of-registration data derived from the sample were almost identical with the data derived from the Quarterly Census, in the sample the absolute number of families migrating to and from certain States was so small as to make graphic illustration difficult.

The maps on the left side of these figures show the movement of migrant families out of the several States or regions represented. The corresponding maps on the right side of the page show the movement of migrant families into the State or region represented.[3]

MOVEMENT BETWEEN STATES

Geographical Scatter

At first glance, these maps appear to show a chaotic geographical scattering of families. The families leaving many States spread broadcast across the map, and many States attracted families from all parts of the country. This tendency is clearest on the maps showing the movement to and from the Northeastern and Midwestern States and is especially marked on the Illinois, Iowa, and Michigan maps.

To a lesser degree the same tendency characterized the movement to and from all other areas. Families from nearly all States found their way into a majority of the other States. On the average, the migrant families in each State on June 30, 1935, included families from 32 different States. At one extreme, families in New York, Illinois, and California transient bureaus came from all the other States. In the New Mexico transient bureaus, filled largely with health seekers, there were families from all States except New Hampshire and Delaware. At the other extreme, the transient bureaus of Maine had only 12 families under care, representing in all 7 States but including families from as far as Oklahoma and Nevada.

Also represented in the broad geographical scatter were such movements as from North Dakota to Virginia, from Montana to New Hampshire, Washington to Maryland, Rhode Island to Idaho. Inasmuch as about 30,000 families were involved, however, some long-distance migrations would be expected. The important fact, as the next section will show, is that long-distance migrations represent the extreme rather than the typical case of family migration.

Distance Traveled

Most of the migrations were confined within the general vicinity of the State in which they originated (figs. 5–10). On the maps this tendency is revealed by the clustering of the largest circles about the particular State represented. It is especially noticeable on the maps showing migration to and from the Eastern, Midwestern, and Southern States.

[3] Because space does not allow all States to be individually represented on the maps, two or more States are sometimes grouped on one map. When such combinations are made, the interchange of families between the States within the group is shown in the lower left corner of the map, as "Interstate, intraregional movement."

FIG.5-STATE OR REGION OF ORIGIN AND OF TRANSIENT BUREAU REGISTRATION OF MIGRANT FAMILIES

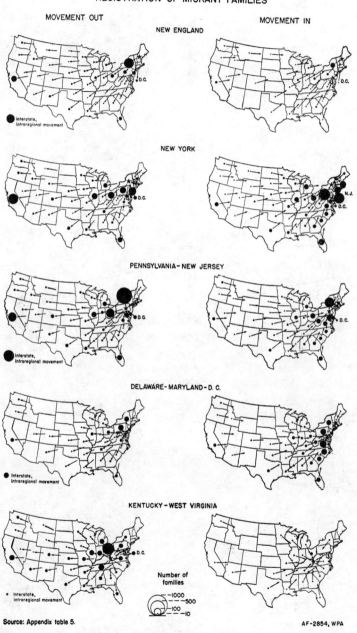

MOVEMENT OUT

MOVEMENT IN

NEW ENGLAND

NEW YORK

PENNSYLVANIA-NEW JERSEY

DELAWARE-MARYLAND-D. C.

KENTUCKY-WEST VIRGINIA

Number of families
—1000
—500
—100
—10

Interstate, intraregional movement

Source: Appendix table 5.

AF-2854, WPA

FIG. 6 – STATE OR REGION OF ORIGIN AND OF TRANSIENT BUREAU REGISTRATION OF MIGRANT FAMILIES

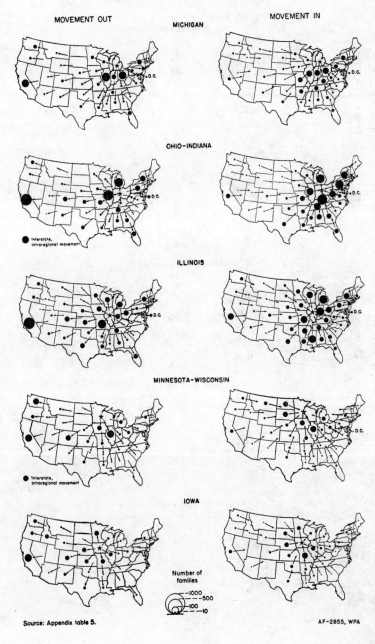

Source: Appendix table 5.

AF-2855, WPA

FIG.7-STATE OR REGION OF ORIGIN AND OF TRANSIENT BUREAU
REGISTRATION OF MIGRANT FAMILIES

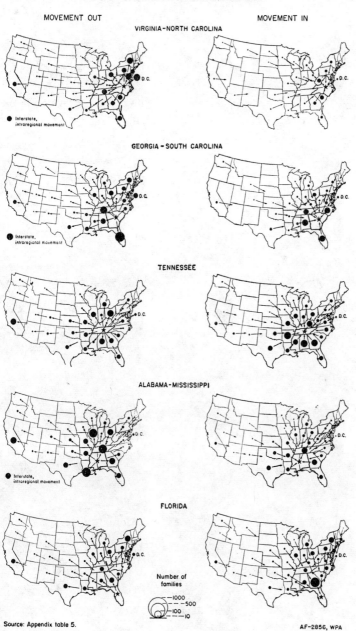

MOVEMENT OUT

MOVEMENT IN

VIRGINIA-NORTH CAROLINA

GEORGIA - SOUTH CAROLINA

TENNESSEE

ALABAMA-MISSISSIPPI

FLORIDA

Number of
families

—1000
---500
—100
---10

Source: Appendix table 5.

AF-2856, WPA

FIG. 8-STATE OR REGION OF ORIGIN AND OF TRANSIENT-BUREAU REGISTRATION OF MIGRANT FAMILIES

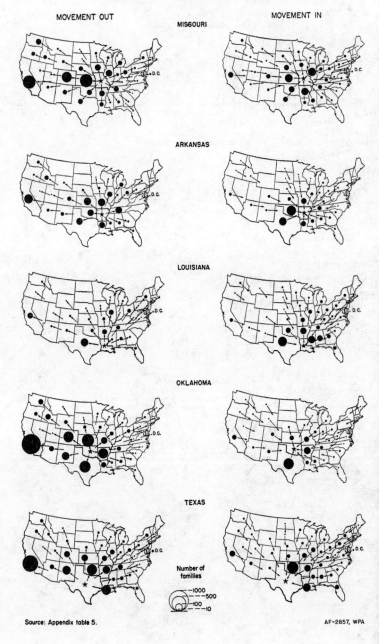

MOVEMENT OUT

MOVEMENT IN

MISSOURI

ARKANSAS

LOUISIANA

OKLAHOMA

TEXAS

Number of families

—1000
—500
—100
—10

Source: Appendix table 5.

AF-2857, WPA

FIG.9-STATE OR REGION OF ORIGIN AND OF TRANSIENT BUREAU
REGISTRATION OF MIGRANT FAMILIES

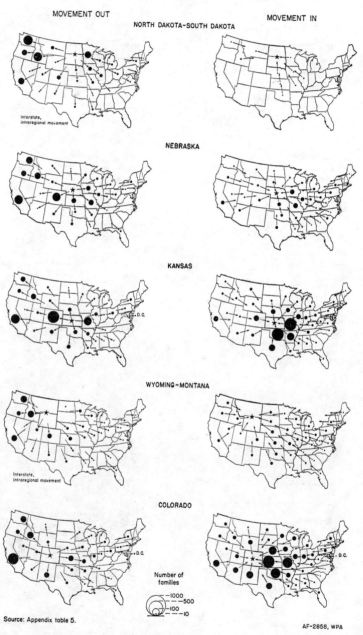

MOVEMENT OUT

MOVEMENT IN

NORTH DAKOTA-SOUTH DAKOTA

Interstate,
intraregional movement

NEBRASKA

KANSAS

WYOMING-MONTANA

Interstate,
intraregional movement

COLORADO

Number of
families

—1000
——500
—100
——10

AF-2858, WPA

Fig.10-STATE OR REGION OF ORIGIN AND OF TRANSIENT BUREAU REGISTRATION OF MIGRANT FAMILIES

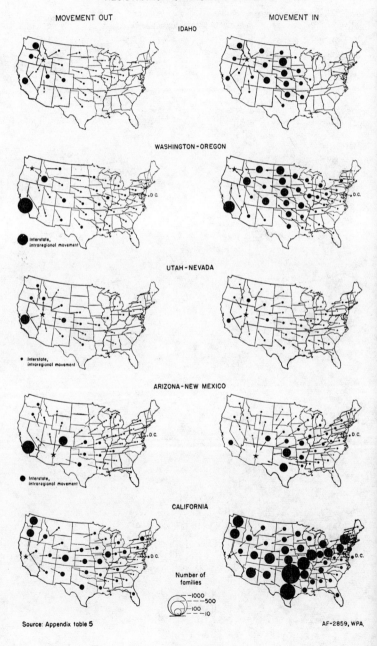

Source: Appendix table 5

AF-2859, WPA.

Statistically this tendency may be measured by a count of the families migrating within the boundaries of uniform zones set up about each State, representing progressively greater distances traveled. Table 5 shows the proportion of families migrating within four such zones, based upon the distance between the geographical center of each State and the geographical center of all other States.[4]

Table 5.—Distance [1] Between State of Origin and State of Enumeration of Migrant Families [2] and of Persons in the General Population 1930 [3] Residing in a State Other Than State of Birth

Distance	Migrant families	General population, 1930
Total	29,885	25,388,100
	Percent distribution	
Total	100	100
Zone 1 (to States 400 miles or less from center of State of origin)	38	53
Zone 2 (to States 401 to 1,500 miles from center of State of origin)	40	31
Zone 3 (to States 1,501 to 2,100 miles from center of State of origin)	19	13
Zone 4 (to States more than 2,100 miles from State of origin)	3	3

[1] Distance is measured in terms of straight line distance from the geographical center of the State of origin (or State of birth for the general population) to the geographical center of the State in which families were registered in transient bureaus (or State of 1930 residence for the general population), Geological Survey, "The Geographic Centers of the Continental United States and of the Several States," mimeographed release No. 22164, U. S. Department of the Interior, Washington, D. C., 1938.
[2] Division of Transient Activities, Quarterly Census of Transients Under Care, June 30, 1935, mimeographed report, Federal Emergency Relief Administration, Washington, D. C., 1935. 419 families from U. S. possessions or from foreign countries are not included.
[3] Bureau of the Census, Fifteenth Census of the United States: 1930, Population Vol. II, U. S. Department of Commerce, Washington, D. C., 1933, ch. 4, tables 32-34.

The first zone includes all the families migrating to a State whose geographical center is within a 400-mile radius of the center of the State in which they originated. Measuring from South Dakota, for example, this zone includes the States of North Dakota, Minnesota, Iowa, Nebraska, and Wyoming, but it does not include Montana.[5] On the average seven neighboring States are included within the 400-mile

[4] The United States Geological Survey's calculations of the center of each State's area were used as the basis for measuring the distance between centers of States.

Distance-traveled tables based upon the distance from State centers were the most practicable of the several that were tried. Zones based upon contiguity of States were abandoned because of the extremely wide divergence in the size of the areas covered. States contiguous to Maine, for example, comprise an area only one-seventieth as great as the area of States contiguous to Oklahoma.

It is interesting to note, however, that the Fifteenth Census classifies birth-residence data according to whether those moving were living in States adjacent to State of birth or living in other States. Of the 25,388,100 persons who, in 1930, were living in a State other than their State of birth, 48 percent were in adjacent States. For migrant families, on the other hand, only 40 percent were registered in States adjacent to States of origin.

[5] When the geographical center of a State comes within a particular zone, the entire State is included in that zone.

radius around any given State. For the next zone, where the radius is 1,150 miles, on the average 23 States are added to those in zone 1. Measuring from South Dakota again, the radius of 1,150 miles includes Virginia on the east, Texas on the south, and California on the west. The third zone includes families migrating within a radius of from 1,151 to 2,100 miles, and adds, on an average, the next 15 States in order of distance. Finally, the most distant zone includes the States whose geographical centers are more than 2,100 miles from a given State, and comprises an average of the three most distant States from a given State.

Each decennial census of population records the number of persons who are residing on the census date in a State other than their State of birth. Although obviously not strictly comparable with the data on migrant families, the census data do reveal the long-time mobile behavior of the American population. Using the census data as a basis for rough comparison, it may be seen that migrant families traveled somewhat greater distances than the persons in the United States population of 1930 who were residing in a State other than their State of birth (table 5). The distance between the State of origin and the State of transient bureau registration was less than 400 miles for 38 percent of migrant families; but the distance between State of birth and of residence was less than 400 miles for 53 percent of the mobile United States population. On the other hand the same proportion (3 percent) of migrant families and of the mobile United States population traveled more than 2,100 miles.

The numerical differences in the two sets of figures, however, should not obscure a general similarity between the mobility of migrant families during the depression and the mobility of the population as a whole. According to the census data short-distance moves greatly outweighed long-distance moves in the birth-residence movement of the total population up to 1930.[6] The same kind of movement, though to a somewhat less extent, was characteristic of migrant families.

The migrant families' tendency to move relatively short distances reflects the fact that a large proportion of families, despite the desperate predicament in which they found themselves at the time of moving, did not venture far beyond the region with which they were familiar. The preponderance of short-distance moves places the

[6] It is impossible to reproduce here for comparison a series of maps parallel with those in figs. 5–10, representing the movement of the total population as recorded in the birth-residence data of the 1930 Census. See Galpin, C. J. and Manny, T. B., *Interstate Migrations Among the Native White as Indicated by Differences between State of Birth and State of Residence*, U. S. Department of Agriculture, Bureau of Agricultural Economics, Washington, D. C., 1934. Galpin's and Manny's technique for depicting mobility has been incorporated into the maps in figs. 5–10.

much-discussed depression movement to the West coast in a new perspective. Although the transcontinental migrations of families were by far the most spectacular, they were actually much less important numerically than the short migrations. Moreover, the tendency of migrant families to remain within the region with which they were immediately familiar shows the error of the frequently-repeated statement that they were chiefly unstable wanderers.

Trends and Reciprocated Movement

The reasons for migration which were reported by the families themselves usually implied no consistent direction of migration. With the exception of the drought, the forces which displaced families from settled residence were generally prevalent everywhere. Although its intensity varied, unemployment—the principal reason for leaving settled residence—was serious in all States; and ill-health and domestic difficulties, among the other reasons, have little relation to geography.

The forces which attracted families were even less localized. Only the migrations of families seeking cheap land and a healthful climate implied migration to particular States to the exclusion of others. Migrations to localities where work had been promised involved many geographically meaningless cross currents of mobility. The large number of families which chose as their destination a community where there were relatives or friends would obviously scatter widely over the country.

As a result, a considerable amount of migrant family mobility consisted of a balanced interchange between the States (figs. 5–10). Very rarely was there a large movement from any given State to another without a substantial counter movement. For example, New York gained 283 migrant families from New Jersey and in return lost 148 migrant families to New Jersey; gained 81 from Florida and lost 57; gained 71 from Ohio and lost 110 (appendix table 5). There was much of this kind of reciprocated geographical mobility, with the result that net population displacement was only a fraction of the population movement.

East of the Mississippi the reciprocated movement of families formed the greater part of all movement. Except for a pronounced net emigration from Kentucky, North Carolina, Mississippi, and West Virginia, the movements in and out of the Eastern and Southern States tended to balance each other. Figures 5, 6, and 7 do reveal two trends of migration in the region east of the Mississippi—one flowing from the South to the industrial North, the other from the Northeastern States westward—but these trends made up a small part of the total movement of the region. West of the Mississippi (figs. 8, 9, and 10) the movement in and out of each State was less evenly balanced. The movement out of the Great Plains States, for example, greatly exceeded the movement in; and the family gains of the Pacific Coast States were far in excess of their losses.

For all the States combined the number of families which were involved in reciprocated migration between States was much greater than the number whose migration resulted in a net population displacement. On June 30, 1935, the number of families in FERA transient bureaus was about 30,000. The population displacement resulting from the movement of these families amounted to 10,524 families, representing the net gain of 16 States and the District of Columbia from the other 32 States. In other words, about two-thirds of all movement resulted in the balance of losses and gains within each of the States and, in terms of net population displacement, was canceled. The remaining one-third of the movement was net displacement (table 6 and appendix table 6).

Table 6.—Net Population Displacement and Reciprocated Movement Resulting From the Movement of Migrant Families [1] and of Persons in the General Population 1930 [2] Residing in a State Other Than State of Birth

Type of movement	Migrant families	General population, 1930
Total	29,885	25,388,100
	Percent distribution	
Total	100	100
Net displacement [3]	35	29
Reciprocated movement [4]	65	71

[1] Division of Transient Activities, *Quarterly Census of Transients Under Care*, June 30, 1935, mimeographed report, Federal Emergency Relief Administration, Washington, D. C., 1935. 419 families from U. S. possessions or foreign countries are not included.
[2] Bureau of the Census, *Fifteenth Census of the United States: 1930*, Population Vol. II, U. S. Department of Commerce, Washington, D. C., 1933, ch. 4, tables 32-34.
[3] Net displacement is the sum of the net gains of States gaining population (or net losses of States losing population). See appendix table 6.
[4] Reciprocated movement is derived by summing (1) the number of movers to all the net-loss States and (2) the number of movers from all the net-gain States. See appendix table 6.

The Significance of Reciprocated Movement

The high proportion of reciprocated movement had an important bearing upon the question of public responsibility for transient relief. Local communities are usually well aware of newly arrived migrants in need of relief, while those distress migrants who depart from the same community are likely to be forgotten. Accordingly, local relief officials are commonly inclined to believe that transiency is a one-way movement in which all other communities are contributors and their own community is recipient. This belief is frequently put forward in defending a policy of extending no aid to nonresidents. Actually, however, the influx of needy migrant families into a majority of the States was either roughly balanced by the movement out or was substantially less than the movement out. A large overbalance of immigration was recorded only for six far Western States and Louisiana, New York, Ohio, and the District of Columbia.

In a limited sense the reciprocated movement is a symptom of mistaken purpose lying behind the mobility of many of the families which eventually turned to transient bureaus for assistance. In the belief that they were moving toward regions of greater opportunity, many of the families actually moved into communities from which families like themselves were at the same time departing because of a lack of opportunity. Thus, it would appear that a large part of the movement studied dissipated itself in "waste" motion. Such a conclusion is not without value in demonstrating the disparity between desirable social goals and the realities of uncontrolled social behavior. Yet, in terms of the concrete realities facing the families in 1934 and 1935, this conclusion is somewhat academic. As figures on relief turnover and duration of unemployment show, it would be difficult to maintain that, by and large, the families would have been wiser had they never undertaken to relocate where conditions seemed better (see chs. IV and VI).

The proportion of net and reciprocated mobility shown in table 6 overemphasizes the confusion of the movement. It does not take rural-urban mobility into account. Moreover, if the trends for each State were measured in terms of interchange with each other *individual* State, rather than in terms of interchange with all States *combined*, the proportion of net movement would be shown to be greatly increased. For a particular State a small net gain or loss may conceal large net gains from certain States and large net losses to others. Thus, Illinois had a net gain, from all States combined, of 251 families. But the sum of its net gains from interchange with Mississippi, Alabama, Indiana, New York, and other individual Eastern and Southern States was 665 families; and from interchange with Missouri, Kansas, Colorado, California, and other Western States, it lost a net of 414 families. In table 6 the eastward net gains and the westward net losses of Illinois are not included and only the difference between the two (251 families net gain) is represented.[7] Because of a general tendency for each of the chain of States from east to west to gain families from its eastern neighbors and to lose families to its neighbors on the west, the method used in table 6 for calculating net geographical change somewhat understates the net geographical displacement of the migrant family population.

In any case it is significant that the rate of net geographical displacement for families registered with transient bureaus was slightly

---

[7] In fig. 11 the net gains and losses are shown on the basis of each State's interchange with each other State individually.

higher than that for persons in the general population who were living outside their State of birth. In so far as this comparison is valid it suggests that, small as the net trends in migrant family movement were, they were nevertheless more pronounced than the trends in the movement of the total population up to 1930. In other words, the migrant families moved more consistently northward and westward than did the total population.

Direction of Movement

The reasons for migration reported by the families rarely showed any awareness of the broad geographical significance of their moves. The many families which told in detail why they had migrated seldom gave explanations that went beyond the immediate reason for the move. Most of the families simply left a community in which they could no longer earn a living and proceeded to another community because of the rumor or hope—usually based upon the presence of relatives and friends—that they would be less insecure. One effect of the unguided action of these families was the seeming geographical confusion which manifested itself in the extent of the scattering of some of the families and in the relative importance of the reciprocated movement of families among the States. When the balanced interchange is canceled and the remaining net movement is traced upon the map a somewhat different picture is revealed. Despite the chaos that might naturally have been expected from the independent and unguided action of the 30,000 families, there were consistent trends of net population displacement (fig. 11).

The flow maps that have been developed after eliminating reciprocated migration show, first of all, that the net movement of migrant families was predominantly westward.[8] The westward flow of families into California, Colorado, Washington, Kansas, Idaho, Oregon, and New Mexico far exceeded all other net movement; and the general direction of the net movement for the entire United States with the exception of the southeastern region was toward the west. Although there was some eastward movement from the Great Plains into Minnesota and Iowa on the north and into Arkansas and Louisiana on the south, by far the greater part of the emigrants from the Great Plains moved westward. Even within the region north of the Ohio River and east of the Mississippi, the States tended to gain from eastern neighbors and lose to western neighbors.

---

[8] The trends shown record the net gain or loss of every State from every other *individual* State, rather than from all States *combined*.

In order to avoid a confusing maze of small lines, all net gains and losses of less than 15 families are excluded. This adjustment eliminated approximately one-fifth of the net movement. Although some of the rejected moves ran counter to the chief lines shown in fig. 11, the majority of them were also net northward and westward moves.

FIG. II – NET DISPLACEMENT OF MIGRANT FAMILIES*
June 30, 1935

NORTH-SOUTH DISPLACEMENT

EAST-WEST DISPLACEMENT

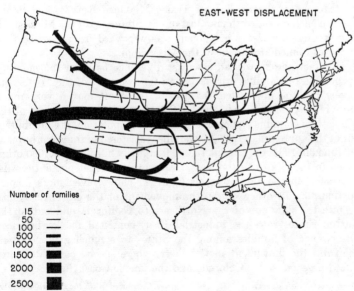

Number of families

15	
50	
100	
500	
1000	
1500	
2000	
2500	

*Net interchange of fewer than 15 families
between States excluded.

Source: Division of Transient Activities,
Quarterly Census of Transients Under Care,
June 30, 1935, Federal Emergency Relief
Administration, Washington, D.C.   AF-2882, WPA

Only the families in the Southeastern States failed to follow the prevailing westward tendency (fig. 11). The contribution of the entire South to the Pacific Coast States was insignificant. Within the southern region itself, there was a slight movement from Georgia, Alabama, and Mississippi into Louisiana. But the greater part of the net loss of the Southern States moved northward into four industrial States—New York, Illinois, Ohio, and Michigan.[9]

This movement, in which Negroes played an important part (appendix B), flowed north along four parallel lines: the first moved up the Atlantic seaboard to the District of Columbia, Maryland, and New York; the second moved from Mississippi, Tennessee, and Kentucky to Ohio and Michigan; the third moved from Mississippi, Alabama, and Georgia to Illinois; and the fourth, starting from Arkansas, culminated in Illinois and Chicago. Within the South, only the movement toward Florida ran counter to the general northward trend.

Figure 11 also shows that the greater part of the net displacement flow of migrant families not only *culminated* west of the Mississippi River but also *originated* there. The excess of outflow over inflow for Oklahoma alone was nearly as large as the total excess that moved westward across the Mississippi River from all States to the east of it. Moreover, the net loss of Texas, Missouri, Kansas, and South Dakota each exceeded the net loss of any State east of the Mississippi. The greatest single net movement was westward from the two tiers of States immediately west of the Mississippi.

This fact emphasizes an essential difference between the mobility of the migrant families originating on the two sides of the Mississippi River. In the first place, families in the West moved very much more readily than those in the East. Although the region east of the Mississippi contains 70 percent of the total population, it contributed, out of the approximately 30,000 families registered in transient bureaus on June 30, 1935, only about 13,000 families, while about 17,000 originated in the States to the west. Moreover, the net population displacement in the West was, as figure 11 shows, even more disproportionate. In other words, the movement of the eastern sections, despite the flow out of the Northeast to California and out of the Cotton States into the industrial East, consisted in the balanced interchange of families among the States to a much greater extent than did the movement in the West, where special conditions produced an exodus into Colorado and the Pacific Coast States.

The Direction of Movement· Migrant Families Compared With the General Population, 1920–1930

A comparison between the displacement flow of migrant families and the flow of the general United States population in the decade

---

[9] There was practically no interchange between Pennsylvania and the Southern States.

from 1920–1930 reveals a striking general similarity.[10] The chief feature of both movements was the predominating westward drift, and the chief destination for both was California. The movement northward out of the Cotton States follows the same general routes in both instances; in both, this movement is distinctly less important than the westward movement. In both, there is a net movement out of the less industrialized Eastern States into the more highly industrialized States: from Arkansas into Missouri and Michigan; from Kentucky into Indiana, Michigan, and Ohio; and from West Virginia into Ohio and Pennsylvania. Other similarities—such as the net movement from Georgia to Florida, from Pennsylvania and New England to New York, and the movement down the coast from the Pacific Northwest into California—might be traced at length.

Within the general pattern of similarity, several important differences between the movement in the twenties and the movement of migrant families appear. The distress movement of migrant families from the Great Plains States was much more pronounced than the general population movement out of these States during the 1920's. In particular, the migration from the southern Plains States to California formed a greater part of the net displacement of migrant families than of the movement of the general population; and two entirely new movements, (1) off the northern Plains into Washington, Idaho, and Oregon, and (2) off the southeastern Plains into Colorado, New Mexico, and Arizona, assumed an important place in the depression migration of families. Moreover, instead of the normal westward infiltration into the Plains States, many migrant families left these States, especially the Dakotas and Oklahoma, and moved eastward, reversing the trend of the 1920's.

In the northeastern industrial States other differences appeared. The migration of the 1920's into Michigan, following the automobile boom, reversed itself for the families studied; and Michigan lost families to both Illinois and Ohio, though it continues to gain from the States south of the Ohio River. Between 1920 and 1930 Illinois gained large numbers of migrants from Iowa and Missouri, probably through rural to urban migrations. For the families studied, however, this trend disappeared.

[10] Thornthwaite, C. W., *Internal Migration in the United States*, Bulletin 1, Philadelphia: University of Pennsylvania Press, 1934, Plate V–A, Plate VI–A (D), and Plate III–A.

The trends in the movement of migrant families (fig. 11) includes the movement of both white and Negro families. Thornthwaite's trend map for 1920–1930 [Plate VI–A (D)] shows the net movement of the native-white population only. The size and direction of the migration of all Negroes born in the South and living in the North in 1930 are shown in Thornthwaite's Plate V–A; and the growth of this migration during each decade beginning with 1890–1900 is shown in Plate III–A.

In the South two States show marked differences. Tennessee lost population to many States in the 1920's and gained from none; but from the interchange of migrant families it gained from Texas, Arkansas, North Carolina, Georgia, Alabama, Mississippi, and Kentucky. North Carolina, on the other hand, gained population in the 1920's from Georgia and South Carolina; but the trend in the movement of migrant families was away from North Carolina to not only Georgia and South Carolina but also to Tennessee, Florida, and Virginia.

Though these differences are important, they should not obscure the close parallels between the displacement of the families studied and the displacement of the general population in the 1920's. The most significant tendency shown in figure 11 is the similarity of migrant family movement to the recent drift of the general population.

Rate of Emigration

The foregoing discussion has considered the interstate movement of migrant families in terms of the absolute number of families moving to and from each State. In order to determine the regions from which the families emigrated most readily, these absolute numbers must be considered in terms of the number of families residing in each State and therefore theoretically likely to migrate.

On June 30, 1935, throughout the United States as a whole, 1 interstate migrant family was under care in FERA transient bureaus for each 910 families in the total population, or 1.08 migrants per 1,000 resident families.[11] Because of the wide variety of social and economic conditions in the various regions of the country, in many States the ratio of families leaving the State to families living in the State fell exceedingly far above and below this national average.

To cite the high and low extremes in the rate of emigration, Nevada and Arizona, which contributed to other States 1 migrant family for each 160 to 200 families in their populations (6.41 and 5.07 families contributed respectively per 1,000 population families) had by far the highest rates (appendix table 7). At the other extreme were New Hampshire and Massachusetts, which contributed only 1 migrant family out of each 5,500 to 3,500 population families (.18 and .30 families contributed respectively per 1,000 population families).

The geographical distribution of the States with high and low migrant family contributions per 1,000 population families is shown in figure 12. This map reveals that the States from which migrant families were most likely to leave were practically all Western States

---

[11] The population data refer to multiperson families as reported in the Bureau of the Census, *Fifteenth Census of the United States: 1930*, Population Vol. VI, U. S. Department of Commerce, Washington, D. C., 1933, p. 36.

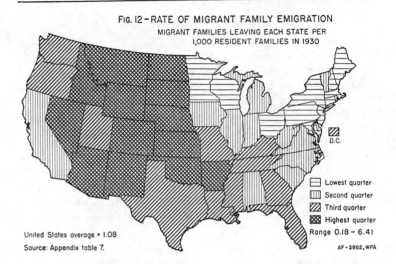

FIG. 12 – RATE OF MIGRANT FAMILY EMIGRATION
MIGRANT FAMILIES LEAVING EACH STATE PER
1,000 RESIDENT FAMILIES IN 1930

D.C.

Lowest quarter
Second quarter
Third quarter
Highest quarter
Range 0.18 – 6.41

United States average = 1.08

Source: Appendix table 7.

AF - 2862, WPA

and that, excepting only California, the entire western United States from the Great Plains to the Pacific Coast States contributed migrant families at a rate above the United States average. All the States with exceptionally high rates were in this region.[12]

Migrant families also tended to emigrate from several States in the South at a rate somewhat above the United States average. This tendency was most marked in the States on the fringes of the South, especially in Arkansas and Florida. In the deep South the rate of emigration was either slightly below the United States average (as in Alabama and the Carolinas) or only very slightly above (as in Louisiana, Mississippi, and Tennessee).[13]

Migrant families emigrated least readily from the densely populated northeastern and north central regions of the United States. All the Midwestern States from Minnesota and Iowa to Ohio were well below the average, and the industrial East from Pennsylvania to Maine contributed fewer migrant families in proportion to its resident population than any other section of the United States.

[12] Appendix table 7 presents the rate of migrant family emigration from the various States in terms of the number of families contributed by each State per 1,000 resident families. The table also shows the rank of each State beginning with the highest: Nevada first, Arizona second, and so on through the entire list of States to New Hampshire, the State with the lowest rate.

In fig. 13 the "highest one-fourth" represents the States with rankings from 1st to 12th, the "second highest one-fourth" represents those from 13th to 25th, etc.

[13] Against the national average of 1.1 migrants contributed per 1,000 population families, the rate for Arkansas was 2.8; for Mississippi, 1.4; for Georgia and Alabama, 1.1. The rate for five Western States, on the other hand, was above 4.0. See appendix table 7.

Emigration and Relief Intensity

The preceding chapter emphasized the basic relationship between distress and migrant family mobility, and it would be supposed that the varying rates of emigration reflect regional differences in the severity of the depression. But if one compares the rate of emigration from the States with the highest percent of unemployed gainful workers—such as Michigan or Pennsylvania—with the rate of migration from the less severely stricken States, the inadequacy of this explanation is quickly revealed. A given degree of adverse economic pressure did not produce the same rate of emigration in all sections of the United States.

Figure 13 shows how the severity of the depression, as measured by the average intensity of general relief during 1934 (excluding rural rehabilitation and other special programs), varied among the States.[14]

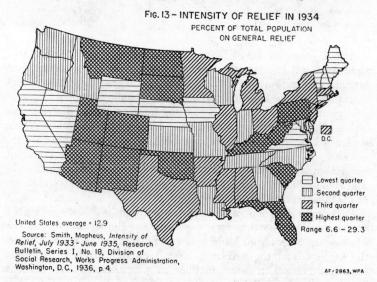

FIG. 13 – INTENSITY OF RELIEF IN 1934
PERCENT OF TOTAL POPULATION
ON GENERAL RELIEF

D.C.

☐ Lowest quarter
▥ Second quarter
▨ Third quarter
▦ Highest quarter
Range 6.6 – 29.3

United States average = 12.9

Source: Smith, Mapheus, *Intensity of Relief, July 1933 - June 1935*, Research Bulletin, Series I, No. 18, Division of Social Research, Works Progress Administration, Washington, D.C., 1936, p. 4.

AF-2863, WPA

Despite obvious limitations these data do after a fashion provide an index of the varying extent of destitution throughout the United States. It is recognized that the intensity of relief is affected not only by the extent of need but also by the availability of funds for relief and by local policies in the administration of relief. The low intensity of relief in the South, for example, is doubtless an inaccurate representation of the actual extent of destitution in that region, and the data for the Southern States must be considered in the light of that

[14] See Smith, Mapheus, *Intensity of Relief July 1933–June 1935*, Research Bulletin Series I, No. 18, Division of Social Research, Works Progress Administration, Washington, D. C., March 25, 1936.

qualification. For most of the United States, however, the index used is reasonably trustworthy. If it be assumed that the intensity-of-relief data represent the varying force of economic pressure in each State, a comparison of figures 12 and 13 will reveal the responsiveness to that pressure among the States.

It will be observed from a comparison between figures 12 and 13 that there was no consistent Nation-wide relationship between relief intensity and the rate of family emigration. It is true that several States with a high relief intensity also had high family emigration rates. Montana, North Dakota, Oklahoma, and South Dakota, for example, fell into the highest quarter-group in both figure 12 and figure 13. Likewise, Connecticut and Maine appear in the lowest quarter-group on both maps. But Nebraska, Wyoming, and Nevada, for example, had extremely high family emigration rates and a very low relief intensity. Pennsylvania, Ohio, and Minnesota were well above average in relief intensity, but all had very low family emigration rates.[15]

The Western States in general had high emigration rates regardless of varying intensity of relief. The Midwestern and Northeastern States, in contrast, contributed in relation to their population few migrant families to other States, even though the intensity of relief was frequently very high. Within the South, also, there appeared to be no consistent relationship between the variations in relief intensity and the rates of family emigration.

Rate of Emigration: Migrant Families Compared With the General Population

Figure 14 shows the rate at which the general population born in the various States had emigrated to other States, according to the birth-residence data of the 1930 Census.[16] A comparison of each State's rank in figure 14 with its rank in figure 12 shows that migrant families tended to emigrate most readily from those States which had normally been contributing the greatest proportion of their native population to other States.

It has been pointed out that the West contained the States with the highest rates of migrant family emigration. The West also con-

---

[15] The coefficient of rank correlation between intensity of relief and family emigration rate was ($\rho = .334$).

[16] Bureau of the Census, *Fifteenth Census of the United States: 1930*, Population Vol. II, U. S. Department of Commerce, Washington, D. C., 1933, ch. 4, tables 32–34.

In fig. 14 the States are divided according to the magnitude of their emigration rates into 4 groups of 12 States each. Those 12 States which had the highest percent of their native population living in other States are represented as the "highest one-fourth" of the States; the 12 States with the next highest percent of natives living elsewhere are represented as the "second highest one-fourth" of the States, etc.

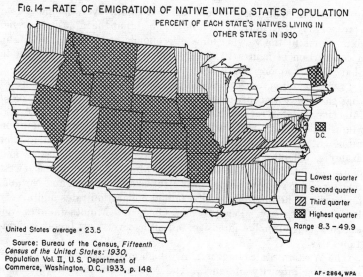

FIG. 14 – RATE OF EMIGRATION OF NATIVE UNITED STATES POPULATION
PERCENT OF EACH STATE'S NATIVES LIVING IN
OTHER STATES IN 1930

Lowest quarter
Second quarter
Third quarter
Highest quarter
Range 8.3 – 49.9

United States average = 23.5

Source: Bureau of the Census, *Fifteenth Census of the United States: 1930*, Population Vol. II, U.S. Department of Commerce, Washington, D.C., 1933, p. 148.

AF-2864, WPA

tained most of the States which had contributed the highest proportion of their natives to other States before 1930. Nine of these States had the same high quarter-group ranking on both maps. In all States in which the quarter-group ranking was not identical the family emigration rank was consistently higher than the emigration rank derived for the general population. Thus, emigration from the Western States, normally very high in comparison with the other sections, became relatively higher among families studied.

In North Dakota and South Dakota, and to a lesser extent in Nebraska, the increase in the relative importance of migrant family emigration resulted from the agricultural depression and the 1934 drought. In all other Western States, however, the direct effect of these two forces was small, inasmuch as the migrants came largely from the urban unemployed.[17] The increased importance of the emigration of migrant families in other Western States appears to have resulted more from the greater susceptibility of newcomers—who form a large part of the population of these States [18]—to unsettling forces intensified by the depression than from the action of any one particular localized force.

In the Midwestern and Northeastern States the relationship between migrant family and general population emigration ranks is the oppo-

[17] See ch. I, fig. 2. Farming failure was an important cause of emigration only for the families leaving the Dakotas. Only 12 percent of all the migrant families from Oklahoma and only 6 percent of those from Texas were farmers who had failed.

[18] See fig. 16, which shows the rate of immigration of the native-born population into these States as recorded in the 1930 Census.

site of that found in the Western States. The Midwest and Northeast as shown in figure 14 have contributed a relatively slight proportion of their native population to other States before 1930; and, as figure 12 indicates, this region also contained most of the States with the lowest rates of migrant family emigration. Eight of these twenty-one States had identically low quarter-group rankings on both maps. In only one State, Michigan, the migrant family emigration rank was higher than the general population emigration rank by one quarter-group, reflecting in all probability the depressed state of the automobile industry after 1930. The rank of each of the remaining States and the District of Columbia was consistently lower in terms of its relative rate of migrant family emigration than in terms of the contribution of its native population to other States before 1930. In other words, the Midwestern and Northeastern States, most of which normally have low emigration rates, were by comparison with the other sections of the country even less important as the source of migrant families.

Chief among the Midwestern and Northeastern States in which the rank in terms of migrant family emigration was lower than the rank of native population emigration were Maine, New Hampshire, Vermont, Minnesota, Wisconsin, Iowa, and Missouri. The low intensity of relief in the New England States offers a possible explanation for the low rate of family emigration by reflecting the lesser pressure of adverse economic conditions. In the Midwest the normal movement to the Great Plains was cut short by the agricultural depression; and Iowa, like the New England States, was less affected by the depression, as its low intensity of relief shows (fig. 13).

A substantial movement of the general population from the States on the fringe of the South was a normal occurrence up to 1930. The relative position of these States in terms of migrant family emigration was much the same as in the emigration of the general population. The relative importance of emigration from Arkansas increased slightly and that from Virginia decreased slightly; while Kentucky and Tennessee maintained the same quarter-group rank on both maps. In the lower South, on the other hand, the rate of emigration of the general population before 1930 was small in comparison with the other States. In all the States from Louisiana to North Carolina, and including Florida, the general population was comparatively immobile notwithstanding the high birth rate of the region, or, indeed, the northward migration of Negroes between 1910 and 1930. These same States became relatively much more important as contributors of migrant families. The rank of Mississippi, Georgia, and North Carolina was raised by one quarter-group and the rank of Louisiana and Florida was raised by two quarter-groups. Although these changes are in part a reflection of a relative decrease in emigration from the Northeast and Midwest during the depression, they nevertheless suggest a growing tendency toward mobility within the lower South. The increase in mobility is particularly noticeable in Florida, where the high rate of migrant family emigration doubtless represents the backwash of the Florida boom.

Rate of Immigration

The constant westward movement of migrant families brought large numbers into California, Colorado, Idaho, and Washington; and a somewhat less marked northward immigration flowed into New York, Ohio, and Illinois. The total number of migrant families in transient bureaus was by no means uniformly distributed in absolute numbers throughout the various States. In terms of relative numbers expressing the transient bureau case load of each State as a proportion of its family population, the variation among the different States becomes even greater.

Appendix table 8 shows the number of migrant families in each State on June 30, 1935, per 1,000 resident families in the State. The table reveals an even wider gap between the State with the highest and the State with the lowest rate of immigration than was discovered to exist between the two extremes in the rate of emigration. Idaho, the State whose rate of immigration was highest, had 1 migrant family for each 100 families residing in Idaho; [19] whereas South Dakota at the other extreme had less than 1 migrant family for each 10,000 resident families (.03 families received per 1,000 resident families).

Inasmuch as the rate of immigration relates the number of destitute, newly arrived families to the size of the resident family population, it provides a rough measure of the varying seriousness of the migrant family relief problem from the point of view of the residents in each State. It is interesting to observe that in June 1935 the problem was most serious in Idaho, followed, as appendix table 8 shows, by New Mexico and Colorado. California, with less than half as many families under care per 1,000 population families as Idaho, only ranked as the fourth highest State. Appearing in order slightly below California were Washington, Wyoming, and the District of Columbia.

Figure 15 shows the migrant family immigration rank of each of the States. In brief, the map reveals that most of the States with the highest rates of immigration and more than half of those in the second highest quarter-group were located west of the Mississippi River. In the East only the District of Columbia and Florida had immigration rates in the highest quarter-group, and 19 of the 26 States [20] had immigration rates in the lowest or second lowest quarter-groups.

---

[19] The migrant family case load of Idaho transient bureaus was not reported in the Quarterly Census of June 30, 1935. Accordingly, the figure reported in the *Midmonthly Census of Transient Activities* of June 15, 1935, was used.

[20] Including the District of Columbia but excluding Vermont which had no transient program.

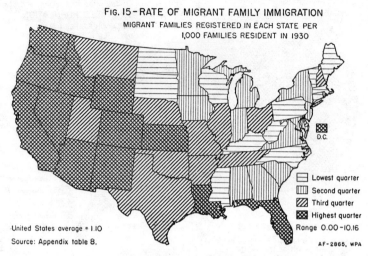

FIG. 15 – RATE OF MIGRANT FAMILY IMMIGRATION
MIGRANT FAMILIES REGISTERED IN EACH STATE PER
1,000 FAMILIES RESIDENT IN 1930

☐ Lowest quarter
▥ Second quarter
▨ Third quarter
▩ Highest quarter
Range 0.00 –10.16

United States average = 1.10
Source: Appendix table 8.

AF-2865, WPA

Immigration and Relief Intensity

A comparison between the rate of immigration map (fig. 15) and the intensity-of-relief map (fig. 13) reveals that there was no consistent relationship between migrant family immigration and relief intensity. Five States had very high relief rates together with very low rates of migrant family immigration; these States were North Dakota and South Dakota, to the west of the Mississippi River, and Pennsylvania, West Virginia, and Kentucky, to the east. At the same time, four other States with very high relief rates—Florida, Colorado, New Mexico, and Arizona—also had very high rates of migrant family immigration. Moreover, some of the States with the lowest intensity of relief had low rates of immigration (for example, Maine, Maryland, and Iowa), while some had high rates (for example, Wyoming, New Hampshire, and Delaware). Clearly there was no general connection whatever between these two factors.[21]

Rate of Immigration: Migrant Families Compared With the General Population

Migrant families did, however, show an extremely great tendency to seek out those States into which the population had largely been flowing during the lifetime of the persons enumerated in the 1930 Census. Figure 16 shows for 1930 the proportion of the residents of each State who were born in other States, in terms of quarter-group rankings. A comparison between figures 15 and 16 reveals very little change in the relative positions of the States.

[21] The coefficient of rank correlation between intensity of relief and family immigration rates was ($\rho = .086$).

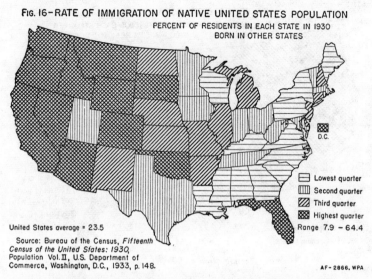

FIG. 16−RATE OF IMMIGRATION OF NATIVE UNITED STATES POPULATION
PERCENT OF RESIDENTS IN EACH STATE IN 1930
BORN IN OTHER STATES

Lowest quarter
Second quarter
Third quarter
Highest quarter
Range 7.9 − 64.4

United States average = 23.5

Source: Bureau of the Census, *Fifteenth
Census of the United States: 1930,*
Population Vol. II, U.S. Department of
Commerce, Washington, D.C., 1933, p. 148.

AF−2866. WPA

In the West the only marked differences on the two maps are for
North Dakota and South Dakota. The 1930 population of these two
States contained a relatively high proportion of the natives of other
States because of the comparative newness of their development as
States and the normally high population turnover in the Plains States.
Migrant families, on the other hand, avoided these two States, doubt-
less because of the drought.

In the Midwest and Northeast the majority of the States had the
same low quarter-group rank on both maps. The principal changes
are the increased relative importance of Illinois, Ohio, and New York
(the States in which the movement of white and Negro migrant families from the South terminated) and the decreased relative importance
of Michigan and of the satellite States close to New York.

In the South the States whose 1930 population contained the highest
proportion of natives born in other States were Florida and Arkansas.
The rate of migrant family immigration into these States remained
high, and Tennessee and Louisiana were added to them. In Alabama,
Georgia, and South Carolina the proportion of 1930 residents born in
other States was extremely low, but the migrant family immigration
rates in these States were somewhat higher. This change suggests
an increase in the mobility of the southern population during the
depression.

RURAL-URBAN MIGRATION

The Quarterly Census of Transient Activities, which permitted the
foregoing analysis of the movement of families between the States,
recorded for each family only the State from which migration began

and the State in which transient bureau registration occurred. It does not supply information about the intervening movement; nor does it distinguish between the families which were at their destination at the time of registration and those which were still en route to their destination. Furthermore, no information was supplied concerning the rural-urban mobility of migrant families. In order to fill in these gaps, it is necessary to turn again to the migrant family interviews upon which the other chapters of this study are based.

An Urban Migration

The origins and destinations [22] of migrant families were both predominantly urban. By and large, the families moved from city to city, rather than from the farm to the city or from the city back to the farm. Urban places, that is, places of more than 2,500 population, were the origin of 70 percent of the migrant families with settled residence; and villages and farms were the origin of 30 percent of the families.[23] Upon leaving settled residence, 76 percent of the families had urban destinations, 17 percent had farm and village destinations, and 7 percent set out with no destination in mind (see table 7).

Table 7.—Rural-Urban Origins and Destinations of Migrant Families

Rural-urban interchange	Migrant families immigrating
Total	4,084
	Percent distribution
Total	100
To city [1]	76
From city	56
From villages and farms [2]	20
To villages and farms	17
From city	9
From villages and farms	8
To no destination	7
From city	5
From villages and farms	2

[1] Places of 2,500 or more population.
[2] Places of less than 2,500 population.
NOTE.—244 families, for which size of place of destination or settled residence was not ascertainable, are not included.

[22] It is necessary to distinguish between the *place of destination*, recorded only for the families interviewed, and the *place of registration*, recorded both for the families interviewed and in the Quarterly Census.

[23] As against this 70 percent urban composition, 58 percent of all multiperson families in the United States as a whole lived in urban places in 1930 and 42 percent lived in rural places. See Bureau of the Census, *Fifteenth Census of the United States: 1930*, Population Vol. VI, U. S. Department of Commerce, Washington, D. C., 1933, pp. 13–15.

A majority of the families moved *from* city *to* city. As table 7 shows, 56 percent of all families had both origins and destinations in urban places and only 8 percent of the families had both origins and destinations on farms or in villages. For 29 percent of the families the first moves from settled residence involved an interchange between urban and rural places. These were composed of 20 percent which left farms and villages for cities and of 9 percent which moved from cities back to villages and farms.

The Back-to-the-Land Movement

The growth and decline of the back-to-the-land movement among migrant families are shown in figure 17. A total of 9 percent of the

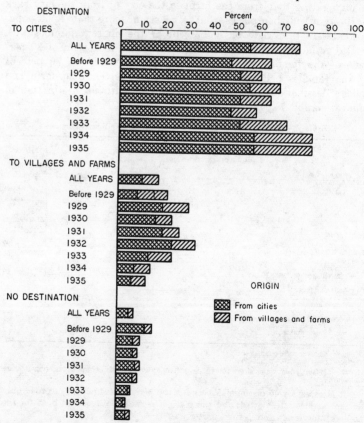

FIG. 17 - RURAL-URBAN MOVEMENT OF MIGRANT FAMILIES
BY YEAR OF MOVE

Source: Appendix table 10.

AF-2626, WPA

first moves from settled residence were from cities to farms and villages. Of the families which left their last settled residence before 1929, only 8 percent moved back to the land. As the depression grew worse, this movement increased until in 1932, 23 percent of the families leaving settled residence moved from cities to farms and villages. Thereafter, as recovery began, it declined rapidly; and in 1935 only 6 percent of the urban families leaving settled residence moved back to the land.

The movement from farms and villages into the cities showed exactly the opposite trend. An average of 20 percent of the moves were from rural to urban areas. Before 1929 the movement was slightly below average size, comprising 17 percent of all moves from settled residence. In 1929 it declined to 9 percent, and in 1932 it was 11 percent. It rose rapidly to 20 percent in 1933, then to 25 percent in 1934, the first serious drought year, and dropped to 24 percent in 1935.[24]

A more detailed classification of rural-urban mobility is presented in appendix table 10. This table shows that the predominant urban movement was itself made up chiefly of movement between the cities of more than 100,000 population, rather than between smaller cities. It also shows that the rural origins and destinations were both about equally distributed between open country and village and that the back-to-the-land movement was thus a movement into villages as well.

Rural and Urban Emigration by State

Recognition of the fact that the movement of migrant families was largely one of city dwellers migrating to other cities is necessary for the proper interpretation of the data on interstate movement presented earlier in this chapter. The predominance of urban over rural migration is characteristic not only of the movement in general but also of the movement involving most of the individual States, even those containing chronically distressed rural areas.

Figure 18 shows for each State by quarter-groups the proportion of the multiperson families which were living in places of less than 2,500 population at the time of the 1930 Census. When this figure is compared with figure 19, which shows the proportion of the migrants who emigrated from places of less than 2,500 population, it may be seen that the proportion of rural families was almost universally low.

---

[24] The rural-urban interchange shown in table 7 and fig. 17 applies only to the moves from settled residence to destination. Accordingly, it includes only one move for each family. But many migrant families changed residence after this first move, and the one-fifth of the families which had no "settled residence" nevertheless changed their "residence." A tabulation of the rural-urban interchange involved in *all* these moves shows practically the same characteristics of those described in fig. 17, except that the back-to-the-land movement constituted 15 percent of *all* moves, as against 9 percent of the moves from settled residence.

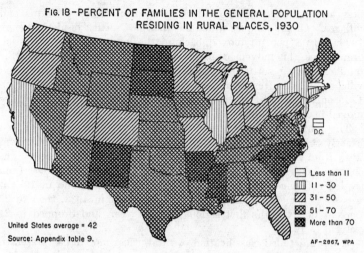

FIG. 18 – PERCENT OF FAMILIES IN THE GENERAL POPULATION RESIDING IN RURAL PLACES, 1930

Less than 11
11 – 30
31 – 50
51 – 70
More than 70

United States average = 42
Source: Appendix table 9.

AF-2867, WPA

Practically all States contributed a smaller proportion of rural migrants than the rural composition of their population would have warranted. In several States the discrepancy is particularly apparent. In most of the Southern States, including Texas and Oklahoma, there was an exceedingly high proportion of the population living in rural places, yet the proportion of rural emigrants from these States was relatively low. Despite the acuteness of the rural problem in this entire area, the families which did leave States within this region tended to come mainly from urban, rather than rural, places. Only in two Southern border States, Kentucky and Arkansas, did the proportion

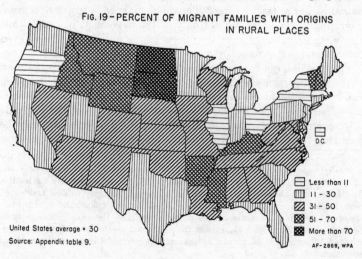

FIG. 19 – PERCENT OF MIGRANT FAMILIES WITH ORIGINS IN RURAL PLACES

Less than 11
11 – 30
31 – 50
51 – 70
More than 70

United States average = 30
Source: Appendix table 9.

AF-2868, WPA

of rural family emigrants approximate the proportion of rural families in the population.

The northern Plains from Kansas to Montana formed the only regional group in which the proportion of migrant families leaving rural places was consistently high. It is significant, however, that even within this region, despite the drought and the long-established tradition of rural mobility within the region, in South Dakota alone were the families leaving rural places overrepresented in terms of the rural-urban composition of the State population (appendix table 9).

Rural and Urban Immigration by State

Figure 20 shows for each State the proportion of the families whose destinations were in rural places. It is obvious from this figure that the proportion of families going to rural places was far less than the proportion leaving rural places. In nearly three-fourths of the States the proportion of families with rural destinations was less than 30 percent of all the families migrating to the State (appendix table 9). Family movement was predominantly urban, not only into industrial States, such as New York, Pennsylvania, and Illinois, but also into many basically agricultural States, such as Kansas, Nebraska, New Mexico, and most of the Southern States. In eight States the *proportion* of families with rural destinations was from 30 to 50 percent of the incoming families. The only States in this group which had a large *number* of incoming families were Arkansas, Oklahoma, and Montana. In only five States did the proportion of families with rural destinations exceed 50 percent; of these, Idaho and Mississippi were the only numerically important States of destination for migrant families.

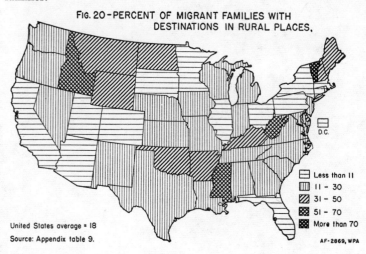

FIG. 20-PERCENT OF MIGRANT FAMILIES WITH DESTINATIONS IN RURAL PLACES.

Less than 11
11 - 30
31 - 50
51 - 70
More than 70

United States average = 18
Source: Appendix table 9.

AF-2869, WPA

Movement Beyond Destinations

It is important to bear in mind that figure 20 is based upon the State of destination of the families rather than upon the States in which families were registered in transient bureaus. Figure 20 thus records only the proportion of the families which intended, when they left settled residence, to take up residence in rural areas in the States specified. By the time these families were interviewed, practically all of them (86 percent) had moved on [25] from their new rural residences and were registered in transient bureaus in urban places. Two-thirds of them were registered in transient bureaus in a State other than the State of destination (appendix table 11).

In contrast, the families which had reached destinations in urban places tended to remain at their destinations. At the time the families were interviewed, 61 percent of those with urban destinations were still in the city to which they had originally set out, and an additional 8 percent were still within the State of their destination. Only one-third of the families with urban destinations were registered in transient bureaus outside their State of destination.

---

[25] Most of this group had arrived at their destinations in rural places and subsequently departed. Of all the families which set out for definite destinations-only 8 percent had not yet reached their destination by the time they were interviewed in September 1935.

Chapter III

THE BACKGROUND OF MIGRATION

IN ANALYZING depression mobility from the point of view of public relief policy, a distinction between wandering and migration is necessary. In so far as public assistance furthers permanent economic adjustment at the same time that it relieves immediate needs, it works toward a solution of the problems growing out of distress migration. Plainly, this end is more easily achieved in assisting migrants than in assisting chronic wanderers.

The essence of the distinction between migration and wandering is the difference in the value that the individual on the road attaches to mobility. At one extreme there is the aimless, "just to be moving" kind of mobility characteristic of persons and families to whom stability has become either impossible or unattractive. Migration, at the other extreme, is the purposeful and socially necessary type of mobility that has stability as its immediate object.

Determining the degree of mobility characteristic of the families studied requires a thorough analysis of the background of the families which turned to transient bureaus for assistance. If the families had developed a long established habit of frequent change of community, or of travel so constant that a residence [1] was seldom established in any community, the evidence would point to the purposeless transiency sometimes observed among nonfamily persons.[2] Con-

---

[1] The term *residence* is used throughout this chapter to mean a stay for at least 30 days in one community without receipt of transient relief. As used here, residence has none of the special and technical connotations that the term frequently has in statutes and legal writings; e. g., legal residence, voting residence, or relief residence. Nor is residence used as a synonym for *domicile;* i. e., a permanent home. For this later purpose, the term *settled residence* has been adopted to represent the particular residence that the family regarded as its last place of settled abode.

[2] See Webb, John N., *The Transient Unemployed*, Research Monograph III, Division of Social Research, Works Progress Administration, Washington, D. C., 1935, pp. 64–74.

versely, if the families had only recently been dislodged from a community where they had maintained a settled, self-supporting existence for a considerable period of time there would be a strong presumption that their mobility was of the nature of purposeful migration.

In order to derive this distinction, the history of these families during the 6 years preceding this study is divided into two periods. One of these periods includes the time between each family's first application for relief at a transient bureau and the date of interview. The mobility of the families during this period is discussed in chapter IV. But family mobility began before that period; otherwise, the families would have been assisted by the resident rather than the transient relief program. Examination of the history of the families during this earlier period will provide information about the mobility of the families during the years preceding their first stay at the transient bureaus. It is the purpose of this chapter to examine this earlier background period. The period under examination begins on January 1, 1929, for all families formed before that date, and it extends forward to the date when the families left the last place of residence prior to their first application for transient relief. For families formed since January 1, 1929, the date of marriage is substituted for the arbitrary predepression date in 1929.[3]

SETTLED AND UNSETTLED FAMILIES

When classified according to their background prior to the period of transient relief the 5,489 families observed in this study disclosed a range from unbroken residence at one extreme to unbroken mobility at the other extreme. By far the larger number of families, however, had few or no changes of residence prior to their transient relief history. A small number had a record of frequent changes of residence, and a few had never had a residence for even as long as 1 month in one locality. Between these two extremes there was a marginal group whose longest stay in one community was less than a year. The proportions of stable, unstable, and marginal families have first been measured in terms of the length of residence in a community; and, second, these proportions have been compared with a report of families' opinions as to whether they had ever maintained a "permanent" settled residence.

Length of Residence

Families Without Residence

To facilitate a detailed examination of the background of migrant families, they were divided into two groups on the basis of whether or not they had, at any time since January 1, 1929, a *residence* as

---

[3] The relationship between year of family formation and degree of mobility is discussed on pp. 68–70.

defined in this study; i. e., a continuous stay in one community for a period of 1 month or more without relief from a transient bureau.

While the existence of a residence according to this definition reveals little about stability, the *absence* of any residence obviously indicates instability. The classification adopted thus separates from the total group these families which were most highly mobile prior to their transient relief history. The distribution of the families according to whether they had ever had a residence is presented in table 8. Only 4 percent of the families had never maintained a residence of as long as 1 month. The remaining 96 percent had one or more residences of durations that represent a wide range of mobility.

Table 8.—Residence Status of Migrant Families

Residence status	Migrant families
Total	5,489

	Percent distribution
Total	100
Residence of 1 month or longer since 1929 or since formation if subsequent to that date	96
No residence of 1 month or longer since 1929 or since formation if subsequent to that date	4

Although the small group with no residence appears to have been almost completely adrift, consideration must be given to the length of time during which it was possible for them to have had residences.

Table 9.—Year of Formation of Migrant Families Having No Residence of 1 Month or Longer Since January 1, 1929 [1]

Year of formation	Migrant families having no residence of 1 month or longer
Total	240

	Percent distribution
Total	100
Prior to 1929	9
1929	1
1930	1
1931	2
1932	2
1933	5
1934	24
1935	56

[1] For families formed since January 1, 1929, the period under consideration begins with date of marriage.

NOTE.—2 families, whose year of formation was not ascertainable, are not included.

About one-tenth of the families with no residence since January 1, 1929, were formed prior to 1929. A closer approach to absolute instability than that represented by these cases is difficult to imagine. But more than one-half of the families with no residence were formed sometime during the 9 months between January 1935 and the date of interview, and an additional one-fourth were formed during 1934 (table 9). Thus, while the existence of families without residence histories implied the presence of a habitually unstable group, their habits in a majority of cases had not been formed over a long period of time.

Families With Residence

When the duration of residences is examined, it is found that between January 1, 1929, and September 1935 over half (56 percent) of the families included among their residences a stay of at least 3 years in one community (table 10). An additional one-fourth (26 percent) had remained in one locality from 1 to 3 years. In judging this evidence, it is necessary to consider that nearly half of all the family groups were formed since January 1, 1929, and that 1 to 3 years would account for all of the time since marriage for many of these families.

In addition to the fact that 82 percent of the families had lived in one place for at least 1 year since the depression began, it should be noted that over 20 percent of all residences other than the longest also lasted at least 1 year. These residences were necessarily maintained by families among the 82 percent whose longest residence was of equal or greater duration.

Table 10.—Duration of Residences of Migrant Families Since January 1, 1929 [1]

Duration of residence of 1 month or longer	Residences	
	Longest residence [2]	Other than longest residences [3]
Total	5,181	11,216
	Percent distribution	
Total	100	100
Less than 1 year	18	79
1–2.9 months	3	28
3–5.9 months	5	27
6–11.9 months	10	24
1–2.9 years	26	19
3 years or more	56	2

[1] For families formed since January 1, 1929, the period under consideration begins with date of marriage.
[2] 308 families, which had no residence of 1 month or longer since January 1, 1929, or since formation if subsequent to that date, and those for whom the duration of longest residence was not ascertainable, are not included.
[3] 208 residences, for which duration was not ascertainable, are not included.

There remains, however, a minority group of families (18 percent) whose longest residence lasted less than 1 year. These families were clearly marginal as to stability. About half of these families had never remained in one locality longer than 6 months and must be considered more mobile than stable. Some of these families, however, were formed during the year the study was made.

It is now possible, in the light of the data that have been given, to establish tentatively the proportions of families having backgrounds of stability. The families clearly unstable do not constitute a large group. They are represented by the families which had no residences at all, plus those whose longest residence was of very short duration.[4] These two groups, comprising one-fifth of all families, were actually unstable or marginal as to stability. But the other four-fifths had a stable background of a residence lasting from 1 to 3 or more years since 1929.

Stability Measured in Terms of Family Opinion

The arbitrary basis upon which the characteristics of stability and instability were measured was realized at the time the study was planned, and a means of verifying or rejecting length of residence as a measure of stability was included. In addition to an account of the duration of their residences, all families were asked whether they had ever had a residence which they considered to be a permanent settlement[5] for the family group. The distinction between length of stay in a community and the families' attitudes toward the permanence of their stay is clearly illustrated in the history of the Allen family:

The Allens lived in Boston, Mass., from 1924 to 1930 where Mr. Allen was steadily employed as a machinist. In 1930 slack work and reduced earnings caused Mr. Allen to take a job as a traveling representative for a mill machinery company. The Boston home was abandoned and the family traveled with the head. After a year the job failed and left the Allens stranded in Memphis.

For 2½ years Mr. Allen supported his family in Memphis by working as a painter. But the Allen family did not consider their stay in Tennessee to be a settled residence because Mr. Allen could not get work at his real trade. The Allens left Memphis at the first opportunity.

Because of situations similar to the one just described, it would be unwise to attempt final judgment about family stability without considering whether or not the families felt that a stay in a particular community represented settlement. To a certain degree, attitudes toward settled residence are independent of time and provide a check upon tentative conclusions based upon length of residence.

[4] The high mobility of the group is qualified in so far as some of the families were so recently formed that a "longest residence" of less than a year would include most of their residence history periods.

[5] *Settled residence* is used to convey the idea of seeming permanence in contrast with the more or less temporary nature of a *residence*. See footnote 1, p. 59.

In the discussion of the reasons for leaving settled residence (see ch. I), it was noted that about four-fifths of all the families interviewed had, according to their individual standards of judgment, *thought of themselves as permanent residents* of some community at some time since 1929. The remaining one-fifth of the families, which considered that they had not been settled since 1929 (or since the date of marriage if the family was formed after that date), were excluded from the tabulations of reasons for migration.[6] According to the opinions of the families themselves, four-fifths thus had a residence that they considered a settlement and one-fifth lacked this evidence of prior stability.

In order to collate this subjective test of stability with the test based upon length-of-residence records, a comparable time-period must be established. The table below provides the basis of comparison by showing when the families which had once considered themselves settled in a given community had left that community.

Table 11.—Year Migrant Families Left Settled Residence

Year of leaving settled residence	Migrant families
Total	5, 479
	Percent distribution
Total	100
No settled residence	21
With settled residence	79
Left prior to 1929	3
Left in 1929	3
Left in 1930	3
Left in 1931	3
Left in 1932	5
Left in 1933	9
Left in 1934	26
Left in 1935	27

NOTE.—10 families, for which date of leaving settled residence was not ascertainable, are not included.

Accepting as a measure of stability the existence of a settlement considered by the family to have been permanent, it may seem at first that the results here are almost identical with those obtained from the data on length of residence. There it was found that 82 percent of the families had lived in one place for 1 year or longer since 1929; but further considerations show that before direct comparison can be made, two adjustments are necessary. In the first place not all of the families which had at one time had a settlement were stable by habit. It seems logical to exclude in table 11 the 3 percent of all families whose last settlement had terminated before 1929, inasmuch

---

[6] See p. 1, footnote 1.

as the lapse of time indicates the rootless type of existence found among chronic wanderers. In addition the 3 percent who left their last settled residence during 1929 should also be excluded in the interest of comparability since few of these families would have maintained a residence for as long as 1 year since January 1, 1929.

If this 6 percent is deducted from the proportion of families which had a settled residence, the original 79 percent (table 11) is reduced to 73 percent; and it is this proportion that may be used to check the earlier provisional estimate of the size of the stable group (82 percent) based upon length of residence. The difference (9 percent) in stability as determined by these two measures is logical. Length of residence as a measure requires that families be considered as stable if they remained in a community for 1 year or more, even though they establish no permanent ties; at the same time, families' opinions as to last place of settlement requires inclusion of those which intended to remain but had no means of establishing lasting ties.

The important point to be noted is not so much the difference as the agreement between the results determined by the two measures of stability. Over half of the families left their last place of settlement in 1934 and 1935 (table 11), and about the same proportion (table 10) had a residence of 3 years or more between 1929 and 1935. It seems possible to conclude from the two sets of data that about three-quarters of the families in the study of transient bureau cases had the characteristics of stable, self-supporting families prior to their transient relief history.

MOBILITY BEFORE TRANSIENT RELIEF

In deriving measures of stability from the residence history prior to application for transient relief, family mobility has been implied as the complement of stability, but has not been fully described. It is worth while to consider the backgrounds of migrant families from the point of view of moves rather than, as heretofore, from the point of view of residences.

To distinguish periods of mobility from periods of immobility, use will again be made of the arbitrary definition of a residence as a stay of 30 days or more in one community. The application of this definition immediately classified 4 percent of the families as extremely mobile, since it has been shown (table 8) that this proportion of families had no residence since January 1, 1929. Nothing is to be gained from further analysis of this small group, and they will be excluded with the warning that their high mobility is in part attributable to recency of formation. The degrees of mobility represented by the remaining 96 percent of the families will be determined by indicating (1) the continuity of residence and (2) the number of residence changes.

.Continuity of Residence

An unbroken sequence of residences, even though there are changes of community over a period of years, may reflect no more than the occasional move that is a commonplace in American life. A break in the sequence, however, specifically indicates periods during which no residence was maintained and consequently reflects some degree of instability. For the purpose of the present discussion, a *continuous* residence history is defined as one in which the time elapsing between terminating a residence (of 1 month or more) in one community and establishing a new residence (of 1 month or more) in another community did not exceed 30 days. A *noncontinuous* residence history is one in which there is a period (or periods) of 30 days or longer between quitting a residence in one locality and establishing it in another.[7]

The results of applying this definition of residence continuity to all families which had a residence history are presented in table 12. Nearly four-fifths of these families had continuous residence histories for upwards of 6 years between January 1, 1929, and the date of quitting their last residence prior to application for transient relief. A break of 30 days or more in the residence histories of the remaining one-fifth indicates the existence of one period or more of protracted mobility.

Table 12.—Nature of Residence Histories of Migrant Families Since 1929 [1]

Nature of residence histories	Migrant families
Total	5, 247
	Percent distribution
Total	100
Continuous	79
Noncontinuous	21

[1] For families formed since January 1, 1929, the period under consideration begins with date of marriage.

NOTE.—242 families, which had no residence of 1 month or longer since January 1, 1929, or since formation if subsequent to that date, are not included.

It must be noted, however, that the distinction between families on the basis of the continuity of their residence histories is incomplete as a measure of mobility. The families with continuous residence histories which had moved from one locality to another several times were obviously less stable than those whose changes of residence were few. Likewise, varying degrees of mobility would be represented among families with noncontinuous residence histories. The fore-

---

[7] The same distinction applies to families whose formation occurred after January 1, 1929. In such cases a lapse of 30 days or more between marriage and first residence constituted a break in residence continuity

going information, therefore, must be supplemented by data on the number of residence changes made by families with continuous and with noncontinuous histories.

Number of Residence Changes

Approximately half of the families had either not changed their community [8] of residence at all or no more than once prior to the migration that led to transient relief (table 13). An additional 18 percent changed their place of residence twice only during the same interval. Thus, according to this measure, the mobility of a large majority of families was clearly restricted during the period examined. Actually, only the very few families which had changed their community of residence five or more times could be considered to have been highly mobile.

Table 13.—Residence Changes of Migrant Families Between January 1, 1929,[1] and First Transient Bureau Registration

Residence changes	Migrant families
Total	5,218
	Percent distribution
Total	100
No change	21
1 change	30
2 changes	18
3 changes	11
4 changes	6
5 changes or more	14

[1] For families formed since January 1, 1929, the period under consideration begins with date of marriage.

NOTE.—271 families, which had no residence of 1 month or longer since January 1, 1929, or since formation if subsequent to that date and those for which the number of residence changes was not ascertainable, are not included.

The analysis of the number of community changes leads to the same conclusion about the mobility of migrant families during the residence history period that was indicated by the previous examination of the length of residence within a community and by the families' opinion as to whether they had a settled residence.

However, some of the families which had changed their residence no more than one or two times also had noncontinuous residence histories. Since a noncontinuous residence history indicates that the process of changing communities involved periods of mobility lasting at least as long as a month, and perhaps much longer, these families were actually more mobile than the tabulation of number of com-

[8] Changes *within* a community are not included among changes of residence.

munity changes shows. The presence of such families does not, however, materially alter the conclusions suggested in table 13. Only 10 percent of the families changed residence no more than twice but had a noncontinuous residence history. This group is more than balanced by 20 percent of the families which moved three times or more and still had continuous residence histories (table 14).

Table 14.—Type of Residence History and Residence Changes of Migrant Families Since January 1, 1929 [1]

Residence changes and type of residence history	Migrant families
Total	5,218
Continuous history	4,145
Noncontinuous history	1,073
	Percent distribution
Total	100
Continuous history	79
No change	19
1 change	26
2 changes	14
3 changes	8
4 changes	4
5 changes or more	8
Noncontinuous history	21
No change	2
1 change	4
2 changes	4
3 changes	3
4 changes	2
5 changes or more	6

[1] For families formed since January 1, 1929, the period under consideration begins with date of marriage.

NOTE.—271 families, which had no residence of 1 month or longer since January 1, 1929, or since formation if subsequent to that date, are not included.

MOBILITY AND YEAR OF FORMATION

Throughout the preceding discussion there have been frequent reminders that nearly half of the families included in this study were formed after January 1, 1929, the date selected for the beginning of the residence histories. The fact that so large a proportion of the families was exposed to the forces causing mobility for less than the full period under examination raises a question as to the validity of number of residence changes in measuring mobility. It may well be asked, for example, whether the large proportion of families—69 percent—which changed community of residence no more than twice indicates a low degree of mobility or simply a short period of existence as families.

The conclusion that at least a substantial majority of the families had a background of stability can carry little weight until the time factor has been examined. It becomes important, therefore, to discover the relationship between mobility and year of formation. The families with residence histories were distributed by year of formation as shown in table 15.

Table 15.—Year of Migrant Family Formation

Year of formation	Migrant families
Total	5,196
	Percent distribution
Total	100
Prior to 1929	57
1929	6
1930	6
1931	6
1932	6
1933	8
1934	8
1935	3

NOTE.—293 families, which had no residence of 1 month or longer since January 1, 1929, or since formation if subsequent to that date, and those whose year of formation was not ascertainable, are not included.

The next step is to examine the number of moves made by families formed in each of the years to discover the source of the large proportion of families with no more than two changes of residence between 1929 and 1935. The results of this examination are presented in table 16.

Table 16.—Year of Formation and Residence Changes of Migrant Families

Year of formation	Total		Residence changes					
	Number	Percent	None	1	2	3	4	5 or more
Total	5,167	100	21	30	18	11	7	13
Prior to 1929	2,928	100	15	31	20	12	7	15
1929	315	100	13	26	17	15	9	20
1930	330	100	15	20	21	15	8	21
1931	304	100	18	29	20	13	9	11
1932	319	100	19	33	17	10	10	11
1933	388	100	29	34	19	8	4	6
1934	423	100	47	37	10	3	1	2
1935	160	100	79	18	3	—	—	—

NOTE.—322 families, which had no residence of 1 month or longer since January 1, 1929, or since formation if subsequent to that date, and those whose year of formation or the number of residence changes was not ascertainable, are not included.

It may be seen that both the number and percent distributions of moves made by families formed in the years 1929, 1930, 1931, and 1932 were much the same. More important, the percent distribution of moves made by families formed in these years was closely parallel to that for all families formed prior to 1929. Referring again to table 15, it will be noted that families formed in years up to and including 1932 comprised more than four-fifths of all the families studied.

Families formed in 1933, 1934, and 1935 did, of course, make fewer moves than families formed in earlier years (table 16). But the difference becomes pronounced only among families formed in 1934 and 1935; and these families make up too small a proportion of all families to bias the results unduly. It follows, then, that the conclusion concerning relatively low mobility of all families is not invalidated by the presence of families so newly formed that they have not yet had time to make more than one or two moves.

Mobility Rate of Recently Formed Families

Table 16 suggests that families formed after 1929 were relatively more mobile than families formed prior to 1929, inasmuch as the percent distribution of moves was about the same, while the time of exposure to mobility was less. In order to measure this increasing tendency to mobility, the moves made by families formed in each of the several years must be adjusted to take into account for the period of exposure. Families formed prior to 1929 can be excluded because they existed during the full period, and the particular year of formation prior to 1929 is not reported. Likewise, the families formed in 1935 must be excluded because they were interviewed before the end of the year (September).

When the mean number of moves made since formation for each year-of-formation group is adjusted for length of exposure—by dividing by the average number of years since formation [9]—a significant trend in mobility is disclosed (table 17).

Table 17.—Average [1] Number of Residence Changes Made per Year by Migrant Families, by Year of Formation

Year of formation	Average number of residence changes since formation	Average number of years since formation to 1935	Average number of residence changes per year
1929	2.85	6.25	0.46
1930	3.08	5.25	0.59
1931	2.28	4.25	0.54
1932	2.08	3.25	0.64
1933	1.47	2.25	0.65
1934	0.83	1.25	0.66

[1] Arithmetic mean.

The more recently a family was formed, the more mobile it was in relation to the length of time it had been formed. The trend disclosed indicates that family mobility tended to be greatest soon after marriage and before the families could gain a foothold in a community.[10]

---

[9] The average number of years since family formation was computed with consideration to: (1) the fact that families formed *during* a given year had an average exposure of half of that year, and (2) the year of interview was three-quarters completed when this study was made.

[10] The coefficient of rank correlation between mean number of moves and year of formation is ($\rho = .94$) a significant value.

MOBILITY OF SETTLED AND UNSETTLED FAMILIES

When changes in community of residence are reduced to annual rates of change,[11] it is found that the rate for all the families as a group increased progressively from 1929 to 1934 (table 18). However, the 1929–1934 trend in the annual rate of change differed significantly according to the families' background during the years preceding their application for transient relief.

Table 18.—Yearly Rate of Residence Change of Migrant Families by Family Settlement Status and by Year of Change

Year of residence change	Migrant families		
	Total	With settled residence	With no settled residence
Total	5,036	4,210	826
Yearly rate of residence change per 100 families			
1929	30	25	87
1930	35	29	96
1931	35	29	94
1932	38	31	93
1933	49	42	98
1934	63	57	94

NOTE.—453 families, which had no residence of 1 month or longer since January 1, 1929, or since formation if subsequent to that date, those formed in 1935, and those whose year of formation, year of residence change, or number of residence changes was not ascertainable, are not included.

The yearly rate of residence change was calculated according to:

$$r = \frac{A}{B + \frac{1}{2}C} \times 100, \text{ in which}$$

A = the number of residence changes made in a given year.
B = the number of families formed prior to that year.
C = the number of families formed during that year. This value is divided by 2 because the average exposure of these families was for ½ of the year in which they were formed.

It will be recalled that when the families' opinion as to whether they had maintained a settled residence was used to measure stability,[12] the families were divided into two groups of unequal size: four-fifths had a residence they considered as settled and one-fifth had no such residence between January 1, 1929, and the receipt of transient relief. Among the first group, families having had a settled residence, the rate of community change was 25 per 100 families in 1929; it rose to 31 per 100 in 1932; and reached 57 per 100 families in 1934 (table 18).

[11] The frequency of the mobility of family groups for any given year was determined by considering the number of community changes made during the year in terms of the number of families in existence that year. It is expressed as an annual rate of community change; that is, as the number of changes during each year per 100 families involved.

The calculation of the yearly rate of residence change is somewhat involved because nearly half of the families were formed during the period under consideration. See note to table 18.

[12] See discussion of Stability Measured in Terms of Family Opinion (pp. 63–65).

Among the families which had no settled residence, the rate showed no such progressive increase. It remained close to 95 for each 100 families and showed little variation throughout the period 1929 to 1934. The comparatively high mobility of the families in this group cannot be explained in terms of the prolongation of the depression, since their rate of residence change was almost as high when the depression began as it was 5 years later.

In part, the consistently high mobility of this group resulted from the nature of the occupations followed by many families. Migratory-casual work, necessitating frequent change of residence as a normal part of the process of earning a living, accounted for many of the families which had never maintained a settled residence.

Doubtless other reasons also played a part in the mobility of this group. Personality defects, alcoholism, and similar conditions, if characteristic of the economic head of a family, affect the ability of a family to maintain itself permanently in a given locality. Many of the families with persistently high rates of residence change presented such problems and could only have been rehabilitated by extremely careful social direction.

By far the larger group of families, however, were displaced by adverse economic pressure. It would seem, therefore, that normal readjustment for such families would require, first of all, the correction of the factor which had been primarily responsible for their migration. Adequate employment would have solved the transient problem presented by the great majority of the families which received assistance from transient bureaus.

The information in this chapter on the background of migrant family mobility leaves little doubt that the majority of the families had been habitually settled and self-supporting in the past. Granted an increase in opportunities for employment, there is no reason for supposing that they would not have shortly resumed their normal way of living.

Chapter IV

MIGRANT FAMILIES AND THE TRANSIENT PROGRAM

FROM THE point of view of the citizens of each community, the out-of-State and out-of-town needy who asked for relief during the depression were not their responsibility. It was soon evident, however, that refusing to assist migrants was of little effect; it neither "prevented" migration nor solved the problem of immediate and pressing need. The fact that the out-of-town applicant may have been the legal responsibility of some other community was of little help, for there were no means by which this responsibility could be invoked. As a result there was a widespread demand that the Federal Government take responsibility for the nonresident in need.

The initiation of a relief program for what came to be known as "transients" was, therefore, a logical development when the Federal Government, through the Federal Emergency Relief Administration, took the leading role in providing direct relief for the unemployed. The FERA first established throughout the United States a uniform requirement of 1 year's State residence for general relief. Then, in cooperation with 47 States and the District of Columbia [1] transient bureaus were established to aid those who could not meet this 1-year requirement. On this basis, the transient program continued in operation from the fall of 1933 until the intake of new cases was closed on September 20, 1935. During this period the transient program assisted approximately 200,000 different families containing some 700,000 individual members,[2] in addition to an even larger number of unattached individuals traveling alone.

---

[1] Vermont did not operate a transient program.

[2] This estimate is based upon the total family intake during the operation of the FERA transient program (in the neighborhood of 300,000 families), adjusted to account for the families registering more than one time. The mean number of stays per family under care was 1.5 (table 22).

After the close of intake the transient program continued to give assistance for well over a year to thousands of cases under care at the time intake was closed. A limited number of cases, principally former registrants, were admitted to care after the intake of new cases was stopped.

Throughout its life the merit of the transient program was the subject of much dispute. To a considerable extent the controversy was based upon the unavoidable confusion that attended the initiation and operation of a totally new relief program. Although the debate over the merits of the program has not completely died away, the confusion has, and it is now possible on the basis of this study to provide some factual analysis of the transient program in relation to the depression migration of needy families.

THE MIGRATION THAT LED TO TRANSIENT RELIEF

Before turning to the record of migrant family mobility within the transient program itself, it is necessary to examine the mobility of the families immediately prior to their first transient bureau registration. Their last residence could have been terminated only under two conditions:[3] either (1) upon departure from the community or (2) upon application for transient relief in the community of last residence. Table 19 indicates the proportion of families whose last residence was terminated by migration and those terminated by application for transient relief in the community of last residence.

Table 19.—Place of First Transient Bureau Registration of Migrant Families

Place of first transient bureau registration	Migrant families
Total	5,237
	Percent distribution
Total	100
Registered in place of last residence	39
Registered in place other than last residence	61

NOTE.—252 families, which had no residence of 1 month or longer since January 1, 1929, or since formation if subsequent to that date, and whose place of first transient bureau registration was not ascertainable, are not included.

The first transient bureau registration of 61 percent of all families was in a community other than the community of their last residence. For these families registration was immediately preceded by mobility. A variety of circumstances necessitated the first registration of these families. Some had run out of money en route to their original destination. Some had reached and departed from their original destination, and had first registered on their way to a subsequent destination. Others, upon arriving at their original destination or at a subsequent destination, immediately found themselves in acute distress when anticipated help did not materialize.

[3] The definition of a residence specified (a) that the family stay at least 1 month in a community and (b) that it receive no transient relief.

Obviously, an essential function of the transient relief program was to relieve this sort of distress. It would be expected that the families which never had a residence and those which were not at their last place of residence would make up most of the cases to whom transient relief would be necessary. In fact, these two groups combined did comprise a substantial majority of the migrant families. But table 19 reveals the existence of another group whose first stay at a transient bureau was in the place of their last residence of 30 days or longer.

In view of the popular concept of transient relief cases as consisting of needy persons en route, it may seem odd that 39 percent of a representative sample of families under transient bureau care should have obtained assistance in the same community in which they had maintained their last residence. Moreover, very few of these families had traveled to other localities and then returned (table 20). For most of them no mobility whatever intervened between last residence and transient relief.

Since a residence was by definition a stay of 1 month or more within a given community, these families did not register for transient relief until they had already lived for at least 1 month in the community where they applied. Actually, a substantial proportion had lived in the community for 6 months or more. Thus, even though these families had been mobile at some time in the past, they had completed their migration at least temporarily before they applied for transient relief.

Time Elapsed Between Last Residence and First Registration

The intervening period between the last residence and the first transient relief involved a lapse of less than 1 month for 73 percent

Table 20.—Time Elapsed Between Leaving Last Residence and First Transient Bureau Registration of Migrant Families, by Place of First Registration

Time elapsed	Total	Registered in place other than last residence	Registered in place of last residence
Total_____	5,170	2,964	2,206
	Percent distribution		
Total_____	100	100	100
Less than 1.0 month_____	73	56	96
1.0–1.9 months_____	14	22	3
2.0–2.9 months_____	3	6	*
3.0–5.9 months_____	4	7	*
6.0 months or more_____	6	9	1

*Less than 0.5 percent.

NOTE.—319 families, which had no residence of 1 month or longer since January 1, 1929, or since formation if subsequent to that date, and whose place of first transient bureau registration or time elapsed between last residence and first transient bureau registration was not ascertainable, are not included.

of the families (table 20).   Practically all of the group which first
registered at their place of last residence had done so within a month
of the termination of their last residence.   Because the last residence
of these families ended by definition with their first transient relief,
the transition in most cases did not involve any lapse of time whatever.   The 4 percent of this group that registered for relief after
1 month had passed represents those who, migrating from their community of last residence to seek employment or help, eventually
returned to their last residence and applied for transient relief.

Those families which first registered for transient relief in a different
community from their last residence were generally mobile for only
a short period of time before applying for relief.   Well over half of
these families had registered for relief within 1 month, and nearly
four-fifths had registered within 2 months of leaving their last residence.   On the other hand, 16 percent of these families did not receive
assistance at a transient bureau until more than 3 months had passed.
Although they may have remained in one locality, or in several, for a
short time before moving on to another place, this entire interval
must be considered one of wandering, since the stopovers were in no
case for as long as 1 month.   Inasmuch as these families were ineligible
for resident relief and did not seek transient relief, they had other
means of support—either reserve funds or, more frequently, migratory work—during this period of wandering.

THE EFFECT OF THE TRANSIENT PROGRAM UPON MOBILITY
"Uncle Sam's Hotels"

The transient program was frequently charged with "encouraging
transiency."   According to one commonly expressed opinion the
transient program subsidized large numbers of undeserving people
who were wandering aimlessly about the country.   Transient bureaus,
it was held, provided free and convenient accommodations for sight-
seers touring the country.   Two editorials illustrate this fairly common
point of view:

The *Times* has not cared for the transient bureau idea nationally.   It has
aggravated, not mitigated the nuisance of wandering, jobless boys, many of them
touring the country for the fun of it, and of professional hoboes doing the same.
This applies to the families also.[4]

In the past two years, transients have been able to travel in comparative comfort
through the aid of "Uncle Sam's hotels" scattered from one end of the nation
to the other.   Most of the itinerants make no pretension of staying at one place.
They blithely skipped from one camp to another, seeing the country while the
government footed the bills.[5]

The acceptance of such opinions is not difficult to understand.
A small part of the migrant family population did consist of chronic

[4] *El Paso Times*, El Paso, Tex., September 16, 1935.
[5] *Pueblo Chieftain*, Pueblo, Colo., November 8, 1935.

wanderers. Although these families were few in number, their seemingly aimless mobility and frequent requests for aid called attention to themselves so forcibly that it was natural, though erroneous, to consider them representative of migrants in general. A small group among the unattached was even more important in creating this impression. An earlier study has pointed out that 7 to 8 percent of the unattached transients receiving aid from the transient program during 1935 reported that a desire for adventure was the reason for their migration.[6] Thus, the extreme case, because of the attention it attracted, was accepted as proof that all needy migrants were irresponsible and undeserving.

Hostility toward all needy migrants was nonetheless the prevailing attitude in most communities. This attitude served to perpetuate or to initiate the "passing on" policy; i. e., overnight care accompanied by an order to leave town the next day, in dealing with these unwanted guests. Indeed, this policy was the only solution, in most communities, that could find support among citizens harassed by the mounting needs of the resident unemployed and the threat of increased taxation to meet these needs. Thus, the attitude of the resident population toward the migrant was in part responsible for the aimless "wandering" that aroused so much criticism.

On the basis of the information obtained in the present sample study, it is possible to test the validity of this criticism.

Turnover Rates

Turnover among migrant families in the transient bureaus can be considered as having two forms. The first consisted of turnover between the different transient bureaus within the national system and is measured by the extent to which families moved about from one bureau to another. The second type of turnover consisted of the process by which the migrant families under care in the entire program were renewed. This type is measured in terms of the rate at which families entered and left the transient program, regardless of moves they may have made from one bureau to another.

The records of the Division of Transient Activities report both types of turnover without distinguishing between them. They report total cases opened, total cases closed, and the number of families under care during a 24-hour period on the 15th day of each month (fig. 21). It is possible to determine from these figures the trends in both types of turnover combined. The migrant family openings rate (the number of cases opened throughout each month as a percent of cases under care on the 15th day of each month) is shown in table 21

---

[6] See Webb, John N., *The Transient Unemployed*, Research Monograph III, Division of Social Research, Works Progress Administration, Washington, D. C., 1935, p. 60 and table 24A.

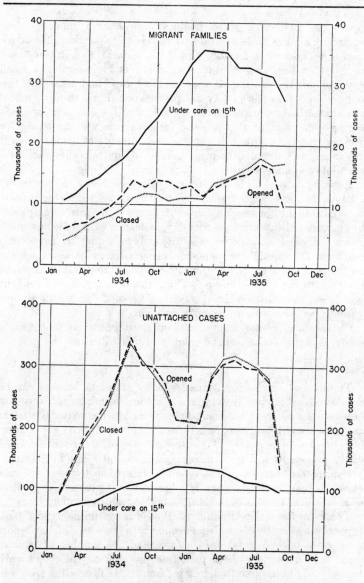

FIG. 21- NUMBER OF TRANSIENT BUREAU CASES OPENED AND CLOSED
DURING EACH MONTH AND NUMBER OF CASES UNDER
CARE ON THE 15th OF EACH MONTH
February 1934 through September 1935

Source: Appendix table 12.

AF 2870, WPA

for the period February 1934 through September 1935, together with the closings rate (the number of cases closed throughout the month as a percent of the cases under care on the 15th day of each month).

Table 21.—FERA Transient Program Openings and Closings of Migrant Family and Unattached Transient Cases During Each Month per 100 Cases Under Care at Midmonth, February 1934 to September 1935

Year and month	Migrant families		Unattached transients	
	Openings per 100 cases under care	Closings per 100 cases under care	Openings per 100 cases under care	Closings per 100 cases under care
1934				
February	56	38	153	146
March	57	43	193	184
April	51	47	234	227
May	59	52	265	255
June	60	52	279	268
July	65	53	301	296
August	72	58	329	321
September	58	53	280	286
October	58	49	256	246
November	51	39	211	203
December	42	37	156	156
1935				
January	39	34	158	156
February	32	31	154	155
March	37	39	211	214
April	40	40	235	242
May	45	46	258	264
June	46	50	264	273
July	53	56	269	271
August	51	53	262	268
September [1]	36	62	140	162

[1] Intake of new cases closed on September 20, 1935.

Source: Division of Transient Activities, Federal Emergency Relief Administration. See also appendix table 12 of this report.

A little consideration will show that if the result of the transient program had been the encouragement of transiency, a *progressive* increase in mobility would be revealed in the rate of opening and closing cases. This point can be demonstrated by reference to table 21. In 1934 the rate of opening family cases at transient bureaus rose from 59 per 100 cases under care in May to 72 per 100 cases in August. Clearly this is a significant increase in mobility, but one that is explained by the fact that the weather during the spring and summer is favorable to mobility. In 1935 a similar seasonal increase in mobility occurred, but it started at a lower point (45 per 100 cases) in May and reached a lower point (51 per 100 cases) in August. The number of families under care increased during this period. Discounting the seasonal factor there is evidence that the rate of openings for migrant families actually declined, whereas the rate would have risen if the transient program had encouraged irresponsible wandering.

The behavior of the rates at which families applied for assistance (cases opened) should, by themselves, provide sufficient indication that transient relief was not the cause of increased mobility. But additional evidence is available from the rates at which families left transient bureaus. If families wandered about aimlessly, using the bureaus simply as convenient stopover points, the closing rates should have risen as rapidly as opening rates and there would have been no such piling up of cases as is shown by the midmonthly count of cases under care. That this was not the case is shown by the behavior of the closing rate which did not equal or pass the opening rate until April 1935 when the peak of the case load had been passed and a voluntary liquidation of the migrant family population had begun.

It is interesting to compare, in figure 22, the opening and closing rates' for migrant families and unattached cases. The higher transient bureau turnover of the unattached person moving about the country without dependents is immediately apparent. Moreover, the rates at which unattached cases were opened and closed increased much more rapidly during the summer than the family rates. From February to August 1934 the opening and closing rates for unattached transients almost doubled. This tremendous increase in mobility is shown by the almost vertical rise of the two curves in figure 22. During the same period of time the opening and closing rates for families rose less than half as much.

For the unattached the marked increase in openings was accompanied by only a slight increase in cases under care on the 15th day of each month (fig. 21). For the families the increase in openings was much less, and the proportionate increase in cases under care by the 15th of each month was much greater. In other words, despite the wide swings in the rates of openings and closings among the unattached transients, the two rates moved together much more closely than the same two rates for family groups.

These comparisons show that there was a decided difference in the transient bureau turnover of the two groups receiving care. The unattached moved more frequently than the family population. It should be noted, however, that the pronounced changes in the mobility of the unattached are associated with the seasons of the year. For neither the unattached nor the family groups is there any evidence that opening and closing rates tended to increase with time; the rate curves did not start at a higher point or reach a higher peak in 1935 than in the preceding year.

The Number of Stays in Transient Bureaus

The use of rates to measure the mobility and turnover of migrant families receiving aid from transient bureaus has the disadvantage of lumping together those who moved within the transient bureau system with those who entered and left the system. Thus, an opening rate and a closing rate of 50 per 100 cases under care could mean that the same 50 families left one bureau and registered at another during

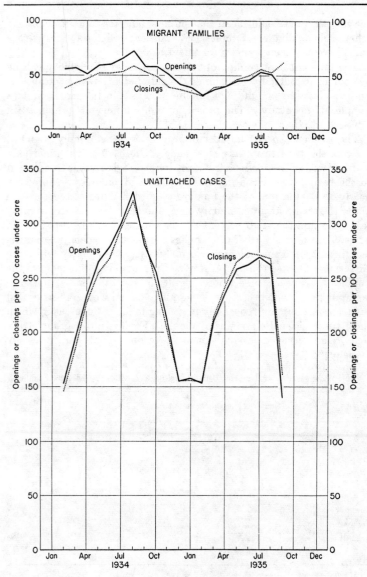

FIG. 22 – RATE OF OPENING AND CLOSING TRANSIENT
BUREAU CASES
February 1934 through September 1935

Source: Table 21.   AF-2871, WPA

the month, or it could mean that 50 new families came to transient relief and 50 different families left transient relief through private employment or some other adjustment.

The inherent shortcoming of rates as an index of mobility can be overcome, in part, by examining the number of stays at transient bureaus made by the migrant families included in the representative sample of this study. The record for 5,489 families is presented in table 22.

The average (mean) number of registrations per family was 1.5; i. e., at the time this study was made each 100 families under care had a record of 50 previous transient bureau registrations in addition to the registration initiating the stay then in progress. Moreover, nearly three-quarters of the families studied had registered for care under the transient program only once, and this stay was still in progress. An additional 16 percent of the families had registered twice. Thus, 9 out of every 10 of the families showed no tendency to use the facilities of the transient program for "seeing the country while the Government footed the bill." Among the remaining 10 percent of the families there were some whose migration was aimless and purposeless; but there were others—the migratory-casual workers—who used the transient bureaus repeatedly in getting to and from areas in which short-time seasonal work was available. For the latter group, transient relief served as a supplement to earnings that were generally inadequate.

Table 22.—Number of Transient Bureau Registrations Made by Migrant Families

Number of transient bureau registrations	Migrant families
Total	5,489
	Percent distribution
Total	100
1 registration	74
2 registrations	16
3 registrations	5
4 or 5 registrations	3
6 or 7 registrations	1
8 registrations or more	1
Average [1] registrations per family	1.5

[1] Arithmetic mean.

An interesting test of the immobilizing effect of transient relief is available from an examination of the stays made by families which had the most unstable backgrounds before the period of transient relief. There were 242 families which had no residence of as long as 30 days in one community from the time of marriage (or January 1,

1929, if formed before that date) until they made the first application for transient relief (ch. III).   Despite this indication of high mobility, nearly two-thirds of these families had stayed in only one transient bureau and were still under care at the time this study was made (table 23).

Table 23.—Number of Transient Bureau Registrations Made by Migrant Families Which Had No Residence of 1 Month or Longer Since January 1, 1929 [1]

Number of transient bureau registrations	Migrant families with no residence
Total	242
	Percent distribution
Total	100
1 registration	64
2 registrations or more	36

[1] For families formed since January 1, 1929, the period under consideration begins with date of marriage.

The stabilization of this group of families is especially significant. The transient relief program provided these families with their first opportunity to get off the road; and the result, as table 23 clearly shows, was for the majority of this particular group the first period of stabilization they had known since their formation into families.

Duration of Stay in Transient Bureaus

Three-fourths of all families had registered only one time for transient relief (table 22). Over one-half of this group had been under care for 3 months or longer (table 24). The median length of stay for families which registered only once was 4 months.

Because the sample study on which table 24 is based was conducted toward the close of the transient program, the proportion of families which had been under care for a year or more was greater than could have been possible earlier in the history of the program. Otherwise, the length-of-stay data may be considered typical of the situation that existed from month to month after the full operation of the program. It is significant that somewhat over one-third of the families with only one stay in transient bureaus had first registered for transient relief within 2 months of interview. This fact explains the relatively high turnover (opening and closing rates) discussed earlier. For at least this proportion of the families, transient relief was needed for only a short time to assist in achieving the purpose of the migration.

About one-quarter of the families obtained assistance from transient bureaus two or more times. The proportion of these families staying

Table 24.—Length of Time Migrant Families Spent at Place of First and Last [1] Transient Bureau Registration

Time spent at transient bureau	Migrant families which registered 1 time only [2]	Migrant families registered 2 or more times	
		At place of first registration [3]	At place of last registration [4]
Total	4,008	1,426	1,410
	Percent distribution		
Total	100	100	100
Less than 1.0 month	22	37	39
1.0–1.9 months	12	15	19
2.0–2.9 months	10	10	10
3.0–5.9 months	18	20	15
6.0–11.9 months	27	14	13
12.0 months or more	11	4	4
Average [5] (in months)	4.0	1.9	1.6

[1] Place of last registration was at place of interview.
[2] 36 families, for which the time spent at transient bureau was not ascertainable, are not included.
[3] 19 families, for which the time spent at transient bureau was not ascertainable, are not included.
[4] 35 families, for which the time spent at transient bureau was not ascertainable, are not included.
[5] Median.

less than 1 month was distinctly higher than among families which had only one contact with transient relief. In part, this difference is the result of families using transient bureaus as stopover points en route to a particular destination, but the group also includes the families whose migrations represented either a regular attachment to migratory-casual work or purposeless wandering.

Table 24 reveals that the last registration of this group of families was of slightly shorter duration than the first stay.[7] This fact does not, however, indicate a progressive increase in mobility between transient bureaus, since the last stay had not yet been terminated at the time this study was made.

The Meaning of the Turnover Rates

With all the evidence in, the effect of the transient program on one aspect of depression mobility may now be seen. The case for the transient program appears clearly in the record of migrant family turnover; i. e., the rates at which families entered and left the transient bureaus.

It has been pointed out that turnover among migrant families was of two kinds. The first consisted in turnover within the national system of transient bureaus or in movement from one bureau to the

---

[7] In measuring the duration of stays in transient bureaus for families receiving aid more than one time, consideration was given only to the first stay and the stay which was still under way when this study was made, since only about 10 percent of the families had more than two stays.

other. The second form consisted in the process by which the migrant family population as a whole was renewed.

As far as the first form of turnover is concerned, the data on the number and duration of stays in transient bureaus permit a definite judgment. This form of turnover was small and was, in so far as it appeared at all, the result of the presence of a small number—not in excess of 10 percent of the total—of highly mobile families. The transient program did not encourage families "to blithely skip from one camp to another"; on the contrary, the program had a stabilizing effect on families, even on those without a prior residence.

As to the second form of turnover—the renewal process—the pertinent data are those showing the rates at which cases were opened and closed at transient bureaus between February 1934 and September 1935, and the duration of stays in transient bureaus by families with only one transient bureau registration.

Monthly opening and closing rates of 30 to 60 families for each 100 under care could mean, over a period of 20 months, only one of two things: the same families were wandering from bureau to bureau, or the migrant family population was continually in process of rapid renewal. Since the evidence from this study is clear that the amount of bureau-to-bureau wandering was small, it must be concluded that the migrant family population was constantly changing in membership. It has been shown that the average number of transient bureau registrations per family was 1.5. If this figure is used to adjust the total opening and closing rates, it may be seen that roughly 20 to 40 percent of the family case load entered and left the transient relief program each month. In contrast, the monthly closings rate on urban *resident* relief in 1935 was only 5.6 percent.[8]

It is true that some of this turnover resulted from the transfer of family cases from transient relief to resident relief. However, the reports of the Division of Transient Activities show that only 8 percent of the 198,039 family cases closed between July 1934 and September 1935 were transferred to resident relief. Accordingly, allowing adjustment for these cases, and even allowing for the possibility that many other families may have received resident relief later, the turnover of transient relief cases through normal economic adjustment would still appear to be many times higher than the turnover rates on resident relief.

In summary, then, the case for the transient program stands as follows: Transient relief was a stabilizing influence upon families uprooted by the depression. It did not encourage wandering. On the contrary, it prevented aimless wandering by relieving the needs which

[8] Unpublished data in the files of the Division of Social Research, Works Progress Administration, Washington, D. C.

are its cause. Stabilization, however, did not imply ·unlimited dependence upon the transient program for support. Transient relief provided necessary but interim assistance to migrants who in most instances had definite objectives and who were frequently only temporarily in need.

The transient program was set up to fill a gap in the relief system, and its first purpose was to relieve distress. That it also assisted in the relocation of families is beyond doubt. Although the rate of turnover of migrant families from transient relief back into private industry cannot be conclusively determined, it is obvious from the data on number of transient bureau registrations and on total cases opened and closed that the rate must have been very high. Probably it was many times higher than the turnover in the resident relief population. In so far as families were enabled to resettle in an environment more favorable to them than the one they had left, transient relief was beneficial, though this effect was in a sense incidental to the basic purpose of the program. The value of the transient program was that it not only provided immediate relief to a distressed group but also assisted materially in working out a solution of the problems that gave rise to the distress.

LEGAL RESIDENCE REQUIREMENTS FOR GENERAL RELIEF

Finally, in judging the value of the transient program, it is necessary to bear in mind that transient relief took over the no man's land which had been created by the legal residence requirements of the various States.[9] The extent of the responsibility which the transient program thus assumed—and the extent of the needs which would have otherwise been largely unmet—can be inferred from a review of the various legal restrictions governing eligibility for resident relief. The requirements in each of the States and the District of Columbia as of January 1, 1936, are set forth in summary form in table 25. This tabulation presents the situation as it existed at about the time the study was made. Two years later—January 1, 1938—the general picture had changed somewhat and a notation of the changes by States are to be found in table 26.

It should be noted that the provisions shown in tables 25 and 26 have exceptions of two kinds. Some State statutes permit or require temporary aid for the needy nonresident. In practice, however, this type of aid seldom amounts to more than emergency medical care for those in ill-health and overnight care for the able-bodied.

---

[9] Legal settlement is a technical term meaning a residence under circumstances which entitle a person in need to assistance from a political unit. Legal settlement, which is based on State poor laws, must be distinguished from the uniform residence requirement of 1 year in all States established under the FERA and from special State regulations governing eligibility for emergency relief.

Table 25.—Residence Requirements for General Relief, January 1, 1936

State	State requirement	Local requirement
Alabama		6 months in county immediately preceding application.
Arizona		
Arkansas		
California	3 continuous years without receiving relief. Time spent in public institution or on parole not counted.	1 year in county immediately preceding application.
Colorado	1 year immediately preceding application and actual physical presence 350 days. Applicant must be self-supporting or the husband, wife, or minor child of a self-supporting person; otherwise, requirement is 3 years immediately preceding application with actual physical presence for 30 months.	6 months in county immediately preceding becoming chargeable.
Connecticut		4 years in a town or 1 year if owner of $500 worth of real estate. Aliens entitled to relief only by vote of inhabitants or by majority vote of selectmen and justices of the peace and inhabitants. The 4 years must be self-supporting.
Delaware	Legal residence	
Florida [1]	Counties between 9,700 and 10,500, 2 years.	1 year in counties between 9,700 and 10,500 or of 155,000 population.
Georgia		
Idaho	1 year immediately preceding application.	6 months in county immediately preceding application.
Illinois		12 months immediately preceding application.
Indiana		Uninterrupted residence of 1 year in township. If supported by governmental agency during first 6 months, such time is eliminated in computing residence period.
Iowa		1 year continuously in county without receiving support from public funds or care in any charitable institution and without being warned to depart. If warned to depart applicant may be considered resident within 1 year of filing affidavit that he is not a pauper.
Kansas		1 year in county.
Kentucky		
Louisiana		
Maine		5 successive years in town without receiving supplies as a pauper.
Maryland		In Baltimore and Prince Georges Counties applicant must be a resident. In Anne Arundel County 1 year's residence is required.
Massachusetts		5 successive years in a town without receiving public relief
Michigan		1 year in township, city, or county without receiving public relief.
Minnesota	1 year. Time spent in public institution or under commitment to guardianship of State Board of Control, or while receiving relief, is excluded in determining residence.	

[1] No State-wide law in Florida.

Table 25.—Residence Requirements for General Relief, January 1, 1936—Continued

State	State requirement	Local requirement
Mississippi		6 months in county.
Missouri	To receive emergency relief applicant must be citizen of State.	1 year in county next preceding time of any order for relief. County court may in its discretion grant relief to any person without regard to residence.
Montana		1 year in county immediately preceding application.
Nebraska	1 year excluding any period during which person received care or relief.	6 months in county excluding any period during which person received care or relief.
Nevada	3 years	6 months in county.
New Hampshire		5 consecutive years in town. Counties must support any person for whose support no person or town in the State is chargeable.
New Jersey		5 years uninterrupted stay in county or municipality.
New Mexico	1 year	90 days in county.
New York		1 year continuous residence in town or city without receiving public relief. Certain counties in which specified hospitals and veterans' homes are located require 5 years residence for inmates of the specified institutions.
North Carolina	3 years, unless at time of entering State person was able to support himself. Time spent in any institution or on parole therefrom is not counted.	1 year continuously in county.
North Dakota	1 year continuously without receiving public relief. Time spent in charitable, custodial, or correctional institution excluded.	1 year in county or if legal resident of State residence in county in which applicant spent major part of preceding year. Time spent in charitable, custodial, or correctional institution excluded.
Ohio		County, 12 consecutive months town or city, 12 consecutive months in county, 3 consecutive months in town or city without receiving public relief.
Oklahoma		6 months in county.
Oregon	4 years. To receive emergency relief applicant must be citizen of State.	6 months in county without receiving public relief.
Pennsylvania		1 continuous year in poor district with intent to establish permanent abode.
Rhode Island	2 years. For home relief or work relief under State financed and State supervised program ending June 30, 1939. State Unemployment Relief Commission may waive these requirements in special cases.	6 months in town for home relief or work relief under State financed and State supervised program ending June 30, 1939. State Unemployment Relief Commission may waive these requirements in special cases. For local relief 5 years in town without aid; or have estate of inheritance or freehold in town and yearly income of $20 clear for 3 years.
South Carolina		3 successive years in county or city. Person must be citizen of some State and must have maintained self and family during 3-year period.
South Dakota	1 year	90 days in county.
Tennessee		1 year in county (applies to poorhouse care only).
Texas	1 year. Funds derived from the sale of State bonds for emergency relief, used only for aid of a person resident 2 years immediately preceding application.	6 months in county.

Table 25.—Residence Requirements for General Relief, January 1, 1936—Continued

State	State requirement	Local requirement
Utah	1 year (applies only to county permanent poor relief program).	4 months in county; minors 1 year. (Applies only to county permanent poor relief program.)
Vermont	State provides for nonresidents of towns who have resided in State 1 year or more.	3 years in town.
Virginia	3 years unless at time of migration person was able to support self; otherwise, 1 year.	12 consecutive months in county, town, or city without receiving public or private relief.
Washington	--	6 months in county immediately preceding date of application.
West Virginia	3 years unless migrant entered State self-supporting.	1 year continuously in county.
Wisconsin	--	1 year in town, city, or village without being supported as a pauper or employed on a Federal work project, an inmate of any asylum or institution, etc.

Source: See Lowe, Robert C. and Associates, *Digest of Poor Relief Laws of the Several States and Territories as of May 1, 1936,* Division of Social Research, Works Progress Administration, Washington, D. C. Additional material will appear in Lowe, Robert C., *State Public Welfare Legislation,* a forthcoming monograph.

Table 26.—Changes in Residence Requirements for General Relief as of January 1, 1938

State	State requirement	Local requirement
Arizona	3 years immediately preceding application. Temporary absence for a total of 1 year does not affect the right for relief.	6 months in county, immediately preceding application; 12 months immediately preceding application to receive hospitalization or medical care from county board of supervisors, except for emergency cases.
Montana	1 year. Aliens illegally in the United States not eligible.	6 months in county. 1 year's county residence for care at poor farm or workhouse.
New Jersey	1 year without interruption immediately preceding May 4, 1936. 5 years without interruption for persons not qualifying under the preceding provision. Time spent in charitable, custodial, or correctional institution excluded.	1 year in municipality or if legal resident of State, municipality in which applicant spent major part of preceding year. Time spent in charitable, custodial, or correctional institution excluded.
Oklahoma	1 year for State funds----------------------	1 year for State funds. 6 months for county funds.
Pennsylvania	1 year immediately preceding application.	
Washington	--	
West Virginia	1 year when funds are specifically available for that purpose, relief may be granted to those who have not been residents of State 1 year.	Actually residing in county.
Wyoming	1 year without receiving public relief, provided applicant has not been absent from State for a period of 1 year or more immediately preceding application.	1 year in county without receiving public relief, provided applicant has not been absent from county for a period of 1 year or more immediately preceding application.

Source: Lowe, Robert C. and Staff, Division of Social Research, Works Progress Administration, Washington, D. C. Additional material will appear in Lowe. Robert C., *State Public Welfare Legislation,* a forthcoming monograph.

Secondly, by January 1, 1936, about two-thirds of the States had passed special emergency relief legislation which altered, in practice, the poor law provisions listed in tables 25 and 26. The majority of these emergency acts did not contain specific residence requirements, and the requirements of the poor laws were applied in some States but not in others. As a result there has been a vast amount of confusion over the meaning and application of residence requirements, and the provisions set forth in tables 25 and 26 may not represent the actual practice of some of the States. These provisions should, however, convey a fairly clear idea of the difficulties which confronted the nonresident family in need of relief.

The requirement for relief eligibility is often much more stringent than the residence requirement for voting purposes. In a majority of States residence of some specified minimum of time has always been a condition for relief eligibility. Laws prescribing a period of residence either in the State or locality, or in both, as a condition for relief eligibility were on the statute books of 43 States and the District of Columbia on January 1, 1936. In the other five States residence requirements were imposed in actual practice.

In 23 States the laws imposed a local (county, town, or city) residence requirement, and in 18 States they prescribed periods of residence in both State and local units. In the latter case, the required period of State residence was usually greater than the required period of local residence. In general, it may be said that the purpose of dual State residence requirement is to provide State-wide "protection" to the local subdivisions against an influx of indigent interstate migrants, while the purpose of the local residence requirement is to establish the responsibility of communities for persons who meet the State requirements. The less stringent residence requirements of the localities, once State requirements are satisfied, permit some intrastate migration without loss of eligibility for assistance in some specific place in the State.

Several States have two sets of State residence requirements. North Carolina, Virginia, and West Virginia had (on January 1, 1936) State residence requirements of 1 year with this interesting exception: a 3-year State requirement was to be imposed unless at the time of migration to the State the applicant was able to support himself. Texas and Rhode Island make one residence requirement for one relief fund and another requirement for other relief funds. Such requirements are clearly intended to disqualify needy interstate migrants from regular State assistance.

Settlement laws in typical States provided that a migrant would not be eligible for local relief unless he had lived within the State continuously, with intent to establish permanent residence, and without public assistance of any sort for at least 1 year; and in 10 States the residence must have lasted from 2 to 5 years.

Residence statutes as of January 1, 1938, do not, on the whole, reveal much progress toward more consistent and equitable laws than those which were in effect on January 1, 1936, though there have been changes in a few States (table 26). Washington has repealed its residence requirement, while Arizona has enacted a statute which prescribes 3 years' residence in the State. Pennsylvania and West Virginia have repealed their local residence requirement and enacted a 1-year State residence law. Montana, Oklahoma, and Wyoming have added State residence requirements to their already existing local requirements. New Jersey has amended its statutes so as to require a 5-year State residence if an applicant has not lived within the State for 1 year immediately preceding May 4, 1936; the earlier New Jersey statute prescribed a 5-year local residence.

The migrant's legal status was further complicated by statutes in 19 States providing for loss of legal settlement in the State of origin. In most of the States making definite provision, legal settlement was lost (as of January 1936) after 1 year's absence regardless of whether it has been acquired elsewhere or not. In two States it was lost after absence of 30 days. These provisions for the loss of legal settlement often caused migrants to lose residence status in one State before acquiring it in another. An earlier study [10] showed that 40 percent of migrant families in transient bureaus in June 1935 were without legal settlement in any State. It is evident, however, that the large proportion of such cases does not reflect any particular degree of mobility among the families so much as it demonstrates the efficiency with which the settlement laws of the States operate to cancel responsibility for needy migrant groups.

When the 48 States are viewed as a whole the complexity of residence requirements for general relief is immediately evident. Not only is the individual migrant family unaware, in most instances, of these requirements but State relief officials are also constantly confronted with borderline cases where judgment must be exercised, as well as official interpretations of the statutes, and a variety of practices that depart from the letter of the statute. A period of self-supporting residence that in one State makes a family eligible for local assistance is completely inadequate in another State. A family which has resided for 1 year without relief in one State is eligible for assistance; in another State the same family would be a transient family, excluded from local benefits.

---

[10] Webb, John N. and Bryan, Jack Y., *Legal Settlement Status and Residence History of Transients*, Research Bulletin TR–9, Division of Research, Statistics, and Finance, Federal Emergency Relief Administration, Washington, D. C., 1935.

General relief involves an expenditure that is borne in whole or in part by the community granting aid, and legislators have not been disposed to add to this expense the cost of caring for those who do not "belong" in their community. Whether or not severe residence requirements do protect a State from an influx of needy nonresidents is still a debatable question. But in many cases, the only reasonable solution of distress is emigration. At this point residence requirements and economic forces meet in a head-on collision that can be avoided only by broadening or abolishing the concept that people actually do belong in a particular place regardless of the fact that the place may not provide the means of making a living.

The more rigid requirements for acquisition of settlement status, especially when coupled with provisions making settlement quickly lost (as in California, Kansas, Minnesota, New Jersey, Oregon, and South Dakota, where specifically less time was needed in 1936 to lose settlement status than to acquire it), were clearly designed to send to other States more needy migrants than are received. Obviously, however, since the other States either try to do the same thing or have at least usually protected themselves against those who do try, the gain arising out of the stringency and confusion of the laws is only at the expense of the migrants in need.

Chapter V

PERSONAL CHARACTERISTICS

A DESCRIPTION of the families which received assistance from the transient program has been deferred until their mobility could be fully explored. Having discovered why and where the families migrated and having examined their mobility before and while receiving transient relief, it is important at this point to consider the families in terms of the standard descriptions of population. As part of the search for factors that explain why some distressed families migrated while others did not, it is particularly important to measure the extent to which migrant families were like or unlike families in the general population.

The comparisons to be presented here show that there is a relationship between particular personal characteristics and migration. For example, the comparative age distribution of economic heads of migrant families and of families in the total population reveals a close relationship between youth and mobility; and an examination of the color and nativity of migrant families indicates that native-born white families are more likely to migrate under adverse circumstances than are foreign-born white or Negro families. Data on the personal characteristics [1] of migrant families make it possible to show further that still other characteristics are not necessarily connected with the fact of migration. Domestic discord, for example, or failure to possess such basic social resources as a common school education were characteristic of migrant families to no greater extent than with families which did not migrate under the same economic stress.

---

[1] An account of the personal characteristics of the heads of migrant families receiving aid from transient bureaus was given in a previous study—Webb, John N., *The Transient Unemployed*, Research Monograph III, Division of Social Research, Works Progress Administration, Washington, D. C., 1935. But because the data there were drawn from a smaller and less representative sample based on 13 cities instead of the 85 cities sampled for this study, this study supersedes the earlier description.

COMPOSITION OF MIGRANT FAMILIES

Migrant families were complete family groups in the great majority of cases. That is, most family groups on the road [2] were identical in membership with the family group before migration. Less than one-tenth of the families had one or more members absent from the relief group, and in only a very small proportion of cases was the economic head [3] of the group among the absentee members (table 27).

Table 27.—Migrant Families Reporting Absence of Members Normally Part of Family Group

Composition	Migrant families
Total	5, 489
	Percent distribution
Total	100
Reporting no absentees	91
Reporting absentees	9
Economic head present	6
Economic head absent	3

Since most of the families left no member behind at the place of last residence, it is suggested that the severance from that community was both complete and final. The small proportion of absentee members is also significant in connection with the families' occupational resources. Because of the fact that nearly all families were complete, their stabilization on a self-supporting basis was dependent upon the human resources of the group at hand.

Not only were most migrant families complete in the sense that all members usually a part of the group were present during migration, but they were also normal [4] family groups. Approximately four-fifths of the migrant families studied consisted of husband and wife (28 percent) or of husband and wife and one or more children (51 percent); and in addition, there was a small proportion (3 percent) of normal families that included some other related or unrelated person (table 28)

[2] Throughout this chapter *migration* refers to the period between leaving the last place of residence lasting 1 month or longer and September 1935.

[3] Because of the presence of incomplete family groups on the road, it is necessary to distinguish between the "economic head" and the "present head" of the group. If the economic head of the family was absent, the present head was some member of the family group other than the person usually responsible for the economic welfare of the group.

[4] Families composed of husband and wife or husband and wife and their children are commonly called "normal families." Families composed of a man and his children or a woman and her children are called "broken families." The terms *normal* and *broken* are used with these specific meanings in this chapter.

Table 28.—Composition of Migrant Families Before and During Migration and Composition of Families in Resident Relief Population, October 1933 [1]

Family composition	Migrant families		Resident relief families Oct. 1933
	During migration	Before migration	
Total	5,489	5,489	2,726,221
	Percent distribution		
Total	100	100	100
Normal families	82	85	81
Husband and wife	28	26	14
Husband, wife, and children	51	55	60
Normal with others	3	4	7
Broken families	18	15	14
Woman and children	14	11	9
Man and children	2	2	3
Broken with others	2	2	2
Other types	*	*	5

*Less than 0.5 percent.

[1] Division of Research, Statistics, and Finance, *Unemployment Relief Census, October 1933*, Report Number Three, Federal Emergency Relief Administration, Washington, D. C., 1935, p. 35. 1-person families are not included.

It is important to observe from this comparison that the proportion of broken families on the road was only slightly larger than before migration, and that no particular type of broken families showed an appreciable increase. The small increase in the proportion of broken families of the woman-children type (from 11 percent to 13 percent) after migration indicates the extent to which male family heads were absent from the relief group. This reflects the small importance of domestic difficulty as a reason for leaving settled residence (table 1). Moreover, the proportion of migrant families which left their children behind was small, since the proportion of families consisting of only husband and wife increased from 26 percent before to 28 percent during migration. Broken families in which the wife was absent (man-children type) from the relief group did not increase at all.

The composition of migrant families receiving aid from transient bureaus did not differ markedly from that of families in the total resident relief population (table 28). The proportion of "other types" of families, i. e., related and unrelated persons not combinations of husband, wife, or children, but living together as family groups, was negligible among migrant families in comparison with resident relief families. This difference is no indication that persons living in this combination did not migrate; but it does mean that if they did, they did not apply for assistance at transient bureaus as family groups. Because of the youth of the family heads, there was a larger proportion of husband-wife families without children among migrant than among resident relief families; but the over-all proportions of normal and broken families were much the same. Although the proportion of broken families was slightly higher after beginning migration than before migration, the agreement with the proportion in the resident relief population is so close that family composition does not appear to have been a selective factor in determining whether or not a family would migrate.

SIZE

Logically, the presence of children and other dependents should tend to restrict the mobility of families under adverse conditions. And, indeed, a comparison between the size of migrant families and families in the resident relief and general population reveals that size of family was one of the selective factors in depression migration.

Table 29.—Size of Migrant Families, of Families in the Resident Relief Population of 1933,[1] and of families in the General Population of 1930 [2]

| Size of family | Migrant families | | Resident relief families Oct. 1933 | Families in general population 1930 |
	During migration	Before migration		
Total	5,489	5,489	2,762,575	27,547,200
	Percent distribution			
Total	100	100	100	100
2 persons	35	32	20	25
3 persons	25	25	20	23
4 persons	17	18	19	19
5 persons	10	11	14	13
6 persons	5	6	10	8
7 persons or more	8	8	17	12
Average [3] size	3.1	3.2	4.1	3.6

[1] Division of Research, Statistics, and Finance, *Unemployment Relief Census, October 1933*, Report Number Two, Federal Emergency Relief Administration, Washington, D. C., 1934, p. 26. 1-person families are not included.
[2] Bureau of the Census, *Fifteenth Census of the United States: 1930*, Population Vol. VI, U. S. Department of Commerce, Washington, D. C., 1933, p. 36. 1-person families are not included.
[3] Median.

Table 29 and figure 23 show two significant facts: (1) Well over one-half of all the families, both before and after migration, contained only two or three persons, and two-person families occurred more frequently than any other; [5] and (2) migrant families were smaller than families in the general population and were markedly smaller than resident relief families.

In considering size of family as a selective factor in mobility it must be remembered that the families in the study were interstate migrants, and the distance traveled, while generally restricted (see ch. I) was obviously much greater than the distance traveled by intra-

[5] See appendix table 13 for a detailed distribution of migrant families by size and family type.

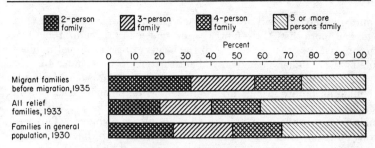

FIG. 23-SIZE OF MIGRANT FAMILIES AND OF FAMILIES
IN RESIDENT RELIEF AND
GENERAL POPULATIONS

Source: Table 29.   AF-2872, WPA

county and intrastate migrants. The conclusion of this report that
size of family is a selective factor in depression migration is therefore
restricted to the instances of interstate mobility. A recent report on
the mobility of the families in the general population [6] of Michigan
shows the need for caution in reaching conclusions on the relationship
between size of family and migration in general.

The Michigan report includes a tabulation of the range of moves
during a period of 57 months (April 1930 to January 1935) classified
by the number of dependent children on January 15, 1935.[7] Despite
its obvious limitations, the Michigan tabulation shows that there is
relatively little relationship between size of family and percent of
moves in intrastate migration, but that there is a definite tendency for
the percent of interstate moves to decline as the number of dependent
children increases.

The comparison of migrant family size first with the size of resident
relief families and second with the Michigan mobility study indicates
that, in this social characteristic at least, migrant families resembled
other mobile groups more than other distressed groups.

AGE

Economic Heads

Youth was a clearly defined characteristic of the economic heads of
migrant families. Among the family groups included in this study,

---

[6] Webb, John N., Westefeld, Albert, and Huntington, Albert H., Jr., *Mobility
of Labor in Michigan*, Division of Social Research, Works Progress Administration,
Washington, D. C., 1937, pp. 31–33 and particularly table 97.

[7] The lack of comparability between moves made at any time during a period
of 57 months and number of children at the end of the period was recognized.
The purpose of the tabulation was simply to explore the possibilities of the data
by using a small sample of schedules preliminary to the complete tabulation of a
larger sample. The lack of comparability mentioned above has been minimized
in the larger tabulation which is being made at the present time (October 1938).

approximately one-half of the economic heads were under 35 years of age, and more than three-fourths were under 45 (appendix table 14). In contrast, less than one-third of the heads of resident relief families in 1933 were under 35, and only about three-fifths were under 45.

The contrast in age is still more marked when the economic heads of migrant family groups are compared with the male heads of all families enumerated in the 1930 Census. Forty-five percent of all male family heads in 1930 were 45 years of age or older. This was true, however, of only 22 percent of the male heads of migrant family groups included in this study (fig. 24 and appendix table 14).

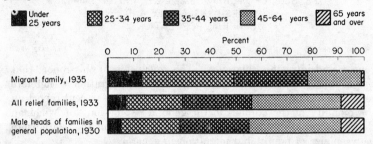

FIG. 24-AGE OF MIGRANT FAMILY HEADS AND OF FAMILY HEADS IN RESIDENT RELIEF AND GENERAL POPULATIONS

Note: Age distribution available only for male family heads in the general population.

Source: Appendix table 14.

AF-2873, WPA

Previous studies have stressed the youth of the depression migrants who received aid from transient bureaus. Unattached transients were found to be even younger than the economic heads of family groups.[8] But youth as a characteristic of migrants is not confined to the depression period or to migrants in need of public assistance. Youth was an important selective factor [9] in the rural-urban migration of the 1920's; and the study of labor mobility in Michigan (1930 to 1935) found "* * * the 20–24 year age group showed a larger proportion of workers moving than any other age group * * * and * * * workers in the most mobile age groups * * * were more likely to have completed * * * longer moves than were those [workers] of other age groups." [10] Accordingly, just as with family size, the age of migrant families was more closely related to the age of other migrants not in distress than of other needy groups that did not migrate.

[8] See Webb, John N., *op. cit.*, p. 24 ff.
[9] Thornthwaite, C. W., *Internal Migration in the United States*, Bulletin I, Philadelphia: University of Pennsylvania Press, 1934, pp. 32–37.
[10] Webb, John N., Westefeld, Albert, and Huntington, Albert H., Jr., *op. cit.*, p. 5.

Age and size of family are related; this relationship qualifies but does not impair the validity of the previous conclusion that size of family, in itself, is a selective factor in migration. The difficulties that stand in the way of distress migration by large families remain regardless of age; and the fact that migrant families are small is in part explained by age and in part by the difficulty of migrating in large groups.

Other Members

In view of the large proportion of young economic heads of migrant families, it is scarcely surprising to find that the age of other principal members of the family groups, mostly wives of economic heads, was even lower. The proportion of other principal members under 35 years of age was 65 percent as compared with 49 percent of economic heads; and the proportion under 45 was 86 percent as compared with 78 percent of economic heads (appendix table 15).

Since over half of all principal members (economic heads and other principal members) were under 35, it follows not only that the number of children per family was likely to be small but also that a large proportion of these sons and daughters would not yet have passed the ages usually associated with common (grade) school attendance. Of the 9,658 individuals apart from economic heads or other principal members of migrant families, nearly one-third were less than 5 years of age and over one-half were between the ages of 5 and 14. Less than one-fifth of all children and other relatives were 15 years of age or older. Thus, not only were the economic heads of migrant families predominantly young but youth was also a characteristic of all members of the family group.

COLOR AND NATIVITY

A comparison of the color and nativity characteristics of migrant families with those of nonmigrant families shows that native-born white families tended to migrate more readily than foreign-born white or Negro families. The proportion of white economic heads was larger among migrant families than among urban resident relief families, although it was about the same as among families in the general population (table 30 and fig. 25).

By comparison with the nativity of the 1930 population, migrant families were composed of a much smaller proportion of foreign-born. Migrant families also included a smaller proportion of foreign-born than the urban relief population.[11] Since a similarly high proportion of native-white persons existed among unattached transients,[12] it is clear that the native-born white, whether families or single indi-

---

[11] Comparable data in the 1933 FERA Relief Census are not available.
[12] See Webb, John N., *op. cit.*, pp. 33–35.

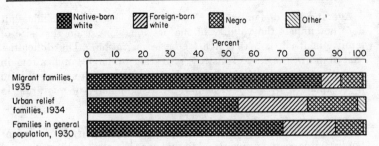

FIG. 25 - COLOR AND NATIVITY OF MIGRANT FAMILY HEADS
AND OF FAMILY HEADS IN URBAN RESIDENT
RELIEF AND GENERAL POPULATION

Source: Table 30.   AF-2874, WPA

viduals, migrated more readily in response to distress than other
population groups.

Two forces tended to stabilize the foreign-born population during
the depression. During the decades since the period of agricultural
expansion, foreign-born white immigrants have settled in large industrial centers and grouped themselves according to racial or national
ties. These ties have acted as deterrents to migration, despite the
pressures arising from limited economic opportunity and recurring
periods of unemployment. In addition, it is probable that local
prejudice outside of the highly industrialized States makes the migration of distressed foreign-born persons both more difficult than for
the native-born and less likely to provide a solution of their economic
problems.

Table 30.—Color and Nativity of Economic Heads of Migrant Families, of Families
in Urban Resident Relief Population of May 1934,[1] and in the General Population
of 1930 [2]

Color and nativity	Migrant families [3]	Urban resi- dent relief families May 1934	Families in general population 1930
Total	5,447	201,994	29,904,663
	Percent distribution		
Total	100	100	100
White	91	79	89
Native-born	84	54	70
Foreign-born	7	25	19
Negro	8	18	10
Other	[4] 1	[4] 3	1

[1] Based on preliminary tabulation of schedules used by Palmer, Gladys L. and Wood, Katherine D., in
Urban Workers on Relief, Research Monograph IV, Division of Social Research, Works Progress Administration, Washington, D. C., 1936.
[2] Bureau of the Census, *Fifteenth Census of the United States: 1930,* Population Vol. VI, U. S. Department
of Commerce, Washington, D. C., 1933, p. 11.
[3] 42 family heads, whose color and nativity were not ascertainable, are not included.
[4] Includes Mexicans.

Negroes showed similar characteristics. In comparison with the general family population, Negroes were underrepresented among migrant families but overrepresented among families on urban resident relief. The overrepresentation of Negro families on urban resident relief is evidence that they were less able to withstand the rigors of a depression. Yet, even though subject to greater economic distress, Negro families were much less likely to migrate than white families.

No doubt custom and prejudice operate to restrict the mobility of Negro families just as effectively as they restrict the foreign-born white.[13] Migration without adequate resources, whether by highway or railroad, is much more difficult for Negroes, and particularly so in the South. Moreover, the employment available for Negroes in any locality is restricted by preference for white labor, and the practicability of migration is limited.

Mexican and other race or color groups were proportionately as numerous among migrant families as among families in the general population of 1930. Among migrant families they were chiefly Mexican migratory workers and Indians who were registered principally in the central and southwestern parts of the country.[14]

The fact that foreign-born and Negro families were underrepresented in the transient relief population justifies a supplementary examination into some aspects of the migration of these two minority groups. Information on State of registration, State of origin, and reasons for leaving settled residence and selecting destinations for both foreign-born and Negroes is presented in appendix B.

CITIZENSHIP

Only 2 percent of all heads of migrant families were without full citizenship status, and half of these had received at least first citizenship papers (appendix table 16). Among the foreign-born family heads approximately two-thirds (66 percent) had full citizenship status. An additional one-sixth had first papers,and one-sixth were without any citizenship status. Of the "others" slightly less than three-fourths were full citizens, and the rest were without any citizenship status.

MARITAL STATUS

In view of the predominance of normal migrant families and young family heads, small proportions of single, separated,[15] divorced, and

---

[13] The fact of the northward migration of Negroes during and after the World War does not invalidate this conclusion, since that migration was in response to an abnormal labor demand which nullified the usual difficulties in Negro mobility.

[14] See Webb, John N., *Transients in December*, TR–3, Division of Research, Statistics, and Finance, Federal Emergency Relief Administration, Washington, D. C., March 1935.

[15] "Separation" as used here refers to separation with intent to live permanently apart, rather than temporary separation arising out of the exigencies of migration.

widowed family heads and other principal members may be anticipated (table 31).

Table 31.—Marital Status of Economic Heads and Other Persons 15 Years of Age and Over in Migrant Families and of Heads of Families in the General Population of 1930 [1]

Marital status	Migrant families		Heads of families in general population 1930
	Economic heads	Other members 15 years of age and over	
Total	5,489	6,481	29,490,174
	Percent distribution		
Total	100	100	100
Single	2	23	5
Married	85	74	79
Separated, widowed, and divorced	13	3	16

[1] Bureau of the Census, *Types of Families in the United States,* special report, U. S. Department of Commerce, Washington, D. C., August 5, 1935, table 1.

The classification of the families' reasons for migration showed that domestic difficulty was a relatively insignificant cause of family mobility. The same fact is reflected in the small incidence of separation, widowhood, and divorce among the family groups. Compared with the returns from the 1930 Census, the proportion of separated, widowed, and divorced heads among migrant families was significantly less than was reported for the total population.

Although the proportion of other persons 15 years of age and over who were married was smaller (74 percent) than among economic heads (85 percent), the actual number was slightly greater. This difference resulted from the presence in a number of family groups of a few married adults other than the spouse of the head. Most of these other married adults were parents or other relatives of economic heads.

SEX

Although migrant and nonmigrant families differed as to age, size of family, and color and nativity, there was little difference in their composition by sex.[16] The economic heads of migrant families

[16] The sex ratio for all members of the migrant family groups included in this study was 97.5 males per 100 females; the ratio for the resident relief population included in the FERA Unemployment Relief Census of 1933 was 103.4; and the ratio for the total population 1930 Census was 102.5. Actually the difference in composition by sex of migrant and resident family groups was less than is indicated by these ratios. Both the FERA Unemployment Relief Census and the United States Census of 1930 included one-person families which were more frequently men than women. Transient bureaus, on the other hand, classified one-person cases as "unattached" or nonfamily persons.

were much more frequently men than women, whereas women were a majority among other principal members. But males and females were about equal in number among all migrants—family heads, other principal members, and children and other relatives (table 32).

Table 32.—Sex and Status in Family of Persons in Migrant Families

Sex	Total	Economic heads	Other principal members	Children and other relatives
Total--	19,978	5,489	4,813	9,676
	Percent distribution			
Total--	100	100	100	100
Male---------------------------------------	49	86	4	51
Female-------------------------------------	51	14	96	49

The slight excess of females among all persons is partly a result of the presence of more migrant families of the woman-children type than of the man-children type (appendix table 13). In other words, most of the male economic heads were accompanied by a wife, but only a few of the female economic heads were accompanied by a husband.

The fact that about one-half of all members of migrant family groups were females is significant by comparison with the other and larger group of depression migrants—the unattached transients. Among unattached transients the proportion of women did not at any time exceed 3 percent of the total unattached transient relief population.[17] The difficulties of travel were alone sufficient to restrict the number of unattached women, but an additional restriction was imposed by social attitudes which disapproved the wandering of lone women. Obviously social disapproval does not apply to the migration of women as members of family groups, although the difficulty of travel without adequate resources does apply.

EDUCATION

Only a small proportion of the heads of migrant families lacked some formal education, and about three-fifths of them had completed at least the eight grades of common school.

It will be observed in table 33 that the younger heads of families were generally better educated than the older family heads, and that this tendency was consistent throughout except for the age group 16 to 19 years. The lower educational achievement of this group is probably the result of an early assumption of family responsibility.

[17] See Webb, John N., *The Transient Unemployed, op. cit.*, pp. 31–32.

Table 33.—Schooling Completed and Age of Economic Heads of Migrant Families

Schooling completed	Total	Age				
		16–19 years	20–24 years	25–34 years	35–44 years	45 years and over
Total	5,437	52	636	2,000	1,567	1,182
		Percent distribution				
Total	100	100	100	100	100	100
None	3	2	1	2	4	6
Grade school:						
Less than 5 years	15	13	8	11	15	21
5–7.9 years	23	23	23	23	22	23
8–8.9 years	26	27	25	28	27	23
High school (9–12.9 years)	28	35	40	32	26	20
College (13–16.9 years)	5	—	3	4	6	6
Postgraduate (17 years and over)	*	—	*	*	*	1
Average [1] years completed	8.4	8.4	8.7	8.5	8.3	8.0

*Less than 0.5 percent.
[1] Median.
NOTE.—52 family heads, whose age or schooling completed was not ascertainable, are not included.

The native-born white heads of migrant families were found to have the highest level of education, followed in order by the foreign-born whites, the Negroes, and the other races (table 34).

Table 34.—Schooling Completed and Color and Nativity of Economic Heads of Migrant Families

Schooling completed	Total	Color and nativity			
		Native-born white	Foreign-born white	Negro	Other [1]
Total	5,405	4,556	357	415	77
		Percent distribution			
Total	100	100	100	100	100
None	3	2	7	9	13
Grade school:					
Less than 5 years	14	12	20	30	26
5–7.9 years	23	23	24	27	32
8–8.9 years	26	27	23	15	13
High school (9–12.9 years)	29	31	19	14	13
College (13–16.9 years)	5	5	5	4	3
Postgraduate (17 years and over)	*	*	2	1	—
Average [2] years completed	8.4	8.5	8.0	6.2	6.0

*Less than 0.5 percent.
[1] Includes Mexicans.
[2] Median.
NOTE.—84 family heads, whose schooling completed or color and nativity were not ascertainable, are not included.

Migrant family heads had a higher level of schooling completed than the heads of either the urban or rural relief population (table 35 and fig. 26).

Table 35.—Schooling Completed by Economic Heads and Other Members 15 Years of Age and Over of Migrant Families and of Heads of Urban [1] and Rural [2] Resident Relief Families

Schooling completed	Migrant families		Heads of resident relief families	
	Economic heads [3]	Other members 15 years of age and over [4]	Urban (Oct. 1935)	Rural (Oct. 1933)
Total	5,441	6,379	6,982	5,333
	Percent distribution			
Total	100	100	100	100
None	4	3	10	8
Grade school:				
Less than 5 years	13	10	22	19
5–7.9 years	23	23	26	27
8–8.9 years	26	27	22	29
High school (9–12.9 years)	29	34	17	15
College (13–16.9 years)	5	3	3	2
Postgraduate (17 years and over)	*	*	*	—
Average [5] years completed	8.4	8.5	7.0	7.6

*Less than 0.5 percent.

[1] Carmichael, F. L. and Payne, Stanley L., *The 1935 Relief Population in 13 Cities: A Cross Section*, Series I, No. 23, Division of Social Research, Works Progress Administration, Washington, D. C., December 31, 1936, p. 9.
[2] McCormick, Thomas C., *Comparative Study of Rural Relief and Non-Relief Households*, Research Monograph II, Division of Social Research, Works Progress Administration, Washington, D. C., 1935, p. 30.
[3] 48 family heads, whose schooling completed was not ascertainable, are not included.
[4] 102 persons 15 years of age and over, whose schooling completed was not ascertainable, are not included.
[5] Median.

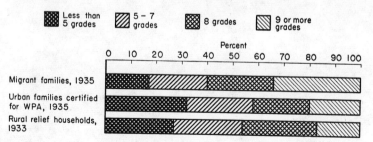

FIG. 26-SCHOOLING COMPLETED BY HEADS OF MIGRANT FAMILIES AND BY HEADS OF URBAN AND RURAL RESIDENT RELIEF FAMILIES

Source: Table 35.

AF-2875, WPA

Some of the difference between the educational attainments of migrant and resident relief families is attributable to the youth of the migrant group and to the underrepresentation of Negroes. In any event, it is obvious that educational attainment was not a selective factor in depression migration.[18]

---

[18] There are no detailed studies of the schooling of the entire population with which the schooling of persons in migrant families may be compared. The Statistical Division of the Office of Education, United States Department of the Interior, in *Biennial Survey of Education, 1932–1934*, p. 14, estimates that 51.5 percent of persons above 21 years of age in 1934 have completed at least the eighth grade, that 13.9 percent have been graduated from high school, and that 2.9 percent have completed college. These figures appear to show that the migrant family heads and the other adult members have had more than average schooling, since 62 percent of the economic heads and 60 percent of the other adult members have completed at least the eighth grade.

Chapter VI

OCCUPATIONAL RESOURCES

A REPRESENTATIVE cross section of the families receiving assistance from transient bureaus necessarily consists largely of families which, at the time of interview, had failed to achieve the purposes of their migration. As soon as migration succeeded, the successful families were no longer a part of the transient relief population and therefore were outside the limits of this study. It is worthy of note, however, that the figures on the turnover among transient families (ch. IV) suggest that migration must have been wholly or partially successful in a large proportion of cases and within a relatively short period of time.

Although this study could not follow migrant families after they left the transient relief population to determine the kind of readjustment that put an end to migration, it is possible to report on three of the most important factors that conditioned the return of migrant families to self-support: (1) employability, (2) usual occupation and industry, and (3) duration of unemployment. For those heads of migrant families who were employable and who, in addition, possessed skills acceptable to industry, it seems reasonable to assume that their return to stability depended chiefly upon an increase in the labor demand of private employment.

EMPLOYABILITY

In this study, employability was determined after a careful consideration of the following factors: (1) interview and case record information regarding the temporary or permanent physical and mental disabilities, temporary or chronic illness, personality and speech difficulties, attitude toward employment, illiteracy, and similar factors bearing on ability and willingness to work; (2) medical examinations, and clinical and hospital reports whenever available; (3) type of work done before migration; (4) age; (5) responsibility for the care of dependent children under 16 years of age; and (6) the interviewers' and case workers' opinions of employability.

107

It was recognized that willingness to work taken in conjunction with an absence of employment handicaps did not assure reemployment by private industry. Any attempt to define employability, or degrees of employability, in terms of probable reabsorption by private industry presumes a knowledge of future developments in economic activity that does not exist. Such factors as age and employment opportunities, to mention only the more obvious, have an important bearing upon the reabsorption of heads of migrant families judged in this study to be employable.

The effect of age on employability has been accounted for, at least in part, by limiting the wholly employable group to economic heads 16 through 50 years of age.[1] But it is clear that arbitrary limits cannot be applied to such intangible factors as the location of families in relation to opportunity for employment. The intricacies of an employability index which would attempt to measure all factors prohibit its use. On the other hand, the practicability of the simple index—absence of bodily handicaps plus willingness to work—justifies its use. The discussion which follows presents an examination of factors which only affect, but do not necessarily determine, the employability of the economic heads of family groups included in this study.

After these factors had been considered by the interviewers for each case, one of the following classifications was assigned: (1) employable; (2) employable with handicaps; or (3) unemployable. The employable group includes those who were under 51 years of age, were willing to work, and for whom no handicaps were reported. In cases where the economic head was 65 years of age and over, was a woman responsible for the care of dependent children, or was definitely listed as unemployable by the interviewer, the head was judged unemployable. In other cases, the seriousness of handicaps was considered so that a judgment could be made as to whether the economic head was "employable with handicaps" or "unemployable."

Employable Heads

In these terms, somewhat over half (56 percent) of the family heads studied appeared to be unquestionably employable; that is, the head was present in the relief group, had no ascertainable employment handicaps, and was willing to work. The problem represented by this group was thus chiefly of reemployment by private industry at a wage sufficient to insure stability (table 36).

It may be thus said that a majority of the economic heads of migrant families possessed the most important qualification for a resumption of stable, self-supporting lives. They were able to work, willing to

---

[1] By definition, an economic head was a person 16 years of age or older who was responsible for the family group.

work, and were within the preferred age range for private employment. Moreover, the majority had other employable members within the family group.

Table 36.—Employability of Economic Heads of Migrant Families

Employability	Economic heads
Total_____	5,426

	Percent distribution
Total_____	100
Employable_____	56
Employable with handicaps_____	33
Unemployable_____	11

NOTE.—63 family heads, whose employability was not ascertainable, are not included.

Heads Employable With Handicaps

The employability of the economic heads of the remaining families offers a more difficult problem of analysis. Clearly some must be judged totally unemployable by any criterion; and the bodily handicaps of others were such as to restrict the range of gainful occupations in which they might engage. However, there were some whose employment handicaps were probably more apparent than real. For instance, age was considered a partial employment handicap for all economic heads 51 through 64 years and a total handicap for all heads 65 years of age and over. This arbitrary procedure probably does some violence to the facts; but it does less violence than would have resulted from ignoring the well-known tendency of employers in hiring workers to discriminate in favor of younger men.

Approximately one-third of the economic heads of migrant families were neither wholly employable nor wholly unemployable according to the criteria used in this study (table 36). That is, one out of every three of the economic heads was willing to work, but there were one or more reasons [2] for believing that his ability to work was limited by handicaps that would impair his success in the labor market (table 37).

Chronic illness was the employment handicap most frequently reported. Among the more important types of chronic illness were, in order of importance: diseases of the respiratory system; heart, circulatory, and blood diseases; and diseases of the stomach and abdomen.

---

[2] In a considerable number of cases a person suffered from more than one employment handicap. For instance, an economic head may have lost the fingers of his right hand and he also may have been 55 years of age. In this case there would be both an age and a disability handicap. For purposes of this report only one handicap was tabulated—the one that most directly affected the employment of the individual. In the case cited above, physical disability would be tabulated rather than age.

Table 37.—Employability and Employment Handicaps of Economic Heads of Migrant Families

Employability and employment handicaps	Economic heads
Total	5,426
	Percent distribution
Total	100
Employable 16–51 years of age	56
Employable with handicaps	33
Physical disability	6
Mental disability	1
Chronic illness	11
Age (51–64 years)	7
Physical injury	*
Temporary illness	1
Institutionalization	*
Women with dependents [1]	2
Illiteracy	2
Other	3
Unemployable	11
Age (65 years and over)	1
Women with dependents	6
All other disabilities	4

* Less than 0.5 percent.

[1] Women whose families required only part-time care, who were able and willing to work, and who had work histories.

NOTE.—63 family heads, whose employability was not ascertainable, are not included.

The proportion of family heads handicapped by chronic illness was considerably higher in this than in a previous study [3] of migrant family groups. The difference is partially due to the fact that the earlier study covered continuous monthly registrations [4] which overrepresented the more mobile and presumably the least handicapped portion of the population. The far more complete examination of employability made in the present study also indicates that handicapped migrant family heads tended in the earlier study to overstate their ability to work,[5] either out of pride or the belief that it would improve

[3] See Research Bulletins Nos. TR–1, 2, 3, 6, and 8, December 28, 1934, to August 26, 1935, Division of Research, Statistics, and Finance, Federal Emergency Relief Administration, Washington, D. C.

[4] Continuous monthly registrations did not take account of the tendency of family groups to accumulate in areas with healthful climates. Thus, among the monthly registrations in Colorado, New Mexico, Arizona, and California, the proportion of family heads suffering from ill-health was probably smaller than the proportion of such persons under care in these States. Since the present study was based principally upon a sample of transient families already under care in transient centers, it may be expected that the proportion of family heads in poor health would be somewhat larger than among family heads currently registered.

[5] The importance of ill-health as a cause of family migration has already been discussed. See pp. 7–8.

their chances of obtaining private employment or employment on the Works Program.

Age was a partially disabling factor for 7 percent of all economic heads and in importance ranked next to chronic illness. Physical disabilities that restricted but did not entirely prevent gainful employment complete the list of the three most important handicaps found among the economic heads of migrant families. These three handicap classifications account for approximately two-thirds of all heads who were considered to be employable with handicaps. Chief among the physical disabilities were: trunk or back injuries; eye injuries; and leg, ankle, or foot injuries. That serious employment handicaps are presented by these physical disabilities under modern hiring procedures is obvious.

Each of the other employment handicaps involved a relatively small number of family heads. Among these other handicaps were the presence of dependent children or invalids who restricted women heads to part-time employment, illiteracy, and other disabilities comprising a wide variety of such circumstances as personality difficulties and unwillingness to work.

In terms of occupational attachment many of the families with heads employable with handicaps were capable of returning to a self-supporting way of life in a new community provided that normal job opportunities were present. Broadly speaking, the usual occupations of these workers (appendix table 17) were such that resettlement would not be unduly difficult in many localities.

It must not be overlooked, however, that many of the families whose economic head was partially handicapped had bunched up in particular localities, where the chances for securing employment adequate to insure a stable self-supporting existence were not promising. For example, many families in which some member was suffering from respiratory disorders migrated to the Southwest, where communities were simply unable to absorb them into private industry. The failure of many of these families to make such an adjustment is evidenced by the large numbers that turned to migratory agricultural work as the only means of remaining in an area believed to be beneficial to the health of the head.

Unemployable Heads

There remain approximately one-ninth of the economic heads who were judged to be totally unemployable (table 37). The most important group among the unemployable heads consisted of women with dependent children requiring their entire time. This group accounted for over half of the totally unemployable heads. Women partially and totally unemployable because of dependent children made up 8 percent of all families and were equal in size to the proportion handicapped and disabled by age.

Next in importance were the family heads who, regardless of age, were so incapacitated by bodily infirmities as to be unfit for gainful employment. Finally, the unemployable group included the economic heads who were 65 years of age and over. Age, however, was the least important of the three factors, accounting for slightly under 1 percent of all economic heads and approximately one-fourteenth of all those classified as unemployable.

It is clear that resettlement of these families on a self-supporting basis was highly improbable. These families contained no members who were either fully or partially employable. In so far as these families were absorbed by communities there was merely a transfer of relief burden from the old to the new place of residence. For many families, particularly the health seekers, such a shift was socially desirable. But the community at their destination is ordinarily reluctant to extend such families aid, and it is seldom that a community of former residence will make any contribution toward defraying the cost of maintaining the family in another locality.

The unemployable family therefore faced the unhappy alternatives of living precariously on what assistance could be obtained in a new community or of returning (or being returned) to a place of former residence where as often as not assistance was no more readily obtained. Though small in number this type of needy nonresident family presents a social problem of great complexity and one that deserves careful and sympathetic consideration on the part of public and private social service agencies. Since the majority of the unemployable heads were mothers who could not work because of the need of caring for young children or invalid dependents, the principal relief problem represented by the unemployable heads was need for aid to dependent children.

USUAL OCCUPATION AND INDUSTRY

About one-ninth of the families lacked an employable economic head, and for this group it seems clear that public assistance was the only means by which stability could be assured. For about nine-tenths of the families, however, employment was necessary for reestablishment. It is worth while, then, to consider their qualifications for employment in terms of the occupation which they usually followed and the industries in which these occupations were customarily pursued.

Because of a pronounced similarity in occupational characteristics between family heads judged to be fully employable and those judged to be employable with handicaps, the two groups have been combined in the discussion which follows. There has been included, however, one summary description of the occupational characteristics of the two groups separately (appendix table 17).

Usual Occupation

In this study the usual occupation was defined as the particular gainful activity at which the economic head of the family had customarily been employed or, in some instances, the activity which the economic head considered his usual occupation by reason of experience or training.[6]

Main Class of Usual Occupation

Broad groups of occupations indicate roughly the general level of skill possessed by workers, and at the same time suggest their economic level. The groupings used in classifying migrant family heads are as follows: (1) white-collar workers, subdivided into professional, proprietary workers (nonagricultural and agricultural), and clerical and salespersons; (2) skilled workers; (3) semiskilled workers; and (4) unskilled workers, who were further divided into laborers (nonagricultural and agricultural) and domestic and personal service workers.

Table 38.—Usual Occupation and Sex of Employable Economic Heads of Migrant Families

Usual occupation	Total	Male	Female
Total	4,729	4,527	202
	Percent distribution		
Total	100	100	100
White-collar workers	28	28	28
Professional workers	5	5	6
Proprietary workers (nonagricultural)	4	4	*
Proprietary workers (agricultural)	8	8	*
Clerical and salespersons	11	11	22
Skilled workers	23	24	1
Semiskilled workers	25	25	24
Unskilled workers	24	23	47
Laborers (nonagricultural)	8	8	—
Laborers (agricultural)	7	8	3
Domestic and personal service workers	9	7	44

*Less than 0.5 percent.

NOTE.—760 family heads, who were unemployable, whose usual occupation was not ascertainable, and those who never worked, are not included.

The employable economic heads of migrant families were almost evenly distributed among the white-collar, skilled, semiskilled, and unskilled workers (table 38). It is interesting to compare this distribution with the broad occupational status of the resident unem-

---

[6] In cases where the economic head had worked at two or more occupations for short periods of time the occupation of his last nonrelief job of 2 weeks, or longer duration was reported as his usual occupation. The number of such cases, however, was small.

ployed in 1935 and of the general population of gainfully employed persons in 1930 (table 39 and fig. 27).

Table 39.—Main Class of Usual Occupation of Employable Economic Heads of Migrant Families, of Resident Relief Families, March 1935,[1] and of Gainful Workers 16–64 Years of Age in the General Population of 1930 [2]

Main class of usual occupation	Employable economic heads of migrant families [3]	Economic heads of resident relief families March 1935	Gainful workers 16–64 years of age in general population 1930
Total	4,729	4,037,709	45,913,404
	Percent distribution		
Total	100	100	100
White-collar workers	28	10	42
Skilled workers	23	18	13
Semiskilled workers	25	24	15
Unskilled workers	24	48	30

[1] Hauser, Philip M., *Workers on Relief in the United States in March 1935*, Abridged Edition, Division of Social Research, Works Progress Administration, Washington, D. C., 1937, p. 26.
[2] Bureau of the Census, *Fifteenth Census of the United States: 1930*, Population Vols. IV and V, U. S. Department of Commerce, Washington, D. C., 1933, pp. 44 ff and 352 ff, respectively.
[3] 760 family heads, who were unemployable, whose usual occupation was not ascertainable, and those who never worked, are not included.

Although the economic heads of the two relief groups are not perfectly comparable with all gainful workers 16–64 years of age in the general population, the differences in the distribution shown in table 38 are of such magnitude that significant tendencies are suggested. The occupational status of migrant family heads, in terms of broad occupational groupings, was clearly higher than that of economic heads of resident relief families. A substantially smaller proportion of the migrant family heads was unskilled, and a larger proportion was skilled and white-collar workers.

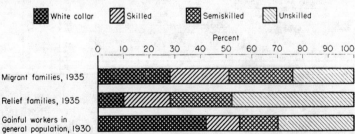

Fig. 27-MAIN CLASS OF USUAL OCCUPATION OF ECONOMIC HEADS OF MIGRANT FAMILIES AND RELIEF FAMILIES IN 1935 AND OF GAINFUL WORKERS 16 THROUGH 64 YEARS OF AGE IN THE GENERAL POPULATION, 1930

Source: Table 39.   AF-2876, WPA

The occupational status of the migrant family heads also compares favorably with that of the gainful workers in the 1930 Census The general population contained a higher proportion of unskilled workers than the migrant family sample. White-collar workers, however, were greatly underrepresented among migrant family heads. The economic heads of migrant families thus occupied a position intermediate between the resident relief unemployed, in which unskilled workers bulked largest, and the total gainful working population, in which white-collar workers were the largest group.

These broad occupational groups fail to carry over the significant detail associated with individual occupations. In order, then, to get a more specific description of the pursuit followed by the economic heads of migrant families it is necessary to consider some of the more important occupations that make up each of the four broad occupational groups (appendix table 18).

White-Collar Workers

Among the professional and technical workers in migrant groups the most important occuptions were: musicians, technical engineers, clergymen and religious workers, and actors. The importance of actors, musicians, and clergymen reflects to some extent the presence of itinerant showmen and revivalists on the road. The most important occupations included under "proprietors, managers, and officials (nonagricultural)" were retail dealers and managers, peddlers, and building contractors. Clerks in offices, bookkeepers, and telegraph and radio operators accounted for most of the office workers; and salesmen, real estate agents, and canvassers accounted for most of the salesmen and kindred workers (appendix table 18).

Skilled Workers

Because of the relatively high proportion of skilled workers among the employable economic heads of migrant families (table 39) it is of particular interest to examine some of the more important types of skills represented by this group. Well over half of these skilled workers were usually employed in the building and construction industry. In order of importance, the skilled trades most frequently reported were: painters, carpenters, electricians, plumbers, engineers, and structural steel workers (appendix table 18). The prolonged depression of the building industry, together with the fact that a considerable number of building trades workers are accustomed to moving about the country in pursuit of their trades, accounts for the relative overrepresentation of skilled construction workers among migrant families.

The remaining skilled workers consisted of craftsmen usually attached to manufacturing industries. Mechanics led the list, with machinists, locomotive engineers and firemen, and printing trades workers following in the order named.

Semiskilled Workers

Workers from the building and construction industries were somewhat less important among the semiskilled than among skilled workers. Truck and tractor drivers in building and construction work were, however, more numerous than any other single group among semiskilled workers, and accounted for nearly three-quarters of the semiskilled from the building and construction industry. Machine operators were the principal group among the semiskilled workers from the manufacturing industries. These workers were usually employed in the manufacture of textiles, iron and steel, automobiles, clothing, and food (appendix table 18).

Unskilled Workers

Economic heads of migrant families following unskilled pursuits came in almost equal numbers from manufacturing and allied industries, agriculture, and domestic and personal service. Unskilled workers usually employed on the construction of buildings, roads, and streets and sewers, together with the traditionally mobile laborers in mines and on railroads, made up most of the unskilled group outside of agriculture. Farm hands, including some migratory seasonal workers who regularly follow the crops, account for the fairly large group of unskilled agricultural workers. Among the domestic and personal service workers, cooks in restaurants, construction camps, and hotels, accounted for well over one-third of the group. Barbers, waiters, and domestic servants made up the second most important group of domestic and personal service workers.

Usual Industry

Table 40 presents a summary account of the industrial attachment of the economic heads, and appendix table 19 presents a detailed account of the specific industries.

Table 40.—Usual Industry and Sex of Employable Economic Heads of Migrant Families

Usual industry	Total	Male	Female
Total	4,663	4,466	197
	Percent distribution		
Total	100	100	100
Agriculture, forestry, and fishing	17	17	4
Extraction of minerals	4	5	—
Manufacturing and mechanical industries	37	37	24
Transportation and communication	13	14	2
Trade	13	13	13
Public service	1	1	1
Professional service	6	5	9
Domestic and personal service	9	8	47

NOTE.—826 economic heads, who were unemployable, whose usual industry was not ascertainable, and those who never worked, are not included.

This distribution of family heads did not depart greatly from the industrial distribution of heads of relief families or gainful workers in the general population. Migrant families represented no particular broad industrial classifications to the exclusion of others. Though a few variations appeared, migrant families' industrial attachment was in general a cross-section of the industrial composition of the resident relief and general populations (table 41 and fig. 28).

Table 41.—Usual Industry of Employable Economic Heads of Migrant Families, of Resident Relief Families March 1935,[1] and of Gainful Workers 10 Years of Age and Over in the General Population of 1930 [2]

Usual industry	Employable economic heads of migrant families [3]	Economic heads of resident relief families 1935	Gainful workers 10 years of age and over in general population 1930
Total	4,663	3,719,074	47,492,231
	Percent distribution		
Total	100	100	100
Agriculture, forestry, and fishing	17	22	23
Extraction of minerals	4	4	3
Manufacturing and mechanical industries	37	39	30
Transportation and communication	13	14	9
Trade	13	9	16
Public service	1	1	2
Professional service	6	2	7
Domestic and personal service	9	9	10

[1] Hauser, Philip M. and Jenkinson, Bruce, *Workers on Relief in the United States in March 1935*, Vol. II, A Study of Industrial and Educational Backgrounds, Division of Social Research, Works Progress Administration, Washington, D. C. (in preparation).
[2] Bureau of the Census, *Fifteenth Census of the United States: 1930*, Population Vol. V, U. S. Department of Commerce, Washington, D. C., 1933, p. 408 ff.
[3] 826 economic heads, who were unemployable, whose usual industry was not ascertainable, and those who never worked, are not included.

Certain differences in the distributions which appear in table 41 are in part a reflection of other causes than the selective factor of migration. Comparability is biased in particular by (1) the relatively small proportion of female migrant family heads and (2) the comparison of family heads in the relief groups with all gainful workers 10 years and over in the general population.

Other differences between the industrial attachment of migrant family heads and all gainful workers appear to have resulted from variations in the distress mobility of particular industrial groups. Agriculture [7] is clearly underrepresented among migrant family heads. Manufacturing and mechanical industries were overrepresented by comparison with the gainful workers in the general population. As appendix table 19 shows, the particular industries contributing most to this overrepresentation were building and construction, automobile repair shops, and sawmills. Transportation and communication

[7] See ch. II, p. 52 ff.

was likewise overrepresented among migrant family heads, particularly in water transportation, automobile trucking, pipelines, and the construction of streets, roads, etc., industries. The overrepresentation in these particular industries is logical, since most of these industries require a mobile labor supply.

It would seem, then, that industrial characteristics were to some degree a selective factor in the migration of the families studied. The differences revealed in table 41 are not, however, great enough to explain migrant family mobility in terms of industrial attachment. While the pursuits which permitted or required mobility were overrepresented, the overrepresentation in most instances was not great.

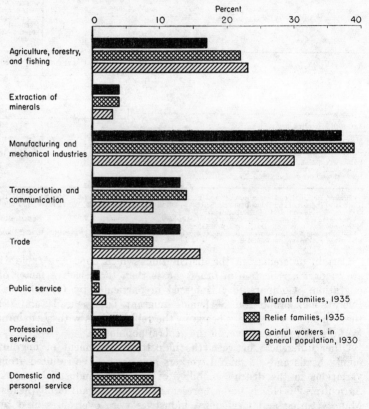

FIG. 28 – USUAL INDUSTRY OF ECONOMIC HEADS OF MIGRANT FAMILIES AND RELIEF FAMILIES IN 1935 AND OF GAINFUL WORKERS 10 YEARS OF AGE AND OVER IN THE GENERAL POPULATION, 1930

Source: Table 41.

AF-2877, WPA

Supposedly sedentary pursuits—such as in the food industries, the clothing industries, the paper and printing industries, trade, professional service, and domestic and personal service—were represented by large numbers of migrant family heads.

Occupation and Industry by Age

Both age and occupational characteristics appear to have operated as selective factors in the migration of families receiving aid from transient bureaus. It may be of interest, therefore, to compare age with occupational and industrial groupings; this has been done for employable economic family heads in appendix tables 20 and 21.

In the two age groups 35 to 44 years and 45 to 64 years the proportions of white-collar and skilled workers were distinctly greater than among the two age groups under 35 years. Within the white-collar group the older age of proprietors, both agricultural and non-agricultural, explains this difference. Among skilled workers the difference is explained to a large extent by the industrial distribution (appendix table 21) which shows that for workers in the building and construction industries the proportions above 35 years were greater than the proportions below this age.

The greater relative importance of youth in the semiskilled and unskilled groups was the result principally of the attachment of youth to transportation industries and to agriculture where these occupational groups predominated.

Education and Occupation

In an effort to discover some significant relationships between educational attainment and occupation these factors were compared in terms of broad educational and occupational groupings. The comparison suggests nothing that goes beyond common knowledge. The proportion of white-collar workers was about two times as great among economic heads with better than a grade school education than among those who stopped at or failed to complete the first 8 years. This situation is reversed among the unskilled and, to a lesser degree, among the semiskilled. The proportions of skilled workers were about the same for these two educational groups (appendix table 22).

DURATION OF UNEMPLOYMENT

Duration of unemployment for migrant family heads has been measured in two ways: first, in terms of the time elapsed since the family economic head was last employed for at least 1 month at his *usual occupation;* and second, in terms of the time elapsed since his last employment (a) for at least 2 weeks and (b) for at least 1 month at *any* nonrelief job. The totally unemployable family heads have been eliminated from the tabulations which follow in order to permit comparison with the employable urban relief workers and WPA project workers.

Time Since Last Job at Usual Occupation

Long unemployment involves a deterioration of skill which lowers the reemployment opportunity of workers without affecting the distribution of their usual occupations. Accordingly, the information on usual occupations in this chapter is conditioned by the lapse of time since the family heads worked at their usual occupation.

The median time elapsed since the migrant family heads' last employment at their usual occupation was 18.5 months. It was accordingly substantially less than the median duration of 30.3 months for the urban workers [8] on resident relief in May 1934.[9] The distributions for both these groups are shown in table 42.

Nearly three-fifths of the migrant family heads had last worked at their usual occupation within 2 years of the time this study was made; and nearly two-fifths had worked at their usual occupation within 1 year. In contrast, only 43 percent of the urban workers on resident relief reported work at their usual occupation within 2 years, and only one-fourth reported a duration of less than 1 year.

For both groups, the workers displaced from their usual occupation since the depression (less than 5 years) comprised an overwhelming majority of the total. But among the migrant family heads the recently displaced workers by far outnumbered the long-time depression unemployed, while among urban workers on relief recent and long-time depression unemployment occurred in approximately equal proportions (table 42).

It is obvious, then, that by comparison with the resident relief population, the deterioration of skills had made less serious inroads upon the occupational resources of the migrant family heads. The shorter duration of unemployment of migrant family heads since

---

[8] The sample of urban workers on relief represents a resident relief group in May 1934, more than a year earlier than the time of the migrant family study. However, this disparity does not invalidate the comparison made. A survey of WPA workers conducted 7 months after the present study shows an even greater median duration of unemployment than was revealed in the urban workers' sample. The median duration of unemployment for the three groups was as follows:

Migrant Family Heads, September 1935_____ 18. 5 months
Urban Workers on Relief, May 1934_____ 30. 3 months
Economic Heads Employed on WPA, April 1936_____ 40. 6 months

See Shepherd, Susan M. and Bancroft, Gertrude, *Survey of Cases Certified for Works Program Employment in 13 Cities*, Research Bulletin, Series IV, Number 2, Division of Social Research, Works Progress Administration, Washington, D. C., 1937, p. 36.

[9] About seven-eighths of the urban workers' sample consisted of family heads.

their last job at usual occupation thus reinforces the conclusion drawn from the broad occupation comparisons in the preceding section. Not only did migrant families tend to fall into higher occupational classifications than urban relief workers, but their experience in the higher classification was also substantially more recent.

Table 42.—Duration of Unemployment Since Last Job of at Least 1 Month at Usual Occupation of Employable Economic Heads of Migrant Families and of Urban Workers on Relief May 1934 [1]

Duration of unemployment since last job of 1 month at usual occupation	Employable economic heads of migrant families [2]	Urban workers on relief May 1934 [1]
Total	4,468	198,130
	Percent distribution	
Total	100	100
Less than 5 years	83	85
Less than 2 years	59	43
Less than 3 months	11	7
3–5.9 months	11	6
6–11.9 months	17	13
12–23.9 months	20	17
2–4.9 years	24	42
Over 5 years	17	15
5–9.9 years	14	11
10 years or more	3	4
Average [3] duration (in months)	18.5	30.3

[1] Based on Palmer, Gladys L. and Wood, Katherine D., *Urban Workers on Relief*, Part I.—The Occupational Characteristics of Workers on Relief in Urban Areas May 1934, Research Monograph IV, Division of Social Research, Works Progress Administration, Washington, D. C., 1936.
[2] 1,021 family heads, who were unemployable, who never worked, and whose duration of unemployment at usual occupation was not ascertainable, are not included.
[3] Median.

Time Elapsed Since Last Job at Any Occupation

Data on the time elapsed since the last job at any occupation provide a basis for comparing the success of migrant families in finding work at any job, both before and after migration to another labor market, with the success of other needy groups which did not migrate. Comparison between the migrant families and the urban workers on resident relief presents a striking difference. Eliminating short-time jobs and calculating for purpose of comparison on the basis of jobs lasting at least 1 month, the median duration of unemployment was 7.8 months. In contrast, the median duration of unemployment for urban workers on relief in May 1934 was 22.7 months; and for WPA workers [10] in the last quarter of 1935 it was 24.0 months, more than three times as long (table 43).

About two-thirds of the migrant family heads had been unemployed for less than 1 year as compared with only about one-third

[10] Ninety-five percent of the WPA workers were family heads.

of the urban workers on relief. This disproportion between groups became even greater for those unemployed less than 6 months and less than 3 months. Among the urban workers on relief 41 percent had not worked since early in the depression as compared with only 11 percent of the migrant family heads.

It is clearly indicated that migrant family heads had been much more successful in finding work outside their usual occupation than the workers on resident relief (tables 42 and 43 and fig. 29). The median duration of unemployment for migrant families dropped from 18.5 months in terms of usual occupation to 7.8 months in terms of any occupation, while for the resident urban relief workers the decrease was only from 30.3 months to 22.7 months. This striking difference suggests that the shorter duration of unemployment of migrant families was the result of their access, through mobility, to another labor market. And, indeed, as table 44 shows, the low duration of unemployment is traceable principally to the jobs the family heads found after leaving settled residence. It should not be overlooked, however, that the median duration of unemployment among the families which did *not* find work after migration (13.1 months) was substantially lower than the median for resident relief workers.

Table 43.—Duration of Unemployment Since Last Job of at Least 1 Month at Any Occupation of Employable Economic Heads of Migrant Families, of Urban Workers on Relief May 1934,[1] and of Urban Workers on WPA October—December 1935 [2]

Duration of unemployment since last job at any occupation	Employable economic heads of migrant families [3]	Urban workers on relief May 1934	Urban workers on WPA October-December 1935
Total	3,997	206,394	347,802
	Percent distribution		
Total	100	100	100
Less than 5 years	97	92	88
Less than 2 years	86	51	50
Less than 3 months	23	8	5
3-5.9 months	20	8	8
6-11.9 months	23	16	13
12-23.9 months	20	19	24
2-4.9 years	11	41	38
Over 5 years	3	8	12
5-9.9 years	3	6	12
10 years or more	*	2	—
Average [4] duration (in months)	7.8	22.7	24.0

*Less than 0.5 percent.

[1] Based on Palmer, Gladys L. and Wood, Katherine D., *Urban Workers on Relief*, Part I.—The Occupational Characteristics of Workers on Relief in Urban Areas May 1934, Research Monograph IV, Division of Social Research, Works Progress Administration, Washington, D. C., 1936, p. 44.
[2] From unpublished data in the files of the Division of Social Research, Works Progress Administration.
[3] 1,492 family heads, who were unemployable, who worked less than 1 month at last job, whose duration of unemployment or occupation was not ascertainable, and those who never worked, are not included.
[4] Median.

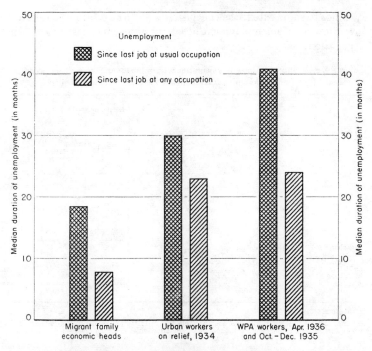

FIG. 29-UNEMPLOYMENT SINCE LAST JOB AT USUAL OCCUPATION
AND LAST JOB AT ANY OCCUPATION

ECONOMIC HEADS OF MIGRANT FAMILIES
URBAN WORKERS ON RELIEF 1934, AND
WPA WORKERS 1935 AND 1936

Sources: Tables 42,43 and Footnote 8, Chapter VI.   AF-2879, WPA

The fact that the short duration of unemployment of migrant family
heads resulted from (1) jobs secured outside their usual occupation
and (2) jobs secured after beginning migration suggests that many
families had turned to migratory-casual employment.   As an earlier
transient study showed, this is what actually took place.   Among
the family heads studied in *The Transient Unemployed* only 3 to 7
percent had usual occupations as migratory-casual workers; but 23
to 33 percent had migratory-casual work as their first job after
beginning migration, and 23 to 38 percent had migratory-casual work
as their last job before registering for transient relief.[11]   This fact not
only implies low earnings but also a lowered occupational status which

[11] See Webb, John N., *The Transient Unemployed*, Research Monograph III,
Division of Social Research, Works Progress Administration, Washington, D. C.,
1935, pp. 54–55 and appendix table 23B.

124 • MIGRANT FAMILIES

qualifies to some extent the conclusion to be drawn from the relatively low duration of unemployment of family heads since last job at usual occupation.

Table 44.—Duration of Unemployment Since Last Job of at Least 2 Weeks at Any Occupation of Employable Economic Heads of Migrant Families

Duration of unemployment since last job of at least 2 weeks at any occupation	Economic heads of migrant families		
	Total	Worked since leaving settled residence	Did not work since leaving settled residence
Total	4,098	2,248	1,850
	Percent distribution		
Total	100	100	100
Less than 3 months	23	35	10
3–5.9 months	20	21	16
6–11.9 months	22	23	21
12–23.9 months	20	16	25
More than 2 years	15	5	28
Average [1] duration (in months)	8.0	5.2	13.1

[1] Median.

NOTE.—1,391 family heads, who were unemployable, who had no settled residence, who never worked, or whose duration of unemployment or occupation was not ascertainable, are not included.

Chapter VII

CONCLUSIONS

THIS REPORT has been concerned with a detailed description of the characteristics and behavior of migrant families which received relief from the transient program during the operation of the Federal Emergency Relief Administration. As such, it has dealt with only one group among depression migrants. This fact should not, however, obscure the broader implications of the information presented. These families were one of the few groups which have left a sufficiently complete record to permit detailed analysis of population mobility during the depression.

The record of the families studied is also significant in its own right. "Mobility in trouble" is one of the most immediate problems related to the internal migration of the American population. In the administration of the broad program of public assistance now being developed by several Federal agencies, distressed population mobility is one of the problems still unsolved. For this reason alone the experience of the transient program warrants careful consideration.

THE NORMALITY OF TRANSIENT RELIEF FAMILIES

Relief for the needy migrant was one of several important experiments in public assistance administration during the depression. Because it departed radically from established procedures, the transient relief program was frequently the subject of criticism. A persistent theme of transient relief's critics, still heard today, is the argument that the transient population includes a large criminal element; that transients are lazy and degraded persons disturbing to settled community life, and therefore are "undesirables." Finally, and particularly during the operation of the transient program, transients were criticized as irresponsible and willful wanderers, out to see the country at the expense of those who would give them relief.

The common element in all these criticisms is the belief that transients are abnormal people. This belief is, on the face of it, highly suspect. The two elements of transiency are mobility and need of public assistance, neither of which is exceptional. The tendency toward mobility is one of the basic characteristics of the American population, as the rapid spread of population across the American continent and the birth-residence data of each decennial census amply prove. Nor can need of public assistance be pointed to as abnormal when it is remembered that, coincident with the operation of the transient program, the relief rolls included as many as 27,000,000 persons at one time. The type of criticism cited appears to be a counterpart of the argument that industrial unemployment exists because "some folks just won't work."

The present study of families registered at transient bureaus provides direct evidence on the normality of migrant families' behavior and characteristics. Comparisons of personal characteristics, for example, suggest that the transient families were, if anything, somewhat "above" the average family on relief. The majority of the families studied were young, experienced, and free from handicaps that would retard their reemployment by private industry.

In terms of ability to find work in a crowded labor market the family heads had been more successful than the great majority of relief family heads. The reabsorption of transient relief families proceeded at a much higher rate than the reabsorption of workers on the resident relief rolls. Family mobility could have been called excessive only by supposing that a small number of highly mobile families was typical of the entire group, which was not the case. Finally, when the motivation of these families is considered it becomes clear that cautiousness rather than irresponsibility governed the families' plans to migrate.

An illustration of the difficulty of depression migration will show the lack of realism in the belief that family migration resulted from a lack of responsibility. The following is a case history of a family on the margin of mobility:

In an industrial city of moderate size the head of a family of five had worked for a millwork manufacturer for 11 consecutive years up to January 1932 when the factory closed. During these 11 years weekly earnings varied, according to business conditions, from $20 to $35 a week. With no more than the average run of expenses incident to a growing family, the head had laid aside some $400 in savings and was carrying two insurance policies of modest size.

During the 5 years following the closing of the millwork plant, the head obtained two full-time jobs lasting about a year each. In between times the family lived on their savings, the proceeds obtained by cashing the insurance policies, on odd jobs, and local relief.

At first, the family had no thoughts of leaving the community because of the persistent hope, supported by recurring rumors, that the millwork factory would resume operations. Gradually the head came to realize that this was not likely to happen, and that his only employment asset—skill as a mill hand—was of little value so long as he remained where he was.

Had the family been willing to move in 1932 and, in addition, had known where to go while they had the means to make a self-supporting migration they might have avoided the "dead-end" in which they found themselves in 1937. With a wife and three children, no money, and an accumulation of debts, migration seemed impossible to the head who continued to realize the need for leaving the community but who found, in his own words, "Going is harder than thinking about it."

This summary illustrates the inertia that must be overcome before the migration of a needy family can occur. Bad as it is, the local situation is known; friends, the church, relief officials, the grocer, milkman, coal man, etc., have been as helpful as possible. How can the family live in another community where such assistance will not exist? The risk seems too great as long as any hope remains that work will be found locally. The transient relief program, however, was evidence that the time did come for many families when all of the real or imagined advantages of remaining where they were did not offset the hopelessness of their predicament. The break was made; families did leave their home communities; and when they came to be in need of public assistance, they learned of the legal concepts of residence and discovered that they were transients.

All these pieces of evidence point in the same direction. While none is conclusive in itself, the sum of the evidence directly contradicts the argument that transient families were "unworthy," "undeserving," and "undesirable."

Future efforts toward providing relief to nonresidents should recognize the fundamental normality of needy migrants. The transient relief problem does not call for special techniques of assistance based on the supposition that migrants in need are essentially different from residents in need. Indeed, the principal difference between migrant and resident is created artificially by legal settlement requirements— requirements that are customarily invoked only in the presence of need. Overemphasis upon the surface distinctions between transients and residents has heretofore been a persistent source of error in attempts to provide transient relief.

TRANSIENT RELIEF AND RESTRICTIONS UPON MOBILITY

Public action has frequently set up barriers against internal migration. Witness, for example, the fact that a number of States have long prohibited employment agencies from sending workers to jobs outside their State borders, and the time-honored use of vagrancy laws and legal settlement restrictions as means of penalizing out-of-State workers. After 1930, because of the intrusion of the relief problem, the restrictions put upon the mobility of needy persons became much more stringent and more generally applied. The border-blockades of Florida, Colorado, and California, as illustrations of such restrictions, have established a particularly dangerous precedent for interfering with the free flow of the American population in the future.

A less spectacular but more serious immobilizing force is the administration of general relief. Resident relief, whether work or direct relief, exacts proof of residence before the grant of assistance is made and continues the grant only as long as the applicant remains a resident. In so far as resident relief is the means of assisting the working population of a community to remain where it may again be absorbed by industry, it acts as a brake on wasteful migration. But when resident relief "freezes" the unemployed workers in a community where industry cannot upon revival reabsorb them, it prevents a desirable migration and perpetuates stranded populations.

During the depression the legal residence requirements for relief benefits placed a severe economic penalty upon the migrant in need of assistance outside his State of residence. Theoretically, however, the social necessity of population mobility during both boom and depression had not been reasonably questioned since the beginning of the nineteenth century. The defense of the residence requirements and the return-to-legal residence procedures has always been in terms of practical necessity in administering limited relief funds and never as a sound contribution to population policy.

One of the indirect results of the transient relief program was to neutralize, during the period of its operation, the tendency of the resident relief program toward penalizing migration already under way or accomplished. The transient program alleviated the distress accompanying population readjustment during the depression by providing relief to needy migrants who would otherwise have been ineligible on the grounds of nonresidence status. Accepting the premise that population mobility is desirable, and accepting the evidence that the families were not irresponsible wanderers, this function of the transient program assumes greater importance than is ordinarily recognized.

TRANSIENT RELIEF AND POPULATION REDISTRIBUTION

Obviously, however, the fact that the transient program neutralized some of the restrictions upon internal population mobility does not necessarily argue its usefulness. Migration as an end in itself has no particular virtue; and "the record of unguided migration," as has been demonstrated,[1] is in part a record of needless waste. The important question is whether any gain accrued from the total movement of the families. Did the families assisted by the transient program tend to migrate from the areas of less economic advantage to the areas of greater economic advantage?

To answer this question in generalized terms, it may be said that the greater part of the movement of the families which registered at transient bureaus produced no population displacement whatever because of the balanced give and take among the various States.

---

[1] Goodrich, Carter and Others, *Migration and Economic Opportunity*, Philadelphia: University of Pennsylvania Press, 1936, pp. 503–519.

Over and above this balanced movement, however, there remained an amount of net population displacement which showed clear geographical trends. These trends were predominantly westward, but also included a northward net movement out of the deep South into the industrial centers of the North.

Accordingly, the most significant characteristic of the net movement was a marked similarity to the net movement of the total American population during the prosperous decade from 1920 to 1930. But the similarity between the displacement of population resulting from the movement of transient-bureau families and the net displacement of the American population during the 1920's is not proof that social gains accrued from the transient bureaus' contribution to population redistribution.

The American "problem areas" have been demarked and recommendations have been ventured as to the desired geographical direction that future migrations should take.[2] The net displacement of the migrant families bears only a partial similarity to the ideal pattern of migration that the Study of Population Redistribution has constructed. This similarity consists chiefly in a large net emigration from the Great Plains and also in net emigration from the deep South northward, though this particular trend among migrant families was exceedingly feeble by comparison with the recommendation for a large scale emigration from the South. The remainder of the net migrant family movement bears little relationship to the ideal pattern, and even runs counter to it.

The movement of migrant families thus appears to be another instance in the record of waste involved in unguided migration and another illustration of the need for planned migration. These judgments are doubtless valid in the long view.[3] Under the exigencies of

---

[2] *Ibid.*, pp. 52–53. See also, Beck, P. G. and Forster, M. C., *Six Rural Problem Areas, Relief—Resources—Rehabilitation*, Research Monograph I, Division of Research, Statistics, and Finance, Federal Emergency Relief Administration, Washington, D. C., 1935.

[3] It may be pointed out, however, that the theoretical need for population redistribution is acceptable only when related to a disparity between the geographical concentration of population and resources. One of the recommendations for population redistribution is based upon the observation of "overpopulation" in the South. But the distress of the South results from existing economic relationships rather than a scarcity of resources. As T. J. Woofter, Jr. has pointed out, "Some observers conclude from the fact that the South ranks low in almost every index of wealth and culture that there are too many people in the area. As the economy of the region is at present organized, this is true, but this condition does not necessarily have to continue. More rational land use, more diversification of production and, above all, an increase in the standard of living of the people through the use of home-produced goods can provide for an increased southern rural population at a higher level of living." (See "Southern Population and Social Planning," *Social Forces*, Vol. 14, No. 1, October 1935, pp. 16–22.)

a severe depression, however, the logic of the long view becomes tenuous, and the blue-prints for the future redistribution of the American population must be set aside until the problem of industrial unemployment has been solved. Outlines of the course population distribution should take, even when postulating normal times, are more convincing in describing where the flow should *originate* than in describing what its *destination* should be. And when millions of gainful workers are unemployed, where does economic opportunity lie?

These facts are of special significance in view of the difficulties which recent experimental attempts at planned migration have already encountered and which any future attempts have to face. A planned migration of any considerable numbers from the stranded populations will involve problems of extreme complication and magnitude— problems of an upset labor market at urban destinations and of an agricultural surplus at rural destinations, not to mention the problems of financing a subsidy for a large number of migrants. The inevitable conclusion must be that the problem of population redistribution, difficult at any time, is scarcely possible of solution during a depression.

If no one can trace abstractly the direction in which depression population movement should flow, no one can appraise abstractly the immediate gains and losses of the depression movements which did occur. Nevertheless, it is difficult to question the wisdom of the individuals who took part in the movement of the families studied here. It must be borne in mind that the families aided by the transient program were by and large normal and responsible groups, and that their migration represented a search for more favorable opportunity. Notwithstanding any appraisal of the geographical trends involved, the migration of transient-bureau families did make sense to the migrants. The extremely high turnover rate of transient relief families is itself sufficient evidence that the families were the best judges of whether they should migrate and of where their destination should be.

IMPLICATIONS FOR THE FUTURE

It remains to consider what bearing the findings of this report have upon the continuing problem of need for public assistance arising out of family group migration. As a factual study of families which were assisted by the one national experiment with transient relief the report should be of some help in looking to the future. Taken as a whole the evidence of the report argues against the need for a separate program of transient relief based upon the assumption that needy migrants are somehow inherently different from needy residents. Specific evidence has been presented to show that families receiving aid from the transient program were in no way unusual except for their mobility; that they were young, with employable heads, in most instances; that their migrations were cautious in nature and were undertaken in an attempt to overcome difficulties caused by the depression; that their efforts at relocation, by and large, were successful and therefore made only temporary demands upon the transient relief program.

In view of this evidence of the essential normality of transient relief families and the additional fact that all States contributed and all States received these migrants, it might seem that the solution of the transient relief problem lies in the complete integration of transient with resident relief by modifying the existing relief procedures and requirements that artificially create the separate category of the "transient."

The experience of the past, however, stands in the way of accepting as likely of realization so simple a solution. States become acutely aware of the inflow of needy outsiders because of the public assistance problem that results, while there is little but the occasional request for verification of legal residence to remind the individual States that the outflow of their own citizens creates a similar problem elsewhere. Moreover, the principle of legal residence which has for so many years governed the attitudes of States and their subdivisions toward relief is based upon the belief that every person "belongs" to some community and should expect assistance only in that specific place. And, finally, there is the obvious fact that some few States have a particular attraction for migrants, with the result that these States receive many more migrants than they give. Such States are prone to insist that by giving relief to nonresidents they only increase the inflow. Yet no one has demonstrated that the hardships and uncertainties of migration are undertaken for the sake of transient relief, and border blockades and the refusal to give any form of assistance have been singularly ineffective in stopping the inflow.

The implications of this report, then, are clear, though its conclusions are neither novel nor startling. The transient relief problem does not originate in, nor can it be confined to, any particular region. All States are affected, but in different degrees. It is difficult to see how a total solution is to be achieved unless there is a coordination of efforts from outside the individual States. The problem is national, and the need of the moment is Federal leadership in achieving a solution which would take account both of the needs of the migrant and the interests of the States.

Appendixes

Appendix A

SUPPLEMENTARY TABLES

Table 1.—Reason Migrant Families Left Settled Residence

Reason for leaving settled residence	Migrant families	
	Number	Percent
Total	4,247	100
Economic distress	2,941	69
Unemployment	1,705	40
Layoffs attributed to depression	1,232	29
Completed job of definite duration	109	3
Locality too small	108	3
Drought	60	1
Migration of industry	16	*
Layoffs attributed to other causes [1]	180	4
Inadequate earnings	308	7
Reduced to part-time work	239	6
Forced into lower occupational status	27	1
Seasonal work only	20	*
Reduced wages	22	*
Unable to work in particular community	113	3
Physical disability	80	2
Personal handicaps	33	1
Farming failure	333	8
Dust or drought	196	5
Floods	13	*
Other failures	124	3
Business failure	142	3
Attributed to depression	135	3
Attributed to drought	7	*
Inadequate relief	146	3
Unwilling to be on relief	46	1
Unwilling to apply	26	1
Unwilling to continue	20	*
Evicted from rented or owned domicile	71	2
Relatives unable to continue support	51	1
Miscellaneous economic difficulties [2]	26	1
Personal distress	1,040	25
Ill-health	448	11
Unhealthful climate	388	9
Inadequate medical care	60	2
Domestic difficulties	254	6
Desertion	34	1
Separation and divorce	128	3
Quarrels with relatives	35	1
Death of breadwinner	44	1
Other domestic difficulties [3]	13	*

See footnotes at end of table.

Table 1.—Reason Migrant Families Left Settled Residence—Continued

Reason for leaving settled residence	Migrant families	
	Number	Percent
Personal distress—Continued.		
Disliked separation from relatives or friends	167	4
Community disapproval	42	1
Social handicaps, prison records, etc	14	*
Illegitimate children	4	*
Other community disapproval ⁴	24	1
Personal dislike of community	86	2
Climate as personal factor	8	*
Death as personal factor	11	1
Boredom and other repulsions	67	1
Miscellaneous personal difficulties ³	43	1
Not in distress	266	6
Job required travel	144	3
Left job	73	2
Left farm	14	*
Left business	22	1
Other ⁶	13	*

* Less than 0.5 percent.

[1] Most of these families reported that new managers brought their own crews or that they were dismissed to make a job for the manager's relatives (see history 1, pp. 21–22).

[2] Includes families whose pension was discontinued, whose scholarship expired, who wished to avoid high cost of commutation, etc.

[3] Includes families in fear of ex-husband, those attempting to secure support of child, those searching for fiance, etc.

[4] Includes families moving because of unpopularity growing out of political campaigns, because of racial prejudice, etc.

[5] Includes families fleeing from revolution, lack of school facilities, fear of earthquakes, etc.

[6] Includes families leaving to look after personal business, to take vacations, etc.

NOTE.—81 families, whose reason for leaving settled residence was not ascertainable, are not included.

Table 2.—Reason Migrant Families Left Settled Residence, and State or Region of Settled Residence

State or region of settled residence	Total number	Reasons for leaving settled residence									
		Percent distribution									
		Total	Economic distress					Personal distress			Not in distress
			Unemployment	Inadequate earnings	Farm failure	Inadequate relief	Other economic distress	Ill-health	Domestic trouble	Other personal distress	
Total	4,195	100	40	7	8	4	9	11	6	9	6
New England	129	100	58	5	4	4	8	7	4	6	4
New York	210	100	41	5	1	1	9	18	4	9	12
Pennsylvania and New Jersey	237	100	40	7	1	2	14	12	9	10	5
Delaware, Maryland, and District of Columbia	66	100	44	8	3	3	9	9	6	14	4
Kentucky and West Virginia	153	100	41	10	4	7	13	5	8	9	3
Michigan	112	100	44	7	4	5	10	9	9	8	4
Ohio and Indiana	212	100	42	10	3	3	8	12	10	5	7
Illinois	213	100	41	6	2	7	12	8	7	10	7
Minnesota and Wisconsin	113	100	42	5	6	6	5	15	7	8	6
Iowa	84	100	47	8	7	3	7	6	8	7	7
Virginia and North Carolina	141	100	45	5	4	3	18	3	6	8	8
Georgia and South Carolina	115	100	39	9	5	3	10	5	11	10	8
Tennessee	100	100	44	10	6	3	14	3	9	5	6
Alabama and Mississippi	149	100	36	13	10	7	11	7	5	7	4
Florida	108	100	44	9	2	5	9	10	5	10	6
Missouri	266	100	41	4	13	7	6	10	5	9	5
Arkansas	142	100	42	5	14	6	7	11	6	6	3
Louisiana	67	100	43	12	4	6	4	9	5	11	6
Oklahoma	281	100	38	11	12	9	5	12	3	6	4
Texas	235	100	43	6	6	4	5	15	5	9	7
North Dakota and South Dakota	94	100	18	5	54	—	13	3	4	1	2
Nebraska	116	100	36	5	20	5	6	8	4	9	7
Kansas	140	100	33	8	17	4	7	13	1	8	9
Wyoming and Montana	79	100	29	4	19	3	15	20	4	6	—
Colorado	115	100	34	10	16	4	2	18	3	7	6
Idaho	53	100	32	7	11	4	8	11	9	10	8
Washington and Oregon	130	100	36	6	2	5	10	13	6	16	6
Utah and Nevada	47	100	38	9	7	2	13	17	6	2	6
Arizona and New Mexico	78	100	39	6	5	3	9	19	4	10	5
California	210	100	44	7	*	3	4	9	4	21	8

* Less than 0.5 percent.

NOTE.—133 families, whose settled residence was in a foreign country or in U. S. possessions and whose State of settled residence or reason for leaving was not ascertainable, are not included.

Table 3.—Type of Contact Migrant Families Had at Destination, and State or Region of Destination

State or region of destination	Total number	Type of contact							
		Percent distribution							
		Total	Definite contact				No definite contact		
			Former residence	Residence of relatives, etc.	Skill of head in demand	Other	Rumors	Advertisement	Chance
Total	3,869	100	12	43	2	23	16	1	3
New England	118	100	12	45	1	26	14	1	1
New York	226	100	17	36	2	22	21	—	2
Pennsylvania and New Jersey	205	100	7	55	2	24	11	—	1
Delaware, Maryland, and District of Columbia	102	100	9	48	4	21	15	—	3
Kentucky and West Virginia	60	100	3	57	10	17	10	---	3
Michigan	108	100	19	42	2	18	11	2	6
Ohio and Indiana	187	100	14	49	2	20	12	—	3
Illinois	174	100	13	50	3	19	12	—	3
Minnesota and Wisconsin	166	100	25	49	1	17	7	*	1
Iowa	50	100	12	60	2	14	6	—	6
Virginia and North Carolina	75	100	15	45	4	20	12	---	4
Georgia and South Carolina	111	100	10	51	6	19	13	---	1
Tennessee	76	100	9	50	3	20	14	—	4
Alabama and Mississippi	99	100	17	54	3	19	7	—	—
Florida	104	100	11	29	5	25	26	1	3
Missouri	177	100	19	41	3	27	16	*	3
Arkansas	89	100	10	33	2	43	11	—	1
Louisiana	56	100	7	32	—	27	32	—	2
Oklahoma	101	100	7	50	4	21	14	—	4
Texas	193	100	10	34	4	29	21	—	2
North Dakota and South Dakota	13	†	†	†	†	†	†	†	†
Nebraska	49	100	6	47	—	31	16	—	—
Kansas	157	100	10	52	3	20	10	*	5
Wyoming and Montana	43	100	7	44	2	30	12	—	5
Colorado	134	100	11	31	2	34	22	—	—
Idaho	121	100	12	43	1	19	6	17	2
Washington and Oregon	264	100	17	38	*	16	19	4	6
Utah and Nevada	57	100	19	25	2	26	26	—	2
Arizona and New Mexico	135	100	8	24	1	53	13	*	1
California	419	100	9	44	1	17	22	2	5

*Less than 0.5 percent.
† Percent not calculated on a base of fewer than 20.

NOTE.—459 families, which had no destination, whose reason for selecting the State of destination, type of contact at the State of destination, or State of destination was not ascertainable, and whose destination was in a foreign country or in the U. S. possessions, are not included.

Table 4.—Objectives Sought by Migrant Families at Destination, and State or Region of Destination

State or region of destination	Total number	Objectives sought								
		Percent distribution								
		Total	Economic betterment					Personal objectives		
			Hope of job	Promise of job	To secure farm	To secure help	Other	Health	To rejoin relatives, etc.	Other
Total	3,974	100	44	14	5	11	5	10	8	3
New England	119	100	42	24	8	10	3	2	9	2
New York	234	100	52	16	—	10	5	5	7	5
Pennsylvania and New Jersey	208	100	34	17	1	19	6	4	17	2
Delaware, Maryland, and District of Columbia	111	100	41	14	1	17	3	4	10	10
Kentucky and West Virginia	61	100	41	13	3	23	3	5	10	2
Michigan	112	100	53	14	2	10	3	3	7	8
Ohio and Indiana	191	100	46	21	3	15	2	1	8	4
Illinois	179	100	45	13	3	13	4	4	13	5
Minnesota and Wisconsin	171	100	37	14	2	25	5	7	6	4
Iowa	51	100	35	16	—	19	4	2	20	4
Virginia and North Carolina	78	100	48	11	1	13	3	6	13	5
Georgia and South Carolina	114	100	47	16	2	16	3	6	7	3
Tennessee	79	100	49	11	3	18	5	5	5	4
Alabama and Mississippi	101	100	35	18	5	17	2	3	18	2
Florida	105	100	43	18	2	8	9	14	1	5
Missouri	178	100	40	18	8	13	5	4	12	*
Arkansas	90	100	45	11	13	10	4	8	7	2
Louisiana	58	100	54	10	3	11	3	9	7	3
Oklahoma	103	100	48	16	7	12	3	1	10	3
Texas	201	100	48	15	1	11	5	11	4	5
North Dakota and South Dakota	13	†	†	†	†	†	†	†	†	†
Nebraska	50	100	42	26	6	8	—	4	12	2
Kansas	158	100	49	13	4	10	7	4	11	2
Wyoming and Montana	46	100	52	22	2	9	2	7	—	6
Colorado	139	100	40	10	4	4	4	33	1	4
Idaho	122	100	31	6	44	4	—	10	4	1
Washington and Oregon	272	100	48	8	11	10	4	8	4	7
Utah and Nevada	60	100	43	20	2	3	7	12	5	8
Arizona and New Mexico	136	100	24	10	3	2	6	50	4	1
California	434	100	47	10	1	6	3	22	6	5

*Less than 0.5 percent.
† Percent not calculated on a base of fewer than 20.

NOTE.—354 families, which had no destination, whose reason for selecting the State of destination or whose State of destination was not ascertainable, and whose destination was in a foreign country or in the U. S. possessions, are not included.

Table 5.—State of Origin and State of Transient Bureau Registration of Migrant Families, June 30, 1935 [1]

State of origin	Total	State of transient bureau registration								
		Alabama	Arizona	Arkansas	California	Colorado	Connecticut	Delaware	District of Columbia	Florida
Total	30,304	417	225	693	6,044	1,847	27	49	379	717
Alabama	596	—	2	16	29	7	—	—	6	38
Arizona	466	—	—	8	239	65	—	—	1	3
Arkansas	1,161	21	15	—	188	39	—	—	1	7
California	1,193	—	14	16	—	103	2	2	8	18
Colorado	838	13	7	14	279	—	2	—	3	2
Connecticut	207	1	—	1	22	2	—	—	3	9
Delaware	53	—	—	—	1	—	—	—	2	—
District of Columbia	119	3	1	2	18	1	2	2	—	9
Florida	534	25	—	8	34	7	1	—	22	—
Georgia	690	48	1	12	25	3	1	1	17	198
Idaho [2]	327	16	1	2	86	25	—	—	1	—
Illinois	1,264	12	10	19	281	53	1	1	12	35
Indiana	685	1	—	6	119	35	—	—	7	11
Iowa	522	1	2	1	126	47	—	—	—	3
Kansas	1,091	—	7	23	193	335	—	—	2	5
Kentucky	657	16	5	11	40	11	2	—	9	11
Louisiana	504	18	4	47	64	6	1	—	2	11
Maine	78	—	—	—	8	—	—	—	1	—
Maryland	209	1	—	—	13	2	—	14	26	7
Massachusetts	284	1	1	—	34	3	2	—	7	15
Michigan	799	14	4	5	127	14	—	—	4	28
Minnesota	334	2	2	1	69	30	—	—	—	7
Mississippi	609	43	2	25	61	4	—	—	4	7
Missouri	1,818	14	10	65	381	235	—	—	4	3
Montana	264	—	1	—	40	2	—	—	4	3
Nebraska	809	—	1	3	160	151	—	—	—	5
Nevada	120	1	1	—	57	9	—	1	—	—
New Hampshire	19	—	—	—	2	—	—	—	1	1
New Jersey	592	—	—	—	52	6	3	6	6	27
New Mexico	369	1	23	5	136	112	—	—	—	1

New York	1,074	4	5	3	255	14	8	5	27	57
North Carolina	409	9	1	1	18	1	7	—	49	31
North Dakota	318	—	—	1	30	17	—	—	—	—
Ohio	843	14	1	4	196	17	2	—	12	36
Oklahoma	2,633	15	51	213	916	228	—	—	1	4
Oregon	503	5	1	1	233	19	—	12	2	1
Pennsylvania	1,140	—	1	3	138	18	1	—	21	27
Rhode Island	59	11	—	1	6	—	—	—	—	2
South Carolina	299	—	—	4	6	1	1	—	29	15
South Dakota	521	—	2	1	65	12	—	—	—	—
Tennessee	687	63	4	39	68	7	1	—	12	32
Texas	1,971	26	32	130	624	79	—	—	10	17
Utah	239	—	—	—	140	33	—	—	—	—
Vermont	86	—	—	—	4	—	—	—	—	1
Virginia	375	7	4	—	17	1	—	2	51	13
Washington	631	12	1	1	300	14	1	—	2	5
West Virginia	341	1	7	1	15	3	—	2	14	8
Wisconsin	318	—	—	1	45	33	—	—	—	2
Wyoming	227	—	1	—	36	43	—	—	—	—
U. S. possessions	119	—	—	—	16	—	—	—	—	—
Foreign countries	300	—	—	—	32	—	1	1	—	8

See footnotes at end of table.

Table 5.—State of Origin and State of Transient Bureau Registration of Migrant Families, June 30, 1935—Continued

State of origin	State of transient bureau registration										
	Georgia	Idaho [2]	Illinois	Indiana	Iowa	Kansas	Kentucky	Louisiana	Maine	Maryland	Massachusetts
Total	393	973	1,525	316	394	1,372	54	820	12	275	80
Alabama	74	—	41	4	—	6	2	66	—	—	1
Arizona	—	7	6	9	13	10	2	5	—	1	—
Arkansas	4	35	60	13	26	124	2	84	—	1	4
California	7	43	81	13	10	56	2	23	—	11	1
Colorado	1	107	19	3	—	69	1	2	—	1	—
Connecticut	—	—	5	2	—	1	—	2	4	2	5
Delaware	1	—	1	—	—	1	—	1	—	3	—
District of Columbia	4	—	6	1	—	1	—	1	—	10	—
Florida	61	—	18	8	—	4	2	28	—	12	2
Georgia	—	—	32	8	1	1	2	29	—	5	—
Idaho [3]	—	—	2	1	2	7	—	30	—	—	1
Illinois	4	7	154	59	46	45	2	4	—	3	3
Indiana	6	—	30	—	9	17	3	6	—	3	1
Iowa	—	35	22	4	—	32	—	6	—	1	—
Kansas	1	72	—	2	20	—	—	—	—	—	—
Kentucky	6	—	40	45	3	7	—	11	—	2	1
Louisiana	4	—	45	1	2	8	—	—	—	3	8
Maine	1	—	1	—	1	1	—	—	—	—	—
Maryland	3	—	10	1	1	3	1	1	2	6	—
Massachusetts	—	—	11	3	2	2	—	4	—	—	—
Michigan	6	7	158	36	8	8	3	11	—	4	1
Minnesota	—	—	28	4	29	7	1	5	—	—	—
Mississippi	5	28	132	3	4	11	—	116	—	3	3
Missouri	4	50	98	17	73	357	3	37	—	2	2
Montana	—	—	2	1	1	12	—	1	—	—	—
Nebraska	—	100	22	2	37	41	—	1	1	—	1
Nevada	—	7	3	—	1	4	—	—	2	—	—
New Hampshire	—	—	—	—	—	—	—	—	1	—	1
New Jersey	5	7	12	6	1	1	1	5	—	—	2
New Mexico	—	—	1	1	—	15	—	2	—	12	—

State										
New York	10	7	77	5	8	5	3	11	1	24	9
North Carolina	28	—	6	1	—	2	2	8	—	23	—
North Dakota	—	28	6	27	1	—	—	3	—	10	2
Ohio	24	—	83	2	7	13	6	12	1	10	2
Oklahoma	4	64	25	2	15	343	—	56	—	2	1
Oregon	—	—	3	—	5	6	—	2	—	40	—
Pennsylvania	5	28	43	11	1	4	1	10	—	1	6
Rhode Island	1	7	2	—	—	—	—	4	—	15	4
South Carolina	53	164	2	1	25	5	2	1	—	—	—
South Dakota	—	—	10	—	—	—	—	28	—	—	—
Tennessee	43	14	53	10	3	15	4	187	—	4	1
Texas	14	21	41	8	13	93	2	—	—	4	1
Utah	2	—	3	—	1	3	—	—	—	—	—
Vermont	8	—	3	1	12	5	1	8	—	52	6
Virginia	3	71	13	1	4	12	1	1	—	—	—
Washington	3	—	15	1	3	4	1	4	—	9	1
West Virginia	—	—	11	6	1	5	5	4	—	9	1
Wisconsin	1	57	80	5	12	5	1	3	—	2	—
Wyoming	—	7	2	1	4	12	1	1	—	—	6
U.S. possessions	1	—	2	—	1	—	—	3	—	—	—
Foreign countries	—	—	8	1	2	4	—	3	—	3	8

See footnotes at end of table.

Table 5.—State of Origin and State of Transient Bureau Registration of Migrant Families, June 30, 1935—Continued

State of origin	Michigan	Minnesota	Mississippi	Missouri	Montana	Nebraska	Nevada	New Hampshire	New Jersey	New Mexico	New York
Total	679	359	128	1,027	99	289	42	131	538	714	1,746
Alabama	14	2	16	12	-	1	1	1	4	5	8
Arizona	-	-	1	6	-	3	2	-	2	42	2
Arkansas	34	1	16	119	-	9	1	-	1	25	4
California	18	12	1	59	5	30	10	2	6	43	40
Colorado	8	4	1	31	1	10	6	-	3	60	5
Connecticut	-	1	1	3	-	-	-	6	9	2	94
Delaware	4	-	-	-	-	-	-	-	6	-	8
District of Columbia	17	1	6	2	-	-	-	1	3	4	14
Florida	17	2	10	6	1	-	-	-	18	4	81
Georgia	-	-	-	3	1	1	1	1	10	3	24
Idaho	1	1	4	3	5	1	2	-	-	3	1
Illinois	77	28	4	161	4	21	1	1	13	13	44
Indiana	81	3	2	21	1	7	-	-	3	5	7
Iowa	4	40	-	36	3	36	1	-	1	13	9
Kansas	1	6	3	149	5	23	-	-	1	30	8
Kentucky	40	2	3	22	1	2	1	-	1	14	9
Louisiana	4	-	8	19	-	2	-	-	1	10	17
Maine	2	-	-	1	1	1	1	22	2	4	10
Maryland	4	-	-	1	-	-	-	-	12	3	24
Massachusetts	5	2	-	3	1	3	-	31	8	1	88
Michigan	13	17	5	16	3	7	-	2	11	7	51
Minnesota	6	-	2	9	2	4	-	-	2	1	5
Mississippi	42	1	-	36	-	4	-	-	1	3	4
Missouri	2	10	3	-	6	42	4	-	2	43	15
Montana	-	16	-	3	-	4	-	1	1	1	2
Nebraska	6	11	-	50	6	-	-	-	1	9	5
Nevada	1	-	-	2	-	-	-	-	1	4	2
New Hampshire	-	3	1	1	-	2	-	-	2	-	5
New Jersey	6	3	1	-	-	-	-	-	-	2	283
New Mexico	5	1	1	8	2	-	-	-	1	-	2

New York	43	5	—	10	1	5	1	14	148	6	—
North Carolina	3	—	—	5	—	1	—	1	17	2	33
North Dakota	1	47	3	1	10	2	2	1	—	1	2
Ohio	90	8	4	17	1	5	—	—	5	12	71
Oklahoma	4	4	3	79	1	13	2	—	1	136	5
Oregon	3	4	3	2	4	3	1	—	1	7	1
Pennsylvania	29	4	1	7	2	7	—	—	182	11	315
Rhode Island	2	—	3	—	—	—	—	4	4	2	12
South Carolina	4	1	—	3	—	3	—	1	9	1	33
South Dakota	4	62	—	11	10	7	—	—	1	2	4
Tennessee	36	3	8	33	1	—	—	—	1	8	14
Texas	12	7	17	50	3	14	1	1	6	148	20
Utah	—	—	—	4	1	2	2	34	—	2	1
Vermont	1	—	—	—	—	1	—	—	3	4	22
Virginia	5	1	1	4	1	—	—	—	22	2	47
Washington	4	8	—	12	10	2	1	—	4	4	3
West Virginia	13	4	—	2	1	2	—	—	6	1	6
Wisconsin	10	34	—	3	3	4	—	1	1	6	11
Wyoming	—	3	1	2	2	6	1	—	—	5	1
U. S. possessions	—	—	—	—	—	—	—	—	—	—	82
Foreign countries	3	1	—	1	2	1	—	5	1	—	192

See footnotes at end of table.

Table 5.—State of Origin and State of Transient Bureau Registration of Migrant Families, June 30, 1935—Continued

State of transient bureau registration

State of origin	North Carolina	North Dakota	Ohio	Oklahoma	Oregon	Pennsylvania	Rhode Island	South Carolina	South Dakota	Tennessee	Texas
Total	48	11	1,480	607	755	594	51	193	5	919	1,073
Alabama	2	—	59	3	4	8	—	14	—	113	28
Arizona	—	—	2	5	12	1	—	—	—	5	20
Arkansas	—	—	23	91	8	4	—	3	—	101	96
California	1	—	31	30	141	13	—	—	—	19	68
Colorado	—	—	10	16	34	3	—	—	—	4	9
Connecticut	—	—	4	1	1	7	—	—	—	—	4
Delaware	—	—	—	—	1	27	—	3	—	6	—
District of Columbia	4	—	7	2	1	5	—	16	—	37	3
Florida	8	—	34	3	1	21	8	40	—	89	35
Georgia	—	—	43	—	—	15	—	—	—	—	19
Idaho [2]	—	3	2	3	42	1	1	2	1	35	4
Illinois	—	1	65	11	20	13	—	1	—	24	34
Indiana	—	—	84	4	7	7	—	—	1	2	14
Iowa	—	—	4	4	22	2	—	—	—	2	12
Kansas	1	1	11	33	24	4	—	—	—	—	25
Kentucky	—	—	217	4	2	7	—	3	—	70	15
Louisiana	—	—	26	17	2	2	3	—	—	30	139
Maine	—	—	3	1	—	1	—	1	—	7	1
Maryland	—	—	13	1	1	38	15	1	—	1	1
Massachusetts	—	—	11	—	2	12	—	—	—	—	1
Michigan	1	1	139	4	10	15	—	2	—	15	13
Minnesota	—	—	5	—	14	4	—	5	—	2	9
Mississippi	—	—	23	15	—	1	—	1	1	59	27
Missouri	—	—	39	51	26	7	—	—	—	51	48
Montana	—	—	1	2	20	—	—	—	—	—	—
Nebraska	—	1	7	6	60	2	—	—	—	1	11
Nevada	—	—	2	2	6	1	—	—	—	1	3
New Hampshire	—	—	1	—	1	—	—	—	—	1	—
New Jersey	1	—	16	—	2	105	2	3	—	4	2
New Mexico	—	—	1	15	2	—	—	—	—	4	13

New York	1	—	110	1	12	92	11	3	—	16	17
North Carolina	—	—	20	1	1	10	—	45	—	32	5
North Dakota	—	—	2	—	36	—	—	—	—	—	2
Ohio	1	—	—	4	5	57	3	2	—	37	13
Oklahoma	1	—	19	—	20	3	—	2	1	27	293
Oregon	—	—	2	3	—	2	—	—	—	—	7
Pennsylvania	—	—	161	—	3	—	3	5	—	11	17
Rhode Island	1	1	4	—	—	3	—	—	—	—	—
South Carolina	18	—	10	4	2	17	—	—	—	21	7
South Dakota	—	1	3	—	30	—	—	—	—	1	1
Tennessee	2	—	94	18	2	3	—	22	—	—	26
Texas	1	—	26	242	21	8	—	5	—	51	—
Utah	—	—	2	—	9	—	—	—	—	—	3
Vermont	—	—	2	—	—	1	—	—	—	—	1
Virginia	3	—	26	1	3	30	2	7	—	23	9
Washington	—	—	4	2	129	3	—	1	1	4	4
West Virginia	1	1	97	3	2	37	—	5	—	14	3
Wisconsin	1	—	10	2	7	1	—	1	—	2	3
Wyoming	—	1	—	1	9	1	1	—	—	—	5
U.S. possessions	—	—	—	—	—	—	—	—	—	—	—
Foreign countries	—	—	1	1	—	—	2	—	—	1	3

See footnotes at end of table.

Table 5.—State of Origin and State of Transient Bureau Registration of Migrant Families, June 30, 1935—Continued

State of origin	State of transient bureau registration						
	Utah	Vermont	Virginia	Washington	West Virginia	Wisconsin	Wyoming
Total	146	—	233	1,394	41	210	180
Alabama			3	1			3
Arizona	1		1	10		2	
Arkansas	1		2	16		2	4
California	26		1	166	1	10	15
Colorado	10			86		3	16
Connecticut			2	2			1
Delaware			1			1	
District of Columbia	2		6	5	1	1	2
Florida	3		6	5	1	3	
Georgia			12				
Idaho ²	25		2	95	2	1	6
Illinois	3		1	24	1	51	6
Indiana	2			14		6	3
Iowa				25		8	1
Kansas	8			53		3	11
Kentucky	1		11	6	3	2	3
Louisiana	1		1	4	1	1	1
Maine				1			
Maryland	1		13	2	2	2	1
Massachusetts	1		2	3	1		
Michigan	2			23		16	3
Minnesota			7	53		23	
Mississippi				1		4	13
Missouri	3		2	61	1	13	5
Montana	2		1	83		6	
Nebraska	2			95		3	10
Nevada	1			3			5
New Hampshire	1						
New Jersey			4	1		2	
New Mexico	4			6			7

New York	2	—	13	10	1	9	5
North Carolina	2	—	51	3	1	—	1
North Dakota	1	—	1	117	9	5	1
Ohio	4	—	5	12	—	6	6
Oklahoma	2	—	1	51	1	3	19
Oregon	4	—	15	150	5	1	3
Pennsylvania	1	—	—	5	—	4	3
Rhode Island	—	—	15	—	3	—	—
South Carolina	—	—	1	—	—	1	1
South Dakota	7	—	—	88	3	2	—
Tennessee	2	—	18	6	3	3	11
Texas	6	—	—	21	2	—	2
Utah	—	—	—	11	—	2	1
Vermont	—	—	—	2	—	1	1
Virginia	1	—	—	2	2	1	—
Washington	2	—	1	6	—	2	3
West Virginia	1	—	34	25	—	1	2
Wisconsin	10	—	—	22	—	1	—
Wyoming	—	—	—	9	—	—	—
U. S. possessions	1	—	—	12	—	3	—
Foreign countries							

[1] Division of Transient Activities, *Quarterly Census of Transients Under Care*, June 30, 1935, Federal Emergency Relief Administration, Washington, D. C. Families registered in State of origin are not included.

[2] Idaho transient bureau case load estimated on the basis of June 15, 1935, *Midmonthly Census of Transient Activities*. Origins of the Idaho case load estimated on the basis of the migrant family sample study.

Table 6.—Net Population Displacement and Reciprocated Movement Through Migrant Family Emigration and Immigration [1]

State	Migrant families		Net displacement		Recipro-cated movement
	Emigrating from	Immigrat-ing to	Gain	Loss	
Total [2]	29,885	29,885	10,524	10,524	19,361
Alabama	596	417	—	179	417
Arizona	466	225	—	241	225
Arkansas	1,161	693	—	468	693
California	1,193	5,996	4,803	—	1,193
Colorado	838	1,847	1,009	—	838
Connecticut	207	27	—	180	27
Delaware	53	48	—	5	48
District of Columbia	119	379	260	—	119
Florida	534	709	175	—	534
Georgia	690	393	—	297	393
Idaho	[3] 327	[3] 966	639	—	327
Illinois	1,264	1,515	251	—	1,264
Indiana	685	315	—	370	315
Iowa	522	391	—	131	391
Kansas	1,091	1,368	277	—	1,091
Kentucky	657	54	—	603	54
Louisiana	504	816	312	—	504
Maine	78	12	—	66	12
Maryland	209	272	63	—	209
Massachusetts	284	72	—	212	72
Michigan	799	676	—	123	676
Minnesota	334	358	24	—	334
Mississippi	609	128	—	481	128
Missouri	1,818	1,026	—	792	1,026
Montana	264	97	—	167	97
Nebraska	809	288	—	521	288
Nevada	120	42	—	78	42
New Hampshire	19	126	107	—	19
New Jersey	592	537	—	55	537
New Mexico	369	714	345	—	369
New York	1,074	1,472	398	—	1,074
North Carolina	409	48	—	361	48
North Dakota	318	11	—	307	11
Ohio	843	1,479	636	—	843
Oklahoma	2,633	606	—	2,027	606
Oregon	503	755	252	—	503
Pennsylvania	1,140	594	—	546	594
Rhode Island	59	48	—	11	48
South Carolina	299	193	—	106	193
South Dakota	521	5	—	516	5
Tennessee	687	918	231	—	687
Texas	1,971	1,070	—	901	1,070
Utah	239	145	—	94	145
Vermont	86	—	—	86	—
Virginia	375	233	—	142	233
Washington	631	1,373	742	—	631
West Virginia	341	41	—	300	41
Wisconsin	318	207	—	111	207
Wyoming	227	180	—	47	180

[1] Division of Transient Activities, *Quarterly Census of Transients Under Care,* June 30, 1935, Federal Emergency Relief Administration, Washington, D. C.
[2] 419 families emigrating from U. S. possessions or foreign countries are not included.
[3] Idaho transient bureau case load estimated on the basis of June 15, 1935, *Midmonthly Census of Transient Activities.* Origins of the Idaho case load estimated on the basis of the migrant family sample study.

Table 7.—Migrant Families [1] Emigrating per 1,000 Families in General Population 1930,[2] by State

State	Families in general population 1930	Migrant families emigrating from State	Migrant families emigrating per 1,000 families in general population
Total	27,547,200	29,885	1.08
Nevada	18,730	120	6.41
Arizona	91,871	466	5.07
Oklahoma	531,183	2,633	4.96
Wyoming	48,441	227	4.69
New Mexico	89,490	369	4.12
South Dakota	146,513	521	3.56
Colorado	237,936	838	3.52
Idaho	95,721	327	3.42
Arkansas	410,454	1,161	2.83
Nebraska	314,957	809	2.57
Kansas	446,437	1,091	2.44
North Dakota	132,004	318	2.41
Montana	114,679	264	2.30
Utah	106,621	239	2.24
Oregon	231,258	503	2.18
Missouri	868,115	1,818	2.09
Washington	371,450	631	1.70
Florida	332,957	534	1.60
Texas	1,293,344	1,971	1.52
Mississippi	436,971	609	1.39
Tennessee	567,100	687	1.21
Kentucky	573,558	657	1.15
Georgia	610,083	690	1.13
Louisiana	449,616	504	1.12
District of Columbia	108,945	119	1.09
Vermont	80,197	86	1.07
Alabama	556,174	596	1.07
Delaware	54.155	53	.98
West Virginia	353,562	341	.96
Iowa	583,638	522	.89
Indiana	779,021	685	.88
South Carolina	343,562	299	.87
California	1,375,607	1,193	.87
Virginia	493,547	375	.76
Michigan	1,098,010	799	.73
Illinois	1,789,581	1,264	.71
North Carolina	615,805	409	.66
New Jersey	923,613	592	.64
Minnesota	560,080	334	.60
Maryland	356,514	209	.59
Connecticut	360,764	207	.57
Pennsylvania	2,095,332	1,140	.54
Ohio	1,569,544	843	.54
Wisconsin	663,089	318	.48
Maine	177,860	78	.44
Rhode Island	153,322	59	.38
New York	2,889,889	1,074	.37
Massachusetts	940,541	284	.30
New Hampshire	105,299	19	.18

[1] Division of Transient Activities, *Quarterly Census of Transients Under Care*, June 30, 1935, Federal Emergency Relief Administration. Idaho emigration estimated on basis of migrant family sample study. 419 families emigrating from U. S. possessions are not included.
[2] Bureau of the Census, *Fifteenth Census of the United States: 1930*, Population Vol. VI, U. S. Department of Commerce, Washington, D. C., 1933, p. 36. 1-person families not included.

Table 8.—Migrant Families [1] Immigrating per 1,000 Families in General Population 1930,[2] by State

State	Families in general population 1930	Migrant families immigrating to State	Migrant families immigrating per 1,000 families in general population
Total	27,547,200	30,304	1.10
Idaho	95,721	973	10.16
New Mexico	89,490	714	7.98
Colorado	237,936	1,847	7.76
California	1,375,607	6,044	4.39
Washington	371,450	1,394	3.75
Wyoming	48,441	180	3.72
District of Columbia	108,945	379	3.48
Oregon	231,258	755	3.26
Kansas	446,437	1,372	3.07
Arizona	91,871	225	2.45
Nevada	18,730	42	2.24
Florida	332,957	717	2.15
Louisiana	449,616	820	1.82
Arkansas	410,454	693	1.69
Tennessee	567,100	919	1.62
Utah	106,621	146	1.37
New Hampshire	105,299	131	1.24
Missouri	868,115	1,027	1.18
Oklahoma	531,183	607	1.14
Ohio	1,569,544	1,480	.94
Nebraska	314,957	289	.92
Delaware	54,155	49	.90
Montana	114,679	99	.86
Illinois	1,789,581	1,525	.85
Texas	1,293,344	1,073	.83
Maryland	356,514	275	.77
Alabama	556,174	417	.75
Iowa	583,638	394	.68
Minnesota	560,080	359	.64
Georgia	610,083	393	.64
Michigan	1,098,010	679	.62
New York	2,889,889	1,746	.60
New Jersey	923,613	538	.58
South Carolina	343,562	193	.56
Virginia	493,547	233	.47
Indiana	779,021	316	.41
Rhode Island	153,322	51	.33
Wisconsin	663,089	210	.32
Mississippi	436,971	128	.29
Pennsylvania	2,095,332	594	.28
West Virginia	353,562	41	.12
Kentucky	573,558	54	.09
Massachusetts	940,541	80	.09
North Dakota	132,004	11	.08
North Carolina	615,865	48	.08
Maine	177,860	12	.07
Connecticut	360,764	27	.07
South Dakota	146,513	5	.03
Vermont	80,197	—	—

[1] Division of Transient Activities, *Quarterly Census of Transients Under Care,* June 30, 1935, Federal Emergency Relief Administration. Idaho Transient Bureau case load estimated on basis of June 15, 1935, *Midmonthly Census of Transient Activities.*
[2] Bureau of the Census, *Fifteenth Census of the United States: 1930,* Population Vol. VI, U. S. Department of Commerce, Washington, D. C., 1933, p. 36. 1-person families not included.

Table 9.—Urban-Rural Distribution of Place of Migrant Family Origin and Destination and Residence of Families in General Population of 1930 [1]

State	Migrant family origin [2]			Migrant family destination [3]			Families in general population 1930		
	Total	Urban	Rural	Total	Urban	Rural	Total	Urban	Rural
Total	4,216	2,934	1,282	3,882	3,185	697	27,547,200	15,975,874	11,571,326
				Percent distribution					
Total	100	70	30	100	82	18	100	58	42
Alabama	100	65	35	100	71	29	100	30	70
Arizona	100	66	34	100	93	7	100	36	64
Arkansas	100	38	62	100	58	42	100	22	78
California	100	89	11	100	94	6	100	76	24
Colorado	100	69	31	100	91	9	100	53	47
Connecticut	100	80	20	100	100	—	100	71	29
Delaware	100	71	29	100	65	35	100	51	49
District of Columbia	100	100	—	100	100	—	100	100	—
Florida	100	78	22	100	90	10	100	54	46
Georgia	100	62	38	100	81	19	100	33	67
Idaho	100	44	56	100	41	59	100	31	69
Illinois	100	91	9	100	94	6	100	74	26
Indiana	100	72	28	100	79	21	100	56	44
Iowa	100	66	34	100	82	18	100	41	59
Kansas	100	58	42	100	82	18	100	41	59
Kentucky	100	47	53	100	54	46	100	33	67
Louisiana	100	69	31	100	82	18	100	41	59
Maine	100	83	17	100	50	50	100	40	60
Maryland	100	56	44	100	89	11	100	61	39
Massachusetts	100	93	7	100	96	4	100	90	10
Michigan	100	85	15	100	86	14	100	68	32
Minnesota	100	72	28	100	96	4	100	51	49
Mississippi	100	47	53	100	46	54	100	18	82
Missouri	100	66	34	100	71	29	100	52	48
Montana	100	45	55	100	61	39	100	36	64
Nebraska	100	51	49	100	76	24	100	37	63
Nevada	100	69	31	100	83	17	100	42	58
New Hampshire	100	45	55	100	59	41	100	58	42
New Jersey	100	89	11	100	86	14	100	83	17
New Mexico	100	63	37	100	81	19	100	27	73
New York	100	93	7	100	97	3	100	84	16
North Carolina	100	68	32	100	71	29	100	27	73
North Dakota	100	26	74	100	60	40	100	18	82
Ohio	100	92	8	100	90	10	100	69	31
Oklahoma	100	57	43	100	57	43	100	37	63
Oregon	100	90	10	100	81	19	100	53	47
Pennsylvania	100	86	14	100	94	6	100	69	31
Rhode Island	100	100	—	100	100	—	100	92	8
South Carolina	100	78	22	100	83	17	100	23	77
South Dakota	100	15	85	100	100	—	100	21	79
Tennessee	100	67	33	100	77	23	100	36	64
Texas	100	72	28	100	79	21	100	43	57
Utah	100	76	24	100	93	7	100	55	45
Vermont	100	41	59	100	25	75	100	34	66
Virginia	100	59	41	100	83	17	100	35	65
Washington	100	72	28	100	83	17	100	59	41
West Virginia	100	58	42	100	32	68	100	31	69
Wisconsin	100	57	43	100	82	18	100	55	45
Wyoming	100	39	61	100	52	48	100	34	66

[1] Bureau of the Census, *Fifteenth Census of the United States: 1930*, Population Vol. VI, U. S. Department of Commerce, Washington, D. C., 1933, State table 5. 1-person families not included.
[2] 112 families, whose State of origin or size of place of origin was not ascertainable or whose origin was a foreign country or U. S. possessions, are not included.
[3] 446 families, without definite destinations, whose State of destination or size of place of destination was not ascertainable, or whose destination was a foreign country or U. S. possessions, are not included.

154 • MIGRANT FAMILIES

Table 10.—Size of Place of Origin and Destination of Migrant Families, by Year of Leaving Settled Residence

Type of residence change	Total	Year of leaving settled residence							
		Before 1929	1929	1930	1931	1932	1933	1934	1935
Total	4,074	143	139	141	167	269	486	1,346	1,383
				Percent distribution					
Total	100	100	100	100	100	100	100	100	100
To urban areas	76	64	60	68	64	58	71	82	82
To metropolitan cities	53	32	31	35	36	33	48	61	61
From metropolitan [1] cities	24	15	19	20	18	18	23	24	26
From small [2] cities	16	10	9	11	11	10	12	20	19
From villages [3]	7	4	2	1	3	4	7	8	9
From farms	6	3	1	3	4	1	6	9	7
To small cities	23	32	29	33	28	25	23	21	21
From metropolitan cities	8	11	14	15	12	11	8	6	5
From small cities	8	11	9	10	10	8	8	7	8
From villages	4	7	2	6	4	4	5	4	5
From farms	3	3	4	2	2	2	2	4	3
To rural areas	17	21	30	23	26	33	23	14	12
To villages	10	11	20	12	15	19	14	8	6
From metropolitan cities	3	1	10	6	7	8	6	2	2
From small cities	3	4	4	2	4	5	3	3	2
From villages	2	3	1	3	2	2	3	2	1
From farms	2	3	5	1	2	4	2	1	1
To farms	7	10	10	11	11	14	9	6	6
From metropolitan cities	2	2	4	5	5	7	2	1	1
From small cities	1	1	2	3	3	3	2	1	1
From villages	1	2	2	—	2	*	1	1	1
From farms	3	5	2	3	1	4	4	3	3
No definite destination	7	15	10	9	10	9	6	4	6
From metropolitan cities	3	6	6	4	3	4	3	1	2
From small cities	2	6	1	3	5	3	2	2	2
From villages	1	*	1	2	1	2	*	1	1
From farms	1	3	2	—	1	—	1	*	1

* Less than 0.5 percent.

[1] Places of more than 100,000 population.
[2] Places of 2,500–100,000 population.
[3] Places of less than 2,500 population.

NOTE.—254 families, whose size of place of settled residence or destination and those for which the year of leaving settled residence were not ascertainable, are not included.

Table 11.—Place of Destination and of First Transient Bureau Registration of Migrant Families

Place of destination and of first transient bureau registration	Total	Migrant families	
		Urban destination	Rural destination
Total_____	3,896	3,190	706
		Percent distribution	
Total_____	100	100	100
Registered in place of destination_____	53	61	14
Registered in State but not at place of destination_____	8	6	19
Registered in State other than State of destination_____	39	33	67

NOTE.—1,593 families, which had no settled residence, had no definite destination, and whose State of destination or size of place of destination was not ascertainable, are not included.

Table 12.—Migrant Family and Unattached Cases Opened and Closed During Month and Number Under Care at the Middle of the Month in Transient Bureaus, February 1934—September 1935

Year and month	Migrant family cases			Unattached cases		
	Cases opened	Cases closed	Cases under care at midmonth	Cases opened	Cases closed	Cases under care at midmonth
1934						
February_____	5,911	4,045	10,522	92,417	88,465	60,577
March_____	6,612	4,933	11,585	136,088	129,812	70,483
April_____	6,929	6,316	13,458	179,660	174,835	76,934
May_____	8,444	7,475	14,289	209,136	200,870	78,771
June_____	9,568	8,204	15,885	240,716	231,079	86,369
July_____	11,301	9,160	17,346	291,148	286,451	96,687
August_____	13,925	11,149	19,235	345,031	335,988	104,789
September_____	12,885	11,886	22,275	302,439	308,984	108,134
October_____	13,999	11,789	24,044	298,262	285,786	116,289
November_____	13,875	10,687	27,391	271,941	260,973	128,686
December_____	12,734	11,071	30,216	213,739	213,506	136,823
1935						
January_____	13,070	11,184	33,124	212,894	210,145	135,051
February_____	11,505	10,930	35,414	207,189	208,272	134,170
March_____	12,967	13,576	35,254	279,632	283,653	132,562
April_____	13,961	14,118	35,019	303,941	312,594	129,249
May_____	14,769	15,174	32,727	310,642	317,035	120,224
June_____	15,122	16,179	32,669	298,034	308,168	112,958
July_____	16,848	17,716	31,791	295,999	298,334	110,094
August_____	15,945	16,588	31,112	275,090	281,814	105,174
September [1]_____	9,769	16,832	27,312	133,797	154,481	95,509

[1] Intake of new cases closed on September 20.

Source: Division of Transient Activities, Federal Emergency Relief Administration. Interstate cases only are included.

Table 13.—Size and Composition of Migrant Families During and Before Migration

Size	Total	Composition			
		Normal with or without children	Woman-children	Man-children	All other types
During migration	5,489	4,343	728	119	299
Before migration	5,489	4,476	589	105	319
		Percent distribution			
During migration	100	100	100	100	100
2 persons	35	35	42	43	15
3 persons	25	24	30	31	30
4 persons	17	17	14	12	19
5 persons	10	10	7	7	19
6 persons	5	6	3	4	8
7 persons	4	4	3	1	4
8 persons	2	2	1	—	2
9 persons	1	1	*	1	2
10 persons or more	1	1	*	1	1
Before migration	100	100	100	100	100
2 persons	32	32	41	37	13
3 persons	25	25	29	28	29
4 persons	18	18	15	13	19
5 persons	11	11	7	14	18
6 persons	6	6	4	6	9
7 persons	4	4	3	1	4
8 persons	2	2	1	—	3
9 persons	1	1	*	1	3
10 persons or more	1	1	*	—	2

* Less than 0.5 percent.

Table 14.—Age and Sex of Economic Heads of Migrant Families, of Heads of Resident Relief Families October 1933,[1] and Age of Male Heads of Families in General Population 1930 [2]

Age	Economic heads of migrant families [3]			Heads of resident relief families October 1933			Male heads of families in general population 1930
	Total	Male	Female	Total	Male	Female	
Total	5,480	4,725	755	204,100	174,042	30,058	26,093,416
			Percent distribution				
Total	100	100	100	100	100	100	100
16–24 years	13	12	19	7	7	5	5
25–34 years	36	37	32	22	23	17	23
35–44 years	29	29	27	27	28	25	27
45–54 years	15	15	14	22	22	22	22
55–64 years	6	6	7	13	12	16	14
65 years and over	1	1	1	9	8	15	9

[1] Division of Research, Statistics, and Finance, *Unemployment Relief Census, October 1933*, Report Number Three, Federal Emergency Relief Administration, Washington, D. C., 1935, p. 36. 1-person families are not included.
[2] Bureau of the Census, *Fifteenth Census of the United States: 1930*, Population Vol. VI, U. S. Department of Commerce, Washington, D. C., 1933, p. 9.
[3] 9 family heads, whose age was not ascertainable, are not included.

Table 15.—Age and Status in Family of Persons in Migrant Families

Age	Total	Economic heads [1]	Other principal members [2]	Children and other relatives [3]
Total	19,935	5,480	4,797	9,658
	Percent distribution			
Total	100	100	100	100
Under 5 years	15	—	—	31
5-9 years	14	—	—	28
10-14 years	11	—	—	23
15-19 years	8	1	8	12
20-24 years	10	12	22	3
25-29 years	10	18	20	1
30-34 years	9	18	15	*
35-44 years	13	29	21	*
45-54 years	6	15	9	*
55-64 years	3	6	3	1
65 years and over	1	1	2	1

*Less than 0.5 percent.

[1] 9 family heads, whose age was not ascertainable, are not included.
[2] In the majority of cases "other principal members" were spouse of economic heads. 2 other groups are also included: (1) parents of economic heads, where the economic head was an unmarried child; and (2) siblings (16 years of age and over) of economic heads.
[3] Includes brothers and sisters under 16 years of age, grandparents, nieces, cousins, aunts, uncles, etc.

NOTE.—43 persons, whose age was not ascertainable, are not included.

Table 16.—Citizenship Status and Color and Nativity of Economic Heads of Migrant Families

Citizenship status	Total	White		Negro	Other
		Native-born	Foreign-born		
Total	5,447	4,578	371	419	79
	Percent distribution				
Total	100	100	100	100	100
U. S. citizens	98	100	66	100	73
Naturalization in process	1	—	16	—	—
No U. S. citizenship	1	—	18	—	27

NOTE.—42 family heads, whose color, nativity, or citizenship status was not ascertainable, are not included.

Table 17.—Usual Occupation and Employability of Economic Heads of Migrant Families

Usual occupation	Total	Employability	
		Employable	Employable with handicaps
Total	4,729	2,995	1,734
	Percent distribution		
Total	100	100	100
White-collar workers	28	26	31
Professional and technical workers	5	4	5
Proprietors, managers, and officials (nonagricultural)	4	4	4
Proprietors, foremen, and overseers (agricultural)	8	7	10
Office workers, salesmen, and kindred workers	11	11	12
Skilled workers	23	25	21
Semiskilled workers	25	27	22
Unskilled workers	24	22	26
Laborers (nonagricultural)	8	7	8
Laborers (agricultural)	7	7	8
Domestic and personal service workers	9	8	10

NOTE.—760 economic heads of families, who were unemployable or who had no experience in any occupation and those whose usual occupation was not ascertainable, are not included.

Table 18.—Usual Occupation and Sex of Employable Economic Heads of Migrant Families

Usual occupation [1]	Total	Male	Female
Total	4,796	4,534	262
Inexperienced persons	67	9	58
White-collar workers	1,308	1,249	59
Professional and technical workers [2]	215	203	12
Actors	17	17	—
Artists, sculptors, and teachers of art	9	9	—
Chemists, assayers, metallurgists	3	3	—
Clergymen and religious workers	23	21	2
Designers	1	1	—
Draftsmen	2	2	—
Engineers (technical)	31	31	—
Lawyers, judges, and justices	1	1	—
Musicians and teachers of music	40	39	1
Nurses (trained or registered)	4	3	1
Physicians, surgeons, and dentists	6	6	—
Playground and recreational workers	4	4	—
Reporters, editors, and journalists	7	6	1
Teachers	13	9	4
Other professional workers	7	6	1
Other semiprofessional workers	47	45	2
Proprietors, managers, and officials (except agriculture)	180	179	1
Building contractors	12	12	—
Foresters, forest rangers, and timber cruisers	1	1	—
Hucksters, peddlers, and junk and rag dealers	19	19	—
Trucking, transfer and cab companies, and garages	8	8	—
Retail dealers and managers (n. e. c.[3])	51	51	—
Other proprietors, managers, and officials	89	88	1
Proprietors, foremen, and overseers (in agriculture)	383	382	1
Farm foremen, managers, and overseers	15	15	—
Farmers (owners, tenants, croppers, etc.)	368	367	1
Office workers	224	203	21
Bookkeepers, accountants, and auditors [2]	57	55	2
Cashiers (except in banks)	3	1	2
Clerks (n. e. c.)	98	91	7
Office machine operators	3	1	2
Office managers and bank tellers	5	5	—
Stenographers, stenotypists, and dictaphone operators	7	4	3
Telegraph and radio operators	16	16	—
Telephone operators	2	—	2
Typists	8	6	2
Other clerical and allied workers	25	24	1

See footnotes at end of table.

Table 18.—Usual Occupation and Sex of Employable Economic Heads of Migrant Families—Continued

Usual occupation [1]	Total	Male	Female
White-collar workers—Continued.			
Salesmen and kindred workers	306	282	24
Canvassers (solicitors, any)	31	26	5
Commercial travelers	28	28	—
Newsboys	3	3	—
Real estate agents and insurance agents	34	32	2
Salesmen and saleswomen (retail stores)	122	106	16
Other salespersons and kindred workers	88	87	1
Skilled workers	1,106	1,105	1
Skilled workers and foremen in building construction	664	664	—
Blacksmiths	25	25	—
Boilermakers	6	6	—
Bricklayers and stonemasons	19	19	—
Carpenters	128	128	—
Cement finishers	24	24	—
Electricians	59	59	—
Foremen: construction (except road)	11	11	—
Foremen: road and street construction	10	10	—
Operators or engineers: stationary and portable construction equipment	45	45	—
Painters (not in factory)	191	191	—
Paper hangers	2	2	—
Plasterers	13	13	—
Plumbers, gas and steam fitters	57	57	—
Roofers	10	10	—
Sheet metal workers	4	4	—
Stonecutters and carvers	4	4	—
Structural iron and steel workers	35	35	—
Setters: marble, stone, and tile	1	1	—
Other skilled workers in building and construction	20	20	—
Skilled workers and foremen in manufacturing and other industries	442	441	1
Cabinetmakers	6	6	—
Cobblers and shoe repairmen	15	15	—
Conductors: steam and street railroads and buses	4	4	—
Foremen (in factories)	18	18	—
Foremen and inspectors (except in factories)	22	22	—
Locomotive engineers and firemen	25	25	—
Machinists, millwrights, and toolmakers	63	63	—
Mechanics (n. e. c.)	171	171	—
Molders, founders, and casters (metal)	12	12	—
Sawyers	13	13	—
Skilled workers in printing and engraving	24	24	—
Tailors and furriers	11	10	1
Tinsmiths and coppersmiths	7	7	—
Metal workers (except gold and silver) (n. e. c.)	4	4	—
Skilled workers in manufacturing and other industries (n. e. c.)	47	47	—
Semiskilled workers	1,189	1,141	48
Semiskilled workers in building and construction	452	452	—
Apprentices in building and construction	1	1	—
Blasters (except in mines)	2	2	—
Firemen (except locomotive and fire department)	27	27	—
Operators of building and construction equipment	23	23	—
Pipelayers	2	2	—
Rodman and chainmen (surveying)	2	2	—
Truck and tractor drivers	327	327	—
Welders	28	28	—
Other semiskilled workers in building and construction	40	40	—
Semiskilled workers in manufacturing and other industries	737	689	48
Bakers	23	23	—
Brakeman (railroad)	18	18	—
Deliverymen	26	26	—
Dressmakers and milliners	7	—	7
Filers, grinders, buffers, and polishers (metal)	12	12	—
Furnacemen, heaters, smeltermen, etc. (metal working)	4	4	—
Guards, watchmen, and doorkeepers (except railroad)	12	12	—
Handicraft workers: textile, wood, leather, metal, etc.	1	1	—
Inside workers (mines)	87	87	—
Operatives (n. e. c.) in manufacturing and allied industries	336	298	38
Chemical and allied industries	9	9	—
Cigar, cigarette, and tobacco factories	9	5	4
Clay, glass, and stone industries	9	9	—
Clothing industries	26	16	10
Electric light and power plants	1	1	—
Food and beverage industries	46	41	5
Iron and steel, machinery, and vehicle industries	65	64	1
Laundries and dry cleaning establishments	20	13	7
Lumber and furniture industries	22	22	—
Metal industries (except iron and steel)	6	6	—
Paper, printing, and allied industries	9	8	1

See footnotes at end of table.

Table 18.—Usual Occupation and Sex of Employable Economic Heads of Migrant Families—Continued

Usual occupation [1]	Total	Male	Female
Semiskilled workers—Continued.			
Semiskilled workers in manufacturing and other industries—Con.			
Operatives (n. e. c.) in manufacturing and allied industries—Con.			
Shoe factories	7	7	—
Textile industries	72	63	9
Miscellaneous and not specified manufacturing industries	35	34	1
Painters, varnishers, enamelers, etc. (factory)	15	15	—
Switchmen, flagmen, and yardmen (railroad)	15	15	—
Taxicab drivers, bus drivers, and chauffeurs	38	38	—
Other semiskilled workers in manufacturing and other industries	143	140	3
Unskilled workers	1,126	1,030	96
Unskilled laborers (except in agriculture)	357	357	—
Laborers in manufacturing and allied industries	68	68	—
Clay, glass, and stone industries	1	1	—
Iron and steel, machinery, and vehicle industries	19	19	—
Lumber and furniture industries	20	20	—
Other manufacturing and allied industries	28	28	—
Laborers except in manufacturing and allied industries	289	289	—
Mines, quarries, and oil and gas wells	32	32	—
Odd jobs (general)	19	19	—
Railroads (steam and street)	29	29	—
Roads, streets, and sewers	39	39	—
Stores (including porters in stores)	12	12	—
Laborers and helpers (n. e. c.) in building and construction	79	79	—
Longshoremen and stevedores	4	4	—
Lumbermen, raftsmen, and woodchoppers	21	21	—
Street cleaners, garbage men, and scavengers	3	3	—
Teamsters and draymen	9	9	—
Other laborers, except in manufacturing and allied industries (n. e. c.)	42	42	—
Unskilled laborers (in agriculture)	356	349	7
Domestic and personal service workers	413	324	89
Barber and beauty shop workers	51	49	2
Bootblacks	1	1	—
Cleaners and charwomen	8	6	2
Cooks and chefs (except in private family)	149	142	7
Elevator operators	10	10	—
Janitors, caretakers, and sextons	22	17	5
Laundresses (not in laundry)	4	—	4
Porters (except in stores)	11	11	—
Practical nurses, hospital attendants, and orderlies	25	13	12
Servants (hotels, boarding houses, etc.) (n. e. c.)	34	31	3
Servants (private family)	37	5	32
Waiters, waitresses, and bartenders	40	27	13
Other domestic and personal service workers	21	12	9

[1] The occupational classification used here differs from the classification in Bureau of the Census, *Fifteenth Census of the United States: 1930*, Vol. V, U. S. Department of Commerce, Washington, D. C., 1933. The basic code used in classifying the occupations was prepared by Palmer, Gladys L., *Occupational Classification*, Section 2, Division of Research, Statistics, and Finance, Federal Emergency Relief Administration, Washington, D. C., July 1935. The arrangement of occupations above is in the main comparable to that used by Hauser, Philip M., *Workers on Relief in the United States in March 1935*, Abridged Edition, Division of Social Research, Works Progress Administration, Washington, D. C., January 1937.

[2] Certified public accountants are excluded from professional and technical workers and are included with bookkeepers, accountants, and auditors.

[3] Not elsewhere classified.

NOTE.—693 economic heads of families, who were unemployable and those whose usual occupation was not ascertainable, are not included.

Table 19.—Industry of Usual Occupation and Sex of Employable Economic Heads of Migrant Families

Industry of usual occupation [1]	Total	Male	Female
Total	4,730	4,475	255
Inexperienced persons	67	9	58
Agriculture	761	753	8
Fishing and forestry	41	41	—
Fishing	8	8	—
Forestry	33	33	—
Extraction of minerals	203	203	—
Coal mines	73	73	—
Copper mines	4	4	—
Gold and silver mines	15	15	—
Iron mines	1	1	—
Lead and zinc mines	15	15	—
Other specified mines	1	1	—
Not specified mines	19	19	—
Quarries	10	10	—
Oil wells and gas wells	65	65	—
Manufacturing and mechanical industries	1,711	1,664	47
Building industry	658	656	2
Chemical and allied industries	43	42	1
Gas works	6	6	—
Paint and varnish factories	2	2	—
Petroleum refineries	17	17	—
Rayon factories	2	2	—
Soap factories	5	5	—
Other chemical factories	11	10	1
Cigar and tobacco factories	11	7	4
Clay, glass, and stone industries	19	19	—
Brick, tile, and terra-cotta factories	2	2	—
Glass factories	8	8	—
Lime, cement, and artificial stone factories	4	4	—
Marble and stoneyards	4	4	—
Potteries	1	1	—
Clothing industries	45	33	12
Hat factories (felt)	7	6	1
Shirt, collar, and cuff factories	3	2	1
Suit, coat, and overall factories	22	19	3
Other clothing factories	13	6	7
Food and allied industries	129	123	6
Bakeries	29	29	—
Butter, cheese, and condensed milk factories	5	4	1
Candy factories	15	13	2
Fish curing and packing	2	2	—
Flour and grain mills	12	12	—
Fruit and vegetable canning, etc	7	6	1
Slaughter and packing houses	46	45	1
Sugar factories and refineries	4	4	—
Other food factories	2	1	1
Liquor and beverage industries	7	7	—
Iron and steel, machinery, and vehicle industries	363	363	—
Agricultural implement factories	6	6	—
Automobile factories	71	71	—
Automobile repair shops	118	118	—
Blast furnaces and steel rolling mills	50	50	—
Car and railroad shops	16	16	—
Ship and boat building	17	17	—
Other iron and steel and machinery factories	79	79	—
Not specified metal industries	6	6	—
Metal industries (except iron and steel)	27	27	—
Brass mills	1	1	—
Clock and watch factories	1	1	—
Copper factories	4	4	—
Gold and silver factories	2	2	—
Jewelry factories	3	3	—
Tinware, enamelware, etc., factories	12	12	—
Other metal factories	4	4	—
Leather industries	14	14	—
Harness and saddle factories	1	1	—
Leather belt, leather goods, etc., factories	1	1	—
Shoe factories	10	10	—
Tanneries	2	2	—
Lumber and furniture industries	103	102	1
Furniture factories	29	28	1
Piano and organ factories	2	2	—
Saw and planing mills	60	60	—
Other woodworking factories	12	12	—

See footnotes at end of table.

Table 19.—Industry of Usual Occupation and Sex of Employable Economic Heads of Migrant Families—Continued

Industry of usual occupation [1]	Total	Male	Female
Manufacturing and mechanical industries—Continued.			
Paper, printing, and allied industries	73	68	5
Blank book, envelope, tag, paper bag, etc., factories	2	2	—
Paper and pulp mills	5	5	—
Paper box factories	2	2	—
Printing, publishing, and engraving	64	59	5
Textile industries	96	87	9
Cotton mills	48	43	5
Knitting mills	4	4	—
Lace and embroidery mills	1	—	1
Silk mills	8	7	1
Textile dyeing, finishing, and printing mills	1	1	—
Woolen and worsted mills	7	7	—
Other and not specified textile mills	27	25	2
Miscellaneous manufacturing industries	130	123	7
Button factories	1	1	—
Electric light and power plants	37	37	—
Electrical machinery and supply factories	14	14	—
Independent hand trades	31	25	6
Rubber factories	7	7	—
Turpentine farms and distilleries	1	1	—
Other miscellaneous manufacturing industries	28	27	1
Other not specified manufacturing industries	11	11	—
Transportation and communication	617	613	4
Air transportation	3	3	—
Construction and maintenance of streets, roads, sewers, bridges	154	154	—
Express companies	1	1	—
Garages, automobile laundries, greasing stations	50	50	—
Pipe lines	15	15	—
Postal service	5	4	1
Radio broadcasting and transmitting	1	1	—
Steam railroads	167	167	—
Street railroads	9	8	1
Telegraph and telephone	22	20	2
Truck, transfer, and cab companies	127	127	—
Water transportation	62	62	—
Other and not specified transportation and communication	1	1	—
Trade	579	553	26
Advertising agencies	19	19	—
Banking and brokerage	21	21	—
Grain elevators	1	1	—
Insurance	32	31	1
Real estate	14	12	2
Stockyards	1	1	—
Warehouses and cold storage plants	8	8	—
Wholesale and retail trade	482	459	23
Automobile agencies, stores, filling stations	50	49	1
Wholesale and retail trade (except automobile)	432	410	22
Other and not specified trade	1	1	—
Public service (n. e. c.[2])	63	61	2
Professional service	250	233	17
Professional service (except recreation and amusement)	111	97	14
Recreation and amusement	133	130	3
Semiprofessional pursuits and attendants and helpers	6	6	—
Domestic and personal service	438	345	93
Hotels, restaurants, boarding houses, etc	249	218	31
Domestic and personal service (n. e. c.[2])	154	99	55
Laundries	22	15	7
Cleaning, dyeing, and pressing shops	13	13	—

[1] The arrangement of industries is in the main comparable to that used by Hauser, Philip M. and Jenkinson, Bruce, in *Workers on Relief in the United States in March 1935*, Vol. II, A Study of Industrial and Educational Backgrounds. Division of Social Research, Works Progress Administration, Washington, D. C., (in preparation). Industries which were reported by no employable economic head of migrant families are not shown in this classification.

[2] Not elsewhere classified.

NOTE.— 759 economic heads of families, who were unemployable and those whose usual industry was not ascertainable, are not included.

Table 20.—Usual Occupation and Age of Employable Economic Heads of Migrant Families

Usual occupation	Total	Age			
		Under 25 years	25–34 years	35–44 years	45–64 years
Total	4.722	548	1,770	1.410	994
		Percent distribution			
Total	100	100	100	100	100
White-collar workers	28	18	24	30	37
Professional and technical workers	5	3	4	5	6
Proprietors, managers, and officials (nonagricultural)	4	1	2	5	7
Proprietors, foremen, and overseers (agricultural)	8	5	6	8	13
Office workers, salesmen, and kindred workers	11	9	12	12	11
Skilled workers	23	11	23	27	26
Semiskilled workers	25	34	30	22	16
Unskilled workers	24	37	23	21	21
Laborers (nonagricultural)	8	10	7	6	8
Laborers (agricultural)	7	17	8	5	6
Domestic and personal service workers	9	10	8	10	7

NOTE.—767 economic heads of families, who were unemployable, who had no experience at any occupation, and whose usual occupation or age was not ascertainable, are not included.

Table 21.—Industry of Usual Occupation and Age of Employable Economic Heads of Migrant Families

Industry of usual occupation	Total	Age			
		Under 25 years	25–34 years	35–44 years	45–64 years
Total	4,656	543	1,752	1,384	977
		Percent distribution			
Total	100	100	100	100	100
Agriculture, forestry, and fishing	17	25	15	14	20
Extraction of minerals	4	4	4	5	5
Manufacturing and mechanical	37	30	37	39	37
Building and construction	14	8	14	16	16
Clothing industries	1	1	1	1	1
Food and allied industries	3	5	3	2	2
Automobile factories and repair shops	4	3	5	5	2
Iron, steel, and machinery industries	4	3	3	4	4
Textile industries	2	3	2	2	1
Lumber and furniture industries	2	2	2	2	3
Paper, printing, and allied industries	2	1	2	1	2
Other manufacturing industries	5	4	5	6	6
Transportation and communication	13	14	15	13	9
Trade	12	12	13	12	12
Public service	1	1	2	1	1
Professional service	6	5	5	6	6
Domestic and personal service	10	9	9	10	10

NOTE.—833 economic heads of families, who were unemployable, who had no experience at any occupation, and whose age or usual industry was not ascertainable, are not included.

Table 22.—Usual Occupation and Schooling Completed by Employable Economic Heads of Migrant Families

Usual occupation	Total	Schooling completed	
		8 grades or less	9 grades or more
Total	4,687	3,034	1,653
	Percent distribution		
Total	100	100	100
White-collar workers	28	21	40
Professional and technical workers	5	2	9
Proprietors, managers, and officials (nonagricultural)	4	3	6
Proprietors, foremen, and overseers (agricultural)	8	10	4
Office workers, salesmen, and kindred workers	11	6	21
Skilled workers	23	24	23
Semiskilled workers	25	27	21
Unskilled workers	24	28	16
Laborers (nonagricultural)	8	10	4
Laborers (agricultural)	7	10	3
Domestic and personal service workers	9	8	9

NOTE.—802 economic heads of families, who were unemployable, who had no experience in any occupation, and whose occupation or schooling completed was not ascertainable, are not included.

Appendix B

SOME ASPECTS OF MINORITY-GROUP MIGRATION

FOREIGN-BORN

AMONG THE families with foreign-born white economic heads Italians formed the largest group with 20 percent of all foreign-born, followed in order by English (13 percent), Russians (9 percent), Canadians (9 percent), Germans (8 percent), Poles, Greeks, Austrians (each 6 percent), and Scandanavians (5 percent). The nationalities listed made up four-fifths of all the foreign-born family heads. Two-thirds of the foreign-born were citizens, and one-sixth had first papers.

State of Registration

The distribution of the 370 families with foreign-born economic heads was extremely uneven among the States. In New York the 308 families in the sample included 108, or 35 percent, foreign-born families. In contrast, the 320 families under care in Kansas included only 2, or less than 1 percent, foreign-born families. The proportion of foreign-born was consistently above the average (7 percent of all families studied) in Northeastern industrial States, such as New York, Massachusetts, Michigan, Pennsylvania, New Hampshire, and New Jersey, and consistently below the average in agricultural States, such as Kansas, Iowa, Oklahoma, and the entire Southeast.

State of Origin

The origin States of these families showed the same concentration. For example, 23 percent of the families whose last place of residence was in New York State were foreign-born, whereas only slightly over 1 percent of the families starting from Kansas were foreign-born. The same States that contributed and received the highest proportions of foreign-born migrant families are also the States that had the highest proportion foreign-born in their total 1930 population. Obviously, then, the movement represented by the foreign-born migrant family was between places of foreign-born concentration. Unlike native white migrant families the migration of the foreign-born was restricted to those communities where previous experience had shown that the conditions for absorption of the foreign-born groups were favorable.[1]

Reasons for Leaving Settled Residence

The reasons for migration reported by foreign-born families indicate that the economic forces operating on them were no less important than in the case of all migrants. Almost three-fourths of the foreign-born families were in economic distress when they set out to find a more favorable location. This ratio is slightly above that reported among all migrant families and is the result principally of the larger proportion of foreign-born reporting business failure as the reason for migration. Inadequate relief was a less important expelling force among foreign-born than among all families. A smaller proportion reported personal distress. Ill-health was the most important personal reason but was less frequently reported by foreign-born families than by all families.

Kind of Contact at Destination

The tendency of foreign-born families to migrate to places where there was already a concentration of the foreign-born is further illustrated in their choice of destinations. As compared with 80 percent of all families, 78 percent of the foreign-born had chosen a community where they had some kind of definite contact. Foreign-born families, however, showed a somewhat greater tendency to return to a place of previous residence than was found among all families. Chance selection of destination was reported only twice among the whole group of 370 foreign-born although rumor and advertising attracted 18 percent of them in contrast to 16 percent of all migrant families.

Reasons for Selecting Destination

As indicated by the reasons for leaving settled residence, economic betterment was the goal of the majority of the foreign-born migrants. Unlike all migrant families, however, a larger proportion sought business and farm opportunities. While 7 percent of all migrant families hoped or expected to obtain a farm or business, 11 percent of the foreign-born were motivated by this desire.

In summary, it may be said that although families with foreign-born economic heads were represented in comparatively small numbers

---

[1] For a discussion of the distribution of minority peoples in the United States, see Young, Donald. *Research Memorandum on Minority Peoples in the Depression*, Social Science Research Council, New York, 1935, ch. III.

among the depression migrants they migrated in response to forces similar to those operating on all transient families. The foreign-born tended to move to communities similar to the ones in which they had been living and showed a decided preference for the industrial States.

NEGROES

State of Registration

It was pointed out in chapter II that, in contrast with the prevailing westward movement of families, the movement from the South was to the Northeastern and North Central States.[2] The importance of the Negro family in this movement is evident in the greater than average proportions of Negroes registered in transient bureaus in such States as Illinois, New York, Ohio, Michigan, and Pennsylvania. Evidence of a movement of Negro families north along the Atlantic coast is found in the higher than average proportion of Negroes in the sample for the District of Columbia, Maryland, Delaware, and New Jersey. The 11 Southeastern States had only 9 percent of all Negro families under care.

State of Origin

The movement of families out of the Southern States, both from the deep South and the Mississippi Valley, included relatively large proportions of Negro families. Mississippi, Arkansas, Missouri, North Carolina, South Carolina, Kentucky, and Georgia were of outstanding importance as origins of Negro families. The 11 Southeastern States contributed 40 percent of all Negro migrant families.

With States in the southeastern section of the country contributing more than a proportionate share of Negro families to the transient relief population, and with States in the northeastern section receiving more than a proportionate share, it is clear that lines of Negro migration established during the 1920's were, in general, being followed during the depression. The attractive force during prosperity was industrial employment in the larger industrial centers. The pre-depression Negro migration undoubtedly influenced southern Negro families suffering from the depression to seek work in the northern cities where in many cases friends and relatives had preceded them.

Reasons for Leaving Settled Residence

Unemployment, domestic difficulties, inadequate earnings, and a desire to rejoin relatives were the more important reasons given by Negro families for leaving settled residence. Unemployment and ill-health were reported less frequently by Negroes than by all families or by the foreign-born; on the other hand, domestic difficulties, inadequate earnings, and inadequate relief were reported much more fre-

[2] See p. 40 ff.

quently by Negroes than by all families or by foreign-born white families.

Kind of Contact at Destination

Negro families had, on the whole, the same kinds of contacts in the community of destination as were reported for all families. The presence of relatives or friends in the place of destination, however, was decidedly of more importance among Negroes than among all families. "No definite entree" was reported somewhat less frequently by Negro families, and fewer Negro families were attracted by rumors and advertisements.

The conclusions to be drawn from this analysis of Negro families are (1) that the most important direction of movement was from South to North, with the large industrial centers as the principal destinations; (2) that economic causes were the chief expulsive forces, with domestic difficulties assuming more than average importance; and (3) that the presence of friends or relatives was an unusually significant factor in the choice of destination.

Appendix C

SCHEDULE AND INSTRUCTIONS

F. E. R. A. Form DRS–216A.

STUDY OF FEDERAL TRANSIENT FAMILY GROUPS

Date of interview................... City and State of registration........... Interviewer..............

Name of present head.. Case number..............

Status of case: ( ) Under care; ( ) Intake.

1. Members of family group:

A	B	C	D	E	F		G	H	
					Place of birth			Education: Grades completed	
Line No.	Relation to head	Sex	Age	Color or race	Marital status				
					State	City or county		Grade and high school	College
1....	Present head.	....	....	....	....	....	....	....	....
2....	....	....	....	x x	....	....	....	....	....
3....	....	....	....	x x	....	....	....	....	....
4....	....	....	....	x x	....	....	....	....	....
5....	....	....	....	x x	....	....	....	....	....
6....	....	....	....	x x	....	....	....	....	....
7....	....	....	....	x x	....	....	....	....	....

(Enter below information for members usually included in family group but not now present)

8....	....	....	....	....	....	....	....	....	....
9....	....	....	....	....	....	....	....	....	....
10....	....	....	....	....	....	....	....	....	....
11....	....	....	....	....	....	....	....	....	....

2. Month and year of last marriage of normal head...

3. Is normal head a U. S. citizen? ( ) Yes; ( ) No; ( ) First papers.

4. Residence history of family group since January 1, 1929, or since date of present marriage if later:

(*List in chronological order all places in which the family resided 1 month or longer, excluding periods when the family received transient relief*)

A		B		C		
Location		Duration		Nature of place (check one on each line)		
State	City or county	From (month and year)	To (month and year)	Farm	Village (under 2,500 population)	Urban (2,500 population or more)

5. Transient relief record since July 1, 1933:

(*List in chronological order all instances in which the family as a whole or 2 or more members of it were registered for transient relief as a family group*)

A		B	C	D
Location		Date of registration (month, day, and year)	Length of stay	Reason for leaving
State	City			

REASONS FOR FAMILY GROUP MOBILITY

(*This section applies to the entire period during which the family group has been in an unsettled condition, beginning before or after January 1, 1929*)

6. Last place in which the family lived a settled self-supporting life; that is, the place at which family group mobility began:

State .... City or county .... Date left ....

7. Reasons for leaving. State fully all the circumstances that caused the family to leave the place entered in question 6:

----

8. Destination at time of leaving place entered in question 6:

   A. State .... City or county ....

   B. Reasons for selection of this place ....

....

....

....

9. Present plans for future:
   A. ( ) Formulated by family group.
      ( ) Formulated with assistance of Transient Bureau.

   B. Nature of plans ....

....

....

OCCUPATIONAL HISTORY

10. Present employment status of *normal head*:
   A. ( ) Not working; ( ) Working on transient relief projects.

     ( ) Other employment (specify) ....

....

   B. Interviewer's opinion as to employability of normal head:

....

   C. Employment handicaps of normal head (specify):

....

....

11. Usual occupations of *all employable persons 16 years of age and over* entered in question 1:

A	B		C	D	
	Usual occupation			Last nonrelief job of 1 month or longer at usual occupation	
Line number of person in question 1 (A)	Occupation	Industry	Total number of years experience	From (month and year)	To (month and year)
Present head........					
Normal head........					
Others........					

12. Last nonrelief job of 2 weeks or longer held by *normal head* at any occupation:

A	B	C	
		Duration	
Occupation	Industry	From	To

INSTRUCTIONS FOR FILLING OUT SCHEDULE DRS-216A

Cases To Be Scheduled

1. Schedules are to be taken only for cases registered as family groups.

2. Schedules are to be taken only for cases classified as *Federal families* (i. e. Federal transients); *do not* schedule cases classified as *State families*.

3. Cases classified as "service only" are *not to be scheduled*.

General Instructions

An interview with a responsible member of the family group, preferably the head, will be necessary in all cases. For cases taken from current registrations, the entire schedule is to be filled by interview. For cases taken from among those under care, the case record will be helpful in providing some information, but an interview will be necessary to answer most of the questions on the schedule. The case record should also be of use in checking some of the information obtained from the interview.

At the time of the interview and before the person interviewed has left, the schedule should be checked to see that there are no omissions or inconsistencies.

Specific Instructions

Name of Present Head

The present head is the person who is registered by the Transient Bureau as the head of the family group.

1. *Member of family group.*

b. *Relation to head:* Enter on lines 1 to 7 the persons now registered as part of the relief case.

Enter on lines 8 to 11 persons normally a part of the family group but not now registered as part of the relief case.

The entries must be in terms of relation to the present head; e. g., wife, son, daughter, sister, friend, etc.

The entries must be in the following order: head, spouse, children in descending order of age, other persons.

If the person who is normally the head of the family group is not the person registered as the present head, enter his relation to the present head on line 8 and add "normal head"; e. g., husband (normal head).

In cases where the husband and wife are permanently separated or divorced, the husband is no longer a member of the family and should never be entered as the normal head.

c. *Sex:* Enter "M" for male, "F" for female.

d. *Age:* Enter age as of last birthday.

e. *Color or race:* Enter "W" for white, "Neg" for Negro, "Mex" for Mexican, and "Oth" for other races.

f. *Place of birth:* In all cases where the person was born on a farm, enter the name of the county followed by the abbreviation "Co."

If a person was born in a foreign country, enter the name of that country according to present day boundaries.

g. *Marital status:* Enter "S" for single, "M" for married, "Wid" for widowed, "Div" for divorced, and "Sep" for separated.

Separated means legally separated or separated with the intention of living permanently apart. The term must not be used to include temporary separation.

h. *Education—Grades completed.*

Grade and high school: Enter the highest grade successfully *completed* in grade and high school; e. g., for a person who completed eight grades in grade school and entered but failed to complete the third year in high school, enter "10."

For persons who entered school but completed no grade, enter "0."

For persons who have not attended school, enter a dash.

College: Enter the number of years successfully completed.

For persons who entered college but did not complete a year, enter "0."

Do not include attendance at so-called "business colleges."

2. *Month and year of last marriage of normal head.*

Enter the date when the normal head was last married. If inapplicable, enter a dash and explain.

3. *Is normal head a U. S. citizen?*

Check *First papers* for persons who have made formal declaration of intention to become U. S. citizens but who have not yet received their certificate of citizenship.

4. *Residence history of normal family group.*

List in chronological order all places in which the family has resided 1 month or longer since January 1, 1929.

Exclude periods when the family, or the two principal members thereof, were receiving transient relief.

If the family was formed after January 1, 1929, give the residence history from the time the principals were married.

a. *Location:* Enter the State and city for each residence.

If the residence was in open country, enter the name of the county followed by the abbreviation "Co."

b. *Duration:* Enter the month and year when each period of residence began and ended.

If at the beginning of 1929 the family was in a place where they had been living for some time previously, record the year their residence in this place began, regardless of the fact that it was prior to 1929. The earliest date entered here can never be earlier than the date of marriage of the normal head (Question 2) since that was the date the family was formed.

c. *Nature of place:* Determine for each period of residence the nature of the place in which the family was living.

Check one on each line.

Farm: If the family was living on a farm.

Village: If the family was living in or near a village with a population of less than 2,500, but *was not operating a farm.*

Urban: If the family was living in a place with a population of 2,500 or more.

5. *Transient relief record since July 1, 1933.*

Enter in chronological order all instances in which the family as a whole or two or more members of it were registered for transient relief as a family group. Include only relief given under the direction of transient authorities established under the provisions of the Federal Emergency Relief Act of 1933.

a. *Location:* Enter every place (State and city) in which transient relief was received.

b. *Date of registration:* Enter for each period of transient relief the date when the case was registered.

c. *Length of stay:* Enter the length of time the case was under care.

d. *Reason for leaving:* Enter the chief reason for the group's going off transient relief in each place listed.

Reasons for Family Group Mobility

This section applies to the entire period during which the family group has been in an unsettled condition, whether beginning before or after January 1, 1929.

6. *Last place in which the family lived a settled, self-supporting life.*

The purpose of this question is to determine the place and time at which family group mobility began.

Enter the name of the last place in which the family lived a settled, self-supporting life. That is, the place which the family considered its permanent place of residence and in which the family was entirely or mostly self-supporting. In cases where the family has moved several times in recent years careful interviewing will be necessary to determine the location of the place, because in one or more of these moves the family may have established a semipermanent residence which properly belongs to the period of family mobility. For example:

Family A—lived in Chicago, Ill., from June 1924 until August 1930. The head of the family was steadily employed there as a machinist. In August 1930 part-time employment had reduced the family income to a subsistence level. The head succeeded in finding a full-time job as field representative for a mill machinery company. The home in Chicago was given up and the family accompanied the head on his movements about the country. A year later the job ended when the family was in Houston, Tex., where the head found enough employment doing house painting to support the family for 2½ years. When this work failed, the family went to Richmond, Va. (birthplace of the head), where it obtained transient relief.

The proper answer to Question 6 in this case is "Illinois, Chicago, August 1930" and *not* "Texas, Houston, February 1934." Careful interviewing disclosed that although the family lived in Houston long enough to gain legal settlement, it did not consider Houston its home, nor its residence there as permanent, because the head could not obtain steady employment at what he considered adequate wages.

If the family has had no place of settled residence since marriage, enter "None" and explain.

If the last place of settled residence was prior to January 1, 1929, enter the name of this place and the date left.

7. *Reasons for leaving.*

Give a comprehensive explanation of all the circumstances which caused the family to leave the place entered in Question 6.

The answer to this question refers specifically to the place and time entered in Question 6 and is not to be conditioned by subsequent events.

Brief entries, such as "seeking work," "unemployment," "visits," "health," and "family trouble," are *not* adequate. The statement of reasons for leaving should be amplified to include both the primary and secondary factors which caused the family to leave a settled abode.

In no case is the answer to this question to be taken from the registration card (Tr–10).

8. *Destination at time of leaving.*

a. *State, city, or county:* The destination to be entered is the place to which the family planned to go *at the time* it left the locality entered in Question 6.

If the family had no definite destination, enter the general area into which it expected to go.

b. *Reasons for selection of this place:* Enter the reasons why the family selected this particular place rather than any other as its original destination.

9. *Present plans for future.*

State what plans for the future have been made by the family alone or by the family in conjunction with the transient relief agency.

Occupational History

10. *Present employment status of normal head.*

a. Check one item to indicate the employment status of the *normal head* at the time of interview.

Check *Other employment* if the normal head has any job other than a transient relief job. Include in this category persons on strike, persons going to a definitely promised job, and persons employed on nontransient work relief projects.

Specify what kind of work and in what industry; whether it is full time or part time; and whether the person is employed by others or working on his own account.

b. *Interviewer's opinion as to employability of normal head:* Enter here a statement of the interviewer's opinion as to whether the *normal head* is readily employable, or wholly or partially unemployable.

c. *Employment handicaps of normal head:* Specify all factors which would seriously handicap the normal head in securing and pursuing steady employment. It is particularly important to note such factors as permanent physical or mental disabilities, chronic illness, temporary disabilities, old age, personality difficulties, household duties, etc.

11. *Usual occupation of all employable persons 16 years of age and over entered in Question 1.*

a. Identify each person by the appropriate line number in Question 1a. If the present head and the normal head are the same, leave the second line blank.

b. *Usual occupation:* (See appendix for supplementary instructions for recording occupation and industry.)

The usual occupation is that at which the person has normally been employed, or the one which he considers has been his usual occupation by reason of experience or training.

If the person has worked at two or more occupations for short periods of time and considers none of them his usual occupation, enter "No usual occupation."

If the person has never done gainful work, enter "Never worked."

The occupation is the specific job or work performed (e. g., cook).

The industry is the specific industrial or business organization in which the job or work is performed (e. g., hotel).

c. *Total number of year's experience:* Enter the total length of time the person has worked at his usual occupation.

d. *Last nonrelief job of 1 month or longer at usual occupation:* Enter the dates of the beginning and ending of the last nonrelief job of 1 month or longer which the person held at his usual occupation Employment on PWA project is to be considered as nonrelief employment; employment on work relief projects is to be excluded.

12. *Last nonrelief job of 2 weeks or longer held by normal head at any occupation.*

This entry should report the *last* nonrelief employment at any job held by the normal head for 2 weeks or longer.

13. *Farm experience of normal head.*

a–b. The purpose of these questions is to determine the number of *normal* family group heads who have had some farm experience; and whether this experience was as farm laborer or as farm operator.

c. *Owner, manager, tenant, cropper.*

Farm owner: A farmer who owns all or part of the land he operates. Include squatters and homesteaders who are farming.

Farm manager: A person who manages a farm for the owner, assuming full responsibility for the crops and their cultivation and receives a salary for his services.

Farm cropper: A farmer who cultivates only rented land and to whom the landlord furnishes equipment and stock; i. e., he is a farmer who contributes only labor and receives in return a share of the crop.

Farm tenant: A farmer who cultivates rented land only, furnishing all or part of the working equipment and stock, whether he pays cash or a share of the crop or both as rent.

d. *Type of farm:* Indicate the type of farm; e. g., wheat, fruit, dairy, stock. In cases where there was little specialization, enter "general."

e. *Number of acres:* Enter the number of acres included in each farm, whether under cultivation or not.

f. *Location:* Enter the name of the State and county in which each farm was located.

g. *Number of years operated:* Enter the number of years each farm was operated.

h. *Date left:* Enter the month and year the person ceased operating the farm.

i. *Reason for leaving:* Enter the reason for giving up the farm; e. g., mortgage foreclosed, dispossession or eviction, drought, operated at a loss, moved to better farm, moved to city to obtain employment.

14. *Remarks on farm experience.*

If the normal head has had farm experience, but is not now capable of operating a farm, explain the circumstance, and specify whether there is some other member of the family group (e. g., son) who is capable.

15. *General comments on case.*

Make free use of this space to explain, amplify, or interpret entries on the schedule and to record other pertinent information.

Appendix D

LIST OF TABLES

TEXT TABLES

179

SUPPLEMENTARY TABLES

Index

INDEX

RURAL
FAMILIES
ON
RELIEF

WORKS PROGRESS ADMINISTRATION
DIVISION OF SOCIAL RESEARCH

Publications
of the Division of Social Research
Works Progress Administration

Research Monographs

I. Six Rural Problem Areas, Relief—Resources—Rehabilitation
II. Comparative Study of Rural Relief and Non-Relief Households
III. The Transient Unemployed
IV. Urban Workers on Relief
V. Landlord and Tenant on the Cotton Plantation
VI. Chronology of the Federal Emergency Relief Administration, May 12, 1933, to December 31, 1935
VII. The Migratory-Casual Worker
VIII. Farmers on Relief and Rehabilitation
IX. Part-Time Farming in the Southeast
X. Trends in Relief Expenditures, 1910–1935
XI. Rural Youth on Relief
XII. Intercity Differences in Costs of Living in March 1935, 59 Cities
XIII. Effects of the Works Program on Rural Relief
XIV. Changing Aspects of Rural Relief
XV. Rural Youth: Their Situation and Prospects
XVI. Farming Hazards in the Drought Area
XVII. Rural Families on Relief

Special Reports

Legislative Trends in Public Relief and Assistance, December 31, 1929, to July 1, 1936
Survey of Cases Certified for Works Program Employment in 13 Cities
Survey of Workers Separated From WPA Employment in Eight Areas During the Second Quarter of 1936
A Survey of the Transient and Homeless Population in 12 Cities, September 1935 and September 1936
Areas of Intense Drought Distress, 1930–1936
The People of the Drought States
Relief and Rehabilitation in the Drought Area
Five Years of Rural Relief
Age of WPA Workers, November 1937
Survey of Workers Separated From WPA Employment in Nine Areas, 1937
Workers on Relief in the United States in March 1935, Volume I, A Census of Usual Occupations
Urban Housing: A Summary of Real Property Inventories Conducted as Work Projects, 1934–1936

WORKS PROGRESS ADMINISTRATION
F. C. Harrington, *Administrator*
Corrington Gill, *Assistant Administrator*

DIVISION OF SOCIAL RESEARCH
Howard B. Myers, *Director*

RURAL FAMILIES ON RELIEF

By
Carle C. Zimmerman
and
Nathan L. Whetten

•

RESEARCH MONOGRAPH XVII

1938
UNITED STATES GOVERNMENT PRINTING OFFICE, WASHINGTON

Letter of Transmittal

WORKS PROGRESS ADMINISTRATION,
Washington, D. C., December 27, 1938.

SIR: I have the honor to transmit an analysis of the social characteristics of rural families receiving assistance under the general relief program. The report evaluates the various characteristics of rural families on relief in terms of their effect on the families' need for aid. The findings of this analysis will be of distinct value to relief administrators in rural areas. At the same time it is a contribution to the general study of rural families in the lower income groups.

Not only are rural relief families found to differ in their characteristics according to their position in the local rural community, but, in addition, even wider differences exist among the various geographical areas of the country. The predominant industries determine the extent to which the head of a family will be able to care for his dependents continuously, and the cultural traditions largely determine the composition and solidarity of the family unit. Four factors are of particular importance in determining the incidence and amount of relief for rural families: (1) The number of employable members in the family and their capabilities; (2) unemployment because of the business cycle; (3) unemployment and underemployment because of the weather cycle; and (4) social action for improving the standard of living.

The study was made in the Division of Social Research under the direction of Howard B. Myers, Director of the Division. The data were collected under the supervision of A. R. Mangus and T. C. McCormick. Acknowledgment is made of the cooperation of the State Supervisors and Assistant State Supervisors of Rural Research who were in direct charge of the field work. The analysis of the data was made under the supervision of T. J. Woofter, Jr., Coordinator of Rural Research.

The report was prepared by Carle C. Zimmerman of Harvard University and Nathan L. Whetten of Storrs Agricultural Experiment Station, with the assistance of Wendell H. Bash of Harvard University. It was edited by Ellen Winston of the Division of Social Research.

Respectfully submitted.

CORRINGTON GILL,
Assistant Administrator.

COL. F. C. HARRINGTON,
Works Progress Administrator.

Contents

ILLUSTRATIONS

Figures

Page

VIII • CONTENTS

Rural Families on Relief

INTRODUCTION

IN 1930 there were approximately 30 million families in the United States.[1] Of these, 17,372,500 were classified as urban; 6,604,600, as rural-farm; and 5,927,500, as rural-nonfarm. Thus, about 42 percent of America's families were classified as rural, 22 percent being farm and 20 percent being nonfarm.

Since 1930 more than one out of four of these rural families have been forced to seek public or private assistance. In January 1935, for instance, almost 2 million of them received general relief grants. The purpose of this study is to give a general description of rural relief families and to point out some of their characteristic features. It summarizes information concerning their occupational origin, their size and composition, the age and sex characteristics of the heads, the marital condition of the heads, the number and types of dependents, the composition of the families from the standpoint of relationship, their fertility rates, their employability, employment, and amount of relief, and the mobility and education of their members. These various factors are analyzed on the basis of geographical distribution. Information is given about the racial backgrounds of the families, their former agricultural experience, and their forms of land tenure if they have been engaged in agriculture.

The data for this monograph are from the records of the Rural Section, Division of Social Research, Works Progress Administration. The materials consist of information gathered by means of a survey

---

[1] "The term *family*, as it is used in the tabulation of the results of the 1930 Census, is limited in the main to what might be called private families, excluding the institutions and hotel or boarding-house groups which have been counted as families in prior censuses. A family may therefore be defined in general as a group of persons related either by blood or by marriage or adoption, who live together as one household, usually sharing the same table. Single persons living alone are counted as families, however, as are a few small groups of unrelated persons sharing the same living accommodations as 'partners.' Households reporting more than 10 lodgers are classified as boarding or lodging houses rather than as families. Two or more related persons occupying permanent quarters in a hotel are counted as a private family rather than as a part of the hotel group." Bureau of the Census, *Abstract of the Fifteenth Census of the United States: 1930*, U. S. Department of Commerce, Washington, D. C., 1933, p. 401.

covering 138 counties, representative of 9 major agricultural areas,[2] and 116 New England townships (fig. 26, p. 112). The data were taken as of June 1935 with the exceptions of those for education and marital condition. These were taken as of October 1935 since items to secure such information were not included on the June schedules.[3]

[2] Eastern Cotton, Western Cotton, Appalachian-Ozark, Lake States Cut-Over, Hay and Dairy, Corn Belt, Spring Wheat, Winter Wheat, and Ranching.

[3] For a detailed discussion of the methodology of the survey, see Mangus, A. R., *Changing Aspects of Rural Relief*, Research Monograph XIV, Division of Social Research, Works Progress Administration, Washington, D. C., 1938, appendix B. For the meaning of terms used in this monograph, see appendix A.

Farm Security Administration (Lee).

On Relief.

SUMMARY

RURAL FAMILIES in the United States were subjected to a number of unusual forces during the period 1930–1935 which resulted in severe economic distress in all sections. Some regions suffered directly from only one force or received the diffuse effects of several. In other regions the full brunt of various forces focused on the area and resulted in the almost complete collapse of normal economic and social activities.

While rural distress was caused in considerable part by long-range factors, the effects of the business depression were nevertheless of great importance in the rural relief situation. The drop in the price of farm commodities, because of cyclical fluctuations in the money market, was only one factor in this situation as it affected the farmer and the village dweller. Included also were price movements resulting from the weather and from crop conditions in foreign countries and the long-time trend in agricultural production and exportation. Thus, all of the agricultural price movements resulted in a decline in prices and sales. This included both the drop in value and quantity of exported goods and the change in the urban market with the depression.

Another force bearing on the rural population and helping to determine relief needs, which can also be identified with the business depression, was the change in nonagricultural work opportunities which accompanied the decline in industry and commerce. This affected primarily the large numbers of part-time farmers who live in densely settled and relatively urbanized areas. These families were forced to a more complete dependence on the soil and to a more self-sufficient type of farm economy.

Partly connected with the business depression and partly dependent upon a long-time trend has been the decline in the utilization of natural resources. Activity in isolated coal and iron mining areas has decreased or stopped entirely, and the lumber industry has been sharply curtailed. These are typical examples of industries which give employment to rural families either on a part-time or full-time basis. In some areas the depression coincided approximately with the exhaustion of natural resources so that the shutdown has been permanent rather than temporary. For the most part rural families suffering under the pressure of these forces are located in mountain and wooded areas.

A factor which was not connected with the business depression was the drought. Short-time cyclical movements of rainfall and dry weather have not been unusual on the plains of the great West, but in 1934 and 1936 there were droughts which have been unequalled for both extensity and severity during this generation. The most extreme effects of the drought were found in a belt running north and south through the two Wheat Areas and bordering both the Corn Belt and Western Cotton Areas, but minor effects of the drought were found in almost every section of the country.

TYPES OF FARM FAMILIES

Aside from their regional incidence, the forces leading to the need for assistance were found to affect rural families in different ways and different degrees according to the type of farming in which they were engaged. Commercial farmers may be accurately described as small-scale entrepreneurs. All of their efforts are concentrated on the production of cash crops, generally only one, and usually they grow comparatively little for home use. They live under relatively the same type of money economy as city people, and their prosperity is determined by the price of these goods in the market. It is also significant that for most of the products included under this type of production the price is largely determined by the surplus which is exported. Since they are goods of relatively inelastic demand and subject to wide fluctuations in supply, such products at times undergo violent fluctuations in price in accordance with weather and economic conditions. Consequently, the business depression and the decline in the exportation of foreign products have been the most important factors in every area in the need for relief of commercial farmers. One governmental action which has ameliorated conditions for these farmers has been the agricultural adjustment program. As a result relief needs have not been as extensive for these farmers as they otherwise would have been.

A second category of farm families may be called noncommercial. It consists largely of those families which combine part-time farming for home consumption with part-time industrial or commercial work and those which lead a relatively self-sufficing life in the more isolated areas. For these families the most important influence has been the decline in industry in the isolated areas together with the depletion of natural resources. This includes also the decline in employment in and around cities. These families are influenced to a certain extent, however, by the decline in the agricultural market since they sell their surplus for cash. These families are helped relatively little by agricultural price-raising.

Cutting across both the commercial and noncommercial groups, a third category of the agricultural population may be called the chronically poverty-stricken. This includes chiefly the farm laborers in all areas and the sharecroppers and tenants of the Cotton Areas. These agricultural groups work for commercial farmers and seldom produce much food for home consumption. They are directly affected by the prosperity of the farmers who hire them so that their prosperity and depression are concurrent with those of commercial producers. Moreover, it is safe to say that in the current situation the troubles of commercial farmers have been passed on to these groups and accentuated in the process.

ANALYSIS OF RURAL RELIEF FAMILIES BY AREA

Although the diversity of occupations and the different types of families within occupations have been repeatedly pointed out, there is still a tendency to think of the rural population as a homogeneous unit. Since *rural* was defined for purposes of this study as including the open country and villages of less than 2,500 inhabitants, it is easy to see that nearly all classes and all occupations were included in one way or another. The rural relief families not only differed in their characteristics according to their position in the local rural community but also even wider differences existed among the various geographical areas of the country. Major differences in the average family on relief in June 1935 were found, for example, between the Eastern Cotton and Spring Wheat Areas. In addition it was found that, when classified on the basis of type-of-farming area, relatively homogeneous groups in the rural population were set up, even if all the occupations were included. Consequently, the average family in different sections of the country was studied on the basis of a regional analysis, resulting in a better understanding of the peculiar problems in each section.

In the Eastern Cotton Area more of the relief families were engaged in agriculture than the average for the country as a whole, but the proportion was still less than 50 percent. However, because of its comparatively slight urbanization, agriculture and family solidarity still set the prevailing tone. The relative multiplicity of social classes within agriculture, including owners, tenants, croppers, and laborers, determines a social stratification which is more pronounced than in other agricultural areas. The relatively small size of the average relief family (3.7 persons) was due partly to the splitting of plantation families and partly to the fact that the median age (43.7 years) of the head of the family was less than for many other areas. Dependent family members were found in about the same proportions as in the country as a whole, but there were more broken families. The excessively high mobility within short distances and the low level of formal education are two of the factors leading to an unusually low material standard of living. Considering all factors, however, this area has preserved its social vitality to a greater extent than have many of the more wealthy sections.

In the Western Cotton Area more of the relief families (54.3 percent) were customarily engaged in agriculture. The average family was a little larger than in the Eastern Cotton Area (3.8 persons) but was still smaller than the average for the country. The splitting of plantation families was probably more widely practiced here than in the older and more traditional East, and here also the heads of families were relatively young (41.7 years of age). Slightly more of these families were normal families consisting of husband and wife or husband, wife, and children than in the Eastern Cotton Area. Although they had more dependents, this did not result from an unduly higher birth rate. In many ways material standards are slightly higher in the Western Cotton Area, but the improvement in material levels has meant a regression or at least no advance in the stability and vitality of social relations.

In the Appalachian-Ozarks is found the best example of self-sufficing farm family living. Four out of ten of the heads of rural relief families were customarily employed in agriculture. Here the average family was the largest (4.3 persons) of any area with the exception of the Spring Wheat Area. The fertility of the rural relief population was the highest of any of the areas surveyed. Although families in this area frequently have a meager existence, a minimum living is assured to them as long as they remain on the land. The chief function of this area continues to be the production of new workers for the cities.

The Corn Belt is a relatively prosperous and highly commercialized area. Here corn is produced either for sale directly or for the feeding of livestock. Commercial production is dominant, and agriculture is on a relatively large scale. The average head of a rural relief family was 43.5 years of age, and 4 out of 10 heads were engaged in agriculture. The tendency toward a small family system is evident; and, although there was a high proportion of normal families, the fertility rate was below the average. In this area farm families as a whole have achieved a level of living seldom paralleled in agricultural history, but the social system does not give great evidence of stability, and the farm family is not maintaining its strength and vitality.

The Hay and Dairy Area cuts through some of the most highly urbanized sections of the country. It forms a belt from the Atlantic seaboard to the fertile lands of Wisconsin which supplies dairy and other products demanded by the highly industrialized and commercialized culture of that section of the country. Only a small proportion of agriculturalists (28.9 percent) was found among the relief families in this area. The median family was about the same size as the average for the country, but the head was about 2 years older on the average. Although 76.0 percent of the rural relief families were normal families, the birth rate was lower than for all areas surveyed. Since most workers gain their living in nonagricultural occupations and since most of the farmers are directly dependent upon the prosperity of the urban market for the sale of their products, the problems of this area are essentially the same as, or are ultimately tied up with, those of the contiguous cities.

The Lake States Cut-Over Area is made up of isolated farming sections and mining communities. Only 26.0 percent of the heads of rural relief families were agriculturalists, and the problems are in many ways different from those in the neighboring Hay and Dairy Area. Its recent settlement, its relative cultural heterogeneity, its isolation, and the depletion of its natural resources are all factors which help to determine its extremely high relief rate, its meager standard of living, and its as yet unstable culture.

Although there are differences between the two Wheat Areas, in contrast with other agricultural areas they present many similarities. A higher proportion of the families is engaged in agriculture than in other areas, with the exception of the Western Cotton Area, and most of this agriculture is of the extensive, commercial type. Like the Corn Belt, the Wheat Areas have had periods of great material prosperity; educational standards are advanced; and material comforts are highly valued. However, the comparatively recent settlement and development of the Wheat Areas, the ethnic heterogeneity, the high rates of social mobility, and the wide fluctuations in climatic conditions are all factors leading to a social instability which markedly affected relief rates.

In the extensiveness of its agricultural production, the Ranching Area is but a step removed from the Wheat Areas. However, mining and lumbering occupations raise the proportion of nonagricultural workers and help account for the large proportion of nonfamily groups in the rural relief population. In many respects this area presents problems which are different from those in other areas, but the probability is that these differences in family statistics are influenced particularly by factors associated with an area of new settlement.

The New England Area represents a further intensification of the factors found in the Hay and Dairy Area. Urbanization has proceeded farther, and the rural culture is even more highly commercialized and industrialized. Only one out of eight of the rural relief families in this area in June 1935 was engaged in agriculture, and the proportion of nonagricultural families in the relief population was higher than in any other area surveyed. This is due both to the large number of local rural industries and to the presence of large numbers of city workers living in the surrounding countryside.

OCCUPATIONAL ORIGIN OF THE HEADS OF RURAL RELIEF FAMILIES

Agricultural occupations accounted for about the same proportion of the heads of rural relief families in June 1935 as did the nonagricultural occupations, 40.6 percent as compared with 41.2 percent. Considering that relief represented only one of four public measures to assist agriculture, it is disheartening that so many farm families had to have this form of assistance. The proportion of agriculturalists among the heads of rural relief families varied from more than two out of three in the Spring Wheat Area to one out of eight in New England.

Among the agriculturalists there were two and one-half times as many farm operator as farm laborer families on relief. This is not surprising since there are considerably more than twice as many farm operators as hired farm laborers in the United States. Within the farm operator group, however, tenant families constituted a greater proportion of the relief cases than did farm owner families although the country as a whole contains about three farm owners for every two tenants.

Unskilled laborers accounted for by far the largest proportion of heads of nonagricultural families. In New England there were also a large number of relief families whose heads were skilled and semiskilled workers.

Families whose heads were nonworkers accounted for 15.6 percent of all relief cases, reflecting the tendency for relief rolls to include a large number of families that for various reasons contain no breadwinner. In 2.5 percent of the cases the head of the family had no usual occupation.

PERSONAL CHARACTERISTICS OF THE HEADS OF RURAL RELIEF FAMILIES

The average head of a rural relief family was in the prime of life, the early forties. Village heads, on the whole, were about 2 years older than those in the open country. The heads of families in New England had the highest average age (46.6 years), while the lowest average age was found in the Winter Wheat Area (39.0 years). The median age of heads of agricultural families on relief was about the same as that of heads of nonagricultural families. Farm owners, however, had the highest average age of any occupational group on relief (46.5 years). On the other hand, farm laborers were the youngest group, averaging only 36.4 years. Among the nonagriculturalists the skilled laborers with an average age of 43.7 years had the highest average of any subgroup. Negro family heads on relief were much older than white heads on the average. In the Eastern Cotton Area the difference was 4.9 years and in the Western Cotton Area 7.5 years.

The western areas of extensive, commercialized agriculture had the smallest proportions of rural relief families with female heads while the southern areas, including the Eastern and Western Cotton and the Appalachian-Ozark Areas, had the highest proportions of such families. An exception to this rule was found in the Ranching Area which ranked with the South in the proportion of families with female heads. Significant differences also existed between village and open country residents in that almost half again as many village heads of rural relief families were women as was the case among open country heads.

Most of the male heads of relief families were married, while most of the female heads were either unmarried or had had their homes broken by divorce, separation, or death. For all areas the highest proportion of female heads married was 15.7 percent for the age group 45–64 years, while the lowest proportion was 0.6 percent for those aged 65 years and over. In contrast, the highest proportion married among the male heads was 90.9 percent in the age group 25–34 years, and the lowest was 61.5 percent in the age group 65 years and over. The proportion of family heads that was married was greater in the open country than in the villages, while the proportion of widowed, divorced, or separated heads tended to be greater in the villages. Differences in marital condition among the areas were consistent with differences in social and economic backgrounds. The greater industrialization of New England and the North has led to a greater participation in industry by women, and consequently the emancipation of women has reached its most advanced stages in these regions. Accompanying this emancipation is a rapidly rising divorce rate and a general disintegration of former social rules which have regulated the distribution of rights and duties of the sexes.

SIZE AND COMPOSITION OF RURAL RELIEF FAMILIES

The problem of the size and composition of relief families is important to relief programs from a number of points of view, but principally because large families, or those with numerous dependents and few gainfully employed or employable, may need relief more frequently and in larger amounts than smaller families or those with relatively more productive units.

The median size of the rural relief family in June 1935 was 3.9 members. The open country families were larger than those in the villages. Averages, however, do not give an adequate picture of the situation with respect to size of family. Of all the rural households receiving relief in June 1935, 9.9 percent were one-person households. This was a 2 percent greater proportion of one-person households than was found for the whole rural United States in the 1930 Census (7.7 percent). Since severe economic depressions usually tend to increase social solidarity, at least for a time, it would seem from these data that the proportion of one-person households receiving relief was very much greater than could be expected from a normal sample of the rural population. Further comparisons with census data suggest that a larger proportion of rural relief families consisted of six persons or more, whereas a larger proportion of families in the general population consisted of two or three members. Families with four or five members were found in about equal proportions among both relief families and families in the general population.

Rural relief families had relatively more young members (children under 16 years of age) than are found in the general rural population, and they contained a smaller proportion of adults of working age.

DEPENDENT AGE GROUPS

Four out of five of the rural relief families contained persons in the dependent age groups, i. e., persons under 16 years of age or 65 years of age and over. Three out of five relief families had children under 16 years of age but no one over 64 years; one-eighth of the families had aged individuals 65 years of age and over but no children under 16; while one out of twenty families contained both children and aged persons. These proportions varied somewhat among the agricultural areas of the country and were related to the type of economy and the "age" of the area.

In general a large number of dependents in a family may be an indication of a prolific population, where a high birth rate results in large families, or it may indicate a high degree of family solidarity. Again there is the possibility, as shown in the Cotton Areas, that there may be a splitting of families so as to place aged persons on relief and to leave the younger employables to fend for themselves without the responsibility for other individuals. All of these factors may operate to increase the number of old or young dependents on relief. The question of dependency and relief is, however, related principally to the basic economic and cultural factors in any particular region. The predominant industries and occupations determine the extent to which the head of a family will be able to care for his dependents continuously, and the cultural traditions to a large extent determine the internal solidarity and cohesiveness of the family unit.

Background factors of an economic, sociological, or even medical nature, when viewed in their full complexity, are agents which determine the number of dependents on relief. Families in the South, including the Appalachian-Ozark Area, for example, are likely to be large as a result of high birth rates; they tend to cling together in a large cohesive aggregate. Loss of economic support, or the injury or death of the chief provider, quickly forces the whole aggregation on relief. Therefore, it is easy to understand why the proportion of families with no persons in the dependent age groups should be smallest in the South, where rural cultural traditions are strong, and greatest in the North, where the strong Yankee traditions are now nearly submerged by the newer mores of an industrialized and urbanized society.

FAMILY STRUCTURAL TYPES

For purposes of analysis family units were divided into three main types—normal families, broken families, and nonfamily types. In the normal group were found 72.5 percent of all rural relief families, while 10.9 percent were broken families and 16.6 percent were nonfamily types. The great majority of the normal families consisted of husband and wife or of parents and children alone, while about one out of nine also had relatives or friends present. Normal families were relatively more frequent in the open country than in the villages, and a larger proportion in the open country consisted of husband, wife, and children, as compared with husband and wife only in the villages. Likewise there were more broken families in the villages than in the open country, and broken families with female heads especially tended to congregate in the villages. Normal families were relatively more prevalent among the agricultural (82.2 percent) than among the nonagricultural (77.4 percent) families.

Broken families occurred most frequently in the southern areas. Nonfamily types were most evident among the Negroes of the South and in the industrial and urban areas of the North and East.

FERTILITY OF RURAL RELIEF FAMILIES

The relationship between fertility and relief is difficult to measure. A comparison of the relief data with the 1930 Census data was made for identical counties, and certain relationships were noted concerning the number of children under 5 years of age per 1,000 women 20 to 44 years of age in the population. The comparison is subject to qualification on several scores, however. One difficulty is the fact that there was a difference of 5 years between the census figures and the relief figures, and the depression of the early thirties had far-reaching effects on marriage and birth rates. Another was that relief practices in certain areas, particularly in the Western Cotton Area, resulted in the splitting of tenant and cropper families and resulted in the placing on relief of aged or unemployable members while the younger and more able members were kept under the care of the landlord. This naturally would tend to affect the size of the relief family. From such data as were available, however, it appears that for the country as a whole the fertility ratio for the relief families was considerably higher than that for the general population. This is to be expected since relief families, for the most part, come from the lower social and economic strata where the birth rates are higher than those in the higher strata. Furthermore, since population traits are well grounded in the mores, relief families with more children may continue, at least for a time, to have children while still on relief.

The relationship between fertility and relief, however, was by no means uniform. In some areas fertility was much higher among relief families than among census families, particularly in the Appalachian-Ozark and Ranching Areas. In other areas the differences were smaller, while in the Eastern Cotton Area the number of children under 5 years of age per 1,000 women aged 20 to 44 years was actually slightly smaller for the relief families than for all families in 1930.

EMPLOYABILITY, EMPLOYMENT, AND AMOUNT OF RELIEF

Employability and employment are directly related to relief and are vital factors in family status in either prosperity or depression. The employability composition of a family sets the outside limits for its employment success, and many families are greatly handicapped by the lack of any capable member between the ages of 16 and 64 years. The plight of many rural relief families can be shown by the fact that one-eighth of them had no employable worker and an additional 7.8 percent of these families had female workers only. These two types of unemployability taken together were relatively most important in the two Cotton Areas. Unemployability was especially high among the Negroes of the South and relatively lower among the whites.

During times of depression work in agriculture is relatively more stable than in nonagriculture, although the past unusual period in agricultural production forced a large number of normally self-supporting agricultural families on relief. However, only 29.2 percent of the gainful workers who had usually been employed in agriculture were unemployed at the time of the survey in contrast with 72.1 percent of the nonagricultural workers. The small proportion of unemployed in agriculture, however, was partly due to the fact that farm operators were arbitrarily defined as employed if they were still on their farms, even if they had no cash income. For the groups that were actually employed within these broad classes, much more occupational shifting had taken place among the nonagricultural occupations. Only 1 percent of the former workers in agriculture had shifted into nonagricultural jobs, but almost 11 percent of the nonagricultural workers were employed in agriculture at the time of survey. This difference was also shown by the fact that 95.8 percent of all the workers in agriculture who were employed were engaged in their usual occupations as contrasted with 55.7 percent of the workers in nonagriculture. In part this reflects a widespread movement back to the farm during the depression, and in part it also represents a reversed current of occupational mobility, which caused a general shifting down the scale for workers at all levels.

When rural relief families were analyzed according to continuity of their relief histories, certain trends were observable. Of all cases on relief in June 1935, 74.3 percent had received assistance continuously since February. Another 14.2 percent of the cases had been reopened between March and June, and only 11.5 percent were new cases. Slightly more new cases appeared in the villages than in the open country. Continuous relief histories were found most frequently among groups of a generally low economic level or among groups especially affected during the depression period by unusual circumstances. The Negroes in the South are an example of the first type, and the farmers in the drought area are an example of the second type.

The average amount of relief per family was influenced mainly by these same factors, low economic levels or unusual conditions of stress. Also of importance in the determination of amount of relief were comparative price levels and costs of living. Lowest amounts of relief were found in the three southern areas, particularly among the Negroes, and the highest amounts were spent in the industrialized areas of the North and East. Indeed, the cost of relief per family in the Eastern and Western Cotton Areas was not more than one-third the cost in New England. Four factors were most important in determining the incidence and amount of relief for rural families: (1) The number of employables in the family and their capabilities; (2) unemployment because of the business cycle; (3) unemployment and underemployment because of the weather cycle; and (4) social action for improving the standard of living.

MOBILITY OF RURAL RELIEF FAMILIES

Only crude measures of the mobility of rural relief families were available. For the most part the families were divided into three groups as follows: *lifelong residents*, referring to those families whose head was born in the county in which he was living at the time of the survey; *predepression migrants*, referring to those families whose head moved to the county at any time prior to 1930; and *depression migrants*, including those families whose head moved to the county some time during the period 1930 to June 1935.

Of the heads of rural families on relief in June 1935, 40.5 percent were lifelong residents of the county; 45.6 percent had moved to the county before the depression; and the remaining 13.9 percent were depression migrants. As might be expected, smaller proportions of the heads of rural relief families were lifelong residents in the more recently settled areas than in the areas of older settlement. The proportion of lifelong residents was 14.4 percent in the Winter Wheat Area, 17.8 percent in the Lake States Cut-Over Area, 22.4 percent in the Ranching Area, and 28.0 percent in the Spring Wheat Area. All of these are areas of comparatively recent settlement. Portions of the two Wheat Areas and of the Lake States Cut-Over Area were settled as recently as the

World War. Proportionately more lifelong residents were found in the South and in other sections of older settlement. Migration during the depression was characterized by two main types. The first was migration because of the drought. This was most noticeable in the Wheat Areas and the Western Cotton Area, resulting in a shifting of population within those areas and also a movement to the villages and to the States in the far West. The second form of depression migration was the back-to-the-farm movement from the depression-stricken cities. This was important in the self-sufficing areas of the Northeast. It was also of great importance in the mountain areas of the South.

Agriculture is an occupation which encourages stability as contrasted with nonagriculture. Within agriculture farm operators were more stable than farm laborers, but among the nonagricultural occupations unskilled laborers were the most stable group. More nonagricultural than agricultural workers had moved during the depression. The depression meant a move to the village for farm operators and a move to the country for nonagricultural workers while many farm laborers simply moved to another location in the open country.

EDUCATION OF RURAL RELIEF FAMILIES

Heads of rural relief families were found to be on a comparatively low educational level since less than 4 percent were high school graduates and only about 35 percent had completed as much as a grammar school education. Wide differences appeared among the various areas, however, as well as between village and open country residents, between agricultural and nonagricultural workers, and between whites and Negroes. In general, the educational level was higher in the more industrialized and urbanized areas than it was in the more agricultural areas. Similarly, within each area the agricultural workers had a lower educational level than the nonagricultural workers. In every area a larger proportion of the heads of village families had completed a grammar school education than had the heads of families living in the open country; for all areas combined the difference reached approximately 11 percent. In the South Negroes were on a lower educational level than whites. The median school grade completed by heads of white relief families in the Eastern Cotton Area was 5.9 years, while for heads of Negro relief families it was only 2.9 years. The median school grade completed for all heads of rural relief families in all areas was 6.4 years.

The contrast between the education of heads and of other family members, particularly of youth and children, reflects the fact that educational levels have been rising during the past generation. This was most noticeable in areas of low standards where the requirements have been raised rather rapidly and are beginning to approximate the standards of the country as a whole.

Chapter I

TYPES OF FARM FAMILIES AND THE INCIDENCE OF RELIEF

THE RURAL population of the United States is not homogeneous according to residence. It is not only distributed among farm, open country nonfarm, and village residences, but it is also broken up into major agricultural regions (fig. 1). The farm population of the United States is unevenly distributed over these regions (fig. 2), being more concentrated in the hilly regions, on poor soils, and in the South than it is in the richer regions of the Corn Belt of the North, in the wheat regions, and in the arid plains of the West. This leads to a differentiation of the farm population into broad categories.

TYPES OF FARM FAMILIES

The first category in the farm population is that of the commercial farmers, including both owners and tenants, who produce most of the products sold from American farms. The importance of this group can be seen from a study of figure 3 which gives the value of the products sold from the farm and used by farm families classified into groups, by values, for the United States in 1929. Farm families having products valued at more/than $1,000 comprised 51.2 percent of such families and produced 89.2 percent of the products sold. These families under ordinary circumstances are relatively well-to-do. They comprise a good part of the farm population in the Corn Belt, the Spring and Winter Wheat Areas, and the Hay and Dairy Area. They also comprise a large proportion of the upper economic classes in the Eastern and Western Cotton Areas and some of the families in the Lake States Cut-Over and Ranching Areas and in certain areas of New England. They comprise only a very few of the families in the Appalachian-Ozark Area (see fig. 1 and fig. 26, p. 112).

These families are commercial producers and consumers and to a large extent are under the direct influence of the export markets of the United States, because of the fact that the prices of their products are determined largely by the commercial surplus which is exported. Relief for these families, and for the regions where they predominate, is determined to a great extent by the fluctuations in quantities and prices

1

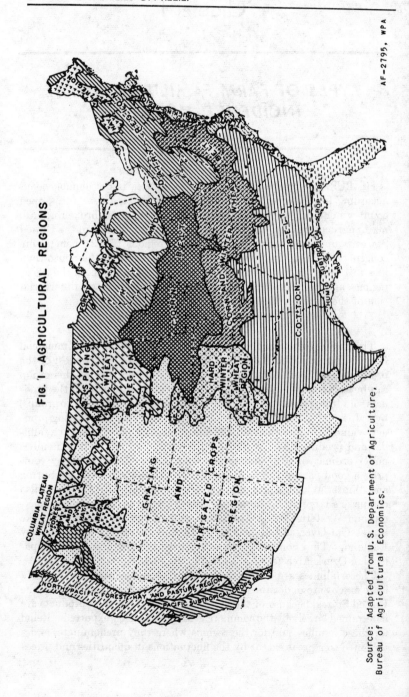

FIG. 1—AGRICULTURAL REGIONS

AF-2795, WPA

Source: Adapted from U.S. Department of Agriculture,
Bureau of Agricultural Economics.

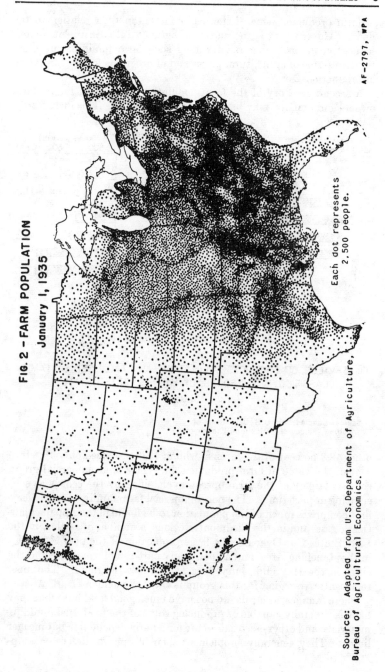

FIG. 2 – FARM POPULATION
January 1, 1935

Each dot represents
2,500 people.

AF-2797, WPA

Source: Adapted from U.S.Department of Agriculture,
Bureau of Agricultural Economics.

of farm products. One of the major factors in their relation to the Federal Government is the matter of agricultural adjustment. Consequently, in discussing relief among such farm families, one must think in terms of agricultural prices and of programs for the limitation of production.

A second category of the farm population, likewise including both owners and tenants, may be called noncommercial. This includes the

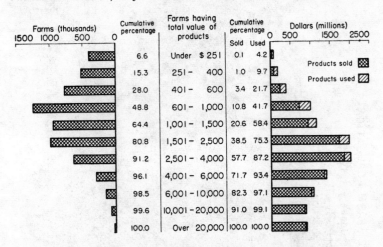

Farms (thousands) 1500 1000 500 0	Cumulative percentage	Farms having total value of products	Cumulative percentage Sold Used	Dollars (millions) 0 500 1500 2500
	6.6	Under $ 251	0.1 4.2	
	15.3	251 – 400	1.0 9.7	Products sold ▨ Products used ▧
	28.0	401 – 600	3.4 21.7	
	48.8	601 – 1,000	10.8 41.7	
	64.4	1,001 – 1,500	20.6 58.4	
	80.8	1,501 – 2,500	38.5 75.3	
	91.2	2,501 – 4,000	57.7 87.2	
	96.1	4,001 – 6,000	71.7 93.4	
	98.5	6,001 – 10,000	82.3 97.1	
	99.6	10,001 – 20,000	91.0 99.1	
	100.0	Over 20,000	100.0 100.0	

FIG. 3 - VALUE OF PRODUCTS SOLD FROM FARM AND USED BY FAMILY CLASSIFIED INTO GROUPS, BY VALUES, UNITED STATES
1929

Source: Adapted from U.S. Department of
Agriculture, Bureau of Agricultural Economics.   AF-2801,WPA

other 48.8 percent of the farmers who in 1929 produced only 10.8 percent of the value of farm products sold. This noncommercial group consists largely of the farm operators classified by the census as self-sufficing or part-time. The noncommercial farm family or subsistence unit comprises much of the population to be found in the Appalachian-Ozark Area and in the Piedmont Regions, a number of settlers in the Lake States Cut-Over Area, a large proportion of the poorer families in the Ranching Area, and a good many part-time farmers around the cities in the Hay and Dairy Area and in New England. The most representative region for this group is the Appalachian-Ozark Area.

These families, as a rule, do not have much good land but what they have is generally capable of producing some of the food, fuel, building materials, and other essentials of life for a fairly dependable but meager living. They generally supplement their income in direct consumption goods from these poor land resources by labor in other occupations, such as those connected with timber and mineral resources and decentralized factories. These families are helped relatively little by agricultural price-raising in the United States since their products are consumed rather than sold and since to some extent they must purchase the products whose prices have been increased by the program. On the other hand, restricted production in the coal, copper, and iron mines and in the factories located in the rural districts has a direct influence upon their living. The depletion of timber resources is also very important. This explains why these families form a category of their own and why they are, to a large extent, to be found in the Appalachian-Ozark Area (with formerly abundant timber and coal resources) more frequently than in the richer agricultural areas. This also explains why they are found in the Lake States Cut-Over Area with its former timber resources and its copper and iron mines and in New England with its decentralized industries. The presence of these families, to a limited extent, in the grazing area is determined by the fact that this is a mountainous region with some timber and mineral resources.

Cutting across both the commercial and noncommercial groups, a third category of the agricultural population may be called the chronically poverty-stricken. Some rural families of this type, both owner and tenant, are to be found in all areas. It includes chiefly, however, the farm laborers in all areas and the sharecroppers and tenants of the Eastern and Western Cotton Areas. In the South relief among them is complicated by the problem of race because a high proportion of the poverty-stricken families are Negro families. A great many of them, however, are white families living under the same economic conditions. As laborers, croppers, and tenants upon farms chiefly in the South, they produce goods primarily for commercial sale. In spite of the fact that they are chronically poverty-stricken, they seldom produce much food for home consumption. This is due partly to the system of agriculture and partly to ignorance, disease, and the fact that they either have lost or have never developed sufficiently the type of culture which emphasizes production of goods for home consumption. These poverty-stricken rural families include also the migratory laborers to be found in the West, particularly in California. During the depression, and especially since the droughts of 1934 and 1936, they have been joined by a number of the former farmers of the drought region [1] (fig. 4). Many of these lost everything they had and migrated westward to join the group of relatively poverty-stricken laborers. Whereas in the South the problem of

---

[1] See Taeuber, Conrad and Taylor, Carl C., *The People of the Drought States,* Research Bulletin Series V, No. 2, Division of Social Research, Works Progress Administration, Washington, D. C., 1937, pp. 45–47.

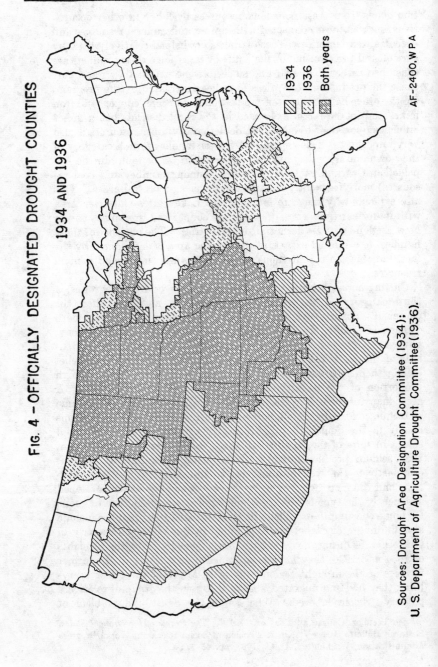

FIG. 4 — OFFICIALLY DESIGNATED DROUGHT COUNTIES
1934 AND 1936

1934
1936
Both years

AF-2400, W P A

Sources: Drought Area Designation Committee (1934);
U. S. Department of Agriculture Drought Committee (1936).

poverty-stricken laborers is complicated by the fact that a great many of them are Negroes, in the West there are many persons of Mexican, oriental, or South European origin.

A large proportion of the poverty-stricken, whether laborers, share-tenants, or sharecroppers, work for commercial farmers. In many cases they live on the farms the year round, but the migratory workers live on them only during the crop season. During the other parts of the year they tend to become attached to the rural-nonfarm population, chiefly in the villages. As a general rule they work solely for wages or for a part of the crop. Supplies are furnished by the land-lord or employer, and they do little subsistence farming for home supplies on their own account. As a result they share the sufferings caused by fluctuations in the business cycle along with the commercial farmer. If agricultural adjustment keeps them on the farms or fur-nishes them employment during a period of production restriction and higher prices, they gain in higher wages and more return for their crop from the change. If, under any process, they are not kept on or re-hired in their former seasonal employment during such a period, they are forced upon relief providing they cannot find alternative opportu-nities for work.

From the point of view of these categories of farm families, three important types of influences came to bear upon rural life in America during the depression of the early thirties. These were, respectively, the decline in prices and sales for the commercial farmers, either the decline in utilization or the disappearance of other natural resources for the noncommercial farmers, and the change in work opportunities for the poverty-stricken laborers, croppers, and tenants. In analyzing the problem of relief and of the depression in any rural area one should consider it in terms of how far the area is influenced by the predomi-nance of one of these broad rural classes on relief.

Another problem in American rural life which has had an influence upon the relief needs of farm families is that of production for domestic consumption or for export. Some farmers specialize in export crops or crops with an export surplus, such as wheat or cotton, and others in producing goods consumed almost entirely by the American wage earner, such as milk and dairy products. The Hay and Dairy Area is representative of the farmer who produces almost entirely for American consumption, whereas the Spring and Winter Wheat Areas and the Eastern and Western Cotton Areas all have high export sur-pluses.

The farmers who produce crops with an export surplus depend, to a considerable extent, upon a foreign market which, at the same time, may or may not be as prosperous or restricted as the American urban market. The people in these regions are generally located at some distance from the large cities and on level agricultural lands more or less devoid of timber and mineral resources. Consequently their opportunities for a part-time farming and industrial combination are more or less restricted. On the other hand, the producers for the domestic urban market are located almost entirely near the large cities in industrial regions where their opportunities for subsidiary income from sources other than agriculture are considerably enhanced. Thus, they have come to depend on these subsidiary sources of income and may suffer considerably from unemployment even though the general prices of agricultural products are fairly stable. Such farmers are in direct contact with the city. As a result, whatever influences urbanization, industrialization, a high rate of mobility, and communication have upon rural family life will be felt most quickly in a region where production for the domestic market predominates. All of these statements apply with particular force to the Hay and Dairy Area and to New England.

Finally, there are the special problems of the farmers in those regions of the United States with restricted rainfall—averaging less than 20 inches per year. These regions are to be found in the Spring and Winter Wheat Areas and in the Great Plains grazing area. Rainfall in these regions fluctuates not only according to the seasons of the year and year by year but also through longer cycles. Many of these regions were densely settled, at least from the standpoint of acreage farmed, during the period of high prices for agricultural products which set in about 1910 and carried on through the World War. This also happened to be a period of relatively good rainfall. Since that time, and particularly during the depression of the early thirties, a period of drought set in. The extensive droughts of 1934 and 1936 are related to this cycle, and any analysis should consider the relief families in those regions from this standpoint.

THE INCIDENCE OF RELIEF

Rural families receiving general relief gradually increased in number from the inauguration of the Federal Emergency Relief Administration early in 1933 to January 1935 when they reached an estimated total of 1,949,000 cases. By the time final FERA grants were determined in December of that year the rural relief load had declined to 401,000 cases (table 1). Part of the decline in the relief load was due to the transfer of thousands of cases to the rural rehabilitation program in the early months of 1935.[2] In the latter part of the year the decline was largely due to the transfer of employable cases to the

---

[2] See Asch, Berta and Mangus, A. R., *Farmers on Relief and Rehabilitation*, Research Monograph VIII, Division of Social Research, Works Progress Administration, Washington, D. C., 1937, p. 18.

Farm Owner Family in the Drought Area.

Table 1.—Rural Families in the United States Receiving General Relief, July 1933 Through December 1935 (Estimated)

Year and month	Number of families	Year and month	Number of families
1933		**1934**	
July	1,270,000	October	1,667,000
August	1,282,000	November	1,753,000
September	1,010,000	December	1,853,000
October	1,113,000		
November	1,333,000	**1935**	
December	1,007,000	January	1,949,000
		February	1,907,000
1934		March	1,858,000
January	1,165,000	April	1,764,000
February	1,227,000	May	1,649,000
March	1,414,000	June	1,427,000
April	1,321,000	July	1,289,000
May	1,453,000	August	1,149,000
June	1,523,000	September	1,039,000
July	1,610,000	October	991,000
August	1,765,000	November	859,000
September	1,725,000	December	401,000

Source: Smith, Mapheus and Mangus, A. R., *Cases Receiving General Relief in Urban and Rural Areas, July 1933-December 1935 (Estimated)*, Research Bulletin Series III, No. 1, Division of Social Research, Works Progress Administration, Washington, D. C., August 22, 1936.

Works Program.[3] Increased employment in private industry and administrative closings further reduced the relief load.

Comparison of the estimated proportion of the rural and urban population receiving general relief between July 1933 and December 1935 reveals two important aspects with respect to rural relief. The first of these is the relative position of the rural population in regard to the incidence of relief (fig. 5 and appendix table 1). For each month of the period covered the proportion of the rural population on relief was less than that of the urban population. The national average was always nearer the urban than the rural ratio because there are about 5 million more urban than rural families in the United States.

A second factor was the fluctuations in relief loads in rural and urban areas. The proportion of the urban population on relief was 15.2 percent in July 1933 and tended on the whole to remain large but with a number of fluctuations throughout the whole period studied. Rural relief was relatively high in some of the early months of 1933. Fundamentally, however, rural relief reached a peak of a little above 15 percent in January and February 1935 and declined slowly after that time. The urban percentages also declined systematically during 1935 from the peak of February. The important point is that the rural and urban relief curves had some elements in common but others which differentiated them. Differences were most significant in the early period while in the later period similarities were outstanding. The dividing point was the late spring of 1934.

Relief rates also varied considerably among the agricultural areas surveyed (appendix table 2). By far the most outstanding relief area

[3] Mangus, A. R., *Changing Aspects of Rural Relief*, Research Monograph XIV, Division of Social Research, Works Progress Administration, Washington, D. C., 1938, appendix table 9.

was the Lake States Cut-Over with the Appalachian-Ozark Area competing with the Spring Wheat Area for second place. The Appalachian-Ozark Area had a generally high incidence of relief, whereas the

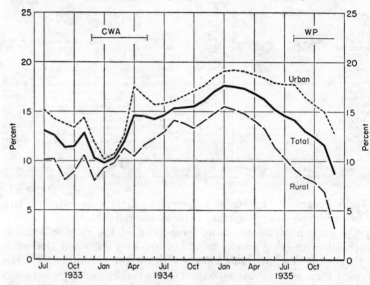

FIG. 5 – INTENSITY OF GENERAL RELIEF IN THE UNITED STATES*
BY RESIDENCE (Estimated)

July 1933 through December 1935

*Percentage ratio of total estimated number of cases
to all families of the same residence class.

Source: Mangus, A.R., *Changing Aspects of Rural Relief*, Research Monograph XIV, Division of Social Research, Works Progress Administration, Washington, D.C., 1938

AF-2802, WPA

Spring Wheat Area had particularly high relief loads following the drought of 1934.

The areas with the lowest relief loads were the Corn Belt and the Hay and Dairy Area.[4] These two regions represented the commercial farmers who received particular aid through the Agricultural Adjustment Administration (Corn Belt) and who produced food crops for domestic consumption (Hay and Dairy Area). Hence, low relief rates for the farmers in these areas are understandable because, if they produced export crops, they were aided by the AAA and, if they produced goods primarily for American wage earners, their markets did not decline as much as did the foreign ones. The maintenance of

---

[4] Comparable data for New England are not available.

domestic markets was due in part to the fact that Federal relief in the cities enabled the urban families, who consumed much of these farm products, to continue to purchase the food produced for such markets.

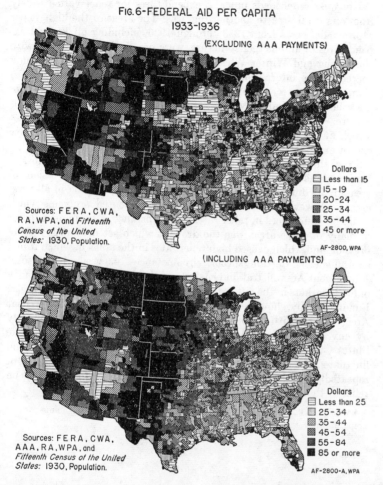

FIG. 6-FEDERAL AID PER CAPITA
1933-1936

(EXCLUDING A A A PAYMENTS)

Dollars
Less than 15
15 - 19
20 - 24
25 - 34
35 - 44
45 or more

Sources: F E R A , C W A ,
R A , W P A , and *Fifteenth
Census of the United
States:* 1930, Population.

AF-2800, WPA

(INCLUDING A A A PAYMENTS)

Dollars
Less than 25
25 - 34
35 - 44
45 - 54
55 - 84
85 or more

Sources: F E R A , C W A ,
A A A , R A , W P A , and
*Fifteenth Census of the United
States:* 1930, Population.

AF-2800-A, WPA

It should be pointed out that the figures on relief intensity do not represent the same families every month. Rural families came on and went off relief at a rapid rate as their fortunes temporarily improved or declined.[5] As a result of the high rate of turnover, it is probable that the actual number of families which received relief for at least 1 month during the period of the FERA was at least 50 percent

[5] Mangus, A. R., *op. cit.*, ch. III.

greater than the number on relief at the peak month. More than one out of every four rural families received public or private assistance at some time during the early thirties.[5]

Not only relief loads but also expenditures for relief varied widely from one rural area to another (fig. 6). The areas of the highest per capita relief costs from 1933 through 1936, including all Federal expenditures of an emergency nature, were practically coextensive with the Spring and Winter Wheat Areas. This region has an economy geared to the international industrial-commercial complex. It is of comparatively recent settlement with but slight accumulations of material goods; and, as yet, it has not developed a strong indigenous culture. Thus, when the combination of drought and a low market struck at the economic organization, the population had no recourse except emigration or dependency.

From this brief summary of the incidence of rural relief a number of factors stand out clearly. First, the general economic depression increased the difficulty that families had in making a living in all rural areas. However, different types of areas presented problems which made for differences in relief rates. For instance, a prominent factor in many of these areas was the drought which set in during the depression and which caused high relief rates in the areas in which it had an influence. Certain special circumstances, such as Agricultural Adjustment Administration benefits and the accessibility and stability of food markets in the cities, tended to lower relief rates for some areas. Fundamentally, however, with the exception of the Spring Wheat Area, sections with the highest relief rates were not influenced directly by any of these factors. In the Appalachian-Ozark and the Lake States Cut-Over Areas rural relief rates were the highest of all and fluctuated the least. Further in this study the analysis will attempt repeatedly to throw light on the particular problems of the families on relief in those two areas.

---

[6] Woofter, T. J., Jr. and Winston, Ellen, *Seven Lean Years*, manuscript in preparation.

Chapter II

OCCUPATIONAL ORIGIN OF THE HEADS OF RURAL RELIEF FAMILIES

THE USUAL occupations [1] of the heads of rural relief families give both a picture of the background of the relief problem and some indication of the kind of breakdown responsible for the relief situation. For purposes of analysis heads of families are classified as agricultural or nonagricultural, as having no usual occupation,[2] or as nonworkers [3] (table 2).

A high proportion of agricultural families was receiving general relief in June 1935 although this was only one of four important public measures for the improvement of agriculture and rural life in operation at that time. The other three were the Agricultural Adjustment Administration, which sought to raise prices and give bonuses to the farmer; the Farm Credit Administration, which sought to lower interest rates and take over mortgages to keep farmers from losing their farms; and the rural rehabilitation program, which sought to remove farm families from relief rolls by advancing credit for subsistence and farming operations so that they could once more become self-supporting.

The agricultural occupations accounted for about the same proportion of the rural relief cases as the nonagricultural occupations (40.6 percent as compared with 41.2 percent). Considering that relief represented only one of four public measures to assist agriculture, it is disheartening that so many farmers had to have this form of assistance.

---

[1] A person was considered to have had a usual occupation if at any time during the past 10 years he had worked at any job, other than work relief, for a period of at least 4 consecutive weeks. If a person had worked at two or more occupations, the one at which he had worked the greatest length of time was considered the usual occupation. If he had worked for an equal length of time at two or more occupations, the one at which he had worked last was considered the usual occupation.

[2] Capable of working and seeking work but not qualifying for a usual occupation under footnote 1 above.

[3] Neither seeking gainful employment nor qualifying under footnote 1 above.

13

Table 2.—Usual Occupation of Heads of Rural Families Receiving General Relief, by Area, June 1935

[138 counties and 116 New England townships]

Usual occupation	All areas	Eastern Cotton			Western Cotton			Appalachian-Ozark	Lake States Cut-Over	Hay and Dairy	Corn Belt	Spring Wheat	Winter Wheat	Ranching	New England
		Total	White	Negro	Total	White	Negro								
Number	62,831	7,732	5,084	2,648	7,208	5,432	1,836	17,016	3,814	8,626	7,512	3,374	1,288	1,886	4,315
Percent	100.0	100.0	100.0	100.0	100.0	100.0	100.0	100.0	100.0	100.0	100.0	100.0	100.0	100.0	100.0
Agriculture	40.6	47.5	47.5	47.4	54.3	56.8	46.7	41.3	26.0	28.9	40.2	68.7	54.3	42.9	12.7
Farm operator	29.3	28.1	31.6	21.7	34.3	36.0	29.4	38.3	22.2	17.3	20.8	61.5	38.5	25.2	6.9
Owner	10.7	6.1	7.6	3.1	4.0	4.0	4.5	15.3	17.4	8.4	5.2	25.6	8.5	15.6	6.4
Tenant	15.4	13.5	15.9	8.9	17.0	18.9	13.5	23.0	4.8	8.9	15.6	35.9	30.0	9.6	0.5
Cropper	3.2	8.6	8.1	9.7	13.2	13.1	11.4	—	—	—	—	—	—	—	—
Farm laborer	11.3	19.4	15.9	25.7	20.0	20.8	17.3	3.0	3.8	11.6	19.4	7.2	15.8	17.7	5.8
Nonagriculture	41.2	31.2	34.4	25.3	24.7	26.1	20.7	43.8	52.8	51.1	44.1	19.1	33.0	34.8	63.7
White collar	3.7	4.1	6.0	0.5	2.9	3.6	0.9	2.1	2.8	4.2	5.8	3.5	5.0	2.3	6.8
Skilled	6.8	4.0	5.3	1.5	2.9	3.8	0.4	3.2	7.8	11.4	8.1	4.6	6.1	4.0	12.5
Semiskilled	6.8	7.9	11.1	1.8	2.9	3.6	0.7	3.6	5.8	9.7	8.5	2.4	4.0	4.5	21.5
Unskilled	24.7	15.2	12.0	21.5	16.0	15.1	18.7	34.9	36.4	25.8	21.7	8.6	17.9	24.0	22.9
No usual occupation	2.5	3.4	4.8	0.8	1.5	1.9	0.4	3.3	1.7	1.0	1.6	3.9	2.3	2.2	3.0
Nonworker	15.6	17.7	13.2	26.5	19.5	15.2	32.2	11.5	19.2	19.0	14.1	8.3	9.9	19.8	20.2
Unknown	0.1	0.1	0.1	—	—	—	—	0.1	0.3	—	—	0.1	0.5	0.3	0.4

Among the agriculturalists [4] farm operators were two and one-half times as numerous on relief as farm laborers. This might be expected because there are considerably more than twice as many farm operators as hired farm laborers in the United States. Within the farm operator group, however, tenants furnished a greater proportion of the relief cases than did farm owners [5] although in the entire United States there are about three farm owners for every two farm tenants.

Unskilled laborers accounted for most of the heads of relief cases among the nonagricultural group. This is partly because they are the most numerous class among rural nonagriculturalists and partly because the incidence of relief is greater at the bottom of the economic pyramid. Nonworkers constituted 15.6 percent of the heads of relief cases, reflecting the tendency for relief rolls at any particular time to include a large number of families which for various reasons contain no breadwinner at all.

OCCUPATIONAL ORIGIN BY AREA

The occupational origins of heads of relief families varied widely by areas (table 2). Agriculture was more important than nonagriculture in the Cotton, Wheat, and Ranching Areas. In the other areas the opposite was true. The greatest proportionate difference existed between New England with only 12.7 percent of its rural relief families engaged in agriculture and the Spring Wheat Area where 68.7 percent were of farm origin. The important factor in New England was probably the extent of urbanization along with decentralized industrial villages. Drought was chiefly responsible for the high proportion of farm families on relief in the Spring Wheat Area.

The proportion of farm laborers on relief in the two Cotton Areas and in the other commercial agricultural regions is one indication of the net results of agricultural restrictions. Under the system of reducing farm production these workers were no longer needed in agriculture, and finding no other alternative they went on relief. Also,

---

[4] Agriculturalists include farm owners, tenants, and croppers, and farm laborers. A *farm owner* is a farmer who owns all or part of the land which he operates. A *renter* or *tenant* is a farm operator who operates hired land only, furnishing all or part of the working equipment and stock whether he pays cash or a share of the crop or both as rent. A *farm cropper* is a farmer who operates only rented land and to whom the landlord furnishes all of the work animals; i. e., a farm operator who contributes only his labor and receives in return a share of the crop. A *farm laborer* is a person who works on a farm with or without wages under the supervision of the farm operator. Children over 16 years of age and wives who work regularly and most of the time on the household farm are included in this definition, whether they receive money wages, a share of the crop, or board and room. Persons who do only incidental farm chores are not included.

[5] Asch, Berta and Mangus, A. R., *Farmers on Relief and Rehabilitation*, Research Monograph VIII, Division of Social Research, Works Progress Administration, Washington, D. C., 1937, p. 51.

part of the excess destitute population in the Cotton Belt migrated and showed up among the laborers on relief in the far West.

For the nonagricultural families on relief the most important additional observation was the proportions of skilled and semiskilled workers on relief in rural New England. With the closing of factories in industrial villages they were forced on relief along with the unskilled. Moreover, the number of white-collar workers receiving relief in the rural districts of New England was almost twice as great as the national average. On the other hand, New England furnished slightly less than the national average of unskilled laborers on relief. This is to be explained by the fact that the industrial population in New England is a highly skilled one as contrasted with the general rural-industrial population in the United States.

The proportion of heads with no usual occupation receiving rural relief was not significant in any area. Nonworkers were important, however, constituting from 10 to 20 percent of the relief load in all areas except the Spring Wheat.

In the Eastern and Western Cotton Areas tenants, croppers, and farm laborers were the important groups to receive relief among the agriculturalists. Among the nonagriculturalists unskilled laborers formed the important group. Thus, occupations at the bottom of the economic pyramid accounted for larger proportions of the relief load than the other occupations. These same conclusions apply also to the Winter and Spring Wheat Areas—other regions which had high proportions of agriculturalists receiving relief. In the Ranching Area more owners than tenants were found on the relief rolls while unskilled laborers from the small mining towns dominated the nonagricultural load. In the areas where agriculture played a lesser role in relief, the predominant emphasis was upon the unskilled laborer. These areas, with the exception of the Corn Belt, formerly had many persons engaged in exploiting timber or mineral resources. Such persons naturally would have had either to turn to subsistence farming for a living or to apply for aid during the depression.

OCCUPATIONAL ORIGIN BY RESIDENCE

About two-fifths of the rural relief load was located in villages and the remainder in the open country. The relief families were most heavily concentrated in villages in the Ranching Area and the Corn Belt and least so in the Appalachian-Ozark Area [6] (tables 3 and 4).

Naturally agriculture played a predominant role in the open country (57.2 percent) as contrasted with the villages (19.7 percent). Nonagriculture almost reversed the proportions with 58.6 percent in the villages and 27.5 percent in the open country (fig. 7). The areas

---

[6] New England is excluded because of the difficulty of distinguishing between the open country and villages.

Tenant Family in the Midwest.

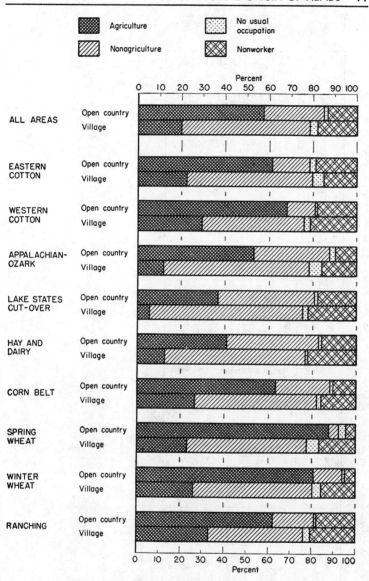

FIG. 7 - USUAL OCCUPATION OF HEADS OF OPEN COUNTRY
AND VILLAGE FAMILIES RECEIVING
GENERAL RELIEF, BY AREA
June 1935

AF-2803,WPA

Table 3.—Usual Occupation of Heads of Open Country Families Receiving General Relief, by Area, June 1935

[138 counties]

Usual occupation	All areas[1]	Eastern Cotton			Western Cotton			Appalachian-Ozark	Lake States Cut-Over	Hay and Dairy	Corn Belt	Spring Wheat	Winter Wheat	Ranching
		Total	White	Negro	Total	White	Negro							
Number	35,802	5,002	3,366	1,636	4,686	3,510	1,176	12,066	2,512	5,028	2,802	2,386	670	650
Percent	100.0	100.0	100.0	100.0	100.0	100.0	100.0	100.0	100.0	100.0	100.0	100.0	100.0	100.0
Agriculture	57.2	61.4	62.6	58.7	68.1	71.4	58.1	53.4	36.6	40.7	63.5	87.6	80.9	62.2
Farm operator	44.9	37.5	41.9	28.4	46.5	48.4	40.8	50.2	32.1	26.5	41.3	81.6	63.0	48.7
Owner	16.2	8.0	9.9	4.0	5.6	5.3	6.5	20.0	25.3	12.9	10.3	35.0	15.2	33.0
Tenant	23.9	17.9	21.1	13.0	23.5	26.1	16.0	30.2	6.8	13.6	31.0	46.6	47.8	15.7
Cropper	4.8	11.6	10.9	11.4	17.4	17.0	18.3	–	–	–	–	–	–	–
Farm laborer	12.3	23.9	20.7	30.3	21.6	23.0	17.3	3.2	4.5	14.2	22.2	6.0	17.9	13.5
Nonagriculture	27.5	17.0	20.1	10.6	12.8	13.9	9.7	34.6	44.0	41.9	24.5	4.4	13.1	18.8
White collar	1.7	1.2	1.9	0.4	1.1	1.4	0.2	1.6	1.6	2.9	2.4	0.8	2.7	1.8
Skilled	3.6	2.1	2.6	0.5	1.6	1.7	–	2.4	5.1	9.6	5.1	0.4	1.2	3.1
Semiskilled	4.1	4.7	6.6	0.6	1.3	2.1	0.2	3.5	5.6	7.9	6.0	0.8	1.8	1.8
Unskilled	18.1	9.0	9.0	9.1	8.8	8.7	9.3	27.1	31.7	21.5	11.0	2.4	7.4	12.7
No usual occupation	1.9	2.6	3.6	0.6	0.9	1.1	0.2	2.5	1.4	1.1	1.2	3.2	3.0	0.6
Nonworker	13.3	19.0	13.6	30.1	18.2	13.6	32.0	9.4	17.6	16.3	10.8	4.8	2.7	17.6
Unknown	0.1	*	0.1	–	–	–	–	0.1	0.4	–	–	–	0.3	0.6

* Less than 0.05 percent.

[1] Exclusive of New England.

Table 4.—Usual Occupation of Heads of Village Families Receiving General Relief, by Area, June 1935

[138 counties]

Usual occupation	All areas[1]	Eastern Cotton			Western Cotton			Appalachian-Ozark	Lake States Cut-Over	Hay and Dairy	Corn Belt	Spring Wheat	Winter Wheat	Ranching
		Total	White	Negro	Total	White	Negro							
Number	22,714	2,730	1,718	1,012	2,582	1,922	660	4,950	1,302	3,598	4,710	988	618	1,236
Percent	100.0	100.0	100.0	100.0	100.0	100.0	100.0	100.0	100.0	100.0	100.0	100.0	100.0	100.0
Agriculture	19.7	22.1	17.9	29.2	29.2	30.2	26.4	11.7	5.4	12.5	26.3	23.0	25.6	32.8
Farm operator	8.9	10.8	11.4	9.9	12.5	13.3	9.1	9.2	2.9	4.3	8.7	12.7	12.0	12.9
Owner	2.7	2.1	3.0	0.6	1.5	1.7	0.9	4.1	2.0	2.1	2.2	3.0	1.3	6.4
Tenant	4.8	2.5	2.6	2.4	5.2	5.8	3.3	5.1	0.9	2.2	6.5	9.7	10.7	6.5
Cropper	1.4	6.2	5.8	6.9	5.5	5.8	4.9							
Farm laborer	10.8	11.3	6.5	19.3	17.0	16.9	17.3	2.5	2.5	8.2	17.6	10.3	13.6	19.9
Nonagriculture	58.6	57.3	62.2	49.0	46.4	48.4	40.3	66.4	69.9	64.1	55.7	54.7	54.4	43.2
White collar	6.2	9.5	14.6	0.8	6.3	7.7	2.1	3.2	5.2	6.1	7.9	10.1	7.4	2.9
Skilled	8.7	7.5	10.0	3.2	5.7	6.8	1.2	5.1	13.1	14.0	9.9	13.0	9.4	5.2
Semiskilled	8.3	13.8	19.8	3.8	5.7	7.2	1.5	3.6	6.1	12.2	10.0	6.3	7.1	6.8
Unskilled	35.4	26.5	17.8	41.2	29.1	26.7	35.5	54.5	45.5	31.8	27.9	25.3	30.5	28.3
No usual occupation	3.2	5.1	7.5	1.2	2.6	3.2	0.9	5.3	2.3	0.9	1.9	5.5	3.9	3.1
Nonworker	18.4	15.4	12.3	20.6	21.8	18.2	32.4	16.5	22.4	22.5	16.1	16.6	15.5	20.7
Unknown	0.1	0.1	0.1	—	—	—	—	0.1	—	—	—	0.2	0.6	0.2

[1] Exclusive of New England.

in which the relief rate was high among agriculturalists residing in villages were those devoted to cotton, corn, wheat, and ranching. In the areas where commercial farming was not so important agriculturalists accounted for smaller proportions of the village relief loads. Likewise, the open country families connected with agriculture and receiving relief were fewest proportionately in the Appalachian-Ozark, Hay and Dairy, and Lake States Cut-Over Areas. The general prevalence of large numbers of nonagriculturalists in these regions is responsible for the difference.

Further differences begin to appear upon examination of the economic stratification within the agricultural and nonagricultural groups residing in the open country and in the villages, respectively. In the open country the agricultural group on relief had over three and one-half times as many farm operators as farm laborers, whereas among the village families farm laborers were more important than farm operators. The predominance of farm laborers over farm operators among families on relief in villages was chiefly due to the residence of farm laborers in villages in the Ranching, Corn Belt, Hay and Dairy, and Western Cotton Areas.

The economic pyramid among the nonagricultural families receiving relief was about the same in the villages as in the open country. About the same relative proportions of relief families were found to be in the unskilled labor classes as contrasted with the other nonagriculturalists. Heads of families on relief in villages who were nonworkers, however, were more numerous proportionately than in the open country. Together with this group the data for heads with no usual occupation show the extent to which the villages in the rural districts are collecting places for broken families and the nongainfully occupied population. It also indicates in part the extent to which these families are separated from plots of land where it would be possible for them to add to their income by keeping cows, chickens, and pigs and by gardening for home consumption.

OCCUPATIONAL ORIGIN BY COLOR

The remaining major problem as to the incidence of relief according to occupational origin applies to color. Since most of the rural Negroes are concentrated in the South, separate tabulations for the whites and Negroes are presented only for the Eastern and Western Cotton Areas (tables 2, 3, and 4).

In general a larger proportion of Negro than of white families on relief had nonworker heads. This category accounted for more than one-fourth (26.5 percent) of the total Negro group in the Eastern Cotton Area and for almost one-third (32.2 percent) in the Western Cotton Area as compared with about one-seventh for the whites in each area. This is related to the fact that a higher proportion of

Sharecropper's Family at Home.

Lunch Time for Cotton Pickers.

Negro than of white households on relief consisted of broken families.[7] The difference is explained by the fact that relief was not given to Negroes as freely as to whites either in amounts or in proportions related to needs. Many landlords gave subsistence only to working members of Negro families, and the nonworking aged members, not able to secure help from their relatives, turned to relief.[8]

On the other hand, a larger proportion of the whites than of the Negroes on relief were represented in most of the other occupational groupings in each of the two areas with the exception of unskilled nonagricultural laborers. In both areas Negroes predominated in this group, chiefly because of the concentration of Negro laborers in the villages (tables 3 and 4). In the Eastern Cotton Area Negro farm laborers were also more numerous proportionately than white farm laborers. One out of every four Negroes (26.1 percent) on relief was a farm laborer as compared with about one out of every six whites (15.9 percent). In the Western Cotton Area the proportions were somewhat reversed with 17.3 percent of the Negroes reported as farm laborers as compared with 20.8 percent of the whites.

[7] See ch. VI.

[8] See Mangus, A. R., *The Rural Negro on Relief, February 1935*, Research Bulletin H–3, Division of Research, Statistics, and Finance, Federal Emergency Relief Administration, Washington, D. C., October 17, 1935, p. 6 and *passim*, for an analysis of the relative proportions of Negroes and whites on relief in these areas; see also Woofter, T. J., Jr., *Landlord and Tenant on the Cotton Plantation*, Research Monograph V, Division of Social Research, Works Progress Administration, Washington, D. C., 1936, ch. X.

Chapter III

PERSONAL CHARACTERISTICS OF THE HEADS OF RURAL RELIEF FAMILIES

THE DEFINITION of heads of families used in this study [1] takes into consideration a number of variables, including age, sex, parental status, economic rights, and social position. Actually, most persons under 21 or over 64 years of age have been excluded, and the person economically responsible for the support of the family has usually been designated as the head.

AGE OF FAMILY HEADS

The average head of a rural relief family in June 1935 was in the prime of life—the early forties (table 5 and fig. 8). Village family heads were about 2 years older on the average than were heads in the open country. When the families were analyzed by agricultural areas, however, certain exceptions were noted in that village heads in the Eastern Cotton, Lake States Cut-Over, and Ranching Areas were found to be slightly younger than those in the open country. The greatest differences were to be found in the Winter Wheat,

Table 5.—Average [1] Age of Heads of Rural Families Receiving General Relief, by Area and Residence, June 1935

[138 counties and 116 New England townships]

Area	Average age			Area	Average age		
	Total rural [2]	Open country	Village		Total rural [2]	Open country	Village
All areas	42. 9	41. 9	43. 9	Appalachian-Ozark	41. 6	40. 6	44. 1
				Lake States Cut-Over	44. 8	45. 0	44. 5
Eastern Cotton	43. 7	43. 8	43. 4	Hay and Dairy	44. 5	43. 7	45. 7
White	42. 1	41. 9	42. 6	Corn Belt	43. 5	42. 6	44. 1
Negro	47. 0	48. 8	44. 8	Spring Wheat	39. 9	39. 1	41. 7
Western Cotton	41. 7	40. 9	43. 1	Winter Wheat	39. 0	37. 1	41. 5
White	40. 1	39. 1	41. 8	Ranching	44. 0	45. 5	43. 2
Negro	47. 6	47. 0	48. 6	New England	46. 6	—	—

[1] Median.
[2] Exclusive of heads of families whose age was unknown.

[1] See appendix A.

23

Appalachian-Ozark, and Ranching Areas. In the Winter Wheat and Appalachian-Ozark Areas the open country heads were younger than village heads by about 4 years, and in the Ranching Area village heads were younger than open country heads by more than 2 years. These differences reflect not only variations in the populations by area but also variations in the factors responsible for relief. In the Ranching Area there is a young working population in the mining villages. In the Winter Wheat Area the drought apparently affected the tenants and the younger families in the open country to a greater extent than the older and retired families in the villages.

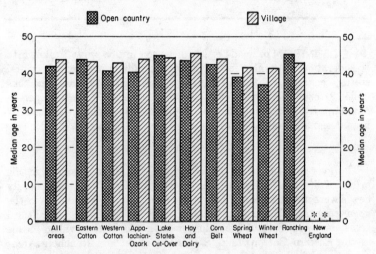

FIG. 8 - MEDIAN AGE OF HEADS OF RURAL FAMILIES RECEIVING
GENERAL RELIEF, BY AREA AND RESIDENCE
June 1935

*New England sampled by townships.   AF-2804,WPA

The smallest proportions of heads of rural relief families in the youngest age group (16–24 years) were found in New England, the Corn Belt, and the Hay and Dairy Area while the largest proportions were found in the Winter Wheat, Western Cotton, and Appalachian-Ozark Areas (appendix table 3). At the opposite extreme the Cotton, Lake States Cut-Over, New England, and Ranching Areas had the highest proportions of heads 65 years of age and over. The Western Cotton Area had both young and old family heads on relief in undue proportions. New England had few young heads and many old heads, reflecting the migration of young people to urban centers. In the Western Cotton, Appalachian-Ozark, and Winter Wheat Areas the high proportions in the younger age groups seemed to be due in part to the lower age at marriage. In New England a higher age at marriage may possibly help to account for the high proportion of older heads. In societies where marriage is usually accompanied by considerable economic foresight, it does not take place as early as in other societies where this is less frequently the case. Societies with a smaller proportion of young family heads of course have fewer chances for the young heads of families to be on relief.

The age distribution of heads of relief families in the open country and in villages varied somewhat inversely. The younger heads tended to be found more often in the open country and the older heads in the villages (appendix table 3). Among the open country families, 56.1 percent were under 45 years of age as contrasted with 51.2 percent in villages. This variation in age between village and open country family heads is explained in part by the degree of industrialization of the population.

The median age of heads of agricultural families on relief was about the same as that of nonagricultural families (table 6 and fig. 9). The

Table 6.—Average [1] Age of Heads of Rural Families Receiving General Relief, by Usual Occupation and Area, June 1935

[138 counties and 116 New England townships]

Usual occupation	Average age										
	All areas	Eastern Cotton	Western Cotton	Appa-lach-ian-Ozark	Lake States Cut-Over	Hay and Dairy	Corn Belt	Spring Wheat	Winter Wheat	Ranch-ing	New Eng-land
All occupations[2]	40.2	40.4	37.9	39.7	41.1	41.3	41.0	38.5	37.3	40.0	43.6
Agriculture	40.0	41.5	38.1	39.4	42.8	41.3	40.9	38.2	36.1	40.7	47.5
Farm operator	41.2	43.2	39.1	40.0	44.4	44.0	43.0	39.3	38.7	43.1	49.5
Owner	46.5	49.9	47.5	45.1	46.3	47.3	50.0	46.3	45.9	46.2	49.8
Tenant	38.0	44.3	39.2	36.1	39.4	40.4	40.7	34.2	37.5	38.5	42.6
Cropper	37.9	39.5	35.5	—	—	—	—	—	—	—	—
Farm laborer	36.4	39.0	36.3	31.5	30.2	36.1	38.2	30.4	31.2	36.9	44.2
Nonagriculture	40.5	38.9	37.9	40.2	40.7	41.5	41.2	39.6	39.0	39.3	42.8
White collar	40.3	40.1	35.1	35.5	40.1	42.9	40.5	38.5	42.8	44.5	41.0
Skilled	43.7	43.0	41.4	44.7	42.4	43.8	44.0	43.8	42.0	37.8	45.7
Semiskilled	38.1	36.9	35.5	35.3	33.8	38.9	38.5	32.8	37.8	33.7	41.8
Unskilled	40.4	38.6	37.9	40.3	41.8	41.0	41.6	39.8	37.5	40.1	42.8
No usual occupation	37.1	39.2	35.6	36.3	24.9	33.5	36.2	38.1	39.5	40.8	43.5

[1] Median.
[2] Exclusive of heads of families who were nonworkers or whose age was unknown.

heads of farm owner families on relief averaged 46.5 years, the highest average age of any occupational group. On the other hand, farm laborers were the youngest group, averaging only 36.4 years. Skilled laborers, who averaged 43.7 years, had the highest average age of any subgroup of nonagriculturalists. By areas heads of agricultural families had the highest median age (47.5 years) in New England and the lowest (36.1 years) in the Winter Wheat Area.

The three occupational groups with the highest proportion of young heads, 16–24 years of age, were those with no usual occupation (22.1

percent), farm laborers (14.2 percent), and farm croppers (9.8 percent) (appendix table 4). On the other hand, only 4 percent of the farm owner heads of rural families on relief were 16–24 years of age. The farm owners, however, had by far the highest percentage in the age group 55–64 years (25.9 percent).

Negro family heads on relief were much older, on the average, than white heads. In the Eastern Cotton Area the difference was 4.9 years and in the Western Cotton Area it was 7.5 years (table 5). Negroes had a larger percentage than whites in the age group 55–64 years in all occupational classifications except that of farm owner (appendix table 5). The whites had more young family heads and the Negroes more older heads.

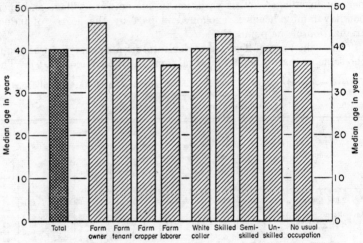

FIG. 9 – MEDIAN AGE OF HEADS*OF RURAL FAMILIES RECEIVING
GENERAL RELIEF, BY USUAL OCCUPATION

June 1935

*16 - 64 years of age, working or seeking work.   AF-2805, WPA

SEX OF FAMILY HEADS

In actual social situations it is usually assumed that the father and husband is the head of the house. This priority is frequently challenged, but there is sufficient basis in fact for the usage followed in this study. Consequently, by definition, a man will nearly always be the head of the family if he is living in the home and active. Thus, the presence of a woman as the head of a household generally indicates an incomplete family unit.

The western areas of extensive and commercialized agriculture had the smallest proportions of rural relief families with female heads while the southern areas, which include the Eastern and Western Cotton and Appalachian-Ozark Areas, had the highest proportions of such families (fig. 10 and appendix table 6). An exception to this rule was the families in the Ranching Area which ranked with families in the South in the proportion with female heads. The differences were

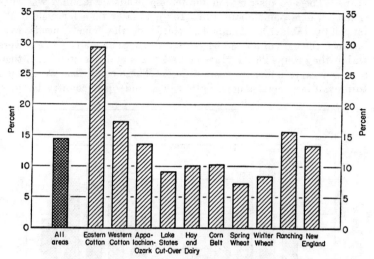

FIG. 10 – PERCENT OF FEMALES AMONG HEADS OF RURAL FAMILIES
RECEIVING GENERAL RELIEF, BY AREA
June 1935

AF-2806, WPA

great from area to area. The proportion of female heads varied from 7.2 percent in the Spring Wheat Area to 29.3 percent in the Eastern Cotton Area.

Significant differences also existed between villages and the open country (appendix table 6) inasmuch as village heads were likely to be females almost half again as frequently as were those in the open country. The differences between villages and the open country were least marked in the Eastern Cotton Area and most marked in the Wheat Areas where female heads appeared about three or four times as frequently in the villages as in the open country.

In spite of the fluctuations between the open country and villages and among areas, it should be noted that the average proportion of families with female heads was only 14.4 percent. Since a higher percentage of females than of males in the general rural population is married in each age group up to 45 years, the proportion of females who were heads of rural relief households was really very small.[2]

---

[2] See Stouffer, Samuel A. and Spencer, Lyle M., "Marriage and Divorce in Recent Years," *Annals of the American Academy of Political and Social Science*, Vol. 188, November 1936, table III, p. 60.

Male heads of families in each area, whether in the open country or in villages, were fairly evenly distributed between the ages of 25 and 54 years (appendix table 7). Usually less than 10 percent were under 25 or over 64 years of age. The peak was at the age group 25–34 years. The age distribution for female heads of families was concentrated at a point about 10 or 15 years later than for male heads (appendix table 8). About two-thirds of the female heads were between the ages of 35 and 64 years, inclusive; about 15 percent were within the groups 25–34 years and 65 years and over; and less than 6 percent were under 25 years of age. These conditions were found to prevail in general among both village and open country families,

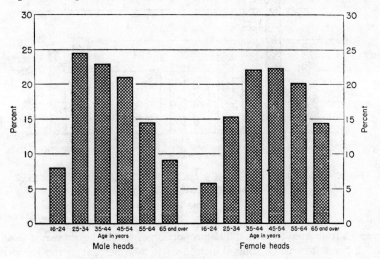

Fig. II - AGE OF HEADS OF RURAL FAMILIES RECEIVING
GENERAL RELIEF, BY SEX
June 1935

AF-2807, WPA

but the age distribution was more regular for females than for males (fig. 11).

There were certain significant differences among the age distributions for male heads of families by areas. Male heads were youngest in the Wheat Areas with the Southern and Ranching Areas next in rank (appendix table 7). The oldest male heads, on the average, were found in New England. Male heads in the open country were slightly younger than those in villages.

The age distribution for female heads of rural families revealed the same general differences by area and residence as the distribution for male heads. However, the clear uniformities found among male heads were not so outstanding for the females and slightly different conditions were apparent. For example, open country and village age distributions showed a greater similarity for female than for male heads.

MARITAL CONDITION OF FAMILY HEADS

The marital condition of the head of the family is, for many purposes, a convenient index of various social and cultural conditions. Conditions which lead to marriage or to the breaking up of marriage through divorce, separation, or widowhood are related intimately to fundamental social conditions. Among these social conditions may be listed (1) the type of industry, which might lead to the employment of large numbers of women outside the home and their "emancipation"; (2) economic conditions, which, because of either poverty or prosperity, might result in delayed marriage or else the complete removal of women from outside occupations; and (3) the social customs which regulate the activities of the sexes and which at times disapprove of households "managed" by women.

Most male heads of rural relief families are married while most female heads either have never married or have had their homes broken by divorce, separation, or the death of a husband [3] (table 7).

Table 7.—Marital Condition of Heads of Rural Families Receiving General Relief, by Sex and Age, October 1935

[138 counties and 83 New England townships [1]]

Sex and marital condition	Total [2]	Age in years				
		16-24	25-34	35-44	45-64	65 and over
BOTH SEXES						
Number	46,722	3,816	11,174	10,874	16,000	4,858
Percent	100.0	100.0	100.0	100.0	100.0	100.0
Single	9.4	24.5	8.8	6.3	7.7	11.9
Married	72.2	69.3	80.5	77.1	70.6	49.1
Widowed	13.3	1.9	4.9	10.3	17.4	34.6
Divorced	1.2	0.8	1.1	1.5	1.1	1.7
Separated	3.9	3.5	4.7	4.8	3.2	2.7
MALE						
Number	39,302	3,334	9,756	9,178	13,168	3,866
Percent	100.0	100.0	100.0	100.0	100.0	100.0
Single	8.8	21.4	7.6	5.7	7.5	12.9
Married	83.9	78.2	90.9	89.8	82.4	61.5
Widowed	5.4	0.2	0.6	2.5	7.5	22.1
Divorced	0.6	—	0.2	0.6	0.8	1.6
Separated	1.3	0.2	0.7	1.4	1.8	1.9
FEMALE						
Number	7,420	482	1,418	1,696	2,832	992
Percent	100.0	100.0	100.0	100.0	100.0	100.0
Single	12.7	46.9	16.5	9.2	8.7	7.9
Married	10.4	7.1	9.4	8.8	15.7	0.6
Widowed	54.7	13.3	34.6	52.4	63.3	83.5
Divorced	4.5	6.6	7.1	6.4	2.5	2.2
Separated	17.7	26.1	32.4	23.2	9.8	5.8

[1] Townships in Connecticut and Massachusetts only.
[2] Exclusive of heads of families whose marital condition or age was unknown.

[3] Data on marital condition were available for October rather than June 1935. See Introduction, p. XII.

For all areas the highest proportion of female heads married was found among those aged 45–64 years (15.7 percent), while the lowest proportion was found among those aged 65 years and over (0.6 percent). Probably in many of these cases the woman became head of the household because of illness or injury of the male head. In comparison, the highest proportion of married male heads was found in the age group 25–34 years (90.9 percent) and the lowest proportion was found in the oldest age group, 65 years and over (61.5 percent). The peak percentage appeared from 20 to 30 years earlier for males than for females.

A note of warning should be given as to the interpretation of the figures for the marital condition of the head of the family; that is, a high proportion of family heads who were single did not necessarily mean a high proportion of nonfamily types. In many cases where a normal family of parents and children was living at home, an unmarried son or daughter may have been designated as the head. The number of such cases could not be determined with accuracy, but it is certain that this was a factor which tended to increase the proportion of single heads of families.

In the various age groups there were important differences by sex in the marital condition of heads of rural families among areas and between open country and village. Over two-thirds of the male heads 16–24 years of age were married in each area except New England (appendix table 9). Practically none of these youthful heads of families were widowed, divorced, or separated.

Only 1 in 14 of the female heads of families aged 16–24 years was married. Practically all of the married heads were in the Eastern Cotton and Appalachian-Ozark Areas. About one-half of the female heads of this age were single while a large percent were already widowed or separated.

Over 90 percent of all male heads of families who were 25–34 years of age were married. The only area in which the proportion fell below 87 percent was New England with 79.9 percent married (appendix table 10). Very few homes headed by males of this age were broken by widowhood, divorce, or separation so that most of the heads who were not married were single. A higher proportion of married heads was found in the open country than in the villages with the exception of the Wheat and Ranching Areas. In the Winter Wheat Area there was a particularly large proportion of single heads in the open country.

Less than 10 percent of the female heads aged 25–34 years were married. Generally the female head of a relief family in this age group was widowed or deserted; in a relatively small proportion of the cases she was single or divorced. Higher proportions of married and widowed heads were found in the open country than in the villages while village

Parents and Children.

heads were more often single, divorced, or separated. The old saying that separation is the poor man's divorce still seems to be true.

About nine-tenths of the male heads of rural families 35–44 years of age were married (appendix table 11). At this age the proportion of widowed, divorced, and separated male heads first became large enough to be significant, but for all areas it was still only 4.5 percent. Male heads of families in the villages were widowed, divorced, or separated slightly more often than those in the open country where a higher percentage of married heads appeared.

Widowed female heads increased from 34.6 percent in the 25–34 year age group to 52.4 percent in the 35–44 year age group. The change was due to a decline in the proportions separated or single. The fact that women outlive men is the important consideration as the groups grow older since a woman has a much greater chance than a man to become widowed.

Over 80 percent of the male heads of rural families 45–64 years of age were married, and most of the nonmarried heads were widowed or single (appendix table 12). There continued to be a somewhat higher proportion of broken homes in the villages than in the open country.

Although the proportion of male heads who were married was still much higher than that of female heads, the proportion of female heads married in this age group had increased for practically all areas. It varied from 1.3 percent in New England to 33.3 percent in the Spring Wheat Area. In each area except the Hay and Dairy Area widowhood was the marital condition of the majority of all female heads.

Among male heads 65 years of age and over, the proportion married had dropped to 61.5 percent (appendix table 13), the smallest proportion for any age group. At the same time, the proportion widowed had increased markedly to 22.1 percent while the proportion that was single (12.9 percent) was higher than for any age group except that 16–24 years. Practically none of the aged female heads were married while five out of every six were widowed.

In summary, male heads were generally married and female heads were widowed (fig. 12). The proportion of male heads married increased until about the age of 40 and then decreased as the wife died or as older male children took over the responsibility for the household. The proportion of heads that was single decreased until about the age of 40 and then increased again. The percent of female heads that was separated increased until 35 years of age and then decreased. As the female heads became older, the proportion of single women decreased and that of widows increased.

The high proportions of married heads of families among females came 10 to 20 years later, on the average, than among males. This can possibly be attributed to the increased probability of injury or illness for the older male heads of families. In such cases the wife

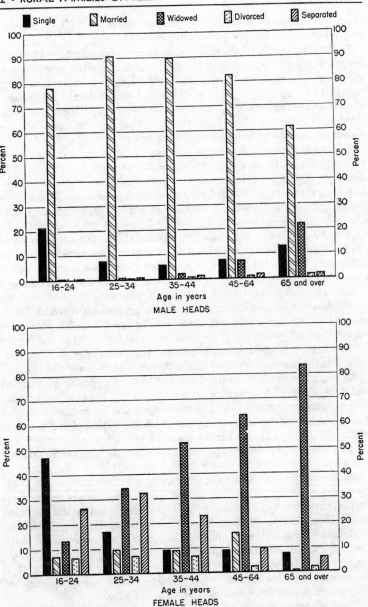

FIG. 12-MARITAL CONDITION OF HEADS OF RURAL FAMILIES RECEIVING
GENERAL RELIEF, BY SEX AND AGE

June 1935

AF-2808, WPA

was almost forced to become the head of the family. Very often she had no usual gainful occupation, resulting in a significant correspondence between high proportions of female heads of families and high proportions of heads of families who had no usual occupation.

Aside from families where the male head was old or incapacitated, the only cases where a female would ordinarily be designated as the head of the household were those in which the home was broken by the death of a husband and father or by separation or divorce. An unmarried female might also be designated as the head of the household in many cases. Thus, it is not surprising that the proportion of broken homes among the families with male heads, although it increased at each age group, was very small. The proportion of widowed male heads increased gradually at each age to 7.5 percent at 45–64 years but was three times as great at the age 65 years and over.

For both sexes there was a well-established uniformity that the proportion married was greater in the open country than in the villages, while the proportion of widowed, divorced, or separated tended to be greater in the villages. In general the same contrasts appeared among the different ages for each area as well as in the total group.

Marital condition also varied for the two races in the South (appendix table 14). The proportion married among white males exceeded the average for Negroes at every age group, while among Negro males larger numbers were widowed or separated than among whites. Divorce was almost completely absent among both groups. In general these differences were found in both the open country and villages.

The proportions of white female heads that were married were small for all age groups in the Cotton Areas, and more Negro than white women were married. None of either race who were 65 years of age and over were married. Even in the youngest age group 1 out of 5 of the white female heads was widowed, and this proportion gradually increased to 9 out of 10 for the group 65 years of age and over. Similarly, large proportions of Negro women were widowed. There was also a high proportion of female heads of families who were separated among both whites and Negroes.

Several factors which are important influences bearing upon the individual and which may affect his marital condition are reflected in the rural relief data. Since these causal influences are interrelated and interdependent, an analysis cannot hope to separate them to show the particular effects of each one. Yet several of the more important can be outlined.

One factor which is important in the analysis of marital condition is its interrelation with the necessity for relief. This, however, is evident only in the background and obviously cannot be separated without more materials than are at hand. From the significant differences between male and female heads in the proportions which were divorced or separated, it is probable that women heads of broken homes found it necessary to seek relief more often than men. Homes broken by divorce or separation were almost completely absent among the families with male heads; yet in every area and at every age the proportion of such homes with a female head of the family was significant. In all cases it was at least two or three times as high as for families with male heads. The explanation seems to be that after divorce or separation the children are more likely to accompany the mother than the father, and that he, as a single individual, is less subject to economic stress, or less likely to receive relief at any rate, than the remainder of the family with the mother as its head. Approximately the same can be said with regard to widowed heads of families except that the shorter life span of the male obviously increases the number of women who are widowed. Yet, even here, the differences between male and female heads were much too large to be accounted for by the comparatively slight difference in the average length of life.

Differences in marital condition among the areas studied were illustrative of certain background characteristics of a socio-economic nature. The greater industrialization of New England and the North has led to a greater participation in industry by women, and consequently the emancipation of women has reached its most advanced stages in these regions. Accompanying this emancipation is a rapidly rising divorce rate and a general disintegration of the former social rules which have regulated the distribution of rights and duties of the sexes.

The differences between open country and village families are partly a reflection of this same phenomenon, but in purely agricultural areas additional influences are present. Since farming is for the most part a family occupation, families which have been broken in any way tend to congregate in the villages, leaving the larger and more normal families in the open country.

One other related variable may be associated with particular areas of the country. According to certain customs and traditions the husband or father is always the head of the house, and a woman is not expected to be forced to assume such responsibilities. In extreme cases where the home is broken for some reason, remarriage is often the normal course. In areas where the sexes are found to be more equalized in their responsibilities, there is a greater tendency for the woman to take over the place of the male head and to continue the family without remarriage. This tradition of the male head of the family is strongest in the South and West and weakest in New England and has helped to keep down the proportion of broken homes in the former areas.

Chapter IV

SIZE AND COMPOSITION OF RURAL RELIEF FAMILIES

THE SIZE and composition of the rural relief family are important from a number of points of view. Large families, or those with numerous dependents and few members gainfully employed or capable of work, may need relief more frequently and in larger amounts than smaller families or those with relatively more workers. Offsetting this is the fact that larger families, other conditions being constant, have more chances than smaller units of having someone who can bring in an income. Also, there is the more general problem of the importance of family solidarity in making for or preventing the need for relief. This applies particularly in a society, such as the contemporary United States, which has gone through a long period of decline in size and of change in composition of its family units.

That the American family has become smaller and smaller since the founding of the country is a well-established fact.[1] Furthermore, the American family varies in size according to a number of characteristics, one of which is its relation to agriculture and another of which is the amount of commercialization in the various areas. In 1930 the average size of all families in the United States was 3.40; whereas that for the urban population was 3.26, for the rural-nonfarm population 3.28, and for the rural-farm population 4.02 (table 8).

Rural-farm families are larger than rural-nonfarm and urban families in all sections of the country. However, the average size is more than four persons for the farm families in the southern divisions as contrasted with less than four persons in the northern and western divisions. The urban and rural-nonfarm families divide the country into two regions on the basis of family size. In the South and West the urban family is the smallest while in the North and Northeast the rural-nonfarm family is the smallest. These differences are due to a number of reasons, but among them commercialization, industrialization, and

---

[1] See Bureau of the Census, *Abstract of the Fifteenth Census of the United States: 1930*, U. S. Department of Commerce, Washington, D. C., 1933, p. 415.

Table 8.—Average [1] Size of Families in the United States, by Division and Residence, 1930

Division	Average size			
	Total	Urban	Rural-nonfarm	Rural-farm
United States	3.40	3.26	3.28	4.02
New England	3.39	3.44	3.15	3.45
Middle Atlantic	3.43	3.42	3.38	3.71
East North Central	3.32	3.27	3.11	3.75
West North Central	3.34	3.14	3.02	3.91
South Atlantic	3.76	3.28	3.66	4.56
East South Central	3.69	3.22	3.52	4.15
West South Central	3.57	3.23	3.38	4.14
Mountain	3.33	3.13	3.23	3.86
Pacific	2.83	2.75	2.87	3.31

[1] Median.

Source: Bureau of the Census, *Fifteenth Census of the United States: 1930*, Population Vol. VI, U. S. Department of Commerce, Washington, D. C., 1933.

regional patterns play very important roles. In addition, the percent of foreign-born in the northeastern cities probably has increased the urban family size at least temporarily.

SIZE OF RURAL RELIEF FAMILIES

The function of relief is to take care of needy families. When relief facilities are limited, it seems likely that the policy of most relief administrators would be to give the money where there are the most mouths to feed. As a result, one would expect to find relief families of a larger average size than nonrelief households [2] (fig. 13). Such differences between relief and nonrelief families have not been very great, however, indicating that the problem of relief is not so much one of large families versus small families as of the difficulties which different types of relatively small families have had during the depression.

Of all rural cases receiving relief in June 1935, 9.9 percent were one-person households (appendix table 15). This was a 2 percent greater proportion of one-person households than was found for the whole rural United States in the 1930 Census (7.7 percent).[3] Since the period 1930–1935 tended by its economic pressure to force a decrease in the number of persons living alone,[4] these data lead to the con-

[2] See McCormick, T. C., *Comparative Study of Rural Relief and Non-Relief Households*, Research Monograph II, Division of Social Research, Works Progress Administration, Washington, D. C., 1935, pp. 22–25.

[3] Since a small number of so-called partnership families were classified as one-person families by the 1930 Census, the difference in the proportion of one-person families would be slightly greater than the data indicate.

[4] A severe economic depression tends at first to increase social solidarity. Persons who live alone, if they continue to be gainfully employed or to have an income, tend to share it with others to a much greater extent than formerly. Furthermore, it is a frequent practice of business firms to lay off last of all, among those of equal merit, the individuals who have families to support.

clusion that the proportion of one-person households receiving relief in rural districts in 1935 was very much greater than could be expected from a normal sample of the population.

The importance of this fact should not be neglected. It is commonly believed that a great deal of relief has been necessitated by rather large families. Such a popular conception is to be expected in a society which is changing from an increasing to a stable or declining population and has not yet become generally aware of the new conditions which exist. It is generally forgotten that family membership is not only a matter of obligation but also a privilege. In a clear-cut case in which a depression would take place in a country with little or no public relief facilities,[5] this would come out more

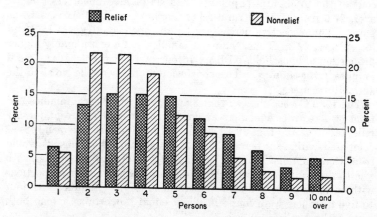

FIG. 13 – SIZE OF RURAL RELIEF AND NONRELIEF HOUSEHOLDS
October 1933

Source: McCormick, T. C., *Comparative Study of Rural Relief and Non-Relief Households*, Research Monograph II, Division of Social Research, Works Progress Administration, Washington, D. C., 1935, p. 24

AF-2809, WPA

clearly than it has in the United States. During a depression isolated individuals who are largely bereft of family membership come under an unusual strain. If they are fortunate and have a source of income, unemployed relatives and other indigent persons of no legal claim upon them generally try to share their livelihood. If the isolated individuals have neither money nor positions, they must either beg,

[5] See ch. IV by Zimmerman, Carle C., in *Problems of the New Cuba*, New York: Foreign Policy Association, 1935, for a description of family behavior in such a case.

starve, or accept relief.[6] Thus, there are other implications to a study of the family on relief than the sole matter of the pressure of the number of mouths to feed upon the formerly employed wage earner.

These generalizations concerning one-person households apply to all areas in the United States. In the Lake States Cut-Over Area more than one-fifth (21.8 percent) of all households on relief in June 1935 consisted of persons living alone (appendix table 15). These were cases of former woodsmen or of isolated individuals who had settled on a piece of land or in a village in the Cut-Over Area when the timber had been cut.

On the other hand, an unusually high proportion of the relief load consisted of large families. According to the 1930 Census 23.3 percent of the total rural population had six or more members. However, 27.9 percent of all rural relief families contained six persons or more. The respective percentage for the open country was 32.2 and for villages, 22.3. Thus, the relief families had a considerably higher proportion of households with six or more persons than the total rural families in the country. This conclusion probably applies to all of the agricultural areas.

The 1930 Census showed that 39.9 percent of all rural families had from two to three members as compared with 33.3 percent for the relief families, and that 29.1 percent had from four to five members as compared with 28.9 percent for the relief families. Thus, it would seem that nonrelief families had higher proportions of families with two to three members, whereas those on relief had higher proportions with only one person or with six persons or more. Families with four to five members were found in about equal proportions among both relief and nonrelief groups.

Open country families on relief were larger than those in the villages (table 9). The largest open country relief families were in the Appalachian-Ozark and Spring Wheat Areas. In the villages only the Spring Wheat Area had disproportionately large families.

The differences in size between the open country and the village families were very important as indicated by the fact that the median-

---

[6] A further study of family solidarity during the depression by Carle C. Zimmerman, J. H. Useem, and Wendell Bash in cooperation with the National Research Project which dealt with industrial towns in New England showed that employment differentiated families so that those which had members with positions would tend to have fewer employables unemployed than those which did not have members with positions. These were cases of industrial wage earners in rubber, woolens, automobile bodies, and other types of manufacturing. The chief wage earner was eliminated from the computation. It was clear in the 4 towns of less than 10,000 population studied that the depression differentiated the common masses of the people, much more sharply than before, into those who did and those who did not have a livelihood. Family solidarity was a factor in this, and in that respect oftentimes counteracted efforts to share the work so that all would have some sort of a livelihood.

After the Children Have Left Home.

sized family was 4.2 persons for the open country and 3.5 persons for the villages. The proportion of relief households which consisted of one-person families was much greater in the villages than in the open country, 12.5 and 7.5 percent, respectively (appendix table 15). Such a conclusion as this hardly applies, however, to the Lake States Cut-Over Area where one-person households comprised 21.2 percent of the open country relief load as contrasted with 22.9 percent of the village load. Neither does it apply to the Ranching Area where one-person households on relief in the open country accounted for 19.4 percent of the total as contrasted with 16.7 percent in the villages. In all other areas, however, the conclusion does apply.

Table 9.—Average Size of Rural Families Receiving General Relief, by Area and Residence, June 1935

[138 counties and 116 New England townships]

Area	Total rural		Open country		Village	
	Median	Mean	Median	Mean	Median	Mean
All areas	3.9	4.3	4.2	4.6	3.5	3.9
Eastern Cotton	3.7	4.1	3.9	4.3	3.4	3.8
Western Cotton	3.8	4.2	4.1	4.4	3.4	3.8
Appalachian-Ozark	4.3	4.7	4.7	5.0	3.5	3.9
Lake States Cut-Over	3.4	3.9	3.4	4.0	3.3	3.7
Hay and Dairy	3.8	4.3	4.1	4.5	3.6	4.0
Corn Belt	3.8	4.1	4.1	4.4	3.5	4.0
Spring Wheat	4.4	4.9	4.7	5.2	3.8	4.3
Winter Wheat	3.9	4.2	4.2	4.5	3.5	3.8
Ranching	3.5	3.9	3.5	3.9	3.5	3.9
New England	3.5	3.9	—	—	—	—

The median size of the agricultural family receiving relief was 4.6 persons as contrasted with 4.0 persons for the nonagricultural family (table 10). This was not due to age differences because the average nonagricultural family had a head 41.0 years of age as contrasted with the median age for agricultural families of 40.5 years (table 6, p. 25).

Table 10.—Average [1] Size of Rural Families Receiving General Relief, by Usual Occupation of Head and Area, June 1935

[138 counties]

Usual occupation of head	All areas [2]	Eastern Cotton	Western Cotton	Appalachian-Ozark	Lake States Cut-Over	Hay and Dairy	Corn Belt	Spring Wheat	Winter Wheat	Ranching
Total	4.0	3.7	3.8	4.3	3.4	3.8	3.8	4.4	3.9	3.5
Agriculture	4.6	4.4	4.5	5.0	4.4	4.8	4.3	4.8	4.2	4.2
Farm operator	4.9	4.6	4.6	5.1	5.3	5.4	4.5	5.0	4.6	4.4
Owner	5.0	4.4	4.5	5.4	4.5	5.1	4.4	5.6	4.5	4.4
Tenant	5.0	5.1	4.9	4.9	5.8	5.5	4.5	4.8	4.6	4.4
Cropper	4.5	4.4	4.3	—	—	—	—	—	—	—
Farm laborer	4.0	4.1	4.3	4.0	2.8	4.0	4.1	3.1	3.5	3.9
Nonagriculture	4.0	3.9	3.8	4.3	3.7	4.1	3.9	4.3	3.8	3.8
No usual occupation or nonworker	2.1	2.1	2.0	2.4	1.0	2.0	2.1	2.3	2.2	1.7

[1] Median.
[2] Exclusive of New England.

However, within the agricultural group farm owners' and tenants' families had a median size of 5.0 as contrasted with 4.5 for croppers and 4.0 for farm laborers. These differences were due, in part at least, to the fact that the heads of the owner families had a median age of 47.0 years as contrasted with 38.4 years and 38.5 years for croppers and tenants, respectively, and 36.9 years for farm laborers. If it be assumed that the average woman is 2 years younger than her husband, the average wife of a farm owner had practically reached the end of the childbearing period while the wife of a cropper, tenant, or laborer had 8 years or more of possible fertility ahead of her.

One-person households constituted a small proportion of the total in each occupational group with the exception of the group in which the head had no usual occupation or was a nonworker. There it reached 30.6 percent (appendix table 16). In the two Cotton Areas more than one-fifth of the white households in this group were one-person families as contrasted with more than two-fifths of the Negro families. Large families of six persons or more were found more often among the agriculturalists than among the nonagriculturalists (37.1 percent as compared with 27.4 percent). Large families were more frequent among owners than among tenants or croppers, due at least in part to the age factor discussed above.

AGE COMPOSITION

Children under 16 years of age were overrepresented in relief families as compared with all rural families in the United States (table 11). This conclusion applied with varying degrees of intensity to all nine agricultural areas surveyed. Youth 16–24 years of age formed about the same proportion of the relief group as of the total rural population although there were considerable variations from area to area. The general population tended to have a higher proportion of adults than did the relief families. This is evidence that a greater proportion of wage earners in families is one factor in weathering a depression. It is in the age group from 35 to 44 years that the general rural population exceeded the relief families most of all. A slightly higher proportion of aged persons was to be found in the general rural population than among the relief families. The really important differences may be summarized by the statement that *relief families have a higher proportion of children and a smaller proportion of adults of working age than does the total rural population.*

Children under 10 years of age were proportionately most numerous in the relief families in the Spring Wheat Area, reflecting the larger average size of family in that area (appendix table 17). New England was characterized by a small proportion of children under 10 years of age and a high proportion of aged persons 65 years and over. This reflects the tendency toward limitation of family size which has been

Table 11.—Age of Persons in Rural Families Receiving General Relief, June 1935, and Age of All Rural Persons, 1930,[1] by Area

[138 counties]

Area and group	Total		Age in years						
	Number	Per-cent	Under 16	16–24	25–34	35–44	45–54	55–64	65 and over
ALL AREAS [2]									
Persons receiving relief	253,636	100.0	43.3	16.3	12.0	9.7	8.0	5.5	5.2
All persons	2,413,676	100.0	37.4	16.5	12.7	11.7	9.6	6.5	5.6
EASTERN COTTON									
Persons receiving relief	31,670	100.0	42.5	15.6	11.9	9.4	7.9	5.9	6.8
All persons	629,355	100.0	41.8	18.3	12.2	10.6	8.7	4.9	3.5
WESTERN COTTON									
Persons receiving relief	30,556	100.0	42.8	16.7	12.5	9.3	7.4	5.1	6.2
All persons	295,280	100.0	37.2	17.4	12.7	10.5	13.2	5.1	3.9
APPALACHIAN-OZARK									
Persons receiving relief	79,508	100.0	44.7	17.2	11.8	9.2	7.6	5.1	4.4
All persons	412,232	100.0	41.7	16.8	12.2	10.7	8.5	5.5	4.6
LAKE STATES CUT-OVER									
Persons receiving relief	14,586	100.0	40.0	17.3	17.2	9.6	8.9	6.1	5.9
All persons	54,807	100.0	36.5	15.3	12.0	12.6	10.8	7.2	5.6
HAY AND DAIRY									
Persons receiving relief	37,004	100.0	44.0	14.9	10.6	10.7	8.9	5.6	5.3
All persons	465,034	100.0	32.2	14.0	12.5	13.0	11.2	8.7	8.4
CORN BELT									
Persons receiving relief	31,130	100.0	40.5	15.6	12.5	10.3	9.2	6.5	5.4
All persons	378,512	100.0	31.8	15.1	13.3	12.8	10.8	8.2	8.0
SPRING WHEAT									
Persons receiving relief	16,472	100.0	46.9	16.3	13.5	9.3	6.9	4.2	2.9
All persons	68,944	100.0	39.7	17.3	13.0	11.6	9.3	5.3	3.8
WINTER WHEAT									
Persons receiving relief	5,388	100.0	40.3	18.3	14.1	11.0	7.5	4.9	3.9
All persons	50,478	100.0	34.3	17.0	14.4	12.8	9.9	6.3	5.3
RANCHING									
Persons receiving relief	7,322	100.0	43.6	15.1	12.0	9.6	7.3	6.4	6.0
All persons	59,034	100.0	33.1	15.7	13.5	13.7	11.0	7.2	5.8

[1] Bureau of the Census, *Fifteenth Census of the United States*: 1930, Population Vol. II, U. S. Department of Commerce, Washington, D. C., 1933.
[2] Exclusive of New England.

carried farther in New England than in the other regions of the United States, even in the lowest economic groups. As the number of children becomes less, the proportion of old persons increases relatively. For a long time these results in New England have been masked by the coming in of new waves of immigrant families, but their birth rates in turn have followed the traditional downward course until the results are now readily apparent.[7]

[7] For proof, see Baker, O. E., "Rural-Urban Migration and the National Welfare," *Annals of the Association of American Geographers*, Vol. XXIII, 1933, pp. 59–126; and Spengler, Joseph J., *The Fecundity of Native and Foreign-Born Women in New England*, The Brookings Institution Pamphlet Series, Vol. II, No. 1, Washington: The Brookings Institution, 1930.

Open country families on relief had a significantly higher proportion of children under 10 years of age than village families (appendix table 17). This was true of all areas surveyed. In contrast the villages had a larger proportion of aged in all areas except the Eastern Cotton.

Negro families receiving relief had many more persons 65 years of age and over than did white families in the two Cotton Areas (appendix table 17). Concerning this difference Mangus has said:

> The practice of "splitting" families may account in part for the smaller relief benefits received by Negro cases in rural areas. In many instances landlords are willing to "take care of" the productive members of their tenant families but shift the care of aged dependent members to the relief agency. Hence, one or two members of the tenant or cropper family may receive small relief benefits while the other members of the household receive support from the landowner. It is probable that white tenants offer more resistance than do Negroes to such shifting of responsibility on the part of the landlord.[8]

Thus, much of the argument over whether agricultural restrictions cause a reduction or not in the number of tenant families on the cotton plantation becomes somewhat clearer when it is recognized that a landlord who furnishes supplies to his tenants can split off the non-productive members and put them on relief. A family of three crop hands can be broken up into a unit of two crop hands with few dependents and another unit with one crop hand and a majority of the dependents. Legally the plantation has as many tenants as before, but economically the landlord avoids the burden of furnishing supplies to a large family and has a smaller number of crop hands for his reduced acreage.[9]

SEX COMPOSITION

Ordinarily, slightly more males than females are born. However, males die more rapidly than females. As a result males tend to predominate in the younger age groups, but the proportion of females increases in the older ages. The sex distribution of the population is also affected by the fact that females tend to concentrate in urban areas to a greater extent than males. The situation is influenced by the fact that long-distance migration, such as immigration into a country, is more of a male phenomenon, whereas short-distance migration, particularly to cities and to an urban environment, is more of a female phenomenon.

[8] Mangus, A. R., *The Rural Negro on Relief, February 1935*, Research Bulletin H–3, Division of Research, Statistics, and Finance, Federal Emergency Relief Administration, Washington, D. C., October 17, 1935, p. 6.

[9] See Richards, Henry I., *Cotton and the AAA*, Washington: The Brookings Institution, 1936, p. 150 ff., for this argument on the influence of cotton restriction on displacement of tenants. For data from the relief standpoint, see Woofter, T. J., Jr., *Landlord and Tenant on the Cotton Plantation*, Research Monograph V, Division of Social Research, Works Progress Administration, Washington, D. C., 1936, pp. 153–161.

A Motherless Home.

In 1930 there were 102.5 males per 100 females in the United States, and this was the lowest count of males relative to females in any census year since 1830 with the exception of 1870 when the ratio of males per 100 females was 102.2. In 1930 there were 98.1 males per 100 females in American urban districts and 108.3 males per 100 females in the rural population. The rural-farm population had 111.0 males for every 100 females as contrasted with 105.0 males per 100 females in the rural-nonfarm population.

In the rural relief population of June 1935, 50.9 percent of all persons were males as contrasted with 49.1 percent who were females (appendix table 18). This was a sex ratio of 104 males per 100 females.

When the rural relief population was analyzed by sex according to agricultural areas, it was found that there were more males than females in all areas except the Eastern and Western Cotton. In the open country population males predominated in all except the Eastern Cotton Area while in the village population males predominated in all except the Cotton and Wheat Areas.

In comparing the sex ratio by age groups for the rural relief population in June 1935 with the general rural population in 1930, the most conspicuous differences were the overrepresentation of females in the relief population for the age groups 10–44 years and the overrepresentation of males in the age group 65 years and over (table 12). Males under 10 years of age and males 55–64 years of age were found on relief in about equal proportions to their numbers in the general population, and males 45–54 years of age were only slightly underrepresented on relief.

Table 12.—Sex Ratio of the Rural Relief Population,[1] June 1935, and of the General Rural Population,[2] 1930, by Age and Residence

Age	Sex ratio					
	Rural relief population			General rural population		
	Total rural	Open country	Village	Total rural	Farm	Nonfarm
Under 10 years	104	105	103	103	103	103
10–24 years	98	101	94	107	112	99
25–34 years	97	98	94	103	102	104
35–44 years	96	99	92	118	103	142
45–54 years	109	111	102	117	118	115
55–64 years	125	136	114	124	137	111
65 years and over	136	146	121	120	139	104

[1] 138 counties.
[2] Bureau of the Census, *Fifteenth Census of the United States: 1930*, Population Vol. II, U. S. Department of Commerce, Washington, D. C., 1933.

Chapter V

DEPENDENT AGE GROUPS

THE TERM *dependent* as used in relief surveys included all persons who were under 16 or over 64 years of age. Detailed information was not recorded concerning dependent persons between the ages of 16 and 64 years nor was any distinction made between those persons 65 years of age and over who were self-supporting and those who were not. Hence, the present chapter deals only with the two arbitrarily defined dependent age groups and excludes dependents within the productive ages, 16–64 years.

DEPENDENTS BY AREA

From the standpoint of dependents relief families were of all types. Some had children or aged dependents and others did not. One out of five of the relief families studied in June 1935 was composed of persons 16–64 years of age only; three out of five had children under 16 years of age but no one over 64 years; one out of eight had aged individuals 65 years of age and over but no children under 16; while one out of twenty had both children and aged persons (fig. 14 and appendix table 19).

The proportions of families having no persons in the dependent ages varied somewhat among the agricultural areas of the country and were related to the type of economy and the "age" of the area. They ranged from 17.6 percent in the Appalachian-Ozark Area to 27.4 percent in New England and 28.9 percent in the Lake States Cut-Over Area. The South was low and the West and North, except for the Spring Wheat Area which was affected by its high birth rate, were high in this respect. The areas reversed their order in the proportions having children under 16 years of age with the lowest percent (55.4) in New England and the Lake States Cut-Over Area and the highest percent (72.3) in the Appalachian-Ozark Area. The Spring Wheat Area was also outstanding with 71.5 percent of its relief families containing children. Similarly, the highest proportions of families having persons 65 years of age and over were found

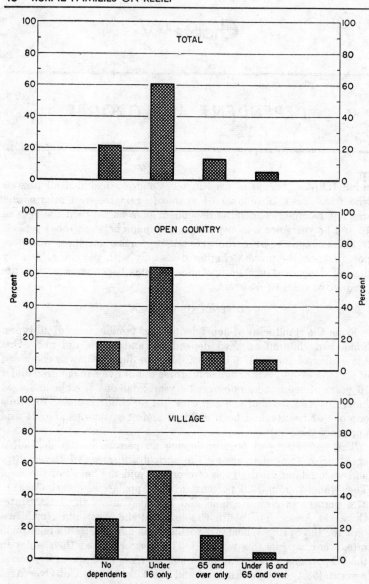

FIG. 14 – RURAL FAMILIES RECEIVING GENERAL RELIEF
WITH PERSONS IN DEPENDENT AGE
GROUPS, BY RESIDENCE

June 1935

AF-2819, WPA

in New England and in the two Cotton Areas. The lowest proportions were in the newly settled Wheat Areas. In general the differences between the open country and villages were consistent with those discussed in previous chapters. In every area there was a higher proportion of families which had children under 16 years of age in the open country than in the villages. Likewise, in the villages there were more families with aged persons and more families having no members within the dependent age groups. In general the areas were ranked in regard to young dependents according to their comparative birth rates, and the areas with the highest birth rates had the smallest proportions of families with adults only.

DEPENDENTS BY COLOR

White and Negro rural relief families in the Eastern and Western Cotton Areas differed significantly with respect to dependents. About 15 percent more of the white families had only dependent children while about 10 percent more of the Negro families had only aged dependents. Also, about 5 percent more of the Negro than of the white families had both children and aged as dependents. This difference may be largely due to the practice of many plantations in the South, previously referred to, of splitting the Negro families so as to keep the able-bodied members on the plantation and to place most of the disabled or aged members on relief.[1]

This is not a complete explanation, however, since the relative differences in the proportions of relief families which had dependent children existed both in the open country and in the villages. Among both whites and Negroes consistently more families with dependent children lived in the open country than in the villages. The tendency to split the Negro plantation family was most evident in the fact that in the open country twice as many Negro families as white families contained both dependent children and aged persons while the proportions were more nearly equal in the villages.

AGED AND JUVENILE DEPENDENTS IN THE SAME HOUSEHOLD

The rural family has remained most united in the Cotton and Appalachian-Ozark Areas as measured by the proportion of relief households having dependents both under 16 and over 64 years of age (appendix table 19). Moreover, 37.5 percent of such families in the Appalachian-Ozark Area had four or more dependents as contrasted with 33.9 percent in all areas (table 13). In the open country of the Eastern Cotton and Appalachian-Ozark Areas 40 percent of these families had four or more dependents. The proportion among the village families of the Corn Belt was almost equally high.

[1] See p. 42.

Table 13.—Rural Families Receiving General Relief With Persons Both Under 16 and Over 64 Years of Age,[1] by Number of Such Persons, Residence, and Area, June 1935

[138 counties and 116 New England townships]

Residence and area	Total		Persons under 16 and over 64 years of age		
	Number	Percent	2	3	4 or more
TOTAL RURAL					
All areas	3,339	100.0	37.3	28.8	33.9
Eastern Cotton	628	100.0	41.7	23.9	34.4
White	322	100.0	39.8	24.8	35.4
Negro	306	100.0	43.8	22.9	33.3
Western Cotton	454	100.0	43.6	27.3	29.1
White	284	100.0	44.3	29.6	26.1
Negro	170	100.0	42.4	23.5	34.1
Appalachian-Ozark	1,066	100.0	30.2	32.3	37.5
Lake States Cut-Over	138	100.0	36.3	33.3	30.4
Hay and Dairy	344	100.0	39.6	26.7	33.7
Corn Belt	332	100.0	36.7	27.1	36.2
Spring Wheat	94	100.0	34.0	29.8	36.2
Winter Wheat	38	†	†	†	†
Ranching	60	100.0	53.3	30.0	16.7
New England	185	100.0	38.9	33.0	28.1
OPEN COUNTRY					
All areas [2]	2,202	100.0	34.7	28.1	37.2
Eastern Cotton	476	100.0	36.1	23.1	40.8
White	236	100.0	32.2	24.6	43.2
Negro	240	100.0	40.0	21.7	38.3
Western Cotton	318	100.0	39.6	28.3	32.1
White	194	100.0	39.2	30.9	29.9
Negro	124	100.0	40.3	24.2	35.5
Appalachian-Ozark	844	100.0	29.9	30.1	40.0
Lake States Cut-Over	96	100.0	39.6	27.1	33.3
Hay and Dairy	210	100.0	37.2	29.5	33.3
Corn Belt	148	100.0	39.2	27.0	33.8
Spring Wheat	62	100.0	32.3	32.3	35.4
Winter Wheat	26	†	†	†	†
Ranching	22	†	†	†	†
VILLAGE					
All areas [2]	952	100.0	42.9	29.6	27.5
Eastern Cotton	152	100.0	59.2	26.3	14.5
White	86	100.0	60.4	25.6	14.0
Negro	66	100.0	57.5	27.3	15.2
Western Cotton	136	100.0	52.9	25.0	22.1
White	90	100.0	55.5	26.7	17.8
Negro	46	†	†	†	†
Appalachian-Ozark	222	100.0	31.5	40.6	27.9
Lake States Cut-Over	42	†	†	†	†
Hay and Dairy	134	100.0	43.3	22.4	34.3
Corn Belt	184	100.0	34.8	27.2	38.0
Spring Wheat	32	†	†	†	†
Winter Wheat	12	†	†	†	—
Ranching	38	†	†	†	†

†Percent not computed on a base of fewer than 50 cases.

[1] See appendix table 19.
[2] Exclusive of New England.

The contrast between white and Negro families on relief in regard to juvenile or aged dependents was again brought out by the number of such dependents (table 13). In the open country the proportion of Negro families with two dependents was larger than the proportion of white families while in the villages the reverse was true. A larger proportion of Negro than of white families in the Western Cotton Area had four or more dependents while in the Eastern Cotton Area more of the white families had this many dependents.

Sharecropper's Widow and Child.

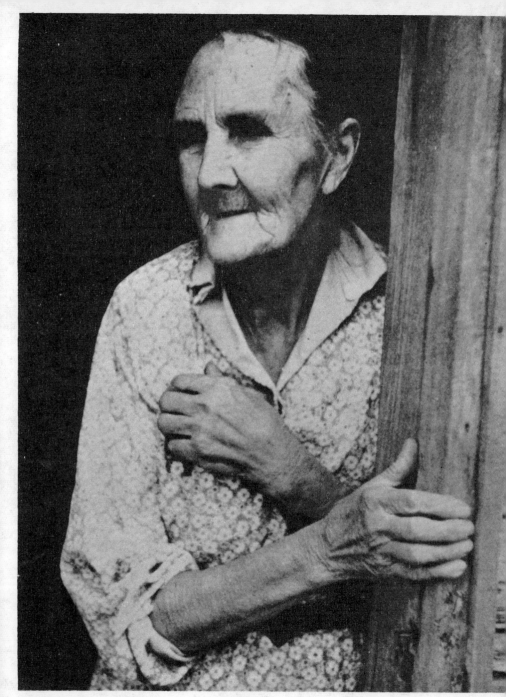

Old Age.

DEPENDENT CHILDREN

Among relief families whose only dependents were children under 16 years of age, the proportion of families which had three children or more increased from 43.8 percent in New England to 52.2 percent in the Appalachian-Ozark Area and to 55.9 percent in the Spring Wheat Area (table 14). With the exception of the Appalachian-Ozark Area the southern areas ranked low and fell below the average for all areas.

Table 14.—Rural Families Receiving General Relief With Children Under 16 Years of Age,[1] by Number of Children, Residence, and Area, June 1935

[138 counties and 116 New England townships]

Residence and area	Total		Number of children		
	Number	Percent	1	2	3 or more
TOTAL RURAL					
All areas	37,975	100.0	26.5	24.1	49.4
Eastern Cotton	4,414	100.0	26.9	25.4	47.7
White	3,182	100.0	26.1	27.5	46.4
Negro	1,232	100.0	29.0	20.0	51.0
Western Cotton	4,362	100.0	26.9	25.0	48.1
White	3,460	100.0	27.7	25.7	46.6
Negro	902	100.0	23.7	22.4	53.9
Appalachian-Ozark	11,232	100.0	24.8	23.0	52.2
Lake States Cut-Over	1,966	100.0	28.6	24.0	47.4
Hay and Dairy	5,224	100.0	26.4	23.5	50.1
Corn Belt	4,354	100.0	28.2	26.4	45.4
Spring Wheat	2,318	100.0	24.3	19.8	55.9
Winter Wheat	802	100.0	26.7	29.2	44.1
Ranching	1,098	100.0	27.1	24.6	48.3
New England	2,205	100.0	30.8	25.4	43.8
OPEN COUNTRY					
All areas [2]	23,138	100.0	24.5	23.2	52.3
Eastern Cotton	2,930	100.0	25.3	24.5	50.2
White	2,176	100.0	24.7	26.1	49.2
Negro	754	100.0	26.8	19.9	53.3
Western Cotton	2,952	100.0	25.5	24.7	49.8
White	2,340	100.0	26.4	25.5	48.1
Negro	612	100.0	22.2	21.6	56.2
Appalachian-Ozark	8,470	100.0	22.9	22.1	55.0
Lake States Cut-Over	1,300	100.0	28.0	23.1	48.9
Hay and Dairy	3,212	100.0	25.5	22.9	51.6
Corn Belt	1,738	100.0	25.9	27.0	47.1
Spring Wheat	1,712	100.0	23.3	18.9	57.8
Winter Wheat	440	100.0	21.8	31.8	46.4
Ranching	384	100.0	28.6	22.4	49.0
VILLAGE					
All areas [2]	12,632	100.0	29.5	25.5	45.0
Eastern Cotton	1,484	100.0	30.3	27.1	42.6
White	1,006	100.0	29.2	30.4	40.4
Negro	478	100.0	32.6	20.1	47.3
Western Cotton	1,410	100.0	29.6	25.7	44.7
White	1,120	100.0	30.3	26.1	43.6
Negro	290	100.0	26.9	24.1	49.0
Appalachian-Ozark	2,762	100.0	30.8	25.5	43.7
Lake States Cut-Over	666	100.0	29.7	25.8	44.5
Hay and Dairy	2,012	100.0	27.8	24.4	47.8
Corn Belt	2,616	100.0	29.8	25.9	44.3
Spring Wheat	606	100.0	27.4	22.1	50.5
Winter Wheat	362	100.0	32.6	26.0	41.4
Ranching	714	100.0	26.3	25.8	47.9

[1] Exclusive of cases with both children and aged persons. See appendix table 19.
[2] Exclusive of New England.

White families on relief had fewer dependent children than Negro families in both the Eastern and Western Cotton Areas. In these areas over one-half of the Negro families and about 46 percent of the white families had three dependent children or more. This reveals again the separation of many Negro households resulting in the placing of disproportionately large numbers of children on relief, but it suggests also that the relief problem for the white family in the South is not one "caused" primarily by large numbers of children or by a high birth rate but by other factors.

AGED DEPENDENTS

Of the rural families on relief which had only aged dependents three out of four had one such person and one out of four had two persons (table 15). Practically none had three persons or more.

Table 15.—Rural Families Receiving General Relief With Aged Persons,[1] by Number of Aged,[2] Residence, and Area, June 1935

[138 counties and 116 New England townships]

Residence and area	Total		Number of aged persons		
	Number	Percent	1	2	3 or more
TOTAL RURAL					
All areas	8,226	100.0	73.5	26.0	0.5
Eastern Cotton	1,096	100.0	72.3	26.6	1.1
White	548	100.0	67.5	31.4	1.1
Negro	548	100.0	77.0	21.9	1.1
Western Cotton	1,074	100.0	71.7	28.1	0.2
White	654	100.0	69.4	30.3	0.3
Negro	420	100.0	75.2	24.8	—
Appalachian-Ozark	1,728	100.0	72.0	27.4	0.6
Lake States Cut-Over	594	100.0	82.2	17.8	—
Hay and Dairy	1,234	100.0	72.0	27.7	0.3
Corn Belt	1,038	100.0	73.4	25.8	0.8
Spring Wheat	292	100.0	73.3	26.7	—
Winter Wheat	118	100.0	62.7	33.9	3.4
Ranching	310	100.0	81.3	18.7	—
New England	742	100.0	76.0	23.7	0.3
OPEN COUNTRY					
All areas [3]	4,082	100.0	71.4	27.9	0.7
Eastern Cotton	762	100.0	68.8	29.9	1.3
White	378	100.0	64.5	34.4	1.1
Negro	384	100.0	72.9	25.5	1.6
Western Cotton	640	100.0	67.2	32.5	0.3
White	396	100.0	66.7	32.8	0.5
Negro	244	100.0	68.0	32.0	—
Appalachian-Ozark	1,088	100.0	70.6	28.7	0.7
Lake States Cut-Over	374	100.0	81.3	18.7	—
Hay and Dairy	626	100.0	72.5	27.2	0.3
Corn Belt	302	100.0	72.9	25.8	1.3
Spring Wheat	140	100.0	70.0	30.0	—
Winter Wheat	50	100.0	56.0	36.0	8.0
Ranching	100	100.0	88.0	12.0	—
VILLAGE					
All areas [3]	3,402	100.0	75.5	24.2	0.3
Eastern Cotton	334	100.0	80.2	19.2	0.6
White	170	100.0	74.1	24.7	1.2
Negro	164	100.0	86.6	13.4	—
Western Cotton	434	100.0	78.3	21.7	—
White	258	100.0	73.6	26.4	—
Negro	176	100.0	85.2	14.8	—
Appalachian-Ozark	640	100.0	74.4	25.3	0.3
Lake States Cut-Over	220	100.0	83.6	16.4	—
Hay and Dairy	608	100.0	71.4	28.3	0.3
Corn Belt	736	100.0	73.7	25.8	0.5
Spring Wheat	152	100.0	76.3	23.7	—
Winter Wheat	68	100.0	67.6	32.4	—
Ranching	210	100.0	78.1	21.9	—

[1] 65 years of age and over.
[2] Exclusive of cases with both children and aged persons. See appendix table 19.
[3] Exclusive of New England.

In the Eastern Cotton Area 29.9 percent of the families in the open country had two aged dependents as contrasted with 19.2 percent of the village families, and in the Western Cotton Area 32.5 percent of the open country families had two aged dependents as compared with 21.7 percent in villages. In the Eastern and Western Cotton Areas about 5 to 10 percent more of the white families than of the Negro families had two aged dependents. The difference between races in the open country of the Western Cotton Area was negligible, however.

The proportion of families with one aged dependent varied from four out of five in the Lake States Cut-Over and Ranching Areas to three out of five in the Winter Wheat Area. These differences were accentuated in the open country, where as high as 88.0 percent of the families in the Ranching Area had one aged dependent. At the opposite extreme was the Winter Wheat Area with only 56.0 percent.

GENERAL SIGNIFICANCE OF DEPENDENT AGE GROUPS

In general a large number of dependents in a family may be an indication of a prolific population, where a high birth rate results in large families, or it may indicate a high degree of family solidarity. In other words, the family clings together to a great extent; and when it is finally forced upon relief, a large number of persons are found in a single unit. Again, there is the possibility, as shown by the families in the Cotton Areas, that there may be a splitting of families with a tendency to push aged persons upon relief and to leave the younger employables to fend for themselves without the responsibility for other individuals. All of these factors operate to increase the number of old or young dependents on relief.

The question of dependency and relief is related principally, however, to the basic economic and cultural factors in any particular region. The predominant industries and occupations determine the extent to which the head of a family will be able to care for his dependents continuously, and the cultural traditions to a large extent determine the internal solidarity and cohesiveness of the family unit. This does not even consider such fundamental problems as sanitation, health, and disease which may through debilitating conditions bring about the need for relief. Background factors of an economic, sociological, or even medical nature, when viewed in their full complexity, are agents which predetermine increased numbers of dependents on relief.

Families in the South, including the Appalachian-Ozark Area, are more likely to be large as a result of high birth rates; they are more likely to cling together in a large cohesive aggregate; and finally, because of the loss of economic support or even the injury or death of the male provider, the whole aggregation is forced on relief. Consequently, it is more easily understood why the proportion of families with no persons in the dependent age groups should be smallest in the South, where rural cultural traditions are strong, and greatest in New England, where the strong Yankee traditions are now all but submerged by the newer mores of an industrialized and urbanized society. These are the extreme cases, and the other areas fall in between.

Chapter VI

FAMILY STRUCTURAL TYPES

TYPE OF family has many meanings since the type depends upon the perspective of the approach. In this chapter families are viewed from the standpoint of constituency. The elements are husband, wife, children, and others. The family units are divided into three categories as follows:[1]

Normal families	72. 5 percent
Broken families	10. 9 percent
Nonfamily types	16. 6 percent

Normal families are divided into four categories:

Husband and wife alone	11. 6 percent
Husband and wife with others not their children	2. 2 percent
Parents and children alone	53. 2 percent
Parents, children, and others	5. 5 percent
Total normal families	72. 5 percent

Broken families consist of one parent and children. These are also divided into four categories:

Father and children alone	1. 9 percent
Father, children, and others	0. 8 percent
Mother and children alone	6. 6 percent
Mother, children, and others	1. 6 percent
Total broken families	10. 9 percent

The nonfamily types are similarly divided:

Male alone	6. 6 percent
Male head and others	5. 0 percent
Female alone	3. 2 percent
Female head and others	1. 8 percent
Total nonfamily types	16. 6 percent

[1] This classification is patterned somewhat after that developed in connection with the Unemployment Relief Census, October 1933, taken by the Federal Emergency Relief Administration.

The present analysis gives a picture of the incidence of relief among different structural types of families by area, residence, occupation, and color.

FAMILY STRUCTURAL TYPES BY AREA AND RESIDENCE

From three-fifths to four-fifths of the families on relief in the various agricultural areas in June 1935 were normal families composed of husband and wife or of parents and children, with or without others (fig. 15). The Eastern Cotton and Lake States Cut-Over Areas

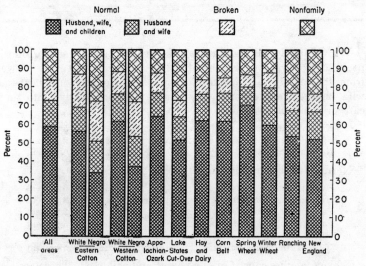

Fig. 15– STRUCTURAL TYPE OF RURAL FAMILIES RECEIVING GENERAL RELIEF, BY AREA

June 1935

AF-2816, WPA

had the smallest proportions of normal families while the Wheat Areas had the highest proportions. These latter were largely drought families. The great majority of the normal families consisted of husband and wife or of husband, wife, and children alone while about one out of nine also had relatives or friends present.

Broken families were found most frequently in the Eastern and Western Cotton Areas and in the Appalachian-Ozark Area. The percentage of broken families composed of fathers and children varied only slightly among areas, but the percentage of families composed of mothers and children was much greater in the South than in other sections.[2]

---

[2] See also ch. III, where the analysis reveals the high proportion of female heads in the South who were widowed or separated and the small proportion who were divorced.

Nonfamily types were rarest in the Winter Wheat and Appalachian-Ozark Areas (12.4 and 12.8 percent, respectively) and most frequent in the Lake States Cut-Over Area (27.6 percent). Nonfamily types with male heads appeared most frequently in the Lake States Cut-Over Area while female heads were most numerous in the Eastern Cotton Area.

Open country families stood out in contrast to village families since 8 percent more of the open country than of the village units were normal families (table 16). Families consisting of husband, wife, and children were found more often in the open country while families of husband and wife only tended to congregate in the villages, but in neither case were the differences particularly great. There tended to be more broken families in the villages than in the open country as broken families with female heads concentrated in the villages. Nonfamily types with both male and female heads were found in the villages more often than in the open country.

The composition of the family was undoubtedly an important factor in relief, but careful analysis of the data indicates that its influence may easily be overestimated.

Table 16.—Structural Type of Rural Families Receiving General Relief, by Residence, June 1935

[138 counties and 116 New England townships]

Structural type	Total rural [1]	Open country [2]	Village [2]
Number	62,809	35,782	22,712
Percent	100.0	100.0	100.0
Normal families	72.5	76.2	67.9
Husband and wife	13.8	12.7	15.2
Without others	11.6	10.5	13.2
With others	2.2	2.2	2.0
Husband, wife, and children	58.7	63.5	52.7
Without others	53.2	57.0	48.5
With others	5.5	6.5	4.2
Broken families	10.9	10.1	12.2
Father and children	2.7	2.6	2.5
Without others	1.9	1.9	2.0
With others	0.8	0.7	0.5
Mother and children	8.2	7.5	9.7
Without others	6.6	5.8	8.1
With others	1.6	1.7	1.6
Nonfamily types	16.6	13.7	19.9
Male head	11.6	9.9	13.2
Without others	6.6	5.3	8.1
With others	5.0	4.6	5.1
Female head	5.0	3.8	6.7
Without others	3.2	2.2	4.5
With others	1.8	1.6	2.2

[1] Exclusive of families whose type was unknown.
[2] Exclusive of New England.

FAMILY STRUCTURAL TYPES BY OCCUPATION

Classification of rural family types according to the usual occupation of the head reveals significant differences between agricultural and nonagricultural families. Among agricultural families 82.2 percent were normal as contrasted with only 77.4 percent among nonagricultural families (fig. 16 and appendix table 20). Although there was considerable overlapping among the occupational levels within these two major groups, similarities existed in the ranking of the different occupational levels within each group. The smallest proportions of normal families were found in the highest strata but the other strata were ranked in descending order. Proceeding from the bottom to the top, for both the agricultural and nonagricultural groups, the proportions of normal families increased, if the upper groups (farm owners and white-collar workers) were excluded. Thus,

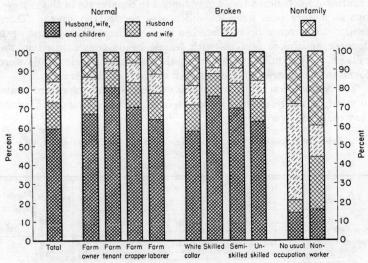

FIG.16-STRUCTURAL TYPE OF RURAL FAMILIES RECEIVING GENERAL RELIEF, BY USUAL OCCUPATION OF HEAD

June 1935

AF-2817, WPA

within agriculture the smallest proportion of normal families was found among owners (75.0 percent) with increasing proportions for laborers (77.8 percent), croppers (83.4 percent), and tenants (89.9 percent). For the nonagricultural group the proportions were white collar, 71.5 percent; unskilled, 74.5 percent; semiskilled, 82.8 percent; and skilled, 88.0 percent. Among the families whose heads were not workers, there was a surprisingly large proportion of normal families (43.6 percent).

Broken families appeared equally as often in agriculture as in nonagriculture. While full proof is lacking, there is some indication that broken homes among agricultural families are caused more often by the death of one parent, whereas among nonagricultural families divorce or separation is a more influential factor. Similarly, divorce or separation is probably more important for the upper than for the lower occupational levels in both agricultural and nonagricultural families. Slightly over one-half of the families whose heads had no usual occupation were broken family types, and most of these consisted of mothers and children. A little less than 17 percent of the families whose heads were not workers were broken with the great majority again composed of mothers and children.

Nonfamily types were found much more frequently in nonagriculture (13.9 percent) than in agriculture (9.1 percent). Nonfamily types with female heads appeared very rarely in agriculture but more often in nonagriculture, particularly in white-collar occupations. Almost 40 percent of the families whose heads were not workers were nonfamily types as compared with 28.2 percent for families whose heads had no usual occupation. The largest proportion of the heads who were not workers consisted of men living alone while the largest proportion of the heads with no usual occupation consisted of unattached women.

FAMILY STRUCTURAL TYPES BY COLOR

The relatively small proportion of normal families in the rural relief population in the Cotton Areas may be largely attributed to conditions among Negroes. Only slightly over one-half of the Negro families in both areas were normal as contrasted with two-thirds to three-fourths of the whites (appendix table 21). Four percent more of the Negro families in the Eastern Cotton Area and six percent more in the Western Cotton Area were broken than was the case among the whites. These differences were most marked in the open country. In general there were more broken homes in the villages for both races. Significantly, for both races, most of the broken families consisted of mothers and children.

The greatest difference between white and Negro households, however, appeared in those groups called *nonfamily* types. In both areas Negro groups of the nonfamily type appeared on relief at least twice as often as white groups of this type. The differences were especially marked in the Western Cotton Area, both in the villages and in the open country. One-third of the Negro families in the western villages consisted of nonfamily types. These Negro nonfamily groups in the Western Cotton Area were about evenly divided between those with male and those with female heads.

Although for the white relief population in the South the proportion of normal families was greater among the farm laborers and the unskilled nonagricultural laborers than among farm owners and white-collar workers, respectively, such was not the case among Negroes. The unskilled occupational groups among Negro families had the smallest proportions of normal families, the farm laborers having only 49.0 percent and the nonagricultural laborers only 51.0 percent (appendix table 22).

An important exception to the rule that Negro families were more likely to be broken than white families was the farm owner group with 20.9 percent of the white families in the two Cotton Areas broken as contrasted with 10.4 percent of the Negro families. However, one-half of these broken Negro families were composed of fathers and children, while only one-eight of the broken white families consisted of fathers and children. In contrast, the proportions of broken homes among croppers and farm laborers were much greater among Negroes than whites.

Of the Negro and white families whose heads were not workers, 56.7 percent and 31.1 percent, respectively, were nonfamily types. A fairly high proportion of broken Negro families had female heads who were not workers.

ONE-PERSON HOUSEHOLDS

One-person households present special problems to relief administrators. Such households may originate as a result of the breaking up of a family, leaving aged persons living alone; or they may be the result of special social and economic conditions which prevent marriage and which keep individuals living as isolated units. One-person households most often consist of men, and cases of men living alone are found most frequently in isolated mining or heavy industrial areas. Although the ratio of males to females is very high in some agricultural areas, one-person households are not found as frequently in such areas because of combinations into family groups.

One-person families constituted less than 10 percent of all rural families on relief in June 1935 except in the Eastern Cotton, Hay and Dairy, New England, Ranching, and Lake States Cut-Over Areas (appendix table 20). The latter areas include a high proportion of one-person families because of economic conditions. In addition to the self-sufficing agriculture in the Lake States Cut-Over Area there has been employment for large numbers of men both in the forests and in the iron mines of Minnesota. The Hay and Dairy and New England Areas include many centers of industry, and the Ranching Area uses many unattached men in its type of agricultural production. As a result, the highest proportions of one-person families that were males were found in the Lake States Cut-Over, Ranching, and New England Areas.

Three times as many one-person families were found among Negroes as whites in the two Cotton Areas, and the difference was especially striking in the Western Cotton Area (appendix table 23). The majority of the white one-person families in these two areas consisted of males, whereas the majority of the Negro one-person families consisted of females. These differences were accentuated in the open country. An additional difference between Negroes and whites was the greater proportion of Negroes who were 65 years of age and over.

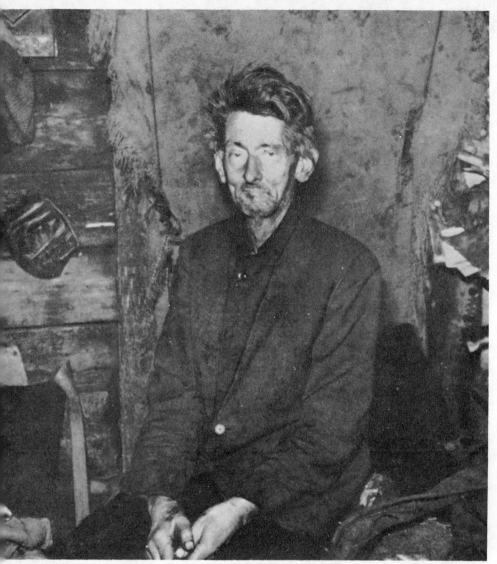

Farm Security Administration (Rothstein).

Homeless.

Farm Security Administration (Rothstein).

Penniless and Alone.

Chapter VII

FERTILITY OF RURAL RELIEF FAMILIES

THE RELATIONSHIP which exists between fertility and the relief problem is important. Other conditions being equal, there is greater *a priori* probability for families with a high birth rate to be on relief than there is for families with a low birth rate. With few exceptions this relationship holds true throughout the country. In addition to the fact that relief authorities may select for their grants those families with the greatest number of dependents, the expectation of a higher than average birth rate for relief families coincides with their general position in the social structure; that is, with fairly constant uniformity the birth rate increases with progressive steps down the social ladder.[1] Since relief families for the most part come from the lower strata, they will tend to have a higher birth rate than the general population. Furthermore, since population traits are well grounded in the mores, relief families with more children will continue, at least for some time, to have children while still on relief. Such relationships, however, are shadowy and difficult to measure accurately because of the fact that during the depression of the early thirties all levels of society were affected to such a great extent. However, the higher birth rate of relief families as contrasted with nonrelief families has been noted by experts.[2]

FERTILITY OF GENERAL RURAL POPULATION

According to available data 444 children under 5 years of age per 1,000 white women 20–44 years of age are now necessary in order to maintain a stationary population. Because of the higher death rates the

---

[1] See Gini, Corrado, "Real and Apparent Exceptions to the Uniformity of a Lower Natural Increase of the Upper Classes," *Rural Sociology*, Vol. I, 1936, pp. 257–280. See also Notestein, Frank W., "Class Differences in Fertility," *Annals of the American Academy of Political and Social Science*, Vol. 188, November 1936, pp. 26–36; and McKain, W. C., Jr. and Whetten, N. L., "Size of Family in Relation to Homogeneity of Parental Traits," *Rural Sociology*, Vol. I, 1936, pp. 20–27.

[2] See, for example, Stouffer, Samuel A., "Fertility of Families on Relief," *Journal of the American Statistical Association*, Vol. XXIX, 1934, pp. 295–300.

number rises to 499 among Negroes in the country as a whole.[3] As shown by the 1930 Census, the fertility rates [4] of the general rural population were highest in the Appalachian-Ozark (838), Spring Wheat (804), Eastern Cotton (752),.and Lake States Cut-Over (737) Areas. The rates were lowest in the Corn Belt (565), Hay and Dairy (605), Winter Wheat (613), and Ranching (644) Areas (table 17). It is clear that the rural population has a birth rate considerably higher than necessary for replacement needs. It is a general phenomenon in civilizations, such as ours, that the rural districts produce a surplus of population which moves constantly to the cities to make up for the deficit caused by low birth rates in urban areas.

Table 17.—Children Under 5 Years of Age per 1,000 Women 20 Through 44 Years of Age in the General Rural Population, by Area and Residence, 1930

[138 counties]

Area	Total rural			Rural-farm			Rural-nonfarm		
	Number of children under 5 years of age	Number of women 20–44 years of age	Number of children under 5 per 1,000 women 20–44 years of age	Number of children under 5 years of age	Number of women 20–44 years of age	Number of children under 5 per 1,000 women 20–44 years of age	Number of children under 5 years of age	Number of women 20–44 years of age	Number of children under 5 per 1,000 women 20–44 years of age
All areas [1]	270,110	387,481	697.1	178,474	236,694	754.0	91,636	150,787	607.7
Eastern Cotton	79,003	105,110	751.6	61,845	75,904	814.8	17,158	29,206	587.5
White	49,141	62,318	788.6	36,253	41,911	865.0	12,888	20,407	631.5
Negro	29,862	42,792	697.8	25,592	33,993	752.9	4,270	8,799	485.3
Western Cotton	33,980	48,830	695.9	26,286	34,772	756.0	7,694	14,058	547.3
White	24,487	36,218	676.1	18,241	24,826	734.8	6,246	11,392	548.3
Negro	9,493	12,612	752.7	8,045	9,946	808.9	1,448	2,666	543.1
Appalachian-Ozark	53,172	63,458	837.9	28,654	33,689	850.5	24,518	29,769	823.6
Lake States Cut-Over	5,638	7,648	737.2	2,737	3,583	763.9	2,901	4,065	713.7
Hay and Dairy	43,396	71,714	605.1	22,478	33,176	677.5	20,918	38,538	542.8
Corn Belt	35,221	62,339	565.0	23,805	39,045	609.7	11,416	23,294	490.1
Spring Wheat	8,501	10,570	804.3	6,255	6,941	901.2	2,246	3,629	618.9
Winter Wheat	5,223	8,526	612.6	3,479	5,288	657.9	1,744	3,238	538.6
Ranching	5,976	9,286	643.5	2,935	4,296	683.2	3,041	4,990	609.4

[1] Exclusive of New England.

Source: Special tabulation by U. S. Bureau of the Census for identical counties used in the Survey of Current Changes in the Rural Relief Population.

[3] Data for fertility of white women from National Resources Committee, *Population Statistics, 1. National Data*, Washington, D. C., October 1937, table 14; data for fertility of Negro women computed by Harold Dorn, based on life tables prepared by the U. S. Bureau of the Census.

[4] The fertility index used here is the ratio of children under 5 per 1,000 women 20–44 years of age. This index is most valuable for a study of this kind since it minimizes differentials in infant mortality among areas. Thus, it more closely approximates a measure of effective fertility than a crude or specific birth rate taken from registration figures. One weakness of this index is under-enumeration of younger children. For example, tests made by the U. S. Bureau of the Census show a short count of considerable size. The size of this omission may be much larger in rural and isolated districts than in cities. There is also the possibility of underenumeration on the schedules used in the sample study, but assurances from field workers indicate that the relief enumeration was more complete than the census enumeration.

The fertility rate for all rural areas sampled was 697 for the 1930 Census population. Since the rate among the rural-nonfarm (608) population was lower than that among the rural-farm (754) population, a closer approximation to the birth rate necessary for a stationary population was found in the nonfarm group. This was particularly true in the Corn Belt, Winter Wheat, Hay and Dairy, and Western Cotton Areas where the rates for the rural-nonfarm population were very low.

Differentials in the rates for the total rural-farm and rural-nonfarm populations were greatest in the Spring Wheat (282), Eastern Cotton (227), and Western Cotton (209) Areas. They were least in the Appalachian-Ozark (27) and Lake States Cut-Over (50) Areas. The largest number of children under 5 years of age per 1,000 women 20–44 years of age in any of the areas studied was found in the rural-farm population of the Spring Wheat Area, where the fertility rate was 901 per 1,000. This high rate may be largely attributed to the families of immigrant stock which have rather recently migrated into the area. The comparatively high rate in the rural-farm population of the Appalachian-Ozark Area (851) may be attributed largely to the isolated and, to a certain extent, self-sufficient economy. The next highest rural-farm rates were found in the two Cotton Areas and the Lake States Cut-Over Area. In these districts a familistic culture is dominant. In contrast, the lowest fertility rates for rural-farm families were found in the Corn Belt, Winter Wheat, Hay and Dairy, and Ranching Areas. In these areas a highly commercialized, mechanized, and extensive agriculture, including some urban influences, is the rule.

FERTILITY OF RURAL RELIEF FAMILIES

The ratio of children to women among rural relief families, as revealed by the enumeration of October 1935,[5] is not the same as that of the general rural population, and the differences between the two enumerations show wide contrasts in the various type-of-farming areas. In the relief population fertility was highest in the Appalachian-Ozark (1,277), Spring Wheat (1,092), and Ranching (1,000) Areas (table 18). The rates were lowest in New England (664), in the Eastern Cotton Area (748), and in the Corn Belt (867). In comparison with the rates for the total rural population the Ranching Area had moved up from a very low rank to near the top and the two Cotton Areas had both dropped down the scale. It is interesting to note that according to fertility rates in the villages the three southern areas ranked at the bottom. Only in the Ranching Area was the rate higher in villages than in the open country.

---

[5] Data on fertility were available from the October rather than the June 1935 tabulations.

Table 18.—Children Under 5 Years of Age per 1,000 Women 20 Through 44 Years of Age in Rural Families Receiving General Relief, by Area and Residence, October 1935

[138 counties and 83 New England townships [1]]

Area	Total rural			Open country [2]			Village [2]		
	Number of children under 5 years of age	Number of women 20–44 years of age	Number of children under 5 per 1,000 women 20–44 years of age	Number of children under 5 years of age	Number of women 20–44 years of age	Number of children under 5 per 1,000 women 20–44 years of age	Number of children under 5 years of age	Number of women 20–44 years of age	Number of children under 5 per 1,000 women 20–44 years of age
All areas	31,434	30,332	1,036.3	22,262	18,164	1,225.6	8,040	10,464	768.3
Eastern Cotton	2,434	3,254	748.0	1,932	2,330	829.2	502	924	543.3
White	1,830	2,454	745.7	1,474	1,788	824.4	356	666	534.5
Negro	604	800	755.0	458	542	845.0	146	258	565.9
Western Cotton	3,256	3,512	927.1	2,556	2,504	1,020.8	700	1,008	694.4
White	2,684	2,894	927.4	2,110	2,054	1,027.3	574	840	683.3
Negro	572	618	925.6	446	450	991.1	126	168	750.0
Appalachian-Ozark	15,382	12,044	1,277.2	12,340	7,912	1,559.7	3,042	4,132	736.2
Lake States Cut-Over	1,516	1,568	966.8	1,108	1,070	1,035.5	408	498	819.3
Hay and Dairy	3,314	3,628	913.5	1,970	2,066	953.5	1,344	1,562	860.4
Corn Belt	1,624	1,874	866.6	686	706	971.7	938	1,168	803.1
Spring Wheat	1,694	1,552	1,091.5	1,180	1,046	1,128.1	514	506	1,015.8
Winter Wheat	444	558	795.7	270	342	789.5	174	216	805.6
Ranching	638	638	1,000.0	220	188	1,170.2	418	450	928.9
New England	1,132	1,704	664.3	—	—	—	—	—	—

[1] Townships in Connecticut and Massachusetts only.
[2] Exclusive of New England.

NOTE.—The fertility rate of the rural relief population for all areas is importantly weighted by the Appalachian-Ozark sample. In the areas not sampled fertility rates were lower than in those represented by the 10 sample areas. See Mangus, A. R., *Changing Aspects of Rural Relief*, Research Monograph XIV, Division of Social Research, Works Progress Administration, Washington, D. C., 1938, table 24.

The comparison of relief families with the general rural population in the same areas according to number of children under 5 years of age per 1,000 women 20 through 44 years of age was affected by various factors.[6] One difficulty in the comparison was the fact that there is a difference of 5 years between the census figures and the relief figures, and the depression of the early thirties had far-reaching effects on marriage and birth rates. For instance, Stouffer and Spencer [7] estimated a depression deficit of 748,000 marriages and possibly over a million births. Following a drop in 1930, 1931, and 1932, marriage and birth rates have risen somewhat again. The fertility rates used here would be affected by factors in the periods 1926–1930 and 1931–1935 so that to measure the depression drop in the birth rate actual births were compared for these two periods.

---

[6] Some of the rates in the Southern States may have been affected by the marked population changes in the period between 1930 and 1935. See Smith, T. Lynn, "Recent Changes in the Farm Population of the Southern States," *Social Forces*, Vol. 15, 1937, pp. 391–401. In this article the relocation of the southern population is brought out and the increase in population in areas adjacent to cities and in the poor-land areas is shown.

[7] Stouffer, Samuel A. and Spencer, Lyle M., "Marriage and Divorce in Recent Years," *Annals of the American Academy of Political and Social Science*, Vol. 188, November 1936, pp. 56–69.

It was found that the chief loss in number of births during 1931–1935 was in regions other than the South.

The expectation that relief families would have a higher birth rate than the census population has been suggested earlier in this report. This was due to the natural expectation that relief would be distributed where need was greatest in terms of mouths to feed. This situation was realized in most areas, but actually in the Eastern Cotton Area the relief fertility rate was 748 as contrasted with 752 for the rural population as a whole. In the other agricultural areas the ratio of children to women for relief families was higher than that for the census population. The difference between relief families and census families was greatest in the Appalachian-Ozark and Ranching Areas.

Differences from area to area in the ratio of children to women in the rural relief population are related to cultural backgrounds. One of the oldest and most firmly rooted rural cultures is found in the South. There tradition and custom play an exceedingly important role, and the habit of mutual assistance is well established.

In the depression of the early thirties these traditions and customs were unifying forces which assisted the families and groups in caring for themselves without outside governmental aid. Many tenants and croppers on the southern plantations were cared for by landlords who advanced them food and clothing throughout much of the crisis period. This was especially true in the older sections of the Eastern Cotton Area and to a lesser extent in the Western Cotton Area. Although the same type of landlord and tenant relationship did not exist in the Appalachian-Ozark or the Lake States Cut-Over Areas, informal mutual aid may also have been a vital factor. In each of these latter areas the tendency was toward a small-scale, noncommercial, and self-sufficient agriculture. The single crop system in the Cotton Areas was concentrated on a cash crop, but the small-scale operations, together with other social and cultural background features, created an affinity with the small farmer in the other two areas.

In contrast to this situation was that found in the more highly commercialized areas where extensive agriculture is the rule. Scattered widely over the landscape, of diverse cultural backgrounds, psychologically absorbed in a money-market economy, these farmers have not built up the body of traditions and customs that determine an integrated culture. True there are scattered communities which are highly homogeneous, and there are nationalities which are extremely clannish. But in general the families in those sections of the United States exist as individualized units, each of which acts independently. Their unity lies in the common concentration on a cash crop and on the commercial exchange markets rather than in a

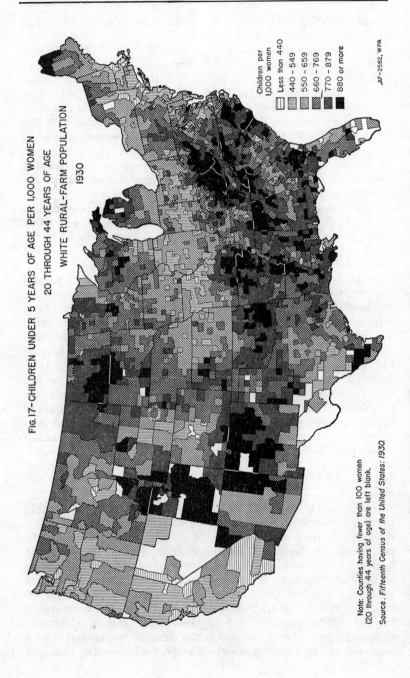

FIG. I7—CHILDREN UNDER 5 YEARS OF AGE PER 1,000 WOMEN
20 THROUGH 44 YEARS OF AGE
WHITE RURAL-FARM POPULATION
1930

Children per
1,000 women

Less than 440
440 – 549
550 – 659
660 – 769
770 – 879
880 or more

AF-2582, WPA

Note: Counties having fewer than 100 women
(20 through 44 years of age) are left blank.

Source: Fifteenth Census of the United States: 1930.

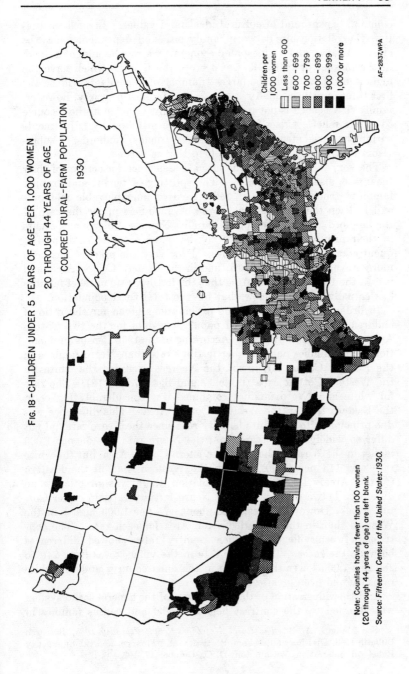

FIG. 18 – CHILDREN UNDER 5 YEARS OF AGE PER 1,000 WOMEN
20 THROUGH 44 YEARS OF AGE
COLORED RURAL-FARM POPULATION
1930

Children per
1,000 women

Less than 600
600 - 699
700 - 799
800 - 899
900 - 999
1,000 or more

AF-2837,WPA

Note: Counties having fewer than 100 women
(20 through 44 years of age) are left blank.

Source: Fifteenth Census of the United States: 1930.

common background of cultural ideals and values. In such a situation the relationship between family size and dependency may be close. That is, given widespread economic distress because of a break in the market or to the loss of a crop, the families which have the highest birth rate and the largest number of dependents will be the first to use up their small reserves. In a familistic society, however, family size as such is not the most important variable in the recourse to public relief. Crises in these areas are met first by adjustments within the social structure, and relatives, friends, landlords, or supervisors may extend the economic help that is needed.

The very fact that landlords provide assistance for certain of their tenants is also of significance. The splitting of tenant and cropper families [8] tended to place on relief aged or unemployable members and to keep the younger and more able members under the care of the landlord. Thus, the normal families composed of young parents in their prime would probably not be listed as relief cases as frequently as other types of families. However, this practice has been more prevalent in the Western than in the Eastern Cotton Area, and it is in the Eastern Cotton Area that the fertility rate of relief families has actually dropped below that for the total rural population.

In order to check further the explanations given for the ratio of children to women in the relief population, data for the two Cotton Areas were analyzed by color. According to the 1930 Census enumeration white families had a higher fertility rate than Negro families in the Eastern Cotton Area, but the Negroes exceeded the whites in the Western Cotton Area (table 17 and figs. 17 and 18). The rate for white and Negro families combined was considerably higher in the Eastern than in the Western Cotton Area. This difference was due principally to the white fertility rate since the Negro rate did not differ so widely in the two areas; the Negro rate was 55 per 1,000 higher in the Western than in the Eastern Cotton Area, but the white rate was 113 per 1,000 lower in the Western than in the Eastern Cotton Area. In the relief population there was practically no difference between the white and Negro fertility rates in either Cotton Area. However, rates were about 175 per 1,000 higher in the Western than in the Eastern Cotton Area for each race. The contrast between village and open country rates showed differences between the races. The Negro rate in the villages was from 240 to 280 per 1,000 lower than it was in the open country and the white rates showed even greater differences.

A further illustration of the importance of the general social system was afforded by the contrast between relief and census families in

[8] See Mangus, A. R., *The Rural Negro on Relief, February 1935*, Research Bulletin H–3, Division of Research, Statistics, and Finance, Federal Emergency Relief Administration, Washington, D. C., October 17, 1935, p. ii.

Table 19.—Children Under 5 Years of Age per 1,000 Women 20 Through 44 Years of Age in the General Rural Population, 1930,[1] and in the Rural Relief Population, October 1935, of 2 New England States

[83 townships]

State	General rural population			Rural relief population		
	Number of children under 5 years of age	Number of women 20–44 years of age	Number of children under 5 per 1,000 women 20–44 years of age	Number of children under 5 years of age	Number of women 20–44 years of age	Number of children under 5 per 1,000 women 20–44 years of age
Total_____	71, 538	154, 942	461. 7	1, 132	1, 704	664. 3
Massachusetts_____	33, 237	70, 264	473. 0	800	1, 228	651. 5
Connecticut_____	38, 301	84, 678	452. 3	332	476	697. 5

[1] Bureau of the Census, *Fifteenth Census of the United States: 1930*, Population Vol. III, U. S. Department of Commerce, Washington, D. C., 1933.

two New England States (table 19). Here the ratios of children to women were considerably lower than they were in the South (tables 17 and 18) and came much nearer approximating merely reproductive needs. In Connecticut the rate for the general rural population was 452 per 1,000, and in Massachusetts, 473 per 1,000. Fertility rates were strikingly higher for relief than for census families. In Connecticut the difference was almost 250 per 1,000, and in Massachusetts it was about 180 per 1,000.

STRONG AND WEAK FAMILY SYSTEMS

As a consequence of these differences in the fertility rates of census and relief families, two major types of families, designated as weak and strong families,[9] stand out clearly. In a familistic social system the families have a larger number of children on the average than those in the weaker counterpart. This does not mean that sterility or small families will be absent in a familistic complex, or that there will not be large families in an individualistic system. Rather it means that the combination of all of the factors which tend to concentrate the attention of the individual on his own wants and desires and to lift from him the burden of support for others results in a steadily decreasing birth rate; and out of this variable mass in which each item differs from the others in almost imperceptible degree, two contradictory typological cases can be segregated analytically. These cases are designated as strong and weak family types.

In the contemporary United States these family types are associated concretely in varying degrees with the different sections of the country; and the analysis can be made in terms of either social or geo-

[9] See Zimmerman, Carle C. and Frampton, M. E., *Family and Society*, New York: D. Van Nostrand Company, Inc., 1935, ch. XVIII.

graphical space. This means that there is a pronounced tendency for the weak family system to be correlated with the extensity and intensity of the diffusion of urbanism. The opposite relation of strong family systems and rural mores is also true. Geographically, the Old South, including the two Cotton Areas and the Appalachian-Ozark Area, approaches most closely a familistic social system. A familistic system was also once present in other sections of the United States, particularly in New England, but there only its traces are left amidst the dense urban and industrial population. A compensating factor in New England has been the strong family mores of recent immigrants, but the process of assimilation tends to wipe out these traditions in a generation or two.[10] In the early period of settlement by New England and southern families the Midwest also corresponded to this type of familism, but the disruption of systems of social relationships through migration, together with rapid urbanization and sudden prosperity, has meant an equally sudden transformation of the family system in that region. Thus, the tendency today in all regions but the South is toward the weak family system, and, if the movement continues, all that is required for its realization is the necessary time for the process to work itself out. Evidence indicates that the South is headed in the same direction, but it has farther to go. In this manner the two family types can be related to the birth rates in specific areas.

Thus, within the strong or the weak family systems the influence of the birth rate, as one of the factors causing relief, may have opposite effects. The weaker the family structure, and correspondingly the weaker the cultural background, the closer becomes the correlation between birth rates and relief. But within a strong family system the factors leading to relief do not appear to be directly related to the birth rate, and the problems of families in these areas cannot be explained merely in terms of a large number of dependent children.

---

[10] In this connection it is interesting to note that in a recent study of relief in rural Connecticut it was found that foreign-born families were not overrepresented on relief and were probably slightly underrepresented as compared with the native-born. See Whetten, N. L., Darling, H. D., McKain, W. C., Jr., and Field, R. F., *Rural Families on Relief in Connecticut*, Bulletin 215, Storrs Agricultural Experiment Station, Storrs, Conn., 1937, pp. 24–25. That the mores of the immigrant groups are rapidly breaking down in certain areas, however, is illustrated by the fact that in a recent study of Montville, Conn., where there are a large number of Polish immigrants, it was found that the foreign-born Polish families had the highest relief rate in town. See Whetten, N. L. and McKain, W. C., Jr., *A Sociological Analysis of Relief and Non-Relief Families in a Rural Connecticut Town*, Bulletin 219, Storrs Agricultural Experiment Station, Storrs, Conn., 1937.

Chapter VIII

EMPLOYABILITY, EMPLOYMENT, AND AMOUNT OF RELIEF

THE DIRECT cause and effect relationship between cyclical unemployment and relief is so obvious that during depression periods it tends to be overemphasized to the detriment of more continuous, long-time factors. Even in the most prosperous times many families are on relief because of the lack of wage earners or because of their illness or injury. These families may be styled *economically disorganized* since their economic organization is completely broken or badly crippled. Families of this type include those with no worker 16–64 years of age and those with female workers only. In addition to these extreme types there are the families which have varying numbers of male workers or both male and female workers.

The employability composition thus sets the outside limits for family employment, and within these limits there may be wide variations. Therefore, under the general heading of employment and relief the analysis consists of a study of (1) employability composition, (2) occupational displacement and shifting, (3) unemployment prior to relief, (4) reason for accession to relief, (5) relief history, and (6) amount of relief.

EMPLOYABILITY COMPOSITION

The serious plight of many relief families is shown by the fact that 12.9 percent of all rural relief families in June 1935 had no worker (table 20 and fig. 19), and an additional 7.8 percent of the families had female workers only. Considerable differences appeared among areas in regard to employability composition. About one family out of six in most areas had no employable member and hence no means of wage income. The Cotton Areas had the highest proportions of families with female workers only, and in those two areas the total of the two categories, female workers only and no worker, accounted for one-fourth to one-third of all rural relief families. All of these families may be called unemployable or potentially unem-

69

Table 20.—Employability Composition of Rural Families Receiving General Relief, by Residence and Area, June 1935

[138 counties and 116 New England townships]

Residence and area	Total[1]		No worker	Female workers only			Male workers only			Male and female workers		
	Number	Per-cent		Total	1	2 or more	Total	1	2 or more	Total	2	3 or more
TOTAL RURAL												
All areas	62,809	100.0	12.9	7.8	6.6	1.2	64.3	53.5	10.8	15.0	8.2	6.8
Eastern Cotton	7,732	100.0	13.9	19.3	15.6	3.7	41.1	35.4	5.7	25.7	16.1	9.6
White	5,084	100.0	9.6	17.0	14.0	3.0	47.7	40.5	7.2	25.7	16.1	9.6
Negro	2,648	100.0	22.4	23.6	18.5	5.1	28.4	25.5	2.9	25.6	16.2	9.4
Western Cotton	7,268	100.0	16.6	10.2	8.9	1.3	61.6	50.7	10.9	11.6	6.1	5.5
White	5,432	100.0	13.0	7.9	6.9	1.0	68.5	56.3	12.2	10.6	5.6	5.0
Negro	1,836	100.0	27.5	17.2	15.0	2.2	41.0	33.9	7.1	14.3	7.3	7.0
Appalachian-Ozark	17,016	100.0	9.1	6.6	5.4	1.2	65.8	53.5	12.3	18.5	10.2	8.3
Lake States Cut-Over	3,792	100.0	16.5	2.7	2.4	0.3	73.0	60.9	12.1	7.8	3.3	4.5
Hay and Dairy	8,626	100.0	15.9	3.9	3.6	0.3	71.5	59.8	11.7	8.7	4.8	3.9
Corn Belt	7,512	100.0	11.5	5.6	5.2	0.4	72.6	61.0	11.6	10.3	6.2	4.1
Spring Wheat	3,374	100.0	6.5	3.5	3.0	0.5	73.0	62.0	11.0	17.0	5.2	11.8
Winter Wheat	1,288	100.0	8.9	4.3	3.8	0.5	79.3	70.0	9.3	7.5	4.7	2.8
Ranching	1,886	100.0	17.1	8.1	6.8	1.3	66.5	59.8	6.7	8.3	3.8	4.5
New England	4,315	100.0	16.7	7.4	6.3	1.1	58.0	46.5	11.5	17.9	9.9	8.0
OPEN COUNTRY												
All areas [2]	35,782	100.0	11.0	6.7	5.5	1.2	66.7	54.5	12.2	15.6	8.1	7.5
Eastern Cotton	5,002	100.0	15.7	18.5	14.4	4.1	40.7	35.0	5.7	25.1	15.4	9.7
White	3,366	100.0	10.8	15.5	12.6	2.9	48.9	41.8	7.1	24.8	15.2	9.6
Negro	1,636	100.0	25.8	24.7	18.0	6.7	23.8	20.9	2.9	25.7	15.8	9.9
Western Cotton	4,686	100.0	15.4	7.8	6.6	1.2	65.1	53.2	11.9	11.7	5.6	6.1
White	3,510	100.0	11.7	5.7	4.9	0.8	72.1	59.2	12.9	10.5	5.2	5.3
Negro	1,176	100.0	26.5	13.9	11.7	2.2	44.5	35.8	8.7	15.1	6.8	8.3
Appalachian-Ozark	12,066	100.0	7.4	6.2	5.0	1.2	66.1	52.7	13.4	20.3	10.9	9.4
Lake States Cut-Over	2,492	100.0	14.8	2.3	2.1	0.2	75.1	61.4	13.7	7.8	3.4	4.4
Hay and Dairy	5,028	100.0	13.8	3.1	2.9	0.2	75.6	61.7	13.9	7.5	4.0	3.5
Corn Belt	2,802	100.0	9.1	2.0	2.0	—	79.4	64.0	15.4	9.5	4.6	4.9
Spring Wheat	2,386	100.0	3.9	1.4	1.1	0.3	77.2	64.7	12.5	17.5	4.1	13.4
Winter Wheat	670	100.0	4.2	2.4	1.8	0.6	85.9	76.6	9.3	7.5	3.3	4.2
Ranching	650	100.0	16.5	6.2	6.2	—	71.7	63.7	8.0	5.6	2.8	2.8
VILLAGE												
All areas [2]	22,712	100.0	15.0	9.4	8.3	1.1	62.2	53.6	8.6	13.4	8.2	5.2
Eastern Cotton	2,730	100.0	10.7	20.7	17.8	2.9	41.9	36.1	5.8	26.7	17.4	9.3
White	1,718	100.0	7.1	20.0	16.9	3.1	45.5	38.0	7.5	27.4	17.7	9.7
Negro	1,012	100.0	16.8	21.9	19.3	2.6	35.8	32.8	3.0	25.5	16.8	8.7
Western Cotton	2,582	100.0	18.8	14.7	13.2	1.5	55.2	46.1	9.1	11.3	6.9	4.4
White	1,922	100.0	15.3	11.9	10.7	1.2	62.0	51.2	10.8	10.8	6.4	4.4
Negro	660	100.0	29.1	23.0	20.9	2.1	35.2	31.0	4.2	12.7	8.2	4.5
Appalachian-Ozark	4,950	100.0	13.4	7.6	6.6	1.0	64.8	55.1	9.7	14.2	8.6	5.6
Lake States Cut-Over	1,300	100.0	19.7	3.7	3.2	0.5	68.6	59.7	8.9	8.0	3.2	4.8
Hay and Dairy	3,598	100.0	18.8	4.9	4.3	0.6	65.8	57.2	8.6	10.5	6.1	4.4
Corn Belt	4,710	100.0	12.9	7.6	7.0	0.6	68.6	59.2	9.4	10.9	7.2	3.7
Spring Wheat	988	100.0	13.0	8.5	7.7	0.8	62.9	55.4	7.5	15.6	7.7	7.9
Winter Wheat	618	100.0	13.9	6.5	6.2	0.3	72.2	62.8	9.4	7.4	6.1	1.3
Ranching	1,236	100.0	17.3	9.1	7.2	1.9	63.9	57.9	6.0	9.7	4.4	5.3

[1] Exclusive of families whose employability composition was unknown.
[2] Exclusive of New England.

ployable [1] since they had no male worker and only in very few cases had more than one female worker. The high proportion of these two types of families in the Cotton Areas was the net result of the

[1] See Hulett, J. E., Jr., *Some Types of Unemployability in Rural Relief Cases, February 1935*, Research Bulletin H–2, Division of Research, Statistics, and Finance, Federal Emergency Relief Administration, Washington, D. C., October 4, 1935, table II, p. 17.

No Breadwinner in This Home.

social environment, the depression, and agricultural restriction measures.

The proportion of all rural relief families having only male workers was 4.5 percent higher in the open country than it was in the villages, while the proportion of unemployable and potentially unemployable families was 6.7 percent higher in the villages. Again it is seen that open country families comprised a more homogeneous group, most of whom were normal families with an employable male head, a wife, and children. The economically disorganized families tended to concentrate in the villages.

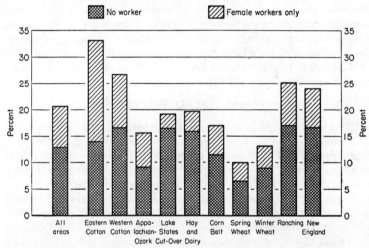

FIG. 19 - RURAL FAMILIES RECEIVING GENERAL RELIEF WITH
NO WORKER OR WITH FEMALE
WORKERS ONLY, BY AREA
June 1935

AF-2810, WPA

The areas did not fall into any clear-cut groups on the basis of families without workers. The highest proportion of families with no worker was found in the Ranching Area, followed by New England, the Western Cotton Area, the Lake States Cut-Over Area, and the Hay and Dairy Area. The smallest proportions were found in the two Wheat Areas and in the Appalachian-Ozark Area.

The explanation for the large number of potentially unemployable families in the Southern Areas was found to be largely attributable to Negro rather than white families (table 20). From two to three times as many Negro as white families had no workers. As high as 29.1 percent of the Negro families in the villages of the Western Cotton Area and 16.8 percent of those in the villages of the Eastern Cotton Area had no workers. White families with no worker varied from 7.1 percent in the eastern villages to 15.3 percent in the western villages. Similarly, more of the Negro than white families had female workers only although the differences did not appear to be as great. However, the summation of these two categories shows that almost one-half of the Negro families on relief in June 1935 had no employable male (46.0 percent in the Eastern Cotton Area and 44.7 percent in the Western Cotton Area). Fewer of the white families were in this situation with the proportions 26.6 percent in the Eastern and 20.9 percent in the Western Cotton Area. It seems that through a number of circumstances rural Negro families had become much more disorganized economically than white families. It is also probable that administrative factors affect the figures. Principally, however, the data reveal that relatively more of the families in the South, especially the Negroes, were on relief because of unemployability and that more of the families in other areas were on relief because of special circumstances associated with the depression.

OCCUPATIONAL DISPLACEMENT AND SHIFTING

Considered according to employment status and occupation, only 29.2 percent of the workers in agriculture were totally unemployed in comparison with 72.1 percent of the workers in nonagriculture (table 21 and figs. 20 and 21). The high proportion in agriculture, however, was partly due to the fact that farm operators were arbitrarily defined as employed if they were still on their farms, even if they had no cash income. Within the agricultural group the proportion unemployed [2] was smallest among farm owners (6.5 percent) and increased steadily at each of the lower occupational levels. Among the nonagricultural occupations the greatest unemployment was in the skilled and semi-skilled occupations while for both the unskilled and the white-collar occupations unemployment was slightly less severe.

Only 1 percent of the former workers in agriculture had shifted into current nonagricultural employment, but almost 11 percent of the former nonagricultural workers were currently employed in agriculture at the time of the survey. In part this reflects a widespread movement back to the farm during the depression, and in part it also reflects the reversed direction of occupational mobility during the depression, which caused a general shifting down the occupational scale for workers at all levels.[3] These occupational shifts are shown

---

[2] The term *unemployment* is used here to describe the situation of both nonagricultural and agricultural workers. A worker was considered employed if he had employment of at least 1 week's duration during the month. Of course employment for a farm operator who may or may not have a cash income is different from that of the urban employed, but the two are combined for terminological consistency.

[3] See, for example, Hogg, Margaret H., *The Incidence of Work Shortage*, New York: Russell Sage Foundation, 1932, diagrams 3 and 4.

Table 21.—Employment Status of Workers[1] in Rural Families Receiving General Relief, by Usual Occupation, June 1935

[138 counties and 116 New England townships]

Usual occupation	Total workers [2]		Employed		Unem-ployed	Total employed workers		At usual occu-pation	At other than usual oc-cupation
	Num-ber	Per-cent	Agri-culture	Nonagri-culture		Num-ber	Per-cent		
Total	80,684	100.0	37.1	7.5	55.4	36,013	100.0	85.5	14.5
Agriculture	37,792	100.0	69.7	1.1	29.2	26,754	100.0	95.8	4.2
Farm operator	18,686	100.0	85.3	1.0	13.7	16,136	100.0	96.3	3.7
Owner	6,789	100.0	92.9	0.6	6.5	6,346	100.0	97.9	2.1
Tenant	9,827	100.0	86.8	1.5	11.7	8,604	100.0	96.6	3.4
Cropper [3]	2,070	100.0	53.6	2.8	43.6	1,168	100.0	85.1	14.9
Farm laborer	19,106	100.0	54.4	1.2	44.4	10,618	100.0	95.1	4.9
Nonagriculture	33,125	100.0	10.8	17.1	72.1	9,251	100.0	55.7	44.3
White collar	3,253	100.0	5.8	28.1	66.1	1,101	100.0	71.0	29.0
Skilled	4,068	100.0	11.1	12.4	76.5	957	100.0	36.8	63.2
Semiskilled	5,729	100.0	8.9	16.1	75.0	1,431	100.0	54.0	46.0
Unskilled	20,075	100.0	12.1	16.6	71.3	5,762	100.0	56.4	43.6
No usual occupation	9,767	100.0	0.1	*	99.9	8	†	—	†

* Less than 0.05 percent.
† Percent not computed on a base of fewer than 50 cases.

[1] Persons 16 through 64 years of age working or seeking work.
[2] Exclusive of workers whose employment status was unknown.
[3] In the 2 Cotton Areas.

even better when workers reporting employment are considered according to whether they were employed at their usual occupation or at other than their usual occupation. Thus, 95.8 percent of the workers in agriculture who were employed at the time of the survey were engaged in their usual occupation as contrasted with 55.7 percent of

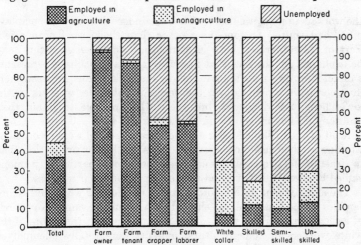

FIG. 20 – EMPLOYMENT STATUS OF WORKERS IN RURAL FAMILIES RECEIVING GENERAL RELIEF, BY USUAL OCCUPATION

June 1935

AF-2811.WPA

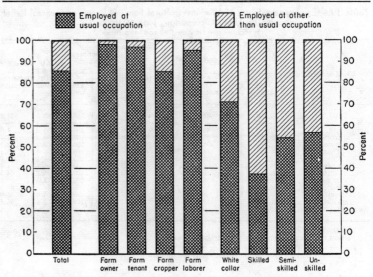

FIG. 21 - OCCUPATIONAL CHANGE OF WORKERS IN RURAL
FAMILIES RECEIVING GENERAL RELIEF, BY
USUAL OCCUPATION

June 1935

AF-2812, WPA

the workers in nonagriculture. The remainder who had some employment had shifted to something other than their usual occupation.
Part of this difference between agriculture and nonagriculture may
be explained by the fact that in many regions agriculture represents
a direct shift down the scale for all occupations. Thus, when workers
in general are moving down the occupational scale, workers in the
lower levels are displaced, but those who are able to retain their
positions do not move any farther down the scale. Therefore, 56.4
percent of the unskilled laborers who were employed were recorded as
working at their usual occupation. This is a higher proportion than
in either of the two occupational levels just above, particularly among
skilled laborers, but not equal to that for white-collar workers.

The employment data according to occupation for white and Negro
families in the Cotton Areas showed that about the same proportions
of agricultural workers were totally unemployed but that more of the
white workers in nonagricultural pursuits were totally unemployed
(fig. 22 and appendix table 24). This was true in spite of the fact
that more of the white nonagricultural workers had shifted into farming, 25.8 percent of the employed white nonagricultural workers being
engaged in agriculture as contrasted with only 4.7 percent of the
employed Negro workers.

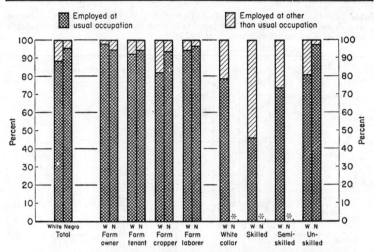

FIG. 22-OCCUPATIONAL CHANGE OF WHITE AND NEGRO WORKERS
IN RURAL FAMILIES RECEIVING GENERAL RELIEF
IN THE EASTERN AND WESTERN COTTON
AREAS, BY USUAL OCCUPATION

June 1935

*Percent not computed on a base of fewer than 50 cases.   AF-2813, WPA

UNEMPLOYMENT PRIOR TO RELIEF

The next question to be considered is the lapse of time between the
last job of the head of the family at his usual occupation and the
acceptance of relief by rural families in their first relief period in
June 1935. The analysis shows in part the effect of reserve accumulations which ward off the necessity of going on relief and in part the
group mores in regard to receipt of relief.

In the case of both agricultural and nonagricultural heads of families,
without current employment at the usual occupation, the period
between the last usual job and the opening of the relief case became
progressively shorter in the lower social strata (table 22). This was
particularly noticeable in the proportion of families whose head had a
job at the opening of the case or who had been out of work only 1 or 2
months. Of the workers in agriculture on relief for the first time, 11.4
percent had a job at the time of going on relief, and of the workers in
nonagriculture, 5.5 percent were employed. Within agriculture the
smallest proportion of these cases was among owners (5.0 percent)
and the greatest proportion among tenants (14.3 percent). Farm
laborers less frequently (12.1 percent) had a job at the opening of the
case, but an unusually large proportion (28.7 percent) had been
unemployed 1 month or less. Among the nonagricultural heads of

Table 22.—Length of Time Between End of Last Job of the Head at Usual Occupation and Accession to Relief of Rural Families in Their First Relief Period, by Residence and Usual Occupation of Head, June 1935

[138 counties and 116 New England townships]

Residence and usual occupation of head	Total[1]		Months between end of job and accession to relief							
	Number	Percent	None (job ended after opening)	1 or less	2	3–6	7–12	13–24	25–36	37 or more
TOTAL RURAL										
Total	15,982	100.0	7.2	22.8	9.3	18.5	11.1	10.3	6.2	14.6
Agriculture	4,681	100.0	11.4	23.5	9.7	21.6	11.3	9.8	4.1	8.6
Farm operator	1,500	100.0	10.0	12.3	7.0	22.1	12.7	15.7	6.5	13.7
Owner	318	100.0	5.0	9.1	6.0	13.5	11.3	16.4	9.4	29.3
Tenant	704	100.0	14.3	12.9	5.1	20.8	14.0	14.0	6.3	12.6
Cropper [2]	478	100.0	7.1	13.8	10.5	29.7	11.3	18.0	5.0	4.6
Farm laborer	3,181	100.0	12.1	28.7	11.0	21.4	10.6	7.0	3.0	6.2
Nonagriculture	11,301	100.0	5.5	22.6	9.1	17.1	11.1	10.5	7.1	17.0
White collar	1,119	100.0	3.6	14.8	8.0	15.8	12.9	13.1	10.0	21.8
Skilled	1,675	100.0	4.8	15.9	9.6	15.5	11.6	11.2	9.0	22.4
Semiskilled	2,056	100.0	5.6	21.9	7.1	16.4	11.0	9.6	7.1	21.3
Unskilled	6,451	100.0	6.0	25.8	9.8	18.0	10.6	10.2	6.1	13.5
OPEN COUNTRY [3]										
Total	6,302	100.0	7.5	23.3	10.0	18.8	9.9	10.4	6.0	14.1
Agriculture	2,574	100.0	13.4	26.7	10.8	23.9	9.2	7.9	3.2	4.9
Farm operator	788	100.0	10.7	13.7	8.6	26.9	12.7	13.5	6.3	7.6
Owner	112	100.0	7.1	8.9	7.1	19.7	10.7	12.5	16.1	17.9
Tenant	332	100.0	15.7	13.9	6.0	26.4	13.9	13.3	3.6	7.2
Cropper [2]	344	100.0	7.0	15.1	11.6	29.6	12.2	14.0	5.8	4.7
Farm laborer	1,786	100.0	14.6	32.5	11.8	22.5	7.6	5.5	1.8	3.7
Nonagriculture	3,728	100.0	3.4	21.1	9.4	15.3	10.4	12.1	7.9	20.4
White collar	258	100.0	1.6	11.6	8.5	8.5	18.6	12.4	10.9	27.9
Skilled	520	100.0	4.6	11.9	7.7	12.3	9.2	14.6	12.7	27.0
Semiskilled	652	100.0	2.5	20.2	8.6	14.7	10.7	11.0	8.3	24.0
Unskilled	2,298	100.0	3.7	24.2	10.2	17.0	9.7	11.8	6.4	17.0
VILLAGE [3]										
Total	7,812	100.0	6.6	23.7	8.8	18.9	12.5	10.8	6.7	12.0
Agriculture	1,848	100.0	10.0	19.8	8.3	19.6	14.2	13.1	5.3	9.7
Farm operator	632	100.0	10.1	10.8	5.7	18.0	13.3	19.7	6.6	15.8
Owner	130	100.0	4.6	7.7	7.7	12.3	15.4	24.6	4.6	23.1
Tenant	268	100.0	13.0	12.0	4.3	15.8	14.1	14.7	8.7	17.4
Cropper [2]	134	100.0	7.5	10.4	7.5	29.8	9.0	28.3	3.0	4.5
Farm laborer	1,216	100.0	9.9	24.5	9.7	20.4	14.6	9.7	4.6	6.6
Nonagriculture	5,964	100.0	5.6	24.9	9.0	18.7	12.0	10.0	7.1	12.7
White collar	684	100.0	4.1	16.7	8.8	17.5	12.3	14.0	9.6	17.0
Skilled	840	100.0	4.8	17.4	11.0	18.0	13.3	10.7	7.9	16.9
Semiskilled	852	100.0	4.9	27.1	5.6	18.3	12.7	9.9	7.7	13.8
Unskilled	3,588	100.0	6.2	27.6	9.4	19.1	11.5	9.1	6.4	10.7

[1] Exclusive of heads who were currently employed at the usual occupation, who were nonworkers, who had no usual occupation, and for whom months between end of job and accession to relief were unknown.
[2] In the 2 Cotton Areas.
[3] Exclusive of New England.

families the proportion became larger in the lower occupational levels for each interval up to 6 months. Thus, 3.6 percent of the white-collar workers were working at the time of first going on relief as contrasted with 6.0 percent of the unskilled workers. There were almost twice as many unskilled workers as white-collar workers who were unemployed 1 month or less before going on relief.

In the case of families whose head had been unemployed more than 3 years before going on relief, the proportions usually became greater with successive steps up the occupational ladder for both agricultural and nonagricultural workers. While in general there was a greater lapse in time for nonagricultural workers than for agricultural workers before applying for assistance, the most outstanding group was the farm owners, 29.3 percent of whom were unemployed more than 3 years before going on relief. Thus, if the lapse of time between first unemployment and relief is correlated with the accumulations of the successful years, agricultural families have smaller reserve funds than nonagricultural families. But the group which holds out longest against relief is the farm owners.

REASON FOR ACCESSION TO RELIEF

When rural families on relief in June 1935 were classified according to the reason for opening or reopening the relief case, loss of employment was found to account for 24.6 percent of all cases, loss or depletion of assets for 33.6 percent, and crop failure or loss of livestock for 13.6 percent (appendix table 25). The other groups were more clearly those which are usually designated as dependent or defective classes in contrast with normal classes which were forced on relief by special circumstances of the depression period. Hence, insufficient income accounted for 12.4 percent of the total group, disability for 5.2 percent, and all other reasons for 10.6 percent.

The differences between open country families and village families in the reasons for going on relief were primarily associated with the differences between agriculture and nonagriculture. Loss of crops or livestock or the depletion of assets was most important in the open country, and the loss of a job or the depletion of assets was most important in villages.

Loss of employment accounted for 35.5 percent of the cases in the Hay and Dairy Area, 34.8 percent in the Ranching Area, and 30.2 percent in the Corn Belt. In contrast it accounted for but 18.0 percent of the cases in the Winter Wheat Area, 14.1 percent in the Appalachian-Ozark Area, and 13.6 percent in the Spring Wheat Area. When analyzed on the basis of residence, these differences were accentuated.

As a factor in the relief situation loss or depletion of assets was not consistently related to any particular type of farming. It accounted for 48.6 percent of the cases in the Appalachian-Ozark Area, 48.9 percent in New England, and 34.2 percent in the Lake States Cut-Over Area as contrasted with 21.2 percent in the Western Cotton Area and 14.8 percent in the Spring Wheat Area.

Insufficient income accounted for 10 to 15 percent of the cases except in the Spring Wheat and Ranching Areas where it was considerably less important as a direct cause of the need for relief. Disability was most important in the areas which tend toward self-sufficient agriculture—Eastern Cotton, Hay and Dairy, Lake States Cut-Over, Appalachian-Ozark, and New England.

Some of the chief effects of the drought period were readily notice-able in that crop failure or loss of livestock was most important in the drought areas. This reason accounted for 81.4 percent of the open country cases in the Spring Wheat Area, 39.7 percent in the Winter Wheat Area, 33.2 percent in the Ranching Area, 31.9 percent in the Corn Belt, and 28.3 percent in the Western Cotton Area. In all of the other areas it accounted for less than 14 percent of the open country relief cases, and it was not a significant direct cause of relief among the village cases of any area.

The two races in the Cotton Areas reported different "causes" of relief (appendix table 25). Negroes were on relief more often because of insufficient income or disability, while whites were on relief more often because of loss or depletion of assets or crop failure. The two races were about equal with regard to loss of job in ordinary employ-ment. These differences no doubt reflect the fact that Negroes occupy a lower economic status than whites. Under ordinary condi-tions they have but very slight accumulations of wealth or property and thus have little to tide them over periods of depression. It is true that whites suffer relatively more from unemployment than Negroes (appendix table 24), but more Negroes who are working are not receiving sufficient pay to provide a livelihood. Negro cases tend more often to conform to the predepression definition of a charity case, while whites are more often of the type defined during the depression as the "new poor"—relief recipients who have for most of their lives been self-supporting.

RELIEF HISTORY

When rural relief families were analyzed according to continuity of their relief histories, certain trends were observable. Of all cases on relief in June 1935, 74.3 percent of the families had received assistance continuously since February (appendix table 26). Another 14.2 percent of the cases had been reopened [4] between March and June, and only 11.5 percent were new cases, coming on relief for the first time. The greatest proportion of new cases in this period was in New England (19.1 percent) and the smallest in the Spring Wheat Area (4.9 percent). Slightly more new cases proportionately appeared in the villages than in the open country.

While 74.3 percent of all relief cases were continuous from February through June, the proportion varied from 66.6 percent in the Eastern Cotton Area to 81.4 percent in the Spring Wheat Area. New cases ranged from 4.9 percent to 19.1 percent, and the fewest new cases were to be found in the drought areas: namely, the Spring Wheat,

---

[4] For definition of reopened case, see appendix A, pp. 110–111.

Drought Victims.

Winter Wheat, and Western Cotton Areas. In these same areas there tended to be high proportions of cases which had been continuously on relief since February, which probably indicates that sufficient time had not yet elapsed for farmers to recover from the drought of 1934.

Also illustrative of the lower economic status of the Negroes in the South was the fact that they more often had continuous relief histories than the whites in spite of differences between the two Cotton Areas (appendix table 26). The difference between Negroes and whites in this respect was greater in the Eastern than in the Western Cotton Area.

A study of the relief history of rural families according to occupation shows that agricultural families were on relief more continuously than nonagricultural families from February through June 1935. There were also fewer new cases in agriculture (table 23). The specific occupational levels within these two major groups were apparently uncorrelated with the continuity of relief history except that there was a slight tendency toward more new cases among the croppers and farm laborers in the agricultural group.

Table 23.—Relief History of Rural Families Receiving Relief, by Usual Occupation of Head, June 1935

[138 counties and 116 New England townships]

Usual occupation of head	Total [1]		Continuously on relief February through June	Opened March–June	Reopened March–June
	Number	Percent			
Total	62,771	100.0	74.3	11.5	14.2
Agriculture	25,524	100.0	75.4	9.5	15.1
Farm operator	18,423	100.0	74.4	9.2	16.4
Owner	6,694	100.0	72.7	9.6	17.7
Tenant	9,705	100.0	75.7	8.7	15.6
Cropper [2]	2,024	100.0	73.6	10.1	16.3
Farm laborer	7,101	100.0	77.9	10.3	11.8
Nonagriculture	25,884	100.0	71.4	14.1	14.5
White collar	2,315	100.0	71.1	17.2	11.7
Skilled	3,801	100.0	75.6	12.4	12.0
Semiskilled	4,287	100.0	66.6	18.1	15.3
Unskilled	15,481	100.0	71.8	12.9	15.3
No usual occupation	1,545	100.0	77.2	12.2	10.6
Nonworker	9,818	100.0	78.8	9.5	11.7

[1] Exclusive of families for which relief history was unknown.
[2] In the 2 Cotton Areas.

AMOUNT OF RELIEF

Among the various factors which may affect the amount of relief needed in individual cases is the severity of economic distress. Here regional variations and rural-urban differences are of great importance since the business depression is primarily a difficulty of a highly industrialized and commercialized economy. Thus, rural sections, and especially those which tend toward self-sufficiency, are less susceptible to the fluctuations of the business cycle, and their need will not be as directly correlated with it.

Another variable is the standard of living in the respective areas. This includes the minimum standard of physical need as defined by the customs and conditions of the community; it includes also the cost of purchasing these items in the open market. In general the higher the material standard of living in an area the higher the relief outlays which are necessary in time of depression. Hence, on this basis also there are variations among areas in the type and quantity of relief that will be granted and in the amount of money that will be necessary for such provisions.

It is not surprising to note that the lowest average monthly amount granted to relief families during June 1935 was found in the Western Cotton Area ($10) (appendix table 27). It was but little higher in the Eastern Cotton and Appalachian-Ozark Areas ($12). The highest average amount of relief was found in the Lake States Cut-Over and Hay and Dairy Areas ($23) and in New England ($37). These areas are either districts of high relief intensity [5] or they are rural areas contiguous to highly urbanized regions where the cost of living is high. It is consistent also that in every area, with the exception of the Western Cotton and Ranching Areas, the average cost of relief was higher in the villages than in the open country. This is probably due in part to the higher cost of living, less subsistence production, and the higher standards of relief in such places, and in part to the probability that more cases were on full relief in the villages than on the farms, where family resources may be greater.

The importance of minimum standards of relief was most noticeable in the South in the contrast between the races. In the Eastern Cotton Area the average white relief family received $14 in June 1935, as contrasted with $8 for the average Negro family. In the Western Cotton Area these amounts were $11 and $8, respectively. The explanation for the racial differences lies mainly in the comparative standards of living. Negro families, on the average, have poorer physical equipment for each occupational level than white families. The average value of the Negro's farm dwelling in the Southeast is usually only about half that of his white neighbor; and Negro dwellings have fewer of the benefits of sanitation, screening, and other household improvements.[6] Thus there are smaller demands on relief officials to supply these meager wants. Further, the caste system makes equal relief grants psychologically impossible in many parts of the South.

That southern families received relatively smaller amounts of relief was shown even more clearly when relief families were classified ac-

---

[5] See ch. I.

[6] See Woofter, T. J., Jr., *Landlord and Tenant on the Cotton Plantation*, Research Monograph V, Division of Social Research, Works Progress Administration, Washington, D. C., 1936, ch. VII.

cording to the total amount of relief (appendix table 28). In the Cotton and Appalachian-Ozark Areas only small percentages of both open country and village relief families received $30 or more in June 1935. The fact that Negro families received smaller amounts of relief than white families, inasmuch as 19 percent more Negro than white families in the Eastern Cotton Area and 9 percent more in the Western Cotton Area received less than $15 for relief, especially needs emphasis.

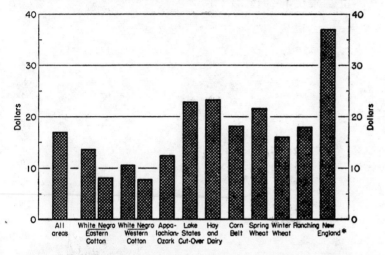

FIG. 23 – AVERAGE AMOUNT OF GENERAL RELIEF RECEIVED
BY RURAL FAMILIES, BY AREA
June 1935

*Townships in Connecticut and Massachusetts only.

AF-2814, WPA

In terms of the average amount of relief per family, the families receiving direct relief were the least expensive and those receiving work relief were next with the average amount almost 50 percent greater for the latter type (appendix table 27). Families receiving a combination of both work and direct relief were most expensive of all. In June 1935 direct relief cost an average of $13; work relief, $18; and the combination of both, $25 per rural family. In the case of all types of relief the cost of relief in New England was on the average over three times that in the South. Similarly, in almost every case the cost of each type of relief was greater in the villages than in the open country.

The average amount granted per family for each type of relief was smallest in the South (fig. 23 and appendix table 27). The difference between the southern and other areas was occasionally as much as 100 percent or more. This was particularly true in direct relief cases where the cost in the Eastern and Western Cotton Areas was only about one-third the cost in the Hay and Dairy, Lake States Cut-Over, and New England Areas. One important point here is the fact that the effect of the drought was not easily noticeable. That is, the two Wheat Areas, the Ranching Area, and to a certain extent the Western Cotton Area experienced the most severe drought. Yet none of these areas ranked consistently high in its average expenditure for each type of relief in June 1935.

Chapter IX

MOBILITY OF RURAL RELIEF FAMILIES

IN MANY respects mobility is an intangible variable, the effects of which are difficult to evaluate. This is due to its many possible inter-correlations with other fundamental sociological factors. However, it is possible to generalize in extreme cases. For one thing, extreme instability, particularly in an agricultural society, is generally considered in the long run to be disadvantageous to economic and social conditions. The frequent shifting from place to place has a tendency to make the individual neglect to develop or preserve his immediate surroundings since he has no interest in their permanent value. A population which is continually on the move has a tendency to neglect the repair of housing, to let landscaping go, and, of even more importance, to be careless about the utilization of land resources. If the continued existence of the family is dependent upon careful hoarding of its resources and frugal habits, reasonable stability is an asset and facilitates the process of accumulating reserves. When the family moves around at frequent intervals, these slow and careful accumulations gradually are wiped out. In addition to this effect, which is primarily economic, there is the psychological effect of long and continued residence in the same place. The power of the hearth and the home in maintaining the stability both of the individual and of the social order has been noted time and again.[1] Frequent mobility often exerts a subtle influence in breaking up the established systems of social relationships. These systems grow and develop at an extremely slow rate and are easily broken. Thus, in a very mobile society the power of group habits and customs may be undermined.

If too great instability is disadvantageous to a society, the reverse is equally true. A society in which the individual members are completely tied down to one locality may easily degenerate since initiative may be discouraged if not actually penalized.

Certainly there are few sections in the United States in which the population might be characterized as exceedingly stable. Many of the

---

[1] See Zimmerman, Carle C., *Consumption and Standards of Living*, New York: D. Van Nostrand Company, Inc., 1936, ch. VII.

newer sections have been settled but a few generations, and in most of the older sections new ethnic groups have been intermingled with the older racial stocks. There is a possibility that some of the isolated sections of New England may have been too stable in the eighteenth century, but that condition has long since been removed by the development of industries and cities and by the immigration of thousands of other Europeans. This situation is also true of the Middle Atlantic States, while in the South the lack of large-scale immigration is more than balanced by the mobility of the tenant and cropper families.

MOBILITY BY AREA

Only crude measures of the mobility of the rural relief population were available. For the most part the families were divided into three groups: *lifelong residents*, referring to those families whose heads were born in the counties in which they were living at the time of the survey; *predepression migrants*, referring to those families whose heads moved to the counties of survey at any time prior to 1930; and *depression migrants*, including those families whose heads moved to the counties of survey some time during the period January 1930 to June 1935.

Of the heads of rural families on relief in June 1935, 40.5 percent were lifelong residents of the county, 45.6 percent had moved to the county before the depression, and the remaining 13.9 percent were depression migrants (table 24). Lifelong residence was correlated rather closely with the period of settlement of the various areas and with the extent of urbanization.

That the more recently settled areas had fewer lifelong residents among the heads of rural relief families was very evident. The proportion of such residents was 14.4 percent in the Winter Wheat Area, 17.8 percent in the Lake States Cut-Over Area, 22.4 percent in the Ranching Area, and 28.0 percent in the Spring Wheat Area. These are all areas of comparatively recent settlement, and, indeed, portions of the two Wheat Areas and of the Lake States Cut-Over Area were settled as recently as the World War. Proportionately more lifelong residents were found in the South and the other sections of older settlement.

In the New England, Spring Wheat, and Appalachian-Ozark Areas only a few of the heads of rural relief families were depression migrants in comparison with much higher proportions elsewhere. Unusual migration from January 1930 to June 1935 may be attributed primarily to one or the other of two "causes," the drought or industrial depression. The extreme drought in the Spring and Winter Wheat Areas resulted in a large-scale migration out of the territory, and the business depression in the cities was the cause of a considerable back-to-the-farm movement.[2] The back-to-the-farm movement was ap-

---

[2] Baker, O. E., "Rural and Urban Distribution of the Population in the United States," *Annals of the American Academy of Political and Social Science*, Vol. 188, November 1936, pp. 264–279.

Moving Time.

Table 24.—Mobility of Heads of Rural Families Receiving General Relief, by Residence and Area, June 1935

[138 counties and 116 New England townships]

Residence and area	Total [1]		Lifelong residents of county	Predepression migrants to county	Depression migrants to county
	Number	Percent			
TOTAL RURAL					
All areas	62,060	100.0	40.5	45.6	13.9
Eastern Cotton	7,684	100.0	48.1	35.0	16.9
White	5,040	100.0	42.9	35.7	21.4
Negro	2,644	100.0	58.2	33.6	8.2
Western Cotton	7,098	100.0	30.0	52.1	17.9
White	5,290	100.0	25.5	52.9	21.6
Negro	1,808	100.0	42.6	50.1	7.3
Appalachian-Ozark	16,972	100.0	59.6	31.3	9.1
Lake States Cut-Over	3,712	100.0	17.8	68.6	13.6
Hay and Dairy	8,602	100.0	34.6	48.9	16.5
Corn Belt	7,470	100.0	36.1	46.2	17.7
Spring Wheat	3,184	100.0	28.0	65.3	6.7
Winter Wheat	1,260	100.0	14.4	57.8	27.8
Ranching	1,858	100.0	22.4	58.5	19.1
New England	4,220	100.0	32.2	59.0	8.8
OPEN COUNTRY					
All areas [2]	35,346	100.0	45.8	39.9	14.3
Eastern Cotton	4,962	100.0	50.3	31.5	18.2
White	3,330	100.0	44.2	32.5	23.3
Negro	1,632	100.0	62.7	29.5	7.8
Western Cotton	4,560	100.0	31.2	50.2	18.6
White	3,404	100.0	26.7	50.9	22.4
Negro	1,156	100.0	44.5	48.1	7.4
Appalachian-Ozark	12,034	100.0	66.8	24.4	8.8
Lake States Cut-Over	2,430	100.0	18.3	66.7	15.0
Hay and Dairy	5,018	100.0	35.9	46.4	17.7
Corn Belt	2,784	100.0	39.4	40.1	20.5
Spring Wheat	2,274	100.0	31.0	63.5	5.5
Winter Wheat	644	100.0	17.7	51.9	30.4
Ranching	640	100.0	13.1	69.7	17.2
VILLAGE					
All areas [2]	22,494	100.0	33.6	52.1	14.3
Eastern Cotton	2,722	100.0	44.3	41.3	14.4
White	1,710	100.0	40.3	42.0	17.7
Negro	1,012	100.0	51.0	40.1	8.9
Western Cotton	2,538	100.0	27.5	55.8	16.7
White	1,886	100.0	23.4	56.6	20.0
Negro	652	100.0	39.3	53.6	7.1
Appalachian-Ozark	4,938	100.0	41.9	48.1	10.0
Lake States Cut-Over	1,282	100.0	17.0	71.9	11.1
Hay and Dairy	3,584	100.0	32.9	52.3	14.8
Corn Belt	4,686	100.0	34.2	49.7	16.1
Spring Wheat	910	100.0	20.4	69.9	9.7
Winter Wheat	616	100.0	11.0	64.0	25.0
Ranching	1,218	100.0	27.3	52.7	20.0

[1] Exclusive of heads of families whose mobility was unknown.
[2] Exclusive of New England.

parently of greatest importance in the self-sufficing areas of the Northeast. It was also of great importance in the mountain areas of the South. This movement from the cities to the farms was of little importance in the areas of commercialized and extensive agriculture. Migration because of the drought came principally from the Wheat Areas and the Western Cotton Area and resulted in a shift of population within those areas and also a movement to the villages and to States in the far West.

The southern areas stand out as areas of comparative stability. Relatively more of the heads of relief families were lifelong residents, and there were relatively fewer recent migrants. It is a known fact, however, that many of the occupational classes in the South are extremely mobile within short distances. The average white tenant, cropper, and laborer family on plantations stays about 5 years on each farm while the average Negro family remains just over 6 years.[3] Most of the mobility of these classes in the South is of such relatively short range that it does not appear in the tabulations on which this report is based.

The greater mobility of white than Negro relief families in the South is demonstrated by the large proportion of white heads that had moved into the county of residence since 1929 (table 24). Between two and three times as many white as Negro heads of rural relief families were depression migrants. These relative proportions held true in both the open country and villages. Almost three-fifths of the Negro heads of families in the Eastern Cotton Area and just over two-fifths in the Western Cotton Area were lifelong residents of the county. In contrast the proportions of white families that were lifelong residents were only two-fifths and one-fourth, respectively.

The contrast between the open country and village families reveals again the fact that villages as a whole stand between the open country and cities in many social characteristics. In all but the Ranching Area a larger proportion of the heads of relief families in the open country than in villages were lifelong residents of the county. The difference was greatest in the Appalachian-Ozark Area where 66.8 percent of the heads of these families in the open country were lifelong residents of their counties as compared with 41.9 percent in the villages. The Appalachian-Ozark, Spring Wheat, and Ranching Areas had slightly more depression migrants in the villages than in the open country, probably for entirely different reasons.

Excluding lifelong residents, rural relief families were considered from the standpoint of the time of migration. Among the migrant families there were more depression migrants proportionately in the Eastern Cotton and Winter Wheat Areas than in the other areas surveyed. The back-to-the-farm movement was evident in the greater proportion of depression migrants to the open country than to villages (table 25). Only in the Spring Wheat and Ranching Areas was there a larger proportion of depression migrants to villages.

The distance of migration during the depression was also reflected in the proportions which came from elsewhere within the same State and from other States. Again migration in the South was seen to be primarily for short distances. The depression movement from the cities to farming areas was probably one of the factors in these migration data. The proportions of relief migrants who came from the

[3] Woofter, T. J., Jr., *Landlord and Tenant on the Cotton Plantation*, Research Monograph V, Division of Social Research, Works Progress Administration, Washington, D. C., 1936, ch. VIII.

Table 25.—Mobility of Migrant Heads of Rural Families Receiving General Relief, by Residence and Area, June 1935

[138 counties and 116 New England townships]

Residence and area	Total [1]		Prede-pression mi-grants to county	Depres-sion mi-grants to county	Predepression migrants to county			Depression migrants to county		
	Num-ber	Per-cent			Total	Dur-ing child-hood	Dur-ing youth or adult-hood	Total	From same State	From another State
TOTAL RURAL										
All areas	36,939	100.0	76.6	23.4	100.0	20.6	79.4	100.0	72.4	27.6
Eastern Cotton	3,984	100.0	67.5	32.5	100.0	19.6	80.4	100.0	72.4	27.6
White	2,878	100.0	62.5	37.5	100.0	18.1	81.9	100.0	71.6	28.4
Negro	1,106	100.0	80.3	19.7	100.0	22.5	77.5	100.0	76.1	23.9
Western Cotton	4,978	100.0	74.4	25.6	100.0	25.5	74.5	100.0	78.6	21.4
White	3,940	100.0	71.1	28.9	100.0	27.2	72.8	100.0	77.4	22.6
Negro	1,038	100.0	87.3	12.7	100.0	20.1	79.9	100.0	89.4	10.6
Appalachian-Ozark	6,862	100.0	77.4	22.6	100.0	20.7	79.3	100.0	78.7	21.3
Lake States Cut-Over	3,050	100.0	83.4	16.6	100.0	17.8	82.2	100.0	57.3	42.7
Hay and Dairy	5,622	100.0	74.8	25.2	100.0	17.9	82.1	100.0	72.8	27.2
Corn Belt	4,770	100.0	72.2	27.8	100.0	18.7	81.3	100.0	75.5	24.5
Spring Wheat	2,292	100.0	90.8	9.2	100.0	29.3	70.7	100.0	62.3	37.7
Winter Wheat	1,078	100.0	67.5	32.5	100.0	20.9	79.1	100.0	73.7	26.3
Ranching	1,442	100.0	75.5	24.5	100.0	20.0	80.0	100.0	61.0	39.0
New England	2,861	100.0	87.0	13.0	100.0	17.6	82.4	100.0	49.3	50.7
OPEN COUNTRY										
All areas [2]	19,142	100.0	73.6	26.4	100.0	22.1	77.9	100.0	73.9	26.1
Eastern Cotton	2,468	100.0	63.4	36.6	100.0	19.8	80.2	100.0	71.5	28.5
White	1,858	100.0	58.2	41.8	100.0	20.0	80.0	100.0	70.6	29.4
Negro	610	100.0	79.0	21.0	100.0	19.5	80.5	100.0	76.6	23.4
Western Cotton	3,138	100.0	73.0	27.0	100.0	26.4	73.6	100.0	76.2	23.8
White	2,496	100.0	69.5	30.5	100.0	27.1	72.9	100.0	74.8	25.2
Negro	642	100.0	86.6	13.4	100.0	24.1	75.9	100.0	88.4	11.6
Appalachian-Ozark	3,992	100.0	73.6	26.4	100.0	21.8	78.2	100.0	80.3	19.7
Lake States Cut-Over	1,986	100.0	81.7	18.3	100.0	18.6	81.4	100.0	54.4	45.6
Hay and Dairy	3,218	100.0	72.5	27.5	100.0	18.3	81.7	100.0	73.1	26.9
Corn Belt	1,686	100.0	66.2	33.8	100.0	18.1	81.9	100.0	79.6	20.4
Spring Wheat	1,568	100.0	92.1	7.9	100.0	31.3	68.7	100.0	61.3	38.7
Winter Wheat	530	100.0	63.0	37.0	100.0	23.4	76.6	100.0	82.7	17.3
Ranching	556	100.0	80.2	19.8	100.0	21.1	78.9	100.0	56.4	43.6
VILLAGE										
All areas [2]	14,936	100.0	78.4	21.6	100.0	19.6	80.4	100.0	72.8	27.2
Eastern Cotton	1,516	100.0	74.1	25.9	100.0	19.2	80.8	100.0	74.5	25.5
White	1,020	100.0	70.4	29.6	100.0	15.3	84.7	100.0	74.2	25.8
Negro	496	100.0	81.9	18.1	100.0	26.1	73.9	100.0	75.6	24.4
Western Cotton	1,840	100.0	77.0	23.0	100.0	24.0	76.0	100.0	83.5	16.5
White	1,444	100.0	73.8	26.2	100.0	27.4	72.6	100.0	82.5	17.5
Negro	396	100.0	88.4	11.6	100.0	13.7	86.3	100.0	91.3	8.7
Appalachian-Ozark	2,870	100.0	82.8	17.2	100.0	19.4	80.6	100.0	75.3	24.7
Lake States Cut-Over	1,064	100.0	86.7	13.3	100.0	16.3	83.7	100.0	64.8	35.2
Hay and Dairy	2,404	100.0	77.9	22.1	100.0	17.5	82.5	100.0	72.2	27.8
Corn Belt	3,084	100.0	75.6	24.4	100.0	19.1	80.9	100.0	72.4	27.6
Spring Wheat	724	100.0	87.8	12.2	100.0	24.8	75.2	100.0	63.6	36.4
Winter Wheat	548	100.0	71.9	28.1	100.0	18.8	81.2	100.0	62.3	37.7
Ranching	886	100.0	72.5	27.5	100.0	19.3	80.7	100.0	63.1	36.9

[1] Exclusive of migrant heads of families whose period of migration was unknown.
[2] Exclusive of New England.

same States were fewest in the Lake States Cut-Over, Ranching, Spring Wheat, and New England Areas. There were more depression migrants among whites than Negroes in the two Cotton Areas, but white families more often came from another State (table 25).

Mobility of relief families may also be approached from the point of view of the number of years of last continuous residence in the

Table 26.—Length of Last Continuous Residence in County of Heads of Rural Families Receiving General Relief, by Residence and Area, June 1935

[138 counties and 116 New England townships]

Residence and area	Total [1]		Years of last continuous residence in county						
	Number	Percent	1 or less	2–3	4–5	6–9	10–14	15–19	20 or more
TOTAL RURAL									
All areas	62,256	100.0	3.4	5.7	5.1	10.2	8.1	8.2	59.3
Eastern Cotton	7,688	100.0	4.3	7.0	5.5	9.1	6.0	6.6	61.5
White	5,042	100.0	5.8	8.8	6.8	10.4	6.3	6.7	55.2
Negro	2,646	100.0	1.7	3.6	3.0	6.6	5.4	6.3	73.4
Western Cotton	7,160	100.0	5.1	7.6	6.0	12.7	9.7	8.8	50.1
White	5,340	100.0	6.5	9.2	6.7	13.5	9.8	9.1	45.2
Negro	1,820	100.0	1.2	2.9	3.8	10.4	9.5	8.0	64.2
Appalachian-Ozark	16,974	100.0	2.9	3.6	2.8	6.3	6.0	7.0	71.4
Lake States Cut-Over	3,744	100.0	1.3	7.3	5.6	11.4	12.0	13.9	48.5
Hay and Dairy	8,612	100.0	3.4	6.0	7.3	13.2	9.9	8.1	52.1
Corn Belt	7,484	100.0	4.2	7.4	6.3	12.9	7.5	6.8	54.9
Spring Wheat	3,222	100.0	1.6	3.2	3.1	8.1	6.2	9.0	68.8
Winter Wheat	1,274	100.0	5.3	10.7	12.9	17.4	8.9	8.0	36.8
Ranching	1,866	100.0	5.4	8.4	5.9	9.9	7.0	9.4	54.0
New England	4,232	100.0	1.8	3.3	4.2	11.2	13.2	11.2	55.1
OPEN COUNTRY									
All areas [2]	35,474	100.0	3.6	5.9	5.1	9.1	6.8	6.9	62.6
Eastern Cotton	4,962	100.0	5.1	7.2	5.9	8.3	5.1	6.3	62.1
White	3,328	100.0	6.7	9.2	7.4	9.7	5.2	6.4	55.4
Negro	1,634	100.0	1.8	3.2	2.9	5.5	5.0	6.2	75.4
Western Cotton	4,606	100.0	5.4	8.1	6.0	12.6	9.7	7.6	50.6
White	3,440	100.0	6.9	9.7	6.7	14.0	9.8	7.7	45.2
Negro	1,166	100.0	1.0	3.4	3.8	8.7	9.3	7.4	66.4
Appalachian-Ozark	12,038	100.0	2.6	3.3	2.9	5.4	4.6	5.1	76.1
Lake States Cut-Over	2,456	100.0	1.4	8.5	5.9	10.7	10.7	13.7	49.1
Hay and Dairy	5,024	100.0	3.3	6.8	7.6	13.5	9.7	7.4	51.7
Corn Belt	2,790	100.0	5.7	8.0	7.0	12.2	6.3	5.7	55.1
Spring Wheat	2,298	100.0	1.7	2.4	2.3	6.6	5.2	8.6	73.2
Winter Wheat	662	100.0	5.4	13.9	13.3	14.8	7.9	6.9	37.8
Ranching	638	100.0	3.1	8.2	6.0	10.0	9.1	11.9	51.7
VILLAGE									
All areas [2]	22,550	100.0	3.5	5.9	5.3	11.7	9.1	9.5	55.0
Eastern Cotton	2,726	100.0	3.1	6.7	4.8	10.5	7.6	7.0	60.3
White	1,714	100.0	4.1	8.2	5.7	11.8	8.5	7.4	54.3
Negro	1,012	100.0	1.4	4.3	3.2	8.3	5.9	6.5	70.4
Western Cotton	2,554	100.0	4.6	6.7	6.0	12.8	9.8	11.0	49.1
White	1,900	100.0	5.7	8.4	6.6	12.6	9.8	11.6	45.3
Negro	654	100.0	1.5	1.8	4.0	13.5	9.8	9.2	60.2
Appalachian-Ozark	4,936	100.0	3.4	4.2	2.4	8.5	9.2	11.7	60.6
Lake States Cut-Over	1,288	100.0	1.2	5.0	5.1	12.6	14.4	14.3	47.4
Hay and Dairy	3,588	100.0	3.4	4.8	6.9	12.9	10.3	9.0	52.7
Corn Belt	4,694	100.0	3.3	7.0	6.0	13.3	8.1	7.4	54.9
Spring Wheat	924	100.0	1.0	5.2	5.0	11.9	8.7	10.0	58.2
Winter Wheat	612	100.0	5.2	7.2	12.4	20.3	10.1	9.2	35.6
Ranching	1,228	100.0	6.5	8.5	5.9	9.8	5.9	8.1	55.3

[1] Exclusive of heads of families whose length of last continuous residence was unknown.
[2] Exclusive of New England.

county. Again the South stands out as being, in general, a region of stable families and of long-time residents in a single county (table 26). Rural relief families in the Eastern Cotton Area were more stable than those in the Western Cotton Area. More long-time residents were found in the Appalachian-Ozark than any other area. In contrast, the Winter Wheat and Lake States Cut-Over Areas had the fewest residents of 20 years or more. Almost the reverse was true of families which had been resident in the county for less than 6 years.

More of these families were found in the Winter Wheat, Ranching, and Western Cotton Areas and fewer in the Spring Wheat, Appalachian-Ozark, and New England Areas.

Again, in the classification according to years of residence, Negroes stood out as a more stable group than whites (table 26). In the Eastern Cotton Area 73.4 percent of the Negro relief families and 55.2 percent of the whites had lived in the county for 20 years or more. In the Western Cotton Area the comparable percentages were 64.2 and 45.2, respectively. Considered according to the proportion of families which had lived less than 1 year in the same county, whites were again seen to be more mobile than Negroes. Indeed, there were three to five times as many white as Negro families in this category.

MOBILITY BY OCCUPATION

Agriculture is an occupation which encourages stability as contrasted with nonagriculture. Of all rural relief families whose heads

Table 27.—Mobility of Heads of Rural Families Receiving General Relief, by Residence and Usual Occupation, June 1935

[138 counties [1]]

Residence and usual occupation	Total [2]		Lifelong residents of county	Predepression migrants to county	Depression migrants to county
	Number	Percent			
TOTAL RURAL					
Total	58,000	100.0	40.9	44.5	14.6
Agriculture	24,746	100.0	47.5	38.3	14.2
Farm operator	17,974	100.0	49.7	38.3	12.0
Farm laborer	6,772	100.0	41.4	38.5	20.1
Nonagriculture	23,014	100.0	36.2	46.4	17.4
White collar	2,008	100.0	33.9	44.1	22.0
Skilled	3,240	100.0	28.6	48.9	22.5
Semiskilled	3,346	100.0	36.4	42.2	21.4
Unskilled	14,420	100.0	38.3	47.0	14.7
No usual occupation	1,408	100.0	53.8	35.8	10.4
Nonworker	8,832	100.0	32.9	58.1	9.0
OPEN COUNTRY					
Total	35,462	100.0	45.7	39.7	14.6
Agriculture	20,306	100.0	49.2	37.3	13.5
Farm operator	15,966	100.0	51.0	37.7	11.3
Farm laborer	4,340	100.0	42.6	35.9	21.5
Nonagriculture	9,792	100.0	41.1	39.3	19.6
White collar	604	100.0	32.5	38.4	29.1
Skilled	1,274	100.0	28.9	43.2	27.9
Semiskilled	1,472	100.0	38.3	35.7	26.0
Unskilled	6,442	100.0	44.9	39.5	15.6
No usual occupation	672	100.0	60.4	29.8	9.8
Nonworker	4,692	100.0	37.7	52.5	9.8
VILLAGE					
Total	22,538	100.0	33.5	51.9	14.6
Agriculture	4,440	100.0	39.3	43.1	17.6
Farm operator	2,008	100.0	39.4	43.1	17.5
Farm laborer	2,432	100.0	39.2	43.2	17.6
Nonagriculture	13,222	100.0	32.7	51.5	15.8
White collar	1,404	100.0	34.5	46.6	18.9
Skilled	1,966	100.0	28.4	52.6	19.0
Semiskilled	1,874	100.0	34.9	47.3	17.8
Unskilled	7,978	100.0	32.9	53.1	14.0
No usual occupation	736	100.0	47.8	41.3	10.9
Nonworker	4,140	100.0	27.5	64.5	8.0

[1] Data not available for New England townships.
[2] Exclusive of heads of families whose mobility was unknown.

were usually engaged in agriculture, 47.5 percent of those in agriculture were lifelong residents of the county in contrast with 36.2 percent of the heads in nonagriculture (table 27). Farm operators were more stable than farm laborers, but among the nonagricultural occupations unskilled laborers were the most stable group. Some differences appeared among these occupational levels in regard to the number who had been migrants before the depression, but the most important differences appeared in the number of depression migrants. More nonagricultural than agricultural workers had moved during the depression. More than one-fifth of the white-collar, skilled, and semiskilled workers and one-seventh of the unskilled workers had moved since 1929. Within agriculture more farm laborers than farm operators had moved during the depression. Among farm laborers and among nonagricultural workers there were more depression mi-

Table 28.—Mobility of Heads of Rural Families Receiving General Relief in the Eastern and Western Cotton Areas, by Color and Usual Occupation, June 1935

[44 counties]

Color and usual occupation	Total [1]		Lifelong residents of county	Predepression migrants to county	Depression migrants to county
	Number	Percent			
TOTAL RURAL					
Total	14,850	100.0	39.2	43.0	17.8
Agriculture	7,514	100.0	41.4	40.2	18.4
Farm operator	4,614	100.0	42.5	41.2	16.3
Farm laborer	2,900	100.0	39.5	38.6	21.9
Nonagriculture	4,186	100.0	36.3	42.2	21.5
White collar	532	100.0	39.9	39.8	20.3
Skilled	518	100.0	28.6	40.1	31.3
Semiskilled	820	100.0	33.9	42.9	23.2
Unskilled	2,316	100.0	38.1	42.9	19.0
No usual occupation	376	100.0	46.8	36.2	17.0
Nonworker	2,774	100.0	36.5	53.1	10.4
WHITE					
Total	10,384	100.0	33.8	44.3	21.9
Agriculture	5,408	100.0	34.5	43.4	22.1
Farm operator	3,516	100.0	37.9	43.1	19.0
Farm laborer	1,892	100.0	28.1	44.0	27.9
Nonagriculture	3,142	100.0	33.0	41.6	25.4
White collar	502	100.0	42.2	37.9	19.9
Skilled	470	100.0	26.4	39.1	34.5
Semiskilled	760	100.0	32.1	43.2	24.7
Unskilled	1,410	100.0	32.3	43.0	24.7
No usual occupation	346	100.0	45.7	37.0	17.3
Nonworker	1,488	100.0	30.2	55.0	14.8
NEGRO					
Total	4,466	100.0	51.7	40.2	8.1
Agriculture	2,106	100.0	59.1	32.0	8.9
Farm operator	1,098	100.0	57.4	35.1	7.5
Farm laborer	1,008	100.0	60.9	28.6	10.5
Nonagriculture	1,044	100.0	46.4	43.8	9.8
White collar	30	†	—	†	†
Skilled	48	†	†	†	—
Semiskilled	60	100.0	56.7	40.0	3.3
Unskilled	906	100.0	47.0	42.8	10.2
No usual occupation	30	†	†	†	†
Nonworker	1,286	100.0	43.7	50.9	5.4

† Percent not computed on a base of fewer than 50 cases.
[1] Exclusive of heads of families whose mobility was unknown.

grants proportionately in the open country, but among farm operators there were more depression migrants in the villages. Thus, the depression meant a move to the village for farm operators and a move to the country for nonagricultural workers, while many farm laborers simply moved to another location in the open country.

The greater mobility of white families on relief in the South was principally a racial difference rather than an occupational difference. This is indicated by the fact that there were more lifelong residents

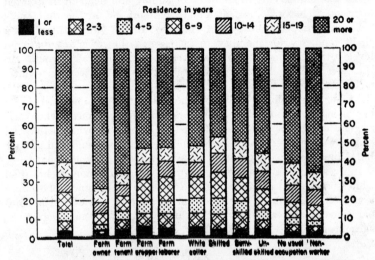

FIG. 24—LENGTH OF LAST CONTINUOUS RESIDENCE IN COUNTY OF HEADS OF RURAL FAMILIES RECEIVING GENERAL RELIEF, BY USUAL OCCUPATION
June 1935

AF-2615, WPA

and fewer depression migrants among Negroes than whites for both agriculture and nonagriculture (table 28). The difference was greater, however, in agriculture than in nonagriculture.

The occupational differences according to length of residence in the county in which they resided at the time of the survey also show that workers in agriculture were in general more stable than those in non-agriculture; 63.2 percent of them had lived 20 years or more in the same county in comparison with 52.9 percent in nonagriculture (fig. 24 and appendix table 29). The stability of the specific occupations within agriculture lessened with progressive steps down the scale as indicated by the proportion that had resided in the same county for 20 years or more. In contrast, stability in nonagricultural occupations increased with progression down the occupational scale with the exception of white-collar workers. The explanation for these differences lies in the fact that the increased responsibility for property in the upper occupational levels of agriculture has a tendency to tie the family more firmly to a particular farm and to increase the interest in improving and developing one farmstead. Farm laborers, however, must necessarily move about frequently from one place to another and do not often identify themselves completely with any particular location. The reversed position of nonagricultural workers in rural areas was due to conditions of labor supply and demand in isolated districts. This was most strikingly brought out in the differences between the open country and villages. In the village there was a slight tendency for mobility to increase in the lower occupational levels although unskilled laborers were a relatively stable group. In the open country, however, the most mobile groups were the white-collar and skilled workers, and mobility decreased successively with the other occupations. This was due to the difficulty encountered by unskilled laborers in finding other work in rural environments when their original occupation was discontinued. In contrast, white-collar and skilled workers were more in demand in rural areas and had greater bargaining power and greater resources in seeking employment.[4]

In every occupational group Negroes were much more stable than whites (appendix table 30). Since Negroes in nonagricultural occupations were less stable than those in agriculture, however, the comparative differences between whites and Negroes were most marked in agriculture.

RELATION BETWEEN MOBILITY AND FAMILY TYPE

Mobility varied greatly among the rural relief families in different areas of the country and had different consequences. As pointed out above, families in some areas were much more stable than those in other areas.

So far as the usual rural migratory movements are concerned, the country may be divided into areas which roughly correspond to the length of time since their original settlement. The rural relief families in the older areas of the East and South, having been settled for generations, were less mobile than those of the North and West where the populations have lived but a comparatively brief time and have not become firmly attached to the soil. Some modifications of this principle were introduced in the Middle Atlantic and New England States where the extensive urbanization and industrialization have increased

---

[4] For a more complete discussion of the difficulties encountered by skilled and unskilled industrial workers in a rural environment, see Zimmerman, Carle C. and Frampton, M. E., *Family and Society*, New York: D. Van Nostrand Company, Inc., 1935, ch. XVI.

Migratory Laborer Family.

the mobility of the population generally.[5] Another factor in the Northeast is the relative importance of foreign immigration in the last 50 years. Thus, mobility is roughly correlated both with geographical regions and with type of agriculture, and one may say that mobility in the rural relief population increases as one moves from the East to the West and from the South to the North.

The small-scale and yet rapid migrations in the South were largely excluded by the definitions of migration which were used in this study. A well-known fact was concealed in so far as residence was considered according to county and not according to farmstead. Since it seems probable that the most important effects of migration are to be found in its social results rather than in its economic results, however, this mobility in the South was really less serious for relief families than that in other parts of the country. Thus, families in the South normally move only a few miles at any one time and probably do not often get outside the bounds of their immediate primary group relationships so that the stability of the social structure is maintained. The principal loss involved in the high rate of mobility in the South is the degeneration of property and other capital goods on the farm and, on another level, there is the psychological effect.

In contrast, mobility in the commercial and extensive agricultural areas, particularly in the Wheat and Ranching Areas, is of a type which maintains economic stability through property ownership or long-term tenantry. At the same time it allows the complete disruption of intimate social relationships, customs and traditions, and cultural values. Most of the areas west of the Mississippi have been settled in a very recent period, and families and groups have not succeeded in sinking their roots deeply into the soil. Of even more importance is the fact that this population is comparatively heterogeneous, and settlement has been an individual rather than a group affair. Migrations in this part of the country have continued to be comparatively frequent, over long distances, and by individuals and families rather than by groups and communities. Under such conditions of mobility there is a tendency, however, for the social structure to become more homogeneous over wide areas and for group loyalty to become more associated with the larger aggregates and less with the immediate and intimate primary group. Yet, since in the long run a system of stable relationships cannot be firmly built upon secondary groups, it is evident that the type of mobility in this section of the country tends to have more important social effects than that in the Cotton Areas. Thus, in the South, the immediate primary group relationships may

---

[5] See, for example, Whetten, N. L. and Devereux, E. C., *Studies of Suburbanization in Connecticut, I. Windsor*, Bulletin 212, Storrs Agricultural Experiment Station, Storrs, Conn., 1936.

be maintained to a greater extent and the fundamental basis of the social order may be kept relatively intact.

Mobility is, then, related to the type of rural relief families.[6] Individualized family groups are usually associated with high rates of mobility; and the family type at the opposite extreme, in the familistic society, is associated with stability. Such mobility may be either a cause of or an effect of individualization. Yet the understanding of the direction of causation is less important than the appreciation of interdependence and of the fact that the final effects are not absolute but relative. The first effects of migration are possibly an increased family unity, and the group becomes necessarily more self-centered if it is to survive. Later, however, if this process continues and is prevalent among other families, a rapid mobility tends to break down all established social relations, including those of the family. In this manner the individualized family has set the prevailing tone of the social structure in the newly settled as well as the urbanized sections of the country. Familism is most evident in the Appalachian-Ozark Area and other areas of stability; and the Cotton Areas, with their short-distance mobile families, fall into an intermediate position. Here the family has indeed become more self-conscious and more self-centered, but the dominant familism of the social system has not been destroyed.

---

[6] For a more detailed study of migration of families during the depression of the early thirties, see Webb, John N., *Migrant Families*, Research Monograph XVIII, Division of Social Research, Works Progress Administration, Washington, D. C., 1938.

Chapter X

EDUCATION OF RURAL RELIEF FAMILIES

EDUCATION AS measured by the number of years of formal school-ing is a valuable index of the socio-economic position of rural relief families. In general it is correct to say that there is a rough correla-tion between social status and the duration of schooling. This is not meant to imply any one-way relationship between the extent of a person's education and his success in life. On the average, however, persons who have the most ability, according to the standards of the culture, tend to remain in established schools the longest. This is true in comparing large numbers of cases within a particular area, but different localities are hardly comparable. Nevertheless, it is very useful to compare the number of years of education for the aggregate population in these different areas in order to gain some understanding of the comparative educational level.

EDUCATION OF HEADS BY AREA

Heads of rural relief families were on a comparatively low educa-tional level.[1] Less than 4 percent were high school graduates and only about 35 percent had as much as a grammar school education [2] (appendix table 31). This means that about two out of three of these heads of families had dropped out of school some time before the eighth grade. In addition, great differences were evident between the open country and the village heads. In every area more of the village heads had completed the eighth grade, and for the country as a whole this difference was 11.1 percent. The areas which stand out as apparently providing the best educational facilities are the urbanized and commercial sections (excluding the Cotton Areas), where almost two-thirds of the heads had an eighth grade education or better. In

[1] For a comparison of the educational attainments of the heads of relief and nonrelief households, see McCormick, T. C., *Comparative Study of Rural-Relief and Non-Relief Households*, Research Monograph II, Division of Social Research, Works Progress Administration, Washington, D. C., 1935, p. 30 ff.
[2] Data on education were available for October rather than June 1935. See Introduction, p. XII.

sharp contrast were the cotton and the self-sufficing areas where very small proportions of the heads had the minimum grammar school education.[3] This was true for both races in the South although Negroes were on a much lower educational level even than whites.

If the length of schooling for heads of rural relief families is expressed in terms of median school attainment, the areas retain the same relative positions but a generally more favorable impression is received. The median for all heads of rural relief families in the United States was 6.4 grades, but in the Corn Belt, Wheat, Ranching, and New England Areas this median was more than 8 grades (table 29 and fig. 25). Progressive changes in educational standards in the United States as a whole are also evident in that the median number of years of schooling was higher for each younger age period. However, since the educational level in New England has been consistently high for over a century, the change was not great in this area, and the median was more than 8 grades for each age group. In contrast, the rapid change in the Cotton South was evident, inasmuch as this median was from 4.5 to 5.7 grades for heads 45 years of age and over and from 5.8 to 8.2 grades for heads aged 16–24 years. Thus, promise is given of a future educational level in the South comparable to other sections of the country.

A low educational level is not a phenomenon peculiar to the South, but it is also prevalent in all areas of the United States where subsistence or small-scale agriculture is predominant. The median school attainment for rural relief heads of families in the Eastern Cotton and Appalachian-Ozark Areas was slightly more than 5 grades, in the Western Cotton Area 6.4 grades, and in the Hay and Dairy and Lake States Cut-Over Areas between 7 and 8 grades. In all other areas the medians were more than 8 grades. This difference was most important, however, for the older heads, and in all areas except the Eastern Cotton and Appalachian-Ozark relief heads 16–24 years of age averaged more than 8 grades.

Differences between whites and Negroes in the South are again evidenced in that the median school attainment for heads of rural relief families in the Eastern Cotton Area was 5.9 grades for the whites and 2.9 grades for the Negroes and in the Western Cotton, 6.7 grades for the whites and 5.3 grades for the Negroes. In the Western Cotton Area the great improvement in education in recent years appeared in the case of the Negro heads whose educational level had been brought up more nearly equal to that of the whites (table 29).

---

[3] Comparison of education in the South and other areas according to years of schooling is made difficult by the fact that in many Southern States a high school education is completed in 11 years and a grade school education in 7 years. Yet this practice is not uniform throughout the South so that no standard can be set for the region as a whole.

Teaching Aunt Nancy To Read.

Table 29.—Average [1] School Grade Completed by Heads of Rural Families Receiving General Relief, by Residence, Area, and Age, October 1935

[138 counties and 83 New England townships [2]]

Residence and area	Average grade completed, by age				
	Total [3]	16–24 years	25–34 years	35–44 years	45 years and over
TOTAL RURAL					
All areas	6.4	7.8	7.4	6.4	5.5
Eastern Cotton	5.2	5.8	5.9	5.3	4.5
White	5.9	6.7	6.6	6.1	5.2
Negro	2.9	4.9	3.5	3.0	1.9
Western Cotton	6.4	8.2	7.0	6.3	5.7
White	6.7	8.3	7.1	6.6	6.1
Negro	5.3	6.9	5.9	5.2	4.6
Appalachian-Ozark	5.3	6.5	6.0	5.3	4.5
Lake States Cut-Over	7.3	8.4	8.4	7.2	5.4
Hay and Dairy	7.9	8.6	8.3	8.0	6.9
Corn Belt	8.2	8.7	8.5	8.2	7.1
Spring Wheat	8.1	8.3	8.3	7.9	8.1
Winter Wheat	8.2	8.7	8.3	7.9	8.1
Ranching	8.4	9.4	8.7	8.3	8.2
New England	8.3	8.5	8.5	8.3	8.2
OPEN COUNTRY					
All areas [4]	6.1	7.2	7.0	6.2	5.1
Eastern Cotton	5.1	5.8	5.7	5.1	4.4
White	5.6	6.4	6.3	5.8	4.8
Negro	2.8	4.8	2.4	3.1	2.0
Western Cotton	6.4	8.1	7.0	6.3	5.6
White	6.7	8.2	7.1	6.5	5.9
Negro	5.4	6.8	6.5	5.5	4.4
Appalachian-Ozark	5.1	6.1	5.8	5.2	4.2
Lake States Cut-Over	7.2	8.4	8.2	7.4	5.3
Hay and Dairy	7.8	8.4	8.2	8.0	6.8
Corn Belt	8.0	8.5	8.5	7.7	5.9
Spring Wheat	8.1	8.3	8.2	7.3	8.1
Winter Wheat	8.1	8.6	8.3	7.8	8.0
Ranching	8.0	8.0	8.3	7.2	7.3
VILLAGE					
All areas [4]	6.9	8.3	8.1	6.7	6.1
Eastern Cotton	5.6	5.9	6.6	5.8	4.8
White	7.2	7.0	7.4	6.9	7.2
Negro	3.1	4.9	5.2	2.6	1.8
Western Cotton	6.4	8.4	6.7	6.4	6.1
White	6.8	8.4	7.2	7.0	6.5
Negro	5.1	†	5.3	4.6	4.8
Appalachian-Ozark	5.7	7.7	6.3	5.4	5.0
Lake States Cut-Over	7.5	8.3	8.6	6.8	5.6
Hay and Dairy	8.0	8.9	8.5	8.0	7.0
Corn Belt	8.3	8.8	8.6	8.3	7.9
Spring Wheat	8.2	8.4	8.5	8.2	7.7
Winter Wheat	8.3	8.7	8.3	8.0	8.3
Ranching	8.6	9.6	9.0	8.5	8.3

† Median not computed on a base of fewer than 50 cases.

[1] Median.
[2] Townships in Connecticut and Massachusetts only.
[3] Exclusive of heads of families whose school attainment was unknown.
[4] Exclusive of New England.

Although the education of heads of families 16–24 years of age was on a higher level than that of any older group of family heads, there is still much which should be done. Among the families studied, less than 9 percent of the youthful heads were high school graduates and more than two out of five were not even grammar school graduates (appendix table 32). For the country as a whole 42.1 percent of these heads in the open country and 58.0 percent in the villages had at least

8 grades to their credit. Relatively small as these proportions may seem, it is encouraging to note that these proportions are much higher than in the case of all heads of families (appendix table 31). In every area the proportion of grammar and high school graduates was considerably higher for heads 16–24 years of age than for all heads.

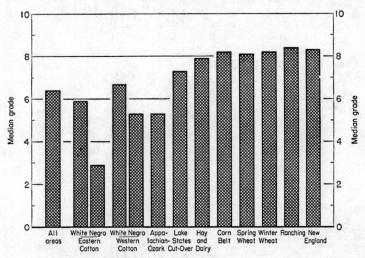

FIG. 25-MEDIAN SCHOOL GRADE COMPLETED BY HEADS OF RURAL FAMILIES RECEIVING GENERAL RELIEF, BY AREA

October 1935

AF-2818, WPA

EDUCATION OF HEADS BY OCCUPATION

The fact that education and social status are roughly correlated can be demonstrated best by the proportion in each occupational group that had completed an eighth grade or a high school education. The proportion of high school graduates among heads of rural relief families was about 2 percent for agricultural workers and almost 7 percent for nonagricultural workers (table 30). In addition, there was a rough stratification within these broad occupational groups.

For the country as a whole education was positively correlated with occupational level within agriculture with the exception of farm laborers. For the last group there were almost as many high school graduates proportionately as in the case of owners, and there were in fact more grammar school graduates. Percentages for owners were apparently unduly weighted in a downward direction by a group with but little education. An example of this is the fact that there were more owners with no formal schooling than was the case among either tenants or farm laborers. The higher school attainment of farm laborers was also due to their lower average age as more of them

Table 30.—School Attainment of Heads of Rural Families Receiving General Relief, by Usual Occupation,[1] October 1935

[300 counties and 83 New England townships[2]]

| Usual occupation | Total[3] | | Last grade or year completed | | | | | | | | | | | | | | Graduate work |
| | Number | Percent | Grade and high school | | | | | | | | | | College | | | | |
			None	1-3	4-5	6	7	8	9	10	11	12	1	2	3	4	
Total	78,886	100.0	7.7	12.8	20.1	10.6	9.5	26.1	4.1	3.3	1.7	2.9	0.4	0.5	0.1	0.2	*
Agriculture	40,014	100.0	8.7	14.9	22.8	10.6	9.6	24.5	3.2	2.5	1.0	1.6	0.2	0.2	0.1	0.1	—
Farm operator	27,244	100.0	8.8	15.0	23.5	10.9	9.6	24.7	2.7	2.1	0.7	1.3	0.3	0.3	0.1	0.1	—
Owner	9,472	100.0	8.8	13.6	22.8	10.1	9.5	25.9	2.9	2.9	0.9	1.7	0.5	0.3	0.1	0.2	—
Tenant	12,820	100.0	7.4	12.9	21.8	11.3	10.1	29.3	2.9	1.9	0.8	1.2	0.2	0.1	—	*	—
Cropper[4]	4,952	100.0	12.5	22.9	29.1	11.6	8.2	11.3	2.1	1.1	0.4	0.6	0.1	—	—	—	—
Farm laborer	12,770	100.0	8.4	14.8	21.2	9.9	9.6	24.5	4.1	3.4	1.4	2.4	0.1	0.1	—	0.1	—
Nonagriculture	31,766	100.0	6.0	10.4	16.5	10.6	9.8	28.4	4.9	4.3	2.4	4.6	0.6	0.8	0.2	0.4	0.1
White collar	2,772	100.0	1.1	2.8	5.2	3.2	5.3	28.3	6.7	5.9	4.4	16.1	5.0	5.6	1.4	4.1	0.9
Skilled	4,746	100.0	2.4	4.4	12.1	10.2	10.8	37.2	6.4	5.6	2.4	6.2	0.2	1.3	0.4	0.3	—
Semiskilled	4,894	100.0	3.7	7.5	13.9	11.4	11.3	32.9	5.5	5.4	2.9	4.5	0.5	0.7	0.3	*	*
Unskilled	19,354	100.0	8.2	13.7	19.9	11.5	9.7	25.2	4.1	3.4	1.4	2.5	0.2	0.1	*	0.1	*
No usual occupation	2,108	100.0	3.9	6.9	20.1	8.6	9.3	26.8	9.1	3.0	4.3	5.3	1.2	1.0	0.1	0.4	—
Nonworker	4,998	100.0	11.6	13.2	21.6	12.1	8.0	22.6	3.6	3.3	1.4	1.9	0.1	0.4	—	0.2	—

* Less than 0.05 percent.

[1] Data by usual occupation and school attainment were not available for the area sample used elsewhere in this analysis. Hence, a larger State sample, taken under the same conditions, was utilized. For a description of the State sample see Mangus, A. R., Changing Aspects of Rural Relief, Research Monograph XIV, Division of Social Research, Works Progress Administration, Washington, D. C., 1938, appendix B.

[2] Townships in Connecticut and Massachusetts only.

[3] Exclusive of heads of families whose school attainment was unknown.

[4] In the 2 Cotton Areas.

have been affected by the increased educational facilities of recent years.

In the case of nonagricultural workers there was a well-marked hierarchy which correlated education and relative socio-economic status. The trend from low education to high education clearly followed the lines from unskilled to semiskilled, to skilled, and to white-collar workers. Here the differences were much more exaggerated than in the case of agricultural workers, and the proportions of high school graduates ranged from 33.1 percent for white-collar workers to 2.9 percent for unskilled workers. White-collar workers as a class were very clearly separated from the rest of the occupations, and all of the nonagricultural occupations were seen to be on a higher educational level than those in agriculture. Unskilled workers, who were on the lowest level among the nonagricultural occupations, were on approximately the same level as the highest group in agriculture.

The educational level of the heads who either were nonworkers or had no usual occupations was also fairly high, inasmuch as from one-third to one-half of them had a grammar school education. This compared favorably with agricultural workers and with workers in the lower levels of nonagricultural occupations.

EDUCATION OF MEMBERS OTHER THAN HEADS

The average school attainment for family members, other than heads, 16 years of age and over was more than eight grades in each area except the Cotton and Appalachian-Ozark Areas (table 31). In contrasting the median number of years of schooling for members falling within the various age groups, it was evident again that educational standards have been raised considerably within the last generation. Because of the longer period of school attendance, youth 16–24 years of age had completed nine grades or more on the average in the Corn Belt, Winter Wheat, Ranching, and New England Areas. Most of the rapid recent improvement in education has taken place in the South, as evidenced by the fact that the average school attainment even for those 45 years of age and over was 8 grades in the New England, Spring Wheat, and Ranching Areas. That the Southern States differ among themselves in educational standards is shown by the fact that the median school attainment for other family members was 7.6 grades in the Western Cotton Area but only 5.8 grades in the Eastern Cotton Area.

Schools in many areas today have relatively high standards and long periods of continuous attendance. This is particularly true in the villages where the average school attainment was almost nine grades in six of the agricultural areas studied. In contrast, the lowest average for any group among the sample families was found in the open country in the Eastern Cotton Area where the median school attainment for persons 45 years of age and over was but 3.7 grades.

Table 31.—Average [1] School Grade Completed by Persons 16 Years of Age and Over, Other Than Heads, in Rural Families Receiving General Relief, by Residence, Area, and Age, October 1935

[138 counties and 83 New England townships [2]]

Residence and area	Average grade completed, by age				
	Total [3]	16–24 years	25–34 years	35–44 years	45 years and over
TOTAL RURAL					
All areas	7.6	8.2	7.4	6.7	5.8
Eastern Cotton	5.8	6.4	5.8	5.6	4.4
White	6.6	7.3	6.3	6.3	5.5
Negro	3.2	3.6	3.9	3.4	1.0
Western Cotton	7.6	8.2	7.4	7.0	6.0
White	7.8	8.4	7.6	7.2	6.6
Negro	6.6	7.2	6.7	5.5	4.6
Appalachian-Ozark	6.3	7.3	6.2	5.4	4.7
Lake States Cut-Over	8.4	8.7	8.4	7.0	5.6
Hay and Dairy	8.4	8.8	8.4	8.0	7.1
Corn Belt	8.6	9.0	8.6	8.4	7.5
Spring Wheat	8.4	8.6	8.3	8.1	8.1
Winter Wheat	8.5	9.2	8.5	8.2	7.7
Ranching	8.8	9.3	8.8	8.6	8.3
New England	8.6	9.0	8.7	8.4	8.2
OPEN COUNTRY					
All areas [4]	7.1	8.0	7.0	6.2	5.4
Eastern Cotton	5.5	5.9	5.6	5.3	3.7
White	6.3	6.9	6.1	5.9	4.6
Negro	2.7	3.0	3.4	1.4	1.4
Western Cotton	7.6	8.2	7.4	6.9	6.0
White	7.8	8.3	7.5	7.0	6.6
Negro	6.7	7.3	6.7	6.0	4.8
Appalachian-Ozark	6.0	6.9	6.0	5.1	4.4
Lake States Cut-Over	8.3	8.6	8.2	6.7	5.1
Hay and Dairy	8.3	8.7	8.3	7.7	6.7
Corn Belt	8.5	8.8	8.6	8.3	7.2
Spring Wheat	8.4	8.5	8.3	8.1	8.3
Winter Wheat	8.5	9.1	8.5	8.1	7.6
Ranching	8.5	8.6	8.5	8.4	8.1
VILLAGE					
All areas [4]	8.1	8.6	8.1	7.6	6.3
Eastern Cotton	6.8	7.7	6.4	6.7	5.6
White	8.1	8.7	7.4	8.3	6.9
Negro	4.4	4.8	4.7	5.3	0.8
Western Cotton	7.7	8.3	7.7	7.3	5.8
White	7.9	8.5	7.9	7.5	6.7
Negro	6.2	6.9	†	†	4.0
Appalachian-Ozark	6.9	8.1	6.7	6.1	5.2
Lake States Cut-Over	8.7	9.6	8.8	8.2	7.0
Hay and Dairy	8.5	9.2	8.5	8.2	7.8
Corn Belt	8.6	9.5	8.6	8.4	7.6
Spring Wheat	8.5	8.9	8.5	8.0	6.9
Winter Wheat	8.6	9.4	8.7	8.5	7.9
Ranching	9.0	9.9	8.9	8.8	8.3

† Median not computed on a base of fewer than 50 cases.

[1] Median.
[2] Townships in Connecticut and Massachusetts only.
[3] Exclusive of members of families whose school attainment was unknown.
[4] Exclusive of New England.

In the South the low standards of education for Negroes dragged down the average for all families (table 31). The greatest difference between Negroes and whites appeared in the Eastern Cotton Area where the median for Negroes was less than four grades at each age up to 45 years and only one grade for family members of that age and over. In the Western Cotton Area the difference between whites and Negroes was only one grade for the two age groups under 35 years and two grades in the age groups 35 years and over. Thus, the improvement in education in recent years in the South was reflected in the school attainments of Negro family members.

In addition the education of many youth in rural relief families was not complete since they were still attending school at the time of the survey. Indeed two-fifths of the number aged 16 and 17 years, other than heads, were still in school as were one-tenth of those 18–20 years of age (table 32).

Table 32.—School Attendance of Youth 16 Through 24 Years of Age, Other Than Heads, in Rural Families Receiving General Relief, by Residence and Area, October 1935

[138 counties and 83 New England townships [1]]

Residence and area	Total				16–17 years			18–20 years			21–24 years		
	Number	Percent	In school	Not in school	Total	In school	Not in school	Total	In school	Not in school	Total	In school	Not in school
TOTAL RURAL													
All areas	25,244	100.0	17.0	83.0	100.0	41.4	58.6	100.0	9.7	90.3	100.0	0.9	99.1
Eastern Cotton	2,364	100.0	15.1	84.9	100.0	34.6	65.4	100.0	10.0	90.0	100.0	1.6	98.4
Western Cotton	2,758	100.0	20.4	79.6	100.0	46.3	53.7	100.0	13.2	86.8	100.0	—	100.0
Appalachian-Ozark	9,934	100.0	12.8	87.2	100.0	31.2	68.8	100.0	7.1	92.9	100.0	1.1	98.9
Lake States Cut-Over	1,632	100.0	17.6	82.4	100.0	48.3	51.7	100.0	8.6	91.4	100.0	0.4	99.6
Hay and Dairy	2,858	100.0	20.8	79.2	100.0	55.6	44.4	100.0	9.7	90.3	100.0	0.4	99.6
Corn Belt	1,492	100.0	22.0	78.0	100.0	53.2	46.8	100.0	14.2	85.8	100.0	0.8	99.2
Spring Wheat	1,470	100.0	14.8	85.2	100.0	32.1	67.9	100.0	12.3	87.7	100.0	1.7	98.3
Winter Wheat	492	100.0	33.3	66.7	100.0	69.8	30.2	100.0	21.1	78.9	100.0+	4.3	95.7
Ranching	568	100.0	31.7	68.3	100.0	67.6	32.4	100.0	15.6	84.4	100.0	—	100.0
New England	1,676	100.0	19.5	80.5	100.0	51.7	48.3	100.0	8.0	92.0	100.0	—	100.0
OPEN COUNTRY													
All areas [2]	15,208	100.0	13.8	86.2	100.0	33.7	66.3	100.0	7.7	92.3	100.0	0.8	99.2
Eastern Cotton	1,756	100.0	11.5	88.5	100.0	26.8	73.2	100.0	6.7	93.3	100.0	1.8	98.2
Western Cotton	1,974	100.0	18.9	81.1	100.0	44.0	56.0	100.0	11.9	88.1	100.0	—	100.0
Appalachian-Ozark	6,514	100.0	10.6	89.4	100.0	25.4	74.6	100.0	6.0	94.0	100.0	0.8	99.2
Lake States Cut-Over	1,194	100.0	17.8	82.2	100.0	47.8	52.2	100.0	7.1	92.9	100.0	0.5	99.5
Hay and Dairy	1,650	100.0	16.4	83.6	100.0	47.1	52.9	100.0	6.9	93.1	100.0	0.7	99.3
Corn Belt	584	100.0	16.8	83.2	100.0	41.4	58.6	100.0	9.2	90.8	100.0	—	100.0
Spring Wheat	1,024	100.0	8.0	92.0	100.0	19.3	80.7	100.0	6.4	93.6	100.0	0.6	99.4
Winter Wheat	316	100.0	33.5	66.5	100.0	66.7	33.3	100.0	19.6	80.4	100.0	4.8	95.2
Ranching	196	100.0	31.6	68.4	100.0	52.3	47.7	100.0	23.5	76.5	100.0	—	100.0
VILLAGE													
All areas [2]	8,360	100.0	22.4	77.6	100.0	53.6	46.4	100.0	13.7	86.3	100.0	1.3	98.7
Eastern Cotton	608	100.0	25.7	74.3	100.0	56.7	43.3	100.0	19.5	80.5	100.0	1.1	98.9
Western Cotton	784	100.0	24.2	75.8	100.0	51.8	48.2	100.0	16.3	83.7	100.0	—	100.0
Appalachian-Ozark	3,420	100.0	17.0	83.0	100.0	42.6	57.4	100.0	9.2	90.8	100.0	1.7	98.3
Lake States Cut-Over	438	100.0	17.4	82.6	100.0	50.0	50.0	100.0	12.8	87.2	100.0	—	100.0
Hay and Dairy	1,208	100.0	26.8	73.2	100.0	65.7	34.3	100.0	13.5	86.5	100.0	—	100.0
Corn Belt	908	100.0	25.3	74.7	100.0	61.9	38.1	100.0	16.7	83.3	100.0	1.4	98.6
Spring Wheat	446	100.0	30.5	69.5	100.0	56.6	43.4	100.0	24.7	75.3	100.0	5.2	94.8
Winter Wheat	176	100.0	33.0	67.0	100.0	76.9	23.1	100.0	23.5	76.5	100.0	3.6	96.4
Ranching	372	100.0	31.7	68.3	100.0	77.6	22.4	100.0	11.3	88.7	100.0	—	100.0

[1] Townships in Connecticut and Massachusetts only.
[2] Exclusive of New England.

Contrasts among areas again appeared, and youth in relief families remained in school most often in the Winter Wheat and Ranching Areas and least often in the Spring Wheat, Appalachian-Ozark, and Eastern Cotton Areas. Opportunities for work in the country, as well as more restricted educational opportunities, were apparent in the fact that youth in the open country were less likely to remain in

Relief Children Go to School.

school than were village youth. In general, however, there was a tendency for rural relief youth to drop out of school rapidly after the age of 16 years, and less than 1 percent of those aged 21–24 years were still in school.

The situation of children 7 through 15 years of age was similar to that of youth, and the proportions in school were lowest in the southern areas and highest in the New England, northern, and western areas (appendix table 33). A small number had dropped out of school at each age until 12.7 percent of those 14 and 15 years old were not in school.

SIGNIFICANCE OF EDUCATIONAL ATTAINMENT

Education among rural relief families was correlated directly with relative social status. This held true for occupational classes within the country as a whole and within each area, and also in comparing one area with another. The principle seems valid that the higher the proportion of nonagricultural occupations the higher is the number of years of formal schooling. In the South the great majority of the population is still in agriculture so the educational level of relief families is low in comparison with the areas which are more industrialized and urbanized. This does not necessarily mean that individuals in the South are less prepared to live successfully within the social order since less formal education is demanded by agriculture and since there is frequently more informal education within the family group among farm families. Nevertheless, as the South becomes increasingly industrialized and as its workers wish to compete with those in other areas, the necessity for higher educational standards will be obvious. In the other areas the average education appears more nearly satisfactory for workers of this level, and the greatest improvement can come in these regions through bringing a higher proportion of the population up to this standard and through raising the quality of this training.

Needless to say, most heads of rural relief families are not illiterate but have had some formal schooling. In general the claim that illiteracy is an all-important factor in relief does not seem to hold. Rural relief families may not have had a great amount of education but in general formal schooling is only one of the various factors necessary to explain relief needs.

Appendixes

Appendix A

MEANING OF TERMS

SINCE MANY of the terms in this study are used not only as the rigid definitions necessary for schedule enumeration but also in their broader significance, a brief discussion of terminology is necessary. Additional terms have been defined as they occurred in the text.

The most important term is naturally the word *family*. Historically it was a Roman law term which denoted the community of producers and consumers in a household, including slaves and other servants as well as members connected by common descent or marriage. The original use of the term family was developed for households which were largely self-sufficing. Other definitions have emphasized the biological or the social aspects of the family, such as blood relationships or status-determining roles. Family is also used in modern times for a unit which has a legal and economic basis.[1] According to any of these bases the family may be larger than the household, or it may exclude certain persons within the household. This present study is primarily socio-economic, and the household is used as the closest general statistical approximation to the family.[2] By household is meant essentially those persons dependent upon the same family budget. In general the members of the household are biologically related to each other.[3]

[1] See Zimmerman, Carle C. and Frampton, Merle E., *Family and Society*, New York: D. Van Nostrand Company, Inc., 1935, ch. II.

[2] For a more restricted use of the word *family* with respect to relief data, see Mangus, A. R., *Changing Aspects of Rural Relief*, Research Monograph XIV, Division of Social Research, Works Progress Administration, Washington, D. C., 1938, appendix C.

[3] The actual definition used in the study was as follows: "*Relief Case:* A relief case consists of one or more related or unrelated persons who *live together* and who *receive assistance* as one unit and are considered as one case by the agency giving the assistance. If two or more families (or nonfamily persons or a combination of families and nonfamily persons) in a household are handled as separate cases, each is a separate case for the purpose of this survey." Form DRS 110–B, Division of Research, Statistics, and Finance, Federal Emergency Relief Administration, Washington, D. C., 1935, p. 4.

The concept *family head* is a socio-legal term based upon privileges and obligations within the family. American law does not emphasize the family head since the legal rights of family members are stated in terms of relations and of individual interests (domestic relations, husband and wife, parent and child). But ordinarily, for economic and social purposes, a family head has the responsibility of providing for the family or seeing that such provision is made. In the normal family of husband, wife, and children, the husband is considered the head. In the broken family consisting of mother and children or father and children, either the mother or the father tends automatically to become the head. In the case where a man or a woman lives with his or her child and the child's husband or wife, with or without others, such as grandchildren and outsiders, the tendency is for the son or son-in-law to become head of the family, chiefly on account of the senility of the other persons. In most cases the family head is determined by the informal organization of the family.[4]

[4] In the statistical study reported here the instructions concerning family head were: "If the household consists of only one family, the head of that family is the head of the household. If the household consists of two or more families, consider the oldest family head as head of the household, unless he or she is 65 years old or over. In such a case consider as head of the household the oldest family head who is less than 65 years old. In determining which member is to be designated as head of a family, proceed as follows: In cases of married couples, with or without children, designate the husband-father as head, except when he is over 64 years of age and is living with a son or daughter between the ages of 21 and 64 who is working or seeking work and who is not a member of another family group in the household. In such a case enter that son or daughter as head. In the case of a widowed, divorced, separated, or single person with children designate the parent as head, except when he or she is over 64 years of age and is living with a son or daughter between the ages of 21 and 64 who is working or seeking work and who is not a member of another family group in the household. In such a case enter that son or daughter as head.

"In cases of households consisting only of single and/or widowed, divorced, or separated persons, without children, designate the person with the largest earnings or property rights as head. In cases in which a male and female are equally eligible to be considered as head of a family give preference to the male. If two or more persons of the same sex are equally eligible to be considered as head of a family give preference to the oldest. No schedule should be filled for only one person under 16 years of age. If such a person is living with adults who are not his parents and if he is the only member of the household who is receiving relief, the members of the family with whom he is living should be entered on the schedule also.

"All members of the head's immediate family and all non-family persons should be shown in their relationship *to the head*. When a second or third group in the relief case constitutes a *family unit*, the head of the relief case must be designated head (1) and the heads of the other families as head (2), head (3), etc., showing also their relationship to head (1). The relationship of the other members of the second family must be shown to head (2), other members of the third family to head (3), etc. * * *." *Ibid.*, pp. 18–20.

The term *relief*, as used in this study, means grants by public and semipublic agencies.[5] Relief generally means an economic consideration given to a needy person without regard to an economic *quid pro quo* or return. In the depression of the last few years the Federal Government has given two types of general relief, *work relief* and *direct relief*. Work relief has usually been given for services of some public nature similar to those widespread under the Civil Works Administration of 1933 and under the Works Program of 1935 and later years. In this case a *quid pro quo* or return of some kind or other was secured by the public or community for the relief given. In some cases work relief has included a situation in which men have been hired to work for themselves, as, for example, in the planting of their own gardens or the building of sanitary conveniences on property which they own or on which they live. It generally is assumed that

---

[5] The exact definition is as follows: "*Relief:* The type of relief received to render a case eligible for inclusion in the study may be one or both of the following:

1. Any form of material relief supported wholly or in part by FERA funds.

2. Unemployment relief in any material form provided it is supported wholly or in part by *public* relief funds, i. e., Federal, State, county, or municipal funds designated for the purpose of giving unemployment relief.

These may include:

(a) 'Direct' relief: Material relief in the form of: cash, orders for food, clothing, fuel, household necessities, rent, medical care given in the client's home or in a doctor's office (but *not* medical care given in a clinic or hospital), transportation, moving expenses, etc.—for which the client is not required to work for the benefits received.

(b) 'Work' relief: Temporary emergency employment through ERA, generally on some specified project undertaken by the municipal, county, State, or Federal Government (or several of these in cooperation).

"In some areas a person working on a particular work relief project may be paid according to a stipulated wage scale, but only up to the limit of the relief agency's budgetary allowance for his type of case. In other places, a person receiving so-called 'direct' relief is required to do a certain amount of work, under direction of the relief agency, in order to be entitled to his budgetary allowance, but which work is not (generally) on a definite work relief project, and for which no wage scale is set. This or any other form of relief given under the requirements that some work be done should be considered 'work' relief, unless it is reported as direct relief to the State ERA.

Do not include:

1. Cases which received *only* services from the relief agency but which received no material aid.

2. Cases which received *only* surplus commodities.

3. Cases receiving Mothers' Pension or other forms of regular assistance which are *not* reported to the State Emergency Relief Administration.

4. Transient cases—interstate and intrastate transient cases do not fall within the scope of this survey.

5. Cases which received only emergency orders pending investigation of their applications for relief *if the application was rejected.* However, if the case was accepted for relief, the date of the emergency order is to be considered the date of first relief." *Ibid.*, pp. 2–3.

these private types of work relief have a public purpose or will help
to bring about the permanent rehabilitation of the family.   Direct
relief is made in the form of gifts to dependent families with regard to
their needs but without expectation of visible return.   The legal basis
of such gifts lies in the concept of "status".[6] in which it is held that a
member of society, no matter how unfortunate he may be, has inher-
ited the right at least to sustenance and to the necessities of life.

The concept *rehabilitation* is related closely to some forms of work
relief.   A special rural rehabilitation program [7] was established in
April 1934 under the direction of the State emergency relief adminis-
trations to assist rural relief families [8] to become self-sustaining.
Rehabilitation differs from relief to the extent that many of the
rehabilitation grants are made in terms of capital goods.   Relief
itself is ordinarily made in money or consumers' goods.   The assumption back of rehabilitation is that the provision of capital goods, such
as a cow, a horse, a plow, a season's rental on a piece of land, or the
adjustment of previous debts, will enable a family to produce sufficiently so that it will have not only consumers' goods for the present
but can also in time accumulate further capital goods in order to regain
complete self-support.   Beneficiaries have been expected to make
repayments in cash, in kind, or in work on approved work projects
for all advances received.[9]   The rural rehabilitation program of the
Federal Emergency Relief Administration was terminated on June 30,
1935, and rural rehabilitation cases became the responsibility of the
Resettlement Administration.[10]   Since September 1937 they have
been under the care of the Farm Security Administration.

For purposes of the schedule enumeration it was necessary to define
clearly the relief status of the family at the time of the survey.   A
family accepted on relief rolls during the month of the survey which
had never before received relief from the agency accepting it was designated as a new or *opened* case.   A family which had been given relief
at some time previously and which was again accepted for relief by

[6] Status is a concept in law used to define rights which cannot be alienated as
can most of the obligations of contract.

[7] Division of Research, Statistics, and Records, *Monthly Report of the Federal
Emergency Relief Administration, June 1 Through June 30, 1936*, Federal Emergency Relief Administration, Washington, D. C., p. 13.

[8] For a statement concerning rehabilitation families, see Asch, Berta and
Mangus, A. R., *Farmers on Relief and Rehabilitation*, Research Monograph VIII,
Division of Social Research, Works Progress Administration, Washington, D. C.,
1937, ch. II.

[9] Division of Research, Statistics, and Records, *Monthly Report of the Federal
Emergency Relief Administration, May 1 Through May 31, 1934*, Federal Emergency Relief Administration, Washington, D. C., pp. 6–8.

[10] Division of Research, Statistics, and Records, *Monthly Report of the Federal
Emergency Relief Administration, August 1 Through August 31, 1935*, Federal
Emergency Relief Administration, Washington, D. C., p. 14.

the same agency after having received no relief for at least 1 full calendar month or after having lost Works Progress Administration employment or Resettlement status was designated as a *reopened* case. A case to which an agency had ceased giving relief from Federal Emergency Relief Administration funds, whether or not the family continued to receive aid from some other Government agency, was considered a *closed* case.

The data included in this study are restricted to the rural population receiving relief. The *rural* population is defined according to the United States Census as persons living on a farm, in the open country but not on a farm, or in a village with less than 2,500 population. A *farm* is defined as having at least 3 acres of land or a productivity valued at $250 or more if it is less than 3 acres in size.[11] *Open country nonfarm* is generally taken to mean residence in an unincorporated region. In this study it includes all nonagricultural families living outside of communities with a population of 50 or more. Conversely, a *village* is defined as a center of population containing 50 to 2,500 persons. Since a community has been defined in terms of house aggregation and density of population on the land, it excludes townships as municipal corporations and other definitions sometimes used for community. In New England townships under the name of "towns" are considered minor public municipal corporations and seldom is there any other type of municipal corporation except a large aggregate known as a city. Since all New England towns are considered incorporated, there is no such thing as a resident who is not in an incorporated region. Consequently, it is difficult, and to a large extent of little value, to attempt to classify New England families as to whether they do or do not reside in villages.

---

[11] "A 'farm' for census purposes is all the land which is directly farmed by one person, either by his labor alone or with the assistance of members of his household or hired employees. The land operated by a partnership is likewise considered a farm. A 'farm' may consist of a single tract of land or of a number of separate tracts, and these several tracts may be held under different tenures, as when one tract is owned by the farmer and another tract is rented by him. When a landowner has one or more tenants, renters, croppers, or managers, the land operated by each is considered a farm. Thus, on a plantation the land operated by each cropper or tenant was reported as a separate farm, and the land operated by the owner or manager by means of wage hands, likewise, was reported as a separate farm. The enumerators were instructed not to report as a farm any tract of land of less than 3 acres, unless its agricultural products in 1929 were valued at $250 or more." Bureau of the Census, *Abstract of the Fifteenth Census of the United States: 1930*, U. S. Department of Commerce, Washington, D. C., 1933, p. 497.

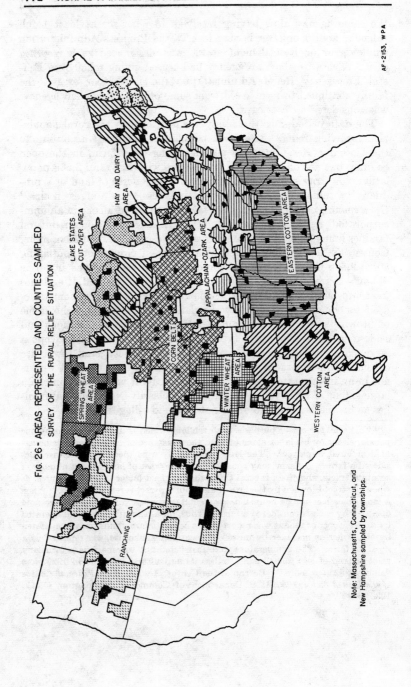

FIG. 26 - AREAS REPRESENTED AND COUNTIES SAMPLED
SURVEY OF THE RURAL RELIEF SITUATION

LAKE STATES
CUT-OVER AREA

HAY AND DAIRY
AREA

APPALACHIAN-OZARK AREA

EASTERN COTTON AREA

CORN BELT

SPRING WHEAT
AREA

WINTER WHEAT
AREA

WESTERN COTTON
AREA

RANCHING AREA

Note: Massachusetts, Connecticut, and
New Hampshire sampled by townships.

AF-2153, WPA

Appendix B

SUPPLEMENTARY TABLES

Table 1.—Intensity of General Relief [1] in the United States, by Residence, July 1933 Through December 1935 (Estimated)

Year and month	Percent of population on relief			Year and month	Percent of population on relief		
	Total	Rural	Urban		Total	Rural	Urban
1933				1934—Continued			
July	13.1	10.1	15.2				
August	12.6	10.2	14.3	November	16.1	14.0	17.6
September	11.4	8.1	13.8	December	17.0	14.8	18.5
October	11.5	8.9	13.4				
November	12.8	10.6	14.4	**1935**			
December	10.3	8.0	11.9				
				January	17.6	15.6	19.1
1934				February	17.5	15.2	19.2
January	9.8	9.3	10.2	March	17.3	14.8	19.1
February	10.3	9.8	10.7	April	16.8	14.1	18.7
March	12.0	11.3	12.6	May	16.2	13.2	18.4
April	14.6	10.5	17.5	June	15.2	11.4	17.9
May	14.5	11.6	16.6	July	14.6	10.3	17.7
June	14.2	12.2	15.7	August	14.1	9.1	17.7
July	14.6	12.8	15.8	September	13.0	8.3	16.5
August	15.3	14.1	16.1	October	12.4	7.9	15.7
September	15.4	13.8	16.6	November	11.6	6.8	15.0
October	15.5	13.3	17.1	December	8.7	3.2	12.7

[1] Percentage ratio of total estimated number of cases to all families of the same residence class.

Sources: Smith, Mapheus and Mangus, A. R., *Cases Receiving General Relief in Urban and Rural Areas, July 1933-December 1935 (Estimated)*, Research Bulletin Series III, No. 1, Division of Social Research, Works Progress Administration, Washington, D. C., August 22, 1936; and Bureau of the Census, *Fifteenth Census of the United States: 1930*, Population Vol. II, U. S. Department of Commerce, Washington, D. C., 1933.

Table 2.—Incidence of General Relief in Rural Areas, October 1933 Through October 1935

[138 counties]

Area	Rural relief cases per 100 rural families				
	October 1933 [1]	October 1934 [2]	February 1935	June 1935	October 1935
All areas	9.0	13.7	15.2	10.5	7.9
Eastern Cotton	12.4	11.3	8.5	5.7	3.3
Western Cotton	6.1	21.2	24.9	11.0	8.4
Appalachian-Ozark	16.5	18.5	19.8	19.6	19.7
Lake States Cut-Over	18.6	32.1	38.9	31.7	26.3
Hay and Dairy	5.1	8.1	11.5	7.6	5.7
Corn Belt	2.8	8.7	12.0	7.7	3.2
Spring Wheat	9.8	32.4	33.5	22.9	14.2
Winter Wheat	12.0	16.4	16.8	10.6	7.0
Ranching	6.8	13.0	16.5	12.3	7.1

[1] Computed from data in *Unemployment Relief Census, October 1933*, Report No. 2, Federal Emergency Relief Administration, Washington, D. C., 1934, table 9.

[2] Data from Survey of the Rural Relief Situation, October 1934, Division of Research, Statistics, and Finance, Federal Emergency Relief Administration, Washington, D. C.

Table 3.—Age of Heads of Rural Families Receiving General Relief, by Residence and Area, June 1935

[138 counties and 116 New England townships]

Residence and area	Total [1]		Age in years					
	Number	Percent	16–24	25–34	35–44	45–54	55–64	65 and over
TOTAL RURAL								
All areas	62,777	100.0	7.7	23.1	22.8	21.2	15.3	9.9
Eastern Cotton	7,730	100.0	7.4	22.5	21.9	20.6	16.4	11.2
Western Cotton	7,266	100.0	9.6	25.1	21.2	17.9	12.4	13.8
Appalachian-Ozark	17,016	100.0	9.1	24.4	23.3	21.6	15.3	6.3
Lake States Cut-Over	3,776	100.0	6.6	22.3	20.9	21.5	15.8	12.9
Hay and Dairy	8,626	100.0	6.2	20.4	23.5	23.2	14.9	11.8
Corn Belt	7,512	100.0	6.3	22.7	23.2	21.7	16.6	9.5
Spring Wheat	3,374	100.0	6.6	30.2	24.8	19.7	13.3	5.4
Winter Wheat	1,288	100.0	9.8	29.7	23.3	18.9	12.1	6.2
Ranching	1,886	100.0	7.3	21.3	22.6	17.7	17.2	13.9
New England	4,303	100.0	5.9	16.0	23.0	24.3	18.5	12.3
OPEN COUNTRY								
All areas [2]	35,768	100.0	8.0	24.8	23.3	20.5	14.6	8.8
Eastern Cotton	5,002	100.0	7.4	22.9	21.0	18.9	16.9	12.9
Western Cotton	4,684	100.0	9.6	27.1	20.8	17.2	12.1	13.2
Appalachian-Ozark	12,066	100.0	9.3	25.9	24.0	20.7	14.8	5.3
Lake States Cut-Over	2,480	100.0	5.9	21.4	22.3	22.7	15.8	11.9
Hay and Dairy	5,028	100.0	6.4	20.7	25.0	23.2	14.4	10.3
Corn Belt	2,802	100.0	7.1	23.6	24.0	22.9	14.3	8.1
Spring Wheat	2,386	100.0	6.0	32.3	25.2	19.9	13.3	3.3
Winter Wheat	670	100.0	10.7	32.8	25.1	17.6	9.6	4.2
Ranching	650	100.0	6.5	19.4	22.1	19.1	19.1	13.8
VILLAGE								
All areas [2]	22,706	100.0	7.4	21.8	22.0	21.7	15.9	11.2
Eastern Cotton	2,728	100.0	7.4	21.7	23.6	23.8	15.5	8.0
Western Cotton	2,582	100.0	9.5	21.8	21.8	19.0	13.0	14.9
Appalachian-Ozark	4,950	100.0	8.6	21.0	21.4	23.9	16.5	8.6
Lake States Cut-Over	1,296	100.0	8.0	24.0	18.2	19.1	15.7	15.0
Hay and Dairy	3,598	100.0	5.8	19.9	21.6	23.1	15.6	14.0
Corn Belt	4,710	100.0	5.8	22.4	22.7	21.0	17.9	10.2
Spring Wheat	988	100.0	8.1	24.7	23.9	19.4	13.4	10.5
Winter Wheat	618	100.0	8.7	26.2	21.4	20.4	14.9	8.4
Ranching	1,236	100.0	7.8	22.3	22.8	17.0	16.2	13.9

[1] Exclusive of heads of families whose age was unknown.
[2] Exclusive of New England.

Table 4.—Age of Heads of Rural Families Receiving General Relief, by Usual Occupation, June 1935

[138 counties and 116 New England townships]

Usual occupation	Total [1]		Age in years				
	Number	Percent	16–24	25–34	35–44	45–54	55–64
Total	52,938	100.0	8.8	26.6	25.6	23.4	15.6
Agriculture	25,522	100.0	9.1	27.2	24.7	22.9	16.1
Farm operator	18,421	100.0	7.2	25.6	25.5	24.6	17.1
Owner	6,692	100.0	4.0	14.1	25.1	30.9	25.9
Tenant	9,705	100.0	8.8	32.2	26.1	21.4	11.5
Cropper [2]	2,024	100.0	9.8	32.0	24.0	19.7	14.5
Farm laborer	7,101	100.0	14.2	31.5	22.5	18.3	13.5
Nonagriculture	25,871	100.0	7.8	26.3	26.5	24.2	15.2
White collar	2,313	100.0	8.1	25.7	27.8	23.1	15.3
Skilled	3,799	100.0	3.2	21.5	27.5	30.0	17.8
Semiskilled	4,284	100.0	8.5	30.9	29.1	20.0	11.5
Unskilled	15,475	100.0	8.7	26.2	25.5	24.1	15.5
No usual occupation	1,545	100.0	22.1	21.9	23.3	18.6	14.1

[1] Exclusive of heads of families who were nonworkers or whose age was unknown.
[2] In the 2 Cotton Areas.

Table 5.—Age of Heads of Rural Families Receiving General Relief in the Eastern and Western Cotton Areas, by Color and Usual Occupation, June 1935

[44 counties]

Color and usual occupation	Total [1]		Age in years				
	Number	Percent	16–24	25–34	35–44	45–54	55–64
WHITE Total	9,014	100.0	10.6	29.3	24.7	21.4	14.0
Agriculture	5,502	100.0	10.9	28.2	23.6	22.1	15.2
Farm operator	3,562	100.0	9.0	27.0	23.4	23.9	16.7
Owner	604	100.0	3.6	11.9	19.5	33.2	31.8
Tenant	1,438	100.0	9.0	26.7	24.8	25.6	13.9
Cropper	1,520	100.0	11.2	33.0	23.7	18.7	13.4
Farm laborer	1,940	100.0	14.2	30.8	23.8	18.9	12.3
Nonagriculture	3,164	100.0	9.9	31.1	26.5	20.8	11.7
White collar	504	100.0	11.5	30.6	24.6	21.4	11.9
Skilled	472	100.0	4.2	25.8	27.5	28.9	13.6
Semiskilled	762	100.0	9.4	35.5	27.0	17.1	11.0
Unskilled	1,426	100.0	11.4	30.7	26.6	19.9	11.4
No usual occupation	348	100.0	13.2	28.2	25.9	15.5	17.2
NEGRO Total	3,192	100.0	8.8	25.1	25.4	23.3	17.4
Agriculture	2,114	100.0	8.1	24.8	25.2	23.1	18.8
Farm operator	1,104	100.0	4.3	25.4	24.1	25.7	20.5
Owner	154	100.0	1.3	13.0	20.8	35.0	29.9
Tenant	446	100.0	4.0	25.6	24.2	26.5	19.7
Cropper	504	100.0	5.6	28.9	25.0	22.6	17.9
Farm laborer	1,010	100.0	12.3	24.2	26.3	20.0	17.2
Nonagriculture	1,048	100.0	9.9	25.6	26.7	23.5	14.3
White collar	30	†	†	†	†	†	†
Skilled	48	†	†	†	†	†	†
Semiskilled	60	100.0	6.7	29.7	27.0	23.3	13.3
Unskilled	910	100.0	10.3	26.4	27.3	22.4	13.6
No usual occupation	30	†	†	†	†	†	†

† Percent not computed on a base of fewer than 50 cases.

[1] Exclusive of heads of families who were nonworkers or whose age was unknown.

Table 6.—Sex of Heads of Rural Families Receiving General Relief, by Residence and Area, June 1935

[138 counties and 116 New England townships]

Residence and area	Total		Male	Female
	Number	Percent		
TOTAL RURAL				
All areas	62,831	100.0	85.6	14.4
Eastern Cotton	7,732	100.0	70.7	29.3
Western Cotton	7,268	100.0	82.7	17.3
Appalachian-Ozark	17,016	100.0	86.4	13.6
Lake States Cut-Over	3,814	100.0	90.9	9.1
Hay and Dairy	8,626	100.0	89.9	10.1
Corn Belt	7,512	100.0	89.7	10.3
Spring Wheat	3,374	100.0	92.8	7.2
Winter Wheat	1,288	100.0	91.6	8.4
Ranching	1,886	100.0	84.4	15.6
New England	4,315	100.0	86.6	13.4
OPEN COUNTRY				
All areas [1]	35,802	100.0	87.3	12.7
Eastern Cotton	5,002	100.0	71.2	28.8
Western Cotton	4,686	100.0	86.7	13.3
Appalachian-Ozark	12,066	100.0	87.7	12.3
Lake States Cut-Over	2,512	100.0	91.4	8.6
Hay and Dairy	5,028	100.0	91.9	8.1
Corn Belt	2,802	100.0	94.1	5.9
Spring Wheat	2,386	100.0	96.2	3.8
Winter Wheat	670	100.0	95.5	4.5
Ranching	650	100.0	88.6	11.4
VILLAGE				
All areas [1]	22,714	100.0	82.7	17.3
Eastern Cotton	2,730	100.0	69.6	30.4
Western Cotton	2,582	100.0	75.6	24.4
Appalachian-Ozark	4,950	100.0	83.3	16.7
Lake States Cut-Over	1,302	100.0	89.9	10.1
Hay and Dairy	3,598	100.0	87.2	12.8
Corn Belt	4,710	100.0	87.1	12.9
Spring Wheat	988	100.0	84.6	15.4
Winter Wheat	618	100.0	87.4	12.6
Ranching	1,236	100.0	82.2	17.8

[1] Exclusive of New England.

Table 7.—Male Heads of Rural Families Receiving General Relief, by Residence, Area, and Age, June 1935

[138 counties and 116 New England townships]

Residence and area	Total [1]		Age in years						Average [2] age
	Num-ber	Per-cent	16–24	25–34	35–44	45–54	55–64	65 and over	
TOTAL RURAL									
All areas	53,740	100.0	8.0	24.5	22.9	21.0	14.5	9.1	42.1
Eastern Cotton	5,462	100.0	8.2	24.9	21.5	20.3	15.1	10.0	42.4
Western Cotton	6,014	100.0	10.5	26.1	21.2	17.9	11.9	12.4	40.8
Appalachian-Ozark	14,704	100.0	9.7	26.1	23.2	20.7	14.2	6.1	40.6
Lake States Cut-Over	3,430	100.0	6.3	23.1	21.5	21.7	15.0	12.4	44.1
Hay and Dairy	7,756	100.0	6.2	21.5	23.7	23.3	14.3	11.0	43.9
Corn Belt	6,738	100.0	6.1	24.1	23.3	21.8	16.1	8.6	43.0
Spring Wheat	3,132	100.0	6.6	30.9	25.5	19.0	13.0	5.0	39.4
Winter Wheat	1,180	100.0	10.3	30.0	22.9	19.3	11.2	6.3	38.7
Ranching	1,592	100.0	7.5	23.1	23.4	18.2	15.5	12.3	42.8
New England	3,732	100.0	5.9	16.7	22.7	24.6	18.4	11.7	46.4
OPEN COUNTRY									
All areas [3]	31,236	100.0	8.4	26.1	23.4	20.2	13.7	8.2	41.1
Eastern Cotton	3,562	100.0	8.3	25.2	20.1	18.9	15.6	11.9	42.7
Western Cotton	4,062	100.0	10.6	27.6	20.9	17.4	11.6	11.9	40.1
Appalachian-Ozark	10,580	100.0	9.9	27.7	24.0	19.5	13.6	5.3	39.7
Lake States Cut-Over	2,264	100.0	5.6	22.3	22.7	22.7	15.4	11.3	44.2
Hay and Dairy	4,620	100.0	6.4	21.4	25.1	23.4	14.1	9.6	43.3
Corn Belt	2,636	100.0	6.8	24.1	24.6	23.0	14.0	7.5	42.3
Spring Wheat	2,296	100.0	6.1	32.7	26.0	19.0	12.9	3.3	38.8
Winter Wheat	640	100.0	11.3	32.8	25.0	18.1	8.4	4.4	36.9
Ranching	576	100.0	6.6	20.1	24.4	18.7	17.4	12.8	44.0
VILLAGE									
All areas [3]	18,772	100.0	7.7	23.4	22.0	21.6	15.1	10.2	43.1
Eastern Cotton	1,900	100.0	8.1	24.5	24.0	22.8	14.3	6.3	41.8
Western Cotton	1,952	100.0	10.1	23.0	21.9	19.1	12.5	13.4	42.2
Appalachian-Ozark	4,124	100.0	9.2	22.0	21.2	23.6	15.9	8.1	43.4
Lake States Cut-Over	1,166	100.0	7.7	24.8	19.0	19.7	14.4	14.4	43.7
Hay and Dairy	3,136	100.0	5.9	21.6	21.9	23.2	14.5	12.9	44.8
Corn Belt	4,102	100.0	5.7	24.0	22.6	21.0	17.4	9.3	43.5
Spring Wheat	836	100.0	7.9	26.2	24.2	18.9	13.2	9.6	41.1
Winter Wheat	540	100.0	9.3	26.7	20.4	20.7	14.4	8.5	41.4
Ranching	1,016	100.0	8.1	24.8	22.8	17.9	14.4	12.0	42.0

[1] Exclusive of male heads of families whose age was unknown.
[2] Median.
[3] Exclusive of New England.

Table 8.—Female Heads of Rural Families Receiving General Relief, by Residence Area, and Age, June 1935

[138 counties and 116 New England townships]

Residence and area	Total [1]		Age in years						Average [2] age
	Number	Percent	16–24	25–34	35–44	45–54	55–64	65 and over	
TOTAL RURAL									
All areas	9,037	100.0	5.8	15.3	22.1	22.3	20.1	14.4	47.5
Eastern Cotton	2,268	100.0	5.5	16.8	22.9	21.3	19.5	14.0	46.8
Western Cotton	1,252	100.0	5.3	20.8	20.9	17.6	15.0	20.4	46.2
Appalachian-Ozark	2,312	100.0	4.9	14.7	23.5	27.3	22.2	7.4	47.0
Lake States Cut-Over	346	100.0	9.8	14.5	14.5	19.7	23.0	18.5	50.2
Hay and Dairy	870	100.0	6.0	10.4	21.6	21.8	20.9	19.3	50.0
Corn Belt	774	100.0	7.8	12.1	21.4	21.2	20.7	16.8	48.6
Spring Wheat	242	100.0	7.4	17.4	16.5	29.8	18.2	10.7	47.4
Winter Wheat	108	100.0	3.7	25.9	27.8	14.8	22.2	5.6	41.8
Ranching	294	100.0	6.1	11.6	18.4	15.0	26.5	22.4	53.8
New England	571	100.0	5.3	11.9	24.8	21.9	19.3	16.8	48.2
OPEN COUNTRY									
All areas [3]	4,532	100.0	5.3	16.5	21.9	22.5	20.8	13.0	47.3
Eastern Cotton	1,440	100.0	5.3	17.5	23.0	18.8	20.1	15.3	46.7
Western Cotton	622	100.0	3.2	23.5	20.6	16.1	15.4	21.2	46.3
Appalachian-Ozark	1,486	100.0	4.7	14.1	24.0	28.5	23.4	5.3	47.0
Lake States Cut-Over	216	100.0	9.3	13.0	16.7	23.0	20.4	17.6	49.3
Hay and Dairy	408	100.0	6.9	12.3	24.0	20.6	18.6	17.6	47.8
Corn Belt	166	100.0	10.8	14.5	15.7	21.6	19.3	18.1	48.7
Spring Wheat	90	100.0	4.4	20.0	6.7	42.3	24.4	2.2	49.0
Winter Wheat	30	†	—	†	†	†	†	—	—
Ranching	74	100.0	5.4	13.5	5.4	21.6	32.5	21.6	55.8
VILLAGE									
All areas [3]	3,934	100.0	6.4	14.5	21.8	22.1	19.5	15.7	47.8
Eastern Cotton	828	100.0	5.8	15.5	22.7	25.8	18.4	11.8	46.8
Western Cotton	630	100.0	7.3	18.1	21.3	19.0	14.6	19.7	46.2
Appalachian-Ozark	826	100.0	5.3	15.7	22.5	25.2	19.9	11.4	47.1
Lake States Cut-Over	130	100.0	10.8	16.9	10.8	13.8	27.7	20.0	52.8
Hay and Dairy	462	100.0	5.2	8.7	19.5	22.9	22.9	20.8	51.8
Corn Belt	608	100.0	6.9	11.5	23.0	21.1	21.1	16.4	48.6
Spring Wheat	152	100.0	9.2	15.8	22.4	22.4	14.4	15.8	45.7
Winter Wheat	78	100.0	5.1	23.1	28.3	17.9	17.9	7.7	42.2
Ranching	220	100.0	6.4	10.9	22.7	12.7	24.6	22.7	52.4

† Percent not computed on a base of fewer than 50 cases.

[1] Exclusive of female heads of families whose age was unknown.
[2] Median.
[3] Exclusive of New England.

Table 9.—Marital Condition of Heads of Rural Families 16 Through 24 Years of Age Receiving General Relief, by Residence, Area, and Sex, October 1935

[138 counties and 83 New England townships[1]]

Residence and area	Both sexes							Male							Female						
	Total[2]		Single	Married	Widowed	Divorced	Separated	Total		Single	Married	Widowed	Divorced	Separated	Total		Single	Married	Widowed	Divorced	Separated
	Number	Per cent						Number	Per cent						Number	Per cent					
TOTAL RURAL																					
All areas	3,816	100.0	24.5	69.3	1.9	0.8	3.5	3,334	100.0	21.4	78.2	0.2	—	0.2	482	100.0	46.9	7.1	13.3	6.6	26.1
Eastern Cotton	450	100.0	35.6	52.9	2.2	1.3	8.0	320	100.0	28.1	71.3	—	—	0.6	130	100.0	53.8	7.7	7.7	4.6	26.2
Western Cotton	438	100.0	17.4	72.1	2.4	0.9	3.2	392	100.0	19.4	80.6	0.5	—	0.3	46	100.0	—	—	—	—	—
Appalachian-Ozark	1,756	100.0	22.1	73.5	1.6	0.6	2.3	1,592	100.0	19.3	79.9	—	—	0.3	164	100.0	48.8	12.2	12.2	6.1	20.7
Lake States Cut-Over	188	100.0	34.0	58.6		2.1	5.3	158	100.0	30.4	69.4				30	100.0	†	†	†	†	†
Hay and Dairy	354	100.0	20.3	75.6	1.1		3.4	328	100.0	19.6	80.4				28	100.0	†	†	†	†	†
Corn Belt	196	100.0	18.4	75.5	1.0	4.1	1.0	176	100.0	16.9	84.1				20	100.0	†	†	†	†	†
Spring Wheat	138	100.0	29.0	68.1			2.9	122	100.0	23.0	77.0				16	100.0	†	†	†	†	†
Winter Wheat	66	100.0	24.2	66.7			2.1	56	100.0	21.4	78.6				10	100.0	†	†	†	†	†
Ranching	92	100.0	26.1	69.6			4.3	78	100.0	17.9	82.1				14	100.0	†	†	†	†	†
New England	138	100.0	44.9	50.8			4.3	114	100.0	38.6	61.4				24	100.0	†	†	†	†	†
OPEN COUNTRY																					
All areas[3]	2,220	100.0	24.0	70.5	2.1	0.5	2.9	1,968	100.0	21.2	78.3	0.2	—	0.3	252	100.0	45.2	10.3	16.7	4.8	23.0
Eastern Cotton	316	100.0	35.4	55.7	2.5	1.3	5.1	240	100.0	28.3	70.9				76	100.0	57.9	7.9	10.5	5.3	18.4
Western Cotton	328	100.0	12.2	78.7	6.1	1.2	1.8	298	100.0	13.4	86.6				30	100.0	49.0	16.3	8.2	4.1	22.4
Appalachian-Ozark	1,042	100.0	25.0	70.9	1.2	0.4	2.5	944	100.0	22.5	76.7	0.4		0.4	98	100.0	†	†	†	†	†
Lake States Cut-Over	148	100.0	32.4	63.5			4.1	134	100.0	29.9	70.1				14	100.0	†	†	†	†	†
Hay and Dairy	194	100.0	16.5	77.3	2.1		4.1	174	100.0	16.1	83.9				20	100.0	†	†	†	†	†
Corn Belt	66	100.0	6.1	90.9	3.0			64	100.0	6.3	93.7				2	†	†	†	†	†	†
Spring Wheat	78	100.0	30.8	66.6			2.6	68	100.0	23.5	76.5				10	100.0	†	†	†	†	†
Winter Wheat	32	†	†	†	†	†	†	32	100.0	†	†				—						
Ranching	16	†	†	†	†	†	†	14	100.0	†	†				2	†	†	†	†	†	†
VILLAGE																					
All areas[3]	1,458	100.0	23.6	68.9	1.8	1.4	4.3	1,252	100.0	20.0	79.7	0.3	—	—	206	100.0	45.6	3.9	10.7	9.7	30.1
Eastern Cotton	134	100.0	35.8	46.3	1.5	1.5	14.9	80	100.0	27.5	72.5				54	100.0	48.2	7.4	3.7	3.7	37.0
Western Cotton	110	100.0	32.7	52.7	7.3		7.3	94	100.0	38.3	61.7				16	†	†	†	†	†	†
Appalachian-Ozark	714	100.0	17.7	77.4	2.2	0.8	1.7	648	100.0	14.3	84.6	0.6			66	100.0	48.4	6.1	18.2	9.1	18.2
Lake States Cut-Over	40	†	†	†	†	†	†	24	100.0	†	†				16	†	†	†	†	†	†
Hay and Dairy	160	100.0	25.0	72.5			2.5	152	100.0	23.7	76.3				8	†	†	†	†	†	†
Corn Belt	130	100.0	24.6	67.7		6.2	1.5	112	100.0	21.4	78.6				18	100.0	†	†	†	†	†
Spring Wheat	60	100.0	26.7	70.1			3.3	54	100.0	22.2	77.8				6	†	†	†	†	†	†
Winter Wheat	34	†	†	†	†	†	†	24	100.0	†	†				10	†	†	†	†	†	†
Ranching	76	100.0	26.3	68.4			5.3	64	100.0	18.8	81.2				12	†	†	†	†	†	†

† Percent not computed on a base of fewer than 50 cases.
[1] Townships in Connecticut and Massachusetts only.
[2] Exclusive of heads of families whose marital condition or age was unknown.
[3] Exclusive of New England.

Table 10.—Marital Condition of Heads of Rural Families 25 Through 34 Years of Age Receiving General Relief, by Residence, Area, and Sex, October 1935

[138 counties and 83 New England townships[1]]

Residence and area	Both sexes[2]							Male							Female						
	Total Number	Total Percent	Single	Married	Widowed	Divorced	Separated	Total Number	Total Percent	Single	Married	Widowed	Divorced	Separated	Total Number	Total Percent	Single	Married	Widowed	Divorced	Separated
TOTAL RURAL																					
All areas	11,174	100.0	8.8	80.5	4.9	1.1	4.7	9,756	100.0	7.6	90.9	0.6	0.2	0.7	1,418	100.0	16.5	9.4	34.6	7.1	32.4
Eastern Cotton	1,148	100.0	9.6	65.3	12.0	0.9	12.2	764	100.0	7.3	90.3	2.1	—	0.3	384	100.0	14.1	15.6	31.8	2.6	35.9
Western Cotton	1,318	100.0	6.7	79.2	8.3	0.9	4.9	1,136	100.0	7.0	91.5	1.1	—	0.4	182	100.0	4.4	2.1	53.9	6.6	33.0
Appalachian-Ozark	4,538	100.0	7.2	84.0	4.4	0.7	3.3	4,054	100.0	5.9	92.9	1.2	0.3	0.7	484	100.0	18.2	9.9	39.2	7.9	24.8
Lake States Cut-Over	598	100.0	10.7	78.6	4.0	0.7	6.0	530	100.0	11.3	87.1	0.8	—	0.8	68	100.0	5.9	11.8	29.4	5.9	47.0
Hay and Dairy	1,294	100.0	9.4	84.6	1.2	1.4	3.4	1,204	100.0	8.8	89.9	0.3	—	1.0	90	100.0	17.8	13.3	13.3	20.0	35.6
Corn Belt	702	100.0	10.5	79.8	2.0	1.4	6.3	624	100.0	7.7	89.5	0.6	0.6	0.6	78	100.0	33.3	2.6	12.8	7.7	43.6
Spring Wheat	602	100.0	7.6	87.1	2.7	0.3	2.3	574	100.0	7.3	91.3	0.7	—	0.7	28	100.0	†	†	†	†	†
Winter Wheat	238	100.0	11.8	81.5	2.5	3.4	0.8	222	100.0	9.9	87.4	—	2.7	—	16	100.0	†	†	†	†	†
Ranching	248	100.0	4.8	88.8	0.8	3.2	2.4	230	100.0	3.5	95.6	0.5	0.9	—	18	100.0	†	†	†	†	†
New England	488	100.0	21.7	68.5	4.1	0.4	5.3	418	100.0	19.6	79.9	—	—	0.5	70	100.0	34.3	—	25.7	2.9	37.1
OPEN COUNTRY																					
All areas[3]	6,752	100.0	7.0	83.6	4.9	0.7	3.8	6,010	100.0	6.1	92.6	0.6	0.2	0.5	742	100.0	14.3	10.8	39.3	4.9	30.7
Eastern Cotton	840	100.0	8.8	67.7	12.1	0.7	10.7	572	100.0	7.0	90.9	2.1	—	—	268	100.0	12.7	17.9	33.6	2.2	33.6
Western Cotton	996	100.0	4.6	82.8	7.6	1.2	3.8	882	100.0	5.2	93.4	1.4	—	—	114	100.0	—	—	56.2	10.5	33.3
Appalachian-Ozark	2,910	100.0	6.7	85.8	4.3	0.5	2.7	2,632	100.0	5.4	93.7	0.2	0.2	0.5	278	100.0	18.7	10.1	43.2	4.3	23.7
Lake States Cut-Over	390	100.0	8.7	85.1	2.1	—	4.1	370	100.0	8.1	89.7	1.1	—	1.1	20	100.0	†	†	†	†	†
Hay and Dairy	756	100.0	6.9	89.9	1.1	—	2.1	724	100.0	6.1	93.3	—	—	0.6	32	100.0	†	†	†	†	†
Corn Belt	233	100.0	5.9	86.6	1.7	0.8	5.0	221	100.0	5.4	91.9	0.9	—	1.8	12	100.0	†	†	†	†	†
Spring Wheat	388	100.0	6.7	90.2	2.1	—	1.0	381	100.0	6.8	91.2	1.0	—	1.0	7	100.0	†	†	†	†	†
Winter Wheat	150	100.0	16.0	80.0	—	2.7	1.3	142	100.0	12.7	84.5	—	2.8	—	8	100.0	†	†	†	†	†
Ranching	84	100.0	4.8	88.1	—	7.1	—	80	100.0	5.0	92.5	—	2.5	—	4	100.0	†	†	†	†	†

VILLAGE [3]																					
All areas [3]	3,934	100.0	10.2	76.8	4.9	1.9	6.2	3,328	100.0	9.0	89.1	0.4	0.4	1.1	606	100.0	17.2	8.9	29.7	10.2	34.0
Eastern Cotton	308	100.0	11.7	59.1	11.7	1.3	16.2	192	100.0	8.3	88.6	2.1	—	1.0	116	100.0	17.2	10.3	27.6	3.4	41.5
Western Cotton	322	100.0	13.0	68.3	10.6	—	8.1	254	100.0	13.4	85.0	—	—	1.6	68	100.0	11.8	5.9	49.9	—	32.4
Appalachian-Ozark	1,623	100.0	8.1	81.0	4.5	2.1	4.3	1,422	100.0	6.8	91.2	0.3	0.6	1.1	205	100.0	17.5	9.7	34.0	12.6	26.2
Lake States Cut-Over	205	100.0	14.4	66.4	7.7	1.9	9.6	160	100.0	18.8	81.2	—	—	1.7	48	†	†	†	†	†	†
Hay and Dairy	538	100.0	13.0	77.0	1.5	3.3	5.2	480	100.0	12.9	84.6	0.8	—	1.7	58	100.0	13.8	13.8	6.9	31.0	34.5
Corn Belt	464	100.0	12.9	76.3	2.2	1.7	6.9	400	100.0	9.0	88.0	0.5	1.0	1.5	64	100.0	37.5	3.1	12.5	6.3	40.6
Spring Wheat	214	100.0	9.3	81.4	3.7	0.9	4.7	190	100.0	8.4	91.6	—	—	—	24	†	†	†	†	†	†
Winter Wheat	88	100.0	4.5	84.2	6.8	4.5	—	80	100.0	5.0	92.5	—	2.5	—	8	†	†	†	†	†	†
Ranching	164	100.0	4.9	89.0	1.2	1.2	3.7	150	100.0	2.7	97.3	—	—	—	14	†	†	†	†	†	†

† Percent not computed on a base of fewer than 50 cases.

[1] Townships in Connecticut and Massachusetts only.
[2] Exclusive of heads of families whose marital condition or age was unknown.
[3] Exclusive of New England.

Table 11.—Marital Condition of Heads of Rural Families 35 Through 44 Years of Age Receiving General Relief, by Residence, Area, and Sex, October 1935

[138 counties and 83 New England townships[1]]

Residence and area	Both sexes							Male							Female						
	Total[2]		Single	Married	Widowed	Divorced	Separated	Total		Single	Married	Widowed	Divorced	Separated	Total		Single	Married	Widowed	Divorced	Separated
	Number	Per cent						Number	Per cent						Number	Per cent					
TOTAL RURAL																					
All areas	10,874	100.0	6.3	77.1	10.3	1.5	4.8	9,178	100.0	5.7	89.8	2.5	0.6	1.4	1,696	100.0	9.2	8.8	52.4	6.4	23.2
Eastern Cotton	1,130	100.0	5.3	64.9	20.0	0.2	9.6	746	100.0	2.7	90.8	4.6	—	1.9	384	100.0	10.4	14.6	50.0	0.5	24.5
Western Cotton	1,286	100.0	5.6	73.6	12.8	1.2	6.8	1,026	100.0	5.5	91.4	1.9	0.4	0.8	260	100.0	6.2	3.1	55.3	4.6	30.8
Appalachian-Ozark	3,970	100.0	5.2	80.0	10.7	0.7	3.4	3,446	100.0	4.8	90.6	2.8	0.2	1.6	524	100.0	7.6	10.3	62.6	4.2	15.3
Lake States Cut-Over	656	100.0	10.7	78.0	4.9	0.9	5.5	608	100.0	11.5	83.6	1.3	1.0	2.6	48	100.0	14.1	10.9	41.3	7.6	26.1
Hay and Dairy	1,428	100.0	6.2	78.6	6.2	3.5	5.0	1,244	100.0	8.2	88.6	1.0	0.3	1.9	184	100.0	9.8	—	33.3	29.4	27.5
Corn Belt	728	100.0	5.5	78.6	6.0	5.5	4.4	626	100.0	4.8	91.4	1.6	0.6	0.6	102	†	†	†	†	†	†
Spring Wheat	542	100.0	5.5	86.4	4.8	2.3	2.2	514	100.0	5.8	90.3	3.1	0.4	0.4	28	†	†	†	†	†	†
Winter Wheat	172	100.0	1.2	83.7	6.8	1.8	3.5	150	100.0	1.3	94.7	1.3	2.7	—	22	†	†	†	†	†	†
Ranching	240	100.0	3.3	75.8	9.2	7.5	4.2	204	100.0	3.9	89.3	2.9	3.9	—	36	†	†	†	†	†	†
New England	722	100.0	9.1	74.3	11.1	2.2	3.3	614	100.0	6.8	87.0	3.9	1.3	1.0	108	100.0	22.2	1.9	51.8	7.4	16.7
OPEN COUNTRY																					
All areas[3]	6,234	100.0	5.4	80.1	9.0	0.8	4.7	5,382	100.0	5.1	91.0	2.1	0.4	1.4	852	100.0	7.5	10.8	53.0	3.3	25.4
Eastern Cotton	790	100.0	3.8	68.4	19.7	0.3	7.8	548	100.0	1.8	92.7	5.1	—	0.4	242	100.0	8.3	13.2	52.9	0.8	24.8
Western Cotton	924	100.0	5.4	79.9	9.1	—	5.6	784	100.0	5.4	93.1	0.5	—	1.0	140	100.0	5.7	5.7	57.2	—	31.4
Appalachian-Ozark	2,472	100.0	4.4	81.0	10.4	1.0	3.2	2,136	100.0	3.8	91.9	2.6	0.3	1.5	336	100.0	8.3	12.5	59.5	5.4	14.3
Lake States Cut-Over	450	100.0	10.2	76.1	5.3	1.3	7.1	418	100.0	11.0	81.9	0.9	1.4	3.8	32	†	†	†	†	†	†
Hay and Dairy	760	100.0	8.2	83.4	3.7	3.3	1.4	700	100.0	8.3	89.4	0.6	0.7	1.7	60	100.0	6.7	13.3	40.0	—	40.0
Corn Belt	304	100.0	5.9	82.9	2.6	3.3	5.3	276	100.0	5.1	91.4	1.4	0.6	1.4	28	†	†	†	†	†	†
Spring Wheat	350	100.0	4.6	91.4	1.7	1.7	0.6	344	100.0	4.7	93.0	1.7	0.6	—	6	†	†	†	†	†	†
Winter Wheat	108	100.0	1.9	90.7	—	3.7	3.7	102	100.0	2.0	94.1	—	3.9	—	6	†	†	†	†	†	†
Ranching	76	100.0	5.3	86.9	2.6	2.6	2.6	74	100.0	5.4	89.2	2.7	2.7	—	2	†	†	†	†	†	†

VILLAGE[3]																					
All areas	3,918	100.0	7.1	73.1	12.0	2.4	5.4	3,182	100.0	6.6	88.2	2.9	0.7	1.6	736	100.0	9.2	7.6	51.7	9.8	21.7
Eastern Cotton	340	100.0	8.8	57.1	20.6	—	13.5	198	100.0	5.1	85.8	3.0	—	6.1	142	100.0	14.1	16.9	45.1	—	23.9
Western Cotton	362	100.0	6.1	57.5	22.1	4.4	9.9	242	100.0	5.8	85.9	6.6	1.7	—	120	100.0	6.7	6.4	53.3	10.0	30.0
Appalachian-Ozark	1,498	100.0	6.4	78.4	11.2	0.3	3.7	1,310	100.0	6.4	88.7	6.1	—	1.8	188	100.0	6.4	—	68.1	2.1	17.0
Lake States Cut-Over	206	100.0	11.7	82.5	3.9	2.7	1.9	190	100.0	12.6	87.4	1.5	0.7	2.2	16	+	†	†	†	†	†
Hay and Dairy	468	100.0	9.9	73.0	9.0	7.1	5.4	544	100.0	8.1	87.5	1.7	2.3	2.2	124	100.0	17.7	9.7	41.9	11.3	19.4
Corn Belt	424	100.0	5.2	75.4	8.5	2.1	3.8	350	100.0	4.6	91.4	5.9	—	1.2	74	100.0	8.1	—	40.6	29.7	21.6
Spring Wheat	192	100.0	7.3	77.1	10.4	9.4	3.1	170	100.0	8.2	84.7	—	—	—	22	+	†	†	†	†	†
Winter Wheat	64	100.0	—	77.9	15.6	—	3.1	48	+	—	†	†	—	—	16	+	†	†	†	†	†
Ranching	164	100.0	2.4	70.7	12.2	9.8	4.9	130	100.0	3.1	89.2	3.1	4.6	—	34	+	†	†	†	†	†

† Percent not computed on a base of fewer than 50 cases.

[1] Townships in Connecticut and Massachusetts only.

[2] Exclusive of heads of families whose marital condition or age was unknown.

[3] Exclusive of New England.

Table 12.—Marital Condition of Heads of Rural Families 45 Through 64 Years of Age Receiving General Relief, by Residence, Area, and Sex, October 1935

[138 counties and 83 New England townships [1]]

Residence and area	Both sexes							Male							Female						
	Total [1]		Single	Married	Widowed	Divorced	Separated	Total		Single	Married	Widowed	Divorced	Separated	Total		Single	Married	Widowed	Divorced	Separated
	Number	Percent						Number	Percent						Number	Percent					
TOTAL RURAL																					
All areas	16,000	100.0	7.7	70.6	17.4	1.1	3.2	13,168	100.0	7.5	82.4	7.5	0.8	1.8	2,832	100.0	8.7	15.7	63.3	2.5	9.8
Eastern Cotton	1,580	100.0	5.2	61.4	28.0	—	5.4	1,008	100.0	3.6	85.1	8.7	—	2.6	572	100.0	8.0	19.6	61.9	—	10.5
Western Cotton	1,624	100.0	6.9	64.3	24.9	1.1	3.9	1,246	100.0	5.1	82.5	10.6	—	1.8	378	100.0	12.7	4.2	72.0	—	11.1
Appalachian-Ozark	5,522	100.0	5.2	74.6	16.9	1.6	2.2	4,694	100.0	4.8	84.5	8.1	0.9	1.7	828	100.0	7.7	18.4	66.9	1.7	5.3
Lake States Cut-Over	1,120	100.0	18.7	61.5	14.5	2.0	3.7	988	100.0	20.9	68.8	6.9	1.0	2.4	132	100.0	3.0	6.1	71.2	6.1	13.6
Hay and Dairy	2,438	100.0	6.9	74.1	10.4	2.7	4.5	2,094	100.0	8.9	81.7	5.4	1.3	2.7	344	100.0	3.9	27.3	40.7	6.4	15.7
Corn Belt	1,114	100.0	9.3	70.6	14.7	2.7	2.7	926	100.0	9.3	82.9	5.2	2.2	0.4	188	100.0	9.6	9.6	61.7	5.3	13.8
Spring Wheat	710	100.0	4.8	79.8	13.2	0.8	1.4	626	100.0	5.4	85.9	7.7	1.0	1.0	84	100.0	9.6	33.3	54.8	7.1	4.8
Winter Wheat	320	100.0	4.4	84.9	6.9	1.3	2.5	286	100.0	4.2	90.2	3.5	1.4	0.7	34	†	†	†	†	†	†
Ranching	388	100.0	6.7	57.7	29.4	3.1	3.1	276	100.0	6.5	80.5	10.2	1.4	1.0	112	100.0	7.1	1.8	76.9	7.1	7.1
New England	1,184	100.0	11.7	69.6	16.0	0.3	2.4	1,024	100.0	11.3	80.3	7.2	—	1.2	160	100.0	13.8	1.3	72.4	2.5	10.0
OPEN COUNTRY																					
All areas [3]	8,714	100.0	5.8	74.6	16.1	1.0	2.5	7,336	100.0	5.3	85.1	7.4	0.7	1.5	1,378	100.0	8.6	19.3	62.3	2.3	7.5
Eastern Cotton	1,014	100.0	4.7	67.1	23.7	—	4.5	700	100.0	2.6	87.4	8.3	—	1.7	314	100.0	9.6	21.7	57.9	—	10.8
Western Cotton	1,042	100.0	5.2	69.8	21.7	—	3.3	852	100.0	2.6	85.0	10.3	—	2.1	190	100.0	16.8	2.1	72.7	—	8.4
Appalachian-Ozark	3,444	100.0	3.4	77.2	16.9	0.8	1.7	2,914	100.0	2.6	87.3	8.4	0.5	1.2	530	100.0	7.5	21.9	63.8	2.3	4.5
Lake States Cut-Over	808	100.0	18.8	65.4	11.4	1.2	3.2	738	100.0	20.1	70.9	6.0	0.8	2.2	70	100.0	5.7	5.7	68.6	5.7	14.3
Hay and Dairy	1,260	100.0	6.0	79.8	9.4	1.9	2.9	1,120	100.0	5.9	85.9	4.5	1.6	2.1	140	100.0	7.1	31.4	48.6	4.3	8.6
Corn Belt	350	100.0	6.9	75.4	13.7	3.4	0.6	312	100.0	7.1	84.5	6.5	2.6	—	38	†	†	†	†	†	†
Spring Wheat	478	100.0	4.6	82.8	11.3	—	1.3	432	100.0	5.1	87.9	6.5	—	0.5	46	†	†	†	†	†	†
Winter Wheat	184	100.0	4.3	90.2	3.3	2.2	—	166	100.0	4.8	91.6	1.2	2.4	—	18	†	†	†	†	†	†
Ranching	134	100.0	4.5	62.6	25.4	4.5	3.0	102	100.0	5.9	82.3	9.8	—	2.0	32	†	†	†	†	†	†

VILLAGE																					
All areas ³	6,102	100.0	9.6	64.9	19.5	1.5	4.5	4,808	100.0	9.9	78.7	7.8	1.2	2.4	1,294	100.0	8.2	13.8	63.0	2.8	12.2
Eastern Cotton	566	100.0	6.0	51.2	35.7	—	7.1	308	100.0	5.8	80.0	9.7	—	4.5	258	100.0	6.2	17.1	66.6	—	10.1
Western Cotton	582	100.0	10.0	54.2	30.6	—	5.2	394	100.0	10.7	77.1	11.2	—	1.0	188	100.0	8.5	6.4	71.3	—	13.8
Appalachian-Ozark	2,078	100.0	8.3	70.3	16.9	1.4	3.1	1,780	100.0	8.3	80.1	7.6	1.6	2.5	298	100.0	8.1	12.1	72.4	0.7	6.7
Lake States Cut-Over	312	100.0	18.6	51.3	22.4	2.6	5.1	250	100.0	23.2	62.4	9.6	1.6	3.3	62	100.0	—	6.5	74.1	6.5	12.9
Hay and Dairy	1,178	100.0	12.2	68.0	11.5	2.0	6.3	974	100.0	12.8	77.0	6.6	0.8	3.7	204	100.0	11.8	24.5	35.3	7.8	20.6
Corn Belt	764	100.0	10.5	68.2	15.2	2.4	3.7	614	100.0	10.4	82.0	4.9	2.0	0.7	150	100.0	10.7	12.0	57.3	4.0	16.0
Spring Wheat	232	100.0	5.2	73.3	17.2	2.6	1.7	194	100.0	6.2	81.4	10.3	—	2.1	38	100.0	†	†	†	†	†
Winter Wheat	136	100.0	4.4	77.9	11.8	—	5.9	120	100.0	3.3	88.3	6.7	—	1.7	16	100.0	†	†	†	†	†
Ranching	254	100.0	7.9	55.1	31.5	2.4	3.1	174	100.0	6.9	79.4	10.3	2.3	1.1	80	100.0	10.0	2.5	77.5	2.5	7.5

† Percent not computed on a base of fewer than 50 cases

¹ Townships in Connecticut and Massachusetts only.
² Exclusive of heads of families whose marital condition or age was unknown.
³ Exclusive of New England.

Table 13.—Marital Condition of Heads of Rural Families 65 Years of Age and Over Receiving General Relief, by Residence, Area, and Sex, October 1935

[138 counties and 83 New England townships 1]

Residence and area	Both sexes							Male							Female						
	Total Number	Per cent	Single	Married	Widowed	Divorced	Separated	Total Number	Per cent	Single	Married	Widowed	Divorced	Separated	Total Number	Per cent	Single	Married	Widowed	Divorced	Separated
TOTAL RURAL																					
All areas	4,858	100.0	11.9	49.1	34.6	1.7	2.7	3,866	100.0	12.9	61.5	22.1	1.6	1.9	992	100.0	7.9	0.6	83.5	2.2	5.8
Eastern Cotton	160	100.0	8.8	38.7	46.2	—	6.3	106	100.0	9.4	58.5	28.3	—	3.8	54	100.0	7.4	—	81.5	—	11.1
Western Cotton	910	100.0	7.3	49.1	40.9	0.9	1.8	662	100.0	10.4	67.7	21.1	0.6	0.6	248	100.0	—	—	93.6	1.6	4.8
Appalachian-Ozark	1,322	100.0	7.0	60.8	29.5	0.6	2.1	1,124	100.0	6.4	71.6	19.2	0.7	2.8	198	100.0	10.1	—	87.9	—	2.0
Lake States Cut-Over	594	100.0	23.2	25.3	43.1	4.0	4.4	504	100.0	25.8	29.8	37.6	4.0	1.1	90	100.0	8.9	—	73.4	4.4	13.3
Hay and Dairy	932	100.0	16.3	46.7	33.0	1.9	2.1	728	100.0	16.8	59.0	21.5	1.9	1.9	204	100.0	14.7	2.0	75.4	2.6	5.9
Corn Belt	390	100.0	9.2	50.9	33.3	1.9	2.6	312	100.0	9.6	63.5	20.5	4.5	—	78	100.0	7.7	+	84.6	+	5.1
Spring Wheat	106	100.0	26.4	50.9	17.0	1.9	3.8	90	100.0	31.1	57.8	11.1	—	—	16	100.0	—	—	—	—	—
Winter Wheat	46	100.0	+	—	—	—	—	36	100.0	—	—	—	—	—	10	100.0	—	—	—	—	—
Ranching	120	100.0	11.7	35.0	43.3	3.3	6.7	78	100.0	17.9	53.9	20.5	—	7.7	42	100.0	—	—	—	—	—
New England	278	100.0	12.2	59.7	24.5	0.7	2.9	226	100.0	10.6	73.4	13.3	—	2.7	52	100.0	19.2	—	73.2	3.8	3.8
OPEN COUNTRY																					
All areas	2,500	100.0	11.7	51.8	33.0	1.4	2.1	2,008	100.0	11.5	62.8	22.7	1.5	1.5	432	100.0	12.5	—	82.0	0.9	4.6
Eastern Cotton	70	100.0	8.6	45.7	40.0	—	5.7	54	100.0	7.4	59.3	25.9	—	7.4	16	100.0	+	—	+	—	—
Western Cotton	562	100.0	5.5	53.8	38.1	1.4	1.4	414	100.0	7.2	73.0	18.8	1.0	—	148	100.0	—	—	91.9	2.7	5.4
Appalachian-Ozark	794	100.0	5.5	66.6	25.9	0.5	1.5	688	100.0	3.5	76.7	18.0	0.6	1.2	106	100.0	18.9	—	77.3	—	3.8
Lake States Cut-Over	396	100.0	24.7	22.7	46.1	3.0	3.5	346	100.0	26.0	26.0	41.6	3.5	2.9	50	100.0	16.0	—	76.0	—	8.0
Hay and Dairy	492	100.0	16.7	47.2	32.1	1.6	2.4	400	100.0	15.5	58.0	22.5	2.0	2.0	92	100.0	21.7	—	74.0	—	4.3
Corn Belt	90	100.0	8.9	68.9	17.8	4.4	+	80	100.0	5.0	77.5	12.5	5.0	—	10	100.0	—	—	—	—	—
Spring Wheat	56	100.0	35.7	46.4	17.9	—	—	54	100.0	37.0	48.2	14.8	—	—	2	100.0	—	—	—	—	—
Winter Wheat	18	100.0	+	—	—	—	—	14	100.0	+	+	—	—	—	4	100.0	—	—	—	—	—
Ranching	22	100.0	+	—	—	—	—	18	100.0	—	—	—	—	—	4	100.0	—	—	—	—	—

VILLAGE																					
All areas³	2,080	100.0	12.1	44.4	38.0	2.1	3.4	1,572	100.0	15.1	58.4	22.5	1.8	2.2	508	100.0	2.8	1.2	85.8	3.1	7.1
Eastern Cotton	90	100.0	8.9	33.3	51.1	—	6.7	52	100.0	11.5	57.7	30.8	—	1.6	38	100.0	†	†	96.0	—	†
Western Cotton	348	100.0	10.3	42.0	45.4	0.8	2.3	248	100.0	14.5	58.9	25.0	0.9	3.7	100	100.0	†	†	100.0	—	4.0
Appalachian-Ozark	528	100.0	9.1	52.3	34.8	6.1	3.0	436	100.0	11.0	63.3	21.1	5.1	2.5	92	100.0	†	†	†	—	†
Lake States Cut-Over	198	100.0	20.2	30.3	37.3	2.3	6.1	158	100.0	25.3	38.0	29.1	1.8	—	40	100.0	3.6	8.9	76.8	3.6	7.1
Hay and Dairy	440	100.0	15.9	45.9	34.1	4.0	1.8	328	100.0	18.3	60.4	19.5	4.3	2.6	112	100.0	2.9	†	88.3	2.9	5.9
Corn Belt	300	100.0	9.3	45.4	38.0	4.0	3.3	232	100.0	11.2	58.6	23.3	—	—	68	100.0	†	†	†	—	†
Spring Wheat	50	100.0	16.0	56.0	16.0	—	8.0	36	†	†	†	†	—	—	14	†	†	†	†	—	†
Winter Wheat	28	†	†	†	†	—	—	22	†	†	†	†	—	—	6	†	†	†	†	—	†
Ranching	98	100.0	10.2	32.7	46.9	4.1	6.1	60	100.0	16.7	53.3	23.3	—	6.7	38	†	†	†	†	—	†

† Percent not computed on a base of fewer than 50 cases.

¹ Townships in Connecticut and Massachusetts only.
² Exclusive of heads of families whose marital condition or age was unknown.
³ Exclusive of New England.

Table 14.—Marital Condition of Heads of Rural Families Receiving General Relief in the Eastern and Western Cotton Areas, by Residence, Age, Sex, and Color, October 1935

[44 counties]

WHITE

Residence and age	Both sexes							Male							Female						
	Total[1]		Single	Married	Widowed	Divorced	Separated	Total		Single	Married	Widowed	Divorced	Separated	Total		Single	Married	Widowed	Divorced	Separated
	Number	Percent						Number	Percent						Number	Percent					
TOTAL RURAL																					
Total	7,614	100.0	7.7	70.3	16.2	0.5	5.3	5,906	100.0	6.3	87.9	4.9	0.1	0.8	1,708	100.0	12.5	9.6	55.4	1.9	20.6
16–24 years	684	100.0	22.2	66.6	4.4	1.5	5.3	548	100.0	18.2	81.4	—	—	0.4	136	100.0	38.1	7.4	22.1	7.4	25.0
25–34 years	1,984	100.0	8.2	75.1	9.1	0.6	7.0	1,592	100.0	7.2	91.4	1.0	—	0.4	392	100.0	12.2	9.2	41.8	3.1	33.7
35–44 years	1,892	100.0	4.3	73.8	14.5	0.7	6.7	1,452	100.0	3.5	93.2	2.2	0.3	1.0	440	100.0	7.7	9.5	55.0	2.3	25.5
45–64 years	2,410	100.0	6.6	67.8	21.8	—	3.8	1,804	100.0	4.5	86.4	7.6	—	1.5	606	100.0	12.5	12.5	64.1	—	10.9
65 years and over	644	100.0	5.3	57.4	35.1	0.6	1.6	510	100.0	5.9	72.5	20.4	0.8	0.4	134	100.0	3.0	—	91.0	—	6.0
OPEN COUNTRY																					
Total	5,364	100.0	6.2	74.8	14.2	0.4	4.4	4,350	100.0	4.8	89.8	4.6	0.1	0.7	1,014	100.0	12.4	10.3	55.2	1.8	20.3
16–24 years	516	100.0	19.8	71.2	3.9	1.6	3.5	436	100.0	16.5	83.0	—	—	0.5	80	100.0	37.5	7.5	25.0	10.0	20.0
25–34 years	1,510	100.0	6.6	78.4	8.7	0.5	5.8	1,242	100.0	5.6	93.1	1.3	—	—	268	100.0	11.1	9.7	43.4	3.0	32.8
35–44 years	1,350	100.0	3.0	79.4	12.7	0.2	4.7	1,100	100.0	2.2	95.1	1.8	—	0.5	250	100.0	4.4	10.4	60.8	0.8	23.2
45–64 years	1,600	100.0	5.0	72.0	19.5	—	3.5	1,256	100.0	2.2	88.1	8.1	—	1.6	344	100.0	15.1	13.4	61.0	—	10.5
65 years and over	388	100.0	3.1	60.8	32.5	1.0	2.6	316	100.0	3.2	74.6	20.3	1.3	0.6	72	100.0	2.8	—	86.1	—	11.1
VILLAGE																					
Total	2,250	100.0	11.3	59.4	21.1	0.8	7.4	1,556	100.0	10.7	82.0	5.7	0.3	1.3	694	100.0	12.7	8.6	55.7	2.0	21.0
16–24 years	168	100.0	29.8	52.3	6.0	1.2	10.7	112	100.0	25.0	75.0	—	—	—	56	100.0	39.3	7.1	17.9	3.6	32.1
25–34 years	474	100.0	13.1	65.5	10.1	0.8	10.5	350	100.0	12.6	85.7	—	—	1.7	124	100.0	14.5	8.1	38.7	3.2	35.5
35–44 years	542	100.0	7.8	59.8	18.8	2.2	11.4	352	100.0	5.7	87.5	3.4	1.1	2.3	190	100.0	11.6	8.4	47.4	4.2	28.4
45–64 years	810	100.0	9.6	59.5	26.4	—	4.5	548	100.0	9.9	82.5	6.5	—	1.1	262	100.0	9.2	11.4	67.9	—	11.5
65 years and over	256	100.0	8.6	52.3	39.1	—	—	194	100.0	10.3	69.1	20.6	—	—	62	100.0	9.3	—	96.8	—	—

NEGRO

TOTAL RURAL																					
Total	2,430	100.0	10.4	49.6	30.1	0.7	9.2	1,500	100.0	12.0	73.5	12.1	—	2.4	930	100.0	7.7	11.0	59.2	1.9	20.2
16-24 years	204	100.0	41.2	48.0	3.9	—	6.9	164	100.0	40.2	59.8	—	—	—	40	†	†	†	†	†	†
25-34 years	482	100.0	7.5	62.6	14.1	2.1	13.7	308	100.0	7.1	89.0	3.9	—	—	174	100.0	8.0	16.1	32.3	5.7	37.9
35-44 years	524	100.0	9.5	54.2	22.1	0.8	13.4	320	100.0	8.7	81.9	6.9	—	2.5	204	100.0	10.8	10.8	46.1	2.0	30.3
45-64 years	794	100.0	4.5	47.9	40.3	—	7.3	450	100.0	4.0	72.9	18.2	—	4.9	344	100.0	5.2	15.1	69.2	—	10.5
65 years and over	426	100.0	10.8	32.9	51.6	0.9	3.8	258	100.0	17.8	54.3	25.6	—	2.3	168	100.0	—	—	91.6	2.4	6.0
OPEN COUNTRY																					
Total	1,518	100.0	10.2	54.6	25.7	1.6	7.9	994	100.0	11.3	77.8	9.3	*	1.6	524	100.0	8.2	11.6	56.2	4.5	19.5
16-24 years	128	100.0	39.1	51.5	6.3	—	3.1	102	100.0	35.3	64.7	—	—	—	26	†	†	†	†	†	†
25-34 years	326	100.0	6.1	64.4	14.1	3.1	12.3	212	100.0	7.5	88.7	3.8	—	—	114	100.0	3.5	19.3	33.3	8.8	35.1
35-44 years	364	100.0	11.0	56.6	18.7	—	13.7	232	100.0	10.3	82.8	5.2	—	1.7	132	100.0	12.1	10.6	42.4	—	34.9
45-64 years	456	100.0	4.8	56.1	33.8	—	5.3	296	100.0	4.0	77.7	14.9	—	3.4	160	100.0	6.2	16.2	68.8	—	8.8
65 years and over	244	100.0	9.8	40.2	47.6	1.6	0.8	152	100.0	15.8	64.5	18.4	—	1.3	92	100.0	—	—	95.7	4.3	—
VILLAGE																					
Total	912	100.0	10.5	40.4	37.3	0.4	11.4	506	100.0	13.4	64.8	17.8	—	4.0	406	100.0	6.9	9.9	61.5	1.0	20.7
16-24 years	76	100.0	44.7	42.1	—	—	13.2	62	100.0	48.4	51.6	—	—	—	14	†	†	†	†	†	†
25-34 years	156	100.0	10.3	58.9	14.1	—	16.7	96	100.0	6.3	89.5	4.2	—	—	60	100.0	16.7	10.0	30.0	—	43.3
35-44 years	160	100.0	6.2	48.8	30.0	2.5	12.5	88	100.0	4.5	79.6	11.4	—	4.5	72	100.0	8.3	11.1	52.8	5.6	22.2
45-64 years	338	100.0	4.1	36.7	49.1	—	10.1	154	100.0	3.9	63.6	24.7	—	7.8	184	100.0	4.3	14.1	69.6	—	12.0
65 years and over	182	100.0	12.1	23.1	57.1	—	7.7	106	100.0	20.8	39.6	35.8	—	3.8	76	100.0	—	—	86.8	—	13.2

* Less than 0.05 percent.

† Percent not computed on a base of fewer than 50 cases.

‡ Exclusive of heads of families whose marital condition or age was unknown.

Table 15.—Size of Rural Families Receiving General Relief, by Residence and Area, June 1935

[138 counties and 116 New England townships]

Residence and area	Total [1]		Number of persons in family					
	Number	Percent	1	2–3	4–5	6–7	8–9	10 or more
TOTAL RURAL								
All areas	62,809	100.0	9.9	33.3	28.9	16.8	7.8	3.3
Eastern Cotton	7,732	100.0	10.3	35.8	29.0	16.5	6.1	2.3
White	5,084	100.0	6.6	34.6	32.5	18.3	6.2	1.8
Negro	2,648	100.0	17.4	38.1	22.3	13.0	6.0	3.2
Western Cotton	7,268	100.0	8.7	35.3	30.0	16.0	7.3	2.7
White	5,432	100.0	5.5	36.1	32.2	16.4	7.4	2.4
Negro	1,836	100.0	18.1	32.8	23.7	14.8	7.0	3.6
Appalachian-Ozark	17,016	100.0	6.1	30.4	30.4	19.5	9.9	3.7
Lake States Cut-Over	3,792	100.0	21.8	29.8	24.2	13.2	7.8	3.2
Hay and Dairy	8,626	100.0	10.3	34.2	27.5	16.6	7.6	3.8
Corn Belt	7,512	100.0	8.8	36.6	30.4	15.2	6.4	2.6
Spring Wheat	3,374	100.0	8.3	28.8	26.8	18.7	10.2	7.2
Winter Wheat	1,288	100.0	6.8	35.7	33.5	15.7	6.4	1.9
Ranching	1,886	100.0	17.6	32.2	26.4	16.0	5.7	2.1
New England	4,315	100.0	15.1	35.5	26.6	14.0	6.0	2.8
OPEN COUNTRY								
All areas [2]	35,782	100.0	7.5	30.4	29.9	18.8	9.3	4.1
Eastern Cotton	5,002	100.0	9.5	33.6	29.3	17.7	7.1	2.8
White	3,366	100.0	5.8	33.0	32.3	19.6	7.0	2.3
Negro	1,636	100.0	17.1	34.8	23.2	13.7	7.2	4.0
Western Cotton	4,686	100.0	7.1	32.7	31.5	17.7	8.0	3.0
White	3,510	100.0	4.2	33.8	33.2	18.0	8.1	2.7
Negro	1,176	100.0	15.8	29.3	26.4	16.7	7.7	4.1
Appalachian-Ozark	12,066	100.0	3.3	27.6	31.6	21.7	11.2	4.6
Lake States Cut-Over	2,492	100.0	21.2	29.8	24.2	12.6	8.6	3.6
Hay and Dairy	5,028	100.0	9.1	32.3	27.6	17.4	9.3	4.3
Corn Belt	2,802	100.0	6.1	32.8	32.8	18.0	7.6	2.7
Spring Wheat	2,386	100.0	7.3	26.2	26.5	20.0	11.0	9.0
Winter Wheat	670	100.0	4.8	31.0	35.8	17.9	7.2	3.3
Ranching	650	100.0	19.4	31.3	24.3	16.3	6.5	2.2
VILLAGE								
All areas [2]	22,712	100.0	12.5	37.5	27.8	14.2	5.8	2.2
Eastern Cotton	2,730	100.0	11.6	40.0	28.4	14.4	4.4	1.2
White	1,718	100.0	8.0	37.7	32.8	15.9	4.7	0.9
Negro	1,012	100.0	17.8	43.7	20.8	11.9	4.0	1.8
Western Cotton	2,582	100.0	11.6	40.0	27.4	13.0	6.0	2.0
White	1,922	100.0	8.0	40.3	30.3	13.5	6.1	1.8
Negro	660	100.0	22.1	38.8	19.1	11.5	5.8	2.7
Appalachian-Ozark	4,950	100.0	12.9	37.0	27.5	14.1	6.8	1.7
Lake States Cut-Over	1,300	100.0	22.9	30.1	24.0	14.5	6.2	2.3
Hay and Dairy	3,598	100.0	12.1	36.7	27.3	15.5	5.2	3.2
Corn Belt	4,710	100.0	10.4	39.0	28.9	13.5	5.6	2.6
Spring Wheat	988	100.0	10.7	34.8	27.7	15.7	8.3	2.8
Winter Wheat	618	100.0	9.1	40.7	31.1	13.3	5.5	0.3
Ranching	1,236	100.0	16.7	32.5	27.5	15.9	5.3	2.1

[1] Exclusive of families whose size was unknown.
[2] Exclusive of New England.

Table 16.—Size of Rural Families Receiving General Relief, by Usual Occupation of Head, Area, and Color, June 1935

[138 counties [1]]

Usual occupation of head, area, and color	Total [2]		Number of persons in family									
	Number	Percent	1	2	3	4	5	6	7	8	9	10 or more
ALL AREAS												
Total	58,454	100.0	9.5	16.2	16.8	16.1	12.9	10.0	7.1	4.8	3.2	3.4
Agriculture	24,976	100.0	2.7	11.2	16.9	17.4	14.7	12.2	9.1	6.6	4.5	4.7
Farm operator	18,126	100.0	2.0	9.5	15.7	17.3	14.9	12.9	9.7	7.3	5.2	5.5
Owner	6,418	100.0	3.6	10.0	14.1	15.2	13.9	13.4	9.6	8.0	5.7	6.5
Tenant	9,684	100.0	1.2	8.4	15.9	18.3	15.7	12.8	10.0	7.2	5.2	5.3
Cropper [3]	2,024	100.0	1.2	13.5	19.6	18.1	14.3	11.7	8.8	5.4	3.9	3.5
Farm laborer	6,850	100.0	4.4	15.7	20.3	17.8	14.0	10.4	7.5	4.7	2.6	2.6
Nonagriculture	23,136	100.0	7.4	14.8	18.4	18.0	14.0	10.4	6.9	4.3	2.7	3.1
No usual occupation or nonworker	10,342	100.0	30.6	31.6	13.5	9.4	6.0	3.6	2.4	1.5	0.8	0.6
EASTERN AND WESTERN COTTON AREAS—WHITE												
Total	10,512	100.0	6.0	17.5	18.0	18.1	14.2	10.8	6.5	4.4	2.4	2.1
Agriculture	5,502	100.0	1.3	12.4	17.1	19.2	16.5	12.8	8.6	5.8	3.3	3.0
Farm operator	3,562	100.0	0.8	10.9	17.5	20.2	15.8	12.7	8.5	6.1	3.8	3.7
Owner	604	100.0	2.6	12.9	14.6	22.6	18.3	13.2	7.9	2.3	2.6	3.0
Tenant	1,438	100.0	0.8	8.1	15.9	19.8	16.0	13.9	8.1	8.3	4.5	4.6
Cropper	1,520	100.0	0.1	12.8	20.3	19.3	14.6	11.4	9.1	5.5	3.7	3.2
Farm laborer	1,940	100.0	2.2	15.1	16.3	17.7	17.7	13.0	8.8	5.2	2.4	1.6
Nonagriculture	3,164	100.0	4.2	16.4	21.1	20.0	14.7	10.9	5.4	3.7	2.0	1.6
No usual occupation or nonworker	1,846	100.0	23.2	34.4	15.3	11.5	6.4	4.9	2.1	1.5	0.4	0.3
EASTERN AND WESTERN COTTON AREAS—NEGRO												
Total	4,484	100.0	17.7	20.8	15.3	13.3	9.5	7.9	5.8	3.7	2.7	3.3
Agriculture	2,114	100.0	4.8	14.1	17.0	16.7	12.3	10.6	8.8	5.7	4.0	6.0
Farm operator	1,104	100.0	2.7	11.2	15.3	15.3	13.9	12.9	9.2	7.2	5.6	6.7
Owner	154	100.0	3.9	11.7	14.3	13.0	14.3	7.8	6.5	6.5		6.5
Tenant	446	100.0	0.4	5.8	12.1	16.7	14.8	13.0	11.2	9.9	6.7	9.4
Cropper	504	100.0	4.4	15.8	17.8	14.3	13.5	12.3	7.9	5.2	4.4	4.4
Farm laborer	1,010	100.0	7.1	17.2	19.3	18.2	10.5	8.1	8.3	4.0	2.2	5.1
Nonagriculture	1,050	100.0	9.0	21.4	17.9	17.1	11.6	9.9	5.3	2.9	3.0	1.9
No usual occupation or nonworker	1,320	100.0	45.1	30.7	10.3	5.0	3.5	2.0	1.5	1.1	0.5	0.3

[1] Exclusive of New England townships.
[2] Exclusive of families whose size was unknown.
[3] In the 2 Cotton Areas.

Table 17.—Age of Persons in Rural Families Receiving General Relief, by Residence and Area, June 1935

[138 counties and 116 New England townships]

Residence and area	Total [1]		Age in years							
	Number	Percent	Under 10	10–15	16–24	25–34	35–44	45–54	55–64	65 and over
TOTAL RURAL										
All areas	270,506	100.0	26.2	16.7	16.3	11.9	9.8	8.2	5.6	5.3
Eastern Cotton	31,670	100.0	25.8	16.7	15.6	11.9	9.4	7.9	5.9	6.8
White	21,686	100.0	25.5	17.1	15.8	12.9	9.7	8.1	5.8	5.1
Negro	9,984	100.0	26.9	15.8	15.4	9.6	8.7	7.4	5.9	10.3
Western Cotton	30,556	100.0	26.4	16.4	16.7	12.5	9.3	7.4	5.1	6.2
White	23,348	100.0	26.8	15.9	17.5	13.2	9.4	7.4	4.8	5.0
Negro	7,208	100.0	26.1	17.9	14.1	10.0	8.8	7.2	5.9	10.0
Appalachian-Ozark	79,508	100.0	27.3	17.4	17.2	11.8	9.2	7.6	5.1	4.4
Lake States Cut-Over	14,586	100.0	23.7	16.3	17.3	12.2	9.6	8.9	6.1	5.9
Hay and Dairy	37,004	100.0	27.2	16.8	14.9	10.6	10.7	8.9	5.6	5.3
Corn Belt	31,130	100.0	25.1	15.4	15.6	12.5	10.3	9.2	6.5	5.4
Spring Wheat	16,472	100.0	30.3	16.6	16.3	13.5	9.3	6.9	4.2	2.9
Winter Wheat	5,388	100.0	24.9	15.4	18.3	14.1	11.0	7.5	4.9	3.9
Ranching	7,322	100.0	27.9	15.7	15.1	12.0	9.6	7.3	6.4	6.0
New England	16,870	100.0	21.0	16.7	16.3	9.7	11.2	10.7	7.7	6.7
OPEN COUNTRY										
All areas [2]	164,854	100.0	28.1	17.0	16.3	12.0	9.4	7.5	4.9	4.8
Eastern Cotton	21,404	100.0	27.2	17.0	15.2	11.7	8.7	7.1	5.7	7.4
White	14,874	100.0	27.2	17.1	15.1	13.1	8.9	7.5	5.7	5.4
Negro	6,530	100.0	27.2	16.8	15.3	8.6	8.1	6.4	5.7	11.9
Western Cotton	20,630	100.0	27.8	16.3	16.7	12.9	8.7	6.9	4.8	5.9
White	15,696	100.0	28.1	15.8	17.5	13.7	8.8	6.8	4.5	4.8
Negro	4,934	100.0	26.9	17.9	14.2	10.2	8.7	7.0	5.6	9.5
Appalachian-Ozark	60,168	100.0	28.8	17.6	17.1	11.9	9.1	6.9	4.6	4.0
Lake States Cut-Over	9,776	100.0	24.2	16.6	16.8	11.7	9.9	9.2	6.0	5.6
Hay and Dairy	22,612	100.0	27.9	17.6	14.8	10.5	10.9	8.6	5.1	4.6
Corn Belt	12,450	100.0	25.8	16.0	16.0	12.8	10.6	9.0	5.4	4.4
Spring Wheat	12,274	100.0	31.6	16.5	16.4	14.0	9.0	6.8	3.7	2.0
Winter Wheat	3,020	100.0	26.9	15.1	18.7	14.9	10.9	6.2	3.7	3.6
Ranching	2,520	100.0	29.3	16.0	13.3	11.2	9.5	8.4	6.8	5.5
VILLAGE										
All areas [2]	88,782	100.0	24.2	16.0	16.3	11.9	10.1	9.0	6.5	6.0
Eastern Cotton	10,266	100.0	23.1	16.0	16.7	12.2	10.9	9.4	6.2	5.5
White	6,812	100.0	21.8	16.9	17.2	12.7	11.4	9.4	6.1	4.5
Negro	3,454	100.0	26.0	14.1	15.7	11.3	9.8	9.3	6.4	7.4
Western Cotton	9,926	100.0	23.6	16.6	16.7	11.7	10.4	8.3	5.8	6.9
White	7,652	100.0	23.7	16.2	17.5	12.3	10.7	8.5	5.6	5.5
Negro	2,274	100.0	23.7	17.9	14.0	9.7	9.1	7.7	6.6	11.3
Appalachian-Ozark	19,340	100.0	22.8	16.9	17.2	11.7	9.5	9.7	6.7	5.5
Lake States Cut-Over	4,810	100.0	22.7	15.9	18.4	13.3	9.0	8.1	6.3	6.3
Hay and Dairy	14,392	100.0	25.8	15.7	15.0	10.8	10.5	9.4	6.3	6.5
Corn Belt	18,680	100.0	24.5	15.1	15.4	12.3	10.1	9.3	7.2	6.1
Spring Wheat	4,198	100.0	27.0	16.8	16.0	11.9	10.1	7.2	5.5	5.5
Winter Wheat	2,368	100.0	22.7	15.7	17.8	13.0	11.1	9.1	6.3	4.3
Ranching	4,802	100.0	27.2	15.5	16.1	12.5	9.6	6.7	6.2	6.2

[1] Exclusive of persons whose age was unknown.
[2] Exclusive of New England.

Table 18.—Sex of Persons in Rural Families Receiving General Relief, by Residence and Area, June 1935

[138 counties and 116 New England townships]

Residence and area	Total [1]		Male	Female
	Number	Percent		
TOTAL RURAL				
All areas	270,752	100.0	50.9	49.1
Eastern Cotton	31,692	100.0	47.5	52.5
Western Cotton	30,566	100.0	49.8	50.2
Appalachian-Ozark	79,518	100.0	51.0	49.0
Lake States Cut-Over	14,682	100.0	55.5	44.5
Hay and Dairy	37,030	100.0	51.4	48.6
Corn Belt	31,134	100.0	51.5	48.5
Spring Wheat	16,482	100.0	51.3	48.7
Winter Wheat	5,388	100.0	50.7	49.3
Ranching	7,322	100.0	51.1	48.9
New England	16,938	100.0	52.2	47.8
OPEN COUNTRY				
All areas [2]	164,970	100.0	51.3	48.7
Eastern Cotton	21,410	100.0	48.4	51.6
Western Cotton	20,636	100.0	50.3	49.7
Appalachian-Ozark	60,176	100.0	51.3	48.7
Lake States Cut-Over	9,860	100.0	55.7	44.3
Hay and Dairy	22,620	100.0	52.0	48.0
Corn Belt	12,452	100.0	52.9	47.1
Spring Wheat	12,276	100.0	52.2	47.8
Winter Wheat	3,020	100.0	51.5	48.5
Ranching	2,520	100.0	52.2	47.8
VILLAGE				
All areas [2]	88,844	100.0	49.8	50.2
Eastern Cotton	10,282	100.0	45.8	54.2
Western Cotton	9,930	100.0	48.9	51.1
Appalachian-Ozark	19,342	100.0	50.1	49.9
Lake States Cut-Over	4,822	100.0	55.0	45.0
Hay and Dairy	14,410	100.0	50.4	49.6
Corn Belt	18,682	100.0	50.7	49.3
Spring Wheat	4,206	100.0	48.6	51.4
Winter Wheat	2,368	100.0	49.6	50.4
Ranching	4,802	100.0	50.5	49.5

[1] Exclusive of persons whose sex was unknown.
[2] Exclusive of New England.

Table 19.—Rural Families Receiving General Relief With Persons in Dependent Age Groups, by Residence and Area, June 1935

[138 counties and 116 New England townships]

Residence and area	Total [1]		Children under 16 years only	Aged 65 years and over only	Children under 16 years and aged 65 years and over	No person under 16 years or 65 years and over
	Number	Percent				
TOTAL RURAL						
All areas	62,809	100.0	60.4	13.1	5.3	21.2
Eastern Cotton	7,732	100.0	57.1	14.2	8.1	20.6
White	5,084	100.0	62.6	10.8	6.3	20.3
Negro	2,648	100.0	46.5	20.7	11.6	21.2
Western Cotton	7,268	100.0	60.0	14.8	6.2	19.0
White	5,432	100.0	63.7	12.0	5.2	19.1
Negro	1,836	100.0	49.1	22.9	9.3	18.7
Appalachian-Ozark	17,016	100.0	66.0	10.1	6.3	17.6
Lake States Cut-Over	3,792	100.0	51.8	15.7	3.6	28.9
Hay and Dairy	8,626	100.0	60.6	14.3	4.0	21.1
Corn Belt	7,512	100.0	58.0	13.8	4.4	23.8
Spring Wheat	3,374	100.0	68.7	8.7	2.8	19.8
Winter Wheat	1,288	100.0	62.3	9.2	2.9	25.6
Ranching	1,886	100.0	58.2	16.4	3.2	22.2
New England	4,315	100.0	51.1	17.2	4.3	27.4
OPEN COUNTRY						
All areas [2]	35,782	100.0	64.7	11.4	6.2	17.7
Eastern Cotton	5,002	100.0	58.6	15.2	9.5	16.7
White	3,366	100.0	64.7	11.2	7.0	17.1
Negro	1,636	100.0	46.0	23.5	14.7	15.8
Western Cotton	4,686	100.0	63.0	13.7	6.8	16.5
White	3,510	100.0	66.7	11.3	5.5	16.5
Negro	1,176	100.0	52.0	20.7	10.6	16.7
Appalachian-Ozark	12,066	100.0	70.2	9.0	7.0	13.8
Lake States Cut-Over	2,492	100.0	52.2	15.0	3.8	29.0
Hay and Dairy	5,028	100.0	63.9	12.4	4.2	19.5
Corn Belt	2,802	100.0	62.0	10.8	5.3	21.9
Spring Wheat	2,386	100.0	71.8	5.9	2.6	19.7
Winter Wheat	670	100.0	65.7	7.4	3.9	23.0
Ranching	650	100.0	59.1	15.4	3.4	22.1
VILLAGE						
All areas [2]	22,712	100.0	55.6	15.0	4.2	25.2
Eastern Cotton	2,730	100.0	54.4	12.2	5.6	27.8
White	1,718	100.0	58.6	9.9	5.0	26.5
Negro	1,012	100.0	47.3	16.2	6.5	30.0
Western Cotton	2,582	100.0	54.6	16.8	5.3	23.3
White	1,922	100.0	58.3	13.4	4.7	23.6
Negro	660	100.0	43.9	26.7	7.0	22.4
Appalachian-Ozark	4,950	100.0	55.8	12.9	4.5	26.8
Lake States Cut-Over	1,300	100.0	51.3	16.9	3.2	28.6
Hay and Dairy	3,598	100.0	55.9	16.9	3.7	23.5
Corn Belt	4,710	100.0	55.6	15.6	3.9	24.9
Spring Wheat	988	100.0	61.3	15.4	3.2	20.1
Winter Wheat	618	100.0	58.6	11.0	1.9	28.5
Ranching	1,236	100.0	57.8	17.0	3.1	22.1

[1] Exclusive of families for which age of members was unknown.
[2] Exclusive of New England.

Table 20.—Structural Type of Rural Families Receiving General Relief, by Usual Occupation of Head, June 1935

[138 counties [1]]

Usual occupation	Total [2]		Normal families					Broken families					Nonfamily types				
	Number	Percent	Total	Husband and wife		Husband, wife, and children		Total	Father and children		Mother and children		Total	Male head		Female head	
				Without others	With others	Without others	With others		Without others	With others	Without others	With others		Without others	With others	Without others	With others
Total	58,454	100.0	73.0	11.5	2.1	53.8	5.6	10.9	1.9	0.7	6.7	1.6	16.1	6.4	4.8	3.1	1.8
Agriculture	24,976	100.0	82.2	8.3	2.1	64.5	7.3	8.7	2.0	0.8	4.3	1.6	9.1	2.3	5.5	0.4	0.9
Farm operator	18,126	100.0	84.0	7.1	2.1	66.9	7.9	7.9	1.8	0.8	3.9	1.4	8.1	1.7	5.3	0.3	0.8
Owner	6,418	100.0	75.0	6.0	2.1	59.0	7.9	11.5	2.0	1.0	6.3	2.2	13.5	2.9	8.3	0.7	1.6
Tenant	9,684	100.0	89.9	7.2	1.8	72.8	8.1	5.0	1.5	0.6	2.1	0.8	5.1	1.1	3.6	0.1	0.3
Cropper [3]	2,024	100.0	83.4	9.5	3.5	63.2	7.2	10.5	2.8	1.3	4.8	1.6	6.1	1.0	4.1	0.2	0.8
Farm laborer	6,850	100.0	77.8	11.5	1.9	58.5	5.7	10.5	2.3	0.6	5.6	2.0	11.7	3.7	6.1	0.7	1.2
Nonagriculture	23,136	100.0	77.4	10.4	1.9	59.7	5.4	8.7	2.0	0.7	5.0	1.0	13.9	6.0	5.0	1.4	1.5
White collar	2,022	100.0	71.5	12.4	1.5	51.7	5.9	10.2	1.6	0.7	6.6	1.3	18.3	3.8	4.5	4.3	5.7
Skilled	3,260	100.0	88.0	10.5	1.7	70.3	5.7	3.2	2.5	0.6	0.1	—	8.8	4.2	4.5	—	0.1
Semiskilled	3,360	100.0	82.8	10.8	2.6	64.4	5.3	8.0	1.5	0.6	4.8	1.1	9.2	3.3	3.6	1.2	1.1
Unskilled	14,494	100.0	74.5	10.2	1.9	57.2	5.2	9.9	2.1	0.7	5.9	1.2	15.6	7.4	5.6	1.3	1.3
No usual occupation	1,414	100.0	20.9	5.8	0.7	12.6	1.8	50.9	0.4	0.3	42.3	7.9	28.2	3.8	8.9	9.1	6.4
Nonworker	8,928	100.0	43.6	24.5	3.1	14.1	1.9	16.8	1.7	0.5	12.0	2.6	39.6	19.4	1.7	14.1	4.4

[1] Exclusive of New England townships.
[2] Exclusive of families whose type was unknown.
[3] In the 2 Cotton Areas.

Table 21.—Structural Type of Rural Families Receiving General Relief, by Residence and Area, June 1935

[138 counties and 116 New England townships]

Residence and area	Total [1] Number	Total [1] Percent	Normal families Total	Husband and wife Without others	Husband and wife With others	Husband, wife, and children Without others	Husband, wife, and children With others	Broken families Total	Father and children Without others	Father and children With others	Mother and children Without others	Mother and children With others	Nonfamily types Total	Male head Without others	Male head With others	Female head Without others	Female head With others
TOTAL RURAL																	
All areas	62,809	100.0	72.5	11.6	2.2	53.2	5.5	10.9	1.9	0.8	6.6	1.6	16.6	6.6	5.0	3.2	1.8
Eastern Cotton	7,732	100.0	62.6	11.0	3.1	41.4	7.1	19.0	2.0	0.7	11.8	4.5	18.4	4.6	3.8	5.7	4.3
White	5,084	100.0	68.8	10.5	2.2	49.2	6.9	17.7	2.2	0.5	11.3	3.4	13.5	3.3	3.9	3.3	3.0
Negro	2,648	100.0	50.7	12.1	4.7	28.5	7.4	21.4	1.7	1.0	12.6	6.6	27.9	4.6	5.1	10.5	6.7
Western Cotton	7,268	100.0	70.4	12.1	2.5	49.0	6.1	13.5	1.9	0.8	8.1	2.0	16.1	3.4	4.8	4.1	2.3
White	5,432	100.0	76.1	12.8	2.9	54.9	6.4	11.9	1.9	0.8	7.7	1.5	12.0	3.4	5.1	2.1	1.7
Negro	1,836	100.0	53.6	12.6	3.0	31.7	5.4	18.3	1.9	1.6	11.4	3.4	28.1	8.0	5.9	10.0	4.2
Appalachian-Ozark	17,016	100.0	76.5	10.1	2.4	57.4	6.6	10.7	2.0	0.8	6.3	1.6	12.8	4.4	5.1	1.7	1.6
Lake States Cut-Over	3,792	100.0	63.9	11.1	1.7	48.2	3.4	8.5	2.3	0.4	5.4	0.4	27.6	19.3	5.0	2.5	0.8
Corn Belt	8,626	100.0	76.0	12.5	1.2	57.3	4.5	7.7	1.6	0.5	5.0	0.6	16.3	7.2	4.7	3.0	1.3
Hay and Dairy	7,512	100.0	76.6	13.3	1.0	56.0	5.3	7.7	1.9	0.6	4.7	0.8	15.4	5.9	5.2	2.0	1.3
Spring Wheat	3,374	100.0	79.8	8.7	2.0	66.4	3.7	6.6	1.8	0.6	3.5	0.7	13.6	6.5	4.5	1.8	0.8
Winter Wheat	1,288	100.0	79.2	17.7	2.2	55.3	4.0	8.4	2.0	0.6	4.1	1.7	12.4	5.1	5.3	1.7	0.3
Ranching	1,886	100.0	67.2	12.0	1.6	50.8	2.8	9.3	1.5	0.4	6.9	0.8	23.5	12.2	4.1	5.4	1.8
New England	4,315	100.0	66.7	12.3	2.5	47.4	4.5	9.6	2.3	0.4	5.9	1.0	23.7	11.0	7.0	4.1	1.6
OPEN COUNTRY																	
All areas [1]	35,782	100.0	76.2	10.5	2.2	57.0	6.5	10.1	1.9	0.7	5.8	1.7	13.7	5.3	4.6	2.2	1.6
Eastern Cotton	5,002	100.0	64.1	10.5	3.1	42.5	8.0	18.7	1.8	0.7	11.3	4.9	17.2	4.3	3.7	5.3	3.9
White	3,366	100.0	70.8	10.3	2.0	51.1	7.4	17.2	2.1	0.9	10.5	3.7	12.0	3.4	3.7	2.4	2.5
Negro	1,636	100.0	50.2	10.9	5.4	24.7	9.2	21.9	1.2	0.4	12.8	7.5	27.9	6.1	3.9	11.1	6.8
Western Cotton	4,086	100.0	74.6	12.1	2.5	53.2	6.8	11.8	2.1	1.1	6.5	2.1	13.6	4.0	4.9	3.0	1.7
White	3,510	100.0	80.5	12.6	2.9	59.0	7.0	9.7	2.1	0.9	5.5	1.3	9.8	3.1	4.5	1.1	1.1
Negro	1,176	100.0	57.0	10.4	4.4	35.9	6.3	17.8	2.6	1.7	9.3	4.2	25.2	6.8	6.0	8.8	3.6

Area	Number	Total															
Appalachian-Ozark	12,066	100.0	80.5	8.9	2.4	61.9	7.3	9.8	1.8	0.9	5.6	1.5	9.7	2.0	4.9	1.1	1.5
Lake States Cut-Over	2,492	100.0	64.3	11.2	1.3	47.8	4.0	8.4	2.2	0.5	5.2	0.5	27.3	19.8	5.4	2.2	0.7
Hay and Dairy	5,028	100.0	78.3	11.7	1.9	59.3	4.5	7.0	1.7	0.5	4.3	0.5	14.7	6.8	4.6	2.2	1.1
Corn Belt	2,802	100.0	83.1	12.3	2.5	62.2	6.1	5.8	1.7	0.6	2.7	0.6	11.1	4.8	4.2	1.3	0.8
Spring Wheat	2,386	100.0	83.6	8.1	0.8	70.8	3.9	4.6	1.9	0.4	1.9	0.5	11.8	6.7	4.0	0.6	0.3
Winter Wheat	670	100.0	83.6	16.1	3.3	58.2	6.0	6.0	1.8	0.3	2.4	1.5	10.4	4.5	5.3	0.3	0.3
Ranching	650	100.0	67.4	11.1	1.5	51.4	3.4	7.4	1.9	0.3	4.9	0.3	25.2	15.1	4.3	4.3	1.5
All areas [2]	22,712	100.0	67.9	13.2	2.0	48.5	4.2	12.2	2.0	0.5	8.1	1.6	19.9	8.1	5.1	4.5	2.2
VILLAGE																	
Eastern Cotton	2,730	100.0	59.8	12.0	3.0	39.4	5.4	19.5	2.4	0.7	12.7	3.7	20.7	5.1	4.0	6.6	5.0
White	1,718	100.0	64.7	10.8	2.7	45.3	5.9	18.8	2.3	0.6	13.1	2.8	16.5	3.3	4.3	4.9	4.0
Negro	1,012	100.0	51.4	14.0	3.6	29.3	4.5	20.8	2.4	0.8	12.3	5.3	27.8	8.3	3.5	9.5	6.5
Western Cotton	2,582	100.0	62.9	14.3	2.3	41.3	5.0	16.7	1.4	0.9	12.5	1.9	20.4	5.6	5.4	6.0	3.4
White	1,922	100.0	68.2	13.5	2.1	47.3	5.3	15.9	1.7	0.7	11.5	2.0	15.9	4.1	5.2	0.9	2.7
Negro	660	100.0	47.6	16.7	2.3	24.0	3.9	19.1	0.6	1.5	15.2	1.8	33.3	10.7	5.8	12.1	5.4
Appalachian-Ozark	4,950	100.0	66.7	13.1	2.3	46.2	4.6	12.9	2.5	0.5	8.5	1.7	20.3	9.7	5.6	3.1	0.9
Lake States Cut-Over	1,300	100.0	63.1	10.9	1.5	49.4	2.0	8.7	2.4	0.1	8.1	0.5	28.3	19.8	4.8	3.1	3.1
Hay and Dairy	3,598	100.0	72.9	13.6	1.7	54.2	4.8	9.3	1.9	0.5	6.1	1.0	17.9	7.7	5.7	4.4	0.5
Corn Belt	4,710	100.0	72.8	14.0	1.6	52.5	4.1	11.3	1.8	0.5	5.9	0.7	18.4	6.5	5.2	4.0	1.6
Spring Wheat	988	100.0	70.7	10.1	1.0	55.6	3.1	11.0	2.3	1.0	7.3	1.2	17.9	6.1	5.7	4.6	1.6
Winter Wheat	618	100.0	74.4	19.4	1.6	52.1	1.9	11.3	2.3	1.0	5.8	1.9	14.6	5.8	5.2	3.0	0.3
Ranching	1,236	100.0	67.1	12.4		50.5	2.6	10.4	1.3	—	7.9	1.2	22.5	10.7	3.9	6.0	1.9

[1] Exclusive of families whose type was unknown.
[2] Exclusive of New England.

Table 22.—Structural Type of Rural Families Receiving General Relief in the Eastern and Western Cotton Areas, by Color and Usual Occupation of Head, June 1935

[44 counties]

Color and usual occupation of head	Total¹ Number	Total¹ Percent	Normal families — Total	Husband and wife — Without others	Husband and wife — With others	Husband, wife, and children — Without others	Husband, wife, and children — With others	Broken families — Total	Father and children — Without others	Father and children — With others	Mother and children — Without others	Mother and children — With others	Nonfamily types — Total	Male head — Without others	Male head — With others	Female head — Without others	Female head — With others
WHITE																	
Total	10,512	100.0	72.5	11.8	2.1	52.0	6.6	14.8	2.0	0.8	9.5	2.5	12.7	3.4	4.3	2.7	2.3
Agriculture	5,502	100.0	80.9	8.8	1.9	61.7	8.5	11.7	2.4	1.1	6.2	2.0	7.4	1.1	4.9	0.3	1.1
Farm operator	3,562	100.0	83.5	7.8	2.0	64.6	9.1	10.1	2.2	1.2	4.6	2.1	6.4	0.6	4.4	0.3	1.1
Owner	604	100.0	64.2	6.6	0.7	43.7	13.2	20.9	1.6	1.7	11.9	6.1	14.9	0.7	7.3	0.1	5.0
Tenant	1,438	100.0	88.5	7.1	1.5	70.2	9.7	6.6	1.6	1.3	2.6	1.1	4.9	0.1	3.8	—	0.3
Cropper	1,520	100.0	86.4	8.9	2.9	67.8	6.8	9.4	3.4	1.7	4.1	0.8	4.2	2.0	5.8	0.2	1.2
Farm laborer	1,940	100.0	76.4	10.7	2.2	56.4	7.5	14.4	2.6	0.7	8.8	2.0	9.2	3.0	6.0	0.2	2.8
Nonagriculture	3,164	100.0	74.5	11.5	2.8	55.3	6.3	13.3	2.6	0.4	9.3	2.0	12.2	3.2	5.1	0.2	2.8
White collar	504	100.0	58.3	11.6	2.2	38.9	6.7	13.1	0.8		11.5	2.8	26.5	3.0	6.0	8.3	9.1
Skilled	472	100.0	89.9	8.7	3.9	67.8	8.1	1.2	0.4		0.4		8.8	0.8	4.2	1.0	0.4
Semiskilled	762	100.0	77.0	11.5	3.4	55.8	6.6	15.7	2.1	0.8	10.5	3.1	7.7	2.0	4.2	1.5	1.3
Unskilled	1,426	100.0	74.0	8.5	1.4	55.8	5.3	15.3	2.1	0.6	10.9	1.7	10.7	1.7	5.0	14.4	2.2
No usual occupation	348	100.0	6.3	1.7		4.6		70.2		1.1	57.6	11.5	23.5	1.7	1.7	14.4	5.7
Nonworker	1,498	100.0	52.6	27.1	2.8	20.7	2.0	16.3	2.0	0.7	10.5	3.1	31.1	15.2	1.5	9.6	4.8
NEGRO																	
Total	4,484	100.0	51.9	12.3	4.4	28.6	6.6	20.1	1.7	1.0	12.1	5.3	28.0	7.4	4.6	10.3	5.7
Agriculture	2,114	100.0	63.1	7.7	4.7	40.2	10.5	22.2	2.3	1.1	12.6	6.2	14.7	2.5	7.2	2.4	3.8
Farm operator	1,104	100.0	76.2	7.6	6.2	48.8	13.6	11.7	2.2	1.6	3.4	3.4	12.1	2.3	7.3	0.7	2.2
Owner	154	100.0	67.5	9.1	9.1	37.6	11.7	10.4	2.6	0.9	3.9	3.6	22.1	14.3	7.6	2.6	2.9
Tenant	446	100.0	80.9	2.7	5.2	51.2	20.7	9.8	1.3	0.9	4.0	3.6	9.3	0.4	7.6	0.8	1.3
Cropper	504	100.0	74.5	11.5	5.2	49.9	7.9	13.9	0.8	0.6	7.1	4.0	11.6	3.6	4.6	0.8	2.4
Farm laborer	1,010	100.0	49.0	12.8	4.2	31.0	7.1	33.7	3.4	0.6	20.4	9.3	17.3	3.6	4.6	4.2	5.5
Nonagriculture	1,050	100.0	54.6		4.1	33.2	4.4	25.5	1.0	1.1	17.3	6.1	19.9	4.4	4.8	4.6	6.1
White collar	48	†															
Skilled	60	100.0	83.4	26.7	6.7	40.0	10.0	13.3	3.3	6.7	3.3		3.3			3.3	
Semiskilled	30	†															
Unskilled	912	100.0	51.0	12.3	4.4	30.8	3.5	27.4	0.7	0.9	19.4	6.4	21.6	4.4	5.3	5.3	6.6
No usual occupation	30	†															
Nonworker	1,290	100.0	19.4	19.4	4.0	6.2	2.0	11.7	3.3	0.6	3.3	3.3	56.7	18.0	2.5	27.5	8.7

¹ Exclusive of families whose type was unknown.

† Percent not computed on a base of fewer than 50 cases.

Table 23.—Rural 1-Person Families Receiving General Relief in the Eastern and Western Cotton Areas, by Residence, Color, Age, and Sex, June 1935

[44 counties]

Residence, area, and color	All 1-person families								1-person families 65 years of age and over								
	Total		Male			Female			Total			Male			Female		
	Number of families	Percent of all families	Number of families	Percent of all 1-person families	Percent of all families	Number of families	Percent of all 1-person families	Percent of all families	Number of families	Percent of all 1-person families	Percent of all families	Number of families	Percent of all 1-person families	Percent of all male 1-person families	Number of families	Percent of all 1-person families	Percent of all female 1-person families
TOTAL RURAL																	
Eastern Cotton	796	10.3	354	44.5	4.6	442	55.5	5.7	378	47.5	4.9	170	21.4	48.0	208	26.1	47.1
White	336	6.6	170	50.6	3.3	166	49.4	3.3	110	32.7	2.2	66	19.6	38.8	44	13.1	26.5
Negro	460	17.4	184	40.0	6.9	276	60.0	10.5	268	58.3	10.1	104	22.6	56.5	164	35.7	59.4
Western Cotton	630	8.7	332	52.7	4.6	298	47.3	4.1	346	54.9	4.8	176	27.9	53.0	170	27.0	57.0
White	300	5.5	186	62.0	3.4	114	38.0	2.1	148	49.3	2.7	100	33.3	53.8	48	16.0	42.1
Negro	330	18.0	146	44.2	8.0	184	55.8	10.0	198	60.0	10.8	76	23.0	52.1	122	37.0	66.3
OPEN COUNTRY																	
Eastern Cotton	476	9.5	214	45.0	4.3	262	55.0	5.2	266	55.9	5.3	128	26.9	59.8	138	29.0	52.7
White	196	5.8	114	58.2	3.4	82	41.8	2.4	78	39.8	2.3	54	27.6	47.4	24	12.2	29.3
Negro	280	17.1	100	35.7	6.1	180	64.3	11.0	188	67.1	11.5	74	26.4	74.0	114	40.7	63.3
Western Cotton	330	7.0	188	57.0	4.0	142	43.0	3.0	178	53.9	3.8	94	28.5	50.0	84	25.4	59.2
White	146	4.2	108	74.0	3.1	38	26.0	1.1	70	47.9	1.1	54	37.0	50.0	16	10.9	42.1
Negro	184	15.6	80	43.5	6.8	104	56.5	8.8	108	58.7	9.2	40	21.7	50.0	68	37.0	65.4
VILLAGE																	
Eastern Cotton	320	11.7	140	43.8	5.1	180	56.2	6.6	112	35.0	4.1	42	13.1	30.0	70	21.9	38.9
White	140	8.1	56	40.0	3.3	84	60.0	4.8	32	22.9	1.9	12	8.6	21.4	20	14.3	23.8
Negro	180	17.8	84	46.7	8.3	96	53.3	9.5	80	44.4	7.9	30	16.7	35.7	50	27.7	52.1
Western Cotton	300	11.6	144	48.0	5.6	156	52.0	6.0	108	56.0	6.5	82	27.3	56.9	86	28.7	55.1
White	154	8.0	78	50.6	4.1	76	49.4	3.9	78	50.6	4.1	46	29.9	59.0	32	20.7	42.2
Negro	146	22.1	66	45.2	10.0	80	54.8	12.1	90	61.6	13.6	36	24.7	54.5	54	36.9	67.5

Table 24.—Employment Status of Workers [1] in Rural Families Receiving General Relief in the Eastern and Western Cotton Areas, by Color and Usual Occupation, June 1935

[44 counties]

Color and usual occupation	Total workers [2]		Employed		Unemployed	Total employed workers		At usual occupation	At other than usual occupation
	Number	Percent	Agriculture	Nonagriculture		Number	Percent		
WHITE									
Total	13,902	100.0	30.1	6.8	63.1	5,130	100.0	88.4	11.6
Agriculture	8,118	100.0	49.7	1.7	48.6	4,176	100.0	91.7	8.3
Farm operator	3,644	100.0	67.4	2.5	30.1	2,546	100.0	89.9	10.1
Owner	622	100.0	86.9	0.6	12.5	544	100.0	97.8	2.2
Tenant	1,474	100.0	75.9	2.0	22.1	1,148	100.0	92.2	7.8
Cropper	1,548	100.0	51.5	3.7	44.8	854	100.0	82.0	18.0
Farm laborer	4,474	100.0	35.3	1.1	63.6	1,630	100.0	94.4	5.6
Nonagriculture	4,290	100.0	3.6	18.6	77.8	954	100.0	74.2	25.8
White collar	738	100.0	1.9	20.9	77.2	168	100.0	78.6	21.4
Skilled	532	100.0	6.4	17.3	76.3	126	100.0	46.0	54.0
Semiskilled	1,100	100.0	3.1	15.5	81.4	204	100.0	73.5	26.5
Unskilled	1,920	100.0	3.9	19.9	76.2	456	100.0	80.7	19.3
No usual occupation	1,494	100.0	—	—	100.0	—	—	—	—
NEGRO									
Total	5,486	100.0	34.1	10.4	55.5	2,444	100.0	95.5	4.5
Agriculture	3,616	100.0	51.3	0.8	47.9	1,884	100.0	95.6	4.4
Farm operator	1,130	100.0	74.2	0.7	25.1	846	100.0	94.1	5.9
Owner	156	100.0	88.4	2.6	9.0	142	100.0	94.4	5.6
Tenant	452	100.0	85.4	0.9	13.7	390	100.0	93.6	6.4
Cropper	522	100.0	60.2	—	39.8	314	100.0	96.9	3.1
Farm laborer	2,486	100.0	40.9	0.9	58.2	1,038	100.0	95.3	4.7
Nonagriculture	1,542	100.0	1.0	35.1	63.9	558	100.0	†	†
White collar	34	†	†	†	†	14	†	†	†
Skilled	54	100.0	3.7	14.8	81.5	10	†	†	†
Semiskilled	66	100.0	3.0	21.2	75.8	16	†	†	†
Unskilled	1,388	100.0	0.7	36.6	62.7	518	100.0	97.3	2.7
No usual occupation	328	100.0	0.6	—	99.4	2	†	†	†

† Percent not computed on a base of fewer than 50 cases.
[1] Persons 16 through 64 years of age working or seeking work.
[2] Exclusive of workers whose usual occupation or employment status was unknown.

Table 25.—Reason for Accession of Rural Families Receiving General Relief, by Residence and Area, June 1935

[138 counties and 116 New England townships]

Residence and area	Total [1]		Loss of employ-ment [2]	Loss or deple-tion of assets	Crop failure or loss of live-stock	Insuf-ficient income	Became unem-ployable	Other reasons
	Number	Percent						
TOTAL RURAL								
All areas	62,829	100.0	24.6	33.6	13.6	12.4	5.2	10.6
Eastern Cotton	7,732	100.0	27.3	22.1	8.4	14.7	10.1	17.4
White	5,084	100.0	27.3	26.1	8.6	11.4	8.1	18.5
Negro	2,648	100.0	27.4	14.4	8.0	20.9	14.0	15.3
Western Cotton	7,268	100.0	28.5	21.2	19.3	11.9	2.7	16.4
White	5,432	100.0	28.9	23.2	19.9	11.3	2.5	14.2
Negro	1,836	100.0	27.5	15.5	17.4	13.5	3.3	22.8
Appalachian-Ozark	17,016	100.0	14.1	48.6	10.7	11.5	5.5	9.6
Lake States Cut-Over	3,814	100.0	27.2	34.2	8.9	10.9	5.1	13.7
Hay and Dairy	8,626	100.0	35.5	29.1	8.4	14.2	6.6	6.2
Corn Belt	7,512	100.0	30.2	30.1	13.2	14.3	1.8	10.4
Spring Wheat	3,374	100.0	13.6	14.8	59.4	5.0	4.8	2.4
Winter Wheat	1,288	100.0	18.0	33.3	22.4	12.0	2.5	11.8
Ranching	1,886	100.0	34.8	26.7	16.5	8.9	2.9	10.2
New England	4,313	100.0	26.2	48.9	0.2	14.5	6.0	4.2
OPEN COUNTRY								
All areas [3]	35,802	100.0	17.7	31.7	22.1	13.1	4.7	10.7
Eastern Cotton	5,002	100.0	23.6	20.9	12.1	15.0	10.3	18.1
White	3,366	100.0	24.2	24.8	11.9	12.2	8.1	18.8
Negro	1,636	100.0	22.4	13.1	12.3	20.8	14.7	16.7
Western Cotton	4,686	100.0	22.4	20.9	28.3	10.3	2.0	16.1
White	3,510	100.0	22.4	22.1	29.1	10.1	1.7	14.6
Negro	1,176	100.0	22.3	17.2	26.0	10.9	3.2	20.4
Appalachian-Ozark	12,066	100.0	9.7	48.3	13.8	13.8	5.0	9.4
Lake States Cut-Over	2,512	100.0	20.4	37.4	12.7	12.9	3.9	12.7
Hay and Dairy	5,028	100.0	30.5	27.8	13.9	15.9	5.9	6.0
Corn Belt	2,802	100.0	21.3	21.1	31.9	16.8	1.0	7.9
Spring Wheat	2,386	100.0	4.4	8.4	81.4	2.4	1.5	1.9
Winter Wheat	670	100.0	9.3	23.6	39.7	12.5	1.5	13.4
Ranching	650	100.0	20.3	25.8	33.2	7.4	2.8	10.5
VILLAGE								
All areas [3]	22,714	100.0	35.0	33.9	2.7	10.9	5.8	11.7
Eastern Cotton	2,730	100.0	34.2	24.2	1.7	14.1	9.7	16.1
White	1,718	100.0	33.2	28.9	2.1	10.0	7.9	17.9
Negro	1,012	100.0	35.7	16.4	1.0	21.1	12.8	13.0
Western Cotton	2,582	100.0	39.8	21.9	2.9	14.6	3.8	17.0
White	1,922	100.0	40.7	25.2	3.2	13.4	4.0	13.5
Negro	660	100.0	37.0	12.4	2.1	18.2	3.3	27.0
Appalachian-Ozark	4,950	100.0	24.9	49.2	3.2	5.9	6.8	10.0
Lake States Cut-Over	1,302	100.0	39.9	27.5	1.4	6.9	7.4	16.9
Hay and Dairy	3,598	100.0	42.6	30.8	0.7	11.9	7.6	6.4
Corn Belt	4,710	100.0	35.5	35.6	2.0	12.8	2.3	11.8
Spring Wheat	988	100.0	35.8	30.2	6.5	11.1	7.9	8.5
Winter Wheat	618	100.0	27.5	44.0	3.6	11.3	3.6	10.0
Ranching	1,236	100.0	42.2	27.2	7.8	9.7	2.9	10.2

[1] Exclusive of cases for which reason for opening or reopening was unknown.
[2] Within 4 months prior to accession. For cases in which the worker lost his job more than 4 months prior to accession to relief, a more immediate reason for opening the case was given.
[3] Exclusive of New England.

Table 26.—Relief History of Rural Families Receiving Relief, by Residence and Area, June 1935

[138 counties and 116 New England townships]

Residence and area	Total [1]		Continuously on relief February through June	Opened March–June	Reopened March–June
	Number	Percent			
TOTAL RURAL All areas	62,823	100.0	74.3	11.5	14.2
Eastern Cotton	7,728	100.0	66.6	14.4	19.0
White	5,080	100.0	62.5	17.4	20.1
Negro	2,648	100.0	74.5	8.8	16.7
Western Cotton	7,268	100.0	80.3	8.3	11.4
White	5,432	100.0	79.1	9.2	11.7
Negro	1,836	100.0	83.9	5.4	10.7
Appalachian-Ozark	17,016	100.0	71.8	11.2	17.0
Lake States Cut-Over	3,812	100.0	73.3	11.3	15.4
Hay and Dairy	8,626	100.0	79.3	10.9	9.8
Corn Belt	7,512	100.0	77.5	11.9	10.6
Spring Wheat	3,374	100.0	81.4	4.9	13.7
Winter Wheat	1,288	100.0	76.7	6.2	17.1
Ranching	1,886	100.0	70.0	12.3	17.7
New England	4,313	100.0	68.8	19.1	12.1
OPEN COUNTRY All areas [2]	35,798	100.0	73.9	10.5	15.6
Eastern Cotton	5,000	100.0	66.5	12.8	20.7
White	3,364	100.0	62.1	15.4	22.5
Negro	1,636	100.0	75.3	7.7	17.0
Western Cotton	4,686	100.0	83.0	6.1	10.9
White	3,510	100.0	81.9	7.0	11.1
Negro	1,176	100.0	83.0	6.1	10.9
Appalachian-Ozark	12,066	100.0	70.1	10.9	19.0
Lake States Cut-Over	2,510	100.0	74.0	11.3	14.7
Hay and Dairy	5,028	100.0	79.7	11.2	9.1
Corn Belt	2,802	100.0	73.4	15.0	11.6
Spring Wheat	2,386	100.0	80.4	5.7	13.9
Winter Wheat	670	100.0	72.8	7.2	20.0
Ranching	650	100.0	70.6	11.8	17.6
VILLAGE All areas [2]	22,712	100.0	76.0	11.5	12.5
Eastern Cotton	2,728	100.0	66.9	17.4	15.7
White	1,716	100.0	63.2	21.4	15.4
Negro	1,012	100.0	73.3	10.5	16.2
Western Cotton	2,582	100.0	75.4	12.2	12.4
White	1,922	100.0	74.0	13.2	12.8
Negro	660	100.0	79.7	9.1	11.2
Appalachian-Ozark	4,950	100.0	76.2	12.0	11.8
Lake States Cut-Over	1,302	100.0	71.9	11.4	16.7
Hay and Dairy	3,598	100.0	78.8	10.4	10.8
Corn Belt	4,710	100.0	79.9	10.1	10.0
Spring Wheat	988	100.0	84.0	2.8	13.2
Winter Wheat	618	100.0	80.9	5.2	13.9
Ranching	1,236	100.0	69.7	12.6	17.7

[1] Exclusive of families whose relief history was unknown.
[2] Exclusive of New England.

Table 27.—Average [1] Amount of General Relief Received by Rural Families, by Residence, Area, and Type of Relief, June 1935

[138 counties and 83 New England townships [2]]

Residence and area	Total [3]		Work relief		Direct relief		Both work and direct relief	
	Number of families	Average amount of relief	Number of families	Average amount of relief	Number of families	Average amount of relief	Number of families	Average amount of relief
TOTAL RURAL								
All areas	57,827	$17	27,117	$18	22,440	$13	8,270	$25
Eastern Cotton	7,026	12	3,092	14	2,524	7	1,410	15
White	4,558	14	2,224	16	1,288	8	1,046	16
Negro	2,468	8	868	10	1,236	5	364	13
Western Cotton	6,892	10	3,616	11	2,408	7	868	14
White	5,152	11	2,942	11	1,510	7	700	15
Negro	1,740	8	674	10	898	6	168	12
Appalachian-Ozark	16,084	12	9,348	12	4,846	10	1,890	19
Lake States Cut-Over	3,538	23	654	24	2,118	18	766	36
Hay and Dairy	8,106	23	2,160	29	5,090	19	856	36
Corn Belt	6,944	18	3,344	19	2,774	14	826	30
Spring Wheat	3,180	22	1,552	19	640	14	988	30
Winter Wheat	1,212	16	762	15	226	13	224	24
Ranching	1,686	18	388	19	1,084	15	214	31
New England	3,159	37	2,201	41	730	21	228	55
OPEN COUNTRY								
All areas [4]	33,476	15	15,950	14	12,838	12	4,688	23
Eastern Cotton	4,530	10	1,764	12	1,918	7	848	15
White	3,044	12	1,372	13	1,040	8	632	16
Negro	1,486	8	392	10	878	5	216	13
Western Cotton	4,480	10	2,340	11	1,604	7	536	14
White	3,352	10	1,920	11	1,010	7	422	15
Negro	1,128	8	420	10	594	6	114	13
Appalachian-Ozark	11,392	12	7,290	12	3,004	9	1,098	17
Lake States Cut-Over	2,318	22	412	22	1,408	17	498	34
Hay and Dairy	4,734	23	1,288	27	2,952	18	494	36
Corn Belt	2,538	17	1,296	16	964	15	278	29
Spring Wheat	2,264	21	1,028	17	458	13	778	30
Winter Wheat	628	14	424	13	108	13	96	19
Ranching	592	18	108	21	422	15	62	33
VILLAGE								
All areas [4]	21,192	18	8,966	18	8,872	14	3,354	26
Eastern Cotton	2,496	14	1,328	17	606	7	562	16
White	1,514	18	852	20	248	9	414	17
Negro	982	9	476	10	358	5	148	13
Western Cotton	2,412	10	1,276	11	804	6	332	14
White	1,800	11	1,022	12	500	7	278	15
Negro	612	7	254	9	304	5	54	11
Appalachian-Ozark	4,692	14	2,058	13	1,842	13	792	23
Lake States Cut-Over	1,220	25	242	26	710	19	268	41
Hay and Dairy	3,372	24	872	31	2,138	19	362	37
Corn Belt	4,406	19	2,048	21	1,810	14	548	30
Spring Wheat	916	24	524	23	182	15	210	33
Winter Wheat	584	18	338	17	118	13	128	27
Ranching	1,094	18	280	18	662	15	152	29

[1] Mean.
[2] Townships in Connecticut and Massachusetts only.
[3] Exclusive of cases opened or reopened during the month and of cases for which type or amount of relief was unknown.
[4] Exclusive of New England.

Table 28.—Amount of General Relief Received by Rural Families, by Residence and Area, June 1935

[138 counties and 116 New England townships]

Residence and area	Total [1]		Amount of relief						
	Number	Percent	$1–$4	$5–$9	$10–$14	$15–$19	$20–$29	$30–$59	$60 or more
TOTAL RURAL									
All areas	58,557	100.0	10.4	24.2	21.9	12.8	15.0	13.9	1.8
Eastern Cotton	7,026	100.0	20.2	29.6	25.5	11.6	7.6	5.0	0.5
White	4,558	100.0	13.5	27.4	27.8	12.9	10.1	7.5	0.8
Negro	2,468	100.0	32.8	33.3	21.3	9.2	3.0	0.4	—
Western Cotton	6,892	100.0	19.3	41.7	22.4	9.4	4.6	2.1	0.5
White	5,152	100.0	16.2	40.8	24.2	10.1	5.4	2.7	0.6
Negro	1,740	100.0	28.6	43.9	17.2	7.6	2.1	0.5	0.1
Appalachian-Ozark	16,084	100.0	11.7	31.7	28.8	12.1	10.9	4.4	0.4
Lake States Cut-Over	3,538	100.0	3.2	18.8	16.8	13.6	19.7	23.9	4.0
Hay and Dairy	8,106	100.0	3.9	13.3	14.9	14.8	24.0	26.8	2.3
Corn Belt	6,944	100.0	8.8	17.7	19.4	16.0	21.5	15.7	0.9
Spring Wheat	3,180	100.0	5.6	14.5	18.8	15.2	23.6	19.2	3.1
Winter Wheat	1,212	100.0	10.4	24.9	21.3	13.0	17.3	12.4	0.7
Ranching	1,686	100.0	2.5	13.2	29.7	19.3	23.6	10.6	1.1
New England	3,889	100.0	1.9	5.4	9.1	8.0	17.3	48.5	9.8
OPEN COUNTRY									
All areas [2]	33,476	100.0	12.1	27.9	24.1	12.5	13.0	9.5	0.9
Eastern Cotton	4,530	100.0	23.2	31.3	24.5	11.2	6.8	2.8	0.2
White	3,044	100.0	16.4	30.3	28.3	12.1	8.7	3.9	0.3
Negro	1,486	100.0	37.2	33.5	16.8	9.2	2.8	0.5	—
Western Cotton	4,480	100.0	17.9	43.1	24.4	9.6	4.7	2.0	0.3
White	3,352	100.0	15.8	41.9	24.2	9.9	5.3	2.6	0.3
Negro	1,128	100.0	24.1	46.6	17.0	8.9	3.0	0.2	0.2
Appalachian-Ozark	11,392	100.0	12.0	33.3	31.0	11.7	8.5	3.2	0.3
Lake States Cut-Over	2,318	100.0	3.7	19.0	18.3	14.0	20.6	21.1	3.3
Hay and Dairy	4,734	100.0	4.1	13.6	15.8	14.9	24.3	25.3	2.0
Corn Belt	2,538	100.0	12.2	19.6	20.4	13.9	18.8	14.3	0.8
Spring Wheat	2,264	100.0	6.4	15.7	19.3	15.0	22.7	18.6	2.3
Winter Wheat	628	100.0	10.2	29.3	24.2	12.4	15.0	8.6	0.3
Ranching	592	100.0	2.4	13.8	25.0	20.3	26.7	10.8	1.0
VILLAGE									
All areas [2]	21,192	100.0	9.4	22.1	20.7	14.1	17.6	14.5	1.6
Eastern Cotton	2,496	100.0	14.8	26.3	27.3	12.4	9.1	9.0	1.1
White	1,514	100.0	7.5	21.8	26.9	14.4	12.8	14.7	1.9
Negro	982	100.0	26.1	32.9	28.1	9.0	3.3	0.2	—
Western Cotton	2,412	100.0	22.1	38.8	22.5	9.0	4.3	2.4	0.9
White	1,800	100.0	17.0	38.9	24.0	10.3	5.7	2.9	1.2
Negro	612	100.0	36.9	39.0	17.6	5.2	0.3	1.0	—
Appalachian-Ozark	4,692	100.0	10.9	28.2	23.2	13.1	16.8	7.3	0.5
Lake States Cut-Over	1,220	100.0	2.3	18.5	14.1	13.0	17.9	28.8	5.4
Hay and Dairy	3,372	100.0	3.6	12.9	13.8	14.7	23.4	28.8	2.8
Corn Belt	4,406	100.0	6.9	16.6	18.7	17.2	23.0	16.6	1.0
Spring Wheat	916	100.0	3.7	11.4	17.5	15.7	26.0	20.7	5.0
Winter Wheat	584	100.0	10.6	20.2	18.2	13.7	19.9	16.4	1.0
Ranching	1,094	100.0	2.6	12.8	32.4	18.8	21.9	10.4	1.1

[1] Exclusive of cases opened or reopened during the month and of cases for which amount of relief was unknown.

[2] Exclusive of New England.

Table 29.—Length of Last Continuous Residence in County of Heads of Rural Families Receiving General Relief, by Residence and Usual Occupation, June 1935

[138 counties and 116 New England townships]

Residence and usual occupation	Total [1]		Years of last continuous residence in county						
	Number	Percent	1 or less	2–3	4–5	6–9	10–14	15–19	20 or more
TOTAL RURAL									
Total	62,256	100.0	3.4	5.7	5.1	10.2	8.1	8.2	59.3
Agriculture	25,296	100.0	3.5	5.6	5.0	9.2	6.7	6.8	63.2
Farm operator	18,277	100.0	3.0	4.6	4.3	7.8	6.1	7.0	67.2
Owner	6,646	100.0	1.0	2.8	3.1	5.9	6.0	7.6	73.6
Tenant	9,633	100.0	3.9	5.4	4.7	8.3	5.8	6.3	65.6
Cropper [2]	1,998	100.0	5.5	7.2	6.8	11.7	8.2	7.8	52.8
Farm laborer	7,019	100.0	4.6	8.1	6.9	12.9	8.3	6.4	52.8
Nonagriculture	25,729	100.0	3.9	6.8	6.1	12.0	9.4	8.9	52.9
White collar	2,296	100.0	5.3	7.6	8.1	11.2	7.8	8.5	51.5
Skilled	3,770	100.0	3.7	8.5	8.8	13.8	9.5	8.4	47.3
Semiskilled	4,272	100.0	4.1	9.1	6.2	12.4	9.9	9.1	49.2
Unskilled	15,391	100.0	3.7	5.5	5.1	11.5	9.4	9.1	55.7
No usual occupation	1,538	100.0	2.2	4.3	3.6	8.7	9.0	11.9	60.3
Nonworker	9,693	100.0	2.3	3.5	3.0	8.4	8.1	9.1	65.6
OPEN COUNTRY [3]									
Total	35,474	100.0	3.6	5.9	5.1	9.1	6.8	6.9	62.6
Agriculture	20,312	100.0	3.3	5.4	4.8	8.6	6.3	6.4	65.2
Farm operator	15,976	100.0	2.9	4.4	4.1	7.4	5.9	6.7	68.6
Owner	5,756	100.0	0.7	2.5	3.0	5.9	5.6	7.5	74.8
Tenant	8,534	100.0	3.8	5.1	4.3	7.8	5.6	6.0	67.4
Cropper [2]	1,686	100.0	5.6	7.7	6.6	10.4	7.9	7.4	54.4
Farm laborer	4,336	100.0	5.1	9.0	7.3	13.0	8.0	5.6	52.0
Nonagriculture	9,798	100.0	4.6	8.1	7.0	11.0	8.0	7.2	54.1
White collar	604	100.0	7.3	9.3	12.6	12.9	8.3	8.3	41.3
Skilled	1,276	100.0	4.2	11.6	12.1	15.4	8.0	8.2	40.5
Semiskilled	1,474	100.0	6.0	12.6	7.6	10.7	7.3	7.3	48.5
Unskilled	6,444	100.0	4.2	6.2	5.3	10.0	8.1	7.0	59.2
No usual occupation	672	100.0	2.1	4.5	3.3	8.6	6.5	9.2	65.8
Nonworker	4,692	100.0	2.8	3.9	3.1	7.8	6.4	8.3	67.7
VILLAGE [3]									
Total	22,550	100.0	3.5	5.9	5.3	11.7	9.1	9.5	55.0
Agriculture	4,440	100.0	4.3	6.8	6.5	11.6	7.6	8.0	55.2
Farm operator	2,008	100.0	4.7	6.5	6.4	10.4	6.5	8.6	56.9
Owner	618	100.0	4.2	4.9	3.6	4.2	4.5	6.8	71.8
Tenant	1,078	100.0	4.8	8.0	7.6	11.5	6.7	9.1	52.3
Cropper [2]	312	100.0	5.1	4.5	7.7	18.6	9.6	10.3	44.2
Farm laborer	2,432	100.0	4.0	7.0	6.7	12.6	8.6	7.5	53.6
Nonagriculture	13,230	100.0	3.8	6.5	5.7	12.8	9.7	9.7	51.8
White collar	1,404	100.0	5.3	7.0	6.7	10.5	7.4	8.8	54.3
Skilled	1,966	100.0	3.8	7.8	7.4	13.1	10.2	8.0	49.7
Semiskilled	1,880	100.0	3.7	8.8	5.5	14.8	9.8	8.4	49.0
Unskilled	7,980	100.0	3.5	5.5	5.1	12.6	10.0	10.6	52.7
No usual occupation	736	100.0	2.7	4.1	4.1	7.9	10.9	14.9	55.4
Nonworker	4,144	100.0	1.8	3.3	2.9	9.1	8.7	9.7	64.5

[1] Exclusive of heads of families whose length of last continuous residence was unknown.
[2] In the 2 Cotton Areas.
[3] Exclusive of New England.

Table 30.—Length of Last Continuous Residence in County of Heads of Rural Families Receiving General Relief in the Eastern and Western Cotton Areas, by Color and Usual Occupation, June 1935

[44 counties]

Color and usual occupation	Total [1]		Years of last continuous residence in county						
	Number	Percent	1 or less	2–3	4–5	6–9	10–14	15–19	20 or more
WHITE									
Total	10,382	100.0	6.2	9.0	6.8	12.0	8.1	7.9	50.0
Agriculture	5,406	100.0	6.0	9.1	7.1	12.8	8.4	7.9	48.7
Farm operator	3,516	100.0	5.5	7.3	6.2	11.8	7.7	7.8	53.7
Owner	602	100.0	2.0	3.7	4.0	6.3	3.7	6.0	74.3
Tenant	1,418	100.0	5.6	7.8	6.1	13.3	8.5	8.7	50.0
Cropper	1,496	100.0	6.8	8.4	7.2	12.6	8.6	7.8	48.6
Farm laborer	1,890	100.0	7.0	12.3	8.7	14.7	9.6	7.9	39.8
Nonagriculture	3,142	100.0	8.0	9.8	7.8	12.3	8.1	7.8	46.2
White collar	502	100.0	8.4	5.2	6.4	10.0	7.6	9.2	53.2
Skilled	470	100.0	8.9	13.6	11.9	10.6	8.1	9.4	37.5
Semiskilled	760	100.0	7.4	11.8	5.5	12.9	8.7	7.9	45.8
Unskilled	1,410	100.0	7.8	9.1	8.1	13.3	8.1	6.8	46.8
No usual occupation	346	100.0	4.0	7.5	5.8	11.6	6.9	11.6	52.6
Nonworker	1,488	100.0	3.4	7.7	3.8	8.5	7.4	7.4	61.8
NEGRO									
Total	4,466	100.0	1.5	3.3	3.4	8.2	7.0	7.0	69.6
Agriculture	2,106	100.0	1.3	3.3	4.3	7.2	6.5	6.6	70.8
Farm operator	1,098	100.0	1.1	2.6	3.8	6.2	6.6	7.1	72.6
Owner	152	100.0	—	—	1.3	3.9	5.3	5.3	84.2
Tenant	444	100.0	0.9	2.3	2.7	3.6	6.3	6.8	77.4
Cropper	502	100.0	1.6	3.6	5.6	9.2	7.2	8.0	64.8
Farm laborer	1,008	100.0	1.6	4.2	4.8	8.3	6.3	6.2	68.6
Nonagriculture	1,044	100.0	1.9	4.6	3.3	11.5	10.2	7.1	61.4
White collar	30	†	†	—	†	†	†	†	†
Skilled	48	†	—	—	—	†	†	†	†
Semiskilled	60	100.0	—	3.3	—	10.0	10.0	3.3	73.4
Unskilled	906	100.0	2.0	5.1	3.1	11.7	9.5	7.1	61.5
No usual occupation	30	†	†	†	—	—	†	†	†
Nonworker	1,286	100.0	1.4	2.0	2.0	7.2	5.1	7.6	74.7

† Percent not computed on a base of fewer than 50 cases.
[1] Exclusive of heads of families whose length of last continuous residence was unknown.

Table 31.—School Attainment of Heads of Rural Families Receiving General Relief, by Residence and Area, October 1935

[138 counties and 83 New England townships [1]]

Residence and area	Total [2]		Last grade or year completed							
			Grade and high school						College	
	Number	Percent	None	1–3	4–7	8	9–11	12	1–3	4 or more
TOTAL RURAL										
All areas	40,234	100.0	8.8	13.8	42.0	24.5	7.4	2.5	0.8	0.2
Eastern Cotton	4,294	100.0	14.4	20.4	43.0	9.2	9.1	1.4	1.8	0.7
White	3,190	100.0	9.2	16.3	46.4	11.3	11.7	1.8	2.4	0.9
Negro	1,104	100.0	29.4	32.3	32.8	3.1	1.6	0.2	0.2	0.4
Western Cotton	4,610	100.0	6.4	12.1	51.1	17.5	10.8	1.3	0.7	0.1
White	3,728	100.0	5.4	10.7	50.6	19.6	11.5	1.5	0.6	0.1
Negro	882	100.0	10.9	17.7	53.8	8.4	7.7	0.5	1.0	—
Appalachian-Ozark	15,736	100.0	12.5	19.7	44.9	18.6	3.2	0.8	0.2	0.1
Lake States Cut-Over	2,422	100.0	9.8	12.1	36.2	27.1	10.8	3.3	0.7	—
Hay and Dairy	5,158	100.0	2.9	5.2	43.0	34.1	9.8	3.9	0.6	0.5
Corn Belt	2,724	100.0	2.4	5.4	33.8	41.1	9.8	6.2	1.0	0.3
Spring Wheat	1,982	100.0	5.2	7.4	31.8	42.2	7.9	4.3	1.2	—
Winter Wheat	790	100.0	2.8	6.3	32.7	41.7	10.9	4.6	1.0	—
Ranching	936	100.0	3.2	6.8	23.9	41.0	13.5	8.8	2.4	0.4
New England	1,582	100.0	3.8	4.6	29.3	39.8	12.8	7.3	2.4	—
OPEN COUNTRY										
All areas [3]	23,530	100.0	10.7	15.1	44.3	22.0	5.8	1.5	0.4	0.2
Eastern Cotton	2,946	100.0	14.5	21.2	45.7	8.8	7.6	0.6	0.9	0.7
White	2,300	100.0	10.3	17.6	49.6	10.6	9.3	0.8	1.1	0.7
Negro	646	100.0	29.7	34.1	22.2	1.9	1.5	—	—	0.6
Western Cotton	3,250	100.0	6.5	12.4	52.2	17.4	9.8	1.1	0.5	0.1
White	2,640	100.0	5.5	11.0	51.8	19.0	10.8	1.2	0.5	0.2
Negro	610	100.0	10.5	18.3	53.7	10.5	5.6	0.7	0.7	—
Appalachian-Ozark	9,828	100.0	14.9	19.5	45.6	17.1	2.3	0.4	0.1	0.1
Lake States Cut-Over	1,684	100.0	10.3	13.3	36.5	26.2	10.0	2.9	0.8	—
Hay and Dairy	2,800	100.0	3.4	5.1	44.4	34.7	8.0	3.6	0.4	0.4
Corn Belt	958	100.0	4.4	6.3	37.8	39.6	7.1	4.4	0.4	—
Spring Wheat	1,292	100.0	4.3	8.4	32.4	45.3	6.2	2.6	0.8	—
Winter Wheat	472	100.0	4.2	7.6	33.9	38.7	11.4	3.4	0.8	—
Ranching	300	100.0	6.7	11.3	31.3	39.4	7.3	3.3	—	0.7
VILLAGE										
All areas [3]	15,122	100.0	6.5	12.9	39.5	26.6	9.3	3.7	1.2	0.3
Eastern Cotton	1,348	100.0	14.1	18.7	36.5	10.4	12.5	3.0	3.9	0.9
White	890	100.0	6.5	13.0	38.0	13.3	18.0	4.3	5.6	1.3
Negro	458	100.0	28.8	29.7	34.2	4.8	1.7	0.4	0.4	—
Western Cotton	1,360	100.0	6.3	11.5	48.6	17.6	13.2	1.8	1.0	—
White	1,088	100.0	5.0	10.1	47.3	21.1	13.4	2.2	0.9	—
Negro	272	100.0	11.8	16.9	53.6	3.7	12.5	—	1.5	—
Appalachian-Ozark	5,908	100.0	8.4	19.9	43.9	21.2	4.6	1.5	0.4	0.1
Lake States Cut-Over	738	100.0	8.7	9.5	35.3	29.0	12.7	4.3	0.5	—
Hay and Dairy	2,358	100.0	2.4	5.3	41.4	33.5	11.9	4.2	0.8	0.5
Corn Belt	1,766	100.0	1.4	5.0	31.7	41.8	11.2	7.2	1.2	0.5
Spring Wheat	690	100.0	7.0	5.5	30.7	36.3	11.0	7.5	2.0	—
Winter Wheat	318	100.0	0.6	4.4	30.8	46.5	10.1	6.3	1.3	—
Ranching	636	100.0	1.6	4.7	20.4	41.8	16.4	11.3	3.5	0.3

[1] Townships in Connecticut and Massachusetts only.
[2] Exclusive of heads of families whose school attainment was unknown.
[3] Exclusive of New England.

Table 32.—School Attainment of Heads of Rural Families Receiving General Relief, 16 Through 24 Years of Age, by Residence and Area, October 1935

[138 counties and 83 New England townships [1]]

Residence and area	Total		Last grade or year completed							
			Grade and high school						College	
	Number	Percent	None	1-3	4-7	8	9-11	12	1-3	4 or more
TOTAL RURAL										
All areas	4,806	100.0	3.1	7.6	33.0	28.7	19.1	7.7	0.6	0.2
Eastern Cotton	448	100.0	9.4	12.5	46.4	7.6	16.1	4.0	3.1	0.9
Western Cotton	434	100.0	1.8	3.7	39.7	26.7	20.7	7.4	—	—
Appalachian-Ozark	1,736	100.0	5.2	14.2	44.7	23.3	10.4	2.0	0.2	—
Lake States Cut-Over	184	100.0	—	4.3	31.5	38.1	18.5	7.6	—	—
Hay and Dairy	350	100.0	—	3.4	17.1	49.8	20.6	9.1	—	—
Corn Belt	196	100.0	—	1.0	15.3	49.1	17.3	16.3	1.0	—
Spring Wheat	138	100.0	—	2.9	34.8	42.1	7.2	11.6	1.4	—
Winter Wheat	64	100.0	—	6.3	18.8	37.4	21.9	12.5	3.1	—
Ranching	88	100.0	—	2.3	25.0	15.9	36.3	20.5	—	—
New England	1,168	100.0	0.7	1.4	17.0	33.2	32.7	14.2	0.5	0.3
OPEN COUNTRY										
All areas [2]	2,188	100.0	5.1	9.7	43.1	26.2	12.1	3.1	0.5	0.2
Eastern Cotton	314	100.0	10.8	10.8	47.8	7.6	18.5	1.9	1.3	1.3
Western Cotton	324	100.0	2.5	4.3	39.5	28.4	20.4	4.9	—	—
Appalachian-Ozark	1,022	100.0	6.8	13.1	52.7	19.6	6.8	0.6	0.4	—
Lake States Cut-Over	144	110.0	—	5.6	29.2	37.5	20.8	6.9	—	—
Hay and Dairy	194	100.0	—	6.2	20.6	56.7	10.3	6.2	—	—
Corn Belt	66	100.0	—	—	12.1	69.7	9.1	9.1	—	—
Spring Wheat	78	100.0	—	5.1	33.3	46.2	7.7	5.1	2.6	—
Winter Wheat	30	†	—	†	†	†	—	†	—	—
Ranching	16	†	—	†	†	†	†	—	—	—
VILLAGE										
All areas [2]	1,450	100.0	1.9	9.5	30.6	28.7	18.9	9.4	1.0	—
Eastern Cotton	134	100.0	6.0	16.4	43.2	7.5	10.4	9.0	7.5	—
Western Cotton	110	100.0	—	1.8	40.1	21.8	21.8	14.5	—	—
Appalachian-Ozark	714	100.0	2.8	15.7	33.6	28.6	15.4	3.9	—	—
Lake States Cut-Over	40	†	—	—	†	†	†	†	—	—
Hay and Dairy	156	100.0	—	—	12.8	41.1	33.3	12.8	—	—
Corn Belt	130	100.0	—	1.5	16.9	38.6	21.5	20.0	1.5	—
Spring Wheat	60	100.0	—	—	36.7	36.7	6.7	19.9	—	—
Winter Wheat	34	†	—	—	†	†	†	†	†	—
Ranching	72	100.0	—	—	22.2	13.9	44.5	19.4	—	—

† Percent not computed on a base of fewer than 50 cases.

[1] Townships in Connecticut and Massachusetts only.

[2] Exclusive of New England.

Table 33.—School Attendance of Children 7 Through 15 Years of Age in Rural Families Receiving General Relief, by Residence and Area, October 1935

[138 counties and 83 New England townships[1]]

Residence and area	Total				7–9 years				10–13 years				14–15 years			
	Number	Percent	In school	Not in school	Number	Percent	In school	Not in school	Number	Percent	In school	Not in school	Number	Percent	In school	Not in school
TOTAL RURAL																
All areas	47,050	100.0	93.8	6.2	13,426	100.0	94.9	5.1	23,022	100.0	96.2	3.8	10,602	100.0	87.3	12.7
Eastern Cotton	4,950	100.0	86.7	13.3	1,778	100.0	88.1	11.9	2,242	100.0	89.4	10.6	930	100.0	77.4	22.6
Western Cotton	5,942	100.0	93.2	6.8	2,102	100.0	91.4	8.6	2,668	100.0	96.4	3.6	1,172	100.0	89.1	10.9
Appalachian-Ozark	16,148	100.0	91.8	8.2	2,780	100.0	93.4	6.6	9,153	100.0	95.0	5.0	4,210	100.0	83.8	16.2
Lake States Cut-Over	2,774	100.0	97.0	3.0	878	100.0	98.6	1.4	1,296	100.0	99.2	0.8	600	100.0	90.0	10.0
Hay and Dairy	6,364	100.0	98.8	1.2	2,230	100.0	98.6	1.4	2,774	100.0	99.6	0.4	1,360	100.0	97.6	2.4
Corn Belt	3,116	100.0	97.2	2.8	1,034	100.0	99.2	0.8	1,494	100.0	98.7	1.3	678	100.0	90.9	9.1
Spring Wheat	2,848	100.0	94.0	6.0	1,010	100.0	97.4	2.6	1,258	100.0	99.1	0.9	580	100.0	77.9	22.1
Winter Wheat	936	100.0	97.9	2.1	312	100.0	98.1	1.9	426	100.0	98.3	1.7	198	100.0	94.9	5.1
Ranching	1,110	100.0	96.0	4.0	394	100.0	93.4	6.6	482	100.0	99.8	0.2	234	100.0	95.7	4.3
New England	2,862	100.0	99.0	1.0	908	100.0	100.0	—	1,314	100.0	100.0	—	640	100.0	95.6	4.4
OPEN COUNTRY																
All areas[2]	27,898	100.0	91.8	8.2	7,018	100.0	93.0	7.0	14,388	100.0	94.9	5.1	6,492	100.0	83.6	16.4
Eastern Cotton	3,808	100.0	84.7	15.3	1,400	100.0	87.3	12.7	1,730	100.0	87.5	12.5	678	100.0	72.0	28.0
Western Cotton	4,324	100.0	92.5	7.5	1,574	100.0	91.0	9.0	1,902	100.0	96.0	4.0	848	100.0	87.3	12.7
Appalachian-Ozark	9,868	100.0	89.8	10.2	632	100.0	87.0	13.0	6,356	100.0	93.9	6.1	2,880	100.0	81.2	18.8
Lake States Cut-Over	1,942	100.0	96.6	3.4	614	100.0	98.0	2.0	916	100.0	98.9	1.1	412	100.0	89.3	10.7
Hay and Dairy	3,708	100.0	98.7	1.3	1,326	100.0	98.5	1.5	1,592	100.0	99.4	0.6	790	100.0	97.5	2.5
Corn Belt	1,294	100.0	96.3	3.7	410	100.0	99.0	1.0	600	100.0	98.7	1.3	284	100.0	87.3	12.7
Spring Wheat	1,946	100.0	92.2	7.8	706	100.0	96.9	3.1	862	100.0	98.1	1.9	378	100.0	69.8	30.2
Winter Wheat	608	100.0	92.7	7.3	208	100.0	96.9	3.1	284	100.0	100.0	—	136	100.0	95.6	4.4
Ranching	400	100.0	90.5	9.5	148	100.0	82.4	17.6	166	100.0	96.4	3.6	86	100.0	93.0	7.0

See footnotes at end of table.

Table 33.—School Attendance of Children 7 Through 15 Years of Age in Rural Families Receiving General Relief, by Residence and Area, October 1935—Continued

Residence and area	Total				7–9 years				10–13 years				14–15 years			
	Number	Percent	In school	Not in school	Total Number	Percent	In school	Not in school	Total Number	Percent	In school	Not in school	Total Number	Percent	In school	Not in school
VILLAGE																
All areas [2]	16,290	100.0	96.4	3.6	5,500	100.0	96.4	3.6	7,320	100.0	98.2	1.8	3,470	100.0	92.6	7.4
Eastern Cotton	1,142	100.0	93.3	6.7	378	100.0	91.0	9.0	512	100.0	95.7	4.3	252	100.0	92.1	7.9
Western Cotton	1,618	100.0	95.2	4.8	528	100.0	92.8	7.2	766	100.0	97.4	2.6	324	100.0	93.8	6.2
Appalachian-Ozark	6,280	100.0	94.9	5.1	2,148	100.0	95.3	4.7	2,802	100.0	97.3	2.7	1,330	100.0	89.5	10.5
Lake States Cut-Over	832	100.0	98.1	1.9	261	100.0	100.0	—	380	100.0	100.0	—	188	100.0	91.5	8.5
Hay and Dairy	2,656	100.0	99.1	0.9	901	100.0	98.7	1.3	1,182	100.0	100.0	—	570	100.0	97.9	2.1
Corn Belt	1,822	100.0	97.8	2.2	624	100.0	99.4	0.6	801	100.0	98.8	1.2	394	100.0	93.4	6.6
Spring Wheat	902	100.0	98.0	2.0	304	100.0	98.7	1.3	396	100.0	100.0	—	202	100.0	93.1	6.9
Winter Wheat	328	100.0	96.3	3.7	101	100.0	96.2	3.8	162	100.0	97.5	2.5	62	100.0	93.5	6.5
Ranching	710	100.0	99.2	0.8	246	100.0	100.0	—	316	100.0	99.4	0.6	148	100.0	97.3	2.7

[1] Townships in Connecticut and Massachusetts only.
[2] Exclusive of New England.

Appendix C

LIST OF TABLES

TEXT TABLES

151

Index

INDEX

157

O

POVERTY, U. S. A.

THE HISTORICAL RECORD

An Arno Press/New York Times Collection

Adams, Grace. **Workers on Relief.** 1939.

The Almshouse Experience: Collected Reports. 1821-1827.

Armstrong, Louise V. **We Too Are The People.** 1938.

Bloodworth, Jessie A. and Elizabeth J. Greenwood.
The Personal Side. 1939.

Brunner, Edmund de S. and Irving Lorge.
**Rural Trends in Depression Years: A Survey of
Village-Centered Agricultural Communities, 1930-1936.**
1937.

Calkins, Raymond.
**Substitutes for the Saloon: An Investigation Originally
made for The Committee of Fifty.** 1919.

Cavan, Ruth Shonle and Katherine Howland Ranck.
**The Family and the Depression: A Study of
One Hundred Chicago Families.** 1938.

Chapin, Robert Coit.
**The Standard of Living Among Workingmen's Families
in New York City.** 1909.

**The Charitable Impulse in Eighteenth Century America:
Collected Papers.** 1711-1797.

Children's Aid Society.
Children's Aid Society Annual Reports, 1-10.
February 1854-February 1863.

Conference on the Care of Dependent Children.
**Proceedings of the Conference on the Care
of Dependent Children.** 1909.

Conyngton, Mary.
How to Help: A Manual of Practical Charity. 1909.

Devine, Edward T. **Misery and its Causes.** 1909.

Devine, Edward T. **Principles of Relief.** 1904.

Dix, Dorothea L.
On Behalf of the Insane Poor: Selected Reports. 1843-1852.

Douglas, Paul H.
**Social Security in the United States: An Analysis and
Appraisal of the Federal Social Security Act.** 1936.

Farm Tenancy: Black and White. Two Reports. 1935, 1937.

Feder, Leah Hannah.
**Unemployment Relief in Periods of Depression:
A Study of Measures Adopted in Certain American
Cities, 1857 through 1922.** 1936.

Folks, Homer.
**The Care of Destitute, Neglected, and
Delinquent Children.** 1900.

Guardians of the Poor.
**A Compilation of the Poor Laws of the State of
Pennsylvania from the Year 1700 to 1788, Inclusive.** 1788.

Hart, Hastings, H.
Preventive Treatment of Neglected Children.
(Correction and Prevention, Vol. 4) 1910.

Herring, Harriet L.
**Welfare Work in Mill Villages: The Story of Extra-Mill
Activities in North Carolina.** 1929.

The Jacksonians on the Poor: Collected Pamphlets.
1822-1844.

Karpf, Maurice J.
Jewish Community Organization in the United States.
1938.

Kellor, Frances A.
Out of Work: A Study of Unemployment. 1915.

Kirkpatrick, Ellis Lore.
The Farmer's Standard of Living. 1929.

Komarovsky, Mirra.
The Unemployed Man and His Family: The Effect of Unemployment Upon the Status of the Man in Fifty-Nine Families. 1940.

Leupp, Francis E. **The Indian and His Problem.** 1910.

Lowell, Josephine Shaw.
Public Relief and Private Charity. 1884.

More, Louise Bolard.
Wage Earners' Budgets: A Study of Standards and Cost of Living in New York City. 1907.

New York Association for Improving the Condition of the Poor.
AICP First Annual Reports Investigating Poverty. 1845-1853.

O'Grady, John.
Catholic Charities in the United States: History and Problems. 1930.

Raper, Arthur F.
Preface to Peasantry: A Tale of Two Black Belt Counties. 1936.

Raper, Arthur F. **Tenants of The Almighty.** 1943.

Richmond, Mary E.
What is Social Case Work? An Introductory Description. 1922.

Riis, Jacob A. **The Children of the Poor.** 1892.

Rural Poor in the Great Depression: Three Studies. 1938.

Sedgwick, Theodore.
Public and Private Economy: Part I. 1836.

Smith, Reginald Heber. **Justice and the Poor.** 1919.

Sutherland, Edwin H. and Harvey J. Locke.
Twenty Thousand Homeless Men: A Study of Unemployed Men in the Chicago Shelters. 1936.

Tuckerman, Joseph.
On the Elevation of the Poor: A Selection From His Reports as Minister at Large in Boston. 1874.

Warner, Amos G. **American Charities.** 1894.

Watson, Frank Dekker.
The Charity Organization Movement in the United States: A Study in American Philanthropy. 1922.

Woods, Robert A., et al. **The Poor in Great Cities.** 1895.